HOMEOWNERS MONEY MANAGEMENT

A Guide to Realizing Your Life Dreams by Controlling Your Financial Plan

by Michael C. Thomsett

 Rodale Press, Emmaus, Pennsylvania

Copyright © 1987 by Michael C. Thomsett

All rights reserved. No part of this publication may be reproduced or transmitted in any form or by any means, electronic or mechanical, including photocopy, recording, or any information storage or retrieval system without the written permission of the publisher.

Printed in the United States of America on recycled paper containing a high percentage of de-inked fiber.

Senior editor: Ray Wolf
Editor: Sandra Oddo
Book design: Denise Mirabello
Illustrations: Michael C. Thomsett

Library of Congress Cataloging-in-Publication Data

Thomsett, Michael C.
    Homeowners money management.

    Includes index.
    1. Home ownership—United States.   2. Investments—United States.   3. Finance, Personal—United States.   I. Title.
HD7287.82.U6T47   1987   332.024   86-26096
ISBN 0-87857-673-8 (alk. paper)
ISBN 0-87857-674-6 (pbk. : alk. paper)

2 4 6 8 10 9 7 5 3 1   hardcover
2 4 6 8 10 9 7 5 3 1   paperback

The examples and case studies used in this book illustrate the general principles that go into the development and implementation of a sound financial plan for the average homeowner. They were prepared based on the laws, rules, and circumstances that were in effect at the time the book was written. However, laws, particularly tax laws, sometimes change and those changes may affect your financial plan. Your state may also have its own laws that must be considered in developing and implementing your financial plan. Finally, the financial goals and needs of every homeowner, just like their homes themselves, are in some way unique. We therefore recommend that you consult with your attorney, accountant, or other financial adviser before making any important financial decisions.

For Linda, Eric, and Mike

Contents

INTRODUCTION	ix
SECTION I TENDING THE ASSET	1
1 WHY YOU NEED A PLAN	2
Definitions	3
The Plan Itself	5
Your House and the Plan	7
Evaluating Your House	8
2 DEFINING THE DREAM	12
Owning Your Home Free and Clear	13
Retiring	15
Making a Career Change	17
Starting Your Own Business	18
Short-term Goals	19
Turning Dreams into Realities	20
3 DOING THE PLAN	28
The Planning Process	29
An Example of a Plan	34
Variations on a Plan	56
4 THE HOMEOWNER'S EDGE—PUTTING THE PLAN TO WORK	60
Building Equity	63
Preserving Equity	66
Using Your Equity	68
Avoiding Common Mistakes	71
5 SHORTCUTS TO BUILDING EQUITY FASTER	76
Kinds of Mortgages	81
Shorter Terms	84

  Formal Acceleration Programs 85
  Designing Your Own Plan 89
  Making the Decision to Accelerate 99

6 COVERING THE FLANKS **100**
  Mortgage Insurance for Homeowners 102
  When Coverage Is No Longer Needed 110

7 FINDING HELP WITH THE PLAN **112**
  Choosing the Right Specialist 115
  Choosing the Right Individual 119
  Other Points to Consider 122

8 WHEN THE PLAN CHANGES **126**
  Life Dreams 126
  Family Status 128
  Tax Legislation 129
  Example of a Modified Plan 131
  How Changes Are Made 133

9 MAKING YOUR HOME FIT THE PLAN **138**
  Buying a Future Homesite 138
  Build or Renovate? 140
  Home Improvement 142
  Improvements That Add Equity 145
  Financing Improvements 146

SECTION II   PUTTING EQUITY TO WORK **151**

10 WHEN YOU SELL YOUR HOME **152**
  Going by the Plan 153
  Selling a House 154
  Selecting an Agent 156
  Coordinating a Buy and Sell 158

11 ALTERNATIVES TO HOME OWNERSHIP **162**
  Financial Advantages and Disadvantages 163

    Condo Living 165
    Co-ops and Renting 168

12 USING EQUITY AFTER RETIREMENT **170**
    The Reverse Annuity Mortgage 172
    The Sale-Leaseback 174

13 HOW HOMEOWNERS INVEST **176**
    Protecting Your Shelter 178
    Types of Investments 179
    Insurance Products 185
    Combining Equity and Know-How 187
    The Diversified Investor 187

14 INVESTING IN PROPERTY **192**
    Becoming a Landlord 195

15 THE FINANCIAL WORLD **204**
    Objectives 204
    Investor Characteristics 214
    Investment Advice 218

16 GETTING HELP WITH YOUR INVESTMENTS **220**
    The Stockbroker's Role 220
    Using an Asset Management Account 225
    Investing on Your Own 228
    Investment Clubs 230
    Making the Most of Your Investments 233

INDEX **236**

Introduction

As an American homeowner, you have a problem. It is a fact that most of us do not really make money on our houses, because the interest we pay on a mortgage more than offsets any gain over time. How can you build and preserve the value of your home, and truly profit from that effort?

You have a second problem: In looking ahead toward retirement, you need to figure out how to save enough money to support yourself. If you are an average homeowner, you will have less than $4,000 saved by your 65th birthday. So your home will be your only significant asset.

These two serious problems have solutions. This book will show you specific ways you can plan now to protect the value of your home in the future. It will show you how to retire with an adequate income, without having to sell your house just to survive. The essential point to be made in this book is: You will succeed if you know what you want, and if you have a specific plan for getting there, a plan that can be put into action.

Planning is a continuous process, since nothing stays the same for long. Your house plays a critical role in this process.

First, a house is a necessity; protecting it should have the highest priority. There are instances when the value of your house can be used to achieve another personal goal, but when that occurs you should be fully aware of what it may mean in terms of your personal security and your prospects for a secure and comfortable retirement.

The planning process is simpler when you are young and starting out with time on your side, but planning is a discipline that all of us can learn and put into effect. It becomes a real challenge when you have just a short time to go before you will retire—only 10 or 15 years.

You will benefit greatly from initiating a plan today, regardless of your age and personal wealth. You will benefit most, however, if you have been living in your home for several years, if you are planning to retire within the next 10 to 20 years, and if you have not yet instituted a concrete plan of action for paying off your home mortgage and creating a comfortable retirement income.

If you belong to this group, you probably share three dilemmas common to people of your age and economic status:

(1) You have started to build substantial equity—the portion of your house that you own free and clear of debt—in your home and feel compelled to "do something with it."

(2) You have little knowledge or experience in financial matters or investing, and are afraid of making a mistake with money you cannot afford to lose.

(3) You have a desire to develop a concrete plan for preservation of your assets and creation of a comfortable retirement base, but are not sure just how to go about it.

None of these dilemmas is too complicated for you to unravel. If you have begun to build equity in your house, you are on the right track and don't need to change that course. On the contrary, you should work toward complete ownership.

Financial knowledge is elusive. If you have investigated the field at all, chances are you have already discovered a wide range of services available, some of which are utterly useless to you. The answer here is research and investigation, the use of qualified professional help when it is appropriate, and a clear understanding of what a particular professional can and should provide. For example, you need the help of a savings and loan institution or other lender in financing a home. But those same lenders may not always work for your best interests in subsequent loans.

A wise way to manage your financial affairs is to view your house as the foundation of your personal wealth plan. The plan itself will fall into place as soon as you define where you are going. That definition is the most critical part.

Like most American homeowners, you have goals that reflect your personal values. You want to own your home free and clear. You recognize that one of life's worst dilemmas is to be elderly without sufficient income or a place to live. You may want to retire before the traditional age of 65, and perhaps start your own business or a second career. And if you have children, you would like to be able to pay for their college education. Do not confuse goals like these with more immediate things you want— a new car or a European vacation, for example.

Developing a long-term, personal, written financial plan helps you to stay on track, to avoid misusing your important assets, and to manage income properly. It will be broken into segments involving many different aspects of financial management—investment, insurance, and savings, to name a few. Coordinated with your goals and put into action, your plan is a blueprint for building what you want and deserve. With it in place, you will achieve what you seek.

This book lays out the steps for achieving your dreams. It begins by explaining why you need a plan. From that, you will gain insights into your personal motivations and goals—the unspoken and undefined desires that motivated you to work hard to buy a house in the first place. The first chapters of the book discuss the nuts and bolts of preparing that all-important plan.

Many professionally prepared "plans" in reality are shallow covers for selling products you may or may not need. Some professionals in the field are truly valuable and sincere, but they are in the minority and difficult to find in a sea of pretenders. You will learn how to look for help.

There are institutions that attempt to distract you from the very things you desire to build. You are promised fast money through easily approved loans or lines of credit, all based on your home equity. Banks, savings and loans, insurance companies, even brokerage houses all would like to encourage you to borrow, because all of those institutions have cash to invest. All investment carries some risk, but one of the lowest risks for a lender is a loan secured by real property. When you borrow and pledge your house as security the lender cannot lose. If you are unable to repay the loan, your house will be sold to satisfy your debt.

At first glance, access to this easy money appears to give you special economic power. You can get a large sum of money in a short time. You are told that it is wrong to let equity sit idle in your home when you could take it out and put it to work. And you are told, time and again and in many ways, that a penny borrowed is a penny earned.

None of that is true. Your house is an asset, and you should not spend your assets as you do your income. If you do, nothing is built over time and the comfortable retirement you envision for yourself dwindles away in interest costs and unwise spending. The profit you could build up in your house is given away to lenders.

The answer is to make a distinction between your assets and your earnings. By protecting your house from unwise exposure to the risk of borrowing, and by spending your income wisely to enhance your personal wealth, you will gain a most important form of freedom—freedom to live your life comfortably, without needing to worry about food, shelter, or debt.

The second section of the book discusses how investments fit into the picture, and how to evaluate and implement the advice that professionals may give you.

You might say that this is a book of definitions. It approaches the frustrating and confusing problems every homeowner faces and proposes a number of logical and practical solutions. Where professional help is needed it should be used, but a great deal of the work is personal, requiring you to put definition into your life. This you can do best on your own. In fact, it is unlikely that any form of professional help can substitute for your knowledge and familiarity with your own personal life dreams.

By the time you are through reading this book you will know why you needn't feel guilty for letting your money sit idle in your home. That idle money is there waiting for your dreams to become realities.

Section I

TENDING THE ASSET

1
WHY YOU NEED A PLAN

"If you don't know where you're going,
any road will get you there."

"The road to self-improvement is always under construction."

"Be careful what you wish for, because you'll probably get it."

Folk sayings

These three bits of folk wisdom can serve as guidelines for what is called broadly "financial planning." A conductor works from a score to lead an orchestra, and to keep tempo, sound, and intensity at just the right level. Without that guidance the music would fall apart. You play the role of conductor for your financial orchestra. You control the timing and bring in the instruments you need to achieve the effect you want. Your financial plan—which you also compose—is your score.

Ask any ten financial planners, advisers, consultants, or other money professionals for a definition of financial planning and you will get ten different answers. Few people agree on what it is. To you, as a homeowner, a financial plan describes the goals you set for yourself in order to be in control of your financial life.

You begin by developing a thorough understanding of the planning process and of your personal goals. What do you want? What do you expect? What resources are available to get the job done? After that, it's merely a matter figuring out how to get to the end result you want.

DEFINITIONS

Before proceeding to show how you can use planning and goals to take financial control, let's define a few terms: a financial plan, goals, and financial control.

A *financial plan* is the complete map of your personal finances, including assets like a house, investments, insurance, and retirement funds, for the purpose of achieving specific goals. A plan is also the measure by which you decide what steps must be taken in order to achieve those goals. A good one can protect you against a number of economic threats: death, disability, and catastrophic loss; income taxes and inflation; changes in the state of the investment marketplace.

The single most important feature of a plan is that it is individual. You are unique, therefore any planning you do should start from the point of view that it will be your plan, and yours alone.

Goals are the future achievements you want to accomplish. Most people never set goals consciously. They have them, but never make them tangible enough to reach. A few set wrong goals because they do not understand what they really want. Goals are very powerful means for achievement. By defining them, you can discover how to get what you want. Knowing where you are going, financially speaking, is the first step in putting together a plan.

There are three elements to setting an effective goal. First, it is specific, something you do not now have that you want to have in the future. Second, achieving it has a deadline. And third, you should be able to believe that you can achieve the goal by taking a series of well-understood steps.

Securities and insurance salespeople will tell you that goals are things like "safety," "liquidity," "preservation of capital," or "tax-free income." These are not goals. They are features that describe specific investments. Making a million dollars isn't a goal. Certainly, having a large amount of money gives you greater flexibility in planning, but it is a simplification to say that your goal is to make money.

Goals are more personal. They may include things like:

- Saving enough money to pay for a child's education
- Free and clear ownership of the family home by age 65
- Establishing a retirement fund that will support you for the rest of your life

Goals are the most important part of a personal financial plan. Without them, you don't know clearly what you're trying to achieve. With them, the entire process becomes understandable.

Financial control is simply being in charge of your financial life. *You* decide where you're going and how to get there. *You* select and modify your goals. And *you* design and put into place your financial plan. Ultimately, as you implement your plan, financial control becomes part of your life-style and personal happiness. That's what the planning process is really all about—personal freedom.

There is much to be said for having all the bases covered—enough income to live on comfortably for an indefinite period, insurance against every conceivable event, and a place to live forever. But that's only part of the picture. Along with that security comes contentment and freedom from worry. The greatest concerns of the elderly, living on fixed incomes, are security, housing, and medical care. As we approach retirement, these are certainly pressing issues. The closer we get, the more obvious it becomes that "freedom" really comes down to financial control. With control over your finances you live your life the way you want. Without it, your standard of living and the activities you pursue are chronically hampered by financial restrictions.

THE PLAN ITSELF

There are many types of plans, but the most practical is one that includes a close and detailed look at each of the elements you need to consider in order to achieve your goal. The complete plan does not need to be a legal document. It can be very simple, as long as it is enough for you to work from.

Documentation is a smart idea. Write it down. The notes you make help you to stay on course; the need to define things in words helps you to focus your goals. You should include the following five elements:

(1) Statement of goals: This fairly simple and straightforward series of statements appears to be the easiest part of the plan. In fact, it should be a summary of the hardest part—defining what you need in the future, concisely and in strong, definite language.

(2) Resources: This is a list of the assets and income you have now. The purpose is to compare your present status with where you want to be in the future.

(3) Investment standards: Here you define where you stand in terms of risks you are willing to take. Risk takes many forms—the risk of having too little cash available when it is needed, excessive tax liabilities, inflation, loss of capital, and inadequate insurance. Defining your personal standards for each type of risk helps to focus your plan.

(4) Specific section headings: There should be one section for each of your status reports on savings, retirement, insurance, investments, and assets like your house.

(5) Summary: Here you present deadlines and specific actions that have to be taken. You will see by the end of the planning process, summarized in figure 1-1, that no series of goals can be achieved simply. The secret is to coordinate all the elements of the plan, set a timetable, and identify the actions that must be taken. In short, you take a complex series of interrelated actions and make them simple.

It sounds like a lot of work—and it is. But when you actually go through the process it isn't all that bad.

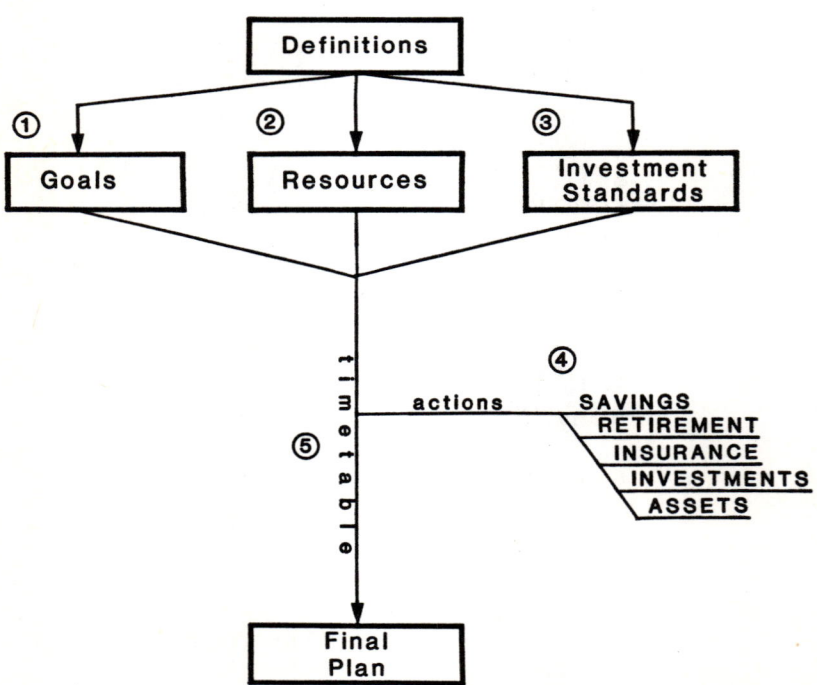

FIGURE 1-1
The Planning Process

Because no one is an expert in all the elements of a financial plan, when you have done your part you should get it reviewed by financial professionals who can present you with alternatives (see chapter 7).

Finally, update the plan periodically. No plan is set in concrete. It must remain a working, changing document that adjusts to your life. The features that make up your financial plan change constantly, and your financial status will change over time. Old goals are achieved or dropped and new ones are put in their place.

YOUR HOUSE AND THE PLAN

Your house is the fundamental resource for your ultimate financial well-being. This is true for a couple of reasons.

First is value. Your house represents the most substantial asset you have, and it needs care and protection. Second is necessity. You need shelter. As you approach retirement your need for a lifelong home becomes more significant.

Those who advise you to borrow, using your house as security, hope that you won't ask yourself the important question: "Would I borrow money to make this investment if I didn't have a house?" Most reasonable people will agree that borrowing to invest is not a good idea, yet people with houses do it every day.

This is partly because taking money out of your house isn't really borrowing—is it? Of course it is, and of the worst kind. You are putting your house at stake and thus risking your family's home.

Yes, your house needs to be protected. There **is** absolutely nothing wrong with leaving your equity right where it is, untouched. There are good, strong cases when borrowing money is advisable, but only after careful evaluation of what that borrowing will do to your overall plan. How will it affect or inhibit your goals? How will it delay your timetable? And how will it harm your ability to stay in control? A large portion of home equity loans would not be requested if homeowners addressed these issues before jumping in.

A much better strategy in many cases is to work toward paying off your home mortgage as quickly as possible, even accelerating payments whenever possible. In chapter 5 you will see how rapid repayment of a mortgage loan is the best way to realize profits from owning your home.

EVALUATING YOUR HOUSE

Most people, myself included, buy their first houses with little or no thought about economic factors. The first time around, we simply buy what we can afford. Later, when value and equity have built up over several years, our perspective changes. For the purposes of developing your financial plan, you must view your house as an economic asset. There are several elements to consider:

(1) Comparisons with other houses: Your house can be compared with others in the same area. Rate it on its number of rooms, general condition and appearance, and location within the neighborhood. For example, a house located on a busy street is exposed to more noise and thus might have less economic value than a house exactly like it that is located one block away on a quieter street.

Other houses in your area may limit its economic value. If the highest sales price in the last two years was $115,000, you will have difficulty getting more than that for your house, even if you have made improvements.

The condition of other houses in the area also affects the value of yours. There is little you can do to make other people mow their lawns or paint, but be aware that these factors will influence the value of your house.

(2) Potential for growth in value: How much will your house increase in value over the next 10 or 20 years? You can decide this by looking at trends in your area. If a lot of new construction is underway, that's a sign that developers see a demand for more residential units. If businesses are moving into your area, demand for housing will certainly be a factor in the future value of your house.

    If business conditions are part of a cycle, how long will it take for the cycle to turn around? The answer to this question—or the lack of an answer—may motivate you to sell and move to an area where houses have more economic potential, if that idea fits with the rest of your plan.

(3) Real costs: The value of your house, by itself, can be a deceptive measure of your net worth. Many homeowners pay so much in interest that they are not likely to realize much profit. The interest they pay simply keeps up with the increase in the value of a house. If the housing market is steady and your house does not increase in value, you actually lose money because of the cost of borrowing.

    Evaluate real costs—interest included—to guide action intended to reduce them, perhaps by looking for loans with lower rates, accelerating your payments to reduce overall costs, and resisting the temptation to borrow.

(4) Maintenance and upkeep: An economic evaluation of a house also includes general maintenance and upkeep. Insulation, air conditioning in hot areas, and the condition of paint and roofing, all enhance the value of your house.

(5) Improvements: You can increase the economic value of your house through well-selected improvements. If you have only one bathroom, the best economic improvement you can make is to add a second bath. Other improvements that almost always add value are modernizing the kitchen or adding an extra bedroom.

By considering each of these points carefully, you can identify the probable market value of your house and, from that, the value of your primary asset. If you know your house would sell for $115,000, and you owe $42,000 on a mortgage, you have equity of $73,000.

But what have you paid in interest on that mortgage? If you have paid more than $73,000, you have not benefited from the growth in market value of your house. In planning for the future, you must determine what interest expenses you will incur, then compare those with what you expect the increase in market value to be. The crucial question is: Will your net worth grow, or will your interest payments take your profit and give it to your lender?

An economic evaluation of your house can give you a realistic understanding of how you accumulate value, and a solid basis for making a workable financial plan based on an intelligent and farsighted comprehension of these issues. Only with such a plan will you be able to take advantage of opportunities to improve your net worth. If you make it one of your goals to realize a profit from your housing investment, there are many ways to achieve it.

2
DEFINING THE DREAM

Planning ahead is the key to reaching financial goals. But before you decide how to plan ahead, decide why. Begin by defining goals, asking questions that focus on what you expect to achieve.

What is the end purpose of accumulating equity in your home? Is it clear ownership? A basis for beginning a profit-making venture in real estate? Sending children to college? Retirement? These are long-range goals.

What future events will require large sums of available cash? This could include your children's college education, changing your career, an early retirement, or starting your own business. Once you have identified why you will need money, it becomes clearer what must be done to save it.

By what year would you like to own your home? If you would prefer to pay off your mortgage sooner than required, you can begin a mortgage acceleration plan (see chapter 5).

When do you want to retire? Do you envision your post-working years as idle or filled with activity? This is not a simple question. I once told a friend, "I'd like to retire early." He asked, "Why?" Retirement means different things to different people, but a good definition of retirement might be that you are able to spend your time doing what you want, rather than what you must do to earn a living. That usually means some degree of financial independence.

What type of house would you like to live in when you do retire? Will you stay in your present house or buy a larger one? A smaller one? Move to a condominium or become a renter? Buy land in the country?

Many people think they're planning when, actually, they're only practicing a form of wishful thinking. We've all heard the expression "If wishes were horses, beggars would ride." If you begin to visualize concrete steps that can be taken—starting today—to make your plan happen, you've stopped wishing and started to act.

Whenever we express a desire like early retirement, we should pause and ask ourselves: "Is this a superficial statement, or is it one of the most important goals in my life?" Upon close examination, I discovered that I didn't really want to stop working but did want to work at something I enjoyed. So the goal wasn't really early retirement, with all its connotations of sleeping in late and spending idle days. The real goal was something I hadn't yet defined for myself.

Tangible, solid thinking. That's the way a real life dream becomes clear. To demonstrate how few people have thought about their goals, ask a friend what he or she wants in 10 years, or in 20. Most people will make general statements about what they'd like to be doing, like mine: to retire early.

The more definition and detail you add to your goal, the better your chances of reaching it. Many homeowners think about one or more of the four goals that follow, with home equity in mind. They are: owning your home free and clear, retiring, making a career change, and starting your own business.

OWNING YOUR HOME FREE AND CLEAR

Total home ownership probably is the most important life dream for American families. But free and clear home ownership should not be an isolated life dream. Rather, it should serve as the foundation for a sensible and farsighted plan.

A lot of secondary dreams—a move to a larger or smaller house, a place in the country, or simply living without the burden of mortgage payments—depend on either a solid base of home equity or the availability of a large amount of money.

Planning for complete ownership will make a difference. With a plan, you can take advantage of opportunities to save thousands of dollars in interest by accelerating your mortgage payment schedule, thereby eliminating mortgage payments a decade or more before schedule. Today, seven of every ten Americans over the age of 65 own their own homes, and most have paid off their mortgages.

Yet the majority of this same group lives on an income of less than $10,000 per year. It's a peculiar dilemma. You can own your home, with thousands of dollars in value, yet be unable to make use of that value without abandoning your most important goal: to live in your house without having to make payments on a mortgage. That's why many retired Americans end up selling houses they'd rather keep, and moving out. People become attached to their homes, and it's an especially sad event when someone is forced to move for purely economic reasons. As a child, I remember how our neighbor, Mrs. Anderson, cried when she saw the moving truck back up to her house. It was obvious that she would have preferred to stay there, where she raised her children and lived with her husband for many decades.

The methods by which you can prevent losing your house eventually include insurance, a retirement plan, investing wisely, preserving your home equity, and paying off your mortgage at the earliest possible date.

Several general principles promote realization of the dream:

(1) Preserve your equity as the strongest link in your financial plan. If you use your house as collateral to borrow money, you only add to your monthly expenses and delay the realization of your life dreams (see chapter 4).

(2) Begin a program to accelerate paying off your mortgage. If you can cut in half the time required to pay off your debt, you have a stronger, financially more secure base, with more flexibility. Imagine the advantage you can realize by eliminating your mortgage from your monthly budget (see chapter 5).

(3) Protect what you are building by insuring against the economic consequences of death and disability. With an appropriate amount of life and disability insurance, your family will be able to keep home and plan intact under unforeseen economic upheavals (see chapter 6).

If you can bring your life dreams into focus and plan realistically to realize them, you have every reason to expect success.

RETIRING

The retirement business has grown in the last century. In 1900 few Americans could afford to retire, but today, with tax incentives, and pensions and profit-sharing plans sponsored by employers, secure and comfortable retirement can be a reality.

More than 20 million people fund Individual Retirement Accounts (IRAs) every year. Participants in employer-sponsored or union-sponsored retirement accounts look forward to a regular source of income after they stop working. And Americans plan for their retirement through savings and investments.

Depending on the details of your life dream, you can look at your house as a source of retirement funds (see chapters 11, 12, and 16).

Define "retirement" for yourself. Does it mean having no need to get up early and go to work? Does it involve working part-time, or in a second career? The key questions to ask yourself are:

- Will you be able to support yourself in the style of life you envision as ideal?

HOW IRAS WORK

The Individual Retirement Account (IRA) is a retirement plan designed for individuals who want to put away money for retirement without having to pay income tax on the money until it is used.

As of 1986, the Internal Revenue Service allows any American with earned income (from salaries and wages, for example) to put away as much as $2,000 per year, excluding that money from gross income. The eligibility for this income exclusion could be substantially restricted in 1987 and beyond.

Once you reach age 59½, you may begin to withdraw the IRA funds, paying tax as you take them out. The funds can be withdrawn earlier without penalty in the event of total disability. If you otherwise take an early withdrawal, you must pay a 10 percent tax penalty and all the money withdrawn is taxed to that year.

- Is your image of retirement realistic, and will you be happy making a drastic change?
- Are there activities you have not considered, that you might like to pursue once your time is your own?

Two income sources that people depend upon are:

(1) Savings: You can build reserves over the years with retirement in mind. Some people believe that interest-bearing savings accounts are the best way to go. Others prefer mutual funds or annuities. The point is to select investments in which money will grow, even slowly, over the years (see chapters 13, 14, and 15).

(2) IRAs: Individual Retirement Accounts are another good place for retirement savings. You are allowed to deposit up to $2,000 every year and in many instances

deduct it from your taxable income. The money is taxed when it is withdrawn.

MAKING A CAREER CHANGE

Understanding why you want to change careers will help to clarify the issue for you. With proper planning and a clear understanding of your goal and its financial ramifications, you can change careers without jeopardizing your home equity.

When you change careers you are likely to earn a lower income, at least for awhile, and as a result you should be prepared financially to survive the transition. For this reason, many career changes are made after a home has been paid in full, and children have grown and left home. At that point, financial requirements are lower and families can afford to live on lower incomes.

The opportunity or the necessity for a career change isn't always convenient, however. If, for example, your employer goes out of business and you'd have to move to stay in the same field, if you're fired and can't find another job in the same field, if technology does away with the kind of job you were doing, or if

---

DECIDING TO START A BUSINESS

Prepare yourself for a midlife career change by finding out exactly what is involved and applying the information to yourself.

Help is available from the United States government. The booklet *Help Yourself to a Midlife Career Change* is published by the United States Labor Department Bureau of Labor Statistics. It lists 20 important questions to ask yourself. Question 15 is the critical one for homeowners: "Exactly what will I be giving up and what will I be gaining to change careers?"

The booklet costs $2.25 and can be ordered from the Superintendent of Documents, United States Government Printing Office, Washington, DC 20402.

the perfect situation for a planned change unexpectedly appears, you may find yourself in your new career suddenly and without time for detailed preparation. The possibility should be included in your financial plan.

With proper planning, you can preserve the equity in your home. Accelerating mortgage payments so that you own your home free and clear sooner is one way to make a change affordable. If you will earn less money in your new occupation, it certainly helps to not be burdened with a mortgage payment. If you suspect the change may be sudden, consider supplementing your income with other work or through your spouse's income. Consider the possibility of a move to a less expensive house so that you can reduce your debt burden. Special attention to savings accounts and other investments is in order.

STARTING YOUR OWN BUSINESS

Being your own boss is a common American dream, perhaps as common as the desire to own a house. Many people are attracted to the idea of going into their own businesses.

If you think being your own boss means fewer working hours and more money, however, you're likely to be disappointed. Starting your own business means hard work, long hours, and often having to live on less money than you could earn working for someone else. Before you quit a secure job to make the move, study the idea realistically.

You should, of course, know a lot about the type of business you will start. Two other questions affect the homeowner headed in this direction: How will you finance the venture—and, can you make a living?

If financing your new business involves start-up money, as it almost always does, how much risk are you willing to take? If you are expecting temporarily to earn less money, using your house as collateral for a loan is not the answer—you'll have the responsibility of an additional loan payment along with lower income. It is a good idea to keep your family's security separate from your business ambitions. Avoid putting your house at risk.

It is almost impossible not to go into debt when you start a new business that needs start-up money. Of course you should have a bankroll saved up, but if the idea is good enough, your homework well done, and your business plan well presented to impress the banker, you probably wouldn't have to put up your house. A business loan becomes part of the business liability—which *must* be clearly separate from your personal finances.

Some people will decide that going into business is a more important goal than preserving home equity. But before borrowing money and reducing equity in your house, take two important steps:

(1) Research the business you intend to start as thoroughly as possible. Know the competition, all the costs involved, and the amount of money you will need to get it off the ground.

(2) Make sure that your income from other sources or your cash reserve is sufficient to make payments on all your debts, including the extra mortgage payment if you borrow against your home equity.

As long as you're willing to remain in debt, there will always be reasons to sign a new mortgage. A new business might last only a year or two, but a mortgage goes on for 15 years or more. Be sure you keep this in mind.

SHORT-TERM GOALS

A comprehensive plan does not aim only toward achieving goals in the far future. It also makes allowances for financial requirements between now and the deadline for your larger life dreams. If you have plans to build a new house or buy a second home, if you want to take a vacation abroad, or buy a new car, your plan must include a division of income between short-term and long-term demands.

This is a difficult task to imagine if you have done no planning in the past. But just as a long-term goal is reached by combining resources, actions, and a timetable, a short-term goal can be achieved by using the same tools. Set aside a portion of your income to reach all your goals, both long- and short-term. Just be careful not to confuse the two.

TURNING DREAMS INTO REALITIES

How do you take an important dream and turn it into a reality? The most important step, summarized in figure 2-1, is to establish a timetable that will coordinate today's resources with tomorrow's goals.

Let's take an example. Suppose you would like to retire in ten years. The most obvious resource that comes to mind is your current salary, and the income from any investments or other sources you may have. Another resource is your assets—savings and IRAs, rental property, and most important, your equity in your house. List all of these.

Estimate known resources for several years into the future. For example, if part of today's income is going into a savings

FIGURE 2-1
Mapping Out Your Goals

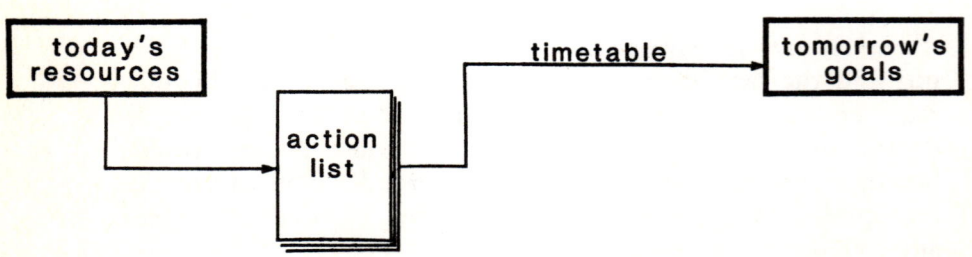

TABLE 2-1

ESTIMATING FINANCIAL RESOURCES

Year	Estimated Income	College Fund	Balance Available
1	$70,000	$4,000	$66,000
2	70,000	4,000	66,000
3	72,000	4,000	68,000
4	72,000	4,000	68,000
5	72,000	0	72,000
6	74,000	0	74,000
7	74,000	0	74,000
8	74,000	0	74,000
9	76,000	0	76,000
10	76,000	0	76,000

account for your children's college education, you know that extra money will be available to you when they have finished college. You can also assume periodic increases in your salary.

Next, you will decide upon what actions you should take to achieve your goal. To retire, you should accumulate money in one or more forms of savings. You will need to consider the effects of income taxes, and you will want to reduce your monthly income requirements enough so that retirement will be affordable.

Accumulating money can take several forms. You can set up an action plan calling for a specific amount to be put into a savings account or a mutual fund each month, for example. If you haven't already, you should investigate IRAs for you and your spouse.

If your interest or dividend income will increase substantially during the next decade, some of your earnings will go toward payment of a higher tax liability.

Your need for monthly income will be reduced in several ways. Once your children are finished with college, you will no longer need to save for college expenses—not to mention food, clothing, and other expenses related to raising a child. Your own requirements may be lower if you no longer need the clothes and transportation related to a job. By planning ahead you can get the mortgage paid off, eliminating monthly mortgage payments.

Imagine, for example, that you have 15 years remaining on your 30-year 12 percent mortgage. You begin a plan to pay it off within 10 years, checking first with your lender to make sure such a plan is allowed by the terms of your contract, and that no prepayment penalties will apply.

If interest rates are lower now than when you took out your loan, it might also make sense to refinance the remaining mortgage for a ten-year term. This and other forms of mortgage acceleration are covered in more detail in chapter 5.

Once resources and actions have been defined, the next step is to establish a timetable. The advantage of a timetable is that it enables you to see immediately whether your goal is a realistic one. For example, if there is simply no way that you can get the money together to retire within ten years, you might have to live with a longer timetable. You won't know, however, until you put it down on paper.

TABLE 2-2

MONTHLY PAYMENTS FOR 10- AND 15-YEAR MORTGAGES

Original Balance	Current Balance	Monthly Payments (10 Years)	(15 Years)
$ 50,000	$42,855	$ 615	$ 514
60,000	51,425	738	617
70,000	59,997	861	720
80,000	68,568	984	823
90,000	77,139	1,107	926
100,000	85,710	1,230	1,029

TABLE 2-3

TIMETABLE: YEARLY SAVINGS AND RETIREMENT PLANS

Year	Savings	Less Taxes	IRA	Total
1	$1,500	$ −525	$4,000	$ 4,975
2	1,500	−525	4,000	4,975
3	1,700	−595	4,000	5,105
4	1,700	−595	4,000	5,105
5	4,500	−1,575	4,000	6,925
6	4,600	−1,600	4,000	7,000
7	4,600	−1,600	4,000	7,000
8	4,600	−1,600	4,000	7,000
9	4,800	−1,900	4,000	6,900
10	4,800	−1,900	4,000	6,900
			Total	$61,885

Tables 2-3 and 2-4 give an example of a ten-year timetable showing yearly savings and retirement plans, and yearly reduction of living expenses. Such a timetable tells you that certain actions must take place at certain times in order for the ten-year plan to work. In this example at the end of the ten years, the following will have been achieved:

- The need to save for college and the need to pay children's living expenses will have ceased.
- In addition to the savings and investments you may already have, you will have accumulated an additional $61,885 plus interest.
- Your yearly living expenses will have been reduced by more than $24,000.
- You will own your house free and clear.

24   Homeowners Money Management

Life dreams are very specific and very individual, but perhaps the best way to understand the process of turning them into realities is to see how somebody else does it. Take the case of Marian Simmons:

Ms. Simmons, age 52, is a widow. For the last ten years she has worked for a manufacturing plant in western Pennsylvania where she earns $1,200 per month. She would like to retire in neighboring Ohio, where she was raised.

When her husband Phil passed away two years ago, Marian received $100,000 from a life insurance policy on his life. With part of this money she paid off the $42,000 still due on the mortgage. Another $12,000 was used to pay off other debts. With the balance of $46,000 invested, and with Marian's salary, she has been able to live comfortably and save her money, while keeping the house.

When she started thinking seriously about going back home, it occurred to her that she could open the pet store she'd always dreamed of owning. So she put her goal down on paper: "I

TABLE 2-4

TIMETABLE: YEARLY REDUCTION OF LIVING EXPENSES

Year	College Savings	Children's Expenses	Home Mortgage	Total Reduction
1	$ 0	$ 0	$ 0	$ 0
2	0	0	0	0
3	0	0	0	0
4	0	0	0	0
5	4,000	0	0	4,000
6	4,000	0	0	4,000
7	4,000	0	0	4,000
8	4,000	0	0	4,000
9	4,000	10,000	0	14,000
10	4,000	10,000	0	14,000
Thereafter	4,000	10,000	10,332	24,332

will buy a small home outside Alliance, Ohio, and open a pet store. I will sell this house and pay all cash for my new house and to start the business."

Marian was surprised at how her resolution became clearer just by writing down these few words. She began to think about the financial possibilities. It could be done. With the equity she and Phil had built up over a lifetime, and the money she'd saved, she would still have enough for a sizable cash reserve. The house was worth $80,000 and Marian's savings added up to $66,000, including the remaining life insurance proceeds. She decided to wait three years. That would give her time to fix up the house and prepare it for sale and start looking into what had to be done to open her pet store.

Marian wrote down a timetable for her goal. It included all the elements necessary: selling her house, finding a new place to live, locating and buying everything she'd need for her new business, and leaving her job.

The schedule was:

- Within 12 months: Research the cost of pet store inventory and locate vendors for supplies.

- Within 18 months: Travel to Alliance to determine available retail space and its cost.

- Within 24 months: Travel to Alliance to view homes and choose preferred living area.

- Within 26 months: Place home on the market.

- Within 30 months: Sign lease on pet store and begin ordering stock for six-month delivery.

- Within 34 months: Complete home sale and resign from job.

- Within 35 months: Purchase new home.

- Within 36 months: Open store.

The planning paid off. She was able to keep to her written timetable once she had a precise and well-focused plan. Knowing what steps were upcoming, Marian scheduled the details. To stock a pet store, she discovered, she would need to invest $15,000 in inventory and spend another $8,000 on permits, business licenses, insurance, and preparation costs. The price of houses in the area in which she was interested ranged between $65,000 and $80,000. The following shows Marian's financial situation.

Available cash:	
Savings	$ 66,000
Proceeds from sale of home (after costs)	75,000
Total	$141,000
Expenses:	
Trips to Ohio	$ 3,000
Investment in pet store	23,000
Cost of new house (after closing costs)	82,000
Living expenses (estimating six months until store is established)	12,000
Total	$120,000
Difference (reserve):	$ 21,000

Marian had a cash savings of $66,000 before going forward with her plan. She had only $21,000 left once the plan was put into action, a reduction of $45,000. But her desire to return to the area where she was raised, and to own a pet store, made the risk worthwhile.

Preparation is the key to making your life dreams happen. You have to be able to visualize the way you would like to live and then execute the steps necessary to get there.

3
DOING THE PLAN

A financial plan is a blueprint for your future. It involves a complete understanding of all aspects of your financial life: building assets, managing debts, increasing your personal net worth, retirement plans, thinking ahead for the tax effect of decisions you make, insurance coverages, and investments.

Financial planning has a lot in common with building a house. First, you decide how many rooms it should have, what materials should be used, where it should be located, and how much money you'll need to build it. Then you draw a very detailed plan, buy materials, and hire workers. Finally, you get down to the business of building it, starting at the foundation and working your way up.

The last chapter dealt with the most important requirement, the definition of personal life dreams. This chapter deals with the construction of a personal financial plan to help realize those dreams. This is the phase where you match goals and plans with financial resources, where the techniques of managing cash and investments are decided, and where insurance requirements are added. A timetable for each step turns your life dreams into completed financial structures.

Successful plans start with a thorough summary of financial priorities. The more you understand about your financial status and the importance of your home equity, the better able you are to formulate the plan.

The first step is to write down a list of basic financial questions and answers. Writing down your answers forces you to think them through.

- In what year will you own your home free and clear?
- By what year *would you like* to own your home?
- What future events in your life will require large sums of available cash?
- By what age do you plan to retire?
- What type of home would you like to live in when you do retire?
- How will your built-up equity be used when retirement arrives?
- If you could retire today, how much money would you need per month to pay the bills?

THE PLANNING PROCESS

The first step (see chapter 2) is a clear and precise understanding of goals, or life dreams. If this plan were a house, that would be the stage in which you decide how large the house will be, where it will be located, and how many rooms it should have. In other words, the blueprint.

Once goals are clear, the specifications must be laid out. In a financial plan, these include control and growth of home equity, savings, future expenses, income taxes, insurance, investments, and provisions for retirement.

The specifications conclude with a timetable, the equivalent of the materials—the nuts and bolts.

With blueprint, specifications, and materials at hand, you are ready to build.

Once a house is built, it can be painted different colors, rooms can be added, and other changes made. A financial plan can also change from time to time, as your circumstances and goals evolve. Flexibility is an important element. The three steps are summarized in figure 3-1.

Two elements every homeowner should understand before preparing a financial plan are safety and risk. Both must be considered carefully as you develop your financial plan.

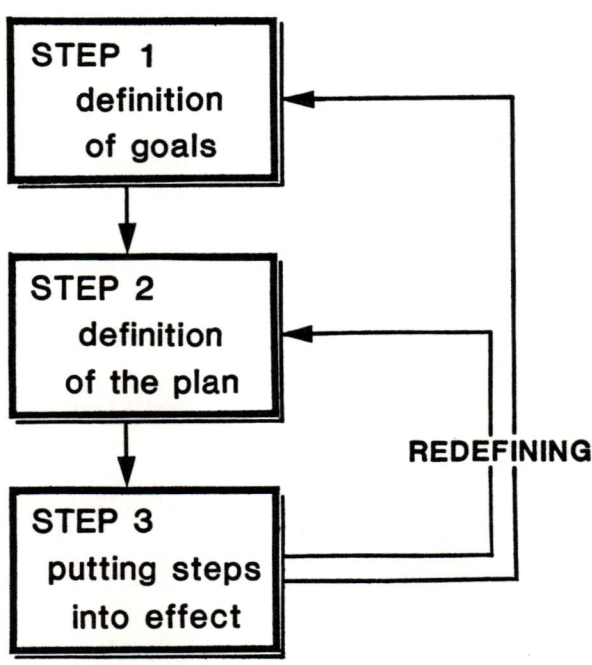

FIGURE 3-1
Reaching Your Goals

THE CONCEPT OF SAFETY

Before you proceed with an actual financial plan, decide how much safety you want and need in your life. The reckless speculator is willing to play the odds. He carries little or no insurance, doesn't look ahead to the far future, and takes chances with money. At the other extreme, the superconservative homeowner takes as little risk as possible, preferring to limit goals rather than risk not reaching them.

Somewhere between these extremes, you can find a comfortable safety level. Here are six rules of thumb for homeowners' financial safety:

(1) Earning income: The word *safety* has its own meaning in the investing world. A "safe" investment is one that will yield a return without decreasing the value of your money, even after income taxes and inflation. A sound investment will earn money for you. Savings accounts are credited with interest, and stocks yield dividends. Your house grows in value over the years, a form of income you can realize when you sell.

(2) Protecting capital: To reduce or eliminate the risk of losing money, seek investments that will grow or, in the worst case, maintain their value.

(3) Maintaining liquidity: You should be able to get your money back from an investment when you want and need it. If you have all of your funds tied up and an emergency arises, you have a problem. Home equity is an example of an *illiquid* investment—you can't simply remove cash as you can from a savings account.

(4) Meeting inflation: Investments should keep pace with the rising cost of living. So investments that give you low interest or dividends and have no potential for growth lose real value over time. If the annual inflation rate is only 3 percent, every dollar you have today will be worth only 54 cents in 20 years.

(5) Minimizing taxes: Your earnings are reduced by income taxes. A "safe" investment will not emphasize tax sheltering above everything else, but you can include protection against taxes with your investments. One advantage is that earnings in IRAs are not taxed. You are not taxed on the market value of your house.

(6) Having insurance: Your life insurance protects the equity in your house. In the event of a wage earner's death, insurance proceeds can be used to pay off a mortgage (see chapter 6). A federally insured bank or savings and loan carries insurance on each account (FDIC and FSLIC). Brokerage accounts are insured by the Securities Investors Protection Corporation (SIPC). United States Treasury securities, considered the safest of all investments, are backed by the "full faith and credit" of the United States. Even with large federal deficits, the United States government owns vast assets in land and resources and has never defaulted on its debts.

THE ELEMENT OF RISK

How much risk are you willing to take with your money? We all have a limit at which we are comfortable, beyond which we feel that we are taking too much risk. Financial planners call this limit *risk tolerance*.

Safety and risk are unavoidably related. The high risk taker may ignore important safety features to chase after a single goal. He may look for high income without protecting capital, or he may seek tax-free income that has no liquidity or insurance protection. The low risk taker attempts to insure against any form of loss. As a result, inflation may overcome investment earnings, and capital may deteriorate over the years.

The elements of risk also can be summarized and compared with those of safety:

(1) Earning income: Earning as much as you can, and compounding your earnings over time, is desirable—but the higher a potential yield, the greater the risk.

(2) Protecting capital: You need to ensure that your investment dollars do not decline in value. If you put funds into a volatile stock, for example, and the price drops from $40 per share to $20 per share, you have lost half your capital. You need to establish a bail-out point, a price at which you will sell in order to cut losses before they become extreme.

(3) Maintaining liquidity: If you do not keep a reserve of cash for emergencies, you can get into a bind. You may risk having to sell other investments in order to meet cash needs, and you will probably lose money. For safety, do not place money into long-term investments until you have established a reserve. Many experts suggest that this should be equal to three to six months' take-home pay.

(4) Meeting inflation: You risk loss of value if your investment is overly conservative. If your yield is 4 percent, inflation is 3 percent, and your tax bracket is 35 percent (federal and state combined), you are losing money. The following shows this in regard to $1,000:

Amount invested	$1,000
4% yield	40
Less: income taxes (35% of 40)	−14
After-tax yield	26
Net	1,026
Less: inflation (3%)	−30
Final value	$ 996

The higher the inflation rate, the more risk you will incur in order to stay ahead. Traditionally, home ownership beats inflation.

(5) Minimizing taxes: You can see from the example above that you also risk losing investment value to income taxes. For many people, this leads to risking more in investment selection, which also exposes you to other forms of risk. In higher tax brackets, tax-free investments like municipal bonds make sense. This risk can also be lessened by investing in an IRA, where taxes may be deferred until you withdraw the money.

(6) Having insurance: Without protection from unexpected losses, your entire financial plan can fall apart. You risk loss when you do not have enough life, disability, health, liability, and casualty insurance. All of these forms of coverage give you safety against potentially catastrophic losses.

The purpose of understanding risk is to decide what type of investor you are. By buying a house, you take risks, but they're low. Apply the six-feature test to every investment you make.

AN EXAMPLE OF A PLAN

In "Financial Plan for Robert and Fran Maher" on pages 36 to 57, these tests are applied to a number of different investments embodied in an example of a financial plan. The income and asset level is above that of the average American family so that a wide range of options could be included. For many families, the plan will be much less involved. Following the example, suggestions are given for those whose income and assets are lower.

The plan follows a logical sequence. First are the definition sections, identifying whose plan it is, goal statements and priorities, available resources, and a clear statement identifying risk and safety standards. Next are the elements to be covered by the plan. Last is the summary of the plan, with a schedule and timetable.

THE SAFETY AND RISK TEST

Take this test with your spouse. Separately, rate each of six safety categories from 1 to 10. A 1 gives that aspect of safety a low priority. A 10 gives it a very high priority.

Earning income	1 2 3 4 5 6 7 8 9 10
Protecting capital	1 2 3 4 5 6 7 8 9 10
Maintaining liquidity	1 2 3 4 5 6 7 8 9 10
Meeting inflation	1 2 3 4 5 6 7 8 9 10
Minimizing taxes	1 2 3 4 5 6 7 8 9 10
Having insurance	1 2 3 4 5 6 7 8 9 10

How far apart are you and your spouse? If you have widely different responses, it's time to sit down and discuss safety/risk factors and come to an agreement. Where are you willing to take high risks? In what respects do you want and need to adopt a safer stance?

FINANCIAL PLAN FOR ROBERT AND FRAN MAHER

The purpose of a financial plan is very simple: You define a few critical goals, dreams that you hold for your life, and then you map out a procedure for achieving them.

Of course, there are several financial matters to consider as part of the plan. These include things like insurance protection and making allowances for future expenses. Without them, the reality of your family situation can interfere with the successful achievement of your primary goals. For example, without adequate insurance an unexpected loss could ruin you financially. Or because you fail to plan for your children's college education the money may not be available by the time you need it.

Figure 3-2 shows the essential purpose of a plan. It includes a series of well-defined goals. You will see exactly how

FIGURE 3-2
Financial Plan Overview

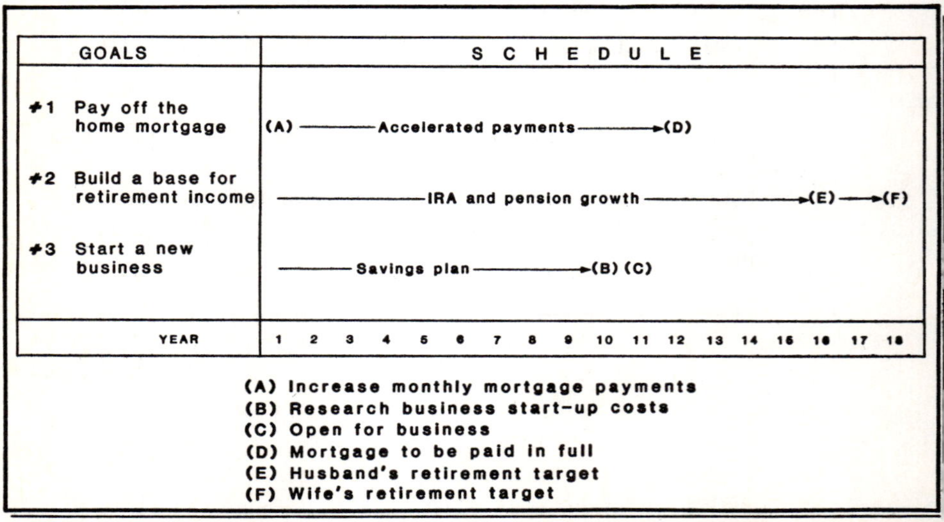

GOALS	SCHEDULE
#1 Pay off the home mortgage	(A) ———— Accelerated payments ————▶(D)
#2 Build a base for retirement income	———————— IRA and pension growth ————————▶(E)——▶(F)
#3 Start a new business	———— Savings plan ————▶(B) (C)
YEAR	1 2 3 4 5 6 7 8 9 10 11 12 13 14 15 16 17 18

(A) Increase monthly mortgage payments
(B) Research business start-up costs
(C) Open for business
(D) Mortgage to be paid in full
(E) Husband's retirement target
(F) Wife's retirement target

FIGURE 3-3

Sections of a Plan

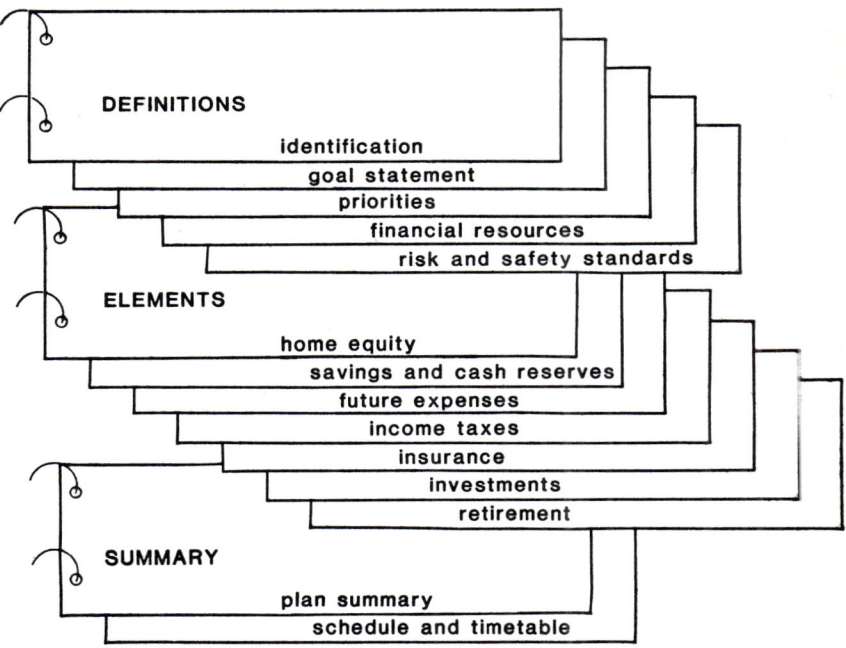

these primary goals are planned for and protected in the full plan that follows.

Meet the Mahers. Robert and Fran are in their forties. They have three children and two jobs. Robert is an engineer and Fran is a loan officer. Together they have mapped out the details of their lives over the next 18 years. Their three primary goals are to pay off their home mortgage earlier than the mortgage contract specifies, to ensure an adequate retirement income, and to start Fran's own business.

A number of points must be addressed in their plan. They will be required to change their investments to match the new definitions they have given to their financial goals. They will need to set money aside for college. And they will need to reexamine their insurance policies and make changes tailored to the plan.

The Mahers have more money than most Americans do, so they have a range of financial options open to them. By following their planning process, however, those with more money and those with less money may see opportunities for their own plan.

SECTION I: DEFINITIONS

Identification:

Date of plan: March 10, 1987

	Name	Age
Husband	Robert J. Maher	44
Wife	Frances A. Maher	42
Address	380 Tenth Street Dallas, Texas	

	Occupation	Employer
Robert	Engineer	Bradley and Speck, Inc.
Fran	Loan officer	Harmon Savings and Loan

	Name	Age
Children	Robert, Jr.	14
	David	12
	Susan	9

Statement of Goals and Priorities

Preliminary definition questions:

1. In what year will you own your home free and clear? *2007*

2. By what year *would you like* to own your home? *1999*

3. What future events in your life will require large sums of available cash? _College tuition and starting Fran's own business_

4. By what age do you plan to retire? _60 (both Robert and Fran)_

5. What type of home would you like to live in when you do retire? _Present house_

6. How will your built-up equity be used when retirement arrives? _Preserved—not to be touched for any reason_

7. If you could retire today, how much money would you need per month to pay the bills? _$4,200_

Statement of goals:

Goal 1: Free and clear ownership of residence at 380 Tenth Street by Robert's 56th birthday

Goal 2: Retirement income and elimination of all debts by Robert's 60th birthday

Goal 3: Open a party planning business within 11 years

Financial Resources

Income:

Robert's annual salary	$38,400
Fran's annual salary	33,600
Investment income	4,400
Total annual income	$76,400
Total assets	$283,710
Total liabilities	100,660
Net personal worth	$183,050

FIGURE 3-4
Robert and Fran Maher's Balance Sheet

ASSETS	
Cash	$ 2,500
Personal property	34,800
Stamp collection	4,000
Art collection	8,000
Automobile	13,100
Investments:	
Savings account	15,000
Stocks	22,000
Mutual fund	18,000
Retirement accounts:	
Husband's IRA	10,450
Wife's IRA	8,300
Husband's pension (estimate)	15,060
Wife's pension (estimate)	22,500
Residence	110,000
Total assets	**$283,710**
LIABILITIES	
Bills due	$ 3,250
Auto loan	9,410
Personal loan	16,000
Home mortgage	72,000
Total liabilities	$100,660
NET WORTH	**$183,050**
Total liabilities and net worth	$283,710

Risk and Safety Standards

Earning income:

Priority 1: Keep house free from debt to avoid paying interest and depleting profits
Priority 2: Improve average earnings from other investments

Protecting capital:

Priority 1: Reduce interest expense by paying off mortgage earlier than terms require
Priority 2: Use investment assets to maintain earnings and flexibility

Maintaining liquidity:

Priority 1: Reduce liquid assets from $55,000 to $27,000

Meeting inflation:

Priority 1: Maintain accounts expected to outperform annual inflation (house and mutual fund)
Priority 2: Reduce or eliminate other assets (savings and stocks)

Minimizing taxes:

Priority 1: Invest maximum allowed in IRAs (if available under current law)
Priority 2: Gift income to children for college education, reducing taxable income for parents

Having insurance:

Priority 1: Increase Fran's life insurance
Priority 2: Maintain present life, disability, health, and homeowner's policies, as well as insured investments

SECTION II: ELEMENTS
Home Equity

Current loan balance	$72,000
Years to pay off	20
Interest rate	13.5%
Monthly payments	$824.70

Alternatives:

Years to Pay Off	Monthly Payments
19	$ 878.56
18	889.38
17	902.07
16	917.05
15	934.80
14	955.96
13	981.36
12	1,012.76
11	1,049.76
10	1,096.39

Mahers' modified plan:

Years to pay off	11
Monthly payments	$1,049.76

Savings and Cash Reserves

	Current Status	Change	New Status
Savings account	$15,000	$ −8,000	$ 7,000
Stocks	22,000	−22,000	0
Mutual fund	18,000	0	18,000
Treasury bills	0	30,000	30,000
Total	$55,000		$55,000

Future Expenses

Year	College Expenses	New Business	Accumulated Total
5	$ 5,000		$ 5,000
6	5,000		10,000
7	10,000		20,000
8	10,000		30,000
9	10,000		40,000
10	15,000		55,000
11	15,000	$20,000	90,000
12	15,000		105,000
13	10,000		115,000
14	10,000		125,000
15	5,000		130,000
16	5,000		135,000
17	5,000		140,000

Income Taxes

Year	Transfers to Children	IRA Deposits
5	$ 5,000	$4,000
6	5,000	4,000
7	10,000	4,000
8	10,000	4,000
9	10,000	4,000
10	15,000	4,000
11	15,000	4,000
12	15,000	4,000
13	10,000	4,000
14	10,000	4,000
15	5,000	4,000
16	5,000	4,000
17	5,000	4,000

Insurance

Life insurance:

	Current Status	New Status
Robert	$200,000	$200,000
Fran	100,000	200,000

Disability insurance:

	Current Status	New Status
Robert	$3,000/mo.	$3,000/mo.
Fran	0	3,000/mo.

Group health:

No change

Homeowner's insurance:

	Current Status	New Status
House value	$100,000	$100,000
Contents	50,000	65,000
Stamp and art collections	0	12,000

Investments

Present assets:

Cash	$ 2,500
Personal property	34,800
Stamp collection	4,000
Art collection	8,000
Automobile	13,100
Investments:	
Savings account	15,000
Stocks	22,000
Mutual fund	18,000
Retirement accounts:	
Husband's IRA	10,450
Wife's IRA	8,300
Husband's pension (estimate)	15,060
Wife's pension (estimate)	22,500
Residence	110,000
Total	$283,710

Planned assets:

	Timing	Value
House (assuming 5% increase in value per year)	17 yrs.	$252,000
Robert's IRA	16 yrs.	113,435
Fran's IRA	18 yrs.	128,737
Personal investments	18 yrs.	140,000
Personal belongings	18 yrs.	100,000
Stamp and art collections	18 yrs.	50,000
Total		$784,172

Retirement

Robert's IRA: Present value $10,450

Year	Annual Deposit	Interest (9%)	Balance
1	$2,000	$1,121	$ 13,571
2	2,000	1,401	16,972
3	2,000	1,707	20,679
4	2,000	2,041	24,720
5	2,000	2,405	29,125
6	2,000	2,801	33,926
7	2,000	3,233	39,159
8	2,000	3,704	44,863
9	2,000	4,218	51,081
10	2,000	4,777	57,858
11	2,000	5,387	65,245
12	2,000	6,052	73,297
13	2,000	6,777	82,074
14	2,000	7,567	91,641
15	2,000	8,428	102,069
16	2,000	9,366	113,435

SECTION III: SUMMARY

Schedule and Timetable

Year	Scheduled Action
1988	Increase mortgage payment from $824.70 to $1,049.76 per month
	Increase Fran's life insurance from $100,000 to $200,000
	New disability policy for Fran, with a monthly benefit of $3,000

Fran's IRA: Present value $8,300

Year	Annual Deposit	Interest (9%)	Balance
1	$2,000	$ 824	$ 11,124
2	2,000	1,181	14,305
3	2,000	1,467	17,772
4	2,000	1,779	21,551
5	2,000	2,120	25,671
6	2,000	2,490	30,161
7	2,000	2,894	35,055
8	2,000	3,335	40,390
9	2,000	3,815	46,205
10	2,000	4,338	52,543
11	2,000	4,909	59,452
12	2,000	5,531	66,983
13	2,000	6,208	75,191
14	2,000	6,947	84,138
15	2,000	7,752	93,890
16	2,000	8,630	104,520
17	2,000	9,587	116,107
18	2,000	10,630	128,737

	Increase homeowner's insurance coverage
	New insurance policy on Robert's stamp collection and Fran's art collection
	Reduce savings to $7,000
	Sell stock holdings
	Open a money market fund
	Invest $30,000 in Treasury bills
	Start college savings plan for Robert, Jr.
1990	Start college savings plan for David

1992   Tuition expense begins for Robert, Jr.
1993   Start college savings plan for Susan
1994   Tuition expense begins for David
1997   Fran: research costs to open business and price shop space
        Tuition expense begins for Susan
1998   Fran to resign her job
        Open party planning business
1999   Free and clear ownership of house
2003   Robert's retirement
        Begin IRA withdrawals
        Receive company pension benefits
2005   Fran's retirement
        Begin IRA withdrawals (possible delay)
        Receive company pension benefits

EXPLANATION OF PLAN
Statement of Goals and Priorities

Robert and Fran have three goals. They want to be free from mortgage payments within the next 11 years. Robert wants to retire from his job by age 60. Fran intends to open her own business.

These three goals involve conflicting requirements. Early full ownership of the house will mean committing money to higher mortgage payments, money that otherwise could be used for either of the other two goals. Retirement by age 60 means a definite limit on future resources for income. And a new business will need start-up capital. In other words, if all three goals are to be realized, a good job of coordination and control must be put into effect.

Because the requirements for each goal are different, a long-range plan should specify deadlines:

Priority	Goal	Deadline
1	Home ownership	1999
2	Retirement income	2003 (Robert)
		2005 (Fran)
3	New business	1999

Financial Resources

The Maher family has $55,000 invested in a savings account, stocks, and a mutual fund.

Both husband and wife put money into an Individual Retirement Account each year. Each also has a pension plan where they work. The total of these assets is $56,310.

The house at 380 Tenth Street has a current market value of $110,000. Total assets add up to a total of $283,710.

The family owes $28,660 in bills and auto and personal loans, and is obligated for a $72,000 mortgage on their house. Their personal net worth (assets less liabilities) is $183,050.

Risk and Safety Standards

Earning income: The Maher home is expected to appreciate in value an average of 5 percent per year. Average earnings from savings, stocks, and mutual fund investments are 8 percent.

Protecting capital: The Maher family has as its first objective full ownership of the house. They view it as their most important asset. They would be justified in paying off the home mortgage sooner than required by the agreed term. The interest rate on the mortgage is 13.5 percent, while their invested funds are earning only 8 percent.

Twenty years remain on the Maher's 30-year mortgage. The monthly payments are $824.70. The Mahers want to pay off the mortgage balance within 11 years. There is no prepayment penalty in the mortgage agreement. They will increase monthly payments to $1,049.76 per month, to pay off the entire balance by 1999.

The average yield of 8 percent on their investments is acceptable to the Maher family. However, the rate could be improved somewhat without sacrificing liquidity or capital protection by shifting a portion of their savings and stocks to other investments.

Maintaining liquidity: There is a balance of $55,000 in highly liquid accounts. This is more liquidity than the family requires. Robert and Fran Maher can afford to reduce their level of liquidity without reducing their capital protection. They should keep approximately $27,000 in available funds (six months after-tax income) and can reinvest the balance elsewhere.

The additional $225 monthly mortgage payment will reduce the amount (an average $500 per month) that the Mahers have been putting into their savings account.

Meeting inflation: The value of the Maher house is expected to grow at a higher rate than the consumer price index. Savings accounts and stocks will not keep pace, in the Mahers' opinion. Their mutual fund investment has outperformed the inflation rate in the past.

Minimizing taxes: The family earns a high taxable income and pays approximately $18,000 per year in income taxes. Both Robert and Fran have opened IRAs and deposit as much as they are allowed per year. In the past, this reduced taxable income. Even without that deduction, though, both plan to keep their IRAs in force and deposit the maximum each year.

Having insurance: The Maher home is insured against casualty and liability. The family carries life, disability, and health policies. Their savings account is protected by federal insurance, and both IRAs are in institutions also carrying insurance protection. Stocks and mutual funds are not insured.

Home Equity

If the Mahers find themselves in a situation where current rates are lower than what they're paying, they should refinance their house to take advantage of lower interest payments. This could advance their timetable. See chapter 5.

Savings and Cash Reserves

The savings account and the mutual fund are the Mahers' cash reserve, representing approximately six months' income.

Savings, stock investments, and mutual fund investments have been supplemented at the rate of $10,000 per year, from the following sources:

Savings deposited	$6,000 per year
Interest and dividends	$4,000 per year

Before structuring their mortgage acceleration plan, the Mahers were saving $500 per month. Now, $250 of that money will go toward mortgage payments. The remaining money will be placed in the mutual fund account. The current mutual fund balance is $18,000. This is the highest yielding of the three investments, averaging 10 percent per year return.

At 6 percent, savings are the lowest yielding investment the Mahers have. So the savings account will be reduced from the present level of $15,000 to $7,000, to be held as an immediate source for emergency cash, and no additional deposits will be made.

Stock investments totaling $22,000 will be sold and, along with $8,000 from the savings account, the funds will be reinvested in three-month Treasury bills (T-bills). These are considered among the safest investments possible, and they yield an acceptable return compared with savings accounts and the stock market. The minimum initial investment required is $10,000, less discounts to reflect the current interest rate. The Mahers plan to place $10,000 in T-bills in three consecutive months. In this way, maturity will occur on some bills every month, once the program is in effect. Each bill will be reinvested as it matures.

Earnings from T-bills and other available cash will be placed in a newly opened money market account, which pays higher interest. The fund itself is not insured, but the majority of investments made by the fund are in institutions carrying federal insurance.

This gives the Mahers more than enough liquidity and a better level of income. It should be noted that investments considered "liquid" by the Maher family are limited to their mutual funds, stocks, and savings account. They do not consider T-bills to be liquid, even though they will be converted to cash every three months.

The Mahers continue to view their home as their best investment and their IRAs as their base retirement accounts. Their other holdings are sources for meeting future expenses.

Future Expenses

The Mahers want to put aside money for two major future expenses. First is Fran's new business, expected to require $20,000 of initial capital by the 11th year from the beginning of the plan. This is a fairly straightforward requirement.

The cost of college educations for each of their three children, anticipated for the fifth, seventh, and tenth years, is not so easy to estimate. The Mahers have made several assumptions:

(1) Each child's college education will cost $40,000 over a four-year period. This is admittedly less than enough for some universities and may be well under actual costs.

(2) While in college, each child will be expected to work to pay a portion of the total cost of schooling.

(3) The cost may be reduced if one or more of the children decides not to attend college, if part of the time is spent in a community college where costs are lower, or if funding is supplemented or replaced with a scholarship.

Even with the relatively high family income, the three children will be of college age in quick succession, and the Mahers have budgeted for what they believe they can afford. The expenditure will fall on the following schedule:

Year	Robert	David	Susan	Total
5	$10,000			$ 10,000
6	10,000			10,000
7	10,000	$10,000		20,000
8	10,000	10,000		20,000
9		10,000		10,000
10		10,000	$10,000	20,000
11			10,000	10,000
12			10,000	10,000
13			10,000	10,000
Total cost to the family				$120,000

Based on current savings, it is possible to achieve both goals—college, and the new business. With savings, plus earnings on their existing balance of $55,000, there is enough of a base.

Income Taxes

Because their combined income is high, the Mahers pay $18,000 per year in income taxes. It would be more, without the interest deduction for their house.

Both Robert and Fran have been paying into IRAs, reducing their taxable income by $4,000 per year. If future tax laws forbid this deduction, it will have a tax consequence, but Robert and Fran would like to keep their IRAs in effect.

The tax situation will be more severe once the mortgage has been paid down. As the plan progresses, interest deductions will become less substantial while income levels remain high.

They could reduce this burden to some degree by transferring funds for college to their children directly. Making such gifts produces no tax advantage in itself, but the money can be invested and taxed at the children's lower income tax level, subject to age limits and earning levels.

This raises the possibility of establishing trust funds, and the Mahers realize that they will need professional help in deciding upon the tax savings and the technicalities of this move.

The tax burden could be reduced even further by seeking tax-free investments (see chapter 15). However, it is more important to the family to maintain their comfort with risk levels, especially for the liquidity of their funds. They have some hefty expenses coming up during the next few years, and this is not the time to abandon a sensible plan simply to escape from taxes.

The Mahers have concluded that they will live with their tax level for several years, expecting relief when Fran starts her new business. At that time, the family's income will be reduced temporarily.

Insurance

The Mahers carry insurance on both lives, $200,000 for Robert and $100,000 for Fran. They plan to increase Fran's coverage to equal Robert's by adding another $100,000.

Robert carries a disability insurance policy through his employer. The group plan will pay him $3,000 per month if he is permanently and totally disabled. Fran does not have disability insurance. She plans to take out a policy that would pay benefits of $3,000 per month. They have decided that a mortgage disability policy is not necessary.

The entire family is covered under group health insurance plans offered by both Robert's and Fran's employers.

The Mahers reviewed their homeowner's policy. It insures the house for $100,000 and its contents for $50,000. They are upgrading coverage, getting rid of their actual cash value insurance on contents that pays only the depreciated value of lost property, and buying replacement value insurance that pays to replace anything lost, in full. Coverage of the contents of the house is being increased to $65,000. The reasoning: The premiums are not much more for this additional coverage, and the Mahers want to be sure they have covered all possible losses. They plan to review their homeowner's coverage every two years.

Other insurance: Robert has a stamp collection valued at $4,000 and Fran collects original art—paintings and limited edition prints. Her collection was worth $8,000 at last appraisal.

For these, a special policy is required. After updated appraisals of each collection, the Mahers plan to acquire additional policies.

Investments

The Mahers are satisfied that their house is the most important investment they have. It grows in value every year at a healthy rate, and none of that growth is taxed. They have invested in the stock market in the past, with poor results.

Their mutual fund and T-Bill investments, supplemented by a local savings account and a money market fund, meet their liquidity and investment income requirements. They assume that salary increases they receive at work will keep pace with inflation.

Upon payment of their mortgage and the children's completion of college, the Mahers will have an additional $1,000 per month to invest. At that time, they will revise their plan for managing investments. Their current thinking is that investments beyond 1998 should be oriented toward their retirement. Accordingly, they will probably seek a high level of capital protection and liquidity.

Retirement

The Mahers have three sources for retirement income: their IRAs, their company pension plans, and Social Security. They will continue to put the maximum allowed into their IRAs each year. When Fran starts her new business, she will also open a Keogh account, in which she will be allowed to place up to 25 percent of her net earnings from self-employment (under current rules). This will substantially increase her retirement income.

Both Robert and Fran will qualify for Social Security and their corporate pension plan benefits by the time they are 65. IRA proceeds can be withdrawn after their sixtieth birthdays.

Robert began his IRA four years ago and its present value is $10,450. It has earned more than 10 percent, but is earning 9 percent now at a local savings and loan. He estimates that at the current rate it will be worth $113,435 in 16 years, his target retirement date.

Fran has had her IRA for three years, invested in a different savings and loan. Her yield is 9 percent. Her current rate, if continued until retirement, will produce an account worth $128,737. Although Fran's current balance is lower than Robert's, she will fund the account for two years longer.

The use of funds during retirement will be the subject of later revisions to the plan. Until then, the Mahers intend to follow this course of action:

VARIATIONS ON A PLAN

In the Mahers' case, clearly understood goals will be reached. The plan is developed from broad ideas, with details filled in. A concise series of steps leads toward the goals. As a result of preparing the plan, the family has improved its insurance coverage, shifted savings to reduce taxes and improve earnings, and the major life dreams of Robert and Fran have become clear, reachable realities.

A financial plan can serve other purposes. For example, if a family has problems meeting their expenses each month, the most immediate problem would be to devise ways to improve cash flow. In that case, a different orientation would be given to the plan.

Families with less income and fewer resources perhaps have a more urgent need for financial planning than the Mahers do. With less available, there is less flexibility—but the ultimate goal, realization of life dreams, can still be achieved. Such plans should emphasize these sections:

(1) The equity in their house will not be used under any circumstances.

(2) Fran will continue to operate her business indefinitely, probably on a reduced schedule after her 60th birthday.

(3) The Mahers plan to support themselves from their IRA proceeds, combined with income from their pensions and Social Security.

(1) Insurance: You need protection from unexpected and catastrophic loss of income and earning power, as well as the effects and expenses of ill health or personal liability.

(2) Savings: You need to make the most of money available to you.

(3) Retirement: This is a critical planning section for every family. Plan to deposit the maximum possible in an IRA, especially if you have no other foreseeable retirement plan.

(4) Housing: You can realize profits and use equity as the foundation for financial security upon retirement. Plan to pay off your mortgage by your intended retirement date.

Some realities must be faced when budgets are tight and income is limited:

- A mortgage acceleration plan will not always be possible. An emergency cash reserve is more important and should be set up before entering into any accelerated payments.
- Future expenses may have lower priorities if other considerations are more important. Children's college educations may depend in part on low-interest college loans and summer jobs.
- A number of insurance policies are essential. It is a mistake to drop insurance coverage you need, although many families do just that when money is tight.
- Investment opportunities are limited by the amount of cash you have available.

Before they mapped out a formal financial plan, the Mahers assumed they would meet their future expenses and accomplish their family goals from their accumulated savings. In doing the plan they could foresee a number of possible problems and opportunities. Now, using the information they gained from the plan, they have reduced risks and taxes, adjusted their liquidity level, and provided a plan to meet their three goals.

Financial decisions are difficult to make, and there's a possibility that the Maher family would benefit from hiring an expert to advise them in insurance, investments, or retirement planning. Now that they have a workable plan, their next step should be to discover what choices are available to them to make the plan a reality.

FINANCIAL PLANNING PUBLICATIONS

The International Association for Financial Planning (2 Concourse Parkway, Suite 800, Atlanta, GA 30328) publishes several useful booklets. Ask for:

A Consumer Guide to Total Financial Independence
Building a Capital Base
The Code of Professional Ethics
Ethics: Issues and Answers

The Institute of Certified Financial Planners (2 Denver Highlands, 10065 East Harvard Avenue, Suite 320, Denver, CO 80231-5942) publishes a code of ethics for professional financial planners. It is especially helpful in selection of an outside adviser.

4
THE HOMEOWNER'S EDGE—PUTTING THE PLAN TO WORK

The most important element of a homeowner's economic system is the value of the home. Of that, the amount that the homeowner actually owns, free and clear, is the key to his or her ability to control an economic destiny. That amount is called *equity*.

Consider how much of your financial plan is affected by this single element. Savings, investments, liquidity, insurance, and taxes are all linked to decisions you make today concerning how you build and preserve home equity. Retirement and the ability to live in a house free of debt are also matters of equity.

Equity represents the total value of your home, except for the amount you owe to your lenders. It is the sum of your down payment, the value of improvements you've made, the amount you have paid on your mortgage, and—most significant—the increase in value that results from growth in the value of real estate.

HOW EQUITY GROWS

As a homeowner, you acquire equity in four ways: your down payment, improvements you make, paying off your mortgage, and increases in market value.

A typical example over ten years:

Purchase price $29,400, with $3,000 down payment	$ 3,000
Second mortgage of $3,000, paid off in three years	3,000
Market value: currently $120,000 less original $29,400	90,600
Amount paid off against original $23,400 mortgage	2,800
Equity after ten years	$99,400

The current value—$120,000—is part equity, part debt. Your equity, or the share of the value that actually belongs to you, is $99,400. The balance of $20,600 (first mortgage of $23,400 less the amount paid off of $2,800) is the amount you owe on the house, or your debt.

Do you remember buying your first home? Chances are, you weren't sure whether or not you'd made a wise investment. But if you're like most people, it turned out to be one of the smartest moves you could have made.

It is doubtful that building equity was an primary motivation when you began to look for a house. I know there were more immediate purposes occupying my thoughts when I made the big move. The excitement and pride of ownership coupled with knowing exactly what my monthly housing costs would be were my major reasons for buying a home. Having a place I could fix up any way I wanted was another.

But real estate grows in value, especially in a good, clean, safe neighborhood where property is cared for and improved over the years. I bought my first house in 1972, at the price of $29,400. I felt uneasy about it then, because I had wanted to spend no more than $25,000. It also irritated me that I had to pay 7.5 percent interest for my mortgage.

Things have changed. Home values have risen from 200 to 500 percent and my fears have vanished. The original idea was to make payments of $161 per month (more than I thought I could afford at the time) for 30 years, amassing value—equity—of $29,400 over the same period of time. That would be the foundation for retirement, or a down payment on a more spacious home.

Along with millions of other homeowners I discovered that the days of modest increases in property values had ended, at least temporarily. In the ten years that followed, values skyrocketed. Interest rates jumped, too. The fixed-rate mortgage at 7.5 percent took on a new appearance—to me, and to the savings and loan institution that granted it. The lender has since offered me "instant cash" and attractive rates if only I'll refinance that mortgage (of course, at a higher rate of interest).

Most people—even homeowners—don't truly understand the power of equity. It may not be apparent when homeowners move into their first homes because it takes several years for equity to become a substantial force. Then it dawns upon them slowly that they actually hold value, real value based on tangible and marketable property.

Every homeowner learns to appreciate that special edge. Inflation works for you. Rising real estate values increase your assets seemingly by magic. Lending institutions court your attention. And goals that seem to you to be worth pursuing come closer and closer to reality as your equity grows.

It's not only a change in interest rates that prompts a lender to make offers. It's also the value currently residing in a home. My original mortgage was only $26,000, but now my equity is suddenly over $100,000. A few years before, I was a renter with no assets to speak of. I now have tremendous borrowing power, which means I have financial flexibility.

BUILDING EQUITY

The real estate cycle is not always on the rise, and inflation cannot be depended upon in the future to add equity consistently. During periods of growth like that in the middle to late 1970s, just about everyone holding property made money. In 1985, a decade later, the real estate market was depressed. At such times, the homeowner must be willing to wait out the cycle while the equity that resides in market value builds slowly or not at all. For example, by 1986 the situation had improved.

The most likely way for a homeowner to accumulate real working capital is through the careful long-term nurturing of home equity. There are alternatives. You may gather a comfortable retirement fund through a company pension or profit-sharing plan, combined with an Individual Retirement Account. For those who are self-employed, there is the Keogh plan. But anyone who is able to hold onto a home—and to the value created as home equity grows over time—will have a definite advantage.

Building value as quickly as possible is a wise policy. The more rapidly you are able to increase your home's value, the greater the strength of your financial plan.

If you understand how value builds, you will see how it can be directed, managed, and made into a working asset, part of a personal plan designed by you and for your own best interests.

There are four primary methods:

DOWN PAYMENT

Lenders insist—at least in traditional financing arrangements—that you have a financial interest, a stake, in keeping your home. Thus, you were required to put up some of your own money, the initial down payment, before they would lend you more.

The down payment demonstrates your intention to maintain your property. Buying a house would be much easier than it is if you didn't need that down payment, but it assures the lender that you will be concerned, both with the condition of your property and the protection of your initial equity.

If you buy a house for $80,000, putting down 20 percent ($16,000), and the house increases in value to $100,000, your initial equity more than doubles in value. This can occur in some market conditions in five years or less. Your original $16,000 has become $36,000—a profitable investment.

IMPROVEMENTS

The second way to make equity grow is through improvements to the property. Additional rooms, a second floor, a swimming pool—a quality improvement adds to equity. If that improvement is financed by borrowing—taking out an additional mortgage—you use the equity you already have in your home as collateral for that second mortgage, making an investment toward acquiring more equity. There's no need to prove your credit beyond the value of your existing equity. This is a substantial edge, one that few other forms of investment can give you.

A second bathroom, a new and modernized kitchen, or an extra room are likely to add value to your home. But some improvements are less valuable. Swimming pools, for example, might take value away from your property if the cost of maintenance, the yard space a pool occupies, and liability insurance cause a potential buyer to hesitate. Other negative improvements might be heating or air-conditioning systems that would add to the routine expenses of the house.

It is possible that a particular improvement won't add to your home's value as much as you thought it would. The wrong improvement will add little or nothing. Too much improvement, if houses in your area are selling within one range of prices and your improvement makes your house cost more, may mean you won't get full value when you sell.

The decision to make an improvement should be based on two factors. The first is the pleasure and convenience you will derive from your planned improvement. If you want features that you can afford, even if no one else would appreciate them, your own preference should come first. Second, however, you should be aware of investment value and of the limits set by general market conditions in your area, the size and style of nearby houses, and the number of years you plan to remain in your house.

For example, if you want a playroom for your children, you might consider converting your garage if leaving the car parked outside poses no big problem for you. But a potential buyer might reject a house without a garage or make a lower offer than you expected.

INCREASE IN VALUE

Simple growth in the value of real estate is the third method by which equity increases. If you hold and maintain a property for a number of years, it will grow in value in most cases. Even without a large down payment or improvements, a well-maintained home in a decent neighborhood will become more valuable over the years.

Inflation and the demand for housing resulting from population shifts or economic growth in your area will certainly increase the value of your house.

The opposite is true, too. For example, if one company employs a substantial number of people in one area, a plant closure or large layoff could mean lower demand for housing and a drop in market values.

Values also rise and fall according to other factors. When interest rates are high, consumers tend to shop for financing rather than price. In the late 1970s, for example, the cost of houses—already high because of double-digit inflation—mattered far less than whether buyers were able to find mortgages they could afford.

RAPID MORTGAGE PAYMENTS

If you pay off your mortgage more rapidly than the terms of your loan call for, you increase equity and reduce interest payments as well. In a 30-year mortgage, one extra month's payment during the first year will reduce your total loan period by as much as one full year. In fact, the earlier during the loan period that extra payments are made, the more substantial the savings overall.

If, for example, you borrowed $80,000 for 30 years at 11 percent, you will pay nearly $275,000 for your house—of which $195,000 is interest. Even if your house increases in value to $250,000, you will have given away all your profits to your lender in interest.

There are many ways to speed up your mortgage payments, and these will be discussed in chapter 5. The point is this: The ability to make additional payments allows you to save money, reduce the term of your loan, and create more equity faster.

PRESERVING EQUITY

Equity can be destroyed much faster than it can be built. It is vulnerable. To protect it, first recognize its value, then make sure you are able to hold on to it.

Proper insurance is important. Losses can be sudden and unexpected. Your equity—and your home—could be lost if your ability to earn a living were lost, either through death or a permanent disability. Your home can be burned to the ground or destroyed by a falling plane. What you have taken many years of hard work to care for could be gone in a matter of moments. Insurance can offset that possibility.

A more common threat to equity cannot be insured against. That is the misuse of equity by the homeowner. If you borrow to the maximum allowed by a lender and use the borrowed money in ways that do not improve your overall financial condition, you invite trouble. Instead of an affordable and comfortable shelter with reasonable monthly payments, you could have a massive, uncomfortable problem.

If, on the other hand, you use money borrowed against equity to improve your home, to purchase additional property, or to invest prudently and wisely, you can increase your personal net worth and build more equity. These actions help to move your financial plan forward. Other needs should be handled through careful budgeting, not use of home equity.

When I had been in my home for about eight years, I convinced myself that it was possible to make a lot of money in the stock market. I took out a $15,000 mortgage and invested the money. For a while I was able to make payments from my profits, but within a year I recognized it had been too big a risk. The investments didn't take off like I'd thought they would.

The big mistake: looking for immediate profits in an unsure investment. The mortgage was to run 15 years. Looking back, I can see how unlikely it would have been to continue to make a stock market profit during that entire period of speculative investing.

How can you protect yourself against this form of loss? By recognizing and acknowledging the critical importance of equity to your financial well-being, developing a plan for its use, and living by it.

What is irresponsible use of equity? Necessity can come into the picture, and each homeowner ultimately must decide what is or is not necessary. Borrowing equity for a vacation, consolidation of other debts, or a new car may be perfectly sound and necessary moves. But to put your home on the line usually is ill-advised. Why? Because the purpose and use of the money does not add to the value of your investment in your home. It subtracts. Speculating in the stock market, as I discovered painfully, is not a sound use of home equity unless you're extremely fortunate.

Begin by deciding whether your equity is to be preserved or not. Is it to be used only when the result will bring back more? Or will you take chances?

With a farsighted plan you can identify actions that will increase value—the right addition or buying rental property, for example. Taking chances, on the other hand, means gambling with equity. That is a threat to your family's plan, assuming you envision retirement without mortgage payments and are attracted to the idea of building your personal net worth over the years.

Make a distinction between assets and income. Unless you believe in taking big risks, you should preserve and use assets wisely, and for other things use income.

Equity can be lessened, too, if you use the value you hold in your home to borrow money at higher interest rates than you are paying on your mortgage. By doing so, you do away with the protective shell of a long-term fixed cost and invite inflation in. A fixed-rate mortgage is an inflation guard. If your mortgage interest rate is variable, wait for a period of low interest rates and do your best to refinance with a fixed-rate mortgage.

If you borrow money at a higher rate, you give away your added value to the lender, who is in the business of selling money at the going rate. With your house as security for a loan, the lender becomes a more successful investor than you are, earning more from the value of your house than you will.

To own your home truly, therefore, you need to control its financial career. This doesn't mean that you refuse absolutely to pledge equity against a loan for any reason. But it does mean you must operate within a plan that looks much farther ahead than a new car, vacation, or the convenience of debt consolidation.

USING YOUR EQUITY

Once you have built up a certain amount of home equity it can be used if you choose to do so—and if you are aware of the dangers. Few other sources of capital are as convenient, but don't feel compelled to borrow when you see ads telling you that your money is sitting idle in your home. Equity is not money. You do not have idle money in your house, only your good credit.

You can view your equity in one of two ways:

(1) I have home equity, which can be used as collateral. This gives me more financial flexibility and an opportunity to borrow money.

(2) Making equity grow is a major benefit of buying a house. If I overborrow by pledging equity, I'll never add value. Therefore I will not use equity as collateral without very serious consideration.

The ease with which you can borrow against your equity is a dangerous trap. Because you have equity, you represent an excellent credit risk to a lender. In the event that you can't repay a loan, the lender can simply sell your house to recover the loss.

A friend wanted to add a room to his house and had gotten estimates of around $15,000 to do the job. I asked, "Where are you going to borrow the money?" His reply: "I don't want to get a loan. I'm taking out a second mortgage."

He was not an ignorant person, simply one of millions who believed the ads. A second mortgage *is* a loan, as simple as that. But when the day arrives that you have tremendous borrowing power because of the equity you hold, your reaction might not be a logical one.

That's why you have a financial plan—to protect you from mistakes. With planning, you can prepare for months and years ahead. A room addition might fit the goals you have set. In that case, the borrowing and the repayment will have been foreseen and scheduled in the plan.

There are other traps lying in wait for the use of equity. One is the misuse of appreciated value. If, for example, your $70,000 house is now worth $140,000, you can borrow almost the whole amount. To you, that appreciated value might be a form of discovered wealth. The equity has grown because of market demand for houses like yours (an intangible element), and now you can get your hands on the cash. That's very appealing.

But if you can avoid the temptation to use that credit, you have an opportunity to work toward putting your dreams into effect. Depending on the goals you have set, you might purchase a larger house and some land, start a business, invest in other real estate, or simply build your net worth in preparation for retirement. The equity gives you tremendous flexibility and freedom to choose your course. The cash may not, particularly later when you are faced with repaying the loan.

Misuse of equity is not always a rash act, but it is often the consequence of poor planning. Consider the case of Ted and Anna Harris, who were in their house for 27 years when it came time to put their son through college. They borrowed $30,000, using their house as security, to pay for tuition.

Three years later, Ted and Anna retired. Their original plan had been to live free of housing costs. The first mortgage was paid off, but now they had to make payments of about $390 per month on the new loan. With a small pension and the modest savings they'd accumulated, they couldn't make ends meet. Ted ended up working part-time to pay off the second mortgage.

Looking back, Ted realized he could have saved the money with more forward thinking. Now, with about 12 years to go on the mortgage, retirement isn't as comfortable as he'd planned.

It is not uncommon for today's homeowner to take out a number of different mortgages, for a variety of reasons, over the years of living in a house. It is not unusual that a new mortgage will be for an amount greater than the previous one. Although you're invariably paying higher rates for the borrowed money than your investment is producing, this can be justified by several reasonable-sounding arguments:

Argument 1: By paying off some other debts at the same time, the mortgage payments are more affordable.
Flaw: Your current debts are short-term and a mortgage is not. Chances are that you will be back in debt for the same or similar bills within a year or two.

Argument 2: For slightly higher payments, we can also afford a new car.
Flaw: You will also need another new car within four or five years. But you will still be making mortgage payments for the money borrowed for this one.

Argument 3: We can put the extra money in the bank for emergencies.
Flaw: Available cash is just too tempting for many people. Chances are that you will pick away at your cash reserve so that when a real emergency does arrive, you will need to go further into debt.

Go back to the plan. It should dictate how home equity should be used. This is a long-range decision. When you bought the house, you might have worried that you wouldn't be able to keep up payments, but it's far more likely that you'll lose money because you can't afford to make payments on subsequent loans, the result of borrowing too freely and pledging equity for it. Every time you borrow, the basic question should be: How will this step enhance the value of the house or personal financial worth in exchange for the loss of equity that occurs when I borrow?

Before you give in, ask yourself:

- Is it a sound investment?
- Will I profit from this decision?
- Is it necessary?

See also chapter 9 for a discussion of shopping for loans.

AVOIDING COMMON MISTAKES

Because homeowners' equity is so tempting, investment counselors and lenders besiege homeowners constantly, urging them to "put equity to work."

One investment salesman made the following argument on a radio talk show:

> I show my clients how they can use the money tied up in their homes to make more money. If you borrow your equity at 12 percent, it's only costing you 6 percent. That's because, in the 50 percent tax bracket, you reduce your taxes by half the interest you pay. If you then invest the money at 9 percent, you're 3 points ahead.

It's a good-sounding argument with some serious flaws. First, very few people are in the 50 percent tax bracket. Your taxable income (which is gross income less adjustments, itemized deductions, and exemptions) has to be more than $169,000 (based on the 1985 tax tables) before you even enter this bracket. But financial "experts" peddling get-rich-quick financial schemes and tax shelters have always favored unrealistic examples.

A second serious flaw is that, if you invest proceeds from a loan at 9 percent, your profit is taxable. So, even in the 50 percent bracket, the unfortunate homeowner who falls for this argument will earn only 4.5 percent after taxes. Instead of being 3 points ahead, he or she is 1.5 points behind.

A counterargument can be made: "But you make the investments in a tax-free municipal bond."

First, and most significant, under tax laws you cannot in some instances deduct the interest expense if you borrow money to invest. In addition, there's no guarantee that you will be able to get 9 percent on a safe municipal bond investment. Besides, there are risks involved. Finally, while your borrowed money is tied up, you will still need cash available to make additional mortgage payments. So a tricky argument that sounds very good turns out to be full of flaws.

The scheme serves the purposes of the salesperson, who depends on commissions, at the homeowner's expense.

There are institutions and individuals in the world who are expert at giving you advice that lines their own pockets, and they won't hesitate to put *your* house on the line to do it. Many banks and brokerage houses offer programs that make borrowing easy if you're willing to pledge your house as security. The plans may give you a lot of convenience, including "free" checks, low annual fees, and minimum monthly payments like the revolving credit plans offered by department stores. All of these increase the danger to your home. Any check you write, for example, in any amount, automatically adds to the balance you owe and the interest you will have to pay and reduces your equity.

What is likely to happen if you fall prey to one of these convenient programs? You can go along for several years, borrowing a little here and a little there, paying interest only. After some time, you will have very little equity left. And quite a bit of money was used for small expenditures along the way. All you really have now is a sizable debt to be paid back, with interest.

Someone else now owns a substantial part of your home. Your equity has been transformed. It now is their equity.

No matter what these plans are labeled, they are forms of mortgage—except that, instead of borrowing a lump sum, you give away your equity a little at a time. Your perspective on what a mortgage really means might be improved when you consider the origin of the word. In the old French, "mort" is death and "gage" is hand—the "hand of death."

It would be revealing for a homeowner to sit in on a board of directors meeting or a management strategy session in an institution that lends money or advises people on investments. Potential sources of capital—cash values in life insurance policies, deposits with banks and savings and loans, pension and retirement funds, and of course, home equity—are constantly reviewed. The discussion centers on how to move money from "them" to "us." Anyone with assets is a target. It doesn't matter whether you need or want to borrow money. For the institution, the trick is to make the program appear so profitable or necessary to you that you will fall for the sales pitch and hand over your equity.

It is ironic that many homeowners regard their personal savings accounts as sacred and wouldn't touch money in the bank except for the most pressing emergency. But at the same time, because home equity is less tangible and harder to understand, those same homeowners will take equity from their homes and use it poorly.

If a deal sounds too good to be true, or so simple that you wonder why it never occurred to you before, investigate it fully. Consult with independent experts who will not profit from giving you bad advice (see chapter 7). Do this *before* you commit your home equity to any program. The safest investment you can make with your home equity is one you've already made—leaving it where it is.

There certainly are instances where home equity can be used for making investments. If you are convinced that pledging equity to borrow money will increase your overall net worth, and if you really know exactly what you are doing, go for it. But be cautious. Be sure you understand the risks and have planned ahead for every aspect, including the effects on your cash every month.

Know your equity for its potential. Be aware and become informed—and remember that charming and seemingly concerned and caring advisers might have their own interests in mind and not yours.

Once you know your equity, protect it within the context of a financial plan. Seek other alternatives for other financial requirements: This is the only way to build personal wealth and to achieve the dreams your plan defines.

5

SHORTCUTS TO BUILDING EQUITY FASTER

Accumulating equity is like rolling a ball down a hill. The speed depends entirely on the shape of the hill. You can, if you'd like, speed the ball up to get it to move faster. Using this strategy toward equity not only saves you money, but also shortens the time before you are a homeowner free and clear.

Anyone who has figured out the total amount of money he or she will pay a lender for a house—the monthly payment multiplied by the number of months the mortgage lasts—knows what effect interest has on the amount.

For example, a $70,000 mortgage at 14 percent, paid over 30 years, totals nearly $300,000. Everything above $70,000 is interest. The principal of that mortgage, after five years' worth of payments, is still about $68,900. The monthly payments of $829.42, an amount that totals nearly $50,000, have been almost entirely devoted to interest.

The majority of first-time homeowners stay in those homes less than five years. They enjoy the advantages of owning a home and, if they have a fixed-rate mortgage, they have fixed housing costs. But during that time, if real estate values have not risen

FIGURE 5-1
Loan Amortization

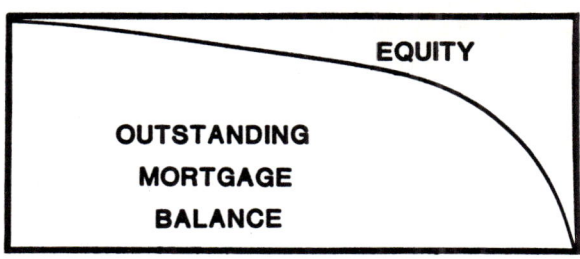

significantly, they have added only $1,100 in equity to their investment.

It is useful to understand the structure of mortgage loans thoroughly, to comprehend *why* it takes so long to reduce the principal, and why we end up paying two, three, or more times the amount we borrow.

Most homeowners think of their mortgage as being made up of equal portions of principal and interest. If this assumption were true, payments on a 30-year loan of $70,000 at 14 percent would be broken down as follows:

Interest	$634.98
Principal	194.44
Total	$829.42

But mortgage interest is not computed this way. Because many people believe it is, they also believe there is no way to reduce the cost of interest, or the term of the loan itself. This assumption also is false.

Mortgages are designed to take the entire loan period to pay off the amount of money you borrow. Most of the interest is paid in the earlier years, because interest is usually computed on the outstanding balance. This means that almost all of the first payments are devoted to paying interest. Each month, the percentage of the payment that represents interest goes down slightly while the percentage that represents principal increases.

This shift in percentages accelerates as the loan ages. In the later years, the outstanding balance falls dramatically as more of the principal is repaid and therefore less and less of each payment is devoted to interest. The arrangement favors the lender, who collects a large amount of interest early. When the homeowner sells—usually before the balance begins to decrease substantially—the lender collects a large amount of principal.

Consider that $70,000, 14 percent mortgage to be paid over 30 years. In the first year of the loan, the homeowner makes

TABLE 5-1

FIRST-YEAR MORTGAGE PAYMENTS OF A $70,000 MORTGAGE AT 14 PERCENT FOR 30 YEARS

Month	Total Payment	Interest	Principal	Balance
				$70,000.00
1	$ 829.42	$ 816.67	$ 12.75	$69,987.25
2	829.42	816.52	12.90	69,974.35
3	829.42	816.37	13.05	69,961.30
4	829.42	816.22	13.20	69,948.10
5	829.42	816.06	13.36	69,934.74
6	829.42	815.90	13.52	69,921.22
7	829.42	815.75	13.67	69,907.55
8	829.42	815.59	13.83	69,893.72
9	829.42	815.43	13.99	69,879.73
10	829.42	815.26	14.16	69,865.57
11	829.42	815.10	14.32	69,851.25
12	829.42	814.93	14.49	69,836.76
Total	$9,953.04	$9,789.80	$163.24	

payments totaling $9,953. But only $163 goes toward repaying the principal of the loan. The balance represents interest on the remainder of the $70,000.

The way a lender calculates mortgage payments is summarized in figure 5-2. There are three steps:

(1) Monthly interest: The loan's beginning balance is multiplied by the annual interest rate. You pay $1/12$ of 14 percent each month, or an effective monthly rate of .0116666 percent, on the amount you still owe.

(2) Principal reduction: The monthly interest is subtracted from the total payment you make that month. What's left is applied toward reducing the principal of your loan.

(3) Your new balance: The portion of your payment representing principal is subtracted from the beginning (outstanding) balance. The result is the new balance, on which you will pay interest next month.

FIGURE 5-2
Monthly Payment Formula

a) beginning balance × (interest rate / 12) = monthly interest

b) total payment − monthly interest = principal reduction

c) beginning balance − principal reduction = new balance

TABLE 5-2

THE SLOW COURSE OF MORTGAGE PAY-OFF

After Year	Percentage Paid Off At:				Percentage Still Due At:			
	11%	*12%*	*13%*	*14%*	*11%*	*12%*	*13%*	*14%*
5	2.8	2.3	1.9	1.6	97.2	97.7	98.1	98.4
10	7.7	6.6	5.6	4.7	92.3	93.4	94.4	95.3
15	16.2	14.3	12.6	11.0	83.8	85.7	87.4	89.0
20	30.9	28.3	25.9	23.7	69.1	71.7	74.1	76.3
25	56.2	53.8	51.4	49.0	43.8	46.2	48.6	51.0
30	100	100	100	100	0	0	0	0

Note: This table shows percentages you actually pay off on mortgages at different rates for 30-year mortgages.

The first payment on that $70,000 mortgage can be broken down as follows:

Interest	$816.67
Principal	12.75
Total payment	$829.42

In a sense, early mortgage payments are not so much a part of the process of buying your home as they are rent on the money made available from your lender. If you pay 14 percent interest for a 30-year mortgage, you still owe half the balance after 25 years of making payments.

The earlier in your mortgage term you begin to speed up your payments, the greater the benefit. When most of your regular payments are going toward interest, extra payments on principal have a substantial impact.

After the tenth year in a 30-year term, the breakdown looks like this:

Interest	$623.20
Principal	206.22
Total payment	$829.42

By that point, the balance of your mortgage is declining much more rapidly.

Most people, upon realizing the relationship between the balance of a mortgage and the interest paid, will be interested in exploring mortgage acceleration. There are several ways to do this, either formally through a regular program or on a do-it-yourself basis.

KINDS OF MORTGAGES

The kind of mortgage you have will affect the acceleration plan you finally decide upon.

With a *fixed-rate mortgage,* the level of your payment and the interest rate do not change during the course of the mortgage. In general, from the homeowner's point of view, these are the best possible loan terms. Fixed-rate loans are in common use today, although rules vary by area and by lender. The more volatile interest rates are, the more nervous lenders become about letting you tie them to a particular interest rate for years.

A new type of loan is the *variable-rate mortgage.* These can be acquired at a lower rate of interest, initially at least. The lender is allowed to increase the rate periodically, typically every 6 to 12 months, according to interest-rate change in a predetermined index. The one-year Treasury bill rate is one popular index. Every time that rate goes up or down, the interest on a variable-rate mortgage is also adjusted.

The holder of a variable-rate mortgage is at a disadvantage. The lender is protected when market rates go up, and the homeowner's cost of housing increases.

It is possible to change from one form of mortgage to the other by refinancing, but doing so will mean paying new closing costs, extra points (each point is 1 percent of the new loan amount), and perhaps a prepayment penalty as well, although in some states lenders cannot charge a penalty if you refinance with the same institution.

For example, one family took out a 13 percent loan with a $60,000 balance at a fixed rate. Two years later, rates were at 10 percent and appeared to be falling. The family replaced its mortgage with a variable-rate loan in the belief that the rates would not climb back to 13 percent, and if rates did fall further, so would those on their mortgage. Their payment level was reduced from $663.72 to $526.55 per month.

The risk here is that rates will rise in the future. This family lowered its payment today in exchange for the risk that future rates could be higher.

When you accept the variable-rate loan, there is also the danger that the rate you are given is a temporary one. In order to attract business, many lenders offer a temptingly low rate called the "teaser" or the "today rate." But if you read the fine print you will find that the low rate is adjusted within a year, and you'll be stuck with a higher monthly payment than you thought.

Another family had seen its variable-rate $75,000 loan climb from 10 to 11 percent, peaking at one point at 13 percent. Rather than live with the uncertainty of future rate increases, they replaced the variable-rate mortgage with an 11 percent fixed-rate loan. (Most lenders charge somewhat higher rates for fixed-rate loans.) For this security, their monthly payment increased by $56.

That extra payment is a form of insurance. The family now knows that the payment will never vary, because of the fixed-rate loan. So while the first family lowered costs and accepted a future risk, this family was willing to accept higher cost to reduce that future risk.

Some homeowners want to build equity in as few years as possible in order to pledge a fully owned house as security for a new mortgage. For them, an alternative is a *growing equity* or *rapid payoff mortgage*. It comes with a fixed rate of interest but the amount paid on the principal is tied to an index that measures an economic change, like the Commerce Department index of per-capita income on an after-tax basis.

You agree with the lender that your payment will change accordingly. If the agreement calls for your payment to increase at the rate of 80 percent of the index change, for example, and the index increases by 5 percent, your payment would go up 4 percent (80 percent of 5). If your mortgage payment was originally $600 per month, it would then increase by 4 percent, or $24 per month.

Because the interest rate is fixed, the change in payment is applied fully against principal. The term of the loan may be set for as much as 30 years, but invariably it will be paid off more quickly.

There are two disadvantages to this type of mortgage. First, the increases in monthly payments won't occur as substantially in the earlier years, where they really count. And second, the program is inflexible. Your increase in payments is made based on an index over which you have no control.

This mortgage will save a lot in interest costs if your income is high enough to cover periodically adjusted payments. And if you can get a lower interest rate by taking out this type of mortgage, that advantage might outweigh its inflexibility. But you can do more on your own with a 30-year fixed-rate mortgage and your own mortgage acceleration program.

Another type, the *graduated payment mortgage,* has a series of increases for the first five or ten years, then levels off for the balance of the loan period. This is suitable for those expecting growth in their personal incomes, but does not give maximum benefits in the early years.

The ultimate form of mortgage acceleration is found in the *zero-rate mortgage*. This is an attractive alternative for those selling a house in which they have substantial equity and buying another with a large down payment.

In a typical case, the buyer puts down one-third of the purchase price. Part of that represents interest. The equal monthly installments for the rest of the purchase price include little or no interest. This type of arrangement is desirable if you have the cash to put up for a house, because the mortgage is paid off quickly once the down payment has been made. But to get such a loan you may also be required to pay a higher purchase price than you otherwise would. You might end up paying more than you would have paid with a less creative and more traditional mortgage.

SHORTER TERMS

The 30-year plan is a popular one, but 15-year mortgages, which today represent fewer than 20 percent of all home mortgages, often are a good bargain. For a relatively small additional payment each month you can cut the mortgage time in half. At 14 percent, a 30-year mortgage for $70,000 costs $829.42 per month. By paying $932.22—an additional $102.80 each month—you could pay off the entire mortgage in 15 years.

This assumes that you can afford the additional payment. In practice, it may be easier said than done. The difference between monthly payments on a 15-year and a 30-year loan can be a burden to the family on a tight budget. When I first bought my home, I wasn't even certain I could afford the payments on a 30-year mortgage. The question of paying *more* never entered my mind.

There's another disadvantage. When you accelerate your mortgage payments, you control how much money is put toward the principal. If you can't afford to make the extra payment for a few months, there's no problem. But if you take out a shorter term mortgage to begin with, you must make the full payment every month.

Shorter term mortgages mean less risk for the lender, especially with fixed-rate loans. So you should be able to trim up to 1 point off the interest rate by agreeing to a quicker payback period. If the going rate for a 30-year fixed-rate mortgage is 11 percent, for example, you may be able to get a 15-year loan for between 10 and 10.5 percent.

FORMAL ACCELERATION PROGRAMS

The leverage you enjoy with a fixed long-term mortgage is not overlooked by the insurance industry. The difference acceleration makes in your overall housing costs signifies an opportunity for an alert salesman: a mortgage acceleration package.

Here's how it works. The insurance salesman first gets your attention: "How would you like to save $100,000 on your housing costs?" Once he has your full attention, he shows you one or more ways to do it, similar to those discussed in this chapter. But there's a catch. Rather than working the additional payment out of your budget, you are told, you will invest money in an insurance and investment program.

Typically, you would set aside a monthly or quarterly deposit and place it in a mutual fund. Part of the profits from this go toward the payment of life insurance premiums (some programs include homeowner's insurance payments as well). The balance is left to accumulate, with dividends reinvested in the program. Then, after several years, a lump sum is withdrawn and applied against the principal balance. Over the period of time you're paying your mortgage, the effect is the same as it would be if you accelerated payments on your own.

The big drawback is that you aren't making the payments on your mortgage for several years. The formal program cannot accommodate the maximum benefit you would get by accelerating payments in the earliest part of a loan.

The advantage of a formal program is that it provides you with insurance—usually a form of life coverage—that you wouldn't otherwise have. If you need this insurance and can still reduce your total mortgage cost substantially, it is a worthwhile program.

But in many cases, you don't really need the insurance. You may already have adequate life coverage through mortgage insurance, policies provided by your employer, and your own policy. In the excitement of saving a large sum of money on your mortgage, this detail might be overlooked. And it might not have occurred to you that you can accelerate your mortgage without that insurance coverage.

For homeowners who can afford to put more cash into payments, mortgage acceleration programs are excellent choices. One benefit of a formal program is the disciplined approach to saving. Like any other insurance policy, you stand to lose what you're building up by allowing it to lapse. So the more time you have contributed to the program, the more there is at stake.

Mortgage acceleration programs coupled with insurance and investment plans are very popular among insurance professionals. But before joining a formal program, compare the cost of getting your own insurance and making your own mortgage acceleration payments (see figure 5-3) with the total cost of the alternative.

One couple wanted to insure both spouses' lives. A formal mortgage acceleration program requiring a payment of $100 a month would provide them with insurance paid from interest

FIGURE 5-3
Acceleration Plan Comparison

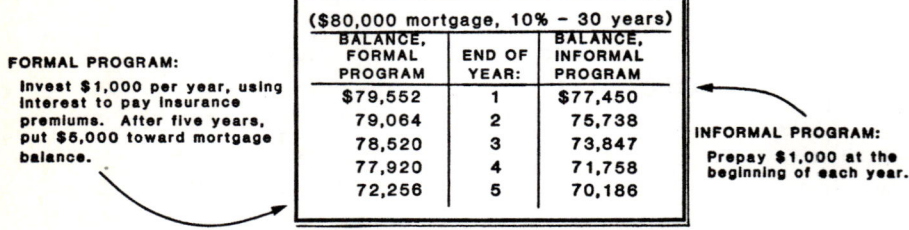

FORMAL PROGRAM:
Invest $1,000 per year, using interest to pay insurance premiums. After five years, put $5,000 toward mortgage balance.

($80,000 mortgage, 10% – 30 years)

BALANCE, FORMAL PROGRAM	END OF YEAR:	BALANCE, INFORMAL PROGRAM
$79,552	1	$77,450
79,064	2	75,738
78,520	3	73,847
77,920	4	71,758
72,256	5	70,186

INFORMAL PROGRAM:
Prepay $1,000 at the beginning of each year.

CONCLUSION:
Earlier prepayments produce more rapid acceleration.

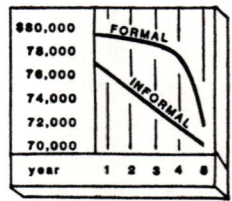

TABLE 5-3

A FORMAL MORTGAGE ACCELERATION PLAN
($100 PER MONTH)

Year	Annual Savings	Earnings (7%)	Cost of Insurance	Accumulated Savings
1	$1,200	$ 84	$73	$ 1,211
2	1,200	169	73	2,507
3	1,200	259	73	3,893
4	1,200	357	73	5,377
5	1,200	460	73	6,964
6	1,200	571	73	8,662
7	1,200	690	73	10,479
8	1,200	818	73	12,424*

*At the end of eight years, $12,424 will be applied against the mortgage balance.

earned on their account, and enable them to save more than $12,000 during the next eight years for eventual payment on their mortgage (see table 5-3).

The alternative would be to buy insurance separately and invest the remainder of $100 per month in accelerated mortgage payments. As long as the mortgage rate is higher than 7 percent (the amount of interest earned by the formal program), this family will be better off.

Assuming a 12 percent mortgage for 30 years (fixed-rate) on a balance of $60,000, monthly payments are $617 per month. Table 5-4 gives the results of the family's paying $717 per month.

Comparing the two plans (tables 5-3 and 5-4), the informal program is more economical:

Ending balance, informal plan	$15,699
Accumulated savings, formal plan	12,424
Net advantage	3,275

TABLE 5-4

AN INFORMAL MORTGAGE ACCELERATION PLAN

End of Year:	Mortgage Balance ($617)	($717)	Accumulated Savings	Cost of Insurance	Ending Balance
1	$59,784	$58,491	$ 1,293	$73	$ 1,220
2	59,538	56,970	2,568	73	2,422
3	59,262	54,874	4,388	73	4,169
4	58,950	52,715	6,235	73	5,943
5	58,596	50,281	8,315	73	7,950
6	58,200	47,540	10,660	73	10,222
7	57,756	44,450	13,306	73	12,795
8	57,252	40,969	16,283	73	15,699

Formal programs are sold with the argument that your insurance is "free," because the premiums are paid from interest. But in fact you will pay more in high mortgage interest than you'll save in premium costs. There is no such thing as "free" insurance.

In making comparisons, be sure to consider whether or not you need the level of life insurance that is to be included. In a good, flexible program, you can choose to take lower amounts if your circumstances make a large life policy unnecessary. For example, if your children are grown and through college and you have enough life insurance to pay off your mortgage, you won't need as much as you did when the children were young. If you have a sizable amount of money coming from a pension plan in which you're fully vested, or you have accumulated funds in an Individual Retirement Account, your life insurance needs, again, are not as great as if your spouse would be left without support. In short, don't end up buying something you don't really need. If you're not concerned with life insurance, you don't have to buy it in order to pay off your mortgage sooner.

DESIGNING YOUR OWN PLAN

As an alternative to a formal mortgage acceleration program, you can design your own plan—without part of the proceeds going to an insurance salesperson's commission.

The easiest way to accelerate payments on your mortgage is simply to make additional payments on the principal.

I applied this principle to the latest mortgage on my own house. During the first year, I increased the required $605 monthly payment by an additional $50. This $655 will reduce the term of the loan by one full year.

The payments are voluntary, but they discipline you to save. You can't get the money back without taking out another loan or selling your house.

Because the idea is your own design, you can start or stop payments whenever you want and even vary the level of your acceleration. You do not need to make special arrangements with your lender in most circumstances. Simply increase your monthly payment and instruct the lender to apply the difference to the principal. Many lenders even include a space for accelerated payments right on the monthly bill. An example follows:

Amount due	$_____
Additional principal payment	$_____
Total enclosed	$_____

If you are not certain about the terms of your mortgage contract or your lender's policies, contact your loan officer and ask about procedures for accelerated payment.

Whether you begin an acceleration program early or late in a mortgage term, you should evaluate the wisdom of the idea with two questions in mind:

(1) Can you afford to accelerate? Before you commit that money, be sure you already have adequate cash reserves (at least three months' take-home pay) for emergencies and other expenses.

TABLE 5-5

ACCELERATION CAN CUT INTEREST IN HALF

End of Year:	Mortgage Balance	
	($829.42)	($900.00)
1	$69,836.76	$68,933.27
2	69,649.41	67,707.23
3	69,433.94	66,298.11
4	69,186.29	64,678.55
5	68,901.65	62,817.09
6	68,574.50	60,677.67
7	68,198.49	58,218.75
8	67,766.35	55,392.60
9	67,269.66	52,144.40
10	66,698.78	48,411.08
11	66,042.65	44,120.24
12	65,288.54	39,132.33
13	64,421.80	33,455.79
14	63,427.20	26,931.43
15	62,280.67	19,432.43
16	60,964.73	10,813.87
17	59,452.26	908.16
18	57,713.92	0
19	55,715.98	
20	53,419.67	
21	50,780.40	
22	47,746.98	
23	44,260.56	
24	40,253.45	
25	35,647.91	
26	30,354.58	
27	24,270.73	
28	17,278.32	
29	9,241.66	
30	0	
Total acceleration:	0	$ 14,350
Total payments:	$298,591	184,519
Total interest:	$228,591	114,519

(2) Is your program sensible? Would you earn a higher rate of return by investing the money elsewhere? For example, if your mortgage has been in effect since before 1974, you probably are paying 7 percent or less. If you can earn 8 percent in a money market fund or in an income mutual fund, that is a better use of your money.

Adding even a little to your monthly payment can make a big difference. In the case of the $70,000 30-year mortgage at 14 percent, what is the effect of paying $900 per month, rather than the required $829.42? Interest is reduced drastically—by half—and the entire loan, originally set for 30 years, will be paid off in 17 years and one month, simply by adding about $70 to each payment. By investing a total of $14,350 in accelerated payments, you save $114,072 in interest. The process is shown in table 5-5.

The additional amount is an investment in equity. Its effect will be seen in every mortgage payment following the extra payment, because interest will be lower from that point forward. The return on your money is going to be better than you can get elsewhere, and the investment resides safely in your equity.

Another popular acceleration method is to pay a 30-year mortgage over 15 years. For a somewhat higher monthly payment, you can save a lot of money. See figure 5-4 to see what this method can accomplish with that $70,000 mortgage.

The arguments against prepaying the mortgage out of special savings accounts are the same ones that can be made against any form of voluntary savings. It's difficult to save money every month without fail when the money is easy to get at, as it is in a local savings account. If you save only what's left over after paying everything else, you are unlikely to save anything at all. And no matter how carefully you budget, there's always at least one unexpected bill each month.

That's why you need to build savings into your budget, so money goes into the savings account *before* anything else is paid. At the same time, the amount you save must be reasonable and affordable. And you still may need to modify what you put in, by

FIGURE 5-4
Mortgage Term Comparisons

$70,000 MORTGAGE

rate of interest	monthly payments		total payments	
	30-year term	15-year term	30-year term	15-year term
8%	$513.64	$668.96	$184,910.40	$120,412.80
10	614.31	752.23	221,151.60	135,401.40
12	720.03	840.12	259,210.80	151,221.60
14	829.42	932.22	298,591.20	167,799.60

rate of interest	difference in:	
	monthly payments	total payments
8%	$155.32	$ 64,497.60
10	137.92	85,750.20
12	120.09	107,989.20
14	102.80	130,791.60

increasing or decreasing the amount that goes toward extra mortgage payments.

It was this reasoning that led me to a strictly planned self-made mortgage acceleration program. When we invest more in our home through such a plan, we solve two problems.

First, we get into the habit of allowing the same amount each month for payment of the mortgage. That payment to the bank—including the extra amount for prepaying the principal—is made routinely.

Second, we can't simply go down to the bank and ask to be given back the extra payments we've made. If we want to get it back, we'll have to take out a loan. That means a delay, closing costs, loan fees, and additional payments. So our savings are truly put away and out of our reach. The prize: They are in one of the safest places they could be, our home. The money hasn't been spent. It remains there in the form of equity.

The only possible objection to this plan is that the money might be needed for an emergency.

A mortgage growth plan should not be done on a scale that endangers a family budget. For a plan to work, it must be realistic and affordable. If you save money in a bank account, you can alter the plan by withdrawing part of it for an emergency. But it's not that easy with mortgage acceleration. So a self-designed plan must contain several elements. It should be long-term. It should be realistic and attainable within your family's budget. It should be flexible enough to provide you with options as your income changes later. It should be designed to avoid prepayment penalties. And it should match your individual goals.

The plan should be long-term. Decide what adjustments you will make if interest rates move up or down. For example, if you are accelerating within a variable-rate mortgage and rates are on the increase, the value of your extra payments is correspondingly greater. This is so because you are reducing interest at a higher rate.

TABLE 5-6

MONTHLY PAYMENTS ON MORTGAGES

Interest Rate	Amount of Loan			
	$60,000	$70,000	$80,000	$90,000
16%	$807	$941	$1,076	$1,210
14%	711	829	948	1,066
12%	617	720	823	926
10%	527	614	702	790
8%	440	514	587	660

In a fixed-rate mortgage, the opposite is true. Let's say you are accelerating a 12 percent mortgage today. If the general market for interest rates goes up, within the next few years, and you could invest your money and earn 14 percent in a money market fund, that would make more sense than mortgage acceleration. By reducing the interest on your mortgage, you are saving the rate in effect at the time you make the extra payment. If you can earn more on the outside, you are wiser to do so.

Your decision to refinance will be based on your savings for monthly payments, versus the cost of refinancing:

$$\frac{\text{Cost of Refinancing}}{\text{Savings per Month}} = \text{Number of Months until Cost Is Offset}$$

Add up the costs and compare them with the amount of time it will take you to break even. For example, if you will save $85 per month in your payments, but the cost of refinancing is $4,500, it will take 53 months to break even, about four and a half years. The decisive question is how long you plan to stay in your house. If you'll move during the next five years, it isn't worth refinancing now. But if you are certain you'll stay way beyond that break-even point, it's a smart move.

If you need to borrow money but like the terms of your first mortgage, and if you have accumulated enough equity, you can arrange a second mortgage instead of refinancing. The interest rate will be higher than for a first mortgage, and the term for paying it back might be shorter. Terms of 10 or 15 years are common. A second mortgage is sensible when:

- Your first mortgage is a fixed-rate long-term contract with a low interest rate.
- You want to borrow only a small amount.
- The cost of refinancing is too high.

The number of mortgages you're willing to carry is a matter of personal choice, your lender's cooperation, and sound management.

Although lenders would naturally prefer that you keep a higher-rate loan, they offer the going rate at any given moment. The lender probably will penalize you for taking a lower-rate loan by charging a prepayment penalty on the old loan and points on the new one.

Watch interest rates over the period that you're accelerating your mortgage. If you plan to borrow money using your equity as collateral at a later date, consider whether your payments on such a loan would be higher than those you're making for your mortgage now.

Knowing exactly what will happen in the future in terms of interest costs and investment opportunities is impossible. The

---

DECIDING TO ACCELERATE: HOUSEHOLD 1

Status: This couple has been married for three years. Together, they earn $47,000. They have saved enough for a down payment on their first house and the wife will be taking a leave of absence in a few months when their first child is expected. This will strain the family's budget temporarily, but she plans to return to work a few months after the baby is born. Within their budget, the family pays for a $50,000 life insurance policy on the husband, whose employer also pays for health and disability insurance.

Decision: Mortgage acceleration should be a low priority for this family until their money and insurance status have improved. With a budget dependent on both incomes, both life and disability insurance will be needed by this family. In the event of either partner's death, there is a likelihood that the remaining spouse could not afford to make mortgage payments on one salary. And with a disability of only a few months, the family's budget would also be strained. Acceleration can wait until the family income allows for more flexibility.

In addition to paying for a new house, they will also have the added expense of another family member. This makes life and disability insurance all the more critical.

DECIDING TO ACCELERATE: HOUSEHOLD 2

Status: A single man has lived in his house for five years and intends to live there until he owns it free and clear. He earns a modest income and has little money saved. He considers his house to be his most important investment.

Decision: Without emergency reserves, it would not be a good idea to put money into an acceleration program. This person should build a cash reserve before considering a rapid payoff program. Then he can consider a rapid payoff program.

DECIDING TO ACCELERATE: HOUSEHOLD 3

Status: This family has a sizable sum of money in investments: two IRAs, the husband's fully vested profit-sharing plan from his employer, and money in stocks and bonds. They also own a vacation home. Their mortgage is for $95,000 and their goal is to move to another area within ten years, when the husband will retire. The new house they have in mind will be custom-built and will cost quite a bit of money.

Decision: This family should think about cutting interest costs and acquiring as much equity as possible during the next ten years. They should compare the yields they can expect from investments with the advantages of increased equity. Also they could probably pay off much of the mortgage within the ten years left before retirement without endangering their liquidity.

DECIDING TO ACCELERATE: HOUSEHOLD 4

Status: A professional couple (he's an architect and she's an accountant) recently purchased a home conveniently located for their short commutes into the city. They both earn good salaries, with a combined family income totaling $80,000.

This is a second marriage for both, and neither has children, so they have been able to save about $25,000 in addition to the down payment they made on their house. They took out a fixed-rate loan at the rate of 11 percent, and their investments are earning between 7 and 9 percent.

Decision: With both earning good incomes, and without the expense of raising children, it makes sense to accelerate their mortgage as much as possible in the first few years they are in their new home.

The rates they are earning on their investments are lower than the cost of their mortgage. Yet, that $25,000 is a nice reserve to hold onto for emergencies. In this case, rather than putting more money into lower-yielding investments, they should increase their monthly mortgage payments. With a high combined income, they'll be able to put several hundred dollars per month toward rapid payment of the principal balance, saving money over the long term.

whole point of mortgage acceleration is based upon two assumptions: First, that it will be desirable to accumulate equity as quickly as possible, whatever your motive for doing so; second, that making payments for a shorter period of time will be to your advantage.

The plan should be realistic. Can you afford the monthly payments to accelerate? The level of payment must work within your budget and be in perspective with your overall financial requirements. If you need liquidity—available cash—but don't have it, build that first, then examine the desirability of mortgage acceleration. See the boxes on pages 95 to 97 for some examples.

The plan should be flexible. It is unrealistic to expect that any financial planning you do today will be completely relevant over the long period of time that it takes to pay off a mortgage. Over those 30 or so years everything about your finances is likely to undergo drastic change: In the years since I purchased my house I have changed occupations, my income has risen, and I've had a second child. Virtually every financial goal I had has changed.

A mortgage plan you enter today does not have to be permanent. It's unrealistic to expect it to be. Mortgages are changed quite frequently in our society. You can replace one mortgage with another—refinancing—or you can add a second and even a third mortgage any time you have the equity and can find a lender who is willing to lend you the money. At the point any of these events take place, those who have accelerated their mortgage have more equity in their pockets, meaning they can borrow more if that's what they want. If you sell, more equity means more cash at the close of the deal. That could mean more buying power for your next house, more money for retirement, or simply more money to bank or hold in equity for emergencies.

The plan should be designed to suit the terms of your mortgage. Every lender has a policy concerning prepayment. Many assess a penalty if you exceed a yearly limit (typically 20 percent of the balance). The penalty may be based on a percentage of the original loan balance.

Most acceleration plans will not exceed a lender's limits, but before starting your own program, check with the institution to make sure you understand its prepayment rules.

The program should match your goals. Plan a mortgage acceleration program in line with your individual objectives. Having clear-cut goals will help you decide whether to enter a mortgage acceleration program.

I had two objectives in starting a mortgage payoff plan: First, to save on total interest; second, to do away with the mortgage long before the terms of the mortgage contract. If you want only to be able to live in your home without owing money to a lender, you have one clear-cut goal. Full ownership without a large monthly payment is tangible and important.

If, on the other hand, your purpose is to pile up equity so that you may borrow against it later, a different goal is in effect. Many homeowners take this approach. The idea is, having equity in your home gives you financial power.

MAKING THE DECISION TO ACCELERATE

Personal financial requirements and tax considerations should be brought into the picture when you assess the most intelligent way to manage your home mortgage.

Your current insurance requirements may change your immediate prospects for mortgage acceleration. Are you covered with enough life, disability, casualty, and health insurance? If not, your insurance should be put in order immediately. If the choice comes down to a budget question of which program you can afford, insurance should be a definite first priority (see chapter 6 for more details). In this regard, a formal program for mortgage acceleration that also provides insurance coverage could be the answer.

Some people argue against mortgage acceleration because mortgage interest payments are deductible on tax returns. This is a weak argument. Why pay $100,000 more in interest to save only a fraction of that amount in lower taxes? For example, if your effective combined federal and state tax rate is 35 percent for every year in which you're paying your mortgage, the maximum benefit you can gain from paying $100,000 more on your mortgage is only $35,000. After taxes, you're still out $65,000.

At most rates of interest available today, with mortgages of $40,000 and above, you can do a lot to reduce your mortgage costs with very little expense. For most people, taking steps to reduce interest costs even a little is better than doing nothing at all. In trying to decide what form—if any—of mortgage acceleration will work best for you, arm yourself with all the information you need to make the right decision. Then go for it.

6
COVERING THE FLANKS

Looking to the far future is only part of the total financial planning picture. What if something unexpected happens tomorrow? If you are disabled or die, will your family be able to keep the house? The majority of homeowners don't plan for loss from these events, at least not adequately. To be complete, a money management program must consider and protect against these losses.

To a great extent you can control the rate at which your home grows in value. But as you are building equity you still need to protect your home and family against events over which you have no control—specifically, death and disability.

Why do we have such trouble keeping insurance up to date? First of all, it's a complex subject. Insurance is boring to most of us, and does not inspire us to action. The vast majority of homeowners have not taken inventory of their belongings and stored the list away from home; they have not reviewed their policies for several years; and they probably have not spoken to their insurance agents in recent memory.

If we listen to insurance agents, we all need a lot more insurance than we have. But like most salespeople, insurance agents are paid on commission, so their motives may be mixed.

"Enough" insurance is different for every family. You need to protect yourself against the economic loss of events beyond your control. You don't need more insurance than is required to achieve this.

Most employees have health insurance provided through an employer's group plan. Many employers also offer life and disability group plans. Follow these general guidelines when reviewing your other insurance needs:

(1) Life: In the event of your death, you should have enough insurance to pay off your home mortgage and all other current debts. If you have a working spouse, he or she should carry the same coverage. It would be unrealistic to try to replace your annual income for an indefinite period as long as your family will continue to have income. If you are the sole supporter of your family, you could also add life insurance to provide income for a limited period, perhaps a year.

(2) Disability: You need to be able to replace lost income if you are injured or become ill and are unable to work for an extended period of time. The cost of medical care not covered under your health insurance should be covered as well.

(3) Casualty: Homeowner's policies must be up-to-date, reflecting the replacement value of what you have. Most of us have more valuable possessions than we think. The traditional casualty policy is set up to insure belongings up to half the value of the house. To find the right level, make a written inventory of your belongings and update it once a year or whenever you buy expensive furniture or equipment. Keep the inventory in a safety deposit box.

(4) Health: To find the right level in your own situation, map out the costs of typical medical expenses, comparing your total out-of-pocket expenses under several variations of a health insurance plan. Try it with a $100, $300, and $500 annual deduction per family member. Compare the differences in annual premiums for different deductible levels.

MORTGAGE INSURANCE FOR HOMEOWNERS

Four forms of coverage are specifically designed to protect homeowners from events that might threaten their ownership and long-range financial plans: mortgage life, joint mortgage life, mortgage disability, and homeowner's insurance.

MORTGAGE LIFE INSURANCE

When you buy most life insurance, you choose the coverage you want in a round amount—$50,000 or $100,000, for example—an amount you believe will replace your ability to bring home an income. Mortgage life insurance is more specific. It addresses the question: "Would my family be able to afford this house if I died tomorrow?"

Mortgage life insurance is designed to pay off the entire amount owed on your mortgage in the event of your death. Unlike most types of life insurance, the amount of coverage is tied directly to what you owe on your loan. It should not be confused with a homeowner's liability and casualty policy.

MORTGAGE INSURANCE/ HOMEOWNER'S INSURANCE

Mortgage insurance is insurance on your mortgage. The amount of coverage in effect at any time is always equal to the amount of money you still owe to your mortgage lender. It is designed for one purpose only: to pay off what you owe on your house if you should die.

Homeowner's insurance is a combination of liability and casualty protection. You are insured against liabilities like injuries to visitors in your home or on your property, or damage to their property by you or a family member. Casualty protection covers fires, natural disasters, theft, burglary, vandalism, and other losses to your property.

The cost of mortgage life insurance is based on three factors:

- Your age at the time you apply for the policy (the older you are, the higher the premium)
- The amount you owe on your mortgage
- The number of years until the mortgage will be paid off and the interest rate you pay

The higher the interest rate and the longer the term, the longer it will take you to pay off the mortgage balance. So for a long-term mortgage at a high rate, mortgage life premiums will be higher than for a short-term mortgage with a low rate.

It is in that third factor—years and interest rate—that mortgage life insurance differs from standard life insurance policies. Because that third factor is a big variable, mortgage life insurance is cheaper than nonmortgage life insurance for some homeowners, and more expensive for others.

To illustrate, compare two different mortgages with the same outstanding balance, $75,000:

(1) At 14 percent and with 30 years to go, the total of the payments due on the mortgage is $319,917.60.

(2) At 11 percent and with 15 years to go, the outstanding mortgage payments total $153,441.00.

Even though the balance is the same on both mortgages, the life insurance company risks twice as much with the 14 percent loan for 30 years. So a much higher premium will be charged for the same coverage.

To demonstrate how the three factors—age, balance, and time/rate—interact to affect total cost of a mortgage life insurance policy, compare the situations of these three households:

Household 1: This family owes $50,000 on a 30-year mortgage and is paying a fixed interest rate of 12 percent. They are interested in a mortgage life policy on the husband, who is 27 years old. One company offered them a policy at a cost of $12.25 per month.

They compared this with rates charged for other life insurance not tied to mortgages, and found that rates were about the same.

One of the other policies was described as a ten-year renewable term policy. Premiums and insurance remained level for ten years, then rates shot up based on the husband's age.

Another policy offered level premiums for either 10 or 20 years but, like mortgage life, the amount of insurance declined each year.

This family decided to buy the mortgage life insurance. Because their purpose is to be able to pay off the mortgage in the event of death, they saw no need to keep the insured amount at $50,000.

Household 2: A single man, age 45, has a 30-year fixed-rate 14 percent mortgage with a balance outstanding of $50,000. He is offered a nonsmoker's rate of $41 per month. While his mortgage balance is the same as that in Household 1, two factors make his insurance more expensive: the interest rate on his mortgage is higher, and he is 18 years older.

His decision was simpler. Rates for nonmortgage life insurance were higher and he chose a mortgage life policy.

Household 3: This family has been making payments on its 30-year mortgage for 22 years. The original balance was $50,000 and they now owe $31,625. The mortgage balance will fall rapidly during the next eight years and, after that, this extra insurance can be dropped.

In this case, a ten-year decreasing term insurance policy is less expensive than mortgage life insurance.

Evaluate mortgage life insurance with your entire financial plan in mind. Remember, the purpose of insurance is to replace lost income or reduce monthly living expenses in the event of death. Your family will need a place to live. If your insurance is adequate to take care of the mortgage and your debts, you do not need more.

JOINT MORTGAGE LIFE INSURANCE

A second form of mortgage life insurance is called joint mortgage life insurance. This is suited for families dependent upon two incomes. When a husband and a wife both work in order to meet total monthly expenses, mortgage included, the death of either partner would leave the survivor with a hardship. The possible result: loss of the house. Therefore, both need insurance. The mortgage will be paid off if either spouse dies.

Joint mortgage life insurance works like single-life mortgage protection, but the cost is higher because two lives are covered.

Even for families with only one working spouse, a joint life policy is worth looking into. The cost of replacing child care and housekeeping services can run high. This extra burden would place a severe strain on the family budget.

The family in Household 1 was quoted a monthly rate of $22.00 for joint mortgage life insurance (compared with $12.25 for the husband alone). The policy they were offered included some attractive features: $7,000 life insurance on their six-year-old son; for example, if the husband died first, insurance would continue for the wife and their child until the end of the mortgage period, free of premiums. Finally, if both died at the same time, the benefit—the amount due on the mortgage—would be doubled, and their son would inherit the extra insurance proceeds.

The family decided against joint coverage, even with the extras. For the ten years or so that their child will still be dependent on their direct care, the family is willing to take a risk, based on their life-style and good health. Even in the event of the wife's death, they believe they would not lose the house because of hardship. Finally, the $22 per month cost is higher than they are willing to pay.

There are no hard-and-fast rules for deciding whether joint mortgage life insurance is necessary in a one-income family. Income, debt, and family assets make every situation unique. When premium costs are compared, some families accept less protection and take on more risk.

Two-income families should look at joint life insurance carefully. In some cases, it isn't the best way to cover two lives.

Household 4: This family has been carrying a joint life policy for many years. Today, their mortgage balance is less than $30,000, and they believe they need to keep coverage in effect, at least on the husband's life. The wife retired a few years ago. The children are grown, and the couple doesn't believe they need insurance on her life. But they can't convert their policy because it is a single policy involving both lives. They don't have the option to drop one person out of it.

They could replace it with another policy, barring two problems. At the husband's age—58—premiums would be much higher than they were when the policy was taken out more than 20 years ago. And even more serious, he had a heart attack last year. He cannot get insurance at standard rates, and many companies would refuse to sell him insurance under any circumstances. Out of necessity, they are sticking with the policy they have. Fortunately for this family, they didn't cancel it before applying for a new one.

Inflexibility can make joint mortgage life insurance more expensive in the long run than two separate policies might be. With standard life insurance you can offset a high premium by carrying a lower amount of insurance on one spouse's life, settling for partial coverage to save money. If one spouse earns less money than the other, there is sensible justification for the lower coverage.

MORTGAGE DISABILITY INSURANCE

A third form of mortgage insurance protects you in the event of total and permanent disability. This form of insurance is often overlooked, but the prospects are dim that your family would be able to keep your home if your income stopped suddenly because of a total disability. Insurance professionals refer to total and permanent disability as "economic death." This morbidly descriptive phrase is quite accurate. With no insurance, a disabled person becomes a source of expense rather than income. The medical and nursing expenses that accompany a serious disability can lead to the loss of not only your house, but everything else you own as well.

In buying insurance many homeowners place too much importance on death benefits and underestimate or ignore the threat of loss from disability. If you do suffer an "economic death," all the life insurance you have will not help. As Mr. Potter tells George Bailey in *It's a Wonderful Life,* you may be worth more dead than alive.

Insurance companies define "total and permanent" disability to mean that you are unable to work in the profession for which you were trained, or in any other profession for which you are reasonably suited. One of two circumstances would make disability insurance critical to protecting your home and family life:

- Both you and your spouse must work in order to afford mortgage payments

- Your employer provides no group disability insurance as an employee benefit (or, if you are self-employed, you do not carry a disability policy)

A disability policy generally provides that you will be paid a preestablished amount of money every month for as long as you are disabled. Mortgage disability insurance is based on the same idea, but the policy will make mortgage payments for you, rather than giving you a check directly. The advantage of this form of coverage is that, regardless of how you fare otherwise, in the event of a disability, your family will not lose your house. It's important to note that because people don't always update their insurance coverage, they can run into trouble even with a mortgage disability policy.

Household 5: One family found that adding additional disability insurance was a smart decision. When they bought their house 14 years ago they bought a mortgage disability policy that would make their payments ($437.07 per month on their $45,000 mortgage for 30 years at 11.25 percent) in the event the husband was disabled. The policy included a waiver of premium provision: If he is disabled, the insurance continues in effect but payments are suspended for as long as he cannot work.

Four years ago, they borrowed another $35,000 to add two rooms to their house. That mortgage runs for 15 years at the rate of 14 percent, with payments of $466.11 per month.

The question of additional disability insurance came up. At first reluctant to pay out yet more money for insurance, the family finally concluded that they should not take chances. They reviewed their situation and defined several points:

- The amount of cash they would need every month to meet expenses, including payments on the two mortgages
- The cost of medical and nursing care for a permanent disability, not covered under their health insurance policy
- Future requirements—including children's education, retirement, the effects of rising prices over the years, and payments for monthly expenses

They decided to take the safe route. It was a smart move: Two years later the husband had his left leg crushed in an auto accident. His employer provides a group disability policy, which pays a small portion of the monthly budget. Their mortgage disability policy takes care of payments on both mortgages.

HOMEOWNER'S INSURANCE

The fourth form of protection is not life or disability insurance: It is protection against the economic losses that would result from casualty or liability.

This is commonly called fire insurance because that is the most common form of loss. The Insurance Information Institute, in its publication *Property/Casualty Fact Book* reports that fire losses in the United States run $5.8 billion per year, the result of more than 600,000 residential fires per year. While the relatively small cost of homeowner's insurance is more than justified by the risks, the same publication reports that 4 percent of homeowners do not have coverage, and another 3 percent don't know whether they do or not.

Besides fires, other perils are covered, the scope depending upon the level of protection taken out. In a comprehensive policy, you are covered from all casualties except those resulting from flood, earthquake, war, nuclear accident, and other perils specifically named in your policy.

The second part of the homeowner's policy is liability coverage. If a person is injured on your property or you damage another person's property, this covers you for medical and other costs. Typical examples are guests tripping over a garden hose or a crack in your walkway; your dog biting the mailman or a visiting friend; or a part of your tree falling and damaging a neighbor's house during a storm.

Both casualty and liability protection are necessary to every homeowner. They are required by lenders as long as the homeowner owes money on a mortgage. Many people make the mistake of dropping their homeowner's policy once they pay off their debt, but they are still are exposed to risk. You should keep your policy in force as long as you own your home.

One important exclusion from most homeowner's coverage is any loss connected with running a business from your home. This exclusion extends to any portion of your property you rent out—even to yourself—which is considered as part of a business. For this you need a separate policy or a rider extending coverage.

There's another homeowner's insurance consideration—room for improvement. Once you have thought through your home improvement and you know exactly what you want to have done, you hire designers and architects, draw plans, and go into action. The improvement was part of your financial plan and you were very thorough. But isn't there something you have forgotten?

In the 1975 fire in Santa Barbara, California, 200 families lost their homes. Eighty-five percent of those families were underinsured, either for the structure and its increased market value, for improvements they had made, or for contents. When you plan to add to the value of your house, check your insurance. From the moment a contractor shows up to start putting materials in, you should be covered.

Gaps in planning cause many homeowners to carry too little of some kinds of insurance and too much of others. Part of the periodical financial planning review that should take place whenever major changes occur is a review of the insurance situation. Even if you have planned well in the past, don't overlook the need to update continuously.

INSURANCE FOR A HOME OFFICE

When you operate a business from your house, you have a special insurance problem. Business assets are *not* covered under standard homeowner's provisions. You need to obtain a separate policy to cover furniture and equipment used for business or attach a rider to your homeowner's policy.

The good news is, the premium to insure desk, chair, typewriter, files, home computer, and so forth, will cost only a few dollars a year if you do attach a rider. One company covers computer hardware up to $4,000 for about $4 per year. In most cases a telephone call to your agent will do it.

WHEN COVERAGE IS NO LONGER NEEDED

There comes a point during the life of your mortgage when special forms of mortgage insurance are no longer needed and should be dropped (see figure 6-1).

If, for example, you start with a mortgage of $50,000, a monthly premium of $12.25 is a reasonable amount to pay to protect your family. Twenty-five years later, when you owe less than half the original balance and have less than five years to go, that premium looks less reasonable.

As a general rule, the point at which mortgage insurance should be reexamined occurs around the 24th or 25th year in a 30-year mortgage, or the 9th or 10th year of a 15-year mortgage, when the balance of the mortgage begins to decline rapidly.

Because you pay a higher premium to insure two lives under a joint mortgage life insurance policy, other circumstances may also indicate when that level of insurance is no longer necessary:

- Each spouse's income has risen enough so that it alone is adequate to cover all expenses, including mortgage payments.

- One spouse has retired and the family is not dependent on that income.
- The children have grown and child-raising costs are no longer an issue.

The need for mortgage disability insurance also lessens as the balance of the mortgage shrinks. If your assets are substantial enough that you could pay off the mortgage even if disabled, or if your employer provides enough disability coverage, you can drop the extra policy.

FIGURE 6-1
Mortgage Life's Decreasing Value

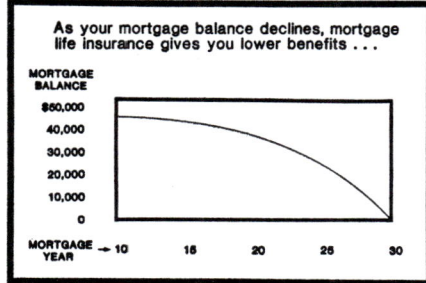
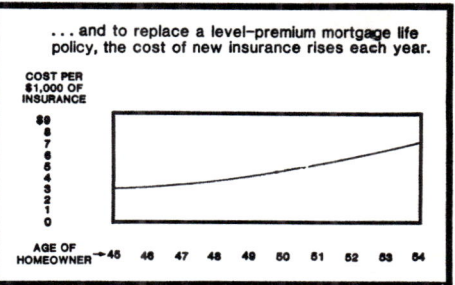

The solution: to identify the point where replacement becomes cheaper than a fixed-cost mortgage life policy.

MORTGAGE YEAR	HOMEOWNER'S AGE	MORTGAGE BALANCE	NEW INSURANCE POLICY		MORTGAGE LIFE PREMIUM
			RATE PER $1,000	ANNUAL PREMIUM	
23	50	$29,135	$5.23	$152.38	$147.00
24	51	26,305	5.72	150.46	147.00
25	52	23,120	6.25	144.50	147.00 ← cross-over point
26	53	19,530	6.84	133.59	147.00
27	54	15,485	7.48	115.83	147.00

7
FINDING HELP WITH THE PLAN

Once a family has put down on paper exactly what they want to achieve, and how they plan to achieve it, they can begin exploring ways to refine the plan, perhaps cutting taxes, improving safety and diversity, and discovering better ways to meet their life dreams. This may involve meetings with financial professionals.

The financial planning industry has undergone interesting changes. In the late 1970s everyone who used to be called something else—stockbroker, salesperson, account executive—suddenly became a "financial planner." It was an exciting new field that held great promise. Public response was good: Finally, professional help available to the average consumer.

Everyone got into the act. Banks opened planning departments. Brokerage firms renamed their salespeople to fit the new image. Large retail chains moved in and marketed financial planning along with washing machines and vacuum cleaners. Small businesses opened up storefront offices in industrial parks and shopping centers, selling financial advice. In the attempt to appeal to a wide segment of the population, service often became secondary to eye-catching advertisements and appealing company names. To make it all glamorous, many stores adopted names like "financial boutique."

To confuse the issue further, the title "financial planner" became so overused that it lost its meaning. Today there are many titles to choose from: financial counselor or adviser, fiscal or money manager are common examples.

Today, about 200,000 people offer financial planning services. Some can be valuable resources for help but many are imitations, trying to sell products disguised as financial services.

Organizations for financial planners attempt to set standards of ethics and practice but can do little to enforce them. The largest, the International Association for Financial Planning, for example, grants membership to anyone who applies and pays annual membership fees. The College for Financial Planning grants the designation Certified Financial Planner and several other schools grant Financial Planner degrees; some states attempt to regulate the industry with varying success—but there are no hard-and-fast regulatory protections for the consumer.

It comes down to this: If you want professional help to explore a facet of your plan or to present you with alternatives, investigate thoroughly to find the best one you can. But because a financial plan is *your* plan, you will have the best chance of succeeding if, first, you define for yourself what you have, what you want, and how long it will take for you to get there. A professional should be able to show you a better way to reach your goals, but should not be allowed to convince you that other goals are more important. Or that what you want is a poor idea.

No one person can possibly be an expert on every phase of financial planning. Many so-called financial planners are people who use the title to promote a product that they understand well. Insurance agents know how to sell insurance; investment professionals often believe the answer to all financial problems is to chase profits and tax shelters; bankers will tell you your money should be put into interest-bearing accounts. All of these steps might belong in a financial plan as part of the picture, but none is the entire answer.

For advice on management of your home equity and control of your financial plan, you certainly can benefit from outside expertise—but don't deceive yourself into believing that a consultant somehow possesses all the answers.

I have met many financial planners during my years as a consultant in the securities industry. Many of them share some common attitudes. First, they tend to believe that most consumers have absolutely no idea as to what they want, or how to go about getting it. Often this perception is true, but that doesn't mean homeowners don't know what's important to them. Your life dreams, your goals, are paramount to you and should be to your financial planner as well.

Second, financial planners tend to believe that their primary value is in directing people toward what they *should* want, not necessarily what they *do* want. Owning your home free and clear, for example, is not only a sensible idea, it is a necessity. When you retire, the burden of a mortgage, or the need to have one, is the ultimate sign of poor planning. The more debt you attach to your house, the further away the life dream of being free of debt is. This goal, unfortunately, probably conflicts with your planner's need to earn a living through commissions on investment sales.

Third, financial planners like to view home equity as a source for money to be used, to be "put to work." You will hear arguments like "The equity in your home is sitting idle. Let's put it to work earning money for you." Many planners have no respect for the principle of owning a home free and clear and even consider it a sign of poor financial management.

The problem with this argument is self-evident. We already know that you don't "put equity to work" by borrowing against it; that only reduces it. And if you will need 15 years or 30 years to repay that borrowed money, how many investments will outpace your interest cost? More to the point, how many safe investments justify risking your home?

Fourth, because these people work with investment and financial subjects constantly, they are not as sensitive to their clients' concerns over risk as they should be. It's a hazard of being too close to one's work, and it can become a blind spot.

For these reasons, you should approach a financial planner with caution. The need to earn commissions or fees for financial planning makes it difficult, if not impossible, for many financial planners to serve you completely.

CHOOSING THE RIGHT SPECIALIST

Let's assume you've gone as far as Robert and Fran Maher have—you've put down on paper the specific steps needed to reach clearly defined goals. These have been given a realistic timetable, and the resources available to you—assets and income—are sufficient to execute the plan. You have mapped a precise series of steps to be taken, decided where money is to be invested, and how much insurance to carry.

You wonder if there might still be a better way to proceed. How do you find out? One of the best ways to use a professional is to request a review and comments on the plan you have already prepared.

If you need help with a specific section of your plan—refinancing, retirement, investments—look for specialists in those areas. Once your plan is down on paper and your goals expressed, you are likely to know where you need help the most. If you are unsure of the best methods to save for college tuition, for example, you may guess that you should consult an expert on trusts. If you understand only enough about insurance to suspect that you need better coverage, it is obvious that you need to find an insurance expert to educate you. Begin by matching each element of your financial plan with the most likely source for help (see figure 7-1).

HOME EQUITY

To explore your alternatives for building and preserving equity, you can check with your banker or lender for acceleration ideas, terms of your existing mortgage contract (such as prepayment penalties), and referrals to other sources. Real estate degrees and designations qualify professionals in sales or advisory roles. These degrees include:

Member, Appraisal Institute (MAI)

Graduate, Realtors Institute (GRI)

Counselor in Real Estate (CRE)

Specialist in Real Estate Securities (SRS)
Certified Residential Broker (CRB)
Certified Residential Specialist (CRS)

SAVINGS AND CASH RESERVES

Banks offer a variety of savings plans, one or more of which should suit your individual requirements. Bankers can also be good sources for information about United States Treasury securities, certificates of deposit, and other accounts. You can also write to the Federal Reserve Bank of Dallas (Station K, Dallas, TX 75222), for such informative free booklets as *United States Treasury Securities*.

FIGURE 7-1
Matching Elements and Specialists

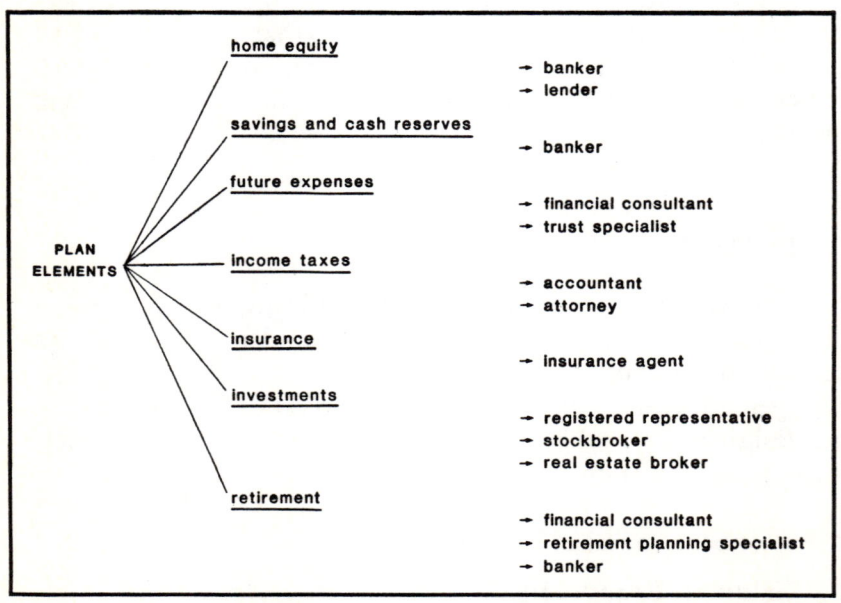

FUTURE EXPENSES

A consultant who specializes in family financial planning can be useful in working with you to design a long-term savings plan or a monthly budget. For more complex requirements, such as setting up a trust for a child's future education, a trust consultant can give you the alternatives and recommend the best way to meet your goals.

INCOME TAXES

An accountant or attorney can be helpful in explaining the planning aspects of tax law. These experts will be able to advise you in methods of planning that minimize the effects of income taxes on your financial plan.

If you have unusual tax or legal questions in your personal financial plan, look for experts in tax preparation and advice. Particularly in this area, you should be willing to spend money on a specialist now, to avoid expensive problems later. Degrees include:

Certified Public Accountant (CPA)

Juris Doctorate (J.D.)

Master of Laws (LL.M.)

INSURANCE

Insurance agents who specialize in individual lines (as opposed to commercial lines) of insurance should review your plan's insurance aspects, including coverage you already have, additional insurance you should carry, and any type of coverage you might have overlooked in your plan. Certifications include:

Chartered Life Underwriter (CLU)

Chartered Property and Casualty Underwriter (CPCU)

Registered Health Underwriter (RHU)

INVESTMENTS

A number of planners, consultants, advisers, agents, and salespeople claim to offer the best possible advice on investments. These include registered representatives affiliated with broker-dealers, stockbrokers (who may now be calling themselves financial planners, along with everyone else), and real estate brokers. Any of these people can help, depending upon the type of investments you want to make. Degrees and certifications include:

Certified Financial Planner (CFP)

Chartered Financial Analyst (CFA)

Chartered Financial Consultant (ChFC)

Registered Investment Adviser (RIA)

Registered Representative (Reg. Rep.)

RETIREMENT

A financial consultant who specializes in retirement alternatives can provide you with valuable information in rounding out your financial plan. A fee will be charged, which could save you thousands of dollars over the years. Look for a Certified Employee Benefits Specialist (CEBS). He or she should be up to date on the latest laws and regulations in the retirement field. For your own IRA, you can speak to your banker, if you keep it in a bank or savings institution, or to an investment counselor or a stockbroker.

Educational credentials help to identify the professional, but should not be the only standard you look for in seeking expert help. Referrals are more dependable. Ask your friends. You can also ask any one specialist to refer you to specialists in other phases of personal financial planning. Many bankers know investment counselors, insurance specialists, or retirement advisers, for example.

You can also ask for referrals from local fraternal organizations or the Chamber of Commerce, or look up experts in the yellow pages. Keep in mind, though, that these are hit-or-miss methods for finding help. Referrals from people who have used a service, or from professionals whose opinions you respect, are more likely to lead you to the right source.

Because you've identified the kind of information you need, your banker, lender, or insurance agent can probably help even without initials after their names. Academic and professional credentials tell you only that the holder has been exposed to a specialization.

CHOOSING THE RIGHT INDIVIDUAL

Once you have located a number of specialists, with or without degrees or designations, you can apply other tests to make sure you have found the right person. Interview each one before you agree to listen to his or her advice. Be very specific about what you do and do not want.

You do want:

- Comments on weak points in your plan and suggestions for what can be done to correct them
- Ideas that will meet your goals more safely, with less expense, or quickly
- Suggestions for goals you may have overlooked but that are apparent to someone else, given the structure and content of your plan

You do not want:

- Product advice
- Arguments about the goals you have established
- Offers for preparation of a different plan

You can cull out a lot of prospects based on their responses to these lists. Find out how long a specialist has been in business, and how long he or she has been providing the kind of service you want. Because anyone can be a "financial planner" (or any of the other popular titles), it is not at all unusual for people to represent themselves as experts when they've only recently passed their exams and have never gone through a plan before. Ask for three references to clients with whom the planner has worked for two years or more. A competent professional will supply this information without hesitation. If you're told, "I can't violate my other clients' confidentiality by giving out their names," look elsewhere. Your rule should be, "I can't work with someone when I cannot verify the quality of their work."

Once the professional gives you the names of other clients, make contact with them. Ask their opinion of the professional help they've received, the rapport they have with the adviser, and whether they'd recommend him or her to you.

What type of clients does this professional serve? If you discover that most clients are extremely wealthy and you're in the middle-income bracket, or that more clients are corporations than are individuals, chances are the professional won't be best suited to your requirements. Some insurance agencies, for example, specialize in business insurance, but know little about personal life, disability, and health lines.

For what part of your plan can the professional offer advice? If someone tells you they know *all* about investments, insurance, retirement planning, real estate, and taxes—be careful. You're much better off working with someone who knows only one or two of these complicated and ever-changing specializations thoroughly.

CHECK LICENSES AND REGISTRATIONS

Federal and state regulation dictates that some professionals must belong to organizations or come under the jurisdiction of a specific agency. Registered investment advisers, for example, are regulated by the Securities and Exchange Commission (SEC). Anyone selling securities is required to be affiliated with a broker-dealer and to pass an examination given by the National Association of Securities Dealers (NASD). The NASD is the self-regulating organization for the securities industry. Regulation is strict within the industry, and both the SEC and the NASD can apply a great deal of pressure on member firms and individuals *after* a problem comes up. The SEC can fine, suspend, or expel violators, or file criminal charges. The NASD can also assess fines, censure offenders, and has the power to suspend members.

For your initial search, these organizations are of no help. Neither will tell you whether someone is under investigation, or has had past offenses or complaints filed against them. But if your financial professional is affiliated with an SEC-registered or NASD-member firm, it means he or she must operate within the strict rules and regulations of the industry.

Certified public accountants are licensed by each state, as are real estate and insurance brokers and agents. Accountancy boards apply strict standards to their members and will respond to consumer inquiries or complaints. Real estate boards, including county-level boards that regulate the activities of licensed individuals and firms, will assist in finding capable brokers.

Insurance commissions audit insurance companies every three years, so that companies can file quarterly summaries and annual reports with state agencies. Unfortunately, the commissions do little in the way of consumer protection. You can verify the current status of a license, but must depend on personal and professional referrals beyond that.

CHECK CREDENTIALS

Too often it turns out, upon questioning, that an "investment adviser" is in fact no more than an insurance agent who has attended a seminar—and who may have one or two pet investments for you, on which the agent will earn a commission.

The price for professional advice ranges from nothing at all for consultations with your banker or lender to sizable amounts for people you retain to perform substantial services. Before you make an appointment, ask what kind of financial commitment you may be asked to make. Many professionals will meet with you for an interview for no consultation fee. Bankers, lenders, and people who are compensated by commissions will probably meet with you free of charge. Insurance agents will gladly review your current coverages and recommend additional insurance if you need it. The key to judging the financial motives behind free advice is simple: Does the adviser first find out what your financial status, income, assets, and goals are, or does he or she rush to the recommendation?

Some advisers charge consultation fees in addition to their commissions; most such fees are between $50 and $200 per hour. Many financial planners charge a flat fee for preparation of the plan itself. This fee can range from $200 to $5,000 or more. Some base their fees on your income or net worth.

Be sure you know ahead of time what you're in for. If you've done your own planning and are now looking only for an expert review, you should not be willing to pay a fee for a complete financial plan. Watch out for those who quote a set fee without having seen your financial status, and without knowing how much or how little help you need.

OTHER POINTS TO CONSIDER

(1) More than any other qualification, the professional you ask to help with your plan should be able to gain your trust. A sense of rapport between client and professional is worth at least as much as any other single qualification.

(2) Watch out for the salesperson posing as a financial professional. For example, a brokerage organization may also sell real estate partnerships. Does this make the people there full-fledged financial planners?

(3) Also look out for people who have only one solution to your financial concerns. If your goal is to save money to start your own business, and a professional suggests you put your money into a mutual fund, ask what he or she would suggest you do to save money for your children's college education or to save for retirement or to own your house free and clear. If the

solution is always the same, you have found a salesperson, not a financial planning service. Ask, "How would you address this goal for someone who earns more money than I do?" If the solution is still the same, it's not financial planning.

(4) Don't let yourself be put in a position where your life dreams are challenged. If you tell the financial professional that your most important goal is to own your home free and clear, that's that. If the response is, "No, you don't want to do that," it's time to look elsewhere. You are best equipped to decide what you want, and why. The adviser's job is to show you how to get there in the best possible manner.

There is an exception to the fourth rule. If your plan is unrealistic or filled with risk, or if your goals appear to be out of line for you, the planner should present you with an intelligent explanation of the problems and suggest alternatives that are in line with your risk and safety standards.

One couple, for example, told their planner that they wanted to mortgage their fully owned home and use the money to buy as many rental properties as they could. They had attended a seminar where they were convinced that this was the best way to get rich.

The planner explained that their idea was risky. He made several arguments:

- They were inexperienced in real estate investing.
- The plan allowed for no cash reserves.
- Their other investments were conservative, while this seemed not to fit their personal risk profile.
- Financial independence comes from planning over many years. Very few people can get rich in real estate in a few years.
- The kinds of properties they planned to buy were foreclosed homes. Valuable investments are seldom given up.

> ## WHEN A PROFESSIONAL DOES THE WHOLE JOB
>
> Some homeowners find it worth paying a fee to have the entire planning process done by someone else. The idea of putting together the many aspects of a financial plan, coordinating the elements, and devising the correct actions at the right time is too big a job for them. If you go that route, be sure to find someone who truly will work within your definitions and meet your life dreams. Look for a planner who will act as a coordinator, locating other professionals who specialize in one area.
>
> Look for someone who will start the process by putting in as many hours as it takes to discover exactly what your goals are. If the professional does not respect your goals and tries to distract you from them by suggesting that they are wrong or not important, you're not getting the kind of help you deserve. Financial planning is so highly personal that, if you are not willing to put your own plan together, the process should be a partnership and you should be the senior partner. Anyone who jumps too quickly to the end—the phase where you put money into a product—isn't working for *you*.

That meant there would be problems to contend with—the need for repairs and maintenance on run-down houses, difficulty in finding reliable tenants, and sliding values of homes in marginal neighborhoods.

By working with this professional, the couple was able to define their goals and develop a plan they could live with. The process probably saved them from losing thousands of dollars.

Have confidence that you *can* do your own financial planning. Look to experts to find ways to achieve your life dreams that are cheaper and safer and that make more sense than your original plan, then incorporate their ideas where *you* think they make sense. Recognize the value of truly expert advice. And keep your mind open, because today's plan won't always work next year.

The process is continuous, and you are in the best position to know when a change is necessary. Use informed outside help where it can benefit you but be sure it remains in your plan, not someone else's.

FINDING A CERTIFIED FINANCIAL PLANNER

The College for Financial Planning in Denver, Colorado, sponsors an extensive study course leading to the designation Certified Financial Planner. You can verify that a professional holds this degree by calling the college at (303) 755-7101 or by writing to 9725 East Hampden Avenue, Denver, CO 80231.

The American College (270 Bryn Mawr Avenue, Bryn Mawr, PA 19010) confers a degree called Chartered Financial Consultant (ChFC). For verification, their phone number is (215) 896-4500.

The Institute of Certified Financial Planners (2 Denver Highlands, 10065 East Harvard Avenue, Suite 320, Denver, CO 80231-5942) has 18,000 certified members and will refer consumers to local professionals who subscribe to their code of ethics. Their phone number is (303) 751-7600.

The members of the International Association for Financial Planning (2 Concourse Parkway, Suite 800, Atlanta, GA 30322) must subscribe to an industry code of ethics. IAFP will also supply names of local chapter members. To get referrals to members of The Registry of Financial Planning Practitioners—limited to those who have passed a qualifying exam—call (404) 395-1605.

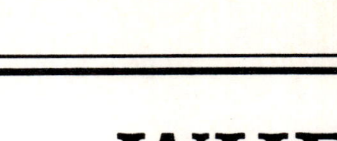

8
WHEN THE PLAN CHANGES

Whether you put a final plan together on your own or use outside professional help, changes must occur periodically. Life goes on; no plan remains intact and unchanged for more than a few years. There are three primary sources for change in financial plans: life dreams, family status, and tax legislation.

LIFE DREAMS

It is unlikely that your life dreams will remain unchanged under all circumstances for your entire life. You will achieve goals and need new ones or outgrow old ones. Perhaps the future expenses you anticipate will change.

Individuals and families move through distinct stages as they grow and age. Note how attitudes toward housing change as life goes on.

> (1) Young singles: Housing is a very immediate need. So an affordable apartment is a common highest priority. Long-range life dreams often are not yet defined.

(2) Newly married: The ultimate life dream at this point might be to save enough for a down payment on a house.

(3) Middle career and child-raising years: Now that equity is building in a house, thoughts about later life begin. Owning a house free and clear, paying off a mortgage more rapidly, or buying a bigger house are common goals. School and college expenses are major future expenses that cause many people to take out second mortgages—often the only alternative when a financial plan has not looked far enough ahead. Unfortunately, this may interfere with other priorities.

(4) Later career years: At this point, the concern is with housing requirements after the children leave. As assets build, thoughts of retirement and mortgage-free shelter begin to predominate. The desire to do those

FIGURE 8-1
Why Changes Occur

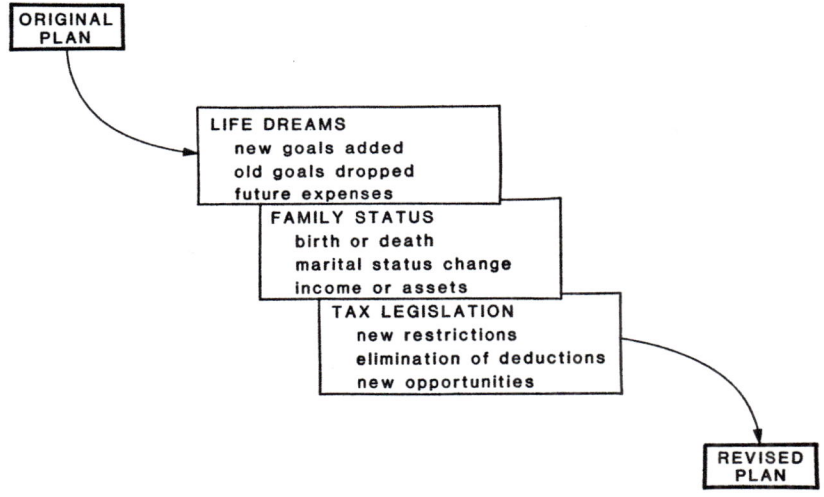

things you have dreamed of all your life—traveling, or buying a luxury car, for example—can become more important. These desires are the most likely causes for borrowing against equity, outside of a financial plan.

(5) Retirement: Once an existing house has been paid for, the priority becomes finding a permanent, practical living arrangement with little or no maintenance, for which no mortgage must be required, of a size that suits a smaller family. Coupled with a desire for lower monthly expenses, people may need to create sources of support from investments and savings, part-time work, or as a last resort, from borrowing.

It is easy to see why American families will see their life dreams grow, become obsolete, or change entirely. If you have not thought about starting your own business, and over a number of years decide you want to go that route, it will mean having to save up money. Thus, a change in your financial plan is warranted. If your child wins a full scholarship and you are no longer required to pay a large sum of money for college tuition, that too will alter the way in which you'll need to plan.

The sections that make up a financial plan cannot be isolated from one another. A change in any one element of your financial plan will be reflected in all of the other elements.

FAMILY STATUS

The birth of a child, a marriage or divorce, or a death will mean the planning process must be done with a different set of restrictions, with greater or lesser monthly expense, or under greater hardships. In an extreme case, a change in family status could mean totally starting over. When the wage earner dies, a plan depending upon years, even decades, of income is no longer valid. Even adequate insurance protection rarely replaces the income that would have been earned over a career's span. Retirement looks much different to the survivor.

Changes in income or family assets will also mean revamping a financial plan. A new job or a substantial increase in pay will alter the monthly budget and potential for savings and investment. If a family member is left a substantial inheritance, or wins a state lottery, financial prospects will change suddenly. More opportunity is likely to make the life dreams of the family more ambitious. Virtually every element of the financial plan alters.

The change could go the other way as well. Imagine how different your financial plan would be if you lost your house and the equity you have built up, without hope of recovering through insurance coverage, by means of earthquakes, hurricanes, tornadoes, or other "acts of God."

There are, of course, less drastic changes that occur. Suppose you have developed a plan to pay off the mortgage on your recently purchased house within 15 years by paying more each month than required by your loan agreement. You can afford to do this, having set aside a cash reserve for emergencies. But your monthly budget is tight and you can't afford a more ambitious plan right now. Then you get the news: In about seven months, your family will be increased by one.

A new child means higher insurance expenses, the need for a higher savings reserve (because your requirements will be greater), and the possibility of higher future expenses. It also means you'll have to modify your plan to pay off your house as quickly as you'd like, possibly reverting to the original loan term and its lower payments, until you've built up a reserve fund. At the same time, you can look for ways to reduce monthly expenses. If your career is promising, income will rise in the future and you'll be able to return to the mortgage acceleration idea in a few years.

TAX LEGISLATION

New federal tax legislation occurs with dependable and deplorable regularity. A major change means that important new rules are added to the already complicated Internal Revenue

Service Code, or significant deductions are eliminated. In recent times, sweeping changes in tax laws have passed Congress with great frequency, often meaning new rules every year or two. Recent tax bills have been the most massive ever enacted and the future will no doubt see more of the same. Whether they begin as reform, simplification, or enhancement, this legislation usually means one thing: an increase in taxes, from the elimination of some deductions, changes in rates, or taxing income that previously was tax-free.

When tax laws change, your status as a homeowner may change, too. If deductions allowed today are reduced or eliminated next year, the economic viability of buying, owning, and selling real estate can be altered.

Another result of tax legislation will be the restriction or elimination of many tax shelters. Investments that reduce taxes first and provide sound economic expectations of a profit second are defined by the IRS as "abusive." Much of the legislation in the past has been aimed at doing away with them. But abusive tax shelters never completely go away; they merely evolve from year to year.

Changes in the tax treatment of profits from the sale of a home would affect the timing and planning of a sale for every homeowner. Residential property transactions have a long history of favorable tax treatment, but we cannot depend upon the protection of tax laws indefinitely. The need for tax revenues, as perceived by Congress, could mean big changes in the future.

New tax legislation may also present opportunities for the homeowner. Recognizing the shortcomings of the Social Security system as a source of retirement income, many economists and legislators encourage individual savings and lend support to broader rules for IRAs and similar tax-deferred retirement accounts. The future could see more of this trend. IRA-like accounts in which earnings are not taxed until proceeds are used might be created to allow families to save money to buy their first home or to fund their children's college tuition.

Every element of your financial plan is likely to be affected by the actions Congress decides to take in the future. Suppose, for example, that your life dream is to own rental property. Your plan calls for the purchase of two or three houses and, perhaps, a duplex over the next 20 years; your income is relatively high, and both you and your spouse work. Part of your motive for investing in real estate will be to reduce your taxes by changing deductions that favor the holders of rental property. Your plan is proceeding according to schedule, but a few years before you intend to put the idea into action, a new tax bill is passed. You will no longer be allowed to deduct those very expenses that made real estate so attractive in the first place.

You could adjust your plan by finding another investment or by proceeding with a revised plan. A wise investment should not be selected or discarded only for tax benefits, and your conclusion might be that the basic idea is a good one but you will have to revise the income tax element. You could accept the inevitability of higher taxes and lower after-tax profits, or you could seek out other ways to shelter part of your income legitimately. You could, for example, put your savings into a tax-free money market fund. As you can see, no plan can be considered permanent and unchanging.

EXAMPLE OF A MODIFIED PLAN

Robert and Fran Maher, introduced in chapter 3, are likely to experience several events that will require modification to their detailed financial plan:

- One of their three children could decide not to attend college.
- The Mahers might decide that, after the children have grown and left home, they would like to sell their house and buy a smaller place outside of town.
- Robert might decide that he would like to leave his job in ten years and, like his wife, start his own business.

Each of these changes would have an immediate effect on the elements of the family's financial plan. Savings and cash reserves would change drastically, as would the allowance for future expenses.

Their original home equity plan—to own their home through accelerated payments within 11 years—would remain intact, but rather than staying in that house, they plan to move. Does this mean taking on a new mortgage for the home they buy or would they have enough in savings and equity to pay cash?

Income taxes would be affected. The Mahers would have a large profit when they sell their house, but if they buy a more expensive house, current tax laws would allow them to avoid tax by repurchasing. Or they could use the once-in-a-lifetime exclusion of up to $125,000 in profits if they're 55 or older.

The Mahers' life and disability policies expire once they each reach their 65th birthday. If they have a new mortgage, they will need extended coverage.

Investment plans would be altered by the change in available cash. The Mahers also must consider that they both plan to

FIGURE 8-2
Changing the Plan's Elements

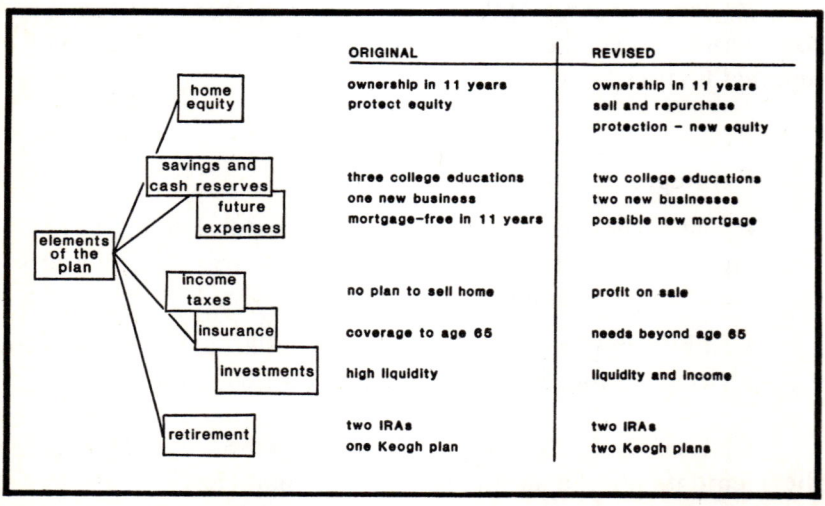

start new businesses at the same time. They would want investments that will help them meet monthly expenses during the time they're both building new income from self-employment.

Once Robert starts his new business, he will be able to have both an IRA and a Keogh account. This increases the funds the family will have for retirement income.

The changes to the Maher family's financial plan are listed in figure 8-2. As each of these changes occurs, the Mahers may check with outsider advisers to seek better ways to realize their now modified life dreams.

HOW CHANGES ARE MADE

These specific modifications to the Maher plan mean recalculating estimated savings, future expenses, insurance requirements, and retirement income for the family, as well as making changes to the plan's timetable.

HOME EQUITY

The Mahers must estimate their home's market value in 11 years, when the mortgage is paid off. When they buy their smaller house they will have some money left over to supplement their retirement reserves. The following shows an assumed rate of inflation and the home's value in 11 years:

Assumed Rate of Inflation	Home Value (11 Years)
2%	$136,700
4%	$169,300

SAVINGS AND CASH RESERVES

Due to the reduction in future expenses, the family will have greater flexibility in their revised plan.

FUTURE EXPENSES

Future expenses are reduced by $20,000:

Reduction: College education	$40,000
Increase: Robert's new business	20,000
Net reduction in requirements	$20,000

INCOME TAXES

With only two of the three children going to college, the Mahers will transfer $40,000 less in income to their children. This means retention of a high level of money to invest and, consequently, higher taxes.

Because both Robert and Fran are starting new businesses, however, higher deductions will be allowed when they each have their Keogh account.

TABLE 8-1

THE MAHERS' FUTURE EXPENSES

	Original Plan		Revised Plan	
Year	College Expenses	New Business	College Expenses	New Business
1	$ 5,000		$ 5,000	
2	5,000		5,000	
3	10,000		10,000	
4	10,000		10,000	
5	10,000		10,000	
6	15,000		10,000	
7	15,000		10,000	
8	15,000		10,000	
9	10,000		5,000	
10	10,000		5,000	$20,000
11	5,000	$20,000		20,000
12	5,000			
13	5,000			

The sale of the family house may result in a tax liability. Profits can be deferred as long as the family buys a more expensive house, but when a less expensive one is purchased the difference in sales and purchase price is subject to tax.

For example:

Sales price (after adjustments)	$155,000
Purchase price of new house (after adjustments)	95,000
Amount subject to capital gains tax	60,000

When they sell their house, the Mahers will decide to take one of two courses. Either they will pay the tax on the profit subject to tax, or they will use their once-in-a-lifetime exclusion, allowing tax-free gains of up to $125,000. The choice will depend on their tax status at the time of the transaction, and their future plans at that point.

INSURANCE

With both Robert and Fran in business, the Mahers probably will keep their life and disability insurance plans in effect after age 65. If they own their new home free and clear, they will not need mortgage insurance. If they do have a mortgage, they will take out a policy at that time.

INVESTMENTS

The Mahers continue to view their house as their primary asset, even after trading for a smaller one. Equity will be preserved as a high priority.

With both Robert and Fran in their own businesses, liquidity will not be as important as they first thought. A higher portion of their capital will be placed in income-producing investments, with less emphasis on liquidity.

RETIREMENT

As owners of businesses, the Mahers will be allowed to deposit up to 25 percent of their earnings from self-employment in tax-deferred Keogh accounts each year. Their retirement income will increase significantly.

Robert will begin his plan in ten years, at age 54, and will keep it until he is 65. He believes his annual deposits will average

TABLE 8-2

ROBERT'S KEOGH PROJECTION

Year	Annual Deposit	Interest (8%)	Balance
1	$5,000	$ 400	$ 5,400
2	5,000	832	11,232
3	5,000	1,299	17,531
4	5,000	1,802	24,333
5	5,000	2,347	31,680
6	5,000	2,934	39,614
7	5,000	3,569	48,183
8	5,000	4,255	57,438
9	5,000	4,995	67,433
10	5,000	5,795	78,228
11	5,000	6,658	89,886
12	5,000	7,591	102,477

$5,000, and that the account will earn about 8 percent interest (see table 8-2).

Fran's account will begin in 12 years, when she is 54. She will also fund the plan until she is 65 and, like Robert, assumes her money will earn 8 percent. She projects annual deposits averaging $4,000 (see table 8-3).

TABLE 8-3

FRAN'S KEOGH PROJECTION

Year	Annual Deposit	Interest (8%)	Balance
1	$4,000	$ 320	$ 4,320
2	4,000	666	8,986
3	4,000	1,039	14,025
4	4,000	1,442	19,467
5	4,000	1,877	25,344
6	4,000	2,348	31,692
7	4,000	2,855	38,547
8	4,000	3,404	45,951
9	4,000	3,996	53,947
10	4,000	4,636	62,583
11	4,000	5,327	71,910
12	4,000	6,073	81,983

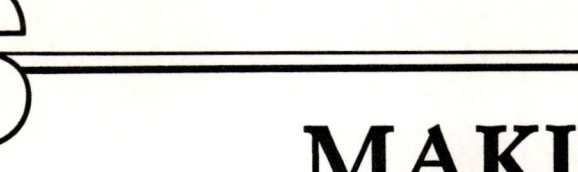

9
MAKING YOUR HOME FIT THE PLAN

For many, the perfect house is the most important life dream of all. Equity can be used to make this happen in two ways: to fund the purchase of land and the construction of the dream house, and to increase and maintain the value and personal comfort of the present house.

Families outgrow their houses for many reasons. Family size grows as children are born and shrinks as children grow and leave. Structures become old. Neighborhoods go through transitions. And people want to make their homes match their dreams, which is possible with planning.

BUYING A FUTURE HOMESITE

Your long-term plan may call for investing in land today, buying it over time, and ultimately building upon it. In making decisions toward this goal, keep investment value in mind even if it is not your first priority.

A sound land investment will grow in value just as your house does. The difficulty, of course, is picking a piece of raw land today that will be viable in the future. The ideal site is one currently not developed (and therefore inexpensive) but potentially desirable. Selecting such acreage is not easy. By the time you can identify the best possible land with certainty, so can everybody else. And the price has risen.

Most people will choose to pay more for a lot in a proven area, to be sure it will hold its value over time. Whether you do, or whether you take a chance on your own instincts, certain factors affect building sites in general:

(1) Shape: Odd-shaped pieces of land mean wasted space and, possibly, a negative impact on value. Traditional square or rectangular lots are more valuable.

(2) Location: Avoid corner lots or lots on busy roads. Look for sites in the middle of quiet streets or in culs-de-sac.

(3) Topography: Check flood zone maps in your area; also avoid areas with sharp drops nearby. Damage from slides and slippage can ruin your land's value and threaten your new home. Also, check to see if the land is such that it can shelter a house from cold or extreme heat.

Never buy a parcel of land you have not seen. Land fraud is big business, and thousands of people have lost their money buying swampland or acreage in the middle of lakes or deserts.

Research prices by checking recent sales for similar lots. This information is public; check with the county recorder or assessor's office.

Start with a fair idea of what it will cost to build a house in the area you are considering. You can get this information from real estate agents, developers, or financing sources. As a general rule, your lot should cost no more than 25 percent of the cost of putting a house on it.

If you buy from a developer, ask for a copy of the property report, which summarizes planned or proposed improvements. Read it carefully—and be aware of the distinction between a planned improvement and a proposed one. Watch out for signs of high-pressure sales tactics and avoid schemes or deals that sound too good to be true.

If you buy under an installment contract, common when buying from developers, be aware that you may not receive title to the land until the entire contract is paid. This depends upon the terms of the contract the developer presents to you. Find out what happens to your payments if the developer goes out of business.

Make sure that any lot you buy will be able to provide these six basic services:

- water supply
- sewage disposal
- paved roads
- drainage system
- garbage collection
- electricity

Look for hidden costs, like taxes, maintenance for the services, or special service district costs.

It is always a good idea to hire an attorney who specializes in real estate transactions to protect you when buying land for a future home site.

BUILD OR RENOVATE?

You take more risks when you buy land than you do when you buy a completed house with the land under it. The decision is highly individual. Will you be happier and better off building, or renovating the house you already have?

> **INFORMATION FOR LAND BUYERS**
>
> Write to the following sources for information on buying land for home sites.
>
> Ask for *The Insider's Guide to Owning Land in Subdivisions* ($2.50) from the following:
>
> INFORM
> 381 Park Ave. S
> New York, NY 10016
>
> Address direct inquiries or complaints about land transactions across state lines to this office:
>
> Office of Interstate Land Sale Registration
> Department of Housing and Urban Development
> 451 Seventh St. SW
> Washington, DC 20410

You can answer that question by defining exactly what you want in a house, an analysis that should be part of your financial plan. Marion and Sam Jaffe, for example, wanted to stay in the town they lived in—but in a house where Sam could have a home office to start his own consulting firm. They sketched out several "ideal" plans and investigated permits, designer and architectural fees, insurance, estimates from contractors, and land appraisals. It became obvious that the project was going to cost more and take longer than they had expected.

Then Marion asked, "Why can't we redesign this house?" Drastic changes were involved but when they considered the plan they saw it could be done. They had plans drawn professionally and obtained several estimates. Their house had a market value of $105,000; the renovation cost less than $50,000—about one-third of the estimated cost to buy land and build a new house.

The cost to build will not always be greater than the cost to buy or to renovate. But it's worthwhile to make some comparisons before you decide.

If you plan to use the equity in your house to construct a new one, the decision must be based on several factors.

First, if the new house will cost more than the equity you have, you will have to finance the difference. Does that fit into your overall plan? Will it interfere with retirement? Can you afford the monthly payments?

Second, will the new house add to your equity? Is it possible that your present house has reached a demand limit? That is, the potential for further increase in value appears to be limited. A new house might appreciate more quickly.

Third, if you plan to move again in several years, you should consider the growth potential for both houses. This means estimating land values, housing demand, and population trends in your area. Areas have been known to double or triple in size in one decade. When this happens, housing values invariably grow at the same time, and most likely at similar rates.

This is happening north of San Francisco, where my family and I live. Typically, a house that cost between $25,000 and $50,000 15 years ago (when we bought) is selling today from $150,000 (on the extreme low end) to $350,000. Housing values have risen to the point where most people cannot afford to buy.

Land has gone up, too. One ad says, "almost an acre—$105,000." Another: "$1/4$ acre, level downslope, $65,000."

Half an hour north of us, the story is different. Planners estimate that the population of Santa Rosa will double by the year 2000, and the rate of construction supports that claim, but the average cost of homes is less by a third or so. Many ads have phrases like "anxious owner," or "priced to sell." If a family from my city wanted to build their dream house and were willing to move 30 minutes farther away, they probably could buy or build more house for the equity they hold now.

HOME IMPROVEMENT

One of the best reasons to tap your home equity is for a home improvement loan to fix up your house—add a new room,

> **FINDING A PROFESSIONAL HOME INSPECTION SERVICE**
>
> To evaluate your own home or a house you are considering buying, have it checked out by an independent home inspector. The person or firm you hire should not, under any circumstances, offer to perform needed repairs or even refer you to a contractor for that purpose. You want someone with completely clear motives. The American Society of Home Inspectors (ASHI), 1010 Wisconsin Avenue NW, Suite 630, Washington, DC 20007 (202) 842-3096, will provide referrals to its members, who are pledged to meet its standards. A home inspector should also have a current contractor's license and should provide a written report on your home. Fees range from $200 to $400.

perform important repairs, repaint, replace the roof, put in new landscaping, upgrade your insulation, or redesign the internal structure.

If you know you will be putting your house on the market, fixing it up will help to sell it more quickly, perhaps for a higher price as well. The more that needs to be done, the wiser it is to spend the money. Potential buyers tend to be more critical than owners themselves. If most houses in your area have two bathrooms, and yours has only one, adding a second one can make a big difference.

Make a distinction between profit-motive investments and the importance of your family's shelter. Improvements done simply to increase values can be a big mistake if you are not planning to move in the near future. Improvements that make personal sense and add to personal comfort should take priority.

You might have bought your house because it was the best you could afford at the time. As more financial security and equity becomes available to you, it is possible to tailor your house to your specifications.

What changes do you need or want to make? The answer to this question changes from one stage of your life to another. As your family grows, you may want another bedroom or another bath. Years later, the need for a home office may be more pressing.

It isn't always another room or so that people want. If your children have grown and left, you might want to take out a bedroom and use the extra space to make a larger living room area. Or your dreams might involve a completely redone kitchen, recreational areas, a different heating or cooling system, or replacement of aging appliances.

Remodeling comes with pitfalls. One is failure to think through the improvement you plan. A family may have the borrowing power—through their built-up equity—to make some very expansive and expensive improvements. It can be as exciting as moving to a new house, and in that fever of excitement, reason can be lost.

Even if you are thinking straight, be careful about the scope of your improvements. The selling prices of other houses in your area helps to determine the market value of your home. So if your improvements result in much more house than your neighbors have, you are likely to lose money when you sell.

That is called overimprovement. If the average house in your neighborhood has three bedrooms, a living room, and one bath, and you end up with a custom-designed house that has four bedrooms and a den, two baths, and a guest cottage, you will be very lucky to break even.

If the average price of those average homes is $145,000, and you improve your home by $65,000 (bringing your basic investment up to $210,000), you have the nicest home on the block. But if the highest sales price for a home in your area during the last two years has been only $150,000, you will have problems getting its worth when you decide to sell. It may not be logical, or even fair. But it's the way the market works.

If you plan to stay in your home indefinitely and can afford the improvements, do them anyway. Your home is shelter, not shares in a mutual fund.

IMPROVEMENTS THAT ADD EQUITY

A common misconception is that your house will be worth $20,000 more if you make $20,000 worth of improvements. It isn't true. Many popular improvements increase in value only by a fraction of their cost to you. In deciding among the possibilities for improvement, consider those first that will add the most to your equity.

The May/June 1985 issue of *Rodale's New Shelter* magazine (which is now *Rodale's Practical Homeowner* magazine) published a list of profitable improvements for the "average" American home in a midwestern suburb—17 years old, 1,600 square feet in area, three bedrooms and one bath before improvements, with a market value of $90,000 (see table 9-1). It is obvious from this

TABLE 9-1

FOURTEEN HOME IMPROVEMENT INVESTMENTS

	Average Cost*	Resale Value*	Percent
Adding a bath	$ 6,800	$ 7,000	103
Adding a fireplace	3,100	4,000	130
Adding a room (15 × 25 ft.)	28,000	17,000	61
Adding a skylight	2,400	1,500	60
Adding a solar greenhouse	10,000	9,000	90
Adding a swimming pool	18,000	5,000	28
Adding a wooden deck	4,300	2,150	50
Adding new roofing	3,350	2,500	75
Adding new siding	6,000	6,000	100
Bathroom remodeling	4,900	2,500	51
Installing insulation	1,200	1,000	83
Kitchen remodeling (major)	16,500	13,000	79
Kitchen remodeling (minor)	5,800	5,000	86
Replacing windows and doors	9,750	6,800	70

*1985 average prices
Source: "Money-Making Home Improvements" by Don Logey, Rodale's New Shelter, *May/June* 1985. Used with permission.

table, that many home improvements increase the resale value of a home. One last word: Don't forget to update your homeowner's insurance for the value of improvements you make (see chapter 6).

FINANCING IMPROVEMENTS

A home improvement loan is perhaps the easiest type of borrowing available. We all know that. We receive junk mail every day telling us we are already approved for equity loans. It's finding the best deal that takes work.

Research the market. Consider the current interest rate, how badly lenders want your money, and what terms you will seek.

When interest rates are moderate to high, fewer people are borrowing, so lenders try to make their products seem more attractive. This can work to your advantage if true bargains, not just gimmicks, are available.

Typical lures include the "no points" loan, or the loan for which the lender promises there will be no appraisal fee. Be careful. The lender has structured the loan to make a profit, so you might find the charges disguised as a higher interest rate, an administrative fee, or other excessive closing costs.

The real bargains are competitive. If you can get a below-market fixed interest rate over 30 years at a time when interest rates seem to be rising, that's a good deal. While it may mean extra costs, they're worth paying.

Variable-rate mortgages often are gimmicks. These are loans in which the interest rate changes each year. Be wary when you sign a variable-rate mortgage contract. Lenders offering no-points loans and competitive rates on this type of mortgage might in fact be inducing you with a "teaser" clause. The low rate may be good for only six months to one year. After that, it jumps significantly, and you're suddenly stuck with hefty payments.

Variable-rate mortgage payments could go out of control if interest rates rise quickly. To protect you, there are two forms of caps in these contracts.

A rate cap limits the top rate the lender can charge you. For example, you might contract for a loan starting at 10 percent, with adjustments in the rate to be made once per year based on movement in the one-year Treasury-bill rates. The contract you sign states that you can never be charged more than 15 percent, regardless of how high interest rates go. Such a contract might include a clause requiring you to make up excess interest—so if rates sit at 16 percent for a while, and you're paying only 15 percent, you might be required to stay there even after the index rate has fallen again.

The second type, the payment cap, can be dangerous. You might express your doubt to a loan officer about the uncertain future of interest rates. He tells you, "Don't worry. The payments start out at $602 per month, but the contract guarantees you will never have to pay more than $750, regardless of the going interest rate." Pretty good clause, at first glance.

In fact, it can do you more harm than any other clause in a mortgage contract. If rates go so high that your maximum of $750 is not enough to cover monthly interest, your loan balance will begin to go up each month instead of down. Your entire payment goes toward interest, but you owe more and more money. This is called "negative amortization," and it's just as frightening as it sounds. It may mean that the profits you are building in your home will pass entirely to the lender.

Variable-rate mortgages are the most desirable for the lenders to sell. But for borrowers the best deal is a 30-year fixed-rate loan. For a home improvement, most lenders will offer shorter terms, perhaps 15 years or only 10.

To get a 30-year loan, you may decide to refinance your whole mortgage. Lenders often offer refinanced mortgages at much lower than the going rates for second mortgages. For example, in mid-1986, interest rates had fallen 3 points from the year before. Fixed-rate first mortgages could be obtained in northern California for 9.5 percent, while second mortgages were averaging 10.5 to 11.5 percent. Points (1 percent of the face amount of a loan) were down from previous periods, too.

Loan marketing lies behind this structure. Consider the case of a family with two mortgages, the first at 7.5 percent and the second at 13 percent. Naturally the family would like to replace the second with a 10 percent loan and leave the first intact. The lender, on the other hand, would prefer that the family replace the first mortgage. If they want the lowest possible rates, they will have to take out a new first mortgage, refinancing all of the debt—including that cheaper loan.

The important point here is to look for the longest possible term. Remember, you can always pay it off more rapidly, assuming prepayment is allowed in your contract without penalty.

Financing is complicated. Many homeowners simply go to one lender, taking whatever loan is recommended. You can do better by investigating alternatives, deciding what you want, and then shopping for your loan.

The biggest mistake a homeowner can make in the effort to acquire the perfect house—through buying land and building, moving, or renovating a present house—is to make the decision without working through the financial plan. You can get exactly what you want while preserving equity but, like other phases of the plan, this means thorough investigation, preplanning, and an analysis of alternatives.

Section II

PUTTING EQUITY TO WORK

10
WHEN YOU SELL YOUR HOME

When you sell and move to another house, the decision is often emotional, based on your like or dislike for the house or changes in the circumstances of your life—a new baby, a new job, a long-planned change in career direction, or retirement. No matter how attached to your home you have become, when you are ready to sell, don't let emotions get in the way of making sensible financial decisions. For the wise money manager, it is an investment decision as well.

Homeowners go through a transition once they decide to sell and move. The home they once considered a deeply personal possession becomes an asset, a thing of value to be disposed of for the highest possible price.

As cold as that sounds, it makes a lot of sense. Evaluating your present home as a seller also helps to make you a better buyer for the next one. Investment value is an important aspect of home ownership—although the emotional attachment you have for your house can be a powerful influence when it comes to dealing with potential buyers and deciding which bid to accept.

GOING BY THE PLAN

John and Lois Browne were guided by the rules they had established for themselves in their plan when they decided to sell their present house and move. They were in their mid-forties and their youngest of three children had recently left home. Some years before they had agreed to sell their three-bedroom, two-bath house at this point in their lives and move to a smaller place. They wanted either a house with two bedrooms or a house with one bedroom and a den, plus two baths.

They also wanted to stay in the same area, close to friends and relatives. Their house, now without a mortgage, had a market value of $105,000. Investigating, they knew they would be able to find the perfect house for $90,000. Their attitude was realistic and they were open to unexpected options.

They had two definite planning points:

- The original plan should be reviewed to see if it still suited their desires.

- The move should make long-term economic sense.

Just because you have made a plan does not mean you are obligated to follow it. You can change your mind; sometimes it is impossible to recognize the best course until you are on the point of taking a less-than-best course. If you think moving might be a mistake, think about it some more. You already have a place to live, so there is no immediate rush to make a decision. You never really miss an opportunity for exchanging houses once you own one. If you fear that prices will rise in the future, meaning you will have to pay more when you do move, remember you also will be able to command a correspondingly higher price for your home. Unless there is a serious flaw in your house, its value will rise and fall with the market in general.

Yes, prices for houses could rise 20 percent during the next year, but such a boom would also include the place you already own. By the same argument, if the value of your home fell 20 percent, other homes would suffer the same rate of decline.

The Brownes reexamined their plan, looking at alternatives: (1) renovating the present house so it would be more fuel-efficient, (2) keeping it as rental property (see chapter 11) and financing a new house by borrowing with their equity as collateral, or (3) simply staying where they were.

(Their second point stated that a move should make long-term economic sense. If your primary reason for considering a move is to free up cash, you may discover you'd be better off staying where you are and refinancing. The result could be no increase in your monthly payment, a shorter term until the loan is repaid, and cash back to you. All without moving.

The difference between the selling price of the Brownes' house and the purchase of a new house would be taken up entirely by closing costs and the expense of moving. But even though no monetary profit would result, money would be saved in the lower cost of maintaining and running the smaller house.

SELLING A HOUSE

The first step toward selling your house is to look at it critically. What's wrong with it? How can you prepare it for sale, making it more attractive, so that you will get the best possible price?

You probably can see some of the most obvious problems yourself. It may need painting or landscaping, a new roof, weather stripping, or plumbing repairs. Your house may need a termite inspection or an engineer's evaluation—more money that must be spent before your house will sell. For a more detailed analysis, you should have an independent house appraisal done by a professional.

Now you must decide what repairs and cosmetic changes to make—a process of economic trade-offs. Will the cost of the repair be offset by the increased selling price of the house? Will an undone repair discourage too many potential buyers? Will some changes *lower* the selling price—as they might if, for example, a potential buyer hated your concept of good landscaping.

The structural condition of a house and the condition of major systems are important. Few buyers will consider a house if the roof is questionable or if the heating system seems unreliable, for example. Also, the buyer naturally expects the house to look its best, so if you spend $2,000 painting the exterior and having a garden service remove weeds, trim hedges, and haul away accumulated trash, the prospective buyer won't necessarily be impressed with your investment. In general, though, the safe course is to do repairs and present the real estate people with the kind of property they love to advertise as "clean," which means the house is ready for new owners to move right in.

The next step is to set a price. Consult your real estate broker and the independent appraisal and compare your price with the prices of houses that have been sold in the last two years in your area. Real estate agents agree that, in general, a house will sell more quickly if you price it below market value, but good financial planning means that you should not feel compelled to take the first offer.

A number of factors will affect the price. If you have one bath while most houses in the area have two, that will hold down your price. If your house is on a quiet street, your price can be higher. A garage can make a difference.

Unusual landscaping can detract from value. If you have replaced lawns with nicely manicured rose bushes or rock gardens, buyers may be fearful of the difficulty of maintaining them.

A swimming pool can reduce the market value of your house and take away from its marketability. Not everyone likes to swim, and pool maintenance costs are high. Pools reduce yard space and pose a threat to small children. And they raise homeowner's insurance premiums.

The price should be both realistic and competitive. Be aware that a real estate agent might disagree with the price you expect. Your opinion as homeowner is not entirely objective, and neither is the agent's, whose motive is to sell the house easily and earn a commission on the sale.

If you want $105,000 and the agent suggests putting the house on the market for $99,950, you must decide whether to comply or to insist on your own price. The agent will make several arguments: setting the price below $100,000 will make the house sell faster, and in a slow market the agent might claim that's the most you can expect to get. Your counterarguments might include the fact that you're not in a hurry, that you would settle for less but want some bargaining room, that the smaller house across the street sold for $105,000 two months ago. Listen to the agent's advice even if you finally decide not to heed it. The truth might be that your house will not command more than $100,000.

If your price is too high for the market, your house simply will not sell. If it is too low, the house will sell quickly and you'll lose some of the profits you might have earned. But if the price is reasonable, the house should sell within a reasonable amount of time, and you will earn that profit.

Be sure you have allowed for unforeseen costs and contingencies as part of your plan. Your most level-headed thinking and planning are useless if you end up in a financial bind with your new house because your equity turns out to be inadequate to cover what you expected it to cover. At that point, financing becomes a necessity instead of a choice.

SELECTING AN AGENT

Agents play a strange role in home sales. They are paid by you and they represent you legally in the transaction. But in reality they are go-betweens, negotiating between buyer and seller.

For example, imagine the following exchange:

Seller: The list price is $105,000, but I'd probably accept an offer as low as $102,000.

Agent: Let's see what offers are made, and you can decide at that point.

Buyer (later): How much below the asking price should I make my offer?

Agent: That's your decision. But I think the seller is really motivated and you could probably offer two or three thousand less.

When you look for an agent, ask friends, neighbors, your banker, accountant, and attorney for recommendations. Then interview the prospects. Select someone with whom you have rapport and sign a listing agreement with them only after you are convinced that they will represent you well.

The terms of the agreement depend on the real estate brokerage's policy and on market conditions. It usually runs from three to six months. If, one month later, you conclude that the agent is not doing a good job, how do you get out of the agreement?

You've signed the contract, but most agents agree that there's no point in keeping you bound if you're unhappy and they will probably release you—with the stipulation that, if you sell the house to someone they originally brought, they are entitled to a commission. You could also insert a clause in the listing agreement, stating that you have the right to cancel it with ten days' written notice. Confident professionals will not object.

Commission rates are negotiable. Successful agents earn every cent of their commissions by their ability to get you the best price possible, but you have the right to talk an agent into a rate lower than the standard 6 or 7 percent.

As an alternative to working with a commissioned real estate agent, you can hire a discount broker or sell your house on your own.

A discount broker will charge a flat 3 percent commission and supply you with all the forms you need, perhaps placing an ad in the paper for you. You will get no help in showing your house, nor in negotiating with potential buyers.

If you're willing to do the research to complete a real estate transaction, you can be a FISBO—real estate jargon meaning "for sale by owner." Inquire at your county recorder's office and ask for help from your loan officer. But FISBOs face real disadvantages. First, many buyers will assume they can offer you 6 or 7 percent less than you ask because there is no real estate commission. Second, you lose the objectivity of a third party in negotiating. And third, potential buyers are often uncomfortable with an owner. They are afraid to ask questions, criticize openly, or point out defects. My wife and I looked at one house where the couple was so anxious to sell that they followed us around, practically wringing their hands and biting their lips. No one wants that kind of pressure.

Once you have a buyer, consider the financing arrangements. The most desirable way to sell is for the buyer to arrange financing and present you with a check at the closing. There are other possibilities, however. If you have an assumable loan at an attractive rate, that makes your house easier to sell. If you are willing to carry a loan yourself, that is even better—from the buyer's point of view. Do not agree to carry a loan just to sell your house. If you feel you must make the sale, it might be necessary to agree to carry part of the loan, particularly if interest rates are high. If the going rate is 13 percent and you are willing to take a $50,000 mortgage at 10 percent, that makes a buyer more than willing to close the deal. But be aware of how this will affect your own financial plan, and of the risk that the buyer will not make payments.

COORDINATING A BUY AND SELL

The greatest difficulty in buying a new house comes from the timing of transactions. You have six possible choices.

First, you can take a chance, hoping that your house will sell at about the same time you buy your new place. The danger is that your house will not be sold for the price you ask, due to any of a number of possible circumstances. Most people do not want to commit themselves to buying a new property until they have determined that the old house will sell. They could end up with two houses and no money.

The traditional method for dealing with this—your second choice—is to make a contingency offer that states, "I will buy your house for an agreed price, assuming I am able to sell my present house by a specified date."

From your point of view as the buyer, a contingency offer is an advantage—and perhaps, for security and peace of mind, a necessity. But it also puts you at one disadvantage: If a seller receives three offers and two of them are contingencies, the seller will be inclined to accept the third, even if it is lower than the other two. Contingencies can fall through. They add an element of doubt to the transaction.

A third idea is to make a contingency offer after a potential sale when your present home has entered the escrow stage. Here, you have the strong argument that the marketability of your house is established and a serious buyer is almost there. In this case, you should have a new house picked out that you want to buy. Timing is crucial. But remember, there are always more opportunities, if you are willing to look for them.

This alternative is practical only when you plan to move to a new house fairly close by. If hundreds of miles separate your old and new homes, the timing is too tricky.

A fourth idea is to place the contingency upon the buyer of your old house, saying, in effect, "I accept your offer to buy my house for an agreed price, assuming I am able to purchase a new home by a specified date." This will work when there are more buyers looking for houses than there are houses available.

The fifth choice is simply to sell your old house and store your belongings, then move to an apartment that you rent on a month-to-month basis, while you look for a new house—for which you will be able to make a cash offer (or an offer with a large down payment and virtually assured financing), free of contingencies on your part. This makes you the most ideal sort of buyer from the seller's and the real estate agent's points of view. The disadvantage is that you must pay for storage and subject your belongings to two moves (probably also meaning a higher cost). You also must live inconveniently "between" houses, but this may be the only practical choice.

If your move is due to a job transfer, your employer probably will pay moving expenses. You may be able to negotiate moving help if you are taking a new job.

There is a sixth idea, which should be considered only if it fits into the context of your financial plan. That is to keep the old property and become a landlord. There are many risks associated with this idea, specifically having to do with the management aspects of renting to someone else. This idea is explored in detail in chapters 11 and 14.

The key planning point to selling a house and coordinating a move is that you will always need a place to live. Put your emphasis on choosing exactly what you want within the context of your plan. Be flexible and keep an open mind to new ideas. And sell your house on terms and for a price that are acceptable to you. As long as the final decisions fit your plan, the choices you make will be the right ones.

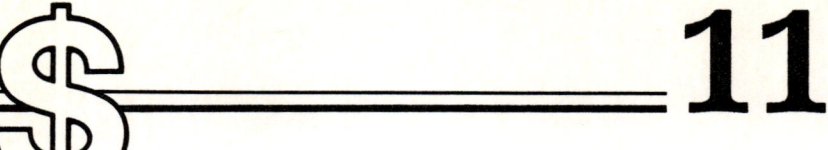

ALTERNATIVES TO HOME OWNERSHIP

There can be life after owning a home. The idea may seem contrary to the entire assumption behind this book: that building and maintaining home equity is critical as a basis for financial well-being.

But remember that the point of a financial plan is to achieve life dreams. At some point in your life, those dreams can change. For some people, retirement means simplicity, low costs, lots of available money. The goal of owning a debt-free house may disappear. You may be ready to move, cash in equity, and live as renters, or owners of a condominium or cooperative.

There are advantages and disadvantages to each situation. Do you enjoy keeping your house in shape? If you do, you will miss it once you move. On the other hand, if you hate that type of work, you can escape most of it by living in a condominium.

It is difficult for many who have lived in a house for years to accept the idea of sharing a wall with a neighbor. You cannot know how significant an issue this might be until you make a move, and by then, it's too late. Look at your style of living now and try to decide how attached you are to your own house.

When my wife and I put in a bid on our first home, the previous owner told the real estate agent that price was a secondary factor: "We want our house to be lived in by a nice young couple with children."

At the time I was surprised, even amused by this illogical standard. But after living there for several years, I began to understand. They had raised their children in the house and had a very personal attachment to it. The only way they could stand to leave was by making sure someone else would continue the tradition.

A move like theirs can come as a result of years of planning. It can also come because lack of planning has forced an emergency adjustment to economic realities. The first, of course, is preferable; the decision is under your control.

That family moved to a condominium. Indirectly, we heard that within a few months they regretted it. Before you make such a major change, remember that your financial plan is the means for reaching personal goals and dreams. Don't move, even if it makes sense on paper, if you think it may prove to be a mistake.

FINANCIAL ADVANTAGES AND DISADVANTAGES

Let's explore some of the financial advantages of selling a house and moving to a rented house, apartment, or condominium. First, maintenance costs will not be your direct responsibility. If you rent, maintenance is factored into your rent. In a condo or co-op you pay for maintenance through monthly association fees, but, because costs are shared, they are usually lower. Not only will you pay less for maintenance but you will also avoid *doing* maintenance: no lawn mowing, no painting, puttering, or trash-removing responsibilities.

Insurance costs for group housing are lower. The biggest part of a homeowner's insurance policy is for property protection. This becomes part of your rent or is handled through the group association.

You can live "rent-free." If you invest the money you receive from the sale of your house, it could yield enough to pay for your rent elsewhere. If your equity is high enough, you could pay cash for a condo or co-op and have enough interest income left to cover the maintenance fee.

It's true that you also live rent-free when you own your home free and clear, but there are important differences. The costs of maintenance and insurance are higher, and the equity is less available for use if it is needed.

To illustrate how home equity could be invested to pay for other housing, let's assume that your sales price is $175,000 and your original cost, after closing, was $55,000.

Selling price	$175,000
Cost	55,000
Profit	$120,000

The profit can be tax-free because of a provision in the tax laws: If you are 55 or older and have used your home as your principal residence for at least three of the last five years, you can claim a once-in-a-lifetime exemption on gains of as much as $125,000.

Do you think this profit, if invested, could earn 8 percent per year? That's $800 per month, without adding the benefits of compound interest. If you paid less than $800 per month rent, the balance could accumulate as an investment or be used for the family budget.

Assume that your $120,000 profit was used to purchase a condo or co-op, for which you spent $75,000. The $45,000 you had left over to invest, at 8 percent, would yield $300 per month, which might be enough to pay monthly maintenance fees.

The decision to give up home ownership also has financial disadvantages. The most important is the issue of rising costs. The owner of a debt-free house, and even the holder of a fixed-rate mortgage, is partially insulated from the immediate effects of inflation on housing. But as property taxes, utilities, and the cost of maintenance rise, so do rents. Increases in monthly maintenance expenses are quickly passed on to condo owners. Changes in management or ownership are also likely to be reflected in increased expenses—and you control very little of the process.

The plan to invest proceeds from the sale of your house also carries several risks. If rents or fees do rise, you have no guarantee that your investment yield will also rise. Even if rents and fees should stay the same, interest rates could fall and your yield could follow.

A second form of risk is loss of capital. Any investment carries some risk. The greater risk you allow, perhaps in trying for a high yield, the greater the chance that you could have money in a losing investment.

Another disadvantage is more subtle. One of the best features of home ownership is that equity is so difficult to "take out." Greater discipline is required once that money is closer at hand in banks or other investing institutions. For some people, the temptation to use just a little is too great. Remember that it is an asset, not income.

While your equity was growing in your house, it was not taxed. Money you borrowed against equity also was not taxed, so even taking out a new mortgage did not raise tax questions. But once that money is invested, it becomes liable to taxation. For this reason, the full yield from your investments is not available for rent or monthly fees. At the end of the year, a percentage will have to go to the government.

CONDO LIVING

If you want the advantages and can live with the disadvantages of selling your house, the next step is deciding which alternative to home ownership you will like best. Condominium living appeals to young families looking for a first home, especially in areas where condos are cheaper than single-family houses, to city-dwelling professionals without children, and to older people whose children have left home.

If you sell your present home and buy a condominium, you are taking a market risk. Demand for units might change in the near future, even if it's high now. That would mean the market value of your investment could level out or decline. This will be a minor concern if the investment value is secondary in importance. Perhaps the simplicity of condo life is appealing enough, and your financial plan does not require increasing market values once you move to a condominium.

Going from a house to a condo offers several advantages and disadvantages for someone used to living in a house. First, condo living means little or no maintenance. You do not actually own the grounds or even the building. You own the "air space" within the walls of your unit, from wall to wall and from ceiling to floor. The rest—the building itself, the lawns and parking lot, recreation room, swimming pool, and any other common elements—are owned by the tenants in common. There is no grass to mow, plumbing to fix, or outside roofing and painting to complete. For this, you pay a monthly maintenance fee set by an association of people living in the development or, in a new development, by a developer.

The association is a form of government run by you and the other owners or tenants. You elect a board, which sets the rules for everyone, as well as the level of maintenance fees to be charged each month. This fee must be high enough to pay the insurance premiums for casualty and other contingent losses, maintenance of the grounds and buildings, and other costs.

Look for the same basic elements in a condo that you would in a house: Is it in a pleasant neighborhood? Are the neighbors people of similar ages, interests, and economic status? Consider the space within a unit. Going from a house of 2,500 square feet to a 900-square-foot condominium will be an adjustment. What is the quality of construction? What grade of materials was used? What is the maintenance record and current appearance of the grounds and units? Pay attention to your own impressions.

As a condo owner, you have the right to lease your unit to someone else, which affords you some flexibility. But note how many other units are being leased. Market values for condominiums populated primarily by resident owners are more likely to maintain their market value and a stable demographic mix over time. Even if you select carefully, you could end up living with people who have nothing in common with you.

Know what to look for in a sales contract. Buying a condominium is more complex than buying a house. In addition to the standard paperwork, condos have a number of special documents. Hire an attorney who specializes in real estate if you are unable to comprehend the full nature of the restrictions under which you agree to live in a condominium.

CONDOMINIUM DOCUMENTS

Master Deed: This can also be called a declaration, enabling declaration, declaration of conditions, covenant, plan of ownership, or restrictions.

The master deed includes a map of the development and a legal description of the property. It describes each unit's area of ownership and the common interests in common areas. It defines the means of governing, sets forth rules for establishing the association, and lists restrictions. If the condominium has not yet been constructed, the master deed should include a full description of all streets, facilities, and parking lots.

Unit Deed: This deed is held by the owner of each unit. It repeats most of the information—plot, legal description, and common element shares—from the master deed.

Bylaws: This often-lengthy document sets forth the rules and restrictions. It may be complex enough to require review by an attorney. It defines how you can use your unit, what you can and cannot do inside or around it, how the governing association operates, how members are elected or replaced and what powers they have. It sets forth methods for assessing monthly maintenance fees, rules of access to common areas, and other rules by which you will have to agree to abide.

Take your time, even if it means losing an opportunity. Do not allow yourself to be pressured into signing an agreement until all your questions have been answered.

Review the management agreement carefully. Be sure that the power to set policy rests with the association's board of directors (consisting of condo owners like yourself) and not with the developer or a property management company.

Check for restrictions before you sign up. For example, most agreements specify that you cannot alter the unit in a significant way without the approval of the board. You probably will not be able to paint the outside without permission and, in some developments, you will not be allowed to plant a garden or put in a deck in a yard (if you even have a yard).

CO-OPS AND RENTING

You do not actually own a cooperative, not even the air space within it (unlike a condo). Rather, you own shares in a corporation, which owns the property. You hold equity through the corporation. Because it is a corporation, you do not have the freedom to sell or rent your unit to anyone you please. The governing board can reject a potential buyer for a number of reasons. The co-op also reserves the right to buy your unit from you before you may offer it outside.

As a renter, your control is even more limited. Except as defined by the terms of your lease, your landlord decides whether to paint, add a swimming pool, or change the drapes and carpet.

There can be a sort of silent agreement between landlords and tenants. The landlord keeps living conditions pleasant, and the rain out of your living room. In return, you learn to live with increases in rent every few years.

Rental units can be taken from you. If the owner decides to convert your place to his own residence, he can force you to leave. Apartment houses are bought and sold. Many for-rent houses are actually perpetually on the market and could sell at any time. A new owner may be under no obligation to keep the tenants who live there at the time. Part of your prerental research should be to determine the prevailing rules governing leases in your area.

You also give up some tax benefits. Interest and property tax deductions disappear. But you do have the ultimate freedom: You can move, usually quickly and easily.

The key to making a decision on giving up home ownership, as with all decisions involving your money, lies in your financial plan. Does it make long-term sense? Does it promote the achievement of your life dreams?

CO-OP DOCUMENTS

Charter: Also called a certificate of incorporation, this document is like the master deed for a condominium. It describes the co-operative without identifying individual units, assigns a par value to shares, and lists the number that will be sold.

Certificate of beneficial interest: Like the stock certificate you receive when you invest in the stock market, this lists the number of co-operative shares you own and how much voting power that gives you.

Proprietary lease: This specifies the expenses for which you will be liable as a co-op resident and the expenses that will be paid by the co-op as a whole through the collection of monthly fees. It also lists penalties and fees for failure to pay your share of maintenance costs, restrictions on sublets or sale of shares, and rules regarding use of common areas, pets, noise, parking, and so forth. Co-op leases commonly run for 99 years or until the date you sell your shares.

Co-op bylaws: This document sets forth procedures for electing the governing board, rights and responsibilities, voting rights, and meeting procedures. Many of the issues spelled out in the proprietary lease are summarized in the bylaws.

12
USING EQUITY AFTER RETIREMENT

Once we have arrived at the age of discretion—somewhere in our forties, probably—we tend to conduct our financial affairs with a retirement target date in mind. After that date, a new set of conditions takes over. The conflict between the need for a continuing income and the need for a place to live causes hardships now for those who have not planned.

Seven out of every ten Americans age 65 and older own their own homes. But 67 percent of Americans in the same group live on less than $10,000 per year. For the homeowner looking ahead to retirement there are alternatives to the either/or choice of remaining in a house and living at a lower standard than you'd like or selling it and having to worry about alternative housing. The typical choices we think about when we view retirement housing are: own or rent.

If you retire on a severely restricted income, the need to own property free and clear is particularly important. But a fixed income often limits even a greatly simplified life-style. With inflation—say 2 percent per year—an income of $10,000 per year diminishes in value in a very short period of time:

Number of Years	Actual Spending Power
1	$9,800
2	9,604
3	9,412
4	9,224
5	9,040
6	8,859
7	8,682
8	8,508
9	8,338
10	8,171

After ten years, your income is worth about $150 per month less than it was when you retired. That becomes increasingly significant as the quality of life you can afford declines year by year.

At the same time, the house you own free and clear might be worth $80,000, $120,000, even $200,000—and in general its value is increasing.

You cannot mortgage the house. If you do, the monthly payments create a larger problem in the long run because you continue to live on a fixed income that has less buying power every year.

Most Americans eventually compromise, sell their homes and move to smaller houses, condominiums, or apartments and put the leftover cash in a safe form of savings to ease their monthly budgets.

It has been my contention all along that you can avoid this kind of problem by working within a financial plan, starting right away. But suppose you are diverted along the way, a business fails, or unforeseen expenses come up? Even with a plan you could end up a cash-poor, equity-rich retired American. What then?

THE REVERSE ANNUITY MORTGAGE

One solution might be a reverse annuity mortgage. An annuity in its traditional form is a type of insurance contract. To buy an annuity, you pay an insurance company a lump sum or the same amount of money each month for a number of years. Then, when you are a predetermined age, the company begins to pay you.

Most annuities promise to make payments for a specified minimum period of time. If you do not live that long, the balance is paid to your heirs. If you live longer, payments continue while you live. Some annuities make payments for the specified period, then stop.

With a reverse annuity mortgage, the payments are drawn from the equity in your house. In effect, you borrow the money, receiving specified payments over a period of time. The mortgage becomes due and is paid from your estate when you die, or at the end of a specified time, depending on your particular reverse annuity mortgage. Many insurance companies offer reverse annuity mortgage contracts, usually to homeowners age 65 and over.

A reverse annuity has two components: the annuity and the mortgage.

THE ANNUITY

The annuity company is gambling that you will not live long enough to exceed the amount of equity in your house. If you do, the insurer will lose money on the contract. Predictions of the average life expectancy for people of your age, sex, and medical background are based on mortality tables that indicate a strong likelihood that the company will profit from the total number of contracts it sells, even if you as an individual surprise them.

This principle is like that applied in life insurance. When a company insures your life, it sets its premiums so that the total amount collected from all its policies will be adequate to pay all claims and still produce a profit. With an annuity, the amount of your equity compared with your life expectancy tells the insurance company exactly how much it can afford to pay you.

Annuity contracts establish the period of time over which the company will pay you and include a specific description of the amount you are to receive. Most contracts include a provision that if you do not live past a certain age, some portion of your equity will be left for your beneficiaries. This ensures you that a large percentage of your equity will not be lost if you die within a short period of time.

That amount varies from company to company but is based on your age and the amount of equity you have in your home.

THE MORTGAGE

As you are paid each month, the amount you receive accumulates as a debt to the insurance company. You are thus relieved from the burden of having to make monthly payments toward a mortgage, although you can continue to live in your house for the rest of your life.

ADVANTAGES AND DISADVANTAGES

The reverse annuity contract allows you to fund your retirement years. It also reduces the equity in your house, possibly to zero. As a homeowner, you can view this in one of two ways. First, using home equity to generate necessary monthly income is a good use of that equity. You have a place to live and you have an income. Your primary concern is no longer building and preserving equity; it is living comfortably.

The second point of view holds that it is still important and necessary to preserve equity. Good financial planning allows you to choose between the two points of view. If your financial plan has not been organized enough, and your income during your working years did not allow you the flexibility to save, you may have to choose the first out of necessity.

The strongest argument in favor of a reverse annuity mortgage is that it enables you to maintain a standard of living, yet gives you the security and shelter you need in the years of retirement.

The biggest negative is that you are spending your assets rather than preserving them. If you plan to stay in your house forever, this will not concern you. But if you decide to move, you will discover that the reverse annuity mortgage has drained away a substantial portion of your equity, perhaps more than a straight mortgage would have done.

By taking out a reverse annuity mortgage you *are* giving up your house. But as a solution, it is worth looking at.

THE SALE-LEASEBACK

Another alternative is to sell your house and to lease it back as a tenant. This type of contract, often made between family members but equally valid between strangers, may solve two problems. The seller needs a place to live but wants access to equity. The buyer wants to build equity within a financial plan or to make a long-term investment.

In this arrangement, you receive all of your equity at once, in cash. The buyer takes out a mortgage and makes payments, treating your home as an investment property. You make monthly rental payments.

If your equity is high enough to produce investment income to pay rent and leave enough so that you have extra money for your monthly budget, this will work.

To illustrate: John and Linda Flores, both age 67, owned their house free and clear. It had a current market value of $145,000. When they entered a sale-leaseback arrangement with their son David, they received that amount in cash and invested it, getting an average return of 8 percent. That added $967 per month to their income.

John and Linda agreed with David on a rent of $750 per month. This left $217 (total interest income, less rental payments) to increase their monthly budget and give them financial flexibility when added to their Social Security and pension income.

David, upon purchasing the property, put down $25,000 and borrowed $120,000. His mortgage payments came to $1,053 per month. After receiving the rent, he was out of pocket $303 per month, which was more than offset by the tax benefits of owning a rental property for which he could deduct interest, property taxes, maintenance, insurance, and depreciation.

ADVANTAGES AND DISADVANTAGES

For the Flores family, a sale-leaseback benefited both parents and son. The arrangement, however, has a number of potential problems both for you and the buyer.

The terms of the contract must be designed so that everyone involved will be satisfied. It must be clear that you will be allowed to live in your home indefinitely, or that your lease can be renegotiated after a certain period of time. The initial rent should be specified and should be in line with rental rates for similar houses in your area. Provision for reasonable increases should be included. Otherwise, the Internal Revenue Service may have strong grounds for calling the entire transaction a tax-motivated one and disallowing tax write-offs for the buyer.

To protect the seller, the contract should also limit rent increases, tying them perhaps to an index like the consumer price index. There should be a clause safeguarding your rights to renew or renegotiate the lease, and the terms under which either party can cancel the arrangement should be specified.

To be sure the IRS does not accuse the homeowner of entering a transaction intended primarily for tax benefits, a tax lawyer should advise him or her on setting one up.

Both the reverse annuity mortgage and the sale-leaseback are opportunities. They help overcome the common problem of retiring Americans: needing a place to live as well as an income. They also bring up special problems that have to be planned for and dealt with before jumping in. Because your financial plan changes after retirement, be prepared to adjust the way you view your real estate investments.

13
HOW HOMEOWNERS INVEST

Once you understand your personal goals and financial requirements and have a family budget under control, it is time to decide how you will handle disposable income—money for investment. There is danger in owning your own home. You have more to lose by taking the wrong path. The best way to insure success as an investing homeowner is to avoid fast money schemes and look for solid, proven investments. This involves detailed investigation before you commit yourself.

The process is similar to buying a house: You look at several properties, compare their features and prices, check financing terms, and make an informed decision. You wouldn't buy a house sight unseen—yet many investors buy investments with little or no investigation and usually without understanding exactly what they are buying.

Your attitude toward investing, as a homeowner with equity available to you, is different from that of someone who does not have equity at his or her disposal. Note that word "disposal." Investment salespeople are interested in getting you to put the largest possible amount of money into products so that their commission income will be higher. Therefore, they may tell you that building equity in your house is poor financial planning, a missed opportunity, and a sign that you don't know how to invest.

If you adopt the view that your house is your most important investment, and that equity is worth building and leaving intact, you will see through these misleading arguments. Money for investment purposes should be free of debt. When you borrow money to invest, you take on more risk and you pay interest, thereby lessening your profit.

It's easy for an outsider to view your home equity as a source of tremendous borrowing power. You will be encouraged by some investment advisers to chase short-term profits by taking on long-term debt.

Using home equity as a source for cash leads to "conveniences" like lines of credit on which you can borrow money whenever you want, just by writing a check. Investment advisers especially like these products because they put so much of your "disposable" income at their fingertips.

If you do think of your home as an investment, a product that must be maintained so that its value will grow over time—leading eventually to a handsome profit—you certainly will not be interested in putting it at risk to take yet further risks with other investments. Borrowing in order to take investment risks is called *leveraging*. Many advisers will tell you to leverage as much as you can, buy as many properties as possible, and never let your equity sit idle while you miss opportunities.

But the homeowner's point of view can be fully appreciated only by someone who owns a house and lives in it. Yes, it's an investment. And, yes, it grows in value over time. But it is also your personal shelter—the place where you raise your children, where you sleep, and where you are protected from the elements. A home, with its equity building over decades of family occupancy and family effort, is a path to life dreams.

That path will be supplemented by the other investments you make. There are good reasons to identify and buy sound investments as part of your financial plan.

First is growth. Compound interest makes money expand over time. This is important to a successful investment, because inflation will cause a stagnant sum of money to deteriorate in value. Consider the effects of only 3 percent inflation per year. Every dollar you have today that is not growing in some form of investment will be worth only 97 cents next year—and 74 cents in ten years.

There are other reasons people are attracted to investing. In its most risky form it is pure gambling, the chance to make a lot of money and the likelihood of losing it all. Playing the odds stimulates some and rouses greed in others. Diverting from conservative investment to speculation is a common mistake. People move to speculation when they lose sight of their original goals.

You need to know when to begin an investment program. Remember that a cash reserve is a first priority. Many financial professionals suggest putting six months' pay aside—which for most of us is more easily said than done. Once this has been achieved, a steady savings program can begin to build capital for future investment.

An insured passbook savings account might be all you will ever need or want, and that's better than nothing saved at all. But with research you will also discover that you can do better by accepting a little risk. No investment should be made without research. The more knowledge you have, the easier it is to pick investments in line with your plan and within the limits of your risk and safety standards (see chapter 3).

You also need to acquire the knowledge to manage your investments or to pay an expert for that knowledge. Retaining a financial planner or adviser can be a smart move, providing the person you choose is able and willing to help within the guidelines you establish.

PROTECTING YOUR SHELTER

As soon as you seek professional help, you will be encouraged to put your equity to work (translation: get that money out of your house and risk it somewhere else!). Prepare yourself by pledging to follow four rules:

(1) Look ahead: Your equity is finite. There is only so much of it available to you, but there are a lot of investment opportunities. If you use up your equity and it turns out to be the wrong way to go, you have a long-term debt and no gain.

(2) Set a standard concerning your home equity: Decide as part of your financial plan that you will not borrow money using equity as security for any purpose other than as a part of your financial plan. Set aside emergency funds, enter an intelligent investment plan that is coordinated within your personal financial plan, and refuse to be swayed by arguments that you should use home equity.

(3) Recognize that risk takes many forms: Every investment has risk, even guaranteed or insured products and accounts. When you borrow against equity you are doubly exposed. First, the investment might not yield as much as you expect or the value of your money could drop. Second is the risk you take by using and exposing your equity. Keep your safety standards in mind.

(4) Make decisions in your own best interests: When you use outside help to make investment decisions, always question it. Try to determine motives and be aware of what an adviser stands to gain by what he or she tells you. If you're not sure whether a commission is involved, ask. A reputable adviser will tell you without hesitation how compensation works.

TYPES OF INVESTMENTS

There are two broad classifications of investment: debt and equity. A *debt investment* is a form of lending money to someone else. Bonds fall into this category. If you buy a bond, you have in effect loaned money to the person or group who sells the bond. The bond is repaid at a predetermined maturity date. In the meantime, you receive interest. Other forms of debt investment are savings accounts (the money you deposit is loaned to others for home mortgages or other purposes), time deposits, and United States Treasury securities through which you loan money to the United States government.

FIGURE 13-1
Debt and Equity

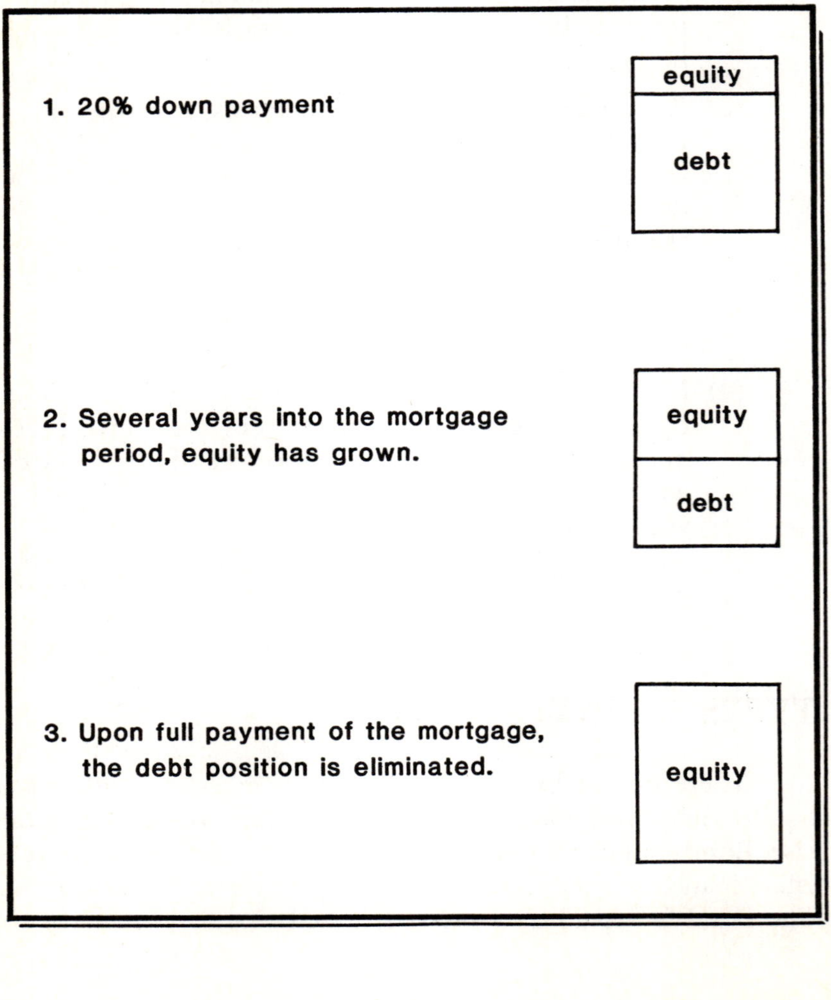

1. 20% down payment

equity
debt

2. Several years into the mortgage period, equity has grown.

equity
debt

3. Upon full payment of the mortgage, the debt position is eliminated.

equity

An *equity investment* is one in which you own all or part of an asset. Your house is a good example. Other types of equity investment include stocks (through which you own a small part of a corporation), real estate partnerships, precious metals such as gold and silver, gemstones, stamps and coins, art and antiques.

When you buy a house, two forms of ownership are at play. Yours is an equity position represented by your down payment, accumulated loan payments assigned to principal, and the increasing market value of your property. Your lender holds a debt position in your house. Until your debt is fully repaid, he has an investor's right to a portion of your house equal to the unpaid balance of the money he has lent to you. The interest you pay to the lender is the return on his investment. This is illustrated in figure 13-1.

DEBT INVESTMENTS

Bonds are the most common form of debt investment. There are three major types:

(1) Corporate bonds: Large companies use bonds as one means by which to raise money to finance their operations, purchase equipment, and expand business. A bond issue is offered for a period of years, with a stated interest rate and sometimes with a conversion feature that allows the holder to convert the bond (debt) into common stock (equity) in the company.

Bonds are traded at premium or a discount. If the fixed interest rate is substantially higher than the current market rate, the bond will be sold at a higher price than its redemption value. That is, a bond worth $1,000 may be sold for $1,100, or "at 110," a premium. But if the current market rate has increased since the bond's original issue date and yield on the bond is now below the market value of the company's stock, it could sell at a discount. "At 98" would mean that the bond is selling at a 2 percent discount, $980 instead of its redemption value of $1,000.

RESEARCHING THE INVESTMENT FIELD

Numerous magazines aimed at investors and homeowners interested in managing their own finances are worth the price of subscriptions. Some include: *Fact, Money, Money Maker,* and *Sylvia Porter's Personal Finance.*

General-interest magazines also run articles concerning money management and investment topics.

The following books can help you to develop a wide understanding of investment products, services, and strategies:

Ady, Ronald W. *The Investment Evaluator.* Englewood Cliffs, N.J.: Prentice-Hall, 1984.

Blume, Marshall E., and Friedman, Jack P., eds. *The Complete Guide to Investment Opportunities.* New York: The Free Press, 1984.

Dougall, Herbert E., and Corrigan, Francis J. *Investments.* Englewood Cliffs, N.J.: Prentice-Hall, 1978.

Harper, Victor L. *Handbook of Investment Products and Services.* New York: New York Institute of Finance, 1977.

Krause, Lawrence A. *The Money-Go-Round.* Emeryville, Calif.: Consolidated Capital Communications Group, 1986.

Money Maker's Complete Guide to Successful Investing. Chicago: *Consumers Digest,* 1986.

Nelson, Wayne F. *Extraordinary Investments for Ordinary Investors.* New York: G. P. Putnam's Sons, 1985.

Skousen, Mark. *High Finance on a Low Budget.* New York: Bantam Books, 1981.

Weaver, Peter, and Buchanan, Annette. *What to Do with What You've Got.* Washington, D.C.: American Association of Retired Persons, 1984.

(2) Municipal bonds: State or local municipalities may place bonds on the market to fund such government projects as public utilities or community buildings. Municipal bonds are exempt from federal income taxes. State-issued bonds also are exempt from tax in the state of issue.

(3) United States Treasury securities: A Treasury bond is issued by the United States Treasury Department for periods of ten years or more, in denominations of $1,000 or more. Other forms of Treasury securities include shorter-term forms of debt. Treasury notes are issued for periods ranging between two and ten years and in denominations of $1,000 or more. Treasury bills are issued for three months, six months, or one year, in initial denominations of $10,000.

Passbook savings accounts and time deposits are also forms of debt investment. You receive interest for allowing the bank or savings and loan the use of your money.

You can also buy debt investments through mutual funds. These are "pooled" investments. The money from thousands of investors is put under the management of a group of experienced trustees or investment managers, who decide which investments to buy and when to sell them.

Mutual funds can specialize in debt or in equity, or even mix the two. Money market funds, bond funds, and unit investment trusts specialize in debt.

Money market funds invest only in short-term, interest-bearing debts like certificates of deposit, bankers' acceptances, and other corporation or government debts. "Short term" means the debts are due within less than a year. Most investments in money market funds are for even shorter periods.

Bond funds invest in bonds issued only by corporations or the government. Bonds are long-term debts, taking one to twenty years or more to mature. Managers of these funds buy and sell in the bond market, seeking the best possible rate of interest for investors.

Unit investment trusts specifically identify all investments before investors pay in their money. The advantage is that you know exactly what you'll earn and how much money you will be paid on what dates. The disadvantage of the unit investment trust is that, without buying and selling in the daily market, the investor does not benefit from new opportunities that come about when interest rates change.

EQUITY INVESTMENTS

The stock market is the best-known form of equity investment. You can buy shares in companies directly, or as part of a mutual fund share. Volume on the New York Stock Exchange has been growing steadily in recent years, frequently exceeding 100 million shares traded daily.

In addition to the New York Stock Exchange, there are a number of regional exchanges. The over-the-counter market for trading stock in smaller companies collectively matches the daily volume of the New York exchange. Trading in international stocks, currency, and commodities accompanies trading in United States corporations.

Your investment in your residence is a form of equity investment. American homeowners hold more than $3 trillion in unmortgaged home equity in the United States today, in 85 million homes.

Property can be purchased as part of equity investment in other ways. You can buy investment property directly (see chapter 14). You can invest in a real estate partnership, a pooled investment that is less liquid than a mutual fund. Or you can invest in a real estate investment trust (REIT), a real estate pool through which you own shares of a trust that, in turn, buys real estate.

A real estate partnership combines your money with other investors' funds to buy properties collectively. Ownership is not flexible. Usually you hold your shares until the partnership is dissolved, which can be years. Costs to enter a partnership are higher than costs to enter a mutual fund, and professional managers take a portion of the profits.

Limited partnerships in real estate are formed for buying, managing, and selling property and for other kinds of speculative investment—oil and gas exploration, equipment leasing, and research and development programs. They contain two classes of equity partners. First is the general partner, the person or company that makes the investment decisions, manages properties, and reports to investors. The limited partner is the group you enter as an investor. You are "limited" in that you have no voice in selection of properties or operation of the partnership. You are also limited in the event of a drastic loss or lawsuit: You cannot lose more than the amount you invest.

Some limited partnerships are designed for tax shelter first, and economic profit second. Many of these have been targeted in recent years by the IRS.

An even more speculative form of equity investment is the so-called tangibles area. This includes the purchase of precious metals, gemstones, or collectibles.

INSURANCE PRODUCTS

Some forms of investment don't fit exactly into either debt or equity classifications.

Insurance is properly classified as an investment as long as it yields a profit to you, protects assets against loss, or is deemed a financial necessity as part of a balanced investment program. Some insurance policies (whole life is an example) allow the building of cash value even though the primary benefit of the investment is protection against the economic consequences of death, disability, casualty, or poor health.

Life insurance with cash value combines insurance protection and savings (equity). In a whole life insurance policy you build cash value over the years. As the value increases, the amount of insurance decreases so that eventually there is no insurance remaining in force—it is entirely a savings account. It is widely agreed (except among those still selling whole life insurance) that this is one of the poorest yielding forms of savings, with most policies paying between 1 and 3 percent over the period of time the insurance is kept in force.

Term life insurance, for a smaller premium, offers no cash value. In a level-term insurance policy the amount of insurance remains the same but premiums increase periodically. In a decreasing-term policy, the premium remains level but the amount of insurance drops each year. Mortgage life insurance (see chapter 6) is one form of decreasing term insurance.

The several forms of annuities and equity investments are also insurance. A fixed-annuity investor places money with an insurance company, either in a lump sum or in periodic payments. The company, while it holds the money, invests it in mutual funds, stocks and bonds, and other investments. At a specified age, the investor begins to receive a fixed monthly (or quarterly) payment.

A variable annuity is similar, but payments to the investor, above a guaranteed minimum, will vary with the market performance of investments the insurance company makes. In most cases variable annuity investments are placed in mutual funds.

Options and commodities don't strictly fit the debt or equity classifications, either. An option is a contract that grants its owner the "right" to buy or sell shares of a stock at a specified price, until a specified date. The value of an option rises or falls with the value of the underlying security. An option can be bought for pure speculation or as part of a coordinated investment plan. A call option is the right to buy shares; a put option is the right to sell. Options are always identified with particular companies.

Options for stock in an entire industry group or index can also be bought and sold. These are called index options.

Commodities are similar to options. The purchaser acquires the right to buy or sell lots of a particular commodity in the future (thus the name "futures contract"). Like the option market, the commodities market is highly speculative and suited only for the most experienced investors.

COMBINING EQUITY AND KNOW-HOW

Making smart investments depends primarily on two factors: knowing enough about a product before you buy it, and basing your decisions on a predetermined financial plan that fits your understanding of your life dreams. The idea that a good investment adviser can steer you toward the best investments is a misconception. Outside advisers can help to educate you, but when an investment is recommended to you, you should first determine how it fits the plan you've already developed. For example, does it provide a means for saving money for known future expenses? with a minimum of risk?

Find out what you can about any investment. This means reading the prospectus and any sales literature you can find. Pay special attention to how an investment is managed—that is, the people or company that handle the money you place with them. They should have a track record, with ten or more years experience in the industry, and a history of guiding successful past programs. Don't take chances on newcomers.

If a financial adviser cannot answer your questions or makes recommendations before he or she understands your financial plan, look elsewhere for help. Outside advice should be informed advice, geared toward meeting your specific goals, not just secondhand information or blanket statements.

THE DIVERSIFIED INVESTOR

Financial advisers love to talk about the principles of diversification. Diversification means spreading risks among different types of investment. If one investment loses or performs poorly, the others should not be affected in the same way.

There are three primary methods of achieving true diversification. First is participation in a pooled fund. A number of investors join to put money into a pool, where it is used for a variety of investments. The most common type of pool is a mutual fund. Another common type is a real estate investment

FIGURE 13-2
Forms of Diversification

pooled funds

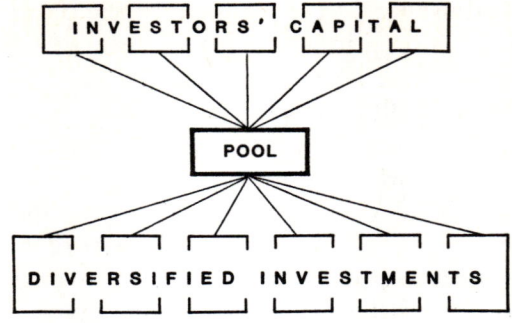

industry groups

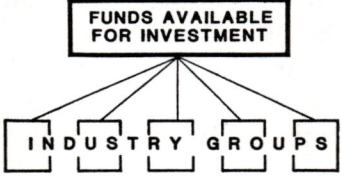

risk spreading

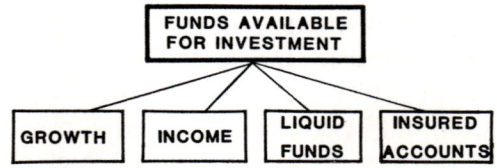

trust. Pools offer excellent means of diversification for anyone with limited funds.

A second type of diversification is investment in unlike industries. If you purchase four or five different electronic stocks or transportation stocks, as some advisers suggest, you are not truly diversified. Industry groups tend to rise and fall in the market collectively. A generally poor trend, as often as not, will affect all the issues within that industry. If you put all your money into transportation stocks, you will suffer if a broad-based decline in transportation values occurs. If you invest only in public utility stocks, which are likely to be hurt when interest rates rise, you do not have diversification. If you buy only real estate, a temporary glut on the market will mean that all of your investments suffer. By putting some money in each area you will not lose across the board because of a single economic setback.

The third form of diversification is more valuable. Risk spreading—the selection of some investments for growth, others for income—can be practiced by the individual investor and can respond quickly to changing situations. Some investments are kept close at hand for emergencies (the liquid portion of your portfolio); others are left in insured accounts.

It isn't prudent to participate in a pooled fund or in different industries if you do not have enough readily available money for your personal requirements. If you leave nothing for emergencies while you look for high profits at the expense of insurance on at least a portion of your funds, you are planning poorly.

Robert and Fran Maher (chapter 3 contains their financial plan) are well diversified in their investments:

Real estate	$110,000
Interest-bearing savings	7,000
Mutual fund	18,000
Treasury securities	30,000

First, these investments are not complicated, nor do they require special knowledge or experience to manage effectively.

Second, the Maher money is invested in different areas—real estate, the stock market (through the mutual fund), savings, and debt securities.

Third, the Maher family has diversified its investments in terms of safety, thus spreading the risks. Their house, especially, is expected to maintain its value over time; the house is one of the best vehicles for minimizing taxes. They have maintained liquidity with their savings, mutual fund, and Treasury securities. Overall, their investments are expected to beat inflation. The family has insurance on its house and savings, and the Treasury securities are backed by the full faith and credit of the United States government.

Real diversification is a mix. A portion of your money should be put into investments that address a particular interest you have within your own financial plan.

There's a lot to remember. Risk, safety, diversification, liquidity, knowledge about different investments. Investing is complex, and made more complex by the insider terminology that frustrates the novice. You cannot become an expert overnight. Inevitably, you can benefit from informed guidance by a professional. But the best way to learn is through individual research and a lot of carefully acquired experience.

As with every aspect of financial planning, choosing investments is a matter of defining what you need in order to reach your goals.

14
INVESTING IN PROPERTY

It is widely recognized that real estate investments are among the safest around. Everyone needs shelter and there is a constant demand for it. Market cycles affect price and demand rises and falls, but the opportunities—and the dangers—are always there.

> ... there were so many cases where people had given up a treasure after getting down within six inches of it, and then somebody else had come along and turned it up with a single thrust of a shovel.
> from *The Adventures of Tom Sawyer,* Mark Twain.

That's how real estate appears to many people: The wealth is there, almost within your grasp, just waiting.

It's true that you can build a base of personal net worth in real estate—but only within a long-range, carefully thought-out plan. Those who proceed recklessly or randomly are playing the odds. Yet slick promoters continue to lure customers into questionable real estate programs and schemes that depend on using home equity to get rich quick.

It sounds so easy. All you have to do is go out and buy real estate (no money down), borrow more money based on that real estate, and buy still more. Within five years you'll be a millionaire. And, if you really want to find out how it's done, send your $250 in to get the kit that gives all the details.

The real situation, of course, is different. Real estate investing is not all that simple. There are risks. It requires research and hard work. Most of all, it requires careful use and management of equity. Real estate *is* the second-best investment around. The best is selling real estate kits telling others how to get rich.

There are a number of reasons why real estate is so popular:

(1) Tax shelter: In the past, real estate was used widely for the tax benefits it offered. It was one of the few investments in which the deduction that could be taken was higher than the amount invested.

Here's how it worked: An investor would join a syndicate and put up a little money, say $5,000. He would also sign a note for $20,000 and get a $25,000 stake in property. Later, by borrowing more money ("leveraging" the investment) still more property could be purchased. Within the first year perhaps $10,000 could be deducted in tax depreciation on the properties. This is an example of an abusive tax shelter.

The IRS decided to go after these tax shelters, and the huge volume of tax-motivated investments in real estate virtually dried up.

But real estate continues to be a viable investment for people looking for good, safe, dependable havens for their money.

Real estate investment trusts (REITs) pool investors' funds. You own shares of a trust that, in turn, buys real estate. A REIT offers the same advantages as syndication, but shares are more easily traded. Investors do not have to tie up their money indefinitely.

(2) Performance: Real estate investments are in demand because of historical performance. Most people recog-

nize that real estate is a necessity of life, and that there will always be a demand for it. Some financial advisers recently have claimed that the validity of real estate as an investment has changed. As prices grew dramatically between 1975 and 1980, many people bought properties and made acceptable profits, but beginning in the early 1980s the market slowed down. Many areas were overbuilt and the market value of properties fell.

It's all part of a cycle. Demand rises and falls over time. Take, for example, these headlines:

"Sharp Curbs on Real Estate Tax Shelters Cleared by House Ways and Means Unit"
—*Wall Street Journal*

"Housing Market's in the Doldrums Again and Isn't Expected to Bounce Back Soon"
—*Wall Street Journal*

"Lenders Are Wounded as Realty Portfolios Are Shot Full of Holes"
—*Wall Street Journal*

"A Nationwide Glut in Office Space Has Hit"
—*Barron's*

While you wouldn't be surprised to have seen these headlines in 1985, these stories all ran during 1974 and 1975.

It is reasonable to conclude that the cycle will repeat itself over the years. It won't always perform at the same rates, and there will be periods of adjustment. But over time, real estate has proven itself.

(3) Familiarity: People understand real estate. Anyone who owns a house knows the benefits of the investment. Many other forms of investing are relatively alien.

> ### REAL ESTATE SYNDICATES
>
> A real estate syndication is like a mutual fund in some respects. Your money is pooled with that of other investors.
>
> There are two forms of this program: specified and blind pools. A specified program identifies specific properties before you put up money, so you can choose an investment based on a type of property (shopping center, industrial park, apartment) and a location. A blind pool identifies the object of the program (for example, "to seek in-demand properties in rapidly growing areas") but not specific properties.
>
> Syndications can be set up by borrowing against equity in the properties they buy ("leveraging"), or they can be all-cash programs. Risks are greater in a leveraged program because a loan must be paid in addition to property taxes and property maintenance costs. There is little risk in an all-cash program.
>
> Getting your money out of a syndicate can be difficult. Syndication units, unlike mutual funds, do not have a ready market, so limited partners must be willing to leave their money in a general partner's hands until properties are sold and the program is dissolved.

BECOMING A LANDLORD

There is one big advantage to investing in real estate through a formal program like a REIT or a syndication: By pooling your funds with other investors and putting management in the hands of knowledgeable professional people, you can diversify among several properties and won't have to worry about managing the properties in the program. Legal issues, relations with tenants, and management of cash and financing all are handled, for a fee, by someone who is in the business full-time.

You can also invest in real estate on your own. In the process of deciding to be a landlord, you should answer two basic questions:

(1) Will my equity earn more by remaining invested in my house, in a rental house, or through outside investment?

(2) Are the potential benefits worth the risks and inconveniences?

The first question is strictly financial. If real estate is not growing in value, keeping your equity in a rental house will not be profitable, at least for the moment. Can you find a zero coupon bond plan that does better? How about a conservative mutual fund with a good history? Even a bank savings account or certificate of deposit might surpass the real estate market and the inflation rate.

Let's say that insured interest-bearing accounts are earning about 7 percent while inflation is about 3 percent per year. At the same time, housing is not growing at all. In this case, a safe insured account carries the least risk. When real estate values begin to rise, if you believe it to be the start of another growth period, you can close out your savings account and buy a rental property. If you are right, your timing will pay off.

But . . . stop for a moment. Do you want to be a landlord? You may find the risks and inconveniences are too great even to consider making the move.

You should be aware of some features that come with the territory. First of all, if you deal directly with tenants, you will receive calls at work and at home, often to request you make minor repairs—the sliding door is stuck, the plumbing leaks, the carpet is wearing thin. You will have to adjust to the responsibility of keeping a property maintained to a tenant's satisfaction. These demands are often more than the standards you set for yourself as a homeowner.

The Simpsons, for example, purchased a second house and rented it. They had always kept their own house maintained but didn't always take care of needed repairs right away. If the budget didn't allow for replacing drapes or carpeting, it waited.

They discovered that tenants want everything fixed immediately. During the first six months they received calls on the average of three times a month. Their weekends and often evenings were spent making repairs that most people would undertake on their own. Even though the house would appreciate in value and the rent paid for the mortgage, they ended up selling and putting their money in a mutual fund. They concluded that landlording just wasn't for them.

It's a matter of temperament. Are you willing to confront tenants who will not pay rent on time? Are you able to continue paying a mortgage when your rental property sits vacant? Or can you see your property deteriorate because tenants neglect the yard and ruin the interior? Probably the ideal landlord is someone who does not need a lot of quiet time and likes to do repairs.

The ideal rental property should be located close enough so that travel doesn't become a chore. It should be where you can also keep an eye on your investment and make sure your tenant is doing his or her part in keeping your property in good shape.

Landlording is not only a personal and financial decision. Community laws vary on tenant and landlord rights. Before making the move, find out whether you will be exposed to complex rules and regulations.

Rent control and procedures for eviction are involved. One homeowner bought a house across the street and rented it. The tenants didn't pay their rent for several months running, so he tried to evict them. He followed the rules to the letter: 30 days' notice in writing, using the language prescribed by local ordinance. But the tenant sued the homeowner and won damages in court. The basis: He didn't have a job or any money so trying to evict him was harrassment.

The fact that a court of law agreed is outrageous, but in some jurisdictions the law favors tenants heavily. A few years later, the trend can shift to favor the landlord. It is a good idea to hire an attorney before becoming a landlord, to find out exactly what *your* rights will be.

Some tenants can be living nightmares, but many rental properties are occupied by people who take excellent care of your investment. Chris and Harry Rollison, for example, had managed to acquire three rental units over the years, the three houses adjoining theirs on a quiet residential block. When Harry died, Chris inherited responsibility for managing them. They had all been occupied for years by the same people, and there had never been trouble with rentals or tenant relations. From Chris's point of view, property ownership was easy, even boring. Why more people didn't get into it, she could never understand.

James Harvey's experience was different. A single man living in a large city, he bought a house in a suburb 30 minutes to the north. It was a sound financial investment with a long-term mortgage, and rental receipts more than made the mortgage payments each month. But because rents were high in the suburb, he could not find a family as tenants. Three or four single people ended up sharing the four-bedroom house. This meant frequent turnover in renters, late payments, and a generally rundown condition. The landlord's weekends were taken up with visits to repair and maintain the property, and every few months he had to clean the place in preparation for new tenants.

Carefully screening tenants reduces risks, although you never avoid them completely. There is no hard-and-fast formula for eliminating trouble or insuring a pleasant experience. Ask for references from a previous landlord and check them. Also check with previous neighbors—and an attorney. You don't want to be accused of discriminatory practices, and innocent inquiries could backfire on you.

SINGLE-FAMILY HOUSING

There are many ways to become involved with rental property. Single-family housing is the one that allows the most freedom of choice.

Many homeowners become landlords not by design, but because they are unable to get the price they want when they decide to move. Whether as an adjustment to an economic reality, or as part of a long thought-out plan, moving out and converting your residence to a rental unit can be profitable and can provide tax benefits. You are allowed depreciation and the deduction of expenses that, as a resident homeowner, you cannot deduct—fire insurance, utilities, and routine maintenance, for example.

You can also use the equity in your present house to finance the purchase of another rental property. There is more risk in landlording when you have to pay back a loan than there is if you rent out a house you own free and clear. Ideally, a rental property should pay for itself.

Compare the cost of owning and maintaining the property and making payments on a loan with the rental income you could earn. If you are unable to keep a tenant in the house, will you still be able to afford the loan payments? Without the financial strength to make it through a difficult period or to meet unexpected expenses, you could lose your investment.

CONDOS AND CO-OPS

The gradual conversion of apartments into condominiums is popular for several reasons. First, it allows owners to sell their property over a period of years instead of all at once, thus spreading out tax liability. It also is an alternative if the present owner is unable to find a qualified buyer for the entire complex.

Investing in a condominium can be risky for the homeowner. Few markets are as inconsistent. In some areas they cannot be constructed quickly enough to satisfy the demand; in others, even the best-built units cannot be sold. As investments, condos have not done as well as single-family homes. In the two years between 1983 and 1985, for example, the value of condominiums dropped between 15 and 30 percent in some areas, according to *Money* magazine (July 1985). During the same period, single-family housing values were flat but for the most part did not fall in value.

Some homeowners choose to invest in condos as rental units because they can be acquired for less money than houses. Of course, since a condo costs less, it will be rented for less. It's also important to note that if there are high vacancies in apartments in your area, your condo investment is also likely to remain vacant. Condos are more closely affected by apartment demand than houses are.

In making a decision on a condo, consider these points:

- Is the development fully sold? If a developer cannot sell all the units, you may have to pay a higher maintenance fee to keep it alive.
- Are the maintenance fees reasonable? Particularly in new developments, some developers understate the initial amount, either because of poor estimates by a governing board or to make it easier to sell units.
- In an established condo, is there excessive "deferred maintenance"—a term meaning that the property has been neglected?
- Is the building as a whole properly maintained?
- How strong has the condo market been in the last five years? The answer could affect your ability to sell when you want.
- If the market is slow now, do you have reason to believe it will improve in the future?

A common problem for condo investors is the unwillingness of many lenders to finance purchases or improvements. A lender generally wants to review the bylaws of the complex before agreeing to lend you money. This will require a legal review, for which you will have to pay.

Be alert, also, for special problems. One apartment building, built on landfill, was converted to condos, and units were purchased mostly by outside buyers. A year after the last unit was sold the new owners discovered that the building was sinking and would have to have its foundation reinforced. Total cost was estimated at more than $45,000. They sued the previous owner for nondisclosure and eventually won, but it was a long and expensive ordeal. Along the way, other "deferred maintenance" was discovered: a nearly broken-down electrical system, an equally poor plumbing system, and window and door alignment problems partially caused by the settling of the building.

For some investors, however, condo ownership combined with landlording works well. The Jones family, for example, moved to a condominium on retirement but decided to keep their house. They wanted to preserve the option of one day moving back and also wanted the tax advantages of being landlords. Even without a tax deduction for interest (their mortgage was paid in full), they showed a cash profit and a tax loss each year:

Total rental income ($500 per month)	$ 6,000
Less expenses:	
Homeowner's insurance	$ 312
Property taxes	1,426
Maintenance (average)	1,135
Utilities	930
Accounting fees	200
Total expenses	$ 4,003
Cash left over	1,997
Less depreciation	3,421
Tax loss reported	$ −1,424

Depreciation was figured on the $90,000 house in the following manner: land, which cannot be depreciated, was valued at $25,000. That left $65,000 for the value of the house. One-nineteenth (the annual allowance for depreciation in the year this arrangement began, 1986) equals $3,421.

Be wary of making the decision to be a landlord solely on tax considerations. Those who invest for tax motives without considering their life dreams will probably regret the decision. If real estate is performing well, perhaps outperforming other investments with equal or greater risk, your peace of mind should still be your primary concern. Let the plan rule. If you have done your preparation you will be able to see the right decision clearly.

There are even greater risks for the homeowner/landlord in buying a cooperative as a rental unit. Cooperative ownership (see chapter 11) is like owning stock in a corporation. If you have 100 shares of IBM you have certain rights. You can vote for the board of directors. You receive dividends. You can use your stock as collateral. But you can't tell IBM how to run the corporation. There are similar kinds of restrictions for the landlord. For example, you are not free to rent your unit to anyone you choose. The co-op board, consisting of your fellow investors, can deny a tenant's application and even deny you the right to rent out your unit at all.

If, therefore, a co-op appeals to you, you should consider living there yourself and making your present home the rental property.

Your intent in considering real estate as an investment should fall within the guidelines of your financial plan. No investment will earn and grow without risks, but future profits look promising indeed if real estate continues to rise as it has in the past.

15
THE FINANCIAL WORLD

To make your financial plan succeed, you must be able to match investments to it, casting each one for its strengths the way a director casts a play. The majority of inexperienced investors make the mistake of choosing investments without a clear-cut idea of what they're trying to achieve. They find out about a promising stock, or a mutual fund that performed well in the past, and they buy into it. Stockbrokers are prone to encourage this method of investing. They call clients and recommend a buy because earnings estimates are high, or a particular company is expanding, or because the price is low compared with a year ago.

OBJECTIVES

Objectives are the characteristics you want in an investment. They describe the levels of risk and safety you are willing to accept, the amount of income you expect to earn, the degree to which you want to protect your capital, the amount of liquidity you require, how insulated you want to be against the effects of inflation and taxes, and whether or not you need insured accounts. Objectives may also be concerned with the specific types of investments you will make—preference for real estate, an absolute rejection of stocks, or belief in the benefits of mutual funds, for example.

Financial planners tend to speak of the safety features of investment (see figure 15-1) as though these were goals in themselves. Many planners confuse their clients by telling them that their investment goals should be to be to protect capital, maintain liquidity, etc. In fact, safety features are characteristics of investments, not goals. Assessing them allows you to place them in an order of preference, in order to judge how they fit into your plan, your life dreams, and your personal comfort level.

Most investments are sold in one of two ways. A person approaches a stockbroker, adviser, or planner to find an investment. The potential client says, for example, "I want to invest $5,000 I have saved up, and add another $100 a month. Where should I put my money?"

The answer often will be, "Here's a mutual fund (or stock or real estate partnership) that we think will perform very well." The intent, of course, is to make a sale, and what is meant by "perform very well" is difficult to define. By presenting himself passively, the potential client has given the salesperson the opportunity to earn a commission quickly and easily.

FIGURE 15-1
What Makes an Investment Safe?

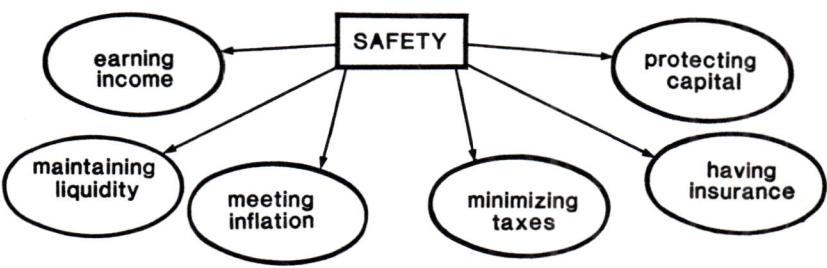

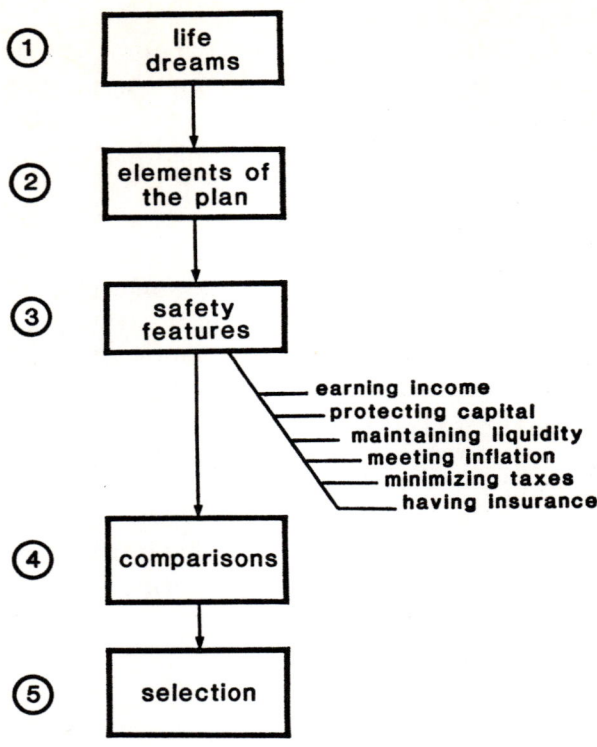

FIGURE 15-2
The Investment Process

Investments are also promoted, through advertisements, mailers, free literature. When you send your name and address to a particular company, the result is a phone call from a stockbroker who will try to get you to open an account and invest. Some common sales openings: "We offer free financial planning for our preferred customers." Or, "I'm looking at one very promising investment right now and I think you should find out about it immediately." Or, "Our customers outperformed the market last year."

The broker or adviser will describe a recommended investment either as "safe" or with the potential for high income or growth, for example. It is not the salesperson's function to consider whether or not a particular investment suits your financial plan and your life dreams. They make a living from commissions.

First-time investors rarely communicate their goals clearly when they approach or are approached by a salesperson. When most people buy a first home they have an idea of how much they can afford, and what they can offer as a down payment. This limits where they can buy, how large a house, and how well constructed and maintained it is likely to be. By the time the same people begin to look for a second house, they know more precisely what is desirable in a house: location, size, quality of construction, and maintenance. The process is the same for investment. The more experience and knowledge you accumulate, the better you'll be able to select the right investment. Lacking experience, you still can be a successful investor if you approach the process correctly.

There are five initial steps (see figure 15-2):

(1) Understand your life dreams, the ultimate outcome of your financial activities.

(2) Develop the elements of your plan. With these worked out, you know precisely how assets must be managed and invested.

(3) Consider safety features, the criteria for seeking an investment with characteristics meeting your standards. Risk is directly related to each safety feature.

(4) Compare different investments with the first three steps in mind.

(5) Select an investment.

Daniel and Sarah Post, for example, approached this initial phase with a simple plan. They wanted to buy a house but had no savings or other investments. Both husband and wife worked but neither had a retirement plan nor an IRA. Their only goal was to establish a savings account. Because they had no experience as investors, other issues were postponed. This is how it went:

(1) Life dreams: Without assets to support a more farsighted plan, the Posts concentrated on getting some money in the bank. This is not in itself a life dream, but personal equity will enable them to formulate detailed goals later.

(2) Elements of the plan: The Posts identified resources and began to manage them by starting a single account.

(3) Safety features: Each of the six features was addressed. For income, the savings account earns a predetermined rate of interest. With the other safety standards in mind, the Posts were willing to accept a relatively low rate of return. For protecting capital, a savings account is the safest possible investment. There is little possibility that the funds will be devalued, as they could be in the stock market or an aggressive growth mutual fund, for example. For maintaining liquidity, a savings account is also best because it is immediately accessible. For meeting inflation, with a low rate in effect, a savings account is adequate. For minimizing taxes—this feature had a low priority for the moment because the Posts are in a moderate tax bracket. For insurance, the savings account is federally insured.

(4) Comparisons: Because the goal was simple—saving money in a liquid account—it was easy to compare investments. The stock market, a real estate partnership, or a speculative commodity venture made little sense under the circumstances. In most cases a minimum investment is required. Partnerships usually ask for a $5,000 minimum, for example. Even if the Posts had a lump sum to invest, they could not afford to give up the liquidity they wanted and needed nor risk losing their initial capital nor invest in an uninsured account.

(5) Selection: After the Posts completed the first four steps, the best choice was obvious.

Once an investment has been made, it must be managed. That is, some form of control must be exercised to help it grow, or at least to help it maintain its value. Professional management groups take responsibility for this in mutual funds and other kinds of investments, but even when someone else is making the decisions on a particular investment, you still exercise control and management over your safety standards and the placement of your capital.

Imagine that you are investing in a mutual fund. You can make management decisions and control your plan by:

- Earning income
- Protecting capital
- Maintaining liquidity
- Meeting inflation
- Minimizing taxes
- Having insurance

EARNING INCOME

For the inexperienced investor, mutual funds are a good way to begin. Your money will grow over time and your rate of earnings, with reinvested gains, will be impressive if you leave your capital on deposit and reinvest all your earnings.

The difference reinvestment can make at 8 percent per year is impressive. For an investment of $1,000, growth will be:

	Without Reinvestment	With Reinvestment
In 5 years	$1,400	$1,469
In 10 years	1,800	2,159
In 15 years	2,200	3,172
In 20 years	2,600	4,661

Mutual funds can lose money, too. There is no guarantee of earnings and you must accept a level of risk (in the tax effect of earnings, lack of insurance, and lack of capital protection).

A popular way to invest in mutual funds is to invest the same amount every month regardless of the value per share. This is called dollar cost averaging. Table 15-1 shows what happens to your capital when you invest this way.

In a falling market, your average cost per share is $18.50 after six months while market value is only $15.00 per share. If you had invested $1,200 the first month, your loss would be much higher. While your investment has lost some value, the loss has been mitigated by dollar cost averaging.

In a rising market, your average cost, $25.50, is below the current market value of $29.00. So you are ahead. If you had invested $1,200 the first month, you would be further ahead, but there is no way to know in advance whether prices will rise or fall. Dollar cost averaging is just one way to insure a consistent return over time and minimize losses in a down market. It also helps you budget.

TABLE 15-1

DOLLAR COST AVERAGING

In a Falling Market

Month	Amount Invested	Market Value per Share	Average Cost per Share
1	$200	$22.00	$22.00
2	200	21.00	21.50
3	200	19.00	20.67
4	200	18.00	20.00
5	200	16.00	19.20
6	200	15.00	18.50

In a Rising Market

Month	Amount Invested	Market Value per Share	Average Cost per Share
1	$200	$22.00	$22.00
2	200	23.00	22.50
3	200	25.00	23.33
4	200	26.00	24.00
5	200	28.00	24.80
6	200	29.00	25.50

PROTECTING CAPITAL

There are many different types of mutual funds. Some offer the opportunity for spectacular gain along with the risk that you will lose money. If you purchase shares in a mutual fund when the market price is $13.00 per share and the price later drops to $10.50 per share, you have lost 19 percent of your capital. The price has to rise back to $13.00 for you just to break even.

You can avoid this risk by looking for a conservative mutual fund. When you are comparing funds, read the "investment objectives" section of the prospectus. Look for funds that emphasize conservative growth or growth and income combinations. Check the performance record, looking for a mutual fund that has performed better than the market in general in both good and bad times, and consistently over the years.

Another way to protect capital is to diversify your money *within* a mutual fund investment. This is possible with a "family of funds" group instead of a single choice. Each fund in a family of funds is managed separately and designed for different safety and risk standards. You can switch money between funds, often by telephone, usually with little or no fee. In one typical family of funds, you can diversify your capital among conservative growth, aggressive growth, growth and income, income, tax-free income, and the money market.

MAINTAINING LIQUIDITY

The family of funds helps you to meet your changing safety and risk standards. If you want a high level of liquidity, you can shift a large portion of your investment into the money market, where you are able to make withdrawals simply by writing yourself a check.

A mutual fund generally is considered a highly liquid investment. You can ask for your money back whenever you want, and usually you will have it within days.

Two problems can arise. First, the market value of shares might have declined between the time of your investment and the time of your withdrawal. Thus, you can lose money. Second, many funds charge a fee if you withdraw funds before a specified number of years (usually five or fewer). Find out these rules before you invest.

MEETING INFLATION

Mutual funds should be considered long-term investments—meaning you should plan to leave your money in for at least two years. It is possible to make large profits in short periods of time, but you should not enter a mutual fund with that goal in mind. The dependable worth of mutual fund investing is the compounding effect of reinvested interest and dividends over periods of time. Historically, funds have beaten the rate of inflation.

Fund investors go wrong by being too opportunistic. If you switch between funds in a family of funds at the wrong time you are less likely to be successful than you are by picking one solid performer and staying with it.

For example, suppose your money is parked in an aggressive growth fund. After a couple of years you think interest rates will rise, causing stocks to fall. You switch your money to a money market fund—but instead of rising, interest rates fall dramatically and the stock market soars (as it did during 1985 and 1986). Now your money is earning a low rate of interest in the money market fund while you miss opportunities in the aggressive growth fund.

By having portions of your money in different funds, you have better exposure to opportunities, and your risks are spread out in case the market does take an unexpected turn.

MINIMIZING TAXES

In a mutual fund you can decide exactly when you will sell. Large gains or losses can be timed so that tax consequences are minimized, or tax advantages taken.

For example, one investor placed $5,000 in one year in an aggressive growth mutual fund. Four years later it had grown to more than $20,000. He believed that the market would level out and, possibly, fall. He wanted to sell, but that year his other income was fairly high and taking the gain would mean paying taxes in a higher bracket. He elected not to sell during that year.

By deferring a decision to sell you also risk losing your profits. If the market does fall, your gain could evaporate. Instead of risking the loss, the solution is to mitigate the tax problem with advance planning. Look ahead, plan the effects of a sale on your tax liability, and look for ways to offset it. If you have other investments that have lost value, you can sell them and use the loss to offset the gain in the market.

For example, let's look at the mutual fund investment mentioned above:

Current market value	$ 20,000
Original value	5,000
Profit	$ 15,000
Less: Losses on other investments	9,500
Balance to be taxed	$ 5,500

So a $15,000 gain could be reduced to $5,550 in this instance, through planning.

A number of funds are designed to provide tax-free income for those in higher tax brackets. Municipal bonds, for example, are exempt from federal taxation. You can also buy shares of funds that are offered in one state only, thus exempting profits from state tax as well.

When you go the tax-free route, yields will be lower than yields in taxable investments, but you could still come out ahead:

Average taxable yield	12.00%
Less: Federal tax (35%)	−4.20%
Less: State tax (8%)	−0.96%
Equivalent tax-free yield	6.84%

If you pay taxes in the 35 percent bracket, a tax-free yield of more than 6.84 percent would be more profitable than a taxable yield of 12 percent.

HAVING INSURANCE

Mutual funds do not give you the insurance protection you would have in a federally insured savings account. However, with the built-in diversification feature, you are virtually insured against sudden loss, so you do have an indirect form of protection.

Consider two cases. The Smiths have all their money in an insured account at a local savings and loan association. Following a state audit the institution is declared to be in violation of minimum reserve requirements and its doors are closed. It may take weeks or even months for the Smiths to get their money back.

The Brown family invests in a mutual fund diversified among different funds in a family of funds and, within each fund, among a number of different securities. In the event of a drastic market downturn, losses will not be as all-encompassing as they would be if capital were invested in a single-issue or a single-objective fund. The family can switch out of volatile accounts and into more defensive ones or withdraw its capital and cut losses.

Both families incur risks. The Smiths may be unable to get their money immediately, while the Browns risk losing in a down market.

INVESTOR CHARACTERISTICS

Just as investment products have different features, so do investors. Some, like the Mahers of chapter 3, look for insurance and liquidity first and high yields second. Others are willing to take bigger risks.

There is a direct relationship between the amount of risk one is willing to take, the importance of life goals, and the age of the homeowner. The more expensive the life goal, and the younger the homeowner, the more risk he or she is likely to be willing to take. Some financial advisers argue that the young *should* take risks. The reasoning: If they make mistakes they have more time in which to offset losses with more conservative investments.

This argument ignores a human element. If you begin by taking risks and succeed, you will be more inclined to take more risks, even greater than before. On the other hand, if you are conservative by nature, you're less likely to take risks at any time.

FIGURE 15-3
The Risk Scale

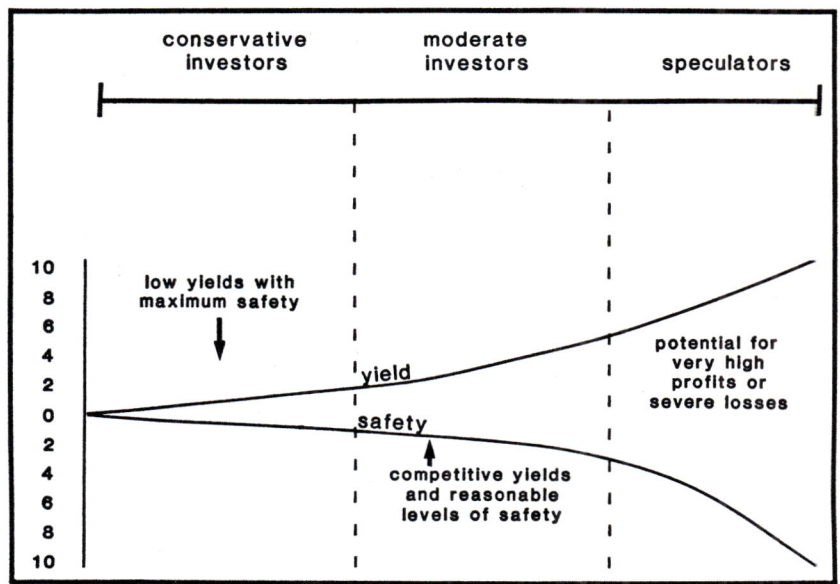

SCALE:
  0 LOWEST YIELDS AND RISKS
  10 HIGHEST YIELDS AND RISKS

Investors set their patterns when they begin to invest and are likely to change only with experience. Most moderate investors have experimented in the past with high risk and have learned through losing money that it usually doesn't pay.

You don't have to find a category for yourself as an investor as long as you invest within the definitions of your life dreams and the elements of your financial plan. It is valuable, though, to be aware of where you stand on the risk scale (see figure 15-3).

Conservative investors will avoid as much risk as possible, looking for maximum safety in their investments. The best possible choice for them: insured but low-yielding savings accounts. They also will invest in securities guaranteed by the United States government, or they will make investments so well diversified that a substantial loss is highly unlikely. An extremely conservative investor actually loses money over time because yields are always lower as risks are reduced, and the buying power of investment dollars is eroded by income taxes and inflation.

Speculators (risk takers) are on the other end of the spectrum. In seeking the highest possible return on their dollar, they will ignore the safety of lower-yielding savings or mutual funds. These people are likely to be attracted to futures contracts and uncovered options and will use leverage whenever possible to increase their positions in the market. This type of investor will mortgage a house to free up money to put into the stock market. Then, using purchases as collateral, he or she may borrow still more money from a broker and invest it, usually in high-risk stocks, options, or commodities. With luck, they'll make a very quick profit and, the theory goes, will then be able to pay off their debts. But in most cases, one of two things takes place: They lose money and never fully recover their financial position; or they do beat the odds and have a profit, which is immediately parlayed in the hopes of realizing still higher profits. Eventually, they almost always lose.

Somewhere between the extremes is a balanced, intelligent plan. The moderate investor seeks the highest possible return within the practical restraint of safety features. This is achieved by diversifying, investing in a number of different products—some in mutual funds, some in real estate or collectibles like stamps or coins. A portion can be committed to risky ventures, options or commodities for example; another to highly conservative ones, like insured savings accounts or United States government securities. The bulk of the portfolio is kept in the middle, in investments that yield a rate above inflation but without so much risk that a big loss is likely.

I have experienced all three investor profiles myself. I began from a very naive position. The first time I had money to invest I walked into a brokerage and asked where I should put my $200. The broker of the day advised buying 10 shares of a computer company stock selling for $18 a share. He told me it could triple in value in a year. I decided not to take that advice, and the stock later fell to about $2 per share. I put my money into a standard passbook savings account where it grew slowly. But it didn't beat inflation.

Several years later I discovered the options market. I saw that if I called the shots right, I could turn very little money into a lot more, quickly. So I thought. Buying options is a very risky business, and the odds are against the speculative buyer. The majority of investors lose. I joined that majority. It was an expensive lesson.

Today, I find myself in the moderate category. Almost all of my investing is in diversified products with a mixture of features. I have IRA funds invested in various places, including a growth mutual fund, a money market fund, a real estate investment trust, and direct ownership of stock. The bulk is committed to the safer choices—the growth fund and the REIT—where returns are higher than could be expected from a savings account, but the risk is higher, too.

You can match investments to investment personality once you understand your own "comfort zone" on the risk and yield scale. If you are willing to accept low yields in return for corresponding low risks, you're a conservative investor. And if you want to make a fast profit even at the risk of losing your money, you're on the opposite end. Most investors are somewhere in the middle.

INVESTMENT ADVICE

Mortgages, home ownership, and all other forms of investment must be chosen realistically, if you want the investment process to do what you want and expect it to achieve. Getting help with your investments is a smart and necessary adjunct. No one can be an expert on every possible financial alternative. Finding good reliable information and professional assistance is as important as it is to find good advice for financial planning.

16
GETTING HELP WITH YOUR INVESTMENTS

You will most likely end up being your own best financial planner, but with knowledge about the different specialists and investment facilities available, you have more chance to design a successful investment program. Knowing when and when not to entrust your financial affairs to someone else is a necessary skill to master.

Once you begin a serious investment program, it is virtually impossible to avoid using professional help completely. If you purchase a security, for example, the transaction must be entered through an exchange. That requires using a brokerage service, but it doesn't mean you should allow a stockbroker to tell you how and when to invest. There is an important difference between allowing an outsider to tell you what to do and working with that same outsider within a structure that you have developed yourself.

THE STOCKBROKER'S ROLE

There are competent and knowledgeable stockbrokers in the world, but it takes luck and knowledge to find them. A few stockbrokers have ventured into true individualized planning. Often, these are the most successful account executives in the business. Their skill and value are recognized.

But consider the way most stockbrokers are trained, and the way they build their client base. To become a stockbroker, the applicant must hold a valid securities license. This means taking a written test administered by the National Association of Securities Dealers. The test is difficult, not because a lot of knowledge is required, but because the multiple choice questions are worded in a complex fashion. The best way to prepare for this test is by studying samples of past test questions, so brokerage firms put applicants through study courses, their own or one given by one of the numerous organizations that exist solely to help people prepare. The week-long classes concentrate on methods for identifying and eliminating wrong answers, and selecting the most likely right ones. Those paying for the study course are guaranteed they will pass.

The young, fully licensed broker who has just passed may have little or no actual experience in the real world of investing and little practical knowledge about investments. When this broker starts out in the business, he or she has to locate clients who will buy and sell actively enough so that the broker earns a commission. That means getting on the phone and prospecting, following leads and referrals all day long, and taking people to lunch to win their accounts. It means serving as "broker of the day," the person in a brokerage office who gets the people who call or come in off the street to find a broker. Most new investors approach a brokerage firm in just that way. When you do so, you are hooked up with the least experienced, least knowledgeable person in the office.

After a while, the broker establishes a base and referrals begin to come in. Clients who are pleased with the level of service they get send in their friends. During this time, brokers learn—often at your expense—what works and what does not.

Do not make the mistake of expecting much real and usable advice from this broker. When a broker needs to earn money, it's time to get on the telephone and call clients. Of course, what they tell you is, "I was thinking about your account, and with today's market condition, I think it would be a good time to move into

INVESTMENT RESEARCH SOURCES

Smart investors are thorough researchers. If that requires help from an outside source, obtain that help. Read all the material you can find about the area you are investigating and use knowledgeable sources.

Major stock brokerage companies publish research papers and brochures that can give you a lot of information. They use this material to locate new customers, so you should also expect a telephone call from a broker. But the information is worth it.

Some examples include Merrill Lynch's *Guide to Tax Investments* and E. F. Hutton's *Financial Alternatives for Today* (Merrill Lynch, 1 Liberty Plaza, New York, NY 10080 and E. F. Hutton, 31 West 52d Street, New York, NY 10019).

Every specialized industry publishes promotional and informational material. The National Association of Real Estate Investment Trusts (1101 17th Street NW, Suite 700, Washington, DC 20036) publishes a comprehensive booklet, the *REIT Fact Book*.

The Federal Reserve System is a good source for free material. You can order from the Federal Reserve Bank of New York (Public Information Department, 33 Liberty Street, New York, NY 10045) the following publications:

---

transportation stocks. I've been watching one issue closely for you...."

Finding a broker whose advice is given with awareness and respect for *your* plan and *your* goals is difficult but worth the effort. Interview, take references, and apply the checking and experience comparisons detailed in chapter 7.

You will not always have an easy time getting the stockbroker you want to take you as a client. The talented, capable professional is in high demand because he or she is a rare commodity. But even if you are a beginner with little money to invest, remember that the successful stockbroker got that way by recognizing the potential for future success in clients.

A Primer on Inflation
The Arithmetic of Interest Rates
The Basics of Foreign Trade and Exchange
Foreign Exchange Markets in the United States
I Bet You Thought...
Money: Master or Servant?
What's All This about the M's?

For younger readers, the Federal Reserve Bank of New York also publishes a series of publications in comic book form, including:

The Story of Banks
The Story of Foreign Trade and Exchange
The Story of Inflation
The Story of Money

Reading and Viewing is a summary of publications available from the Federal Reserve Bank of New York.

The Federal Reserve Bank of San Francisco (Public Information Office, P.O. Box 7702, San Francisco, CA 94120) publishes *Money in the Economy*.

You attract the stockbroker you want in one of three ways:

(1) When you have a plan: The person you want recognizes the absolute need for a personal financial plan. The key to his or her success has been in working with goal-oriented people, those with more common sense than the average investor.

(2) When you are referred: Ask your banker, accountant, attorney, or other professional to introduce you.

(3) When you insist on the best: You can start by making an appointment with a brokerage's branch manager.

List your criteria: Preferably five or more years of experience and exposure to a wide range of different investments; the most successful broker in the branch in terms of customer satisfaction and loyalty, not necessarily in terms of volume of business.

If a particular brokerage house is unable or unwilling to give you the help you need, look elsewhere.

If you have questions about the practices of a firm or a stockbroker, either during your search or after starting to work with someone, ask the individual and, if necessary, the branch

AGENCIES AND ASSOCIATIONS

Regulatory agencies are especially useful for inquiries and complaints or literature.

Write with complaints about practices of stockbrokers or brokerage companies to the following:

Securities and Exchange Commission
Office of Consumer Affairs
450 Fifth St. NW
Washington, DC 20549

The following is the self-regulating organization for the securities industry; they will send, upon request, two booklets entitled *Arbitration Procedures* and *Code of Arbitration Procedures* and also invite complaints about practices of your broker:

National Association of Securities Dealers, Inc.
Two World Trade Center
98th Floor
New York, NY 10048

The Federal Trade Commission enforces the Truth in Lending Act and handles consumer complaints concerning deceptive advertising:

manager. If you are not satisfied, contact the resources listed below in "Agencies and Associations."

USING AN ASSET MANAGEMENT ACCOUNT

In the securities business, the more money the firm can place in accounts it controls, the more they have to work with. A popular method for attracting money is through an asset manage-

---

Federal Trade Commission
Bureau of Consumer Protection
Sixth St. and Pennsylvania Ave. NW
Public Reference Rm. 130
Washington, DC 20580

If you want more information about stock exchange policies or practices, or need to complain or inquire about a member brokerage firm, the two largest exchanges are:

New York Stock Exchange
11 Wall St.
New York, NY 10005
    and
American Stock Exchange
86 Trinity Pl.
New York, NY 10006

You can gain a great deal of knowledge about the theory of investing and protecting yourself by reading the literature available from regulatory agencies, investor assistance clubs and associations, and a large variety of industry associations.

ment account, a device that makes it convenient for you to track your investments. It offers you features that vary from one firm to another but may include a single statement, the sweep, check-writing privileges, and a debit card.

(1) A single statement: Convenience is the major selling point of asset management accounts. Even if you have a number of different accounts, the entire package is reported to you on one statement. The importance of a single statement is overemphasized. You may find it easier to keep statements separate by type of investment. The convenience, in fact, may be the broker's, not yours.

(2) The sweep: The term "sweep" refers to the instant placement of all available money—from dividends and interest, for example—in income-producing accounts. The theory is that with a number of investments some of your money will not always be at work earning interest. The sweep puts funds to work between investments, even if for only a few days.

For most investors, these funds are minimal and the impact of the sweep is not substantial. For example, if the combined money from your interest, dividends, and funds being transferred is $100 for the year, and the rate is 6 percent, you will earn $6.

(3) Check-writing privileges: You can write checks to withdraw part of your cash. Your money continues to earn until checks are presented for payment. This is, essentially, a form of interest-bearing checking.

(4) Debit card: Some brokerage firms also give you a debit card. This is like a credit card. When you want to use some of your money in the asset management account to purchase something in a store, you present your debit card. When the voucher is presented to the brokerage for payment, your account is reduced accordingly. But unlike a credit card, for which you use a line of credit that is, in effect, a form of borrowed money on

which you pay interest, a debit card makes use of money you already have. A form of debit card familiar to most of us is the card used to get money out of a bank account through an automatic teller machine. The largest full-commission firm, Merrill Lynch, and the largest discount broker, Charles Schwab & Company, both offer VISA debit cards within their asset management accounts.

When asset management accounts were introduced in the 1970s, they found immediate and widespread acceptance by the public. For the brokerage firms, they brought millions of dollars under management. And for many consumers, they provided the convenience that they promised.

Most firms require a minimum initial deposit to establish an asset management account—$5,000 or $10,000 in most cases, sometimes as much as $25,000. Most firms also require that you use firm accounts for money you intend to invest.

For investors with a limited amount to put into the market, asset management accounts are of little use. If you have a number of large and complicated accounts, regular transactions and interest and dividend income from many sources, this account can be a great convenience.

Fees range from nothing up to $100 or more per year for the privilege and convenience. The brokerage makes its money from the difference in the spread between the rate of return they make and the rate of return they pay. For example, if the average rate of return to you is 7 percent, and the firm can earn an average of 10 percent, they have a 3-point spread.

For many people, the convenience of simplified account management makes use of a brokerage firm worth the expense. For others, having someone to validate investment decisions is tremendous security, even when it comes with a price.

That price can be high. Many firms offer asset management accounts not only to bring money under management but also to make it easy for you to borrow.

For example, if you own securities that you do not want to sell right now, but would like money for some other purpose—a vacation, a car, Christmas shopping—you can borrow from your brokerage with securities pledged as security.

This is exactly like borrowing against your home equity. Assets you have invested should be viewed as part of your capital base within a financial plan. Like home equity, these assets should not be pledged or spent carelessly.

INVESTING ON YOUR OWN

Once you begin to understand the logical approach to investing and you know how to apply the selection process, it is time to move on. Stockbrokers are useful only if you are willing to trust their advice, and many are capable, honest people who truly do help. But what if you no longer need that support?

At this point, investigate a discount broker. On May 1, 1975, the Securities and Exchange Commission repealed the fixed commission rates it enforced under the Securities Act of 1933. Most brokerage firms raised their rates that day but a few people saw an opportunity to start a new form of business, one specializing in the placement of investment orders. Within a couple of years discounting had established itself in spite of dire predictions from the more established industry members.

There proved to be a strong market demand for minimum service. The Securities and Exchange Commission reports that the market share of business from individual investors grew between 1977 and 1983 from 3.5 percent to 9 percent of total transactions.

Discounters offer one basic service: They buy and sell securities for you. They offer no research, no advice, and no personal service. Some provide services like asset management accounts, and most are set up for IRAs. But beyond that, you are on your own. Discounters' rates are lower by 50 percent or more because no salespeople are involved in the transaction.

Full-commission firms predicted that discounters would find it impossible to stay in business with discounted charges, but the industry has grown and today, there are more than 3,000 such

SOURCES OF INFORMATION

Associations, regulatory agencies, and stock exchanges can also provide help. The New York Futures Exchange (20 Broad Street, New York, NY 10005) publishes *Your Hedge on the Future*. And the Commodity Futures Trading Commission (2033 K Street NW, Washington, DC 20581) will send you *Basic Facts about Commodity Futures Trading* and *Glossary of Trading Terms*.

One of the most useful books to send away for is *What Every Investor Should Know*, which costs $1.25 and is published by the Securities and Exchange Commission (order from the Superintendent of Documents, United States Government Printing Office, Washington, DC 20402—refer to document number 046-000-00137-1).

A number of investor services are available on a subscription basis. Some of the material is available in libraries. For stock market investing, send for literature available from Value-Line, Inc. (711 Third Avenue, New York, NY 10017). This is a comprehensive weekly service that rates and follows a number of different stocks.

A similar service is offered by Standard and Poor's Corporation (25 Broadway, New York, NY 10004). These two organizations are the largest and most complete reference sources for investors.

---

firms. Charles Schwab & Company, the largest discount broker, attracts more than 250,000 new accounts per year. The total market share grows yearly, too. Discounters attract four out of every ten new brokerage accounts and transact about one-fifth of the total retail volume on the major stock exchanges.

Since 1981, following rulings by the Comptroller of the Currency, banks, insurance companies, and other financial institutions have been purchasing or starting their own discount services. The companies involved are not small operations. In

1983, for example, Bank of America acquired Charles Schwab & Company, and Chase Manhattan Bank bought Rose & Company. With 3,000 depositing institutions in the country now offering brokerage services, banks have definitely entered the investment business.

Why the growth? Because discounting is a bargain. Trading 100 shares of a $50 stock typically costs you $360 at a full-commission firm. It runs $132 at the Schwab organization.

If you have a strong and successful relationship with a full-commission broker, if the advice you are getting is good, there is no reason to leave. But many investors maintain accounts at both a full-commission and a discount brokerage, the first for personal service, and the second for savings.

Discounters advertise in the investment newspapers and magazines, and most offer toll-free numbers. Look for a company that has a nearby office so that you do not need to invest at a distance and over different time zones. Compare the services offered by several discount brokerage firms, paying less attention to the comparative rates they each charge than to convenience of location, toll-free availability, and other extra services they offer.

INVESTMENT CLUBS

Another way to get help with your investments is to band together with other investors and form an investment club. Belonging to an investment club is similar to investing in a mutual fund, but on a smaller, more personal scale. A mutual fund pools the funds of many investors under one management group; a club does the same thing but offers its members more control.

The average investment club member invests $34 per month, according to the National Association of Investors Corporation (NAIC), a nonprofit group that assists new investment clubs in organizing. NAIC's membership invests $3.5 million every month through club affiliation.

A club offers you two forms of flexibility:

(1) Combined effort: Working in a group gives you access to more information. A group decision is likely to be better informed because you will have available the results of research conducted by the members at large.

(2) Pooled funds: Investing with the combined resources of a number of people gives you a real edge in placing your money, and deciding how much to buy and to what degree you can diversify. If each of ten members invests $100 per month, you have $12,000 per year to invest for the entire group.

Most clubs are formed as partnerships. At the end of each year, one partnership tax return is filed, showing how profits are to be divided among the members. In most forms of partnership, if one partner leaves or a new one joins, the entire organization must be dissolved and another formed under Internal Revenue Service regulations. But the IRS allows investment clubs to continue to exist as long as a majority of the partners remain for the full year. NAIC can show new clubs how to organize and keep records.

According to NAIC, the ideal group size for an investment club is between 10 and 15 members. The first year of a club's existence is critical. Most clubs that disband do so during the first 12 months. The most common reasons are lack of similar interests among members, lack of investment standards with which the entire club agrees, and an unfair distribution of work.

Setting investment standards from the beginning is a crucial step. If you do not have consensus, you will debate every investment decision. If half the club wants to take risks, and the other half wants to be assured of a safer, more conservative level of income, no one will be satisfied. Put as much effort as needed into coming up with a group financial plan and making sure that members are completely comfortable with it.

A group plan is quite different from a personal financial plan. In the group you must agree on how your collective funds will be managed, what investments to make, and what kind of risks you will take. The process is one of defining risk and safety standards that everyone in the club can live with. Each of the six safety features—earning income, protecting capital, maintaining liquidity, meeting inflation, minimizing taxes, and having insurance—must be rated in order of priority and relative importance before you will be able to put your club into action successfully.

The club goal should be written down and agreed upon by all members, and should be as specific as possible. As your attitude about investing changes, so can your club goal. You might outgrow your club and want to leave, or it might become stagnant as some members lose interest. These possibilities should be considered and covered in the plan. The following are some examples of club goals:

(1) Conservative: Capital will be preserved through investment in insured accounts with at least two-thirds of the total amount available. An additional 10 percent of total club assets will be kept in a money market fund for liquidity and flexibility. Minimizing taxes is not a goal. Meeting inflation, with today's low rate, is not a priority.

(2) Moderate: The club will invest one-fifth of total funds in a conservative growth mutual fund and will reinvest all earnings. An additional one-fifth of assets will be left to accumulate in a money market fund. Once per year, the club will select by consensus a real estate investment trust or partnership and will purchase shares with between $2,000 and $5,000 of club assets. The balance of funds will be used to select common stock issues, seeking income. We seek favorable tax treatment from producing long-term capital gains and also expect to outperform inflation. With diversification, insured accounts are not sought by the club.

(3) Aggressive: The club has been formed to earn income as its solitary purpose. We will invest in new-issue common stocks of companies with volatile price move-

ment, which we believe are at the low point in their cycles, seeking the highest possible income in the shortest possible time.

In most groups of people, 20 percent do 80 percent of the work. This might be unavoidable, but the wider participation you have, the better. If you and one or two other people are carrying the other members, the entire experience is less enjoyable.

MAKING THE MOST OF YOUR INVESTMENTS

Whether you invest through a broker, a club, or on your own, you will want to maximize your efforts within the guidelines you have set for yourself. Maximizing does not always mean going for the largest profit possible. On the contrary, it often means avoiding the risks associated with big gains and settling instead for moderate return and risk in return for peace of mind.

This in turn means using your safety and risk standards as guidelines for the decisions you make. If you are seeking basic safety for your original capital, you will want to avoid high-risk issues. If you want liquidity, keep all of your assets in ready cash accounts.

The idea of owning part of a Texas oil field or a new shopping center appeals to many people. But a mutual fund or certificate of deposit might yield you more profits in the future and lower your risks today. Those investments are rather boring compared to the oil field, but if your risk standard calls for regular income over a period of years, and you cannot afford to lose money, stay away from the oil exploration program. Keep the sure and steady mutual fund.

One experienced financial professional summarizes investment strategy with the question, "Do you want to invest to eat well or to sleep well?"

Losing peace of mind is not maximizing your investment. You cannot look merely at the black-and-white possibilities,

INFORMATION FOR INDIVIDUAL INVESTORS

Thousands of specialized newsletters make recommendations and predictions on the economy and every phase of the market. Investor services and newsletters can be contacted through newspaper and magazine ads. Listed below are organizations that assist investors.

The following group helps an individual to formulate an investment strategy, holds regional seminars, and offers a variety of publications to members:

American Association of Individual Investors
612 N. Michigan Ave.
Chicago, IL 60611

This organization helps people form or locate investment clubs and assists with procedural forms and documents, newsletters, and referrals:

National Association of Investors Corp.
1515 E. Eleven Mile Rd.
Royal Oak, MI 48067

You can obtain a brochure entitled *A Guide to Mutual Funds* (for $1), which lists most major mutual fund addresses, phone numbers, and investment objectives, as well as other publications from the following institute:

Investment Company Institute
1660 M St. NW
6th Floor
Washington, DC 20036

The following group insures customers' investment funds in the event a member brokerage firm suffers bankruptcy or major losses:

Securities Investor Protection Corp.
900 17th St. NW
Suite 800
Washington, DC 20006

future profits, and increase in your net worth. You also have to consider how a decision will affect your personal life and your ability to sleep at night.

Whether your financial plan is devised when you have two or three decades to go before retirement, or you begin planning in your last working year, the essential point is this: with a plan, your life dreams can be realized. If you set goals and devise strategies to meet them, you will succeed.

The plan you come up with may be an impressive document. You can bind it in leather if you'd like. But the real plan itself is not the pieces of paper. It exists in your mind. The paper upon which you write down and map out your finances is only the guide you use, to be reviewed constantly and revised at any time your status changes.

Some people postpone making plans because "I don't want to find out how bad off I really am." Others fear putting concrete objectives down on paper as a way of documenting failure if the goals cannot be achieved. Neither fear is justified. The only way to insure that you will meet your life dreams and, ultimately, find security and peace of mind is to cover the bases, consider all the hazards, and protect yourself against them.

When the producer of an exceptionally bad movie was asked what mistakes he made that he would avoid in the next film, he replied, "Next time, I think we'll try it with a script." The same is true for you. Write your script and stick to it until you come upon a scene that needs to be changed to create a happy ending.

Index

A
Accelerated growth payments, 65–66
Accountants, 117, 121
American Association of Individual Investors, 234
American College, 125
American Stock Exchange, 225
Annuities, 172–73, 186
Asset management account, 225–28
Attorney, help from, 117

B
Bankers, help from, 116
Blind pool, for real estate, 195
Bond funds, 183
Bonds, 179–80, 181, 183, 213–14
Building a house, 138–42
Business, starting own, 17, 18–19
Bylaws, for condominium, 167

C
Career change, making, 17–18
Casualty insurance, 101
Certificate of beneficial interest, 169
Certified Employee Benefits Specialist (CEBS), 118
Certified Financial Planner, 113, 125
Charles Schwab & Company, 227, 229, 230
Charter, for cooperatives, 169
Chartered Financial Consultant (ChFC), 125
College for Financial Planning, The, 113, 125
College fund, 20–21
Comptroller of the Currency, 229
Condominiums, 163–64, 165–68, 199–201
Conservative investors, 215, 216
Contingency offer, 158–59
Co-op bylaws, for cooperative, 169
Cooperatives, 163–64, 168–69, 202
Corporate bonds, 181

D
Debit card, 226–27
Disability insurance, 15, 101
Discount broker, 228–30
Dollar cost averaging, 210
Down payment, equity growth by, 63–64

E
Equity, 14, 60–99, 132, 133, 181, 184
    home improvement adding, 145–46
    insurance protecting, 32
    preserving, 14, 66–68
    specialists assisting with, 116–17
    using, 68–71, 73, 74, 178–79
Eviction procedures, 197

F
Family of funds group, 211
FDIC, 32
Federal Reserve system, 222–23
Federal Trade Commission, 224, 225
Financial plan, 2–10, 29–34, 69–70
    elements in (*see* Equity; Future expenses; Income taxes; Insurance; Investments; Retirement; Savings and cash reserves)
    example of, 34–59
    for limited income and tight budgets, 56–59
    publications for, 59
    risk and, 32–34, 35
    safety and, 31–32, 35
    selling a home guided by, 153–54
Financial planners, assistance from, 7, 112–14, 125. *See also* Professionals, assistance from on financial plan
Financial resources, 5, 20–21, 39, 49
Fire insurance. *See* Homeowner's insurance
FISBO, 157–58
Fixed-annuity, as insurance, 186
Fixed-rate mortgage, 81, 94
Formal acceleration programs, 85–88
FSLIC, 32
Future expenses, 43, 52, 116, 117, 132, 134

G
Goals, 3–4, 5, 12–26, 30, 37, 38–39, 48–49
    financial plan changes and, 126–27
    investments considering, 208
Graduated payment mortgage, 83
Growing equity mortgage, 82–83

H
Health insurance, 101
Home, 7–10, 15, 31
    free and clear, 13–15

236

Home improvement, 9, 64–65, 142–48
Home office, insurance for, 109, 110
Home ownership alternatives, 162–69
Homeowner's insurance, 102, 108–10
Homesite, buying a future, 138–42

I
Income taxes, 32, 34, 43, 53–54, 132, 134–35, 205, 212–14
Individual Retirement Accounts (IRAs), 15, 21, 46–47, 55–56, 63
Inflation, 31, 33–34, 205, 212
Informal mortgage acceleration plan, 88
Institute of Certified Financial Planners, 59, 125
Insurance, 100–111, 116, 117
    annuities, 186
    casualty, 101
    changes made in, 132, 135
    disability, 15, 101
    in financial plan, 44, 54–55
    formal mortage acceleration program and, 85–88
    health, 101
    investments in, 185–86
    investments and equity protected by, 32, 34, 66, 205, 214
    life, 15, 32, 34, 101, 185–86
    mortgage, 102–11
Insurance agents, 117, 121
Interest, on mortgages, 78, 90, 91
International Association for Financial Planning, 59, 113, 125
Investment clubs, 230–33
Investment Company Institute, 234
Investments, 44, 55, 176–90
    capital protected by, 31, 33
    changes made in, 132–33, 135
    in commodities, 186
    debt, 179–80
    diversification in, 187–90
    equity, 73, 180, 181, 184–85
    equity protection and, 178–79
    formal acceleration program for, 85–88
    information on, 222–23, 224–25, 234
    information sources on, 182, 187
    insurance and, 32, 34, 185–86
    leveraging for, 177
    objectives of, 204–9, 233, 235
    in options, 186
    process of, 205–6, 207–9
    professional assistance with, 116, 118, 218, 220–35
    regulatory agencies for, 224–25, 228
    requirements for, 177–78
    for retirement income, 16
    risk scale of investors and, 214–17
    safe, 31–32
    safety features of, 205, 206, 208–14

J
Joint mortgage life insurance, 104–6, 110–11

K
Keogh plan, 63, 134, 136–37

L
Land, buying for homesite, 138–42
Landlord, 159–60, 195–98
    of condos, 189–201
    of co-ops, 202
    of single-family housing, 198–99
Leveraging, for investment, 177
Life insurance, 15, 32, 34, 101, 185–86
Limited partnerships, 185
Liquidity, 31, 33, 205, 211–12
Loan amortization, mortgages and, 77

M
Master deed, for condominium, 167
Merrill Lynch, 222, 227
Moderate investors, 215, 216–17
Modified financial plan, 126–37
Money market funds, 183
Mortgage acceleration programs, 8, 14, 15, 18, 22, 76–99
    fixed-rate mortgage and, 81
    formal, 85–88
    graduated payment for, 83
    growing equity or rapid payoff for, 82–83
    informal, 88
    mortgage loan structure and, 77–80
    self-designed, 89–99
    variable-rate mortgage for, 81–82
    zero-rate mortgage for, 83–84
Municipal bonds, 183, 213–14
Mutual funds, 183, 187, 211

N
National Association of Investors Corporation (NAIC), 230, 231, 234
National Association of Real Estate Investment Trusts, 222
National Association of Securities Dealers (NASD), 120–21, 221, 224

New York Futures Exchange, 229
New York Stock Exchange, 184, 225
No points loan, 146

O
Options, investments in, 186
Over-the-counter market, 184

P
Payment cap, 147
Pooled funds, 183, 187, 188, 189
Professionals, assistance from on financial plan, 112–25
Proprietary lease, for cooperatives, 169

R
Rapid payoff mortgage, 82–83
Rate cap, 147
Real estate agent, 156–57
Real estate investments, 65, 192–202
    limited partnerships as, 185
    property purchase as, 184
    real estate investment trusts as, 184, 187, 189
    real estate partnerships as, 184–85
    syndication, 195
    as tax shelter, 193
Real estate partnership, 184–85
Refinancing, 22, 94
Rental units, 163–64, 168–69
Rent control, 197
Retirement, 12–13, 15–17, 20–22, 24–26
    changes made in, 132, 133, 136–37
    equity used after, 170–75
    in financial plan, 46–47, 55–56
    fixed income during, 170–71
    savings for, 16, 21. *See also* Individual Retirement Accounts (IRAs); Investments; Keogh plan
    specialists assisting with, 116, 118–19
Reverse annuity mortgage, 172, 173–74
Risk, 32–34, 35, 41, 49–50
Risk spreading, 188, 189
Rose & Company, 230

S
Safety, financial plan considering, 31–32, 35, 41, 49–50
Sale-leaseback, 174–75
Savings accounts, 183
Savings and cash reserves, 42, 51–52, 116, 132, 133
Second mortgage, 94–95
Securities and Exchange Commission (SEC), 120–21, 224, 228, 229
Securities Investors Protection Corporation (SIPC), 32, 234
Selling a home, 152–60. *See also* Home ownership alternatives
Single-family housing, 198–99
Standard & Poor's Corporation, 229
Stockbrokers, 220–25
Sweep, 226
Syndication, real estate, 195

T
Tax legislation, 127, 129–31
Tax shelter, real estate as, 193
Tenants, landlords and, 197–98
Term life insurance, 186
Time deposits, as debt investment, 183
Timetable, in financial plan, 20, 22–23, 24, 46–48
Trusts, 117, 183, 184
Truth in Lending Act, 224

U
Unit deed, for condominium, 167
United States Treasury securities, 32, 180, 183
Unit investment trusts, 183, 184

V
Value Line, Inc., 229
Variable annuity, as insurance, 186
Variable rate mortgage, 81–82, 93, 146–47

W
Whole life insurance, 185–86

Z
Zero-rate mortgage, 83–84

Rodale Press, Inc., publishes RODALE'S PRACTICAL HOMEOWNER™, the home improvement magazine for people who want to create a safe, efficient, and healthy home. For information on how to order your subscription, write to RODALE'S PRACTICAL HOMEOWNER™, Emmaus, PA 18049.

DIVES AND PAUPER

DIVES AND PAUPER

A FACSIMILE REPRODUCTION
OF THE PYNSON EDITION OF 1493
WITH AN INTRODUCTION AND INDEX
BY FRANCIS J. SHEERAN

SCHOLARS' FACSIMILES & REPRINTS
DELMAR, NEW YORK
1973

DIVES AND PAUPER

A FACSIMILE RE-EDITION PUBLISHED BY
SCHOLARS' FACSIMILES & REPRINTS, INC.,
P.O. BOX 344, DELMAR, NEW YORK 12054

REPRODUCED FROM A COPY IN
AND WITH THE PERMISSION OF
THE HENRY E. HUNTINGTON LIBRARY
SAN MARINO, CALIFORNIA

© 1973 SCHOLARS' FACSIMILES & REPRINTS, INC.
ALL RIGHTS RESERVED
PRINTED IN THE UNITED STATES OF AMERICA

Library of Congress Cataloging in Publication Data

Main entry under title:

Dives and pauper.

    A facsim. of the ed. published in London; before 1900 attributed to H. Parker.
    Includes bibliograhpical references.
    1. Commandments, Ten—Early works to 1800.
I. Parker, Henry d. 1470. II. Title.
BV4655.D56   1493a   241.5'2   73-17391
ISBN 0-8201-1111-2

INTRODUCTION

Dives and Pauper is a long exposition of the Ten Commandments in dialogue form, given by Pauper, a poor religious, to the rich man Dives. As a general introduction to the specific demands of the commandments, Dives and Pauper first explore rather heatedly how the rich may enter heaven. Dives argues that the rich have greater use of God's gifts, and thus can practice charity more concretely. They will fare better than the poor who force themselves upon the charity of others. But by skillful argument, Pauper forces Dives to admit that he not only doubts the spiritual worth of riches, but also despairs of even understanding and fulfilling many points required by the commandments themselves. Pauper graciously assents to teach him the duties expected of the Christian so that he might attain heavenly bliss after death. One by one the commandments receive exposition in sufficient detail from Canon Law, Scripture, popular devotional literature, and experiences of everyday life. In the main text, Pauper tends to lecture, while Dives progressively fades, merely suggesting topics, raising a few questions and occasional objections, and ultimately assenting to Pauper's indoctrination. When the commandments are finished, Pauper gives a final and extended emotional plea for his listener to put into practice what he has learned. He reviews the homiletic commonplaces on the pains of hell and the joys of paradise.

Authorship

Except for occasional cataloguers, *Dives and Pauper* has received scholarly attention for only the last hundred years. Before 1900, authorship was gratuitously assigned to Archbishop Henry Parker, a young friar in 1464, because his name is copied into two of the eight extant manuscripts (the Royal manuscripts). Parker is first mentioned by John Leland as a Carmelite associated with several speeches on poverty.[1] John Bale, another early bibliographer, follows this lead and attributes to Parker the authorship of this work: "Dialogum diuitis ac pauperis, Lib. I. Diues (Pauper obuiaerunt sibi.)."[2] H. G. Richardson, who has surveyed the problem, finds that "Pitts, Fabricius, Tanner, and others, including the 'D.N.B.' which in turn is followed by 'The Cambridge History of English Literature' (vol. ii, p. 321,)" all accept Parker as the author of *Dives and Pauper*.³ In 1897, Cardinal Gasquet first raised the question about Parker's authorship, pointing out that the work seemed earlier than the dates of Parker's life.⁴ Following Gasquet's suggestions, Richardson, in 1911, presented several reasons from internal evidence for dating *Dives and Pauper* some fifty years before Parker's time.⁵ Gasquet's view that Parker could not be the author is now fully accepted, but true authorship has not been established.

It is possible that parts of *Dives and Pauper* were composed at different times. The anthological nature of this work (and all such works) masks date differences in the general, traditional passages. But interwoven with this commentary is contemporary social comment containing a number of rather specific references which enable H. G. Richardson confidently to date the composition between 1405 and 1410.⁶ In the First Commandment, Chap. 67, Pauper notes that the kalends of January had fallen on Thursday in 1400; and as he is writing, the kalends have again fallen on Thursday. This occurred next after 1400 in 1405 and then in 1411.⁷ So it is reasonable to date at least this part of the text some time after 1 January 1405, and considerably before 1 January 1411. Richardson, in the same place, also cites many contemporary allusions that would be current around 1405. One of the more telling is the account of the "wonderful comet" (First Commandment, Chap. 29), which appeared on Epiphany and lasted until two weeks after Easter in 1405. Sister M. Anselm Gage gathers a full list of contemporary reactions to the event in her master's thesis, pp. 30-45. J. H. Wylie's *History of England Under Henry IV*, 1:274-75, and 4:280, also presents a convenient summary of the event. This comet raised many forebodings that the country would be translated to some other tongue. Relating to this portent, in the Second Commandment, Chap. 28, Dives fears that the realm may against revert to the Britons or that the English would be forced to speak some other tongue (for instance, because of Glendower's rebellion). Another contemporary allusion occurs in the First Commandment, Chap. 60, where Pauper observes that the English have made many martyrs and that they spare neither their king nor their bishops. They have slain St. Thomas and would have slain their king. These references probably relate to Richard II, who was deposed in 1399, and to Scrope and Sudbury who were put to death, the first executed in 1405. This thought is further developed in the Fourth Commandment, Chap. 27, where reference is made to the rebellion of the poor against their sovereign, probably referring to the revolt of 1381. Other references with historical implications appear in the Fourth Commandment, Chap. 11, and in the Sixth Commandment, Chap. 3, with possible references to Bishop Arundel's *Constitutions* prohibiting vulgar biblical translations. As well, in the Sixth Commandment, Chap. 3, and in the Fifth Commandment, Chap. 4, Dives notes that "this land" is being brought "in bitter bales," possibly referring to the general oppression of England under King Henry IV. These political references, all of the same nature and scattered through the First, Second, Fourth, Fifth, and Sixth Commandments, indicate that these parts of *Dives and Pauper* were written by 1411. The last three Commandments are treated in a somewhat different way, but there is no reason to assume a different author. Apologetics gives way to a more meditative development, and Dives becomes more quiet. The explanation may be that the debate format became too limiting or that the author's inventiveness had merely played itself out. The author hurries through to the end, incorporating his favorite homiletic bits rather than employing the debate technique further. And the meditative tone found in the Ninth and Tenth Commandments, though different than the tone in the treatment of earlier commandments, is quite appropriate in its place. After gaining knowledge of what the man of the world must do to get to heaven, the sinner still has to be moved emotionally to want to do what is required. Significantly, it must be noted that none of the surviving manuscripts (which are discussed later), gives any evidence of extensive additions or of multiple authorship.

Although the author is unknown, and the dates of composition fairly narrowly defined, no one has questioned that the work was not originally composed in English. Much in the text implies Latin fluency in Scripture and the Fathers and thorough acquaintance with commentaries on Scripture and Canon Law, but every text mentioned by the author can be found in England by 1400.[8] The author does a fair amount of biblical translation and paraphrasing but only to illustrate his teachings. His mildly conservative vein is also evident in that he accompanies his translation with Vulgate incipit. The work, however, is clearly Anglo centric. Besides the political unrest already mentioned, Dives gives a capsule history of England from the time of the Britons through the Normans, claiming that the present times are filled with the same sort of perjury as found in those dark days (Second Commandment, Chap. 8). English Franciscans—Robert Grosseteste, Thomas Dockyng, Richard Middleton, and Alexander of Hales—are quoted along with Bede. English attitudes toward wedlock are deplored when Pauper refers to the letter of Pope Boniface III to the king of England in which the Pope laments that the English people despise the laws of wedlock (Fifth Commandment, Chap. 3). Pauper continues in his own voice in the same place that the English are notorious throughout Europe for their lechery that is "accused against us that have been in France and Italy, and heathen men reprove us that the English people despise the laws of wedlock." In another vein, in the Fourth Commandment, Chap. 11, and in the Sixth Commandment, Chap. 3, Pauper comments that no "lewd folk" should meddle with God's law, nor should have the Gospel in their mother tongue. These observations likely reflect the writer's immediate response to Bishop Arundel's *Constitutions* against the Lollards enacted at Oxford in 1407 and reenacted in London in 1409.

Other references of a secular nature also point to English composition. In the First Commandment, Chap. 22, we are told that only the king is allowed to mint coins in "this country," and that "this country" is six hundred miles long and two hundred miles wide.[9] Also in the First Commandment, Chap. 28, Pauper compares the tides of the West Sea that go about Britain and Ireland to those of the other far seas, like the Greekish Sea, in which there is no ebbing and flowing. Only four placenames besides Rome are given, each in connection with a local anecdote. Kent—associated with the grave of St. Thomas—Chap. 15 of the Second Commandment; London, Chap. 1 of the First Commandment; Colchester, Chap. 4 of the Fourth Commandment; and Oxford, Chap. 11 of the Fifth Commandment. Finally, Robin Hood's gests are mentioned in Chap. 51 of the First Commandment.

Franciscan Tone

Having had to reject one Englishman, Henry Parker, as living too late to have written *Dives and Pauper*, it is still impossible as yet to isolate another likely candidate for authorship. A few clues suggest that he was a Franciscan preacher. As mentioned above, many of Pauper's authorities are Franciscans. Grosseteste, Docking, Mediavilla (Middleton), and Hales were English. Continental Franciscans referred to are the ubiquitous Bonaventure, Bartholomaeus Anglicus (the Master of Kinds), and Nicholas de Lira. Pauper insinuates the superiority of the Franciscan sandal over the Dominican's boot, one of the more notorious petty quarrels upon which sects staked a salvation or damnation. Pauper says that "Commonly all apostles have been painted barefoot in token of innocence and penance. Nevertheless, they went not always fully barefoot, but sometimes with galochis, a sole beneath and a fastening above the foot."[10] In another place, Chap. 7 of the Fourth Commandment, Pauper draws upon Bonaventure's *Life of Saint Francis* to illustrate charity, where Francis takes altar cloths to give to the poor.

More intrinsic in the work is Pauper's embodiment of the Franciscan ideal. The most prominent piece in *Dives and Pauper,* the "Prologue on Holy Poverty," encompasses this ideal in glowing terms. H. G. Pfander also notes one passage in *Dives and Pauper* that matches almost in length and totality of spirit a section of the Franciscan rule. Pauper says, "Every true preacher sent of God is called God's mouth. It belongs to the preacher of God's word to commend virtues and despise vices, to choose truth and prevent falsehood, to commend heavenly bliss and ghostly things, and reprove pomp and pride of this world."[11] In the earlier version of "Holy Poverty," which has never been printed, Pauper says, "I have made me a servant to all men rich and poor, to serve them of soul. And for my travail, I beg my meat and my clothing. Other hire I ask none, but what they will freely give for the love of God."[12] And Pauper's description of preaching, found on the next folio of MS Douce 295, also represents the Franciscan attitude: "It was God's will to save mankind by such preaching that seemed folly to the world, and by such preachers that the world set not by the poor men and needy, not by the rich men, but by poverty and lowness, not by pomp, pride and richness of this world." Pauper also disapproves of "this curious knacking sung by vicious ministers in the church, and especially in great and rich churches, for it is often seen that the singers in such places are full proud gluttons and lechers also."

Although Pauper condemns "these men of holy church that buckle their shoes with buckles of silver," he approves of costly sepulcher and high churches, if built for devotion and not for pride. Costly burial in Franciscan churches was long a cause of common attack against the Friars.[13] Pauper also speaks like a Franciscan when he says that "it is more profitable to hear God's word in preaching, than to hear any mass, and rather a man should forbear his mass than his sermon." Also the emphasis on poverty, so reminiscent of Franciscans, permeates the whole work—such as when Pauper so poignantly describes himself in the "Prologue on Holy Poverty": "I that am a poor simple caitif and with little set by, holding the prosperity of them that are rich, and the disease [discomfort] that I and other poor men suffer, am many times stirred to grouch and to be weary of my life." Not only is he poor for God's sake, he explains, but he has the continual opportunity to see the rich, which makes for even more baleful contrast to his situation. One in a cloistered order would not often come into contact with the world as Pauper obviously does; and for this reason, especially, it seems that Pauper is characterized as a wandering poor Franciscan preacher, or at least as a preacher who fully embodies the Franciscan spirit. The whole of *Dives and Pauper* is controlled by Pauper's viewpoint which must be a viewpoint totally shared by the author of the work.

Two Major Influences

Dives and Pauper, a vernacular treatise ostensibly written for a wealthy male layman, has its roots in two areas of the English Church's written tradition. The first is the holdover of mystical influences still strong in the early fifteenth century; the second is the continuing proliferation of the standard treatises on the sacraments, prayer, and Ten Commandments. *Dives and Pauper* is a most elaborate mingling of these two strains. Thus, both of these sources need brief attention to enable us to relate *Dives and Pauper* to the body of religious literature most common in England in the late fourteenth century. The mystical writings so popular in late fourteenth-century England[14] did not fulfill all the needs of lay readers. Anti-intellectual in tone,[15] they demanded that one aspire to perfection without benefit of an organized or rational approach. While Majorie Kemp is a notorious example of results of the approach among the laity, the mystical works seem to be written as much for the cloistered religious as the layperson. To better oneself on the terms of the mystical treatise seems to be a practical impossibility for, say, the shrewd businessman, even if he could be led to give intellectual assent to the directions. Although schooled in a tradition idealizing mysticism, the wandering preacher like Pauper profits by the expansion of learning occurring in all religious orders.[16] Well versed both in canon law and popular religious writings (or oral tradition) as well as his informal mystical training, Pauper can bring his knowledge to a practical level when instructing Dives—whose life is filled with the many complications of reconciling idealized religious practice with the active life. While a reaction to the emotional appeal of mystical development dictates the tone of *Dives and Pauper*, the second root, the practical needs of the layman, determines its content.

The remote origin of the book of practical instruction lies in the genre known as the manual of devotion,[17] a lengthy and all-inclusive summary of the Faith. Derived from these manuals are more specialized treatises emphasizing only one or two elements of the manuals.[18] Some treatises (and many other religious writings) were in dialogue form, and the author of *Dives* chooses this treatment. Many religious writings before 1400 were in English and were directed to laymen.[19] *Dives* follows all these innovations: the manual-like content, the debate style, and the English language. A few details concerning previous mystical works and treatises enable us to construct quite adequately the historical genesis of a work like *Dives and Pauper*.

The first point that demands discussion is a comment of Dives. He states that "Twenty years ago I spoke with a man of your estate that was full like you in speech and person. But he spoke of so high perfection as you now being to do, that unto this day, I could never attain thereto." The first question which arises is what work might have appeared twenty years before (around 1385) by one of Pauper's estate, on "High Perfection." I have been unable to identify any single work to fit this description by an author who also could have authored *Dives and Pauper*. If *Dives* is of Franciscan or mendicant origin, there are other Franciscan and mendicant works dating around 1380 of a mystical nature. A representative mystical writing illustrates the attitude which Dives refers to. If the date of (at least) part of *Dives and Pauper* is established as somewhere between 1405 and 1410, one is attracted by the *Scale of Perfection*, written in English about 1381 by Richard Hilton (d. 1396), an Augustinian canon of Thurgarton in Nottinghamshire. Composition in the English language might also serve to define limits. W. A. Pantin finds that "perhaps the most remarkable characteristic of all [concerning the mystical tradition] is the vernacular element in fourteenth-century English mystical literature."[20] The work which Dives refers to would have to be a work in the vernacular like Hilton's, which could attract the interest of a worldly, rich layman who is able to read English. Hilton's approach to sin and conversion from sin is contemplative and mystical—both difficult for a laymen to comprehend or master. Dives finds mystical treatises like Hilton's *Scale of Perfection* too abstract or ideal, and he fears a reiteration of the same material in Pauper's "Prologue on Holy Poverty." Joseph Milosh explains that although "Hilton does differentiate between physical and spiritual sins and subordinates the former to the latter, he provides only one remedy for both kinds of sin, the contemplative remedy appropriate to his reader's goal."[21] This remedy would not fit the pressing needs of the rich secular layman like Dives. Pauper, however, is characterized as wise enough to see that Dives needs more practical advice on merely following the Commandments before he is able to rise to the contemplative's degree of perfection. Dives is characterized in a way pointedly reminiscent of the rich man who could not follow Christ in perfection because he could not give away all his material possessions.

If *Dives and Pauper* is the work of a mendicant less than forty-five years of age, he would have been a novice much under the influence of the mystical teachers and writings popular in the 1380s. But he would be practicing his active ministry out among the reading public who were more and more determined to acquire on their own the knowledge of what they could and could not get away with. Several borrowed passages in *Dives* are devotional in the mystic sense, but these come late in the work after almost all the formal requirements of Canon Law are spelled out. One is a meditation of the Crucifixion, and another is a lament by the sinner on the loss of Christ. And both passages are from vernacular texts of the 1380s. The conclusion of *Dives* centers on the pains of hell and joys of paradise, and is a commonplace of the final steps of mystical exercise. One trained in mystically-influenced meditation as Pauper is, carries his attitudes almost subconsciously into the world of daily teaching. For example, Pauper's preference of preaching to hearing mass reflects the mystic's attitude toward the sacraments. Father Conrad Pepler notes that "They [the contemplatives] seem to have forgotten the full significance of the sacramental life of the Church. Indeed such things always seem to fade in a mystic era; or rather they are taken for granted, as the foundations performing their essential function unseen."[22] Pauper himself fails to give any detailed exposition of the Seven Sacraments common in the religious manuals in the fourteenth century.

Richard Hilton would approve of Pauper's more mundane instruction of Dives as an initiation to higher goals, for the *Scale of Perfection* really treats of three major parts of contemplation. Hilton holds that the first part of contemplation consists of the common or reasoned knowledge of God possessed by men. It is gained by studying Scriptures, by discussion, by instruction, and by logic. These resources are all used extensively in *Dives and Pauper,* and are directed to the interest of laymen. It would seem that the author of *Dives and Pauper* is very much in the traditional heritage of the mystics' schema for perfection. But the resources of *Dives and Pauper* are also methods of speculative theology, which Hilton relegates especially to "lettered men and great clerks who by long study and travail in Holy Writ come into this knowing." (*Scale of Perfection*, 1:iv). That Pauper himself has reached this stage of spiritual development is not only amply illustrated by his own learning, but by Dives' own observation that "thou art a lettered man." At the same time, we can see why Dives thinks that such a "high way" would only waste his time. Pauper's task in *Dives and Pauper* is to start the doubtful rich layman on the road to perfection.

Another aspect of Hilton—his moderation—is equally true of the thinking of the author of *Dives*. Milosh says,

> If a single quality were to be attributed to Walter Hilton's teachings on the three Christian lives and on the three levels of contemplation, it would be the one which some modern critics see in Hilton's work in general and which Hilton himself constantly emphasizes: moderation. In *The Scale* Hilton's moderation exists partially in his refusing to adhere to a plan at all costs, in his refusing to agree consistently with a tradition when he thinks parts of it unreasonable.[23]

Like Hilton's, the moderation by the author of *Dives and Pauper* has been pointed by Priscilla Barnum, who concludes that "a strain of middle-of-the-road reformism is thus characteristic of Pauper's discourse. Yet the reformism he preaches is limited to Church reform."[24] Pauper attacks the new-fangled observance of Lady Day Fast[25] and deplores pompous clerics. And on interpreting the Scriptures for Dives, he says that his interpretation seems correct to him, but if any clerk can say beter, let him do so. But as a wandering mendicant, the author of *Dives* soon realizes that the perfection envisioned by the mystic is not practical for men in the active secular life, at least until the rudiments of the Faith are first entrenched. Thus he creates a fiction in which Dives tells Pauper that he cannot follow the "high way" that he had heard advanced twenty years before, but that he still wants someone to expound to him the facts necessary for the layman's salvation.

Pauper's method for bridging this gap between idealized perfection and reality is used in about the same way in another anonymous work of the late fourteenth century, *Poor Caitiff*.[26] This treatise, too, Pantin finds "particularly instructive for our purpose in showing the link between didactic [literature like the manuals] and mystical literature, for it begins with simple elementary instructions of the creed, the commandments, and the Lord's Prayer, and these lead on to a number of short tracts of a more mystical character exciting men to heavenly desire."[27] This last feature is likewise found in *Dives*, though it has never been noted by writers, showing that the writer of *Dives* is preeminently in the tradition of *Poor Caitiff*. Actually, the prologue of *Poor Caitiff* is very much like that of *Dives*:

> This treatise compiled of a poor caitiff and needy of ghostly help of all Christian people, by the great mercy and help of God, shall teach simple men and women of good will the right way to heaven, if they will busy themselves to have it in mind and work therafter without multiplication in many books. And as a child, willing to be a clerk, beginneth at the ground, that is his A B C, so he who thus desires to speed the better beginneth at the ground of health, that is the Christian men's belief [i.e., "Creed"] . . . but for as much as the belief of itself is not sufficient to man's salvation, without good works of charity, as Christ saith by His Apostle St. James, therfore he purposeth with God's help ensuingly to tell the commandments of God, in which the charitable works be contained that belong to the belief[28]. . . . And for it is hard to purchase aught of God in prayer till a man verily believe and live after His behests, as He Himself saith in the gospel: Whereto say ye ye, Lord, Lord, and do not thilke things that I say: . . . for thus it behoveth to stigh up as a ladder of divers rungs, fro the ground of belief unto the keeping of God's hests, and so up fro virtue to virtue till he see God of Sion reigning in everlasting bliss.[29]

The "ABCs" of *Dives* are not the elementary prayers but rather the principles of Canon Law and one's Christian role in the secular world.

To some degree the author of *Poor Caitiff* agrees in method with the exposition of the author of *Dives and Pauper,* but the author of *Dives* does not go "fro virtue to virtue" because Pauper's antagonist, Dives, asks for something less ideal. The author of *Dives* does end with the standard, impassioned perjoration enjoining Dives to strive for heavenly bliss (Chap. 3, Tenth Commandment). The main difference between the two works is that *Dives*' author relates his many parts by adhering ostensibly to the Ten Commandments. The short tracts of *Poor Caitiff* are not unified in this way. Within the framework of the commandments, however, the author of *Dives* expands and amplifies his outline.

Both include, for instance, the "horse and rider" *figura*: in *Dives* it is forced into the exposition of the Tenth Commandment, while in *Poor Caitiff* it is a separate piece. The same is true of a comparison of the active and the contemplative life, which *Dives'* author fits into the "Prologue on Holy Poverty." Thus, *Dives and Pauper* remains in the realm of practicality for the most part, relegating the more emotional and mystical passages to the later pages in a rhetorically effective perjoration.

The name "poor caitiff" is also used in *Dives and Pauper* and is in rather wide use near the end of the fourteenth century. Miss Deanesly has cited several titles in this respect, which all play on the theme of "poor man." She first corrects a mistaken atribution by Bishop Reginald Pecock (c. 1395-1460) about the author of *Poor Caitiff*. Pecock thought the author a "certain friar," who wrote it "pro suo defensorio." But whatever the motivations, this description cannot apply to the contents of *Poor Caitiff*. Pecock much more likely alluded to another work altogether, Friar Peckham's *Liber Pauperis contra insipientem novellarum haeresium confectorem*, against William de St-Amour, or possibly to the *Protectorium Pauperis* of the Carmelite Richard Maidstone.[30] Also, "poor caitiff" was a self-attribution of the Lollards as well as the clergyman in *Dives and Pauper*. Deanesly gathers a list of self-descriptions used by Purvey, the learned Lollard, who was writing shortly before the time of *Dives and Pauper*. In Purvey's "General Prologue" to the Lollard Bible, he calls himself a "simple creature of God," and writes "For this cause a sinful caitiff having compassion on lewd men" and "this poor caitiff setteth a full sentence of the text together."[31] To describe oneself as a "poor caitiff" is not enough to suggest whether *Dives and Pauper* was regarded by its readers as orthodox, or whether it is the work of a Franciscan. The author's self-description reflects an attitude common to many viewpoints.

In order to put *Dives and Pauper* into its historical and intellectual context, a few representative mystical and mystical-didactic texts written shortly before the time of *Dives* have been examined. One author already mentioned is especially pertinent as a logical and chronological successor to the author of this work, Bishop Reginald Pecock. He is commonly thought a writer too academic and too unemotional to appeal to the humble Lollards, but he emphasizes teaching and persuasion in dealing with them, rather than threats and burnings. Thus his moderation in surviving English language works is similar to the author of

Dives and Pauper. Although he was trying to bridge the gap between Church teaching and layman's needs, he himself was finally condemned for heresy and after 1457 went into long exile.[32] A. R. Myers claims that "Bishop Pecock, for example, ventured on to new ground when he wrote theological and philosophical treatises in English."[33] But by discrediting the attribution of *Dives and Pauper* to Parker, *Dives* predates Pecock's writings by over twenty years. Pfander gives a much sounder judgment: *"Dives and Pauper* is, so far as I know, the only elaborate didactic treatise, written originally in English prose and built on a framework of the Ten Commandments that has been presented to us from the Middle Ages."[34]

The author of *Dives and Pauper* worked during the growth of independent lay searching. His work is both a result of and a reaction to narrow mystical influences. Working within the Church, he is willing to instruct laymen in practical terms of their Faith. By examining some of the works of the period which are organized on a Ten Commandment schema, the core of this sort of instruction, the uniqueness of *Dives and Pauper* lies in its particular treatment of content rather than in any innovation of contents.

To find the remote English origins of treatises on the Ten Commandments, of which *Dives* is a late and peculiarly English product, we find a religious compilation known as the manual. This genre came into being with the decree of Canterbury's Archbishop John Pecham in 1281, which said that the laity were to be instructed four times a year in six points—the Articles of Faith, the Ten Commandments, the works of mercy, the seven deadly sins, the seven virtues, and the seven sacraments. These points were soon written out in Latin for the clergy, and were known as *The Institutes*. This work was intended for the unlearned or hurried clergyman, but the Latin of course proved too difficult for some preachers. So *The Institutes* was turned into English by several hands at several times. Soon many variations in content and length replaced the specific formula of *The Institutes*. As translations multiplied, some copyists took whole sections of other ready-made materials into their own works. *Dives and Pauper* is a late example of one section of *The Institutes*, expanded and Englished, which is a repository for materials found in other works of spiritual instruction. Though no part of *Dives and Pauper* is based on Pecham's decree in a literal sense, the Archbishop is responsible for originating one of the several traditions for long works including comment on the Ten Commandments, intended to instruct laymen through a preacher. Dives asks Pauper for precisely this instruction about the requirements of his faith. But he is doing the inquiring himself.

Two other long manuals also serve as ancestors to works like *Dives and Pauper*, *The Summae de Viciis et Virtutibus* by Peraldus and the *Summa Casuum Conscientiae* by Pennaforte.[35] Pennaforte's omnibus anthology includes many legends, fables, and miracles for the use of the preacher inclined to this type of material. These teaching aids were never imagined by Pecham. Most writers who followed Pecham, Peraldus, and Pennaforte continued to intersperse among the more formal elements of the Faith these popular but instructive diversions. Pauper includes many, such as the lives of the saints, bits of poetry, local anecdotes, animal analogies, and fuller narration of favorite biblical stories, in his own instruction to Dives. But he is not fully committed to secular stories, lest they be told for their own sake. He attacks the person who would rather hear a tale of Robin Hood or a Gest of Charlemagne than learn about the faith. Chaucer's Parson, for the same motives, warned the Canterbury Pilgrims that "ye will get no fables from me."

Although deeper examination of individual religious manuals is not within the scope of this study, an outline of the progress of the three manual-type writings mentioned will indicate the wide dispersal and tenacity of the genre over several centuries. The first, Pecham's *Institutes*, had several Latin versions derived from it at various times. The renewal of Pecham's decree by Archbishop Thoresby in about 1320 gave the decree additional impetus into the fourteenth century. Peraldus' *Summa de Viciis et Virtutibus*, written before 1261 led directly to *Les Manuel des Peches* by Waddington (c. 1272), and this work was supplanted by Robert Brunne's *Handlynge Synne* in 1303. By 1343 *Handlynge Synne* appeared in many versions throughout England. Also deriving from Peraldus is *Somme des Vices et des Vertues* (*Somme le Roy*), an Anglo-French manual by Friar Lorens in 1279. This was supplanted in part by the English *Ayenbite of Inwit* by Dan Michel in 1340. Besides these more formal lists and practical how-not-to handbooks, there is a third main branch of practical religious writing, Pennaforte's *Summa Casuum Conscientiae*, written after 1215. Derived from this is the *Oculus Sacerdotis* by William de Pagula in 1340, and *Regimen Animarum*, an anonymous work from about 1343. The latter work is arranged for transmission to the laity of the points of baptism, ritual, marriage, ethical Christian business practices, and especially confession. The second section of the work is a particular treatment of the Deadly Sins and Temptations.[36] *Dives and Pauper* is like *Regimen Animarum* in that it includes, besides the title matter of the Ten Commandments, a distinct orientation to the needs of the layman on points of faith and morals that he would be concerned with, Christian business practice, marriage, the fine points of Canon Law on tithing, and swearing oaths.

Although like the manuals, especially *Regimen Animarum*, *Dives and Pauper* is in many respects closer to a more limited form of moral exposition, the treatise. The treatise, shorter than the manual, is more narrowly focused, treating only one or two of the subjects in Pecham's decree. With this narrower concern, a section of a manual and an entire treatise could be almost identical. A number of English treatises focusing on just the Ten Commandments exist from at least as early as 1300.[37] *Dives* does have a much longer treatment than one would find in the treatises, judging from the sparse outlines of other treatises.[38] In this lengthy amplification lies one of *Dives and Pauper's* chief claims to attention. There is time and space to follow up the interesting sidepaths of the Faith.

Finally, two related features of *Dives and Pauper* have precedents in other manuals and treatises. First is the continued popularization of self-instruction in religion. Originally, manuals were intended for the priest to use in instructing the layman. But Robert Brunne's manual *Handlynge Synne* was written for "laymen to read in devoutly." And Don Michel's *Ayenbite of Inwyt* gives directly to the layman what was formerly directed through the priest.[39] *Dives and Pauper* assumes initially that the reader is a layman who has been instructed in primary considerations, but goes on to satisfy that layman's need to explore on his own refinements and specifics of the codes. Secondly, to excite the lay reader's interest, some of these works were given a dramatic cast. Chaucer's "Parson's Tale" is narrated by a fictional character, although there is little dramatic content within the tale itself. *Ayenbite of Inwyt* gives the elements of Christian faith and practice a more dramatic form which is developed in a number of more specific treatises, such as *A Disputison By-twene a Cristemon and a Jew* and *Dialogue Betweene a Secular and a Friar*. And in *Clensyng of Mannes Sowle* "vanity of dress" and other vices are personified, with acts of the will playing against their opposites.[40] *Dives and Pauper* is noteworthy for being the longest of the debates. Contradictory views are dramatic in the confrontation of different value systems represented by a clergyman vowed to poverty and a successful business man.

Therefore, although it introduces no new element into treatise-like writing in Medieval England, *Dives'* combination of characteristics is unique. Longer than other treatises on the Ten Commandments, it includes within its framework a prologue on "Holy Poverty" and many ideas more pertinent to a narrow class of wealthy, learned laymen. It is composed in English, written for the layman to read himself. It enhances its content by including popular moral stories and other teaching materials. And it is cast in dialogue form. By the synthesis of these characteristics, it stands as a major and representative work of its period.

The Learning in Dives and Pauper

As has already been noted, the mendicant preachers were becoming more and more learned as more specialized training for preachers increased at Oxford. Canon Law became more important in their formal training. The author of *Dives and Pauper* is especially learned in all of Canon Law as it applies to laymen and their relationship to the clergy, and he uses this knowledge to build up the content of about one half of the text of *Dives*. Most often cited by the author are *"Raymond"* and *"Ex.,"* Raymond Pennaforte's *Summa Confessionis,* and the *Extravagantes,* the main collection of Canon Law with its fourteen major subsections. The other four books of Canon Law are referred to from time to time by number when Dives and Pauper discuss the discipline of the Church.[41]

More works than have been noted by previous scholars working on the text are also cited in the work. Among these are non-canonical writers who also touch upon points covered by Canon Law. Especially popular with the author is Hostiensis (Henricus de Seguisa, or Susa), Guido in Rosario, Peter Tarentinus, Grosthede (Grossteste), Durandus, Haymo, Halis, and Isidore. Two works of Aquinas are also cited, *In quaedam questionis* and *De veritate theologie.*

A sample of *Dives and Pauper* shows the method of composition. In a discussion of the repair of churches, first the "gloss" on Canon Law is cited. Then an opinion of Guido in Rosario is added which says that men must heed the customs of the country. The *Extravagantes* is cited again, that men must pay tithes to even bad priests. This statement can be qualified, however; and Hostiensis is cited by book, chapter, and distinction. The law is then cited on the general topic of sinful clergy being forbidden office. Rosario is next cited, then Book Three of Canon Law, that one cannot pay his tithe to whomever he wishes. The author then turns to a related matter, showing from *Extravagantes* that one having care of a parish must serve it himself. Raymond's *Summa Confessione* is then cited, saying that men must pay intentionally-delayed tithes even if goods are subsequently stolen. Dives, the budding legalist, would want to know what the loopholes are. The method of developments progresses generally in this manner, supporting and modifying various authorities in the discussion of the formal laws of the Church.

But then a new chapter of *Dives* will start, and attention is completely turned to Scripture. This usually runs for several chapters, with the pertinent instance covered in rather full detail through several chapters. The author has a firm grasp of Scripture, citing both text and line for most of his quotations, though supplying his own English translation.[42] He cites the "Gloss" often, and mentions many biblical commentators by name. Among these are Bede on Acts, Pope Gregory's *Moralium* on Job, Dockynge on Deuteronomy, and Augustine on Corinthians, Thessalonians, Genesis, and other books of the Old and New Testaments. The author of *Dives* is cautious enough to stay always in good orthodox company as he delivers sizeable portions of Scripture in English to the layman. Sister M. Anselm Gage has counted 432 references to and quotations from the Old Testament, 299 from the New Testament, and 73 from the Apocrypha, for a total of some 700 citations. She finds all but thirteen correctly cited, attesting to the good text that the author had access to.[43] So extensive is his knowledge that Sister Anselm gives special attention to the possibility that the author of *Dives* might be a Wycliffite, and examines the second Wyclilff Bible for corresponding peculiarities in wording But when *Dives* and Wycliff agree, both are also close to the Vulgate, proving no dependence of our author on the Wycliffites. Sister Anselm also suggests that the author translated the biblical quotations himself. In this opinion she agrees with Miss Deanesly,[44] who finds that Purvey (a Wycliffite) is sometimes even closer to the Vulgate, and that the author of *Dives* sometimes telescopes its matter, That *Dives and Pauper* has so much biblical quotation, despite the prohibitions of biblical translation by Bishop Arundel, is explainable. The author of *Dives* does not set out to translate the Bible literally and place it in the hands of the laity. Rather, he merely quotes passages for their moral instruction. He traps himself into translating into English to be understood by his readers, and he gives, in effect, dozens of biblical stories with full amplification from the glosses.

The debate of whether laymen should or should not have close acquaintance with the Bible enters into *Dives and Pauper*. Dives says "But now men say that there should no lewd people teach themselves of God's law nor of the gospel, nor of holy writ, neither to learn it, nor to teach it" (Fourth Commandment, Chap. 2). Pauper's reply, misinterpreted perhaps by Miss Deansely,[45] emphatically states "This is a foul error, and full peryllous to man's soul. For every man and woman is bound after his degree to do his business to know God's law, that he is bound to keep." The author's unquestionable interest in Scripture lies both in the moral truth and in his interest and ability to tell a good narrative story.

His stock of good stores extends far beyond the Scriptures. Named sources for stories recounted in *Dives and Pauper* include *Vitas Patrum*, events in *The City of God*, the *Life of Barlaam*, Bonaventure's *Life of Saint Francis*, Pseudo-Turpin's *De Gesta Karoli*, the Master of Kynde (Bartholomaeus Angelicus), and *Gesta Romanorum*.* Among the saints cited for edifying incidents and miracles are Gregory, Thomas à Becket, Clement, Nicholas, Francis, Cecilia, Catherine, Agnes, and Lucy. From his manner of citation, he must have had a significantly large library at his disposal during the entire time that he composed *Dives*. The author also delights in telling anecdotes from his own observations or from sermon handbooks—what has recently happened near Colchester, and what "people" say on almost every subject, prodigies recently born in the neighborhood, current superstitions, magic beliefs. Since he uses Pauper as his persona, Pauper has almost all of the narrative parts. Dives is expected to listen dutifully.

Another and final branch of the author's special knowledge lies in what shall be loosely called "devotional" or "mystical" writing, although these writings would not generally be his major interest in his instruction of Dives, even if Dives did not protest the apparent "uselessness of the higher way" in the Prologue. The author cities by name Jerome's "Epistle to Paula and Eustocia," "Ad Nepocianum," and "Ad Rusticum Monachum." Especially noteworthy are the longer "Meditation on the Passion" and "Epistle ad Monacho" by Saint Ber-

---

* *Gesta Romanorum: A Record of Aunciend Histories* (1595) reprinted by Scholars' Facsimiles & Reprints in 1973.

nard, eminent among mystics. Many of Augustine's more spiritually oriented sermons are cited besides the devotional *City of God*. These include almost the entire "De decem Cordis" with its useful metaphor on the Commandments, and the "Epistle ad Letum." After Canon Law itself, Augustine rivals Hostiensis in the number of citations. But we can attach little significance to this, since Augustine was the most popular and universal of the Fathers in England, widely cited by writers of all orders.

Other authors cited in *Dives*, such as Boniface, Popes Leo, Gregory, and Innocent, can be found mentioned often enough in Glosses on Canon Law and in other spiritual writers. Also probably encountered in secondary sources are Aristotle's *Ethics*, sections IV and V, 'Tholomeus," and Seneca. Durandus and Nicholas de Lyra, however, are almost contemporaries to our author, indicating that not all material was derived out of source books and summaries. All of these materials reflect upon the wide interests of *Dives*' author. The book is then almost an encyclopedia of Church-laity relationships in England in 1405. For the laymen, a cross-section of their more practical religious concerns are covered. All that they really need to know of Canon Law is covered since it, like the Scriptures, was unavailable in book form. He can check up on his parish priest's adherence to the Law, instruct his wife in her behavior, test the honesty of business relationships, and at the same time find that he has been led to conform his life with the will of God. To this extent, the "Ten Commandments" framework as well as the possibility that *Dives* has interest only as a debate about the rich versus the poor way of life both mislead the medievalist and historian of English society. It is really a very practical handbook, a shortcut to years of study.

Manuscripts and Editions

Dives and Pauper is extant in eight longer manuscripts and one fragment, and in a number of copies of the three printed editions. The manuscripts can be classified into two groups, based on two versions of the prologue,[46] "Treatise on Holy Poverty." The early manuscripts, MSS Royal 17 C. XX and 17 C. XXI, in the British Museum, Bodleian MS Douce 295, and at University Library, Glasgow, Hunterian MS 270, have a longer (c. 7,500 words) version of "Holy Poverty." A fragment, in the Bodleian Library, known as MS Eng.th.e.1, "Scraps," is just a leaf answering detail for detail the Bodleian's Douce MS 295. We can assume that it would likewise have the longer "Holy Poverty."[47]

One manuscript, British Museum MS Harlian 149, is condensed, and has no prologue whatsoever. The remaining three manuscripts and all three printed editions have a shorter prologue (c. 5,600 words). Manuscripts are Bodleian MS Eng.th.d.36, Chapter Library, Lichfield, England, MS 5, and an uncatalogued manuscript at Yale University, New Haven, Ct. The printed editions are by Richard Pynson in 1493 (Pollard and Redgrave #19212; Proctor #9782), Wynken de Worde in 1946 (Pollard and Redgrave #19213; Proctor #9706), and Berthelet in 1536 (Pollard and Redgrave #19214).

The relationship of the manuscripts is discussed elsewhere in considerable detail. One of these, Bodleian MS Eng.th.d.36, is of special importance because it is the source of Pynson's printed edition. This manuscript is described in *A Summary Catalogue of Western MSS* in the Bodleian Library at Oxford.[48] The manuscript of *Dives and Pauper* is incomplete as it now stands. The "Table" begins with "iii c. What Veniaunce hath fallen for false couetise" and the text breaks off on f. 212v at the beginning for the section on the Tenth Commandment: "DIues Me thenketh thi spech skilful good." That "Table" is in single columns, but the text is written in double columns of thirty-seven lines each. No signatures are used, but after the "Table" leaf, a full quire does begin. Catchwords are used at the foot of the verso of every eighth folio. The handwriting is remarkably clear and well formed, reminding one of the print types used in many incunabula. The printer Pynson used this manuscript when he printed the text.[49] Later Wynken de Worde used Pynson's edition as his copy text, and Berthelet in turn used De Worde's

Richard Pynson's edition of *Dives and Pauper* begins with a title-page with a large woodcut of a poor man in rags approaching a well-dressed rich man. Over the top of the picture is the caption, in large letters, of "diues & pauper."[50] Folio a2r starts the "Table of Contents," folio [13] is blank, and folio [14r] starts the "Prologue on Holy Poverty." The last page of the text is folio [243v]. The colophon is on this page, folio [244r] is blank, and [244v] has Pynson's device #1.[51] The collation reads a-b⁶ a-u⁸ A-I⁸. There are then 244 leaves.[52] Signatures are used on the first half of each gathering on the recto, running "ai"— "aiii," etc., in the first lower case alphabet, "ai"—"aiiii" in the second and, in upper case, third alphabets. Only "c" in the second alphabet is signed "ii" to "v," though on the correct first four leaves. A few capital letter "Ds" are used to indicate *Dives*' parts. Running headlines mark off sections of the text, half on each side, except when a new section starts. Like the manuscript that Pynson's compositors worked from, the "Table of Contents" is in single columns, and the text itself is in double columns of 36 or 37 lines, when content spacing permits every line possible to be used.

Dives and Pauper is printed in blackletter or gothic character, in a rough transitional *lettre de forme*.[53] In general this book is crammed with many inconsequential mechanical errors of many varieties. Misspellings abound, running headlines are not changed when they should be, and chapter headings are misnumbered. However, this poor workmanship is better than that of Berthelet, who was also designated a Royal printer. Six hundred copies of *Dives and Pauper* were printed by Pynson[54] at the request of John Russhe, half of which, printed and bound, were sold to Russhe at the wholsale price of four shillings each.[55]

The Other Printed Editions

Wynken de Worde printed a second edition of *Dives and Pauper* in 1496 at Westminster, attesting to the popularity of the work printed just three years earlier by Pynson. The title page is the same woodcut of a poor man approaching a rich man used as the title page in Pynson. This woodcut is also found on f. [10v], sig. B4v, between the "Table" and "Holy Poverty," and again on the verso of the last leaf.[56] On the verso of the title page is another large woodcut, this of Saint Jerome seated on a dias with an open book, with a courtly crowd including the Virgin and Child before him.[57] On the recto of the last leaf is a woodcut of the Virgin and Child first occuring on the title page of the *Scala Perfectionis* (1494), also printed by De Worde. Nothing is known of the price that Wynken de Worde charged for his book, though it would most likely be close to Pynson's four shillings wholesale, especially if Pynson had copies remaining to sell. Neither is the number of copies printed known. Ronald McKerrow estimates that six hundred or fewer copies was the usual number for Caxton and Pynson, with Pynson's largest known press run, a special book, reaching no more than one thousand copies.[58] Over twice as many copies of Pynson are known by this writer, twenty-seven versus De Worde's thirteen. But I assume that those foundations and individuals most interested in books and with the best commercial connections would have purchased the first printing. These first purchasers are the very people whose libraries survive.

Wynken de Worde derived his edition entirely from the edition of

Richard Pynson,[59] without having in hand any manuscript. Even when De Worde has different readings than Pynson, the variation can always be accounted for. Most often, changes in spelling, the rearrangements of phrases, the deletion of a few words, the substitution of synonyms, or even the addition of a few words to fill out the bottom of a page are solutions to mechanical problems by the typesetters. At times, De Worde corrects obvious Pynson misspellings, and renumbers obvious sections where the correct sequence is clear. Neither of the printers shows acquaintance with any wording variations found in the manuscript tradition.

Forty years after De Worde's edition, Thomas Berthelet printed the last edition of *Dives and Pauper* in 1536. The title page appears as follows: a simple frame, with columns, a cherub above, which enclose the words "DIVES / AND / PAVPER" in the upper section and "Londine in aedibus Tho. / Bertheleti regli im- / pres. excus. / (ornament) / 1534."[60] in the lower, the date being part of the border itself. I wish to locate a copy with the last leaf, sig. v4, which should contain Berthelet's device, "a figure stabbing herself, with a landscape in the distance and an Architectural framework."[61] Otherwise, no complete copies are known among the nine surviving. The volume is small octavo, printed throughout in single columns of thirty-four lines of small gothic character type. No illustrations are used.

Father Tahney notes that the "Table" lists ten chapters for the "Prologue" while there are eleven in the text.[62] This can be explained by collation with the Wynken de Worde edition. De Worde omitted "Chapter 4" in the "Table" entirely, though he carries the listing through "Chapter 11." Berthelet notices the jump from chapter number three to chapter five, renumbers the chapters five through eleven, assuming that De Worde merely misnumbered. Thus, he labels chapter five as chapter four, chapter six as chapter five, etc. Berthelet has two innovations besides printing in single column. He moves all the scriptural citations and references to the Church Fathers, Canon Law, and other texts to the margin, permitting the reader to proceed right through the text. At times, when De Worde follows the tradition exactly giving only author, Berthelet gives the complete source, sometimes both in Latin and English. This is really the first addition to the text since the second version of the prologue on "Holy Poverty" was composed. He also streamlines the bulky "Table" to make it more of a quick location guide than summary. But despite these well-considered improvements, his is the most careless printing job of the three. He has a number of lacunae in sentences and hundreds of misspellings. De Worde has the fewest errors, correcting some of Pynson's and patching a few as best he could, while still repeating others. Pynson had the most difficult work in printing, because he had to work from manuscript copy, while the other two printers could see what the finished book would look like and could improve upon format and introduce modern synonyms.

Textual Editing of the Present Edition

The text chosen for reproduction is that of the Huntington Library, San Marino, California. Not only are all printed pages present, but the well-preserved text shows no ink bleed-through. The Huntington copy lacking the elusive woodcuts, these are supplied from a Wynken de Worde copy, cleaned of hand-written notes. Two pages were carelessly transposed by the compositors,[63] sigs. [t8r] and [t8v]. The running headlines were correct, so the pages' contents have been reversed for correct reading. Since no signatures appear on either the verso or recto of the folio, the error was perhaps never noticed. De Worde repeats the error of the switched leaves, merely changing the punctuation. But his type spacing makes the erroneous break come well down in a column. Berthelet noted something wrong, changed wording and punctuation, and preserved the wrong ordering. It would be almost impossible to know what might have gone wrong if someone in Berthelet's shop was unable to consult any of the manuscripts.

While no stop-press corrections are known in De Worde and Berthelet, Pynson apparently had made extensive changes. I have just one illustration of the changes, the last phrase on sig. [m7r] and the first on sig. [m7v], pp. 200-201. In fol. [m7r], one state of the form reads

>   kept
>   al his cõmaundemētis: therfore
>   the kynred of ionadab shal not;[64]

And in another state appears

>   þe kired of ionadab shal not fail.[65]

A third reads:

>   the kynred of ionadab shal not[66] (no semicolon)

The text reproduced here reads:
> þe kired of ionadab shal not fail (no period)

On the top of sig. [m7v] are found three readings:
> his cõmaundemẽtes. Therfore
> the kynrede of Ionadab shall
> nat fayle.[67]

The second reads:
> his cõmaundemẽtes. Therfore
> the kynrede of Ionadab shalle (*shalle* for *shall*)
> nat fayle/[68]   (/ for .)

The reading in this edition is:
> his cõmaundemẽtes. Therfore
> the kynrede of Ionadab shulle (*shulle* for *shall*)
> nat fayle/

The problem is obviously caused by two compositors, each working on a section of text. Both changed their readings as the press run continued, but without success. Wynken de Worde, printing from Pynson's edition, followed the second version from [m7v] adding more corrections, or checking the reading against an English translation of the Bible. His reading on [k4rᵃ] is:

> & kept all his cõmaũdementes
> therfore yᵉ kynrede of Ionadab shall
> not fayle/but all dayes that kynrede
> shall be in my syght[69]

The complete Wynken de Worde edition is reproduced in my dissertation, cited above. Against it is collated the Pynson printing. All variations are substitutions of synonyms, minor changes in word order to make the text fit the printer's column, and corrections (at times) of spellings.

The problems of *Dives and Pauper* are now mainly in the area of sources. To what extent is it composed from books of summaries, and to what extent is it composed from primary sources? And who had the energy to put it all together for a rich secular layman. His anonimity is usual for works of this kind. Hope Emily Allen's *Richard Rolle of Hampole* is a huge listing of anonymous and misattributed manuscripts of the same period. While Rolle's style is often the deciding clue to authorship, the writer of *Dives* masks his personality even more. The writer certainly flattered laymen, giving them large parts of Canon Law and the Scripture so that they could guide themselves.

Acknowledgments

I wish to thank the Henry E. Huntington Library, San Marino, Calif., for permission to reproduce their superb copy of Richard Pynson's *Dives and Pauper*. I also acknowledge the help of the Marquette University Research Council for aid in this study. Professor John W. Robinson first introduced me to bibliographical history; without his initial interest, this effort would have never been undertaken.

FRANCIS SHEERAN

Milwaukee, Wisconsin
September 1973

NOTES

1. *Commentarii de Scriptoribus Britannicis*, ed. A. Hall (1709), 2:452. Sister M. Anselm Gage traces the problem in detail in the first fifteen pages of her master's thesis, "A Commentary on the 1536 Edition of *Dives and Pauper*," Columbia University, February 1947.

2. *Scriptorum Illustrium Majoris Britanniae Summarium* (1559), ed. R. L. Poole (Oxford: Clarendon Press, 1902), p. 609.

3. *N & Q*, ser. II, 4 (21 October 1911): 321. *CHEL* has not been corrected during its many reprintings. The *Gesämt Catalogue* apparently is headed for a listing under "Parker."

4. "How Our Fathers Were Taught in Catholic Days," *The Dublin Review* 4, ser. ii, 120 (April 1897): 245-65.

5. Parker is called "the yong fryer" in 1464 in *Historical Collections of a Citizen of London*, ed. William Gregory, Camden Society no. 17 (London: Nichols and Son, 1876), p. 230.

6. Richardson, *N & Q*, p. 322.

7. H. G. Pfander, "*Dives et Pauper*," *The Library* 4, ser. xiv (1933): 299-300.

8. Margaret Deanesly, *The Lollard Bible* (Cambridge, 1920), pp. 392-98, gives a long list of these books, all of which are actually listed in English wills.

9. These measurements are a bit generous, but fit no other European country. Bede lists the measurements as 800 by 200 miles. *Ecclesiastical History of the English Nation*, trans. J. Stevens and J. Giles (London, 1910), p. 4.

10. Pfander studies the controversy between the Franciscans and Dominicans over footwear. The Dominicans were attacked for wearing boots in a continuing controversy (Pfander, p. 307).

11. Pfander quotes the Franciscan Rule in Latin from MS Bodley 52, f. 110v-111r (Pfander, pp. 306-7).

12. Modernized from MS Douce 295, fol. 7v. This and the following quotations are in the alternate and never-printed "Prologue on Holy Poverty," which I am editing in another paper.

13. Pfander gives details of Franciscan sepulture, p. 305.

14. Cf. W. A. Pantin, *The English Church in the Fourteenth Century* (Notre Dame, 1962), chap. 11, pp. 244-62.

15. Ibid., p. 251.

16. Ibid., p. 150.

17. Ibid., chap. 9.

18. Ibid., chap. 10.

19. Albert E. Hartung, *A Manual of the Writings in Middle English: 1050-1500*, sec. 7, "Dialogues, Debates and Catechisms," pp. 699-716, and sec. 3, "Wyclyf and His Followers," pp. 360-77.

20. Pantin, p. 252.

21. *"The Scale of Perfection" and the English Mystical Tradition* (Madison, 1966), p. 160.

22. *The English Religious Heritage* (St. Louis, 1958), p. 33.

23. Milosh, p. 49.

24. "A Preliminary Edition of the 'Table,' The Prologues of 'Holy Poverty,' and 'Commandment I' of *"Dives and Pauper,"* Ph.D. diss., Syracuse University, September 1967, p. 16.

25. For a discussion of the history of this fast in England, see Pfander, p. 301, n. 1.

26. Dated by Pantin, p. 249. The work is "sometimes attributed to the school of Wyclif, but apparently without foundation." (Sister Bradley has a remarkable study of texts, with edition, forthcoming from Catholic University of America Press.)

27. Ibid.

28. Quoted from Pantin, p. 249.

29. Quoted from Deanesly, p. 347. No edition is available, thus the composite nature of the citation. Like *Dives*, this treatise's prologue has several variations. For more text, see Vaughan's *Life of Wycliffe* (London, 1852), p. 382 ff.

30. Deanesly, p. 346, n. 5.

31. Ibid., p. 276 and n.

32. *England in the Late Middle Ages*, 2d ed., the Pelican History of England no. 4 (London, 1963), pp. 152-53.

33. Ibid., p. 173.

34. Ibid., p. 299.

35. Both of these works have been suggested as sources for Chaucer's "Parson's Tale." Cf. Germain Dempster, "The Parson's Tale," *Sources and Analogues* (New York, 1951), pp. 723-29. These two works are quoted in part on her pp. 729-45. But more recent critics have shown that while passages of the tale resemble parts of both works, neither can be the source of the tale.

36. For details I am indebted to H. G. Pfander, "Some Medieval Manuals of Religious Instruction in England and Observations on Chaucer's Parson's Tale," *JEGP* 35 (1936), 243-58; Gerald R. Owst, *Preaching in Medieval England* (London, 1926), p. 290; and Dempster, p. 273, n. 3.

37. Pantin describes in detail the contents of MS Burney 356 in the British Museum, pp. 277-80. Another is in the Bodleian, MS Fr. f.1, which goes from Confession to the Seven Deadly Sins and their branches, the Ten Commandments, methods of combating temptation, and returns again to Confession.

38. Treatises were often not much more than four to ten folios of outlines for the preacher to expand upon, and to consult while preparing or giving sermons.

39. Owst believes that all major English language treatises were composed for laymen and nuns. (Owst, p. 223).

40. Pfander, *JEGP*, p. 250.

41. H. G. Richardson finds no reference to Canon Law beyond Book Six, *N & Q*, p. 322. Since there were only six books in existence, the author of *Dives* had access to all there was. The next canon-like book came out during the Council of Trent (1545-63).

42. Gage, "A Study of the Scriptural Material in *Dives and Pauper*," pp. 33-65, presents a full study of his habits in quotation and translation.

43. Gage, p. 40. She is quoting from the Berthelet printed edition. His work has both compounded errors from the earlier editions and a new start at corrections.

44. Deanesly, p. 345. Also Richardson, p. 34.

45. Deanesly, p. 327.

46. The manuscripts are described in detail in Francis Sheeran's "An Edition of Wynken de Worde's *Dives and Pauper*, Collated with Pynson's Edition, MSS Yale, Eng.th.d.36, and Lichfield 5; With the Alternate Prologue on 'Holy Poverty' in Hunterian MS 270, Collated with Royal MSS 17 C. XX and XXI, and MS Douce 295," (Ph.D. diss., University of Nebraska, 1970), pp. xxxii-1. Other accounts of the manuscripts are also discussed, including early cataloguers', Barnum's and Tahney's. Cf. Rev. Shane Tahney, O.Carm., "The Manuscripts and Editions of *Dives and Pauper*, A Medieval Treatise on the Ten Commandments," master's thesis, Catholic University, Washington, D.C., 1950.

47. Bodleian MS Douce 295 merits more explanation, as published information on it is so far from reality. It is foliated throughout in a hand after the several leaves had disappeared. Numbered are 221 leaves, #11 being omitted, and #71 appearing twice, first in order, and then again after #72. The first folio of the "Table" begins with Chap. 39 of the First Commandment, and continues until Chap. Eight of the Second Commandment. A folio is next missing that should include the end of Chap. Eight of the Second Commandment until Chap. Three of the Fourth Commandment of the "Table." This omitted folio is not mentioned in the Catalogue. The manuscript has some fire damage on the edges, and fire might also account for the missing last folio. Some confusion has arisen about the nature of the "Prologue on Holy Poverty" in this manuscript because of the early study by H. G. Pfander, who claims that "Douce 295 compresses approximately the first five chapters of the Royal manuscripts, in the prologue on Holy Poverty, into two chapters" (Pfander, p. 302). He

lists a portion of Chap. Six, all of Chaps. Seven and Eight, and a portion of Chap. Nine as missing. If this were so, we would have a distinct new rendition of the Prologue with which to deal, since the others divide into just two types. Actually, the remaining fragments of the "Prologue on Holy Poverty" match their counterparts in the two Royal manuscripts with only minor differences. The manuscript does, however, lack the last few lines of Chap. Three, all of Chaps. Four through Eight, and the first part of Chap. Nine. The "Table of Contents" is no help as a cross-check on contents, since the first folio of the "Table" which would include the "Prologue" is missing. Either the manuscript copied from was deficient, or the scribe omitted the passage.

48. Vol. 7, 1953. For extended discussion of this manuscript, see Margery M. Morgan, "Pynson's Manuscript of *Dives and Pauper*," *The Library*, 5th ser., vol. 8, no. 4 (1953): 217.

49. Miss Morgan's argument that MS Eng.th.d.36 is Pynson's printers' copy follows: "The whole of the text of the manuscript has been marked off in sections which correspond to the pages of Pynson's edition. A large cross in the margin . . . marks the point at which each fresh gathering in the printed book starts; pages within the signature are counted off and the divisions marked by a number, sometimes the letter of the signature accompanying it, with either a point beside it or a pen-scratch running into the appropriate line. Pynson's table of contents is in sixes, the rest of the book in eights, and each folio sheet is signed once only: on the recto of leaves 1 to 3 in the table and of leaves 1 to 4 elsewhere. The marginal numbers in the manuscript run to 12 in the part of the table that remains and to 16 within each signature through the rest of the work" (p. 217).

50. Error has arisen in descriptions of the title page, and needs to be dispelled. Pynson began numbering the text of the manuscript MS Eng.th.d.36 on the first leaf with the number "3." This indicates that he did not intend to print the text on the first folio of his own copy, but planned another use for it. Information in all catalogues states that the first folio is blank. (The verso in all cases is.) Ames, in *Typographical Antiquities* (London, 1785), 2, #468, p. 401, states that, because the first signature is a², "no doubt it had a titlepage, perhaps with a cut." In his thesis, Father Tahney reports that from examination of the Pierpont Morgan, New York Public Library, and Folger Shakespeare Library copies it seems that though Pynson may have intended to insert a titlepage, he never actually did. The copy that Ames had in hand evidently lacked the first leaf also. However, Miss Margery Morgan has found that the Douce copy of Pynson has the woodcut used later by Wynken de Worde. She also remarks that either the space is empty or a blank leaf is inserted in "so many of the extant copies of Pynson's book" (p. 218). It is easy to imagine why one would want to remove the woodcut from extant copies for separate framing. But why it appears in some Pynson and some Wynken de Worde copies is only open to conjecture. Since the woodcut is useable for only *Dives and Pauper* because of the title being carved into the wood, it must have been specially commissioned by Pynson. It probably arrived too late to be used in all the press run. When De Worde came to print the same text three years later, the woodcut was still sound, and being of no further use to Pynson, he was able to purchase it. But he went over to get it after his own press run started,

or else Pynson was unable to locate it in his shop when De Worde was ready to start.

51. Father Tahney reports that the Morgan and New York Public Libraries do not have this leaf, and that the Folger copy has what cannot be the original, since the chain lines do not match (p. 45). He also criticizes Ames' description, cited in n. 50, which describes the last leaf. William Lowndes, in his *Bibliographer's Manual of English Literature*, ed. Henry Bohn, new ed. (London, 1857), 2:652, posits the last leaf as described above. His description is attacked in an unsigned article in *Notes & Queries*, ser. 2, vol. 5, no. 106 (January 1858): 38, which says "Such is not the case in the copy in the British Museum, or in that sold here [Messrs. Southeby and Wilkinson, London] during the month of August last." But Father Tahney is wrong in saying that "No extant copy of *Dives and Pauper* contains this final leaf of the last gathering" (p. 46). The Huntington Library copy, used for this facsimile edition, has this leaf.

52. Tahney counts 241, denying the existence of "blank" leaves (p. 46). The British Museum *Catalogue* lists 243, since its copies lack the last leaf. Gordon Duff, *Fifteenth-Century English Books*, lists 232 leaves, forgetting the collation a-b[6] which precedes the a-u[8] alphabet, making his description of collation just twelve leaves short.

53. Daniel B. Updike, *Printing Types: Their History, Forms, and Use* (Cambridge: Harvard University Press, 1927), 1:122.

54. Surviving copies of the three printed editions are listed in Sheeran, "An Edition . . .," pp. xxxi-xxxii. Some are listed in nn. 64, 65, and 66 below.

55. H. R. Plomer, "Two Lawsuits of Richard Pynson," *The Library*, ser. 2, no. 10 (1909): 126.

56. The John Rylands Library copy has all five woodcuts. The Morgan Library copy lacks the first three. The Bodleian's S.Seld.d.14. lacks the last two. As far as other material omitted from De Worde texts is concerned, I rely on information received by Tahney from A. R. Domer of the J. Pierpont Morgan Library, which states that the McGill University copy lacks the whole "Table" and also the last two woodcuts. Tahney quotes Maggs' *Catalogue No. 402* (1921), Item 8, which says that almost all known copies do not contain the "Table" or last leaf. He also reports that the Morgan copy lacks the last leaf of the "Table" (p. 54, n. 31).

57. This woodcut is also found in Wynken de Worde's *Vitas Patrum* and in *Polichronicon*, both printed in 1495. Of the woodcuts, only "Dives and Pauper" was to see service once in his shop. Edward Hodnett, *English Woodcuts, 1480-1535* (London, 1935), p. 245.

58. *An Introduction to Bibliography for Literary Students* (Oxford: Clarendon Press, 1928), p. 131.

59. Tahney, pp. 57-63, gives a number of parallel passages, and concludes (before Morgan's article appeared) that "De Worde based his text primarily on Pynson's version" (p. 62). Mrs. Barnum concludes the same, p. 51. H. G. Richardson had asserted a bit strongly that De Worde's 1496 edition is very different from Richard Pynson's 1493 edition (*N & Q*, p. 323). Morgan is right in saying that "De Worde's text of 1496 is a reprint of Pynson's," p. 217.

60. The discrepancy in dates is explained by H. R. Plomer, *Wynken de Worde and His Contemporaries* (London, 1925), p. 226, as follows: "The well-known architectural border with the date, 1534, cut in the bottom panel, was brought into use by the printer in that year. It was continued to be used unaltered until 1560, and has been the source of a great deal of error in dating his later work." E. Gordon Duff, *The Printers, Stationers, and Bookbinders of Westminster and London from 1476 to 1535* (Cambridge: At the University Press, 1906), p. 180, says the same. Note that the error is repeated on the filming card in the Edwards University Microfilms STC Project, Case 3, Carton 18.

61. This is suggested by Cyril Davenport, *Thomas Berthelet* (Chicago, The Caxton Club, 1901), p. 49.

62. Tahney, p. 66.

63. Francis Sheeran, "Printing Errors in the Texts of *Dives and Pauper*," *Papers of the Bibliographical Society of America* 65, no. 2 (1971): 151-54, has more detail and discussion.

64. B.M. (IB. 55492); Bodleian (all 3 copies); U.L.C. 4196; Hunterian; Exeter College, Oxford; J. R. L.; and Westminster. Morgan, p. 223.

65. B.M. (C.11.c.11); Lambeth; U.L.C. 4194 and 4195; King's College, Cambridge; York; and Oscott. Morgan, p. 223. She examined some of the copies herself, while others were examined for her.

66. Curt F. Bühler, "Further Notes on Pynson's 1493 *Dives and Pauper*," *PBSA* 65, no. 4 (1971): 391, reports on the copy in the Pierpont Morgan Library.

67. This is the reading in all copies listed in nn. 64 and 65.

68. This is the reading of the Pierpont Morgan copy.

69. This is the reading of the Bodleian Library copy, S.Seld.d.14.

Riche and pore haue like cūmpnge into this worlde. & lyke outgoyng/ but their liupng in this worlde is vnlike. What shulde consort a pore man apenst grutchyng/ and what wychednesses. folowe louers of richesses.   the first chapter
¶ Of thre maner lordshippes & of whiche lordship it is vnderstōde þ god gaue mā lordship ouir fisshes/ briddes & beestes   ca. ii.
¶ Howe this scripture is vnderstonde. It is more blissfull to yeue than to taue. & howe sūme wylsful pore man yeueth more thanne a riche couetous man so stondyng may yeue.   ca. iii.
¶ That riche & pore either is necessarie to other/ and that the riche man nedith more than the pore.   ca. iiii.
¶ Why richesse is cleppyd a deupsship of wychednesse/ and one epposicion of this texte It is more easy a camel to passe by a nedlis iye thanne a riche man to entre the kingdome of heuene.   ca. v.
¶ Howe men shuld haue them to richesses whan god yeueth them. & whanne god takith theym away/ and in what maner eche man must forsake al that he hath. also the litterall epposicion of this text bifore seide. It is more easy a camel &c.   ca. vi.
¶ Riche men be nat lacked or blamed in scripture for they be riche but for their couetise and mysuse. Ne pore mē praised for wāityng or lackynge of richesses/ but for gode wyll and pacience/ of diuerse maners of pore men. and hou richesse is occasion of synne more thanne pouert.   ca. vii.
¶ Howe this text of salomon is vnderstonde. yeue nat me richesses and beggery.   ca. viii.
¶ Of ii. maner of pfections/ sufficient and excellent. He reherspth the x. commaundementes.   ca. ix.
¶ Why crist enfourmed more the ponge riche man in the preceptis of the secounde table/ than of the firste. and why more the secoūd precept of charite thanne in the firste.   ca. x.
¶ Of ii. lyues cōteplatif & actif/ also other causes of epssinge of the preceptis of the secoūde table to the pong mā bifore seid.   ca. xi.
    ¶ The firste precepte.
¶ Hou pmagerye is lefull/ and howe pmages were ordeyned for thre causes.   cap. i.
Howe the people shulde rede in the boke of pmagery.   ca. ii.
¶ Howe the people shulde do worship & logись to god & to seintes.
    a ii

to god and to seintes bifore ymages/ and nat pptrly shulde suche worship be do to suche ymages.   cap. iii. & iiii.

⸿ Crist is the crosse & me crepe to on godefriday. & Why such crepig is thā do bifore any ymaged crosse/ & hou crist is worshiped on palmesūday whā the peple is drawe vp bifore the rode.   ca. iiii.

⸿ What foly it is to speke to ymages/ or to do seruice to thē. & why crosses be set vp by the high weyes & crosses borne ī pcessions.   ca v.

⸿ What peynture of ymages bitokneth in special. Ensample of the ymage of oure lady/ of peyt. poule. Johny euangeliste/ Johny baptist/ and so of other seyntes.   ca vi.

⸿ What peynture of ymages bitokneth in general/ as y all the apostles ben peyntyd/ bare foote in mantels. and roūde thinges vpon their hedes/ and that the peynture of ymages may be considred on two wyse.   ca. vii.

⸿ What the peynture of aungelis signifieth in liknesse of yong mē with wynges.   ca viii

⸿ Why the iiii. euangelistes ben peynted in the liknesse of a man. of a lyon/ of an oxe/ and of an egle/ and why they ben peynted in foure parties of the crosse/ and of an house.   ca. ix.

⸿ Why ymages be hyled or shulde be hiled in lenten.   ca x

⸿ What seruice & worship we owe to god & What to mā/ what diuyne worship is/ & hou it is shelwyd to god by hert spech & dede/ & hou mē & wymē shulde be worshippyd & why.   ca. xi. xii.

⸿ Howe worship is taken diuersly for worship of adoracion ppre & vn ppre/ also for worship of veneracion/ & so on many maners: for the vnknowyng wherof many men falle in doutes & erroures whan they rede of worshipyng of ymages   ca xiii

⸿ Offering is nat made to prestes but to god by the hōdes of prestis/ & I shrift mē knele to god bifore the preest   ca.xiiii

⸿ Sēsyng may be done in ii. maners/ wᵗ encēse halowed/ & withe encense nat halowed/ & what encense bitokneth   ca. xv

⸿ Diuerse causes why cristen people pray & worship god/ comonly eestwarde/ and that the sūne ne the mone be nat to be worshiped of men as sūme fooles doo.   ca. xvi

Of ye falshed of iudicial astronomy & hou it blasphe' god   c. xvii

⸿ What seruyce planetis and the bodies aboue doo to mankynde and how god doth with them what he wole. Ensample of a smyth

and his gryndinge stone. ca. xviii.
⁋Men may nat knowe by the course of the planetis the doomes of god ne certeynly what is to come/ & holy god chaungith his sentence/ as men chaunge their lyf into gode or wycked. ca. xix
Skilles apene false excusacions of iudicial astronomers. c. xx.
⁋Dyuerse skilles why one is inclined to gode or enyl/ sekenesse or helthe more thanne a nother. ca. xxi
⁋Causes why one man is disposed to this state or this craft/ and a nother man to a nother state or to a nother crafte. ca. xxii.
⁋That ther is no destenye/ & of the sterre of epiphanie ca. xxiii
⁋Howe the iii. kinges knewe the birth of crist by the sterre/ & þ the science of iudicial astronomye is pyrtly no science. ca. xxiiii.
⁋Howe iudicial astronomye is repreuyd in olde lawe/ and in the newe lawe, and by the lawe of holy churche. ca. xxv
⁋Of the folye of them þ dyuyne by astronomye. & of the mischyf. of them þ truste in þ craft/ & þ the planetes and bodies aboue. been tokenes of thinges to cume and nat causes. ca. xxvi.
⁋Examples how the bodies aboue been suche tokenes and nat alway causes. ca. xxvii.
How the sunne & mone be tokenes to creatures here bynethe whan they shuld do their kynde/ & of diuerse wondres I kynde. ca. xxviii.
⁋What it bitokneth whan any sterre or comete appyrith apene comen course of kynde/ and what other wondres appere & fall apon comen course of kynde. ca. xxix.
⁋Diuerse wiles wherby astronomers and faitoures that ben clepyd soth sayers and other wycches knowe thinges that ben doone/ or that ben to be done. ca. xxx
⁋Diuerse caes why feldes can tel thinges þ ben pryuely done. or thinges þ be to be done. & on what maner they tel such thinges c. xxxi
⁋The feende may neither say ne do but as god yeueth bileue. He is euer a lyer say he sothe say he false. and why god suffreth him to tempte men. ca. xxxii.
⁋Witches & iapers that coniure feendes/ conuell nat feendes as it semyth that they do/ ne the feende is nat closed in a rynge/ nathelees by holy coniuracions ordeyned of holy churche ben feendes caste oute of men. ca xxxiii
⁋Howe wicchecrafte is forboden by the lawe canon & lawe impial
a iii

⁋ What peynes longe to witches & to her fautoures. ca. xxxiiii
⁋ It is vnlefull to trust that a man is a theif, or to sle him for a wit che saith a psone to be a thref. ca. xxxv.
⁋ Wytches vsyng prayers and dedes of holynesse, and hose thynges in her wicchecraftes, in somoche they worship the feende the more. and the more they dispise god. also why wytchecraft is moost vsed amonge olde folke. ca. xxxvi.
⁋ That god forbediȝ al maner spy by the first gmaude. c. xxxvii
⁋ How it is lefull to vse lottes, and thou nat, and so of pleiynge at the dyce. ca. xxxviii.
⁋ What wicchecrafte is, and of synne to seyne witchecrafte, also of feynyng of myracles by ypocrisy. ca. xxxix.
⁋ Of charmyng of adders, and how it is vnlefull and perilous to man to charge his freende to cume ayen after his dethe. and shewe him his astate. ca. xl.
⁋ How after mennys deth sumtyme feendes go seyynyg them to be spirites of suche men, and sumtyme the soules of dede men appere and why. ca. xli.
⁋ Howe the newe fast clepyd oure lady fast hath no grounde, neither it is of auctorite. ca. xlii
⁋ Diuerse causes of dremys, and that it is pilouse to bileue in dremys. To trust in dremys is forboden in scripture, and why it is harde to knowe what dremys betoken. ca. xliii. & xliiii.
⁋ Stiryngnes to godenesse ȝ a man hath in his dremys. may he folowe. so that it be done warly. and what harme cumeth to theym ȝ had leuer dreme of the feende than of god. ca. xlv.
⁋ Of the foly of them that had leuer mete with a tode than with a knight, or with a man of religion, and of theim that wene to fare better if the puttok fle ouir the wey. ca. xlvi
⁋ Of the folye of them ȝ diuyne what shal falle in the yere folowyng for cristmasse day, or the first day of January fallith on a sunday or on a munday, and so forth. also of the foly of them that may be them wise what shal falle in the yere suyng for it thundreth in this moneth, or in this. Also what foles they be ȝ diuyne of the yere folowyng by the xii. daies in cristmasse. ca. xlvii. & xlviii.
⁋ Of the foly and falshede of lapers that ben clepyd multipliers. of golde and siluer, and why god suffrith couetouse men to be be-

gpled of sucһe fepłoures.   ca. xlix
⸿Oŋ Wнat maner mē of нoly churche sнulde be no нunters/ and of them that Whan they mete mē of нoly churche and namely sterps. they putt them oŋ the left нonde.   ca. l.
⸿Argumentes Why it is to drede ꝑ solemne makynge of churches and goode arrayng of them/ and that faire seruyce is done iŋ churches of Englonde/ is more of pompe and pride thanne to the worsнip of god.   ca. li.
⸿Gode causes Why it was boden Exodi xxx°. the riche.⁊ the pore pay elyhe to the tabernacle.⁊ ꝑ after diuerse circūstaunces sūtyme it is more conuenient to make churches than to нelpe pore meŋ/ ⁊ sumtyme apenwarde.   ca. lii.
⸿Howe that many that grutche ayenst making of churches ⁊ thinges longyng to churches ben lyke Juda ꝑ grutched Whan malk Delepne anoynted crist. and that Waaste costes and pompe iŋ suche thinges beeŋ to be repreupd   ca. liii.
⸿Hou it is Bnostde ꝑ crist saith/ Whā thou sнalt ꝑy ētre thy chābre ⁊c. ⁊ нou wt eueŋ charite bett is to ꝑy i churches thā out of churchis ⁊ so the prayer of many is bett thā of one alone.   ca. liiii.
⸿Hou ꝑcessions don for to ꝑy for the peas be nat do wt due circumstaūcis ⁊ gode/ ⁊ therfore oure prayer is nat нerde/ ⁊ ꝑ the people is leuer to pay tayes to нaue werre than peas.   ca. lv.
⸿Howe it is Bnderstonde ꝑ short prayer thirleth нeueŋ/ ⁊ that sūtyme it is to pray only iŋ нert/ and sūtyme with mouth. ⁊ ꝑ distinctly. neither to faste ne to treate. cause Why.   ca. lvi.
⸿Hou it is Bnderstonde that Criste bad that men sнuld nat speke moche iŋ prayer. and causes Why principaly men sнulde praye iŋ churches.   ca. lvii.
⸿Why mē pray to god nat withstōdyng ꝑ нe is Bncнaūgeable· ⁊ of ii. maner prayers/ one comē/ another singuler· and dyuers shyples Why men sнulde pray by mouthe.   ca. lviii.
⸿Why iŋ the begynnyng of нoly churche was nat so grete solēpnite. of diuyne seruice as nowe is iŋ churches Also suples Why sōge ⁊ melodye was ordeyned iŋ нoly churche.   ca. lix.
⸿It is a sнame to a londe to нaue many martires Whiche the people of the same londe нaue slayne/ and of vengeaunce cūmynge to the people that sleeth martires.   ca. lx.

7

⁋Why myracles be nat nowe so comeny as they were in the begynnyng of cristen feith. and that the multitude of miracles signifye.
Vnstablenesse in the feith. and rather shewith that the peple is maliciouse thanne gode. ca. lxi.
⁋Doynge of miracles is noo siker preef of holynesse. of the dedis
of ypocrites/ and why that god suffreth false men to do woundres
and myracles to begile the peple. ca. lxii.
⁋Comen solempnite of cristen buriyng is nat to be forsaken and
of the dignite of mannes body and womannes. ca. lxiii.
⁋Feyres and marchettes to be holde in sanctuarie is vnseful/ and
of harmes that come therof. ca. lxiiii.
   ⁋The secounde precepte.
⁋In thre maners is goddes name taken in veyne/ crist is oure principal godfader/ for after criste we be cleped cristen men/ and if we
lyue nat cristenly/ we take the name of Criste in veyne for my lyuynge. ca. i.
Goddes name is taken in veyne by my speche in many maneres.
in scornynge/ in lapyng/ in erroneus techinge/ in couetous or en-
uyous prechyng/ in banyng of waryng/ in lewde vowes makig
and in brekyng of lefull vowes cap. ii.
⁋Vowes shulde be made with a gode aupsement. that Iept synned in his vowe makinge/ and that wycked vowes and wycked
bihestes ben to be broken. ca. iii.
⁋Goddes name is taken in veyne by blasphemy/ by gruchyng a-
yens god/ by ouirhope and wanhope/ and by veyne swerpng and
what harme cumeth of customable swerynge. cap. iiii.
⁋Thre false excusacions of other/ and aunswers to the ii. firste
excusacions. ca. v.
⁋In vii. cases it is lefulle to swere/ and in euery othe shulde thre
thinges be kepte/ & so aunswere to the thridde false excusacion.
Also true vnderstonding of textes of the newe lawe that speke of
swerynge. ca. vi.
⁋Of ii. maner sweringes/ of attestacion & execracion/ and why
it is forboden to swere by creatures on the first maner. ca. vii.
⁋How perilous the seconde maner swerpng is & what it is to say
so helpe me god at the holy dome. & why men swerpng bifore a iuge ley their hondes on a boke. and kysse it. ca. viii.

⁋ They that begyle men with their subtel othes been forsworne. though they say sothe / for in ii. maners may a man be forsworue. in swerpng sothe.　　　　　　　　　　　　　　　　　　　　ca. ix.
⁋ In vi maners may a mā be forsworst / also he þ doth a nother to swet witpng welþ he wote for swere him synneth gretly　　ca. x.
⁋ Howe grete synne it is to swere by goddes body / by godes herte. and other parties of Criste / and how they shulde be punysshed by lawe canon / and lawe imperial.　　　　　　　　　　　　　ca. xi.
⁋ Howe they synne that swere npce othes / as by cok. by our lukē. by bode kepat. and suche other Also that þhe truly / and nay truly. been none othes.　　　　　　　　　　　　　　　　　　　　　ca. xii.
⁋ It is more syn a mā to forswere him by god thā by any creature A mā suerpng a leful thing by his bode is bounde to kepe his oth. A cristen mā may lefully take an othe pstpd of an hethen man / þᵗ suerpth by his false goddes / But he may nat stire him to swere soo. On what wyse seruauntes ben bounden by their othes to be true to their maisters.　　　　　　　　　　　　　　　　　　　ca. xiii.
⁋ Successoures be bounde to kepe þ their predecessoures bonde thē to by othe. Howe a man may be vnbounde of his othe & howe nat A vowe byndeth harder than an othe. though a man be clene shre / upn of dedly stnne / yit may he nat swere sikerly þ he is nat giltpe. and cause why / A man swerpnge ii. contrariouse othes / shal kepe the firste if it be lefulle / If he make ii. vowes contrarie / the greter vowe shalbe kept.　　　　　　　　　　　　　　　　　　ca. xiiii.

⁋ What vowe is. of vowes made in disease / of wyues vowes. of childrpnes vowes / of seruauntes vowes / A dede done with a vowe is more medeful thanne the same thinge doone withouten vowe / of vowes made vnder condicion. For foure causes a man is vnbounde of his vowe. A mayden that vowyd chastite and after is corrupte / pit she is bounden to contynence. in asmoch as she may. and so it is of other vowes / that may nat fully be kepte. Of vowes of nede and of vowes of free wylle. Rightful cause and auctorite of the soueraigne been necessarye in dispensacion. or chaungyng of a vowe.　　　　The husbonde ne the wyf may nat entre into religion / but if that the other make perpetuel vowe
　　　　　　of contynence. Which vowe is solempne.

and howe it settith matrimony Brekyng of fast in siknesse is nat brekyng of abstinence. ca p̄ v
⁋Of othes made in hastinesse/ and of childrens othes and whyche othes. ca. p̄ vi.
⁋Periury is gretter synne than manslaughter/ & causes why p̄ piurty is cause of moche manslaughter/ and of many grete harmes y͡t come of forswerpng. ca p̄ vii
⁋What penaūce songith by the lawe to forsweters/ and why so grete penaunce/ also what vengeaunce hath fallen in Englonde for periury. ca. p̄ viii.
Goddes name is taken in veyne by misserpng and that in diuers maners. ca pix.
⁋Goddes name is taken in veyne by brekyng of couenaunt made in goddes name. & cōfermyd by swerpng in goddes name. Of the othe of gabonytes made to Iosue/ and howe y͡t piurye is cause of hungre & many myscheups. ca. pp̄

⁋The thridde precepte.
⁋On what maner god restyd the seuenthe daye/ and vi. skylles why god badde the seuenth day to be halowyd. ca. ix
⁋Of thre maner preceptis cerimonyal/ iudicial/ and moral/ also diuerse skylles why the halowyng of the sabott is chaungyd from the seuenthe day vnto the sunday. ca. ii.
⁋Faire declarpng how halowynge in the saturday was cerymonial/ and why it ceasyd. ca. iii
⁋Alle the feestis of the newe lawe been feestis of tabernacles. and why the sunday is principaly halowed. ca. iiii
Of thre maner sabotis. and skylles why god bad vs haue mynde to halowe the sabott day. ca. v.
⁋What holy occupacions men shulde haue on sunedayes/ and on other feestis. ca. vi.
⁋Another skille why god badde haue mynde to halowe the holyday. For mē shulde so ordepne their occupacions on werke daies. y͡t they shuld nat nede to breke the holiday/also whiche been scrupule werkes. ca. vii.
⁋Why god badde man & beest to rest on the holiday/ & hou it is vnderstonde y͡t god fulfilled his werk in the vii. day/ and that mercy is fulfilling and pfeccion of all goddes werke ca. viii.

Of foure maner sabotes / & what they betoken.   ca. ix.
⸿ Why the sabot i the olde lawe was more solempne thā other festis of other of ꝥ tyme / hou al the festis of the newe lawe ben daies & sa botes of oure lord / specialy the sūday Causes why more solempny te is made and iṅ sūme other feestis / than iṅ comen sūdayes / & hy the thursday is nat halowyd as it was sumtyme / and of the ꝓcessiō that is done on sundaies.   ca. x.
⸿ Halidaies that holy churche hath ordeyned ben to be kept & hou the sūday though it be the viii. day / yit it is the vii. daye iṅ obser uaunce of the precepte.   ca. xi.
How the nombre of six is a parfyte nombre / and therfore god ma de the worlde iṅ vi. daies; and made iṅ the sixte daye. and the vi. age of the worlde he bicame man.   ca. xii.
⸿ Shyples why god had rest on the vii. day. and of seuyn blisses. that men shal haue iṅ heuene.   ca. xiii.
⸿ Howe longe the haliday shulde be halowyd / and why men ryng iṅ vigiles at mydday. and howe greate nede & pite excuse werkes done on halidaies / and what maner folke be excused though they trauayle on the haliday.   ca. xiiii. et xv
⸿ Howe it is leful to begynne iourneys on holidaies / or to traueil aboute makinge of churches. and hou nat. Ditaylers and other chapmen shulde nat ryde fro towne to towne to vse their market tes on halidaies / for suche markettes shuld nat be holden on sūne daies. neither iṅ sanctuarie. What houre so euensonge be saide on vigilies or halidaies / the haliday is to be kept from euene to euen Howe men shulde axe doutes of their curates. and what ignorāce excusith.   ca. xvi.
⸿ In what maner the seruaunt is excused of his trauayl on the ha lidaies by the biddinge of his soueraigne / and to the soueraigne is halowynge of the haliday principaly boden. In what maner pley es and daunces. been lefull on the halidayes.   And in what manere men shulde bothe mourne. and also make myrthe on ha lidayes.   cap. xvii.
⸿ Where it is groundyd iṅ holy wryt ꝥ men may make mery / and fare wele on halidaies. and why fasting is defendyd on sundaies. Why it shuld nat be moch vsed i pasthe tym. holy wryt shewith suffi

daūces ⁊ songes to be plesaūt to god/ ⁊ þ these ii. thinges sadnesse. ⁊ gladnesse shulde be kepte in goddes seruice.　　　　ca. xviii.

⁋Whiche ben the ꝑceptis of the first table. ⁊ which of the ii. ⁊ why ⁊ howe the x. ꝑceptis be ophhendyd in the ii. ꝑceptis of charite Hou the iii. first ꝑceptis ben applied to the iii. psones in trinyte after declaring of this firste ꝑcept of charite. thou shalt loue thy lorde god with al thyn hert. w' al thy soule.　　　　ca. xix.

⁋Also howe we shulde loue god with al oure hert ⁊ with al oure soule. ⁊c. Howe by the iii. first cōmaūdemētis we be taught feith. hope and charite. and how these thre ꝑceptis teche vs to loue god, in herte worde and dede.　　　　ca. xx.

　　　　⁋The fourthe precepte.
All the preceptes of the secoūde table be knyt in the secoūde ꝑcept of charite/ why the ꝑcept of worshiping fader ⁊ moder. is the first. of the secoūde table/ ⁊ howe they shuld be worshiped/ also of peyn þ cūmeth to them þ worship nat fader ⁊ moder. Ensample of chã the sonne of Noe.　　　　ca. .i.

⁋What mischeif compth to children þ hynder fader and moder for their gode. and of them that ben vnbuxum to fader ⁊ moder Ensample by absolon and adonye.　　　　ca. ii.

⁋By ensample in kynde we ben taught to worship fader ⁊ moder as of the storke ⁊ of the pellicane.　　　　ca. iii.

⁋Helpe at nede is cleppd worship in holy wryt/ ⁊ þ owith the child to fader and moder/ what peryl it is ⁊ foly man or woman to dismytte them of their gode. in trust of their children.　　　　ca. iiii.

⁋In what maner the child owith to hate fader and moder/ and to forsake theym/ and howe fader aud moder shulde helpe the childe and the childe them at nede. Ensample by the rote and the croppe of a tree. but the fader and the moder. haue more kyndely loue to their children thanne ayenwarde.　　　　ca. v.

⁋In what maner men of religion shulde helpe fader. and moder. att nede.　　　　ca. vi.

⁋The godes of holy churche been the godes of pore men and nedye. howe seint Benet gaue godes of his couent to pore men. seīt fraunces badde the same.　　　　ca. vii.

Godes of religion shulde be more comen thā other menys godes.

to helpe nedy folk/of the abusion of some proude religious men & their ypocrites excusyng fro peuyng of almesse.　　　　ca. viii.
☞Textis of holy wryt hou children shulde be obededient to fader & moder/& þ godes liuyng of the child is worshyp to fader & moder. & their euyl lyuyng is shenshyp to fader & moder·　　　　ca. ix.
☞Missuffraunce of children in their youthe is their sheshyp and be-conyng to al their kyn. that men shulde chastise their children. and te che them to serue god.　　　　ca. x.
☞Euery man & woman is bounde after his degre to do his besy-nesse to knowe goddes lawe that he is bounde to kepe/& hou eche man in same maner shulde teche goddes lawe/hou the child shuld worshyp fader & moder whā they ben dede.　　　　ca. xi.
Hou we shuld worshyp god as principal fader & moder　　ca xii.
Oure gostly faders be to be worshiped/& why they ben cleppd gost ly faders. what harme cometh by them? ben cleppd curatis bothe to them self & to the people· for they do nat their deuer　　ca. viii.
Oure elders þ be our faders & modes in age be to be worshiped/ olde mē þ ben custonied I synne shulde be harde repuyd·　　　　ca. xiiii.
☞Kinges & al soueraignes owe to be faders to their subgettes & of them to be worshipped/hou & why seruauntes shulde obey to ther lordes/& howe lordes shuld do to their seruauntes　　　　ca. xv.
How wycked men & tirauntes been goddes seruauntes. & why god suffreth wycked folke to be in this worlde.　　　　ca. xvi.
God geueth lordship & power to wicked mē for syn of the peple/to whō mē owe to obey & to do the worshyp for their dignite.　c. xvii.
☞How and in what ordre mē shuld obey to their soueraignes & in what thinges/In what thinges knightis/bonde mē/wyues & chil drē eche ben bounde to obeye to their soueraignes/& in whiche th[i] ges they ben nat bounden.　　　　ca. xviii.
☞In whiche thinges subgettes been bounde to obey to their pla tis & in whiche nat/though placy or lordship be occupied ayēs the comē lawe/yit is it gode to obey. what a preest shulde do if the bus shop bydde him curse a man whom he holdith vngilty　　ca. xix.
☞In what maner officers of the king shulde obey to the iuge I ma ter of mēnes deth In whiche thinges a religious man is boūde to obey his plate/& I whiche thiges nat In what maner thiges a plate

B i.

of religion may dispense ꝛ in sũme thinges nat. ca. xx.

⁋ In what thinges a clerke is bounde to obey his busshop. howe the wyf is bounde to her husbõde in brekyng of her vowe. Sũme thinges been gode of the self. sũme bed euyl of the self. ꝛ sũme indifferent In whiche thinges indifferent stondith pirly obedience to men that ben soueraignes. ca. xxi.

⁋ Alle men of state and dignity ben clepyd faders, and owe to be worshiped of lower men. ca xxii

⁋ Angels ꝛ seintes in heuene ben oure faders, and be to be worshyped, how aungelis kepe and defende vs. ca xxiii.

⁋ Patrones of churches ben faders of the same churches On thre maners bicometh a man patrone. ꝛ what righte longith to prones. also of presentacion of psones to churches. ca. xxiiii.

⁋ Euery man owith to holde other his fader ĩ sũme degre, for ther ben many maner faders, and so by this cõmaundmẽt we be bounde to helpe al nedy folke upon oure power. ca. xxv

Why this cõmaũde' is pouẽ w' a bihest of welfar ꝛ mede ca xxvi

⁋ Pride rebellion ꝛ vnbuxũnesse of the peple ayẽ their soueraygnes, ꝛ þ they wole enmet the ꝛ detnyne euery cause of the londe, ꝛ of the churche is cause of destruction of reames. ca xxvii.

⁋ The fyfte precepte.

⁋ Vnleful manslaughter is done by hert, by mouthe, by dede. and how a bacbiter sleeth thre at ons. ca. i.

⁋ Thre maner of flateringes in which is manslaughter ꝛ dedly syn also of peyn of flaterly both by goddes lawe ꝛ mans. ca. ii.

⁋ What mischeif cometh of flateringe, and to them that haue lyking in flatering. ca iii.

⁋ A musterer or whisterer is a preuy rownere ꝛ a preuy spyer, who is a double tunged man, the flatering tũge is the thridde tunge that doth moche woo. ca. iiii.

⁋ Flatering of false prophetis and prechoures, ꝛ other false men. distroyeth citees ꝛ kingdomes Ensample by scripture, and howe the flatering tũge is a gilous tunge. ca. v.

⁋ On iiii. maners may a mã be slayne vnrightfully. ca vi

⁋ Nigardes þ wole nat helpe pore folk at nede, also tyrantes and extorcioners þ take fro men their skynnes ꝛ their flesshe fro the bo

nea be manstcers/ What is vnderstonde by these thre skyn flesshe.
and boone. ca. vii.

⸿ Men that witholde seruauntes their hyre. ben māquellers/ why
crist saide to petyr thries pasce. fede. Men of holy churche spēde
amys godes of holy churche/ and wole nat help the pore nedy folk
been manquellers. ca viii.

⸿ Alle ꝑ drawe folke to synne by mys entisyng or wyche ed ensam﹍
ple or mys counseyl or false lore. & namely men of holy churche be
manquellers/ also al that yeue occasion of sclaundre/ howe prela﹍
tes. and their officers shulde haue them self in their visitaciouns.
withouten what deuocion prayer is dede· ca· ix·

Al that lett men of their gode dedes of their gode purpos & mys te
chers ben māsleers/ as the feend is a cōtynuel māquellers Also men
of holy churche ꝑ withdrawe or lett goddes worde to be pched ben
māquellers/ & ꝑ goddes worde shulde highly be worshiped/ & what
pfyt it is to here goddes worde. ca· x

⸿ Curates ꝑ repreue nat their subgettis of their synnes/ also they ꝑ
defraude & take away holy churche godes/ been māquellers/ and
so be the prestis that denye the sacrament of penaunce to repentāt
men in their last ende/ what peryl it is to trust to moche on goddes
mercy· ca· xi·

⸿ He that doth a nother man wyttyngly to forswere him/ also he
ꝑ consentith to dedly synne. & who so doth any dedly syn is a man
sleer/ why god gaue the cōmaundementis in the nombre of x. & yit
ben they al knytt in one precept of kinde. how goddes lawe is lik﹍
ned to a sautrie/ and to an harpe. ca. xii.

⸿ Declaracion of this texte. He that offendith in one/ offendithe
in alle. ca. xiii.

Hou ꝑceptis of the firste table be obseydyd in the ꝑcept of kynde &
of vengeaunce of māslaughter & of murdre. ca· xiiii·

⸿ God defendith nat sleyng of beestis. But only manslaughter w͡t
outen gilte· how men may synne in sleyng of beestis· ca. xv.

In what maner and to whom manslaughter is leful/ god and
the lawe slee wycked doers/ and iuges slee as goddes mynistres. &
his officers. ca. xvi

⸿ why the swerd was grauntyd to pstis & mynistres of the old lawe
why ꝑ swerde of shedyg of blode is forbode pstis of the newe lawe

B ii

also what the sacrament of the auter represētith.   ca. xvii
⁋ How the lawe punyssheth clerkes/ sheders of blode. Many ca∣ses of irregularite for manslaughter/ wymen þ do myscraftis. or vnleful craftis to let themself fro beryng of children/ & all þ come to se though they se nat/ be manslers   ca. xviii
Many other cases of irregularite for manslaughter   ca. xix
⁋ An exposicion of this text he þ hath nat a swerde selle he his cote and by him a swerde ꝛc. and of the dethe of many/ and sayth it al seint petyrs wordes.   ca. xx.
⁋ A iuge knowyng a man vngilty shal nat dampne þ mā though the queest or the wytnesse say that he is gilty & what the iuge shall do in suche a case.   ca. xxi
⁋ Skilles why it is vnleful in any case a man or a woman to sle themself.   ca. xxii
⁋ Why it is more syn to sle a rightous mā thā a wyched mā/ what maner it is vnleful a man to sle his wyf for auoutry/ & þ it is more syn a man to sle his fader or moder than his wif.   ca. xxiii
⁋ Why god suffreth werre and batayle. Thre thinges be nedefull þ a batayl be rightful. How clerkes & other men may defende themself. How subgettes ben excused of fightyng by precept of their prynce and soudeoures also. and how nat.   ca. xxiiii.

The sixte precept.
⁋ Nyne spices of lechery. and in how many maners a man may synne with his wyf   ca. i.
⁋ Why matrimony was ordeyned/ & of the iii. gode thinges of ma∣trimony. What nurture bitokneth & the weddig ringe.   ca. ii.
⁋ What myschefe cūmyth of auoutry. & what vengeaūce god hath do therfore in holy wrytte. Of the prophecye of Boneface matter of the lechery of englonde/ and how the grounde & the begynnyng of euery peple is lauful generacion. in wedlok.   ca. iii.
⁋ Whan god made matrymony & gaue lawes. A gode declarīg of these wordes of adā/ This bone is nowe of my bones ꝛc why wo∣mā was made of the ryb of mā & nat of erth as adā was   ca. iiii
⁋ Auoutry is more greuous syn in the husbōde than in the wyf. A grete ꝑcesse of seint austyn rebukyng men auouters.   ca. v.
⁋ Seint austyn aunswerith to the false excusacions of mē lechou∣res/ howe crist sayd the woman taken in auoutrie they þ shuld

punyssħe spy/ sħulde be vngilty i ŷ synne cases i whicħ the husbōd may nat accuse his wyf of auoutrie. ca. vi.

⁋In what maner a man may forsake his wyf for fornicacion. of the irregularite of a man knowyng his wyf after ŷ he knowith yͭ sħe hath do fornicacion Only deth deptith & brekith the bonde of true matrymonye/ & of ii. maner dethes. of ētre ito religion of wed dyd folk bifore they knowe to gidre flesshly/ the wif hath as grete occasion in ŷ that togith to seith of matrimonye apen her husbond as her husbonde apenst her/ and cause why. ca. vii.

⁋Symple fornicacion is dedly synne. These wordes. Crescite et multiplicamini/ ŷ is Wexe ye & be ye multiplied were spoken only to man & woman weddyd to gidder/ & why crist wold his moder be weddyd or he were concepued. ca. viii.

⁋Weddyd man and woman may lyue chaast if it lyke them both. For manye causes ordeyned god man and woman nat to knowe to gidder flesshly. But in wedloke. What synnes a woman auou‑ tresse doth he. ca. ix

⁋A Woman lecchoure is the feendes snare/ & a man lechour is the feendes nett. Comonly more malice is in men than in wymen/ of excusacion of adam/ and why he synned more than eue. Why crist bicame man and nat woman. ca. x.

⁋Sampson· dauid· & salomon· discepued themself or wymē dis‑ cepued them. Petyr whanne he forsoke criste was more in defaute than the woman that spake to him Men lechoures diffame chast wymen ŷ wole nat assent to them. ca. xi.

⁋Blamyng or lackyng of wycked wymen· and prisynge of gode wymen/ & that the wyne is nat to blame/ though the glutone ther of do lecherie. Neither the beaute of a woman is blame thoughe a mā by occasion therof be stired to hir. the misuse is to blame c. xii

⁋Of manes array & womanes array· Cause why wymē ben ofte more stable in godenesse than men. Of men ankers and wymē an kers/ ŷ womannes counseyl cūmeth oft of god. ca. xiii.

Diuerse remedies ayēs lechery/ ensāple of rosamond/ & of the bau son & the foy/ & of vnclene & lecherous thoughtes ca. xiiii.

Mynde of cristis passion/ redyng i holy wryt & thinkig of the pey nes of hell ben also remedies ayēst lechery. ca. xv.

⁋Wi̇geāce ŷ god hath taken for fornicacion/ for auoutrye/ for

B iii.

mysuse of a mānes owne wyf/ for inceſt/ and for synne of sodomy
Wȳp wymen and children were puniſſhid in the subuerſion of sodo
mye. ⁊c.　　　　　　　　　　　　　　　　　　　　　　　ca. xvi.

☞ Of lechery of pſtis/ deknes and subdekyns/ ⁊ peynes sett in the
salve for suche synnes/ ⁊ whan a man of holy churche is cleppd in
the salve an open notorie lechoure.　　　　　　　　　　　ca. xvii.

Shyplies why lechery in clerkes is more greuous. thanne auoutre
in seculers.　　　　　　　　　　　　　　　　　　　　　　ca. xviii.

How men falle in bigamye. ⁊ why they ben irreguler by bigamye.
⁊ þ bigam' ſhal nat haue the priuelegis þ longe to clerge.　ca. xix.

Women deliuered of childe may entre holy churche what tyme þ
they wole. and ben of power. Neither huſbonde ne wyf may yeue
leue the one to the other. to take a nother woman or a nother mā.
Eycuſacion of abraham and of Iacob. that had at onys diuerse
wyues.　　　　　　　　　　　　　　　　　　　　　　　　ca. xx.

☞ In what maner elues þ ben seldis ben seyd to do lechery. wᶜ mā
womā ⁊ beeſt/ ⁊ of monſtres or wonder thinges so gendryd　ca. xxi.
☞What is goſtly fornicacion and goſtly auoutrie.　　　　ca. xxii.
An anſwere to an argumēt þ the syn of eue was more greuous thā
the syn of Adā oft tyme the leſſe is punyſſhid harder in this worlde
thanne the more.　　　　　　　　　　　　　　　　　　　ca. xxiii.

Grete argumētis ⁊ reſones þ god punyſſhed harder adā thā he did
eue/ for his synne was more greuouse. for that was the oppinion
of him that drewe this boke.　　　　　　　　　　　　　ca. xxiiii.

　　　　　　　Ⅽhe seuynthe precept

By this precepte is defendyd al theft ⁊ al the meanes to theft Of
diuerse maners of theft/ ⁊ diuerse punyſſhing of theftis.　ca. i.
Of them þ robbe folk of their gode name ⁊ fame.　　　　ca. ii.
Falſe bechoures, feyners of falſe miracles/ they þ withdrawe true
prechyng of goddes worde/ bechoures for couetiſe of the worlde or
for veyne worſhip/ ⁊ erzetikes been theups.　　　　　　　ca. iii.
Of many maner theftis/ wrōg gettinges/ Vnrightful occupyng
wrong witholdyng/ ⁊ how by the lawe of kynde thinge be comen.
and why god forbadde theft.　　　　　　　　　　　　　　ca. iiii.
Of thre maner lordſhippes/ ⁊ thre maner propirties/ ⁊ howe þ god
wole nat þ pore folke take any thing without leue of the propre
diſpenſatour' that is cleppd lord therof.　　　　　　　　ca. v.

In iiii cases may a man take of the lordes godes & owith it without
ten his witing / & thou wyues may geue almesse.   ca. vi.
⁋ Of restitucion of thingis lost & founde / & thou children stele whi
le they be yonge shulde be chastispd.   ca. vii.
⁋ Many cases of theft in lenyng borowyng hiring & wedde leying
of restitucion making of stolen thing / also of stolen thing bought
i market.   It is nat to stele fro a nygarde or any vsurer to geue al
messe / & of almesse youen of false purchased gode   ca. viii
⁋ Cristen men may nat stele hethen children to cristene them ayen
the wyl of fader & moder / howe wyues shulde make restitucion of
stolen thinges Cases in whiche the lorde may put out his fermour
oute of his ferme.   ca. ix.
A man y byy gile doth a nother man to selle a thing y he thought nat
to selle / or to sell it lesse than he thought to haue solde it / synneth.
Many cases of biyng & selling / & what is the iust price of a thinge
Of begilyng wᵗ false money of gyle. Of restitucion in diuerse ca
ses in biyng or selling Whanne the seller is bounde to telle defau
tes of thinges that he sellith Of depose that is to say / of thing y is
bitaken a man to kepe.   ca. y.
⁋ In thre maners may a thinge be euyl goten / & of whiche maner
euyl goten gode a man may do almesse. In what maner the false
baily y dyd fraude to his lorde was prised Thre causes why riches
ses of this worlde ben richessis of wychednesse.   ca. xi
⁋ Riche nigardes ben mansleers & theues / Wherof riche men shulo ye
ue almesse / & thou the more lordship in this worlde / the more nede
men of holy churche myspending holy church godes be theuys / & yᵗ
holy church is endowyd to helpe pore men / ayen proude siluerne and
golden harneys of prelatis & of men of religion / thou suche myspenders
ben bounde to restitucion Of them y spende holy churche godes on
their kyn & on riche folk / of them do nat their duetie for their bñfi
ces / though they haue Vicaries or parisshe prestis / Of men vnable to
cure. Whiche resceyue benefices / & of nonresidenteris for couetise or va
nitie. Of clerkes proprietarie. Why men of holy church bē clepid cler
kes & of their crownes. Of clerkes hauyg prymony of their owne.
⁋ What is sacrilege / & in how many maners it is done   ca. xii.
Witholders of tithes been theuys / and of what thynges men been
bounde to tith. and howe.   ca. xiii.

⁋ To what churche tithes shulde be paied/ & tithes & godes of the churche shulde be spendyd in iiii. parties if nede were. To open le‍choures or open malefactoures tithes shulde nat be paied. To whom tithes where suche euyl curatis ben shulde be paied or kept & to what ende. Of tithes of busshoppes or religiouse houses to be youen in case to curates of perisshynes.   ca yiiii
⁋ Diuerse doutes in tithing/ & of custõ of tithinge/ & why god bad more the tenthe part to be paied than a nother part.   ca yv
⁋ That symony is theft/ & what symony is Cases of resignacion of benefices/ wherof came the name of symonye/ & why they been cleppyd comonly rather symonistis than giezitis Symonye is do‍ne in thre maners/ and of many other cases of symony.   ca yvi.
⁋ Fyue cases in whiche it is lefulle to yeue giftes in mater of spiri‍tueltie.   ca. yvii
⁋ What peyne longith to symony by the lawe/ & of diuerse customes i the churche/ in whiche satymes is symonye·   ca· yviii·
Cases in whiche confederatoures/ ministers of buriyng & of bap‍tym/ patrones and sellers of patronages/ precheoures and pardo‍ners do symonye·   ca. yiy.
⁋ Of yeuyng of money whan a psone is rescepued ito religion/ of yeuyng of money to preestis for annuel/ for yereday/&c. or elles to collegis·hou symony is done in suche thinges and hou nat. And of the statute what a parisshe preest or an annueler shulde take by yere.   ca. yy.
Couenãt makith oft symony y shuld elles be none Of theÿ bynde the to say speal messis. of the goldẽ trental & of fals faitourie in y mater/ & y seint gregory ordeyned it neuir   ca. yyi. yyii.
⁋ The grounde of sanctuarie may nat be sold to buriyng nor to chep men For symony god takith moche vengeance Of sellyng of sy‍uersoils out of abbeys & other speal places.   yyiii.
⁋ What is usury & I what thing it is done/ of ii. spices of usurie/ & I what maner god suffred the iewys to take usury.   ca. yyiiii·
⁋ Many diuerse cases of usury.   ca yyv.
⁋ Other cases of usury and diuerse synnes of byers & sellers. Why londes lawe suffreth usury Of notaries y make istrumentes up‍ couenauntes of usurie.   ca.yyvi.

⊕What peyne longith to vsurers by the lawe/ of their heires Of theire seruauntes/ of their counseilours/ of their ofspynges/ of a ieue vsurer to a criste mā/ of ther punysshing þ suffre vsurers duel l their lordshlp or houses A spcal case l Which the byer doth vsury. Hou god reuueth vsurers rauenours ꝗ theups l holy   ☧ ca. xxvii Wryt of fals mē of lawe. Theups do apens iii. lawes/ the lawe of kynde. the lawe writen/ ꝗ the lawe of grace For theft ꝗ other synes mē of armes haue no spede ne grace/ of the wel of sardyn ꝗ hou co uetise blyndeth men. of euyl iuges temporal ꝗ spital.   ca. xxviii.
⊕The eight precepte.
⊕Lesyngmongers and spders of treuthe by stylnesse whan treuth shulde be saide/ brekyng this cōmaundemēt· of thre maner stylhede wyched and synful   ca. i.
Of viii. maner lesynges cōprehendyd iŋ thre/ ꝗ which lesynges be dedly synne And what peryl it is for mē of holy churche to be iape or custoable spers iŋ bourde.   ca· ii.
⊕Aunsweris to auctorities of holy wrytt by whiche men excuseŋ lesynges.   ca iii
⊕Nat alfeyned dedis be lesinges but alfeyned speche. for disceit is lesyng/ what feynyng of dede is synne and what nat.   ca iiii.
⊕Of falshede of the sayer ꝗ falshede of the thing þ is saide. And iŋ what maner it is syn to bileue thing þ is fals It is more synne a man to prise him self falsly/ than to lache or blame him self falsly. Whiche ben cleppd false wytnesses by the lawe   ca. v.
⊕What maner folke may nat bere wytnesse iŋ dome by lawe. By false wytnesses crist ꝗ seyntes were slayne Hou false wytnesses be bounde to restitucion Flaterers and bacbiters breke this cōmaunde ment ꝗ why they be lykned to a best camelion Gode spekers þ beŋ euyl doers breke this precept   ca vi
⊕Hou iŋ many maner false men of lawe ꝗ beyne precourers and false/ ben false witnesses   ca. vii
⊕Alle wyched clerkes ben false wytnesses Hou the vestmentis of prestis and of busshopes betokeŋ cristes passion/ and what they be tokeŋ morally.   ca. viii.
⊕What the busshopes crosse ꝗ the ptie therof betokē Al false syuers þ be cristned ben false wytnesses Hou witnesses shulde haue them l dome to bere wytnesse. ꝗ hou amā shuld bere wytnesse.   ca. ix

⁋ To whom the wytnesse shal make restitucion of mede takē to bere wytnesse After ẏ the cause is/ ⁊ after the dignite of the psone apenst whom wytnessis ben brought. must be the nombre of witnesses· In what maner cases one wytnesse suffiseth/ whanne the wytnesse shal say in certeyne ⁊ whan in doute. ca. x.

⁋ Of kepyng of counseyl of thing ẏ a man knowith by pryue telsyng Many thinges requyred in wytnesse/ and of diuerse iugemēt after diuersite of wytnesses/ of atteyntyng of wytnesses A man may be wytnesse in dome apenst him self/ But nat for him self Cf wytnesse of eretikes ⁊ of hethen men. ca xi

⁋ What penaunce longith by the lawe to false witnesses ⁊ to them that procure false wytnesse/ and to alle that assent to false witnes Many other thinges requyred and to be consideryd in this mater of beryng wytnesse. ca xii

⁋ Of thre wytnesses. god/ oure conscience. ⁊ eche creature· Howe we shulde deme oure self in the courte of consciēce/ of a gostly ghst. and of mysusyng of creatures. ca xiii.

How crist shal come to dome. ⁊ thou he shal deme c. xiiii ⁊ xv
⁋ Of two domes special and general And of sodeyne cūmyng to the laste dome· ca. xvi.
⁋ Crist may nat be discepued in his dome/ and what strept teknyg shalbe there. And of foure diuerse peoples that shalbe att that doome. ca xvii.
⁋ Howe harde the dome shalbe to riche men/ and to them ẏ haue rescepued many piftes of god. ca. xviii.

⁋ Tho nynthe precepte·
⁋ Couetise rote of al euylles is forbode in these laste ii. preceptis· How cursed false purchasoures been. ca. i.
⁋ A story of naboth/ ⁊ another of seint Beatrice· apenst false purchasoures. ca. ii.
⁋ Heires ben bounden to restore thing mypurchased of their fads A sereful story apenst them that wole nat restore· ca iii
⁋ What vengeaūce hath fal for fals couetise I holy wryt, of iiii. wys domes nedsul to al mē/ which the nightyngale taught cc. iiii·
⁋ How the storye of Balaam is remeuyd to false couetise/ and ẏ the god of couetyse is betokned by the ymage of golde· that Nabugodonosor dyd make. ca. v.

℃Whiche folk ben holpen w'their gode after their deth Of iii. toknys of warnyng to riche folk by ensample of Balames asse Riches of this worlde is lykned to a iogloures horse. ca. vi.

℃ False borowers and false executours. ben lykned to shepe that go from their felowes And y no thing sauets more a cōpntie thā feithfulnesse & keping of true biheest. ca. vii.

℃ Two thinges shuld abate couetise of mānes hert This worlde is lykned to iiii. thinges ful vnstable. to a whele. to a ship/ to a rose. to a shadowe. also to slider weye. ca. viii & ix.

℃ Mynde of deth shuld let fals couetise/ by ensāple of the foxe. Almesse do bifore deth is moche bett thā almesse done after ca. x.

℃ Ensamples apēst false executoures. ca. xi.

℃ A parable of thre freendis/ and howe almesdede is the best frend whanne other frendes fayle. ca. xii.

℃ To whome men shulde do almesse/ and how feestis shuld be made to riche men Also what ordre shulde be kepte in yeuynge of almesse. And of the diuersite of pore men to whom almesse is to be youen. ca. xiii

℃ Men ben diuersly pore apens their wyl And to al is almesse to be youen/ why crist shal clepe pore wyched people his bretherne at domes day. And howe crist shal thanke men at the dome. for almesse done to the gode and to the wyched. And howe goddes mercy and pyte shalbe shewyd that day. ca. xiiii

℃ All pore and nedy must be holpē by almesse/ but principaly wilful pore Also nedy prechoures. ca. xv

℃ In yeuyng of almesse a man shulde take hede to y thinges. & in what cases a man shalle rather yeue to one pore man thanne to another. And that a riche man shulde take crist as one of his children. Also they that wole nat forsake synne/ do nat almesse plesaunt to god. ca. xvi

℃ The tenthe precepte.

℃ What maner couetise is forboden in the nynthe precept and what in the tenthe. Assent to dedly synne/ is dedely synne/ why the x. commaundementes that forbede the dede of lechery/ and of theft stōde bifore the commaundementes that forbede wycked wyll of lechery and thefte. ca. i.

⊂ Cause of diuersite whṗ the ii. last preceptis been transposed, exodi. xx°. and Deutro. quinto. ca ii.

⊂ Mynde of cristis passion is remedy apenst temptacions of lecherẏ. Ensample bẏ the pellicane. Of the loue of Crist. and howe it quenchith vnclene loue. ca. iii.

⊂ Dyuerse remedies apenst lecherẏ, and remouẏng of occasions. Ensample bẏ ii. holẏ wẏmen. ca. iiii.

⊂ A man shulde rule his flesshe as a knighte doth his horse. And of gostlẏ sadẏl. brẏdel and spores. ca. v.

⊂ Howe a cristen man is lẏke a bridde & is cleppẏd a bernak. How euerẏ cristẽ mã is a knight, & wt what armure he shuld be armẏd. As moche as a man kepith goddes cõmaũdmētes so moch he is in goddes sight & no more. Alle ꝑ brehe goddes cõmaũdmentis been acursed bẏ the grete sentence of god. ca. vi. & vii.

⊂ Of mischeups and curses temporel and endlesse ꝑ shall come to the brekers of goddes lawe. Comen mischeẏf fallith nat to a comẽ tie. But for sẏnne of the compnte. Whẏ tho vi. sonnes of Jacob. that were assigned to blesse. were assigned to that office, and whẏ the other sixe to curse. And that prelates shulde nat curse butt for greate nede. ca viii.

⊂ Of welthe & blessing tẽporel & endlesse ꝑ is bihight to the kepars of goddes lawe, and of the ioẏe and blisse that is in heuen c. ix.

⊂ Heuene is lẏkned to a cẏte. Of the worthẏnesse of the people of this cite and of the blisse ꝑ is therin. ca. x.

⊂ Heuene is vnderstonde bẏ the cite ꝑ seint John spekith of in the apocalips. and of the gostlẏ expownẏng therof. ca. xi. & xii.

⊂ Whẏ that men haue no sadde feẏth to bileue that ther is so grete blisse. Bẏ ensample of a childe borne in prison. A lẏtel taste of heuẽ blisse turneth al erthlẏ ioẏ to bitternesse. Ensample bẏ petyr and poule, and moẏses.

Of holy pouertie.
The firste chaptre.

Iues & pauper obuiauerūt sibi: vtriusq; operator est dns. Prouerbi. xxii.

These ben the wordes of Salomon this moche to say i englissh The riche and the pore mette to themself/ the lorde is worcher of euiteither This texte worshipfulle Bede expowneth thus. A riche man is nat to be worshipped for this cause only that he is riche/ ne a pore man is to be dispysed. Bicause of his pouertye. But the werk of god is to be worshippyd in them bothe/ for they bothe been made to the ymage. & to the lyknesse of god. And as it is writen. Sapiencie. vii. ca. One maner of entring into this worlde/ and a like maner of out wendyng fro this wrechid worlde is to alle men bothe riche and pore: For bothe riche and pore comen ito this worlde naked and pore/ wepyng and weilynge/ & bothe they wenden hens naked and pore with moche peyne Natheless the riche and the pore in their spuynges in this worlde in many thinges been ful vnlyke For the riche man aboūdeth in tresoure gold and siluer/ & other richesses he hath honours grete and erthly delices/ where the pore creature lyueth in grete penury. and for wantyng of richesses suffreth colde and hunger/ and is ofte in dispyte. Pauper. I that am a pore caytyf symple & lytel set by. biholdynge the prosperite of them that been riche. and the disese that I suffre and other pore men like vnto me an many a tyme sterpd to grutche. and to be wery of my lyf. But thanne renen to my mynde the wordes of Salomon bifore reherspd/ howe the lorde made as wele the pore as the riche. And therto Job witnessith/ that noo thinge in erthe is made withouten cause. Job v. Thanne I suppose within my self that by the preuy domes of god that be to me vnknowen/ it is to me profitable to be pore. For wele I wote that god is no vpgarde of his giftes. But as the apostle sayth. Rom. viii. To them that been chosen of god alle thinges worchen to gydre into gode. And so sithen I truste throughe the godenes of god to be oon of his chosen/ I can nat deme but that to me it is gode to be pore. Moreouir seint Poule. i. Thymoth. vi. writeth in this maner They that wylle or desire to be made riche falle into temptacion & into the snare of the deuyl.
ii a

and into many desires. Unprofi
table & noyous. For couetise
of richesses more than is bihoue
ful a man for to haue/is rote of al
cursses. Experience accordeth
with this sawe of the apostle.

For lesynges/ and piuries/
fals sotelties and gyles and ma
ny other wyckednesses/ been as
comon as the cart weye with su
che inordinate louers of richesse
Whiche synnes brynge theim to
endlesse perisshinge/ But if they
be wasshen alway bifore the out
of deth/ With greate and bytter
penaunce It is an olde prouerb
He is wele at ese þ hath ynough
and can say ho He hath enough
holy doctoures sey to whom his
temporalte godes be they neuir
soo fele e suffisen to hym and to
his/ to fynde them that them ne/
dyth. Wel I know that as poul
saith in the place bifore reherced
and Job sayth the same Job. i.
Naked we come ito this world
we brynge noo richesse with vs.
ne none shalle we bere with vs/
Whanne we shalle passe fro this
world as is also bifore seid Na
theles wriches we yue here we
may nat vtterly caste alle temp
al godes alwey/ Wherfore after
the iformation of this holy man
Poule in the same cheptre/ haue
I belynge and symple liuelode
I purpose through goddes gra

Of holy:

ce. to holde me content/ & neuyr
bisye me to kepe to gider aboun
daunce of worldly richesses.

The seconde Cheptre

Diues. Thou arte the mo
re fole But it is a comon
prouerbe. A foles bolte is sone
shotte Abyde and aunswere & I
wol sey an hundryd poude that
I shalle preue the by gode argu
mentis that he is but a fole whi
che wyl nat bisye him to be riche
And that thou be nat in dout of
what richesse I speke/ worldly
richesse or gostly. I do the oute
of doute I speke of worldly ri
chesse. Pauper. I wyl neither
stryue ne leye wageours. But if
it lyke your benignite/ to carpe
with me a symple captyf/ I wyl
softly admyt your compnynge
Saye what ye wole. Diues.
God made Adam and mākynd
lorde of erthly thinges Whanne
he sayde. Gen. i. Dominamini
piscibus maris &c. Be ye lordes
he sayde of the fysshes of the see.
and of the birdes of the eyre and
of alle thinges that lyue & styre
vpon erthe. Nowe to a lorde it
longith to be riche Sithen than
lorshyppe pertenyth by kynde
vnto man/and so supyngly to be

Pouertie

riche how maiſt thou deny but þ he is a fole. that wole nat beſpe him to be riche. For who is a more fole than he that wol nat beſp him to kepe goddes ordenaūce. What canſt thou ſay to this.
Pauper. Lordſhyppe is taken in diuerſe maners Ther is naturel or kyndely lordſhippe Ther is also ciuyle or ſeculer lordſhip And ther is lorſhyppe pretenſe. Of naturel lordſhip ſpekith the ſcripture that ye allegyd. For god ordeyned in the ſtate of innocencie man kyndely to haue ſoueraynte ouir beſtes fiſſhes and byrdes And this maner of lordſhyp ordeyned by wey of kynde may a iuſte man haue without aboūdaunce of worldly richeſſe To ſeculer or cyuyle lordſhyp. introducte by occaſion of ſynne preyneth worldly richeſſe/ which maner lordſhyp longith to kyngges/ dukes/ erlys/ and other lower lordes/ If I that am a pore wretch ſhulde beſy me to gete ſuche lordſhyp/ of holy ſcripture ne of holy doctours I wote wel priſyynge gete In one Dominium. or lordſhyp ptenſe haue tyrauntes and falſ oppeſſoures ouir the people/ Whiche maner of lordſhip god forbede that euir I deſire. Sir if ye marke wele this diſtinction and this ſimple ſhorte aunſwere ye ſhalle clerly

ſe that your argument is but feble & preupth nat me to be a fole bicauſe that I beſy me not to be worldly riche.

The liii. chaptre.

Diues. What ſayſt thou thanne to this Criſte iheſus ſaythe thus Beacius eſt magis dare q̄ accipere. act xx. It is he ſaith more bliſſful to yeue thā to take But the riche man may bett yeue than may the pore/ for he hath more wherof Ergo it is more bliſſful to be riche. than to be pore But he that wole nat biſye him to haue the better parte. is a fole Ergo nunc tibi concluditur. Nowe thou art cōcludid.
Pauper. That criſt ſaith may nat be falſe But ye riche men take ful moche and yeue oftentyme ful ſkytel for the loue of god Ɛye take the grete and yeue the ſmalle/ ye take moche more thā takith the pore. And the more that ye take the harder ye be boū den/ and the harder rekenynge ye mnſte yeue/ For as ſaith Gregory. Quanto bona creſcunt tā to creſcunt raciones donorum. The more that giftes encreaſe. the more encreaſe rekenynges of giftes/ & ſeint poule ſayth to the riche mā Quid hes q̄ nō accepiſti. What haſte thou. þ thou haſt
a iii

Of holy:

nat receyued of god Right nought but synne. So þe riche men been alle on the takynge syde, ⁊ lytel or the peuynge syde. The pore man takyth but lytel, and peueth fulle moche. For one peny peuyn of the pore man is more in goddes sighte in case, than twenty pounde peuen of the riche. And therfore Criste sayth in the gospel Luce. xxi. that the pore wydowe whiche offryd but ii. myytes in the teple, that ben but one ferthynge, she offryde more than dyd alle men and wymen þ day, and yet it was fulle greate offrynge. For as Criste sayth she offride al that she hadde to lyue by. Other men myghte haue offryd moche more than they dyd and not haue be the worse. And as touchyng cristes wordes whiche ye allegge. Beacius est dare ꝛc. It is more blissfulle to peue thanne to take. Worshypful Bede sayth vpon the same text. act xx. The lorde he sayth preferryth natt by thyse wordes tyche men þ peue almes, bifore theym that forsake al thyngis and sue Criste But Criste commendith them most Whiche forsake worldly richesse and trauayl natheles with their hondes with suche lytel, as they may get iustly to help the pore nedy Or ellis it may be vnderstonde thus That to

euery man be he riche be he pore if he haue any thinge whiche he may forbere, it is better to hym with suche as he may to helpe other that been pore ⁊ nedy, than hym self to take yeftes of other men.   Moreouir sithen the pore wydowe that offryd but ii. myytes yaf so greate a gyfte. Bicause of her gode wylle. A man that forsakyth the worlde, and peueth away alle that he hathe. for the loue of god, and also for sakith therwith couetyse of hauynge, saue only that him bare nedyth be, Bicause that he soo dischargyd of worldsly besynesse, may be the more goostly occupied peueth a fulle grete gyfte, ye so greate a gyfte that a riche man as he kepith his richesse with couetyse may nat peue soo moche as suche a pore man peueth Ergo sir by poure owne wordes suche a pore man is more blyssed, thanne many that ben ful riche.

The iiii. chaptre.

Diues. If alle men were as pore as thou arte thou shuldest fare ful euyl. Pauper. If alle men were as riche as ye been, ye shuld fare moche worse who shulde tile your londe, sold your ploughe, repe youre corne, kepe youre bestes, whoo shulde

Pouertie

shape your clothes or selwe them what inswarde wold than grinde your corne/ what baker bake poure brede/ what brewer brewe youre ale/ what coke dighte youre mete/ what smytß or carpenter amende your house/ & other thingis necessary/ ye shuld go sholesse and clothelesse/ & goo to poure bed meteleße Al muste ye than do alone If ye had a wif moche wo shulde she haue. And if ye hadde none ye shuld be wreche of alle wrecches Ther shulde no man welle do any thinge for you. Therfore saith seynt austyn/ y dives & paup sunt duo sibi necessaria. The riche and the pore been ii. thinges fulle necessarye eche to other: And I saye moreouir the riche mā hath more nede than the pore. Diues. How preuyst thou that. Pauper. Haue a pore man simple lyuelode/ simple mete/ sipse drink and other symple thynges/ and felw'e necessaries to him/ it sufficeth to his persone and to his astate He carith nat but for him self or for felwe mo But the rich man carith for his psone for his astate/ for his greate meyne/ for his worshyppe for his godes He hath nede of moche gold and siluer. moche meyne/ many bitayles He hath nede of many mennys helpe/ of seruauntes/ of la-

bourers/ men of craft/ of men of lawe/ of grete lordshyp without whiche/ he may nat mayntene his state ne his richesse The pore nediþ but sytel of alle this. He that moche hath moche bihoueth And he that lesse hath/ lesse bihoueth The riche man muste peue to his frendes to haue their assistence/ and their helpe He peueth his enemyes to let their malyce And so of moche richesses he peueth but sytel to help wʹ itħ his soule. The pore man of sytel may peue sytel and hath moche thanke of god So the riche mā nediþ more and hath more nede and myscheif thāne hath the pore man. For the more that he hath/ the more him nedyþ & in more myscheif and in perel he is day and nyght For as the hous that stondiþ highe on a hylle is in more tempest thāne the hous in the valy So men of high dignite and greate richesses in high worshippes been in moost drede and moste disease And therfore god sayth to the proude couetous riche man/ Thou holdest the ful riche/ thou seest that thou haste nede of no gode/ and thou knowest nat howe wrecched thou art howe myscheuous/ howe blynd pore and nakyd. Apoc. iii.

The v. chaptre

a iiii

Of ħoly:

Dives. Thou magnifiest moche pouertie Pauper Cristes wordes muste nedes be true. Beati pauperes quoniam vestrum est regnum celoꝫ Luce. vi. Blessyd he sayth be ye pore men/ for poures is the kingdome of heuyns And in a nother place he sayth thus to the pore/ ye that haue haue forsake al this worldly richesses for loue of me and haue folowed me/ shalle sytt on twelue trones at the day of dome/ ⁊ deme the twelue kynredys of israel That is to say al that shalbe demyd quycke or dede/ And therfore riche men do ye as Criste biddeth you in the gospel. Make ye the pore men your frendes of the deuelsheue either richesses of wyckednes/ that the pore men may resceiue you into duellynges of endlesse blisse Eyther ye must be pore or begge he uyn of the pore/ if ye wole come to heuyn. Dives. Why clepyth Criste richesse richesses/ or a deuelsheue of wyckydnesse. Pauper. For couetyse of richesse makith folk to serue the deuyl/ and bryngeth them to synne and shrewdnesse. Dives. This is fulle wounderfulle to the riche folke to here. Pauper. We fynde ma theu. xix. þ ther came a yongman to our lorde and ayed him what

he shulde do to haue the lyf that euir shalle laste. Cryste aunswerd. Serua mandata. Kepe comaundementes. Slee no man/ Do no foly by no woman/ Stele nat/ Bere no false wytnesse/ worshippe fader and moder and loue thy neighboure/ as thy self Lorde sayde he/ alle these haue I do. What lackith me yit Tha sayde Criste. If thou wylt be parfite. go and selle al þ thou haste and yeue it to pore folk/ ⁊ come and folowe me But as saith the gospel whan he herde these wordes he went away fulle sory for he hadde many possessiones and moche richesses. Thanne Cryst sayde to his disciples/ It is ful hard the riche man to entre into the kingdome of heuynes It is more easy sayde he a camele to posse þ the nedles iye/ thane the riche man to entre the kyngdome of heuynes. Thanne his disciples sayde to Cryste Lorde who may thanne be saue. Cryst aunsw erpd and sayde That as anentes man it is ipossible But to god alle thinge is possible. Dives. These wordes sounde fulle harde to myne vnderstondynge/ and some may bryng me and suche other in dispayre/ I praye the declare me this maner of speche if thou canne.

Pauper. Some expositoures of the wordes of Cryste/ say þ in Jerusalem was a lytel priue gate whiche for straytnesse was clepyd the nedyl. Whanne the cameles came ycharged to this gate they myght nat entre but they dyd alwaye their burdeynes and theire pachys. And so by these wordes Cryste excludyth nat you riche men from heuyn/ But he techyth you howe ye may entre the gates of heuyn. For as he sayth in the gospel The gate and the weye that ledith to lyf & blysse is ful strayte/ and fewe passe therby. And soo by this nedyl is vnderstonde the entre of heuyns blysse. By the camel chargyd/ the riche men that ben chargyd with the rychesse of the worlde/ whiche charge as longe as it is fast vpon theym/ Soo longe they may nat entre in to heuyne blysse. For Cryste sayth in the gospel. Nisi quis renunciauerit omnibus que possidet/ non potest meus esse discipulus: But a man forsake alle that he hath/ he may nat be my disciple ¶And therfore if thou entre the straite gate of heuyn/ thou must vnbynde and louse thy charge/ of richesse from the/ and ley it besydes the vndre fote. Soo that thou be lorde and maister of thy rychesses/ and natt richesses thy maister.

The .vi. chaptre.

Diues. Howe shulde I louse my richesses fro me. Pauper. As the prophete saith Diuicie si affluant nolite cor apponere/ If richesse and welthe falle to the/ set nat thyne hert to moche theron. Loue theym nat to moche Be redy to thank god whanne he sent theym the/ And as redy to thank him pacientely/ If he take theym fro the/ And sey as Job sayde. Nudus egressus sum de vtero matris mee. Nakyde I came into this worlde. oute of my moders wombe/ and nakyd I shalle wende hense. Sithen we haue taken goodes/ of richesses and of welth of goddes honde/ why shulde we natt suffre paciently wo and disease if he sende them to vs. God yaue me godes/ and god hathe taken awey/ as god wolde so is it done/ Blessyd be goddes name. Job. primo. Vnlouse so thy rychesses from the/ that in goddes cause thou be redye/ to forsake alle that thou haste/ rather than thou shuldyste offende thy god. Soo that for no wynnynge/ ne for noo losse/ thou woldyste

Of holy

doo any dedly synne. A man be redy rather to forsake thy godes thanne thy god And on this maner muste every man forsake al that he hath if he wol be Cristes disciple/ that is to saye he muste with drawe his herte and his loue from alle that he hath/ so that he loue no thing as moch as god ne in setting of his loue ne of his worshyppe. ⁋For lo to that wose be sayd he muste be pore in spirite and in wylle And therfore sayth Criste in the gospel Beati pauperes spiritu quoniam ipsorum est regnum celorum Blessyd been they that ben pore in spyrite and in wylle. For theires is the kyngdome of heuynes. Alle though this exposicion as touchyng the moralle sense be fulle true and faire Natheles doctor de lira bicause it hath noon autoritie of holy scripture/ that ther was such a yate at Jerusalem/ that was clepyd a nedle/ expowneth the wordes of Cryste in another maner and sayth that Criste spekith in that texte of riche men that sett their blysse and their truste in richesse Wherfore this is the menynge of the text as lire saith As it is impossible a camele to passe through a nedys ire So it is impossible a man that settith his trust and his blysse in richesses/ to en-

tre into the Realme of heuyn. But if he cast from him suche inordinate loue and trustynge in richesse. And that thies wordes of Criste shulde be thus vnderstode/ the same doctour preuith by Cristes owne wordes in another place/ Mark. x. Where oure lorde sayth thus How harde it is ỹ men trustyng in richees entre into the Realme of god It is easyer or lighter. ỹ a camele passe through a nedles iye/ thanne ỹ a riche man entre into the kyngdome of god/ that is to say so trustynge in his richesses/ inordinatly theym louynge.

⁋The vii. chapter.

Dues. I assent to this exposicion I was aferd that god hadde nat louyd riche men: Paup. Abraham Isaac and Iacob the holy patriarkes wer ful riche men/ and yet god louyd them fulle wele Dauyd/ ezechie. and Iosye were kynges of goddes peple/ moche louyd and pryted of god. Ioseph Danyel teusers of realmes wer of god chosen Iob zachee Ioseph of Aramathie were fulle riche men/ and nowe ben fulle high in Blisse. For the riche men be nat lackyd in holy wryt for their richesses/ But for her wykyd couetyse and myswylle of richesse And therfore sayth seint Abrose ft luca. ỹ the faute is nat in the richesse/ but in them that can nat vse their richesse in due maner.   And therfore sayth he that right as richesse is letting of vertu: to wycked men/ soo it is helpingt of vertue to gode men Ne pore men be nat pryssede soo moche in hole wrytte for waunting of richesse/ ne for myscheif y they been in/ but for their gode wyl and their loue that they haue to god.   Whanne for his loue they forsake richesse/ and put them in pouert and mischeif to serue ther god the more frely wt oute settynge of worldly couetyse for more shrewys fynde I none than pore beggers that haue no gode that the world hath forsake/ but they nat the world Diues. Therfore me thynketh alway that it is better to be rich thanne pore for pouerte & myscheif drawe many a man to robbery/ manslaughter and lechery & other synnes many moo And therfore sayth Salomon propter inopiam multi deliquerunt: Ecclesiastes. xxviii. Pauper Some be pore and nedy by ther gode wylle/ and some agenst their wylle/ And they that be pore agenst their wylle/ some haue pacience/ and some haue no pacience/ and they bicause of myscheif lightly falle in synne. But neither pouert wilfully taken/ for the loue of god/ ne pouert y falleth to man agenst his wylle bringeth man to synne if he haf pacience More ouir I say that couetyse of richesse is more cause of synne thane is pouert And therfore sayth seynt Poule that couetyse is rote of al maner wickydnes And the pore man dare nat/ ne may nat synne ne meyntene his synne/ as the riche man may.   For he may soner be punysshed and chastised thane the riche man Also ther is nede of pouert and nede of couetise for as Salomon sayth/ the coueto' man hath neuir ynough But for myscheif of herte he lesith his soule. And of this myscheif and nede. speketh Salomon the wordes y thou alleggist.

The viii. chaptre

Diues. Here by thy talkynge thou arte a settyd man/ what canst thou sey to the wordes of Salomon prouerb. xxx. where he prayde thus. Mendicitatem et diuicias ne dederis michi/ ne egestate compulsus plure nomen dei. Lorde he saith yeue me neither grete richesse ne beggery y I be nat constreyned by nede to forswere my goddes name/ & holy chirche singith & saith Diuicias & paupertates ne dederis Lord saith he yeue me no gret

Of holy

richesse ne grete pouerte Wherby as me thynkith eche man shuld be besy to flee pouerte beggerye and myscheif. Pauper. I pray the be as besy to forsake thy rychesse by ensample of Salomon as thou arte to forsake pouertie and beggery/ For in his prayer in whiche be contepned mo wordes thanne thou rehersist/ he forsoke bothe richesse and beggery: But thou doiste as many men doon/ Thou allegyst the scripture as the syste/ and applyest it to thy fantasye/ & leupst behynd what the liste whiche is ayenste thy fantasye. The hole prayer of Salomon is this/ Mendicitatem et diuicias ne dederis michi Tribue tantum victui meo necessaria Ne forte saciatus illiciar ad negandum. et dicam quis est domin⁹. et egestate compullus furer et periurem nomē Dei mei. Beggerye he sayth & richeos ne yeue thou nat to me/ yeue thou only to my lyuelode ne desful thinges Lest parauenture/ I fulfylled be drawen to denye. and sey who is the lorde/ And through nede constreyned stele/ & forswere the name of my god. After the exposicion of Bede/ & Lyre. in this texte. Salomon prayeth to god that he be nat so fylled with richesses/ that he for pride and aboundance of world

ly godes forȝet his god & en blesse godes/ Also on that other syde that vnpacience of pouert compelle him nat to stele/ neither to forswere him. In whiche prayer he refusith no more pouertie/ thanne he dothe aboundaunce. of richesse. But his prayer indifferently biholdith grete richesse and moche pouertie. Also sir sauf thy pacience/ thou rehersist the wordes of Salomones yper with false englisshe and nat conuenyent. For he saide nat yeue me neither richesse ne beggerye. as thou saydest But he sayde yeue me richesse and beggery. That is to saye/ yeue me nat richesse with nygardshyp & straytnesse of herte and couetyse/ whiche make the riche man alway. to begge and craue. For as I saide. Ecclesiastes. the V. c. the nygard hath neuir enough And so by these wordes he prayeth to god that if he yeue him richesse. that he shuld gyue him therwith largenesse of hert/ and grace to spende them to goddes worshyp and to haue gode of his gode by his lyf. For as he sayth Ecclesiastes vi. It is a greate myscheyf and a greate vanytye that god gyueth a man richesse. and godes ynough what he wol haue And with that he yeueth him no power for nygardshyp to

Pouertie.

haue parte therof/ But kepith them to the straungere/whiche shal deuoure al that he gettyth. With moche care Amen this mys/cheyf and beggery of couetyse. Salomon made his prayer sayenge to the lorde. yeue me nat richesse and beggerye to gyder. For suche nygartshyp: and beggerye/ makith riche men to forsake their god. So it is vnderstonde of beggery and pouertie that cometh of mysconetyse/ nat of pouertie and begery that compth of nede and wantynge of gode. For the riche man nedith more to begge bodily thane the pore. Diues. That is false. Pauper. I preue it. Dauyd þ worthy kynge sayde. Ego autem mendicus sum et pauper: I am sayd he a begger and a pore man/ where the glose saith thᵒ Beggynge is to axe thynge of another that he hath not of him self/ But the riche man nedyth more thane the pore to axe help of other/ as I shewyd here afore Ergo it nedith him more to beg thane the pore man. Diues. Al thoughe we axe helpe of other men as vs nedith al/ yit we pay them for their trauayl and for their gode. And therfore it is no beggery/ But a couenauntle makynge/ payinge/ byeng and sellynge. Pauper. Fulle ofte ye

paye fulle euyl. Thou askyste for the loue of the penye/ and a pore nedy man axith for the loue of god. Thou profryst men of whom thou axist bodily help the peny totheir nede/ and god þ seryth him self to mede to theim that helpe pore men. Diues. Al we be begers gostly as saith seynt austyne/ for we haue noo gode gostly but of goddes gifte Pauper. Ergo we be alle beggers bodily/ for we haf no gode bodily but of goddes gyfte.

The ix. chaptre.

Diues. Thy speche is skilfulle/ but nat moche plesaunt to many riche folk I pray the what is thy name. Pauper. why askyst thou.

Diues. Twenty yere agoo I spake with a man of thyn astate/ that was fulle lyke the in speche and persone But he spake of so high perfection as thou nowe begynnest to do/ that vnto this day I coude neuir ateyn therto And he tolde me the same tale of that yonge man that thou toldest me nowe Pauper. Of whiche yonge man Diues. Of hym that asked Criste what he shulde do to haue the blisse without ende. To whom Cryste.

37

taught hym that pfection / that thou spekest of And yit he dyd it not no more than I do. Paup Ther is two maner of pfectons of whiche Criste spake & taught that yonge riche man / Ther is perfection lesse. and perfection more The firste is nedeful and sufficient The secounde is a pas synge holynesse and fulle excellent. Of the firste god sayth. Perfect⁹ eris sine macula. Glosa. Criminali. deut. xviii. Thou shalt sayth he be parfyte without spotte of dedely synne Of this parfection spake Cryst to that yong riche man whanne he badde him kepe the comaudementes Of the secounde parfection that is so excellent / he sayd to him. Si vis perfect⁹ elle, &c. If thou wylt be parfyte go and selle alle that thou haste and yeue it to the pore folk and come folowe me. Diues, The same tale tolde me thy broder twenty yere paste. But we spake than moste of the hiesse parfection of excellencie I praye the let vs nowe speke a while of the lesse pfection that is nedefulle to alle. For sithen I may nat atteyn to the more parfection. I wold as me muste / kepe and holde wele the lesse parfection / Pauper. Do thanne as Criste taughte ye yonge riche man. Serua mans

data. kepe wele the commaude metes Haue one god in worshyp Take nat his name in ydelnes / Halowe thyne holidaye. Fadre and moder worshyppe and paye Sle no man / Doo no folye by no woman / Loke that thou nat stele. And no false wytnesse that thou bere Couepte thou nat thy neighbours gode with wronge house ne londe Desire nat his wyf ne his childe / ne his seruaut ne his beest / ne ony thinge that to him longith. These ben the .x. commaundementes whi che god wrote in two tables of stone / and toke theym to Moyses / for to teche theym to the people. The thre firste preceptes were wryten by theym self in the firste table / For tho principally teche vs howe we shuld worship oure god / and loue hym aboue al thinge And therfore they ben cleppd the thre preceptes / of the firste table. The other vii. been cleppd of the secounde table / for they were writen in the secound table And they teche vs how we shulde worshyppe and loue our euyn cristen as oure self.

And so alle the ten commaundementes been compreheNded. in the two preceptes of charite. Diues. Whiche been tho. Pauper. The first is that thou shalt loue thy lord god w' al thynhert

Pouertie.

with alle thy mynde. With alle thy might: The seconde is that thou shalt loue thy neighboure as thy self, that is to saye, thou shalt loue him to the same blisse that thou louest to thy self, and do to him as thou woldest men dyde to the, and nat do to hym but as thou woldest men dyde. to the, as longe as he kepith the lawe of charite For and if he for sete and do ayenste charite, it is charite to chastise hym and punysshe him. tyl he wyl amende him, for saluacion of his soule. and ensample of other In these ii. cōmaundementes as Cryste sayth in the gospel, hangith al the lawe and alle the prophecy. And therfore seint Poule saith þ loue and charite is fulfillyng of alle the lawe.

☙ The v. chaptre.

Dives. Me merueylith moche why Crist taught more that yonge riche man the commaundementis of the seconde table: than of the firste, and why he taught hī more how he shuld loue his neighbour, thā he shuld loue his god For neither Criste spake to him of the firste precepte of charite, howe he shulde loue his god aboue al thing, ne how he shulde haue one god in wor-

ship. ne howe he shulde flee piuury, ne þ he shulde halowe the holidaye And yet without keping of these may no man be sauyd. Pauper. Whanne Crist badde him kepe the preceptes in general he badde him kepe the v. cōmaū dementes of the ii preceptes of charitye, a al goddes hestes a his lawes But he specifyed more the preceptes of the seconde table thā of the firste, a more the seconde precepte of charite than the firste. not þ he was more bounde therto But for he was more enclyned. Bicause of pouthe, of richesses, a of lordship, to forsete ayenst tho preceptes than ayenst the other of the firste table For pouthe is enclyned to wrathe, hastynesse. fighting, and so to manslaughter to stelery, auoutrye, to spenge, a so to false wytnesse, to theft, to pryde a rebellion, to indignacion to dispyte of his elder, And so in many wyse offendith his neighboure a his euyn cristen And namely whan pouthe is vnderset with richesses, a is at his owne rule withoute drede of punysshinge. as that yonge man was. For he was fulle ryche, and he was a prynce leder and ruler of the cuntre. as sayth Seint Luke. in his gospelle. And therfore Criste moste soueraȳ leche. not only taught him how

Of holy

he shulde lyue withouten ende. But more ouir he warned him to what seknesse he was moost disposed to/ wherby he myghte lese that lyf and die withouten ende & taught him medicynes apenst tho seknesses/ whan he bad him nat sle/ do no licherp/ no thefte. bere no false witnesse/ worshyp fadre and modre/ and in his refrayng loue his neighbour as him self/ and doo to him as he wolde men dyde to him. Diues. why specified nat criste to him the ii. laste preptes of the secounde table whiche be apenst fals couetise. Pauper. For ponge folk be he nat so moche enclyned to couitise as they be to other synnes Diues. That is sothe/ for couetyse reigneth moost in olde folk And so as men wexe in age/ soo encresith ther couetise And whan al other synnes forsake man for elde and feblenesse/ than couetyse is moost breme Pryde is first in pouthe/ couetyse laste in age Saye forth what thou wylt.

Pauper Euirmore thou shalt understonde þ ther be ii. manere of lyues by the which man may be sauyd The firste is contemplatyf/ the secounde is actyf. The first stondith principally in besinesse to knowe god and goddes lawes/ & to loue him aboue alle thinge. The secounde stondith

principaly in gode dedes & gode reule/ and helpe of our euyn criste The thre first preptes of the first table belongith to alle/ But principaly to them that been in lyf contemplatyf that haue forsake the worlde and worldly besynesse for the loue of god. The vii. preptes of the secounde table also longen to alle/ But principally to theym that ben in lyf actyf & in besynesse of the world The lyf contemplatif is in ease & rest of hert. The lyf actyf is in doynge & trauayl and besynesse of body & soule And of this lyf spake þ ponge riche man whane he seyd. Lorde what shal I do. how shal I lyue to haue the lyf withoutē ende And crist taught hi what gode dedes he shuld do what mysdedes he shulde fle/ if he wolde kepe wele the lyf actyf Also thou shalt vnderstonde for this speche of crist and many suche other/ that crist & the gospel & hole wrytte by exāple of the lesse preueth & shewith the more As whanne he saith þ men shuld be sauyd at the day of dome for they haue mete to the hungrye. drynke to the thrusty/ moche more than shuld they be sauyd þ passe al that they hadde or myght haue for the loue of god. and hem self to serue god night and daie. body and soule/ and put them to

The firste precepte

the dethe for his loue. And they also that fede mannys soule wt brede of goddes worde And sith they shalbe dampned þ wole natt yeue to pore follre mete & drynk for goddes sake, Moche more shuld they be dampned that robbe men of ther lyf & lyuelode. & they that done lecherye, auoutrye, ma[n]slaughter, robberye, and other or rible synnes. And on the same maner whanne cryste specifyed to that riche man, the preceptes of the secounde table, and these counde precepte of charitye, he shewith that sithen tho were soo necessary to haue the lyf without en ende, Moche more the precep tes of the firste table and the first precept of charite been necessarye to alle that wole haue the lyf wt outen ende. Diues. Therfore wolde I fayne kepe theym bet ter thanne I haue done. But I se many doubtes therin þ I can nat kepe theym. Paup. What doute haste thou therin.

The firste chaptre.

Dues. In the firste commau[n]dement as I haue lernyd, god sayth thus. Thou shalt haue noon other straunge goddes bifore me. Thou shalte make to the no grauyn thynge, no mawmet, no lykenesse that is in heuyn aboue, ne that is by nethe in erthe, ne of any thinge that is in the water vnder therth Thou shalte nat worshypp them with thy body outewarde, ne wt thyn hert inwarde. Exodi. xx.c. Soo by this me thinketh þ god defendeth makynge of ymages and worshipppynge of them, and yit men do make ymages, these dayes grete plente, bothe in chur che and out of churche And alle men as me thynk worshyp yma ges: And it is fulle harde to me But I do in that as al men done And if I worshyp them me thin keth I do ydolatrie ayenst god, des lawe. Pauper. God forbe dith nat men to make ymages, For he bad moyses make yma ges of ii. angelys, that be clepyd cherubyn. in the lyknesse of two yonge men, as we fynd Exodi. xxvii.c. And salomon made suche and many mo therto i the temple, to the worshypp of god. the iii. boke of kingis vii.c. And god bad moyses make his taber nacle & al that longith therto, af tre the example and the lyknes. þ was shewyde to hym vpon the hylle, whanne he was there with god xl. daies & xl. nightes. Ex odi. xxv. And therfore god for bedith nat vtterly the makynge

B i

The firste

of ymages/ But he forbediþ ši
terly for to make ymages for to
worship them as goddes/ and to
sette their faith/ their trust/ their
hope their loue/ & their bileue in
them For god wole haue man
nys herte hole knytt to him alo
ne/ for in him is al oure help & al
oure saluacion And therfore we
muste worshyp him & loue him
& truste in him aboue al thynge.
& no thynge worship but him or
for him. That alle the worshyp
that we do to any creature be do
principaly for him. & arectyd to
him. For he sayth. Gloriam me
am alteri non dabo/ et laudem
meam sculptilibus. psal. xlii.
I shal nat yeue my worshyppe
my blisse/ my glorye/ to none o
ther/ ne my prysynge to grauyn
ymages/ ne to paynted ymages

And in the same chaptre
he saith Shamfully shent mote
they be alle that set their truste i
grauen ymages. Diues. Wher
of serue these ymages/ I wolde
they were brent alle/ Pauper.
They serue for thre. thynges/
For they be ordeined to stere m̄
nys mynde to thynke on cristes
incarnacion/ and on his passion
& on his spurnge/ & on other sein
tes lyuynge Also they ben ordei
ned to styre mannys affection.
and his herte to deuocion For
ofte man is more sterpd by sight

than be herynge or redynge. Al
so they be ordeyned to be a tokē
& a boke to the leude peple/ that
they may rede i ymagery & pain
ture/ that clerkes rede i the boke
as the lawe sayth. de cōsecra. dis
tinct. iii. p latū. Where we fynde
that a bisshop distroied ymages
as thou woldest do/ and forsen
dyd that no man shuld worship
ymages He was accused to the
pope seynt Gregory whiche bla
myd him gretely for that he had
so distroyed the ymages/ But ši
terly he prised him for he forsen
dyd them to worshyp ymages.

The ii. chaptre.

Diues. How shuld I rede
in the boke of peynture.
& of ymagery. Pauper. Whāne
thou seest the ymage of the cruci
fixe/ thynk on him ý died on the
crosse for thy synne and thy sake
and thanke him for his endelesse
charite/ ý he wolde suffre so mo
che for the Take hede by the y
mage howe his hede was crow
ned with a garlonde of thornes
til they went into the brayne/ &
the blode braste oute on euery si
de/ for to distroye the bigh synne
of pryde/ that sheweth moste in
mannys hede and womans and
make an ende of thy pride Tak
hede by the ymage howe his ar
mes were spradde abrode & dra
wen ful strayte upon the tre. tyl

Preceptꝭ

al the veynes and the synowes crakyd/ And howe his hondes were naylyd to the crosse and strenyd oute blode/ for to distroye the synne that Adam and Eue. dyd with their hondes/ Whanne they toke the apple ayenst goddes forbode/ Also he suffryd this to distrope the synne of wycked dedys and wycked werkes/ that men and wymmen do with theire hondes/ & make an ende of thy wychyd werkys. Take hede also howe his syde was openyd/ & his herte clouen in two with the sharpe spere/ and how he shedde blode and water/ to shewe that if he had had more blode I his body more he wold haue yeuen for mannys loue. He shedde blode to raunsome of our soules/ & that to wasshe vs from our synes Also he suffride this for to distrope the synne of pryde/ couetise enuye. hate wrathe and malyce. þ reigne in mānes hert & womans

Take hede & make an ende of thy pryde/ of thy false couetise/ of hate/ enuye wrathe & malice/ & forgeue thyn euen crysten/ for his loue þ forgaue his deth. Take hede also by the ymage/ how his feet were nailed to the crosse and strempd on bode/ to distrope the synne of sleuth I goddes seruice. And make an ende of sleuthe in goddes seruice/ and haste thy fot

to goddes house & to goddes seruyce/ Take hede also by the ymage howe his body was to rēt and al to torne/ with tho sharp scourges þ fro the sole of the fote vnto the toppe of the hede/ ther was no hole place on his body. & that was to distrope the synne of lust and likyng of the flesshe. glotonye & lichery. Which regne in mannys body and womans. and make an ende of glotony & lychery. Take hede how naked & pore he henge vpon the crosse/ for thy synne & thy sake/ and be thou nat asshamyd to suffre pouertie & myscheif for his loue.

And as seynt Bernarde by doth take hede by the ymage how his hede is bowed doun to the redy to kysse the and come at one wt the/ See how his armys and his hondes been spradde abrode on the tree/ in token that he is redy to halse and clyppe the/ & kysse the/ and take the to his mercy. Se how his syde was opened. and his herte clouen on two/ in token that his herte is all ape open to the/ redy to loue the and to forgyue the alle trespasse/ yf thou wylte amende the and aye mercy/ Take hede also how his feet were naylyde fulle harde to the tre. in token that he wyl nat fle away from the. But abyde wt the and dwel with the withoute

G ii

43

The friste

ende. On this maner I pray the rede thy boke and falle down ne to grounde / and thanke thy god that wolde do so moche for the / and worſhyp hym aboue al thynge / nat the ymage / nat the ſtocke / ſtone / ne tree / but hym ẏ dyed on the tree / for thy ſynne ꝛ thy ſake. So that thou knele if thou wylt bifore the ymage. nat to the ymage. Do thy worſhyp afore the ymage nat to the yma ge. Make thy prayer bifore the ymage. But nat to the ymage. For it ſeeth the nat / ſeryth the the nat. Vnderſtondeth the nat Ma ke thyn offrynge if thou wylt bi fore the ymage / But nat to thy ymage. Make thy pilgramage nat to the ymage ne for the yma ge. For it may nat helpe the / but to him and for him that the yma ge repreſentith to the. For if thou doo it for the ymage / or to the ymage thou doſte ydolatry.

The iii. chaptre

Diues. Me thynkith that whãne men knele bifore the ymage pray and loke on the ymage / with wepyng teres / bū the or knocke theire breſtps / wᵗ other ſuche countynaunce / they do al this to the ymage / and ſo wenyth moche peple. Pauper. If they doo it to the ymage / they ſynne gretly in ydolatry a penſt reaſone and kynde / Butt as I ſayde bifore / they may doo alle this bifore the ymage ꝗ nat to the ymage. Diues. Howe myght they do al this bifore the ymage / and nat worſhyp the y mage. Pauper. Oft thou ſeeſt that the preeſt in the chirch hath his boke bifore him. he knelyth he ſtareth. he loketh on his boke he holdith vp his hõdes And for deuocion in caſe he wepith / and maketh deuoute prayers / To whome wenyſte thou the preeſt dothe alle this worſhip / Diues to god ꝗ nat to the boke. Pau per. On the ſame maner ſhulde the lewde man vſe his boke that is ymagery and painture nat to worſhyp the ymage / But god in heuyn and ſeintes in their degre And that alle the worſhyp that he doth bifore thy mage / he doth nat to the ymage / But to him ẏ the ymage repreſentith.
Diues. this enſãple is gode / but knoweſt thou any better / Pau per. Whanne the preeſt ſaith his meſſe at the autre / comonly ther is an ymage bifore him / ꝗ com ly it is a crucifixe ſtone / or tree / or portrayed. Diues. Why mo re a crucifixe than any other yma ge. Pauper. For euery meſſe ſyngyng is a ſpecial mynde ma kynge of criſtes paſſion. And

therfore he hath bifore him a crucifixe to doo him haue the more
fresshe mynde as he owith to haue of cristes passion. Diues.
The skylle is gode, say for the.
Paup. Bifore this ymage the
preest sayth his messe, & makith
the highest prayers þ holy chirch
can deuyse, for saluacion of the
quyche & of the dede. He holdith
vp his hondes, he louteth, he knelyth in case, & alle the worshyppe
that he can do he doth. Durmo-
re he offreth vp the highest sacrifyce & the best offrynge that any
herte can deuyse, that is Cryste
goddes sonne of heuyne, vndre
fourme of brede and wyne. Alle
this worshyp dothe the preest at
the messe bifore the ymage, and
yit I hope that ther is no man ne
woman so lewde, that he wolde
say þ the preest syngith his messe
ne maketh his prayer, ne doth þ
worship, ne offrith vp goddes sone criste hym self to the ymage.
Diues. God forbede that any
man or woman shulde saye soo
or byleue. That were erroure
moste of alle erroures. Pauper.
On the same maner, shulde the
lewde man do his worshyp bifore
the ymage. Make his prayer bifore the ymage and nat to the y-
mage.

The iiii. chaptre.

Diues. Contra. On gode
fryday ouir al in holy chirche, men crepe to the crosse and
worshyp the crosse. Pauper. þ
is sothe, but nat as thou menyst
The crosse that we crepe to and
worshyp so highly that tyme, is
criste him self þ died on the crosse
that day for oure synne and our
sake. As sayth Beda lib 20 iii. de
gemma anime. For the shap of
a man is a crosse. And as he heng
vpon the rode he was a very cros
He is that crosse as alle doctoures saye, to whome we praye, &
say O crux aue spes vnica. Hail
be thou crosse oure only hope, en
crease thou to the meke her right
wisnesse this passion tyme, and
yeue pardone to theym that ben
gylty. He is that crosse brighter
than al the sterres of the worlde
as holy churche syngeth & sayth
O crux splendidior. cunctis as-
tris mundi, &c. And as Bede
sayth for asmoche as cryste was
moste dispised of mankynde on
gode fryday, therfore holy churche hath ordeyned þ on gode fry
day men shuld do him most wor
shyp. And for this skyl we do þ
high worshyp that daye, nat to
the crosse that the preest holdith
in his honde, but to him þ dyed for
vs al þ day vpon the crosse. For
oftyn þ cros þ the preest holdith
in his honde is fulle vnthende.

criste hymself/cristes passion/cri
stes deth/cristes spuynge/in erth
fulle of peyne & wo/the crosse þ
he dyed on & euery syknes of the
crosse is clepid cristes crosse But
the syknesse of a thynge o witche
nat to be in as moche reuerence/
& worship as the thinge himself
And euery lorde & knight hath a
special token in his armes or el
les besides his armes wherby he
is knowen/& ofte beryth the na
me of his token/& by the name
of his token his dedys ben tolde
of heraudes & gestours þ knowe
nat their name ne their persone.
Right so Criste in holy wryt oft
tymes is cleppde a crosse/for the
crosse is his special token And so
sumtyme we speke to the crosse as
to crist him self Sumtyme we spe
ke of the crosse only/þ he henge
vpon And so we speke oft in ho
ly churches seruyce to the crosse as
to criste him self/& anone we tur
ne the worde only to the crosse/þ
he died on And so sumtyme we spe
to the crosse & of the crosse/as to
him & of him þ the crosse betoke
neth Sumtyme we speke of the
crosse only as of his token/& the
crosse þ he died vpon/and so one
worde is referred to diuerse thin
ges And this blindith moche folk
in their redynge For they wene
that alle the prayers that holy
church maketh to the crosse/that

he maketh theym to the tre that
Criste died on/or elles to the cro
ce. in the churche/as in that an
teme. O crux splendidior. And
so for selfwdnesse they been decey
ued/ and worshyp creatures as
god him self. Diues. On pal
me sunday at procession the prest
draweth vp the peyple bifore the
rode/& falleth downe to grounde.
With alle the people/and sayth.
thries. Aue rex noster. Hayle
be thou oure kynge/ and soo he
worshipeth that ymage as king
Pauper. Absit. God forbede.
He speketh nat to the ymage/þ
the carpenter hath made and the
peyntour painted But if the þste
be a fole For that stocke or stoo
ne was neuer kynge/ But he spe
kyth to him that dyed on the cro
ce. for vs al/to him that is king
of alle thynge.

The 8. chaptre.

Diues. I assente/for this
is ayenst scrypte and reson
and kynde/that man whiche is
nere of kyn to god that is very
man and our brother. shuld wor
shyp in that maner either stocke
or stone For they may neither
here ne se. ne helpe themself And
therfore who so worshyppeth y-
mages i this maner/doth grete

disshonoure to man that is so noble in ordre of kynde/ & moche more to god that toke mankynde. & bicame man/ & in oure mango de is aboue alle mankynde. Pauper. If the kinges sonne. knelyd to his churle or to his page & worshyppyd him as his soue rayne and prayed him of grace. that only the kyng might graūt and dyd him the same worshypp. he shulde do his fader the king it were a grete disshonoure bothe to the sonne and to the fader. And therfore it is repreef to gentylles to be outr homely w' boyes apenst gode norture. But moche more disshonoure. doo we to god & to oure self also/ sithen we be the kinges children of heuen. so nygh of kynne & heires of the kyngdome of heuyn/ if we worshyp stockes or stones or any other ymages/ or done theim any seruyce/ as sayth the lawe. De consecrac. di. iii. Venerabiles. Diues. This is open enoughe that thou sayst for the ymage. neither can ne may help at nede for it hath no vertue at alle It is nothyng elles but a boke or a tokē to the lewde peple as thou saidest first to stire hem to think on god & on seyntes in heuen/ & so to worshypp god ouir al thing and seyntes in their degre Pauper. For this shylte been crosses made by the wey/ that whanne folke passynge se the crosse/ they shulde thynke on him that dyed on the crosse. & worshyp him aboue alle thinge. And for the same skylle is the crosse borne bifore l procession/ that alle that folowe & mete with the crosse shuld wor ship him þ dyed on the crosse and thanke him for his endeles cha= rite. Also the crosse is borne bifore. in token þ in al oure spuyng & alle oure dedys/ We shuld haf tye & hert to him that died on the crosse. as to oure kynge oure hede/ oure lord/ our leder to heuen blysse. And therfore Salomon saith. Oculi sapientis in capite eius. The iyen of the wiseman been alway in his hede. þ is Je= su Criste. Whiche is hede of holy churche/ and of al cristen peple.

The 81 chaptre

Diues. Sithen ymagerye is but a token & a boke of the lewde peple/ teche me yit a litel bettre to knowe this boke & to rede therin Paup. Imagery shewhat betokneth in special. & what in comen & general In special token the ymage of oure lady is paynted w' a childe in her lefte arme/ in tokē þ she is modre of god/ & with a lylie or elles w' a rose in her right honde/ in tokē þ she is mayden withouten ende & floure of alle wymen And soo of other seyntes/ whose ymages haue diuerse signes in their hondes and other places/ for diuerse vertues & martirdomes þ tho seintes suffryd & hadde in their lyf

The ymage of seint petyr is paynted with keyes in his hond in token þ criste betoke seint petyr the keyes of holy churche/ & of the kingdome of heuene But pit afterwarde/ Criste gaue tho keyes to al the apostles/ as the gospelles wytnesse. M'. xviii. & io. xx. c. Seynt poule is peynted with a swerde in his honde/ I toke þ he was beded w' a swerd for cristes sake/ & also in token/ þ sutyme he pursued holy church with the sw erde/ Seynt John/ the euangeliste is peynted with a coupe in his honde/ & an edder þ rin/ in token þ he dranke dedly venym/ & through the vertue of the crosse it loste his malice. and dyd him none harme. And in his other honde he be: eth a palme. in token that he was a martyr & hadde the palme of martirdonie/ alse though he were natt slayne for his wylle w as to dye for goddes sake Seynt John Baptist is peynted in a camelys shynne at the peintoures wylle in token that his clothyng was fulle harde and sharpe/ made of camelys here He berith a lombe w' a crosse in his left honde: and

his fyngere of the righte honde. ther tolwarde/ in token þ he shewyd goddes lobe goddes sonne þ dyed for us on the crosse w han he seyd to the people. Ecce agnus dei/ ecce qui tollit peta mūdi. Se goddes lombe/ se hym þ doth awey the sines of the world Seynt Kateryne is peynted w' a whele in the one honde/ in token of the orrible wheles w bich the tyraunt maxence. ordeyned to rente her lith from lithe But the aungel distroyed them & many thousandes of hethen peple. And so they dyd her noo harme. She hathe a swerde in the other honde/ in token þ her hede was smyten of with a swerde for cristes sake/ Seynt margarete is paynted w' a dragon vnder her feet/ & with a crosse in her honde in token that whane the dragon deuoured her/ she blessid her and by the vtue of the crosse/ the dragon brast and she came oute of him in helth & hole And so forth of diuerse ymages of other seyntes/ whiche ymages be made to represente to man the vertuous lyuyng of seintes/ & the holy endynge of their temporal lyf.

The vii. chaptre.

Dives. What betokneth ymagery in gnal or comō Pauper. Comonly alle the apostlis ben peynted bare fote in

token of innocence & of penaū
ce Natheleſſe they wente nat al
way fully barfoote/ but ſūtyme
wt galoches/ a ſole bineth & a fa
ſtnynge aboue the fote Of what
the galothes ſeynt bede ſayth
in his original The aūgel ſpak
to ſeynt Petyr. ſayinge. Calcia
te caligas tuas. Do on thy ga=
loches or ſandalynes as ſaythe
ſeynt Marke in his goſpelle Alſo
the apoſtles comonly and other
ſeyntes ben peynted wt māteles
in token of the vertue & pouer=
tie Whiche they had For as ſaith
ſeynt Gregorye. Al theſe world
ly godes ben nought elles but a
clothinge to the body And a mā
tele is a louſe clothyng nat faſt
to the body but louſe. & lightly
may be done awaye Righte ſoo
the godes of this world wet but
a mantel to apoſtles & other ſel
tes. For they were alway ſo
louſe from their herte þ they paſ
no grete tale therof/ nor to leſe
theym. They were nat faſte ne
cleuyd nat to them by noo falſe
couetyſe/ but alway they were
redye to forſake alle for criſtes
ſake. Diues. What betokneth
the rounde thinges peynted on
their hedes Pauper. The blys
þ they haue withouten ende Of
Whiche the prophete pſaie. ſpe=
kyth Leticia ſempiterna ſup ca
pita eorum. pſa: lj. c. Diues.

Precepte.

they were nat ſo gay in clothing
as they be peynted Pauper.
That is ſothe For many of them
were clothed in fulle harde clo=
thyng and pore/ as ſeint Poule
ſayth. Circuierunt in melotis
pellibus caprinis anguſtiati.
They wente aboute in broche
ſkynnes/ in ſkynnes of gete ne=
dy anguyſſhed Natheleſſe yma
ges ſtondynge in churches may
be gſydered in ii. maners/ either
as they repreſent the ſtate of ſel
tes of Whome they be ymages/
as they lyued in this lyf/ and ſo
they be to be peinted in ſuch ma
ner clothing as tho ſeintes vſed
Whiles they lyued here Or elles
they may be conſiderd as they
repſet the ſtate of endleſſe bliſſe.
In Whiche ſeyntes be nowe/ & ſo
they be to be peynted rpaly and
ſolenmely/ as the cherubynes þ
reſſentyd the aūgelles þ been in
heuene were made of golde Ex
odi. xxv. Natheles in al ſuche
paynture an honeſt meane nei=
ther to coſtly bicauſe of this cō=
ſideracion/ ne to vile bicauſe of
the former gſideracōn me thīketh
is to be kept The viii. chapt
Diues. Why ben aūgelles
peynted l liknes of yong
men ſith they be ſpirites & haf no
bodies Paup. Ther may noo
peyntoure peynte a ſpirit in his
kynde And therfore to the bettre

representacion they be peynted. in the lyknesse of a man/ whiche in soule is moofte accordyng to aungellys kynde And thoughe the aungel be nat suche bodily. as he is peynted. he is nathelesse suche goftly/ & hath suche doing & beyng spirituel. They be peynted lyke yonge men berdlesse/ in token ῷ they ben endeles & elden nat/ ne feble natt/ but alwey in one ſphynge/ in one ſtate. alwey mighty and ſtronge/ And alſoo they be peinted with crulled here in token ῷ their thoughtes & ther loue ben ſette alwey in right ordre/ and turne alway vp apen to god/ thanking him and worship pyng him in alle thinge. For by the here of the hede in holy wryt beeth vnderſtonde thoughtes/ & affectiones of the hert. Alſo they be peynted with rowelles about their neckes/ in token that they be alway redy to ſerue god & mā at goddes bidding. And therfore they been clepyd. Adminiſtrato rii ſpūs.. Ab hebre. i. c. That is to ſay. ſpirites of ſeruice. For they ſerue to god/ in ruſhyng of mākynde/ & gouernance of this worlde/ They been peynted feſ theryd & with wynges/ in token of lightneſſe & deſpuerneſſe I her werkes. For in a twynklyng of an iye they may be in heuyn & in erth/ here & at rome/ & at ieruſalē

They be peynted wᵗ whelys vn dre their feet I token ῷ they meue & rule the rounde bodies. the whe les & the circles/ in heuene/ & the cours of the planetes/ as the phi loſopher ſayth/ & alſo in token/ ῷ as the whele turneth alway a boute the centre. & his myddes/ ſo the augelles doyng is alway aboute god/ & alwaye ben nighe him where euir they be. Alſo ſum nie they be peynted armed with ſpere ſwerde & ſhelde/ in token ῷ they be redy for to defēde vs fro the fendes ῷ been beſy night and day to leſe vs. For but if holy au gellys holpen vs & defende vs & kepte vs. letting the fendes ma lyce. we myghte nat withſtonde ne be ſauyd. And therfore righte as euery man and woman hath a wycked aungel aſſigned to hī by the fende to tempe him/ Soo hath he a gode aungel aſſigned to hym of god/ to ſaue him if he wyl folowe his rule.

The ix. chaptre.

Ques. why ben the iiii. eu āgeliſtes peynted in ſuch diuerſe liknes ſith they were mē al iiii. Pauper For diuerſe ma ner of writig & teching/ matheu is peynted in ſyknesse of a man/ For he principaly wrote & tauʒt the māhode of Criſte and tolde.

howe he bicam̄ mā. And most specially and most opēly wrote his genologie. Seint John that wrote In principio erat verbū. is peynted in lyknesse of an egle. Whiche of alle foules fleeth hig̃hest/ ā in sig̃hte is sharpest. ā may se the ferthest. Soo seynt John spake and wrote higheste of the godhode/ and hadde more insig̃ht ā vnderstondynge in the godhede. than the other euāgelistes. Seint luke is peynted in the lykenesse of a calf or an oxe/ bicause that he spekith moost openly of the passion of cryste that was offryd vp to the fadre of heuen/ on the altre of the crosse on gode fryday/ as the oxe or the calf: was offryd on the aulter in the tēple. By the lawe/ for saluacion of the people/ which offrynge was tokenynge of cristes passion. And for that seint luke spekith moste openly of cristes passion. Whiche was betokned by the sacrifice of the oxe. Therfore he is paynted ā presentyd by the lykenes of an oxe. Seynt marke is peynted ī lyknesse of a lyon/ bicause that he spekith moost openly of cristes resurrection/ how he rose frō deth to lyf/ for whan the lyonesse hath whelpid they lye dede iij. dales ā iij. nightes tyl on the thirdde day/ the lyon their fader cometh ā maketh an hidous cry

ouir them. And anoon wᵗ the voice a crye they quyckne ā waken/ ā in maner ryse from deth to lyue. And for this skille is seint mark presented by the liknesse of a lyon. For he spake more openly of cristes resurrectōn. And therfore his gospel is rede on ester day. Also thou shalt vnderstonde þ Criste was god ā man/ ā preest ā kyng. Mathewe spake moost openly of his manhode/ and began att his manhode/ and therfore he is paynted in the lyknesse of a mā. Seint John spake moste of his godhode/ and began at his god hode. And therfore he is painted in the liknes of an egle as I said firste. Seynt luke spake mooste of his presthode/ and therfore he is paynted in the likenesse of an oxe or of a calf. For that was the principalle sacrifice that the prestes by the olde lawe offryd ī the temple. Seynt mark spake most of his kyngdome/ shewing hym kynge of alle thynge. And therfore he is paynted in the lyknesse of a lyon/ that is kynge of vnreasonable bestes. Diues. Why ben they so painted in four endes of the crosse. Pauper. In token that he þ died on the crosse is kynge of alle thynge. For the Egle is kyng of al foules. The lyon is kynge of alle wylde bestes vnreasonable.

The firste

The oxe is kynge of tame bestes/helplich to mankynde. Man is kinge of alle bestes & of al visible creatures/that were made for him But criste is kyng of al thynge visible and vnvysible. And in token therof the foure euangelistes been peynted aboute him on the crosse in dyuerse lyknes of iiii. diuerse kinges I kynd as foure kynges heraldes blasynge his armes/ & the grete batayl & victory that he did ayenst the fende/ for mankynde vpon the crosse/ Diues. Why be they paynted in houses in foure parties of the house. Pauper. For the same skylle and for deuociō & for knowlechynge of his high lordshyp that alle we haue of hī and ayenst tempestes and wycked spirytes that fle the euangelistes set I maner of a crosse/ and been ashamede and abasshed of the crosse/ and specially of Crystes passion. By the whiche they were alle disconfyt.

The x. chaptre

Diues. Why ben ymages hyd in Lenten from mānes sighte Pauper. In token. that whyle men ben in dedly syn they may nat se goddes face/ ne seyntes in heuyn And in tokenynge þ god & al the court of heuyn hyde their face from man & woman/ whyles they be in dedly synne/ tyl the tyme þ they wole amende them by sorowe of herte & shryfte & satisfaction. Diues why been they more hyd in lentē than in other tyme Pauper the tyme of Lente betokneth the tyme of Adams syn/ for the whiche we loste the sight of goddes face/ & god & the courte of heuen hydde their faces from mākynd vnto the tym of cristes passion. & in token therof in lyp. Whā holy churche begineth to make mynd of Adams synne/ he leuyth songes of myrthe/ as Gloria in excelsis. Te deū. & Alleluya For through the synne of adam/ our ioye was turned in sorowe & wo Diues. I holde it wele done to hyde ymages in Lenton to lette men from ydolatry. Nathelesse ymages of comon offrynge ben selden hyd in lenton/ for lettyng of lucre. Pauper. Seynt poul sayth that couetise and namely of prestes is cause of moche ydolatrye. Auaricia est ydolorum seruitus. Coloc. iii. c. For ne were couetise tho ymages shuld be sette as lytel by as other and as sone hiled and hyd Diues. I suppose þ seintes I erth were nat arayed so &ap with stone of syluer/ and wᵗ clothes of baudkyn

rynges & broches & other iewel-
les as ymages be nowe. And sutyme thou seydest þ by the feet is
vnderstonde mannes loue & his
affection. And therfore me thynketh that the feet so shode in syluer shewe that the loue & the affection of prestes is moche set in
golde & siluer & erthly couetyse
for suche richesses of clothynge
of the ymage is but a tollyng of
more offrynge & a token to the
lewde people/ where they shulde
offre and what/ for they had lyuer a broche or a rynge of syluer
or of golde than a peny or a half
peny/ though the broche or the
rynge be but of easy pryce. And
comonly they shoe none ymages
ne clothe them so richely/ but yf
they erne firste their shone & ther
clothes/ but if it be to tolle folk
to offrynge. Pauper. leue this
mater for it is odiouse to the coueitouse prestys þ wynne great
richesse by suche ymages. And
therfore let suche wordes passe
at this tyme and speke we of ʃt
what elles more to purpose.

The xi. chaptre.

Dives. Cryste saith in the
gospelle: Dñm deū tuū
adorabis. & ei soli seruies. Mt.
iiii. c. Thou shalte worship thy
lorde god & serue him alone. And
it is of the firste cōmaundment
as holy wrytte shewyth. Wele.
Deut. vi. c. Howe might I kepe this that I shulde no thinge
worshyppe ne serue but god. I
muste worshyp my kynge/ my
prelate/ my souerayne. & serue
them as myn astate axith/ and
do to them my dueties homage/
and felftie. & seint Poule saithe
Per caritatē seruite inuicem/ Ad
gala 5 c. Serue ye to god ech mā
other by charitie. And seint Petyr sayth: Serui subditi estote.
dñis ðris/ non tantum bonis et
modestis/ sed eciam discolis.
The seruauntes be ye subget to
your lordes/ nat only to the gode and the meke/ but also to tyrauntes. And in the same place
be byddeth vs worshyp alle mē
He biddyth vs also. drede oure
god & worshyppe oure kynge.
Pauper. As clerkes say ther is
ii. maner of seruice and of worshyp. One that longyth only to
god and to noo creature/ and is
cleppyd Latria. oñ latyne that is
to saye diuyne seruyce and dyui-
ne worshyp/ for it longith only.
to god A nother is a seruyce & a
worshyp comon/ to god & to creature resonable & intellectual þ
is to say to man womā & angel.
& it is cleppyd Dulia. oñ latyne:
The firste seruyce and worship
that is cleppde Latria. dyuyne.

The firste

seruice longith only to god And on this maner setupce spekyth Criste Whanne he sayth tho wordes Dominum deum tuum. &c. Thou shalte worshyp thy lorde god and serue him alone with diuyne seruyce/ and dyuyne worshyp. that is to say. Thou shalt do no Latriam. no diuyne worshyp ne diuyne seruyce to no creature. But only to god/ And therfore who so doth any diuyne seruyce that is cleppd Latria. to any creature to any ymage. or any fourme or figure. he doth ydolatry. For ydolum. on latyne is cleppd a fourme and an ymage. on englisshe. And therfore who so doth diuyne worshyp that is cleppd Latria. to any ymage he doth ydolatrye. Diues. What clepist thou propyrly latriam. diuyne worshyp and seruyce that longith only to god Paup. As sayth a grete clerke Antisidoren sis in summa sua. libro tercio. Latria is a prestacion & knowlecchyng of the high maiestye of god p he is souerayne godenesse. souereyne wysdome/ souerayne myghte. souerayne trouthe/ souerayn largenesse. shaper and sauer of al creatures. ende of euery thynge. & al that we haue we haue of him/ & without him we haue right nought. & noughte may haue ne do. Withouten him

we. ne none other creatur/ This knowlecchynge & prestacion is done on thre maners/ By hert By speche/ By dede By hert p we loue him as souerayne godenesse. & loue him as souerayn wisdom & souerayn trouth p may nat discepue/ ne be discepued/ & hope & truste i him as i souereyn might p may best help at nede/ & as souerayn largenesse & lorde p beste may yelde vs our mede/ & as souerayn sauyour moste merciful & moste redy to forgyue vs oure mysdede By mouth & spech this knowlecchynge & this seruyce is doon/ Whan we swere by his name worshipfully & truly i thing of charge. & fle ydel othes/ foul othes false othes/ & in our spech do worship to his holy name/ & swere nat by creatures. But only by his holy name For he saith in the gospelle. Reddes dno iuramenta tua. Thou shalt yelde thyn othes to thy lorde god & to no creature Also it is done By vowes makynge For it is nat lefull to make a vowe to any creature And therfore he sayth Reddes. dno vota tua. Thou shalte yelde thyne avowes to thy lord god. and to no creature. And the prophete saythe/ Douete et reddite domino deo vestro. Make ye vowes/ and yelde ye youre vowes to youre lord god

nat to the ymagis stock eo ne sto
nes Also it is done with prayer.
a prisynge of the mouth For we
muste praye him and pryse him
as souerayne might, souerayne
wysdome, souerayne godenesse
souerayne treuthe, as alle right
fulle and merciful. as shapper a
sauer of alle thing, a lorde of al
a souerayne helpe in euery nede.
And on this maner may we nat
praye ne prise any creature And
therfore they b make their pray
ers and ther prisinges bifore the
ymages, a say their Pater nost.
their Aue maria, and other pray
ers a prisynges, vsed comonly of
holy churche, or any suche other
if they do it to the ymage, a spe
ke to the ymage they doo open
ydolatrye And they be nat excu
syd alle if they vnderstonde nat
what they saye. For their sighte
a their other wyttes, a their yn
ner wyt also, shewyth wele that
ther owith no suche prayer pry
synge ne worshyp be done to no
suche ymages. For they may
nat here them, ne se them, ne help
them at nede.

The xii. chaptre

Also this ptestacion and
knowlechyng is done by
dede, as by offryuge, a sacrifice

making whiche longe only to
god. For what man offreth or
maketh sacrifice he knoulegith
him peuer of grace. a maker of
holynesse, sauyour a forgeuer of
synne, athis may no creature do
Also it is shewyd by tokenys of
the body, as by knelyng loutyng
lyftynge vp of hondes, by bun
chynge of the brest, whiche toke
nys may be do bothe to god and
to resonable creatures, but other
wise to god than to resonable cre
atures. For as saith a clerke Ri
cardus de media villa sup terciu
sentenci. dist. ix q̄ne Vltimī
whāne we knele to god, in þ we
knowlege that we may nat ston
de in vertue, in godenesse, nc in
wele but only by him, whāne we
fal al downe to grounde to god
we knowlege that but he helde
vs a kept vs, we shulde falle al
to noughte And whāne we hold
vp oure hōdes to hym, we know
lege that we may right noughte
do withouten hym, a that we be
al in his power, and that he may
do withouten vs what he wole,
a so we put vs only in his grace
Also by that we knowlege. that
al that we haue of any godenes
we take it of his honde, and of
his yifte. Whāne we bunche
oure brestys, we knowlege vs
gyltye arenste him in herte, and
in dede. And that we haue done.

The firste

moche synne/ Whiche only god knowyth For only he knowyth mannys herte and mānes wylle Also we bunche oure self on the Breest in token of sorowe of hert for oure nypsdedys/ and that we repente Us sore of our nypsdedes These toknes of reuerēce be do also to reasonable creatures/ as to angel/ man & womā/ But nat in this maner: For whānne we knele or loute. or fal downe to grounde/ or holde vp oure hondes to any creature/ we knowlege that ther is some souereinte & some vertue in him that we knele to/ wherby he may helpe vs. nat as principal helper/ but as secundary with the helpe of god And therfore these dedys of worshyp and reuerence shuld not be done to ymages/ stockes/ or stones/ ne to none suche other For they haue no suche vertue ne souerayntie aboue man ne womā. ne right nought may helpe them at nede/ ne themself neither So that these dedys of reuerence principally ought to be done to god. secundary to angel man or woman/ But on no wise to noon other vnreasonable creatures/ ne to none suche ymages And as sayth a grete clerke. Doctor hālies iu summa sua. To god men shulde knele with bothe the knees/in token that in him is al our

principalle helpe/ But to man only with the one knee. Soo leue frende ye shal vnderstonde that the worshyp which is clepid Latria. shalbe done only to god. The worship that is clepid Dulia. is comon bothe to god & mā For we shulde worship man woman and aungel. nat for theim self But principally for god/for that they ben made to goddes ymage For they be goddes seruātes and goddes mynistres. For ther is no lorde/ ne tyraūt/ ne prelate/ man ne woman so wicked But that he serupth god in some thynge. And alle though he be nowe wycked/ we woote neuir howe sone he shal amende hym. and be oure brother in blysse. as sayth seint Austyn vpon the sauter But to the fende shuld we do no worshyp/ for he is dampned withouten ende/ and ther is no hope of his saluacion.

The viii. chaptre

We shulde worship man & woman/for he is made to the lyknesse of god/ for his office/ for the worshyp of god/ & dispyse his syn And therfore sayth seynt petre. Omnes honorate. worshyp ye alle men and wymē Honore inuicem preuenientes. Be ye besy/ who soo may euery

Precepte:

man worſhip other Diues. me
netueyleth moche why men be
so besy to do the people worſhip
ymages Pauper. Couetyſe of
men of holy churche and leude
neſſe bothe of them and of the
people ben cauſe of ſuche ydola
trye. Diues. I haue herde ſay
that many grete clerkes holden
therwith & ſay that men ſhulde
worſhyppe ymages Paup.
worſhippe is a large word and
comon to diuyne worſhyp. and
ſerupce that is cleppde Latria.
and to worſhyppe that is cleppd
Dulia. Whiche longith propyr
ly to ſpeke only to reſonable cre
ature For as ſayth the philoſo
phre. quarto ethicor. Worſhyp
is mede of Bertue And it owith
nat to be done to any creature.
But that creature haue ſome go
denes of Bertue moral & of gra
ce or elles ſome office to lede &
brynge folke to moralle Bertue
Diues. Thanne to the ymage
ſtocke or ſtoner golde or ſyluer/
longith none ſuche Worſhyppe
For whanne it is ſo ſere and dry.
& worme eten/ it hath no Bertue
at alle/ But for to brenne ſoner'l
the fyre than a grene tree But
whanne it weyt vpon the erthe.
it hadde Bertue to wey & ſpryng
& to brynge forth grene leups &
floures to conforte of mannys
lyfe & fruyte, to helpe of man and

beeſt And yit wole no man wor
ſhip ſuche grene trees ne pcious
ſtones ne crops alle if they haf
grete Bertues and wonderfulle
for they haue no Bertue moral.
⸿ Moche more men ſhulde nat
Worſhyppe ſere drye trees/ that
haue no Bertue at alle/
Say forthe what thou wilte.
Pauper. Alſo worſhyp is cleppd Beneracion that ſtondith l
honeſt & ſiker heppnge/ honeſte
handlynge/ clene dighſtynge/ in
ſtondyng/ in ſyttynge/ in place
ſettyng And this maner of wor
ſhyp may be done & ought to be
done to euery holy thynge þ lon
gith to god. and holy church as
bothe chalyce Beſtment/ belles &
ymages. in aſmoche as they be
ournamentes of holy churche/
and the lewde mennys boke.
But this Worſhyp and Benera
cio is no ſeruice ne ſubiection of
hi þ doth it to the thyng þ he doth
it to/ but it ſhe wyth ſubiection/
& ſerupce of the thinges ſo wor-
ſhyppd to him that putteth it ſo
in worſhyp. ſo kepith it & ſo ſa-
uyth it And on this maner the
lawe clepith ymages Benerable
& Worſhypful/ for ther ſhuld no
man diſpyſe them ne defoul hē.
Brenne them ne breke them De
conſecrac. di/ iii. Denerabiles.
& for this maner of Beneracion.
and Worſhyp ſayth the lawe in

c ii

the same place/ ⁊ sūme boctou‍res/ that ymages boke or vest‍ment and chalice/ may be wor‍shypped with dulia. But they take that dulia. fulle largely/ ⁊ fulle vnpropirly/ For such wor‍shyp ⁊ veneracion/ is no seruice ne subieccion as I saide bifore. And propirly to speke dulia. is a worship þ longith only to god and to resonable creatures/ And principally and excellently/ to oure lady seint mary. and to the manhode of criste. whiche wor‍shyp is cleppd. ypdulia: propir‍ly said Also to the crosse that cri‍ste dyed vpon/ if that men had it as clerkes saye longith ypdu‍lia For of al thinges that want syf/ the cros of criste ow̄ith most to be worshippd/ and be in most veneracion and reuerence But that veneracione is cleppd ypdu‍lia. vnpropirly Also frende ther is worshyp that the subget doth to his souerayne/ knowlechyng hym his sourayne/ by worde or by token/ as by knelynge lou‍tyng ⁊ suche other/⁊ this maner worshhip is cleppd propirly ado‍racion Other worshyp that is cleppd honoracion/ ⁊ veneraci‍on is coūenpent bothe to the so‍uerayne ⁊ to the subget For a lord honoureth his seruaunt by yiftes/ by promocions in office. in dignitie/ Also a lorde wor‍

The friste

shyppeth a pore man whanne he settith him at his owne table or aboue other that been of higher degree thanne he/ and yit adou‍reth he him nat/ ne doth him the worshyp of adoracion/ Nathe‍lesse adoracion is taken sūtyme fulle vnpropirly/ for comon ho‍noracion and veneracion/ And for asmoche as al these maners of worshyp so diuerse ben clepid with one name of worship in en‍glisshe tunge. ⁊ ofte the latyne. of worshhyp is taken and vsed. vnpropirly and to comonly. Therfore men fal in moch dout and errour in redyng ⁊ nat wele vnderstonde what they rede

The yiiii. chaptre.

Dives. This distinccion. and declaracion of wor‍shyppynge howe it is taken/ and vsed in diuerse maner/⁊ howe it is cleppd with one name in en‍glisshe/ hath auoided many argu‍mentes and scruples which I thoughte to haue made apenste the/ I am oute of doute. I can aunswere therto my self by thy declaracion/ But ii. thinges as me thynketh thou saidest nat al trouthe Pauper. Whiche be tho Diues. Thou seydest that mē shulde nat offre but only to god Ne knele on bothe knees but only to god. And we se at þe ꝫ mē offre to the preest i the church a knele on both kneis to the pste i sheriste. Pauper. Men offre nat the preeste but only to god. as I saide firste by the hedes of the pste. For the preest is goddes mynistre ordeynede to resceyue thinges þ been offryd to god/ as tithes & deuociōs/ & lyue therby honestly & dispende the remenāt to nedy folke/ & to worshyp of god & helpe of holy churche. Ne men knele nat on ꝫ maner/ to the pste/ but to god bifore the preest. for the reuerence of god & of the sacramētes of holy church But whan man kneliþ to tem poral lordes plates or pstes/ or any other psone/ for reuerēce of his psoone or of his dignyte/ he shuld knele only wᵗ thone knee But as saith seynt Austyn de ciuitate dei. li°. p°. c. ß. By flatery and outcolwnesse of the peo ple & ambicion of the souereyns many worshyppes þ longed sū tyme to god alone/ ben nowe ß sed in the worshippyng of synful man & woman. And though it be do to man or woman for the worship of god as I saide firste it is suffrable: The yß chapt

Jues. Thurification.
Of encensyng was by olde tyme an high diuyne worshyp. And many seyntes were putt to the deth for they wolde nat en cense ymages/stockes ne stones But nowe clerkes encense yma ges & other/ preestes & clerkes & selwde people also. And so as me thynke they do ydolatrie. Pauper. In euery lawe thurificaciō & encensyng hath been an highe dyuyne worship. þ ought nat to be done to any creature by wey of offrynge. Neuirtheles it may be done on ii/ maners. Firste by weye of offrynge wᵗ couenient tokynynge & so it may nat be do to any creature. For on this ma ner it owiþ nat to be done butt only of a preeste/ & at any auter. halowed or with a supaltare ha lowed/ so þ prestes lefuly may sey there their masse. For by the encensour is vnderstonde man nys herte/ by the encēse holy py er/ by the fyre charitie. And so su the encensyng and thurificaciō betokneth that right as the pste offriþ vp in the encensoure en cense. swete smellyng by hete of the fyre. So the preest & the peo ple by the preest offre vp her her tes to god and her prayers quyc ned by the fyre of charite. And pray that their bedes and theire praiers and deuociones may be plesaunte to him for that enbles charite that he shewyd to man kynde/ whanne he dyed for vs alle vpon the crosse/ whiche cha

c iii

The friste

ritye is presentyde in the sacrament of the autre. For alle the masse syngyng is a special mynde makynge of cristes passion/ And right as Cryst was meane in his passion bitwene god and mankynde/ so is the preest i his messe saynge/ and sacrifice makynge and offrynge and encensynge/ meane bitwene god and the people. And therfore only a preest shulde encense at the autre/ and with halowed encense/ and with holy prayer sayng on this wyse for him selfe & for the people. Dirigatur oratio mea sicut incensū in conspectu tuo. Lorde make my prayer go right vp in thy sighte as encense Also thurificacion may be done only for sterpng to deuocion & for to kenynge And so it may be done to the clergie and to the people. in token that as the encense vp hete of the fyre smellith swete/ & styeth vp to heuen warde/ Soo shulde they lyft vp their hertes/ with deuocion/ and make their prayers in charite y they might be plesaunte to god/ and wende vp to god. For but the preest and the peple be in charite/ elles their prayer pleasith nat god/ ne gothe nat vp to god as it shuld elles do. & therfore is no man wor thy to be encensed but if he be in charite And whan the clergye in the quere or the people is encensed/ they shulde sowte sowe/ for reuerēce of god/ and take it nat as for worshyp done hem but as sterpnge to deuocion/ & as a token/ what deuocion they shuld shewe to god/ & by soutyng shewe sowenesse of deuocion that sterith them to For withoute deuocion and sowenesse of hert our prayer goth nat vp to god But as saith the wiseman The prayer of him that soweth him in his prayer thirlith the cloudes The mysſalle and the gospel is encēsed in token that the praiers writen therin profit litel or noughe But if they be made with deuocion and i charite And ther shuld no man preche the gospel. Butt with deuocion and for charitye & alle his spede and alle his profyte referre vp to god/ and alle his prayers put in his wylle At buryinge men encense the dede bodies/ in token that he dyed in charitye. & in his dyenge he had his hert vp to god/ by hope feith charite & deuocion/ for elles he is nat worthy to be buryed in cristen buryelles. Also in token/ he shalle quychen ayen and ryse vp from deth to lyf at the dome and wende vp to heuene for his charite whiche he had by his lyf as the encense stieth vp by the hete of the fyre/ And for the same

60

precepte.

ſcryſly is the graue encenſed ī to ken that he ſhalſe awake and ryſe from deth to lyf Alſo the body ī the graue ben encēſed/ in tokē that it is pleſaunt to god þ holy churche pray for hym. But this maner of encenſyng done to the clergye to the people & to the dede bodies to the graue ſhulde be done with encens nat halowed ne bliſſed. for it is noon offryng And as touchynge encenſynge. done in the preſence of ymages. as it ſempth to me it is nat done propirly to the ymages/ But bifore the ymages in diuerſe ſignificaciones or tokynynges/ For whāne encēſyng is done bifore a peinted ymage þ repreſentith criſte whiche is very god & man. It ſempth to me that the encēſyng ſignifieth þ al deuocion & charitable prayer which is betokned by encence/ ſhulde principally. ſtye up to god/ & whā encēſyng is done bifore any ymage of our lady or of other ſeyntes/ it may ſignifye that the prayers of ſeintes which pray for us wrecches in erthe ſtye up by their grete charite to the maieſty of god.

Diues. Sith encenſyng is nat done to the peple by wey of worſhyppyng/ why encence they firſt the ſouereynes more thanne the ſubgettys. Paup. For in alle thinge muſt be kept ordre in do

ynge And alſo in token ꝑ as they ben principal in ſtate & dignite. ſo ſhulde they be principal in deuocion & charite/ and yeue other gode enſample.
The .yvi. chaptre.
Diues. Why worſhyp we god and pray to him more in the eſt than into the weſte. ſouthe and northe. Pauper. Eeſt and weſt ſouth and north and ouir al it is leſul and medeful to worſhyp god/ as him þ is ouir al/ lorde of al thynge. But for to drawe criſtē peple to one maner doynge/ & to ſle difformite. Therfore holy churche hath ordeyned þ men ſhulde in chirche & other places if it may be wele done/ worſhyp god pray him & pryſe him in the eeſt/ as the lawe ſhewith wele/ Diſtinct ꝑt. eccleſiaſtica. And that for diuers ſkyples Firſte for criſt upon the croſſe dyed into the weſt/ & therfore in oure prayer we ſhuld turne us ito the eeſt/ to ſee how criſt for us henge upon the tree/ & ſo to haue an ye to his paſſion/ & worſhyp him þ dyed for us alle. Upon the tree Alſo to ſette the peple to ſue the iewys in maner of worſhyppyng For all goddes or denaunce they worſhypped weſtwarde in token þ their lawe and their maner worſhippyng ī their cerymonies ſhulde ſone paſſe &

c iiii

The friste

go downe & make an ede as the day endith & passith a way into the west And also in token þ for any worshyp or pryspnge or pyer þ they dyd/ yit they shulde go downe to hel/ tyl the newe lawe came Whan criste dyed for vs al And for the same skylle criste di ed west warde/and in his dyeng saide. Consumatum est. That is to say It is endyd/ For in his deth the olde testament endyd & wente downe as the sonne And the day goth downe in the west And therfore we cristë peple wor ship into the Eest/ By techynge of the holy goost/ in token þ our lawe shal sprynge & sprede as the day climpng of the sonne riseth & sprpngeth oute of the eest. and as alle the sterres ben moste bri ghte in the est. & whan they wende into the west alle they begynne to dymme & derk/ so was tholde lawe ful dymme & ful derk/ But the newe lawe is open brighte & clere Also we worshypp Cryste most in the eest for he was most dispispd in the Eest whanne on gode friday he heng on the crosse turned into the weste/ whan the iewes stode bifore him & passide bifore him w' many scornes & di spytouse wordes/ w' mowes & many a iape they seyde. vath q destruis templū dei: Cprut for the þ distroyest goddes temple.

And for he was moost dispysed into the Eest of the iewes & he: then peple/ Therfore cristen pe ple therayenst worshyp hī most into the eest And for he was most dispysed for vs on gode frydaye Therfore we worship him most on gode fridaye And on this ma ner as moche as we may/ al his dispyte we turne to worshyp of him Also we worship god in the eest in token bright as the sonne ryseth vp in the eest/ so we byle ue that criste rose vp from dethe to lyf/ and in that we worshypt him as him that rose from dethe to lyf/ & shal lyue withoutē ende Also in token that we longe to come ayen to the blisse of para dyse þ we loste in the eest/ & pray god þ we may w' his mercy/ co me ayen therto. Diues. These skylles ben gode But why wer thanne the yp s. men blamed of god for they w' orshippd estward at the risyng of the sonne/ as we fynde. ezechielis. viii.c. Pau per Mat for they worshiped god estwarde For danyel & many o ther worshypped god Estwarde. weste.. southe/ & northe/ as he is worthy to be worshypped ouir al A solis ortu vsq; ad occasū lau dabile nomē dn̄i. From the sōne rysynge vnto the goyng downe goddes name is prisable & wor shipful But they were blamed for they worshypped the sonne in his rysynge/ & dyd diuyne worship therto in dispyte of goddes temple/ & of goddes lawe as many foles yit do these daies worshippynge the sonne in his rispyng & the newe mone in his firste shewynge. Diues. They worship him y made the sonne & the mone. Pauper. If they do so they do wele/ But I drede nat al do soo And as saith a greate clerke Leo papa i a sermone/ for asmoche as it hath a lykenesse of ydolatry & custome of hethen peple. men shulde abstepne them therfro For the people is ful moche enclyned to foly & to ydolatrye.

The xvii. chaptre.

Diues. That is soth For these daies men doo worshyp to sonne/mone/ & sterres/ y for to worshyppe the sterres and the planetes & the crafte of astronomye. they wole put oute god of his maiestye. out of his kingdome & his lordship/ & out of his fredome/ & make him more bonde to sterres/ than euir was any kynge or any lorde/ or any man ypon erth They wole be of goddes pryue counseyl/ wyl god nyl god/ & rule his domes his dedys his werkes/ & al by their wyttes & by the course of the planetes in somoche y as they say ther shall no man ne woman be hole ne seke/ foule ne faire/ riche ne pore/ wyse ne fole, gode ne wycked. But by the worchynge of the bodies aboue & by their wyttes soo y they can tel it afore Ther shal falle no myschepf ne welthe neither to persone ne to comunyte/ But by her wyttes & by the cours of the planetes None hungre no rayne ne tempeste. no sekenesse no warre shal falle But by theire wyttes & by the worchyng of the bodies aboue For as they saye/ the bodies aboue rule alle thing here bynethe And thus they wol make god more thralle & of lesse power than any kynge or lorde ypon erthe. For why oure liege lorde the kinge god saue his lyf hath power & fredome of a page to make a yoman/ of a yoman a gentylman/ of a gentylman a knyght/ of a pore man a greate lorde/ Without leue or helpe of the planetes And if a man trespasse ayest him & be taken with treasone/ he is of power to do hi to be hanged & drawe/ & to take from him & his heires the heritage & make him ful pore And he is of power to make his true liegeman riche though he be right pore This fredome and this power hathe oure liege lorde/ oure kyng Where so the planetes ben or in what signe/ i what respect or in what costellacion or con-
c⸗v

The fristė

iuction our kyng may do al this
& are the planetes no leue The i
may nat let him Ne al the astro
nomoures wᵗ al their calculaciō
though they watch & stare/ after
the sterres/ tyl they lese their he=
des may nat let him/ ne saue oo
mannes lyf y the kinge wol haf
dede Moche more thā the king
of heuyn y made sonne & mone/
& sterres & al thing of noughte &
ruleth gydeth & weldith al thing
at his wyl may make riche and
pore/ faire & foule/ hole & seke/
wyse and fole/ gode or wyched
whom he lyketh wᶜouten helpe.
of the planetis And if any psone
or cōmunyte trespas ayenst him
he may chastise him by hungre/
by moreyne/ by sekenesse/ by tē=
pest/ by swerd. by pouṫe. by losse
of catel & what wyse he wole/ &
he may rewarde his true seruan
tes as hym liketh/ bothe in this
world & i the other world ayıng
the planetes no leue/ ne coūseyl
of astronomours The yᵉViii c.

Þ Auper. As we fynd i tho/
ly wrytte Geñ. i. c. At the
begynnyng of the worlde whan
god made al thinge of noughte
yᵉ iiii. day he made sōne & mone
& sterres & set hem i the firmamēt
to yeue light to the creatures he
re byneth/ y the sonne principal/
ly shulde shyne & yeue lighte by
day/ mone and sterres by night.

More ouir as saith the boke he
made them & ordeyned them for
to yue the day from the nyght/ &
they shulde be in tokenys/ & ty=
mes daies & yeres. y by the toke
nys of yᵉ bodies aboue mē shuld
knowe the day from the nighte
& one day from anothėr/ & wytt
what day it were/ & what tyme
of the day/ what nighte & what
tym of the night/ what yere and
what tyme of the yere/ what mo
neth & what tyme of the moneth
Also god ordeyned them & made
them y by the tokenes & by the bo
dies aboue. men shulde knowe
whan it were tyme to slepe & ty
me to wake/ tyme to trauayl/ &
tyme to rest/ tyme to halowe/ &
tyme to labour/ tyme to ete and
tyme to faste. tyme to sette & to
sowe: tyme to ere tyme to repe
to molwe And therfore salomon
saithe Ecclesiastices iii. c. y alle
thinge hath his tyme/ & al thing
vndre heuyne passith alway by
space of tyme. And so god made
thᵉ firmament aboue wᵗ brighṫ
bodies y been therin to serue mā
kynde. & other creatures also of
light & tyme Of lighte as a lan
terne that may nat be quenchyd
Of tyme as an orloge that may
nat fayle God made hem to ser
ue man/ nat man to serue them
He made them for man. nat mā
for hem He made hem nat to go

uerne man/ But he haue man. ⁊ woman wytter discrecion to go uerne them selue w'his grace by the light ⁊ wissyng of tyme/why che he hath of the bodies aboue/ that by their light they may see to worche. ⁊ by theire stirynge ⁊ their cours they may wyt whan it is tyme to worche And therfo re saith the lawe xx Di. ḥ. B. Nō licet. in glosa. That the bodies aboue ben tokenes ⁊ nat causes of thinges here bynethe And as a lampe or an orloge ben neces sary to religious by nyght wher by they may ryse and rule them self/ in goddes seruyce/soo serue the bodies aboue to makynde þ we may haue of them bodily li ghte And by their mouyng kno we oure tyme to serue oure god eche man ⁊ woman in his degre And as the lampe ⁊ the orloge i the dortoure rule nat the religi ouse But the religiouse rule hem by the lampe and by the orloge/ ⁊ in cites and townes men rule them by the cloke/⁊ yit propirly to speke/ the cloche ruleth natt them But a man ruleth the clock Right so mā ⁊ womā/ beest and byrde ⁊ other creatures rule hem self by the bodies aboue/⁊ the bo dies aboue rule nat theym And therfore they shuld nat be clepid gouernoures of this worlde/for

they gouerne nat this worlde. They be nought elles but istru mentes of goddes gouernaunce For it farith by god ⁊ the bodi es aboue/ as it dothe by the smy the ⁊ his gryndyng stone/by the wright ⁊ his axe: by the orloger and his orloge. Diues. I pray the shewe me wele this Pauper Thou seest at iye that whanne the smyth grindeth a knyf or an axe or a swerde on his stone/ the stone dothe nought but goth a boute in one course. And as the smyth that sytteth aboue wole dispose and holde/ so gryndeth the stone.   If he wole grynde sharpe it shal grynde sharpe If he wole grynde blunte and play ne/it shalle grynde blunt ⁊ play ne Right as he wol that it gryn de. so it gryndeth. If he take a waye the knyf axe or swerde the stone gryndeth right nought/ ⁊ yit it goth about the same cours as it dyd bifore/Right so it is of god and the bodies aboue. For the planetes ⁊ the bodies aboue gone alway about in one cours certeyne/⁋ whiche god ordeyned theym at the begynnynge of the worlde/whiche course they shal kepe vnto the dome.   And as god wole þ they worche/ soo they shalle worche If god wole þ they grynd sharpe/ ⁊ cause mo

The firste

reyne seƂznes a tēpestes hungre a werze a suche other they shalle do so. If he wole þ they grynde playne a smothe a cause helthe of body, faire wedyr a holsome, plentie of corne a vitayles, pees a rest, they shal do so. Righte as god wole þ they worche soo they shal worche. So þ god may doo with the planetes what he wole a he may do withoute the planetes what he wole. In what signe in what cōstellacion, cōiūction, or resp̄c þ they be, they be alway redy to fulfyl the wyl of god.

Dives. Sithen god maye do with the bodies aboue what he wole a whan he wole, a sithen god is so fre in his doyng, a nat artid by the planetes ne by none other creature, how shulde any man knowe goddes domes by the course of the planetes, or deme therby, or telle what god wyl do in tyme comynge, or by upne of thinges þ be to come.

Paup. Thou mayste nat kno/we by the axe what the wrighte wole worche ne whan. Ne thou mayst nat knowe by the orloge what tyme the orloger wole set it ne knowe the orlogers wylle. Ne thou maist nat knowe by the gryndstone what the smyth wol grynde, ne what maner ne whā.

Dives. It is soth. Pauper. No more may we knowe by the bo/dies aboue ne by the cours of ye planetes what god wol do, ne what he wole ordeyne of mā or of woman, or of any coniunyte sonde, realme, cuntre or cite, for the planetes a the bodies aboue ben nought elles but goddes in strumētes, a the course of the planetes is nat chaungeable ne va/riable, but it is put ī certeyn me upnge and styrynge whiche they maye natt flee ne chaunge, for they haue no fre election ī theire doynge. But god is souereyn iu/ge moste rightful, moste merci/ful moste free, to punysshe a to spare. For he is moste of mighte a no thinge may him withstōde a therfore his domes a his wer/kes be nat nedyd ne artid by the planetes, but aft þ mē chaunge her lyuyng so chāgith he his do/mes, to punysshe or spare to wel or to wo, to heuyn or to helle. He demyd the sinful cite of nynyue, bicause of synne to be distroyed within xl. daies, but whan they repētyd hem a amēdyd theym a cryde after mercy, he chāged his dome a sparyd the cyte, a distroi/ed it nat as tellith Jonas the p̄/phete, a yit the planetes chāgyd nat her cours for non amēdmēt of the peple. Also we fynd i holy wryt the fourth boke of kinges þ god sende the p̄phete Isaie to the kig ezechie whā he had sined

Precepte.

and badde hym make his testa‍ment for he shulde dye a no len‍gre lyue Anone the kinge repen‍tyd him/ a wepte ful sore a ayed mercy/ And anon god badde the pphete Isaie þ yit was i the hin‍ges halle to wende ayen to the kinge a say to him þ god had ac‍cepted his repentaunce/ a herde his prayer/ a þ he shulde nat dye than/ But he shuld lyue yv. yere lengre. Lo leue frende how sone the dome of god was chaunged al to mercy And though the pla‍netes yit þ tyme kept forth their course. they chaugyd nat for al the kinges weppynge Diues. Anone aft the son chaungyd his cours a turnyd ayen ito the eest a began a newe day Pauper. The turnyng ayen of the sonne was natt cause of the mercye of god. ne of chaugynge of his do‍mes/ for god chaugyd his dome bifore or the sonne turnyd ayen So the turnyng ayen of the son was noughte elles/ But a token of mercy to the kynge ezechie/ a to alle synful wrecches þ wolde amede hem For right as the son chaugd his course after the re‍pentauce of the kynge Right so god chaugith his sentence anon as man or woman repētith him of his syn/ a is in wyl to amede him).   Therfore saith the lawe De penitenc. di. i. sufficiat No

uit deus mutare sentenciam/ si tu nouis emēdare delictū: God can chaunge his sentence a his dome anone as thou canst ame‍de thy trespasse Also it was a to‍ken to the kyng þ goddes bihest to him shulde be fulfylled Butt alle the astronomours that euir were coude nat telle bifore of þ wounderful token in the sonne. For it was al ayenst the comon course of kynde/ a þ and suche o‍ther shewe wele that god is nat ruled by the course of the plane‍tes/ But that god ruleth the pla‍netes and nat the planetes him/ ne his domes ne his werkes. But god ruleth demeth and go‍uerneth al mankynde psone a co‍munyte after that they deserue/ and as him thynketh moost spe‍deful to his worshyp a to the co‍mon proufyt of his Realme/ in heuen in erthe a in helle/ whose domes and ordenauce passe ma‍nes wyt And therfore seint poul sayth. Quis cognouit sensū dñi aut quis consiliarius eius fuit/ who saith he hath knowe y wyt of god/ or who was his counse‍loure. Forsothe nat the astrono‍mīures ne wycches/ for they ben fooles of alle foles/ and put fer thelte oute of goddes counseyl/ as folke that god moste hatyth Seint poule sayth/ þ the domes of god ben incōphēsible/ no mā

The firste

may knowe them ſe ele/ no man may traſe his weyes ℭho been his wonderful domes/ they ben ſo medled with mercy ⁊ rightfulneſſe þ they paſſe mannes wytte ℭherfore the prophete Dauyd ſayth. Vniuerſe vie dñi mia et Veritas: Alle the weyes of the lorde been mercy and treuthe. Judicia dñi abiſſus multa. The domes of god been a moch depneſſe/ ye ſo depe that no mānes wytte may ſehe to the depeneſſe/ ne knowe wele the cauſe. ne ſtryſſe of his wonderfulle domes And therfore ſuche aſtronomoures ⁊ wycches that enterinet them ſo high of goddes domes/ ⁊ wonderful werkes ⁊ preſume to diuyne of thynges that been to come and make theym wyſe/ as if they were goddes felowes. and knewe alle his preuy counſeyl/ they ben foles of alle foles. Viues. Therfore clerkes ſaye. that they may no thynge tel for certayne But they may tel wher to may or Woman or comunyte is encleued by the Worchyng of the Bodies aboue Neuirtheleſſe as they ſaye/ man and woman may by Vertue outrcome the planetes/ and ſoo euery wyſe man is lorde and maiſter of the planetes And therfore ptolomeus the greate aſtronomoure ſaith. Dū Sir ſapiens dñabitur aſtris.

The .xx. chaptre.

Alſo as they ſay by aſtronompe they may knowe whan men ben iclyned to werre or to peas And whan by comon courſe of kynde ſhulde falle morepn/ hungre/ tempeſt/ drought and ſuch other. But as they ſay one holy prayer may chaūgye euery dele And though it fal nat in one cūtre it falluth in an other cuntre. Pauper. Sithen they can nat telle for certeyne/ what ſhalle bifalle but al in doute/ ⁊ their ſalues ⁊ their domes maye ſo l̄ghtly be chaūgyd ⁊ brought to nought/ it is a greate folye to ſette any truſt to their tales For ſo may euery fole telle what he wole and excuſe euery leſynge. This maner of ſpech is nought elles but a mayntenynge of leſynges and of faytrye and of bydynge of folye and a ſynful excuſacion of ſynne/ ⁊ a nett to cache w‘ womānes ſoul. ⁊ a ſtrēge to drawe men to helle/ ⁊ to drawe mānes hert his loue his truſt from god They wolde fayne be holde wyſe ⁊ nye of goddes coūſeyl But they wote nat howe for they be founden ſo falſe. Ꝙe ſhalle vnderſtonde leue frende. that ther is but one ſonne ⁊ one mone/ and other fyue planetes/ Saturne Jubiter Mars Venꝰ and Mercury. Whiche w‘ other.

sterres gone aboute alle ertħ wᵗ the firmament euery day naturel/ ⁊ so passe alle the londes/ alle realmes/ psones: al ertħe al waters/ al a pte in xxiiii. oures. that is clepid day natural/from sōne ryse to sonne ryse/ from none to none And sithen they passe alle londes ⁊ al psones so euenly/ ⁊ make no more duellyng ouir one than an other Why shuld they more enclyne one lode than another/ or one psone more than another to vice/ or to vertue/ to warre or to peas/ Diues. For some ostellacion or some respect in her passinge falliþ vpon one londe more than a nother. And as folk ben borne vndre diuers constellacions or coniunctiones dyuerse respectes in dyuerse signes ⁊ vndre diuerse planetes/ so ben they enclyned in diuerse maner ⁊ to diuerse thinges; vice or vertue/ werre or pees/ belthe or sekenes/ pouerte or richesse and suche other. Pauper. Whanne the kinges sone is borne/ in the same tyme in the same costellacōn respect planete ⁊ syne/is the bondemannes sone borne. And yit haue they nat boþ one inclinacion/ ne one disposicion For the kinges sonne is disposed by his heritage to be king after his fader The bonde manys sonne.

is disposed by his birthe/ to be a bonde man alle his lyf as his faders haue been bifore him hundryd yeres/ ⁊ no planete mighte auoide their bondage/ne fro the kinges theire dignyte. In the same tyme and in the same constellacion ⁊ vndre the same planete and signe that one childe is borne been many borne ⁊ yit haue they nat alle euyn inclinacion ne euyn disposicion For some of them ben enclyned to godenesse and sūme to wyckednes sūme to sekenesse/ and sūme to helthe/ Sūme been fulle angry and sūme be nat soo. Sūme be wyse/ sūme be foles/ sūme foule some faire sūme riche some pore sūme shupnge longe/ sūme byfulle sone/ Esau and Iacob hadde boþe oone fadre and one modre Isaac and rebecca. Boþe were bigoten at ones/ as saythe seynt Austyn/ and boþe borne at ones/ and yit were they noo thynge lyke For Iacob was a gode man/ esau a shrewe Iacob was loued of god Esau was hatyd for his wyckednesse/ Iacob was smothe of body with lytel here. Esau fulle of here as a beest Iacob was a true symple man Esau a rauenoure/ and a maliciouse shrewe. Iacob was peasible/ Esau a saytoure a baratoure. Soo thou myghte wele se that diuerse inclinacion of man & woman stondeth nat in the planetes ne in the tyme of the byrthe.

The xxi. chaptre.

Dives. What elles may be cause of suche dyuerse inclynaciones. Pauper. For a damys/ syn & original syn b we be alle conceyued in we ben alle iclyned to synne And therfore god saith. Gen. viii. That the wytte & thought of mannes hert is iclyned to euyl fro his pouth. Sensus et cogitacio cordis humani in malum prona sunt/ ab adolescencia sua. And therfore salomon saith. Prouerbi. xx. c. That no man may saye. I am pure and clene withoute synne. Neuirtheles al be nat enclyned alyke moche to synne ne to sekenes/ but some more some lesse/ & b for many diuers causes Sultyme for wycked suffraunce b chyldren be nat chastised in her pouthe. For as salamon saith Prouerbi. xxix. c. The childe b is suffryd to haue his wyl shal shame his modre & al his kynne/ Sultyme for wycked company b they been in/ & wycked example of their elders & mys informacion/ Sultyme for mys vse in pouthe

For salomon saith. puerbi. xxii. b a man in his elde goth nat lyghtly fro the wey of his pouthe. Dives. And yit it is a comon puerbe. yonge seint olde deuyl. Paup. It is a synful puerb to drawe men to synne fro vertue. fro god to the feende/ For holy wrytte saith. Bonū e hoī cū portauerit iugū dñi ab adolescēcia sua. Tren. iii. c. It is ful gode. saith he to a mā whāne he hath borne the yok of oure lord from his pouthe/ And as a poete saith Quod noua testa capit inuetera ta sapit. Whiche as the potte or the vessel taketh whan it is new such it sauoureth whan it is old And therfore in holy wryt seynt John baptist/ toby. ieremye/ sā pson/ samuel/ & many other ben prised for their holynes in theire pouthe For comōly they b been gode & loue god & godenesse in her pouthe they make a fulle gode ende/ al if for a tyme they fal in synne & ben ful peyne God suffreth them to fal for a tyme for they shulde elles be to proude of their godenesse/ & haue disdeyne of other synful wreches Also sū tyme one is inclyned to one syn more than a nother/ for he was conceyued and begoten in more syn thāne a nother/ al if he were begote & borne in wedloche For the man & the wif may synne to

Precepte.

gyder fulle greuously, either by mysusyf of their bodies, or by intemporance if they passe maner and mesure, or if they comen to gydore in vntyme, as in the tyme of seeknesse, or in holy tyme withouten drede or reuerēce of the tyme: ne wose nat spare for the tyme. Natheleesse the synne is in the ayer nat in the yelder. Also they may synne by wicked intencion, as if they doo it for a wycked ende, or only to fulfyl the luste of the flesshe, nat to fle fornicacion. ne to yelde the dett of their body, ne to bryng forth children to the worshyp of god. But only take hede of her owne luste. Also if they coueite children nat to the worsshyp of god, but for the world to be grete, and to make their children grete in this worlde. Also men ben enclyned to synne on entore thā an other by excesse of meete and drynke. By mysheppyng of his fyue witt es. And for these same causes one is Iclyned to bodily seknes. more than a nother. For syn oft tyme is cause of bodily seknesse. Also by mysdietynge of the modre whyle she is with child, or by mys disposicion of the fadre, or of the modre, or of both. Whāne the childe is bigotē, or by mysseppyng of the childe in the youthe. For children & youth wose assay

a handle welnigh al thing, And so oftyme they ete & drynke & receyue inwarde moche vnthrifty thynge & enuenym her self & but te themself in many wyse & but the gode aungel kept hem they shuld perisshe Also god smyteth hem w' seknesse of mysscheif Sū tyme for the faders synne, & the modres, for they loue theym to moche, & wose go to helle to make hem rich & grete in this worlde Sūtyme he smyteth them with sekenes to shewe his might & myracle, as we fynde in the gospel of seynt Johny .ix.c. of him that was borne blynde & the might of god might be shewyd in hym in yeuyng him sight Otber causes ther ben ful fele whiche passe mānes wytte. for we may natt knowe alle goddes domes. Ne these causes here assigned be nat alwaye generalle. For sūtyme a fulle gode man hath a ful shrewyd child, sūme gode sūme bad And sūtyme a fulle wycked mā hath a fulle gode childe. For if the children folowed alway the fader & the modre, in godenesse, or in wyckednesse, alle the godenesse shulde be arettyd to the fadre and to the modre and nat to god. And they shuld be proude, both fadre, modre & the child & compne to gidre flesshly to mo che And i the same maner al the

71

shrewidnesse shulde be arettyd to the fadre and modre al if it come on other bihalf/ and shulde they be euir sory. and falle in dispeyr and nat wyl yelde to them to goddre the dette of their body And therfore god medlyth so one with an other/ & so modifieth his domes that the gode shulde nat presume of himself ne be to proude/ but thanke god of alle. ne the wycked be to sory and so fal i dispair/ but truste in god þ so of the wycked makith the gode and of the unclene makethe the clene

The xxli chaptre

Iues. They say that as children be borne under diuerse synes/ so ben they enclyned and disposed to diuerse craftes & diuerse states If he be borne under some signe they say he shalbe a fisher/ & undre some a monpour/ & undre some a clerk undre some a man of armes.
Pauper. Many cuntries know no monpours ne money neither

And many cuntries alyf haue money/ yit they haue no monyoures For in a ful grete realme of syxe hundred myle on length & it. hundryd of brede be no monyoures but in one place assigned by the kynge. nat by the sig

nes ne by the bodies aboue The kinge assigneth bothe the place and theym that shalle make the money/ nat the bodies aboue And if any wigght make money but tho that the kynge hath ordeyned/ he shalle be slayne as a traytoure. the signes ne the planetes shal nat saue his lyf: And they that be borne nygh the see. or nigh some grete water/ yeue them to fisshynge and their chyldren also. nat for the synes that they be borne in/ but for mooste oportunyte of their lyuynge. Whiche they haue by the water: that is so nygh. They that ben borne fer from the see yeue hem to tylthe of the londe. Sumtyme to clothe makinge if ther be plety of wolle Sume been shepherdes/ some monyours/ some byndoures. some of other craftis as the cuntree axith/ nat aftre the signes ne the bodies aboue. Whanne a man hath many children he putteth thym to dyuers craftes to gete her lyuynge Men of armes put their children to armes And comonly euery man þ can oughte or hath oughte wher by he may lyue/ he puttith some of his children in the same degre to gete her leuyng. And thou maiste wele se that suche diuersitye in crafte. in lyuynge stondith more in the childes fadre &

his frendes that ordeyned so for him than it doth in the signes or in the planetes For if they shuld abyde the ordenance of the planetes they shuld dye for hungre for they teche hem right nought ne ordeyne more for one thanne for another. Diues. Sith such iclinacion stodith lytel or nought in the planetes/What is that destenye that men speke so moche of/ And as they say al thing falleth to man & womā by destenye.

The xxiii chaptre

Pauper. Foles speke as foles. For as sayth seynt Gregory in his omely of the epiphanye ther is no suche destyne Absit a cordibus fidelium Vt aliquid esse fatum dicant. God forbede saith he that any cristen man or woman/ shulde byleue/ or say that ther were any destyne But god sayth he that made mannes lyf of nought/ he ruleth & gouerneth mannys lyf & womannes after that they deserue/ and as his rightwysnesse/ & his mercy axith And man sayth he/ was nat made for y sterres/ But the sterres were made for man. Diues. The gospel is ayenste the For we fynde in the gospel/ that anoon as criste was borne. of the mayden/ his sterre apperyd in the Eest/ in token þ eche man & woman is borne vndre a certeyn sterre/ & vndre a certeyn constellacion Whiche is cleppyd his destyne. for alle his spyvng a st folowyng is gouerned ther by/ as sayen these astronomoutes. Paup. To mayntene foly they say many folies & ben natt asshamed to lye. For that sterre hadde no maistrye ne lordshyppe vpon that blessyd child But the childe was maister and lorde of that sterre The sterre gouernyd nat the childe/ but the childe gouernyd the sterre. The childe sought nat the sterre/ But y stet the childe The childe serued nat the sterre/ but the sterre seruyd the child/ & dyd him ful high worshyp & fulle wonderfnl seruyce/ And therfore it was cleppyde the childes sterre/ for the childe was lord of the sterre as he was of al other For he was and is lorde of sonne mone & alle sterzes & of al thynge/ and they may nat conferme their sayynges ne the false domes of astronomoures/ By þ sterre. For it was no planete ne sterre of the firmament/ as saith seynt austyn & other doctoures/ of holy churche/ and scrypture and reason shewith it. Diues. How Pauper. For as seyn these clerkes. Minima stella fixa maior & tota terra. The leest sterre set

b i

The friste

faste in the firmamente is more than alle the erthe within the see & withouten the see/ & euery planete also is more than al therth outake the mone & mercury whiche be sumdele lesse than al erth And therfore sumtyme they lese their light that they haue of the sonne by the shadowe and the vmbre of the erthe/ whan it falleth right betwene the sonne & theim And if that sterre hadde ben soo moche or any such sterre it shuld haue ouirwhelmyd al erthe/ for it went full lowe nygh the erthe to lede and to wysse the kinges/ in their weye Also the sterres of the firmament and the planetes folowe the course of the firmament/ and ryse vp in the eest and goo down in the west euery day naturel That sterre dyd nat so. for it was aboue the erthe bothe nyght and daye/ & folowed nat the course of the firmament/ But it helde his course as the wey led best into the cite of Bethleem for to wisse the kinges in their weye to the sonne of rightwysnesse/ & there rose out of that clere firmament the mayden mary/ & as the sonne from vnder the erthe Also the sterres in the firmament shyne by nyght and nat by the daye That sterre shone bothe nyghte and day Also the sterres of the firmament shewe them to alme

comonly both pore & riche yong and old That sterre aperyd nat but to the thre kinges/ and their cumpany Also the sterres of the firmament been perpetuel and alwaye lastyng/ that lastyd but a lytel while/ twelue monethes atte moste/ as sume clerkes say and sume say but fourtene dayes or lesse. Oiues. What maner sterre was it than Pauper. Some clerkes sayen that it was an aungel in the liknesse of a sterre For the kinges hadde no knowynge of aungelles/ butt toke alle hede to the sterre Sume say that it was the same childe that laye in the oxe stalle/ whiche aperyd to the kinges in the lyknes of a sterre/ and so drewe theym & ledde theym to him self in Bethleem And therfore holy churche syngith and sayth. Iacebat in presepio et fulgebat in celo. He laye full lowe in the cratche and shone full bright aboue in heuene But the comon sentence of clerkes is that it was a newe sterre newly ordeyned of god to shewe the byrthe of cryste And anoon as it hadde done the office that it was ordeyned fore it turnyd ayen to the mater that it come fro.

The xxliii. chaptre.

Diues. Howe myght they knowe by the sterre that suche a childe was borne/ for ye sterre coude nat speke to theym ne telle no suche tales/ Pauper. That is sothe/ & therfore saythe seynt Austyn openly in a sermone. þ the sterre dyd nought elles/ by his apperynge but broughte them in wounder and grete studye to wytte what it myghte amounte And whanne they were at their wyttes ende and knewe wele þ her craft seruyd them nat thanne god shewyd theym by inspiracion inwarde or elles by an aungel what it betokenyd/ and badde them folowe the sterre. And the same sayth seynt Johñ with the gylden mouthe. Upon Matheu. They knewe wele by Balames prophecy that suche a childe shulde be borne/ but they knewe it nat by the crafte of astronomye/ ne myght knowe by their crafte/ neither the tyme of his birthe ne the place. as the gospel shewyth wele. Diues. Why sayth thanne seynt austyn/ and other clerkes/ that the science of iudicial astronomye of children byrthe was lesul vnto the tyme of cristes birthe sith they myghte natt by that science/ knowe his birthe. xxBi. q. iiii. igitur. But as they say it was nat lesulle ne grauntyd after his byrthe.

Pauper. Seynt austyn sayth nat that the crafte was lesul or graunted to do. ne that it was lesul to truste therin. For it was alwey false and repreued of god and of philosophers by scryptse & resone But he sayth that the scyence of the crafte was lesul and grauntded of god/ nat the doyng that by the science men might repreue the crafte/ and the science also. & shewe by their owne principalles and groundes that the crafte is false. and that the science is no science pprtly to speke. But open foly/ as it was wel preuyd in cristes byrthe. And for it was so openly preuyd fals i his byrthe/ therfore aftre his byrthe it is nat lesul to vse it ne to cũne it. But only to repreue the folye of them that vse it The doynge of the crafte was vnlesul bothe bifore and aftre   The science was suffryd of god bothe bifore and aftre to repreue foly/ as the lawe shewyth wele. di. xxxvii. De mensa.

The xxviii. chaptre

Diues. Whet fyndest thou that god defendeth the iudicial of astronomye. Bifore cristes byrthe. Pauper. Exodi xx. c. In the firste precepte of ye first table. of whiche is now our speche/ where god bad that men

b ii

The friste

shulde make them no lyknesse / is in heuyn But suche astronomoures make them self lyke as moche as they may to god in heuyn / in as moche as they take to theym that longith only to god. For only god knowyth whan suche thinges as they make theym wyse of shulde falle and howe & where And therfore god repuyth theym and sayth to theym. Nunciate que ventura sūt in futurū / et sciemus qr dii estis vos. psale xli°. c. Telle ye vs thinges that been to come after this & thanne shal we knowe that ye be goddes And therfore sayth p̄c salue. xxvi. q̄. iiii. igitur. That they clepid themself diuynes as they were ful of god and knewe alle goddes counsell and by fayre and fals hode coniecte & tel to the peple thinges that ben to come / as they were fulle of godhode and goddes felawes. And on this maner they and alle suche trespasse fulle highly ayenst the firste precepte For they make them lyke to god in heuyn / and the worshyp that longith only to god they take it to them selfe. Suche psumption & pryde coste aungelles kynde / and mākynde also. For as we fynde. psaie xiiii. c. Lucifer saide in his hert that he shulde stye vp vnto heuē & set his feet aboue the sterres / &

sytt in the mout of the testamēt And that he shulde wende vp aboue the highte of the cloudes / & is to say aboue alle aungelles & be lyke to him that is highhest. But anon he felle downe to hel. and so shalle suche astronomoures & wytches / But if they amend them. For they sett their wyttes and their studye and their fayth so moche in the sterres. that they wole passe the sterres and al creatures and be like god that is highhest They wole also sytte i the mout of the testament / for they wole be ayenst goddes lawes / & haue for the their domes / wylle god nyl god For if their crafte were true the testament of goddes lawe shuld serue of nought. & so goddes lawe / holy churche lawe / scripl and reson shulde serue of nought For ther is no mā worthy to be punysshid for a syn that he may nat fle / ne worthye to be medid for a gode dede that he may nat leue. But for that man doth wele whan he myght do amys / therfore he is worthy mede And for that he dothe euyl whan he might do wele / & might leue his mysdede and wole natt therfore he is worthy moch peyne But if he were nedyd by p̄ bodyes aboue to vertue or to vyce he were worthy neither meed ne peyne. This pryde & psumpciō

76

Precepte:

loste also Adam & eue & al man kynde For whanne the feende bight theym that they shulde be as goddes knowynge gode and wycked/ they assentyd to him/ & ete of the apple/ apenste goddes forbode For they wolde haue be as goddes and like god cūnyng gode and wycked/ & haue knowen what was to come Also we fynde Deut°. xviii. c. That whanne god led the children of israel oute of egipt ito the londe of bihest/ he forfendyd them the iudycyal of astronomy, and alle maner wytche craftes/ and bad they shulde axe no counseil of none suche dyuynoures ne wicches For I shal saith he distroye the nacions that ye gone to for they haue vsed such craftes/ and if ye vse hem I shal distroy also you ¶ We fynde also Isaie. xlvii. c. that god repreuyd the people of Babilonye & the caldeis of their wytche craftes and of their astronomy that they trusted mooste in/ for of alle naciones they ha ue theym moost that tyme ther to/ & sayde to them on this wyse Wydowhede & barenhede shal come to the bothe in one day for the multitude of thy wytches/ & for the hardenesse of thy charme tys/ And for thou haddest truste in suche malice thy cūnyng and thy science hath discepued the

Disease and Wo shal falle to the & thou shalte nat wytt fro whēs it cūmyth Sodeyne myscheif shal falle to the and thou mayst nat fle Stonde saith he with thy charmers and with the mul titude of thy wytches/ in whiche thou haste trauayled. from thy youthe Loke if they may ought helpe the or strenght the apenste thyn enempes. Thou hast say led and thou shalte fayle/ in the multitude of thy counseyles that thou haste taken of suche sothe ¶ Lete nowe saith he thy dyuynou res of heuyn stonde and saue the if they may. They that stare so apenst the styrres and loke after the planetes/ and calculen/ and cast peres daies and monethes/ to telle the thinges that been to come/ they shalle nat helpe the. they may natt helpe the.

For as seynt poule sayth Ther is no counseyl apenst god. Also this crafte of astronomy. is reb uyd Sapienc. viii. by the wyse Salomon/ where he repreuyth them that weende and sayd that sonne mone and sterres were god des of this world/ for gouernau ce cōgith to none vnwytty thlg. as sonne and mone and sterres. been But gouernaunce longith only to wytty thynges sensyful. and reasonable and vnderston dyng/ as to god that is souereyn

b iii

wysdome to aungel and man vnwitty bodies with their vertues and their might/ and theire kindes be nought elles but istrumentes of goddes gouernaunce and also of all gestes gouernāce. and of mannys also if they can wele vse them Also suche iudicial of astronomy is repreuyd by the lawe of holy churche/ xxvi. q. iiii. igitur. ⁊ distinct. xxxvii. legimus. ⁊ c. qui de mensa. Also seynt poule repreuyth such crafte of astronomye. Ad galathas iiii. c. Ye kepe saith he dayes and moncthes yeres ⁊ tymes. as hethen people doth And therfore I drede me saith he. that I haue trauelyd in veyne aboute you to conuerte you alle And yᵉ glose i the same place repreueth suche crafte of astronomy fulle harde Suche science god repreuyth. as sayth seint poule in his epystole/ i. ad cor. iᵒ. c. I shalle sayth god/ lese the wysdome of the wyse/ ⁊ the slight of the sligh ⁊ of theim that truste so moche i their cūnynge/ Where moreouer seynt poule saith thus/ Where is nowe the wyse man that setyth so wele by his wyt/ Where is now the man of lawe with al his syghtes/ Where is nowe the seher of nature ⁊ of the cours of kynd of this worlde/ God saith he hath turned the wisdome of this

The friste worlde into folye.

The xxvi. chaptre

Dives. Suche science and wysdō so for to diuyne of thinges to come which stondeth in the wyl of god/ and ofte i the free wyl of man or woman I lete grete folye Ther can none astronmoure by his crafte tel me my thoughtes/ ne what I purpose me to do in tyme cōmynge ne how I shal lede my lyf They knowe nat my counseyl/ alle if they se me and speke with me. Howe shulde they knowe goddes counseyl or what he wolde in tyme cūmynge/ sithen they se him natt/ and they speke neuyr with him They can nat telle bifore ne beware of her owne myshappes Howe shulde they telle other men or women. or warne theym by their crafte of their auenture For comonly suche dyuynoures of astronomye ben in grete myscheif and myshhap as moche as other or more/ ⁊ they knowe it nat tyl it falle/ And yᵉ more that they worche by theire crafte the worse they spede.

Pauper. That is no wounder For the more that they truste in their crafte/ the lesse they truste i god. And the lesse they truste in god in whome is alle our welth.

the worse they shal spede And the more that they trust in their crafte the more they truste in foly. And the more that they trust in foly the more foly & mischeyf shal folowe him. Ther. Wole no wyse man wryte his counseyl & alle that he thynketh to do in y⁹ yere folowyng in the roof of his halle, ne aboute on the walles. Where alle men may see it & knowe it. No more wose god wryte his coūseil ne what he thynketh to do in tyme cūmyng aboue in the firmament, there al foles might knowe his coūseyl his thoughtes and his domes Cryst hyd many thingis from his apostles and sayde to them Non est vrm nosse tēporā vel momēta q̄ pater posuit in sua potestate, actuum primo. c. It longith nat to you to knowe tymes momētes and stoundes Whiche the fadre. of heuyn hath reserued in his power And he sayde by the prophete. Secretum meū michi, secretum meum michi. psa. xxiiii. c. I kepe my pryupte to me I kepe my pryupte to me. And sith he reserud suche counseyl and pryupte from his frendes & were so nygh of counseyl Mochmore he reserud his counseyl from his enmyes fole synful wreches Diues. These clerkes say that they may by craft of astronomy lefully telle and dyuyne of drought, of rayne of tēpest. for they falle by comon course of kynde and therfore they may by comō course of nature knowe theym, and telle them bifore Pauper.

As I saide firste, the course of kynde and of planetes stondeth alle in the wyl of god & do therwith what he wole, as the instrumente stondeth in the werkmannys wyl what he wole do therwith And therfore they may nat knowe by their crafte, ne by the course of the planetes as by cause, neither of drought ne of wete ne tempeste cūmynge But they may knowe by the bodies aboue, as by tokenys bothe of drought, of wete of tempest, froste, snowe wynde, thundre, and suche othere, and so knowyth the shepeherde in the felde. the shypman in the see, the birde in thair the fisshe in the water, beestes in the wode, bettre than alle the astronymoures in this londe,

¶ The xxvii. chapter.

Dives. Howe may the bodies aboue be tokenes of suche thinges and nat causes Pauper. Fallynge of soote in houses is token of reyne sone cōmyng, and yit it is nat cause of

Tħe friſte

tħe rapne/ But tħe repne is cauſe of tħe ſote fallynge For wħāne tħe apre weýitħ moiſte/ tħe ſote by moiſture of tħe apre weýitħ heuy and falliþ dowñe And ſo tħe fallynge of tħe ſote is token of grete moiſture in tħe apre Alſo ſwetynge of water on tħe ſtone is token of repn/ and ýit it is nat cauſe of tħe rapne But repne and moiſture of tħe epr is cauſe of tħe water Alſo meltinge of ſalte wħan it turnetħ into water is token of rapne cūmynge But nat cauſe. Alſo ſmoke in ħouſe wħan it paſſitħ nat redily oute. is token of repne For tħe apr is ſo tħycke and ħeuy of moiſture that tħe ſmoke may nat ſtye by ſo redily as wħanne tħe apre is dry. and clere Alſo tħe brougħe or circle aboute tħe candel ligħt is token of repne And tħe blewe glowynge of tħe fyre/ is tokene of tħe froſte. But nat tħe cauſe Tħeſe and ſuche other ben tokenes of wedyr cūmynge But natt cauſes For tħey ſħewe diſpoſicion of tħe apre Wħedyr it is diſpoſed to drougħte or to wete. And on tħe ſame maner tħe bodies aboue been tokenes of wedyr cūmynge For by their ligħt & maner of ſhynynge tħey ſħewe diſpoſicion of tħe apre wete or dry froſt or ſnowe/ tħudre ligħnyng

wynde and ſuche other. And as tħe ligħte in tħe laterne ſħewitħ diſpoſicion and coloure of tħe laterne/ and ýit is nat ye ligħt cauſe of ſuche diſpoſicion ne of tħe coloure of tħe lanterne. And as tħe ligħte of ſonne or mone ſħewitħ diſpoſicion of tħe glaſſe/ it paſſitħ by wħetħer it be wħyte or blake/ blewe or rede/ ýelowe or grene And ýit is nat tħe ſonne tħe mone cauſe of tħe colour. Rigħt ſo tħey ſħewe tħe diſpoſicion of tħe apre/ and ýit ben tħey nat alway cauſe of ſuche diſpoſicion And tħerfore tħe mone in one lunacion and in tħe ſame tyme ſħewytħ in one cuntre grete tokenynge of repne and ſo it falliþ/ and twentye myle tħens it ſħewytħ grete tokynyng of drougħte and ſo it fallitħ/ and ýit is it tħe ſame moone and tħe ſame lunacion And tħerfore tħe cauſe of tħat diuerſite is nat in tħe mone But in tħe apre. For tħe apre in one cuntre is diſpoſed to rapne/ and in tħe otħer to drougħte

Alſo in one cuntre it ſħewytħ wynde and tempeſt. in an otħer cuntre nat ſoo. Some cuntre is fulle ħote by ſhynynge of tħe ſonne/ ſome cuntre is nat ſo ħote One day is fulle ħote. and tħe nexte day aftre is fulle colde. Tħe ſone ſħewitħ ħis ligħt one

Precepte.

tyme of the day/ and another tyme of the day it shewith nat/ which the diuersite stondeth nat in the sonne/ But in the ayre and other causes For the sonne in hymself as sayne these clerkes is alle way at one and shyneth alway alike it is nether hote ne colde But suche diuersite falleth by dyuersite of the ayre/ and other diuerse meanes and causes Whiche passen mannes wytte. Sumtyme suche auenture of hungre of moreyne/ of tempest/ of droughte. of wete falle by the ordenaunce of god for mannys synne/ or for to shewe his might and his worshippe. Sumtyme by worchyng of aungellys gode or wicked at goddes byddynge. Sumtyme without mene only at his wyl and his byddynge. Sumtyme by the worchynge of the bodies aboue at his byddyng For as I sayde firste he may do wyth the planetes what he wole/ and he may do without them what he wole. And therfore by the course of the planetes. may we nat knowe suche auentures as by causes But as by tokenys. For god made theym to be tokenys to man/ Beest. Byrde/ fisshe/ and other creatures/ as I sayde firste And therfore we shulde take hede to them only as to tokenes nat to causes. Ne dyuyne by hem as by causes For we wote nat whanne they been causes of suche thinges/ ne whan natt.

The xxviii. chaptre

Diues. The mone as clerkes sayne is cause of flowynge/ and ebbynge of the see. for it folowith the course of the mone. Pauper. It may wele be so But wele I wote the course of the mone is token whanne the see shal ebbe and flowe. and the see kepith his tyme of ebbig and flowynge/ after the course. and the tyme of the mone in one cuntre suner/ and in another latter And yit euery see doth nat so But only one parte of the Weste see that goth aboute Britayne & Irelonde/ and other nygh londes Bicause of tho But in other ferre cūtrees ne in the grekes see is no suche ebbyng ne flowyng. So it semyth that there be other causes of that ebbynge and flowynge thanne the mone allone

But sothe it is that man beest and byrde/ fysshe/ the see the ayre/ tree and grasse/ and other creatures vse and kepe their doynge in kynde/ and worchen in tyme that god hath ordeyned to theym. Whiche tyme they

The firste

knowe wele by the course of the sonne mone and sterres. For as salomon saith Ecclesiastes iii.c Alle thynge hath his tyme ordeined of god by wey of kynde whi che tyme they knowe and kepe. By the course of the bodies abou= te/ whiche been tokenys to hem shewyng what tyme they shuld do their kynde that they ben or= deyned to And therfore god saith By the prophete Jeremye viii.c. The puttok in the ayre saith he knolwith his tyme/ the turtyl. ꝓ the swalowe kepe the tym of her cummyng/ But my peple knowe nat the dome of oure lorde god. For these dayes men take none hede to goddes domes/But alle to the domes of astronymoures and to the cours of the planetes The kynde of euery creature is ordeyned by the dome of god. ꝓ What tyme he shal do his kynde whiche tyme they knowe/ and fele. By the course of the bodies aboue For as sayth the phylosophre/ the bodies aboues mesure alle thinge here bynethe as an=tes tyme And therfore sayth Dauid/ that by nyght whan the son is dolwne/ than in derknesse be= gynne bestes of rauepn to walk and seke their prey ꝓ their mete. Whan the sonne rysseth they wend ayen to her dennes ꝓ byde theim than go men oute to worche tyl

it be nyght Nat that the sonne ne the mone cause hem to do so/ But only the lalw of kynde ordeyned of god techich he so to do ꝓ to ke pe their kyndly tyme In the da= wynge ꝓ spryngynge of the day Byrdes begynne to synge/ floures to sprede and spryng that by nyght were ful close May/ birde and beest begynne to glade/ for ioye of the light/ and for the ty= me of their myrthe and of theyr kyndly worchyng cometh ayen By the presence of the sonne/ whi che serueth theim principally of light and of tyme The sonne ru leth them nat proprly to speke. But kynde ruleth them in tyme. By the cours of the sonne and by the course of the bodies aboue We fynde in holy wrytte Gene= sis i°.c. that the erthe at the byd= dynge of god brought forth tre= es grasse and erbe Trees and er bes brought forthe their frupte/ eche in their owne kynde The thridde day er god made sonne/ mone and sterres And bad the er the and gaue it vertue and na= ture to brynge forthe grasse and frupte of many ꝓ dyuerse kynde He gaue nat the sonne ne the mo ne/ne the sterres that nature.

He made theym the fourthe. daye to shyne/ and to be in toke nes of tyme to alle creatures he re bynethe in erthe.

Precepte.

God haue graue trees and erbes dyuerse vertues & wounderfulle nature, to bud and brynge forth leues faire and grene in dyuerse fourme, floures faire blossomes bright of dyuerse shappe and of dyuerse coloure that no man by crafte can deuyse. Also he haue them nature to brynge frupt faire and fyne some in in wynter & sume in somer. Sume he ordeyned in tyme to lese their leups & their grenehede. Sume to be grene wter and somer as forel. Boye hol me pue: and many mo, whanne other herbes sere & drye by than in the colde wedyr saffrone begynneth to sprynge and wᵗ his floures bryngith his frupt. Suche dyuersite in hynde in tre and gras in beest fisshe and foule, vertues so dyuerse in stones & other thinges deuysed neuir ne made the sonne ne mone ne the sterres, but he that made sonne mone and sterres and al thinge I hynde he made and ordeyned, & he gouerneth and kepeth alle this erth in his owne hynde, and hath assigned eche creature here bynneth his due tyme, his nature to doo and to shewe. In one londe falleth bugre, in any other place plentye of alle godes. In one londe is plentye of wyne, in a nother none. In oo cuntre is plentye of wolle gode and clene, & a nother

lytel and ful vnthende: In one cuntre plentye of golde & siluer, and of other metalle, in an other lytel or noughte. Sumtyme is moreyne generalle sumtyme pᵉcial. in oo cuntre and nat in an other. Sumtyme in oo towne & nat in the next. Sumtyme in pᵉ one syde of the strete and nat in that other. Some householde it takith vp al hole & in the nexte it takith noon. Sume dye in youthe. and sume in elde, sume in myddel age, sume wele sume eupl, sume with lytel peyne sume with moche peyne. Howe shuld men knowe or telle al ÿis dyuersite by the bodies aboue or assigne causes therto, or to such other withouten nombre by the course of the planetes.

The ꝓꝓlv. chapitre

IVes. It passith manes wytte Duly god that made al he knowith al. They ben his domes his ordenaunce And therfore I sete greate folye that men entremette them so high of goddes domes, and namely of thinges that been to come.
Butt I praye the telle me if the wounders that fal ayenst kinde in the bodies aboue betokenen.
Cor shewe any auentures.

83

The firste

that been to come. **Pauper.**
That fallith apen comō cours
of kynde betoknethe that some
thynge is cūmynge passynge co
mon course of kynde, be it wele,
be it woo. But comonly suche
wounders falle more apenst wo
thanne apenst welthe. as come-
tis and sterres brennynge castel
les in the ayre. Eclipses of the
sonne or mone apenst kynd, me
in the ayre armyd or fightynge.
the raynbowe turnyd vp so dow
ne, myshape thinges in their bir
the apenste kynde. These and su
che other that falle apenst comō
cours of kynde, betoken that ye
people where they appere, done
apenst kynde, and that lorde of
nature is offendyd with theym.
& alle creatures redy to punysshe
them. **Diues.** It may wele be
as thou sayst for many such haf
apperyd within a fewe yeres, ne
vyt so many I trowe in so lytel
while. And moche sorowe and
woo folowyth after, as we fele
here and see. But I pray the
what betokned that wounderful comete and sterre which apperyd vpon this londe, the yere
of oure lorde a thousande foure
hundryd and ii. from the epipha
ny, tyl two wekes at after ester,
that was the myddel of Apryll.
Pauper. It was open token
of the grete offence of god. With

the peple of englonde, and that
harde wreche was cūmyng but
they wolde amende them of her
falsehode and traytorye, plutye
murdre, mysprydre. I euery degre
& ouirdone, couetyse, erroures &
herises, blasphemye, and ydola
trye, lechery and lesynges withouten shame, and other synnes.
many moo. nat only pryuy but
open to alle cristendome & sclaū
dre to alle cristen people.
And for that men repent theym
nat ne wole nat amende theym.
but putte synne to synne. And
by synne of falsehode, murdre, &
manslaughter, trauayl to mayn
tene their olde synnes, therfore
vengeaunce fallith as the sterre
betoknyd. God of his mercy
smyteth nat alle at onys, but ly
tel and lytel, that by the lytel me
shulde be war of the more. But
allas and welaway that no man
wole be ware, no man amende
hi, but alway do worse & worse.

They yeue no tale of goddes
swerde, but euery cytee is glade
of others disease, vnnethes any
man or woman hath pyte on other
but nyghe euery man is glade
of others wo. And so I drede me
that god wylle make an ende
of this londe, for we soue no pees
we seke no mercy. Butte
alle oure sythynge is alle in wer

& in woo, in murdre and in

shedynge of blode/ in robbery/ ⁊ falshode/ and oure besynesse/ is by nyght/ and day is to maynte/ ne synne and to offede god And more so welalway they haue or/ deyned a comon lawe that what man speke w'the treuthe ayenst their falshode/ he shalbe hanged drawen ⁊ behedyd Diues. Thy salues been ful soth and open at the Euery state ⁊ euery degree. in this londe. is nowe youen to synne ⁊ besy to maynten synne But I pray the what saye cler/ kes of such cometes and sterres/ so apperynge ayenst the comon cours of kynde Pauper They saye that whanne it apperyth. it signifieth moreyne or chauns gynge of some grete prynce/ or distruction of some cuntre/ or cha gynge of some realme. or greate werre or hunger or/ wounderful tempest. Diues. Werre hunger and tempest and moreyn we ha ue hadde grete plentye/ ⁊ many cuntrees in this realme ben dis/ troyed. and chaugyd into other lordshypp ⁊ nacion sithen y' sterre apperyd. And it is ful lyke that in shorte tyme bothe the kynge. and al the Realme shalbe chaun ged and distroyed. Pauper. Salomon sayth that for gyle ⁊ traytoury and dyuerse wronges and dispites done to god and to holy churche/ realmes be chaun gyd fro nacion to nacion This mater is ful heuy and dolefulle Speke we of sumwhat elles.

The xxx. chaptre.

Diues. Al if it be soo y' the iudicyal of astronomye. be reyuyd of god ⁊ of holy chur/ che/ yit experience shewith that oft they telle many treuthes of thin ges that been to come and of thi ges preuy that ben done Paup Sumtyme they happen to saye suche sothes/ as the blynde man hest the staf And sumtyme they knowe suche thynges/ by other waye than by astronomye/ and that they knowe by other weye they saye that they knowe it by astronomye For they wolde fayner be holden wyse/ and ne/ rer of goddes counseyl/ thanne any other. Diues. Howe may they knowe any suche thinges. on other half. Pauper. Sum/ tyme by boke of prophecy. sum tyme by coiecture of diuers cau ses and disposiciones that gone bifore As if ma yeue him to wic kyd cumpanye/ or use suspecte places/ men that wote it. wole coniecte therof and saye that in

The firste

tyme cũmynge it shalbe his confusion. Also yf a man mys dyete him and ete & drynke oute of mesure/ & thing that is nat conueniēt to him/ men wol say that he shalbe seke therof And if a man yeue hym to false the kyn ges seal or the kinges money/ other wyl saye that he shalbe han gyd and drawne/ and comonly it falleth so Also they knowe thinges that been to come by coniec tynge of dyuerse tales and speche in the people/ as if comõ clamoure of the people be ayenste their kinge whan their king trusteth vpon them/ it is a token y the peple shal vndo him or he beware And on this maner these daies the moost parte of the peo ple been prophetes and tel thyn ges y been to come/ whiche thin ges they ben about to pfourme. in bert worde and dede And children also by that they here. theire elders speke ben andhaue been pphetes nigh i euery hous Also they knowe suche thinges/ by discuryng of counsepl or kno wynge of counsepl of them that purpose suche thinges And siltyme they be of the same counsepl and of the assente and helpynge therto. And on this maner these faytoures that been cleppd soth siggers and astronomoures/ sũ

tyme telle thingis preuy and do come ayen thinges that be stole or loste For comonly suche ben theupys/ or of these assent And by one sothe sawe or two which they knowe on this maner/ they blynde the nyce people and make theym to leue al theire sayn ges And therfore if any such say toure byd any thyng come ayen that were stolen/ he shulde be ta ken as a theef or a theuys feere. And comonly suche faytoures & iapers haue maisters to haue pt of their wynnyng/ as tauerners Brewers hostelers/ & nedy werke lesse men that go so gay & spend grete/ whiche aspy aftre thinges that been done in the cuntree/ & that yit ben to be done/ and telle them to the faytours to do them haue a name And ofte they that shulde moste kepe counsepl. dis cure counsepl And soo that men wende were counsepl is no cou sepl And comonly suche faytou res be slye spekers/ & slyghly can oppose the shepherde & the plow man i the felde or sũme olde sim ple folke or children at the tow nes ende/ and ayen howe stou dith it amonge neyghboures/ & aboute in the cuntree. And after that they telle theim they make hem wyse/ as if they knewe it by astronomye. or by prophecye.

Precepte.

or by nigromancye And for as moche as they be vnknowen, ⁊ telle sothes that men knowe, the peple wenyth that they knowe alle thinges, and myght knowe what they wolde, and so leue in them tyl they ben alle disceyued Sumtyme suche faytoures tel sothes nat by their crafte But by techyng and flaushyp of the feend Whiche is allway redy if god suffred hym to seche foles for to disceyue them and other by them

The xxxi. chaptre.

Dives. How may the deuyl knowe thinges that ben to come or any pryue thyng **Pauper.** Better than any man For as saith seynt Austyne, de natura demonũ. xxbi. q. iiii. sci endum. The feend is more sotyl of wytte and feirer can se ⁊ coniecte than any man. Also he is more lyght and delyuer in stertyng and passinge For he is ten folde lyghter than any foul & his fleynge. Also he may lyghtly knowe what is done in dyuerse cuntrees and londes He is so sotel in kynde that ther may noo dore ne walle shytte hym out of counseyl And so he may here and se what men ⁊ women do though it be ful pryue Also by longe experience, for they haue lyued so longe they can telle ⁊ coniect by wey of kynd many thinges þ be to come, ⁊ can do many thinges þ passe mannys wytte Also oftetymes that haue leue of god for mannys synne for to do woundres, to cause hidous tempestes to enfecte and enuenym the ayr and cause moreyne ⁊ sekenesse, hungre ⁊ droughte, discension, and werre by distruction of charite. By mysprynde couetyse licherye, wrathe and enuye, and suche thinges as they done, and pursue them to do and haue done aforne ⁊ made other to do they can ne telle bifore Also by the signes of the body outwarde, they knowe disposicion of man and woman inwarde, signes to helth or to sekenesse, to byce or to vertue or oft by tokne outwarde they knowe mannes thought Iward But for asmoche as they maye nat nat knowe for certeyne suche thinges, for only god knoweth for certeyne thinges þ ben to come, ⁊ ofte tyme god lettyth them of their malice, whan men wole amende theym. Therfore the proude spiryte wyl nat telle suche thinges to the people ymediatly by hymself, but medyate by other that sett theire feythe, ⁊ their truste in hym, as ben wytches faytoures astronomoures þ if her sawes be foulde fals, they

The firste

shal haue the belonpe If it be solde true. the feende shal haue the worshyppe Also they may knowe the thinges that been to come by boke of prophecy whiche they vnderstonde by naturel wytte bettre than any man.

The xxxii. chaptre.

Diues. Sothe it is ynugh euery synne be it neuir so preup/ it is done by the techyng a tysyng of the feende And therfore wonder it is that any lichery thefte and mycchery/ murdre/ lesinges or other synnes may be hydde a kepte preup/ sithen the feende knowith it so wel/a may knowe thinges that been so preup by soo many weyes as thou haste nowe seyde. Pauper. Fulle fayne wolde the feend discure mennys synne and womānes to brynge theym to shame a belonpe. and so to distroye'chastitie and make euery man to sle other But god of his mercy lettith him. for he may nought do. ne telle But as he hathe graunte of god And therfore as we fynd in the gospel M^t. viii. c. The feend myghte nat entre into the swyne that wente ther bisydes/ to drenche hem/ tyl he had graūt of criste Also he might nat disese Iob neither I his body/ ne in his

catel. tyl he hadde graūt of god. Iob. i°. a ii°. c. And alsue he coude disceyue kinge Achab wt lesynges a faire biheftes/ to doo him to fight there'he myght alyued in peas/ pit he might nat do it tyl he hadde graunte of god. The thrid boke of kinges xxii. chapt He knoweth moch thing by the suffraunce of god/ but he may nought do withoute graūt a pmission or suffraunce of god. The feende is so feble a so faynt þ he may ouircome noo man ne woman by temptacion/ butt he wole be ouircome of him/

Ne he may nat dere the leeste childe in the weye but if he haue graunte of god. Whiche sulpme grauntyd him power therto/ for the syn of the fadre a the modre. Diues. Why suffreth god hym so moche to tempte mankynde. Pauper. To morynge or encresynge of oure blysse and of oure mede for as saith seynt poule Ther is noman worthy to haue the crowne of lyf/ but he withstōde the feende in gostly stryf And as he sayth i an other place/ god suffreth him nat to tēpt vs/ But as we may wele withstonde/ if we wole And if we falle he hath ordeyned to vs remedye of penaunce/ sone to ryse ayen a better to fight if we wol And al our tēptacion shal turne vs to mede

if oure wyl be to wiþstonde.
Diues. Siþen þe feende kno
weþ soo many treuþes & wote
what is done/ for he is at euery
wycked dede. me merueileþ mo
che why he is so redy to lie & why
he is so false. Pauper. For he
hatiþ god þat is soueraȳ treu
þe/ & for he miȝte nat be euȳ
wiþ god in souerȳte of treu=
þe/ ne haf þe name of souerȳ
treuþe þat is god/ þerfore his
liuyng and his trauayl is to be
souerayne falshede & souerȳly
false. And þerfore Cryste sayþ
in þe gospelle þ þe feende stode
neuyr in treuþe/ for þer is noo
treuþe in him/ whan he speketh
he spekiþ lesynges/ by weye of
kynde/ for he is a lyer and fader
of lesynges. Jo. viii. c. And soo
wheþyr his tale be true or false
say he soþ or false. alwaye he is
false/ alway a lyer. Diues.
Howe may he say treuþe & yit
lye. for if he say treuþe me thin
keþ he spekþ nat. Pauper.
What so euir man or feende doth
or spekiþ aȝenst gode conscien
ce and aȝenste þe plesaunce of
god in wyl and intencion for to
disceyue may woman or childe.
it is a lesynge. and he is a lyer þ
doþ it or sayþ it. And þerfore
þe lawe sþe wiþ wele. xxii. q. ii.
holes. & c. is aut̄. Þat if a mā
say a treuþ whicħe treuþ he we

nyth be false if he say it for to di
sceyue his euyn crist̄/ in þat he
speþ. And so wiþ a soþe salwe/
a man or þe fende may lie. as if
J say to þe þat it were nat day
to let ye of thy iourney wenyng
my self þat it were nat day alle
þougħe it were as J sayde yit J
lyed. And in þe same maner þe
feend telliþ treuþis of þinges
þat been to come/ and oþer so=
þes also/ wenyng him self þat
þey be false. And so in his soþe
salwes he speþ/ for he saytħ þat
treuþe vnwyttyngly for disceit
and wenyþ to say false. And if
he say any treuþe wyttyng and
wyttyngle/ he saitħ it only for to
disseyue men. and for a wycky d
ende/ and for to do for þe wᵗ one
soþe salwe leeue an hundryd le=
synges/ and so he is alway fals
and disseyuable. And sumtyme
he is compelled by þe miȝte of
god to telle treuþes aȝenst hys
wylle/ to shame and shenshippe
of him and alle his/ as we fynde
in þe gospel Mᵗ viii. mar. i. Lu
ce iiii. & vii. c. But for suche so=
þe salwes is he neuyr þe trewer.
But alway a false lyer/ for suche
soþe salwes ben aȝenst his wyl
and if he may he wole turne hem
alle to dissayte/ and make men
for suche soþe salwes lꝛ þan þey
falle to leue al his lesynges And
þerfore he is clepid in holy wryt

Spiritus mendax spiritus fal∷
lax That is to say a spirite lyer
a spiryte dissepuable And therfo∷
re as the fendes hadde sayde the
treuthe that crist cōpellyd thein
to saye/ anon he put them to si∷
lence/as sayth the glose in the sa∷
me place/ for they wold elles vn∷
dre that sothsawe haue told ma
ny lesynges

The xxviii. chaptre

Dives. Whanne he is con/
iuryd he is so bounde. By
vertue of holy wordes þ he must
nedys say trouthe which he kno
weth if it be ayed him Pauper
Suche wyches and charmours
tapers and faitoures that vse su
che craftes haf no power to byn∷
de him ne to cōpelle him to telle
suche sothes/ ne righte noughte
for to do ne for to telle. For he
may noughte do ne telle without
en the graunte of god And ther
fore suche tapers and wytches/
bynde nat the feend But the feed
byndeth them ful hard in his ser
uage/ and kepith them thralles
to him passynge al other/ whose
bondage is fulle harde to theym
for to escape withouten a specy
al grace of god. Dives. Cōtra
Ofte men knowe þ clerkes close
hem in rynges and in other thin
ges & make hem ther to tel & do

The friste

many wōders Pauper. The
The fende fayneth hl to be boū
de with suche tapers wordes for
to dissepue them & other by them
And yit is he nat closed ne boun
de/ But he goth abrode as he did
bifore/ and whanne he is cleppyd
he is sutynte redy to aūswere for
he is fulle swyfte/ sutynte he is
nat redy to aunswere/ ne to doo
their wylle/ and ofte though he
wolde he may nat for god wole
nat suffre him. Dives. yit con∷
tra te Men wote wele that i ma
ny londes prestes & clerkes with
holy cōiuracions and holy pray
ers ordeyned of holy churche ca
che wychyd spirytes oute of mē
and wymen Paup. That is
sothe and nat only gode spuers.
But wychyd spuers in many lon
des cat he feendes oute of men
and wymen and children by ver
tue of goddes worde/ and holy
coniuracions and holy prayers
ordeyned of holy church/ and so
ner a gode man or a gode womā
shal do that thanne a wych yde.
Suche bynde the feend/ and do
him lese his power and his lorde
ship to shame and shenship of hl
and alle his Suche seke the wor
ship of god and shenship of the
feende and helpe of manes soul
And therfor they haue power of
god to bynde him & to compelle
him But yit as sayth the glose.

90

Precepte:

mar. b. c. sup illud Quod ē tibi nomē. They that ben so trauey sed with the feende must first be clene shreuen as fer as they may and knowe and telle al the maner of the feendes doynge/ and of the temptacion that they haue either wakynge or slepynge by sight by herynge by felynge. or by any of their wyttes/ or by any thought or fantasye/ & disdiscure elle the feendes counseil But these wytches faitours and iapers. seke the fendes worship nat goddes worshyp/ They seke helpe of the feende and forsake goddes helpe/ and do sacrifice to the feend and forsake god and take the feend to ther lorde and make him their god And so the feend hath power ouir them nat they ouir the fende.

The xxxiiii. chaptre

And therfore saith the lawe xx ði. q. vii. non obserue/ tis. That alle suche wytches/ & alle that axe any counseil or help of them/ or sett any feyth i them or bryngeth them to their houses. or go to their houses to haue helpe or counseyl of them/ and alle that take hede to dysmale dayes/ or vse nyce obseruaunces in the newe moone/ or in the newe yere as setting of mete or drynk

by nyght on the benche/ to fede Albolde. or gobelyn. Ledynge of the plough aboute the fire as for gode begynnyng of the yere þ they shulde fare the better alle the yere folowyng/ or take hede to the iudicial of astronomy or to diuynaciones by chyrpynge of byrdes/ or by slepynge of foules/ or assente to any suche nyce obseruaunces/ or dyuyne a mannes lyf or deth by nombres and by the spere of Pythagoras/ or make any dyuynyng therby/ or by sonquary or sompnarye. the boke of dremes/ or by the boke that is clepid the apostles lottis or vse any charmes in gadering of herbes/ or hangynge of scrowes aboute man or woman or childe or beest for any seknesse. wᵗ any scripture or figures and carectes/ But if it be pater nost. Aue or the Crede/ or holy wordes of yᵉ gospel/ or of holy wryt for deuocion nat for curioustie. and only with the tokene of the holy crosse/ and alle that vse any maner wicchecraft or any mis bileue/ that alle suche forsaken the feyth of holy churche/ & their cristēdome/ and bicome goddes enmyes and greue god sulle greuously/ and falle into dampnacion withouten ende/ But they amende theym the soner/ And therfore the lawe cōmaundeth þ

c ii

The friste

busshopes shulde be besy to distroye alle maner wychecraftes. And if they founde any man or woman that gaue them to wytche craft but they wold amende theym/ they shulde chace theym oute of their busshopryke. with open despyte. xxvi. q. v. epi. And in the same place the lawe saythe that tho wymen whiche wene by nyghte to ryde on dyuerse bestes and passe diuerse lodes and cuntrees and folowe a glorious quene that is cleppyd Diana/ or elles herodiana. or any other name and wene þ they been in her seruyce bodilye with moche myrthe/ suche wymen ben al dissyeued and blent wᵗ the feend whome they serue And therfore the feende hath power for to dysceyue them) And that they suffre only by fantasy/ by dreme/ & by iapery of the feende They wene it were so bodily & in dede & it is nat so And al tho that say or leue that men or wymen myghte by wychecrafte be turnyd ito bestes/ or into lyke nesse of beestes or byrdes bodily been worse tha any paynym And they þ for hate or wrathe that they bere aȝenste any man or woman take awey the clothes of the autre and clothe the autre with dolefulle clothynge/ or bisette the autre or yᵉ

crosse aboute with thornes/ and withdrawe light oute of the chirche/ or synge. or do synge masse of Requiem for them that been alyue. in hope that they shulde fare the worse and the soner dye the preest shulde be degradyd/ & Bothe the preest and he that steryd hym therto for to do it shulde be exiled for euyr And alle maner wytches and al that leueᵒ on wytche crafte shulde be acursed solenely/ But they wolde amede them. as the lawe sayth in the same place/ and in the next chaptre folowynge. & cᵒ si quis. As the lawe saythe there: c. Contra. If the wytches were bonde men and wymen/ they shulde be bete harde and sore If they were free they shuld be punysshed i harde prison And by the lawe iperialle vt .C. de maleficiis nullus. & l. nemo. & l. culpa. And by yᵉ law canon. xxvi. q. v. qui diuinacones. in glosa. Suche wytches shulde be hedyde and brent and their fautoures exiled. and alle theire godes eschetyde And by the lawe of holy churche alle that leue in theym or mayntene them shuld do fyue yere penace. xxvi. q. v. Non liceat. & c. Qui diuinationes. Also it is defendyd by the lawe as wytche craft for to do thinges come ayen. by scripture in boke or in tables or by astrolabie. ext. li. v. ti. xxvi. c. i° & ii°. Diues. I sete it a full gode dede to take a theif. w‘ his thyfte by what crafte that a mā may for saluacion of the people and to punysshe or sle a theif by the lawe for ensample of other.

The xxxv. chaptre

Pauper. It is nat leful to any man for to sle a theif agenst the kinges lawe and withoute processe of londes lawe and withouten auctorite of his liege lorde. ne without a lauful iuge ordeyned of his liege lorde. & yit is ye theif worthy to die. Diues. that is sothe For if euery man might sle a theif at his owne wylle and by his owne doome / men shulde vndre coloure of theif sle many a true man for wrathe couetyse. and hate. Pauper. Sithen men do somoche reuerence to the kinges lawes and londes lawes to sle mysheueps that shulde falle but if the lawes were kepte.

Moche more reuerence shulde they do to goddes lawe & holy churche lawe / and eschewe to forfete ther agenst / sithe goddes lawes and holy churche lawes ben as resonable & as gode. as the kinges lawes of englond

Natheleffe the kinges lawes if they be iuste they be goddes lawes. And asmany pereles and mo shulde falle if men toke theups by witchecrafte agenst goddes lawes and holy churche lawes, as if they slewe them agēst the kinges lawes and the lōdes lawes. Diues. Shewe me that. Pauper. If a man sle a theif nat him defendante agenst the kinges lawe. he forfetith agenste his kynge and is worthy deth And if he make him a iustice by his owne autorite. though he kepe other processe of lawe he is a traytoure to his kynge.

And asmoche and more forfetiȝ he agenst the kynge of heuyn / þ taketh a theif with wicchecrafte. agenst goddes lawe / sithen god and holy churche hathe forbode it; as dothe he that sleeth a theif agenst the kinges lawe. And sithen he maketh the deuyl and the wytche that been moost goddes enemyes his iuge / and worcheth by their doome in despyte of god that hath forbode it hem he is a ful highe traytour to god And soo he doth ten folde more synne / and is worthy to be hanged more thanne a theif. More ouir in asmoche as the feende is a lyer alway / redy to lye & w‘ lesynges disseyueth the mankynde.

eiii

93

The friste

and bringith men to murdre and to shedyng of blode/ and rather to sle innocentes thanne theues If suche wytchecraftes were v/ syd/ many innocentes and many a gode man and woman shulde be taken and slayne and theues goo free. For the feende is more fauourable to theues/ maquel/ lers/ licchoures and to other spy/ tufte wretches/ thanne he is to a ny gode man or woman/ & mo/ re lykynge he hath to sle a gode man or woman if he mighte/ than to sle a theif. Also god sayth in the gospel that the feend hath euir been a lyer/ and stode neuir in treuthe. and that he is a man queller/ and fader of lyers/ and of lesynges. And therfore al tho that yeue fayth to his tales and doo therafter/ as moche as is in theym/ they make god fals and forsake theire god that is soue/ rapne treuthe/ and take theym to the deuyl/ that is souerapne falsehode/ and so they worshyp the feende and dispyse god And if such craftes were suffred euery man myght accuse other. of what synne he wald/ and say that the feend or the wyche told it hym And on this maner euery man might hytte other. And therfore for these skylles & many moo and to sle these perelles

and many other/ god hath for/ boden alle maner wytchecrafte for it is nat done without helpe of the feend. But these dai es god of his mercy suffreth nat the feend but fulle selden to so/ thesalwe. for if he suffryde hym to soothsalwe/ englisshe people. shulde forsake god alle at onys and sette their truste and theire fayth alle in the feend. For nat withstandynge that they fynde the feendis tales and his craftis ful false. By greate and ofte ex/ perience/ and spende fulle grete therabout. and lese al that they doon and myshappen/ yit wole they nat cease for noo losse/ for noo precehynge/ for noo shame/ ne for no punysshynge. Neuirtheleffe it is no grete won der. for the fende holdith theym fulle harde bounde. in his boon des as his churles and his thral les. For alle suche doon a pas/ synge homage/ sacrifice and ser uyce to the feende/ and forsake god as I sayde firste.

The xxxvi. chaptre

Iues. Suche craftes & coniuraciones with holy

prayers and they that done hem ben holden fulle gode lyuers, ҭ and ȝeue theym to fastynge, penaunce doynge, bedys byddyng and to many other gode dedys: and therfore men ȝeue the more fayth to them. and leue them yᵉ better. For it is nat semely that the feendes craft shulde be done with suche holynesse Pauper. The more holy thynge and the more hooly prayer that man or woman ȝsyth in the feendes seruyce. the more worshyp and the more plesaunce they doo to the feend. and the more dispyte and offence do they to god For the worshyppe and the prayer and the seruyce. that they shulde doo to god they doo it to the feende. And thinge that is ordeyned only to goddes seruyce, they spend it in the deuylles seruyce. And therfore they that ȝse holy wordes of the gospelle. Pater noster Aue. or Crede. or holy prayers ĩ their wycchecraftes, for charmes or coniuraciones, and alle that ȝse holy water of the fonte, holy crysme, messes syngynge, fastly contynence, wolwarde goynge and suche other in their wycchecrafte they make a fulle high sacrifice to the feende It hath ofte been knowen that wycches with ſaying of their Pater noster. and

droppynge of the holy candel in a mannys steppes that they hatyde hath doon his feet rote of. Diues. What shulde the Pater noster. and the holy candel doo therto. Pauper. Right nought But for the wycche worshyppeth the feende so highly with the holy prayer, and with the holy candel and ȝsyth suche holy thinges in his seruyce, in dispyte of god Therfore is the feende redy to do the wycches wylle, and to fulfylle thyng that they done it for. ҭ so it stondeth only in the deuyl ҭ in mysbyleue of the wycche nat in the Pater noster. ne in the hooly candel, and yit the fooles wene otherwyse. For the feende wold nat do their wylle But they do him suche high sacrifice.

For whanne that they lighte yᵉ candel and say Pater noster, to that ende, they do it nat to god. But to the feend. And in that they forsake god. and worshyp the feende as god. and claymne the feende to theire fader, sayng to him that they shulde sey only to god. Pater noster qui es in ҭc. Oure fader that art in heuenes. halowyde be thy name And alle that folowyth they sey it to the feende. And therfore the feend may claymne hem for his childrē. and god may skylfully forsake

e iiii

The friste

them and say to them þ he sayde to the ielwys. Vos facitis opera patris vestri/ vos ex patre diabolo estis. et desideria patris vestri vultis facere. io. viii. ye done saith he the werkes of the feende youre fadre/ ye been of the fader the deuel. and the desires of your fadre ye wole doo And on the same maner their chastite/ their fastynge her penaunce doyng is i asmoche as they do it to plese þᵉ feende and for a wycked ende/ it is a seruyce and a sacrifice to the feende And ful felwe men or wymnen wose do so moche penauce for the loue of god/ as wytches do for the loue of the fende/ and to please the feende/ in so moche that sumtyme they cutte theym self with knyues/ and pryke hē self with launcettes/ and soo ofte their flesshe and their blode i sacrifice to þᵉ feend/as we fynde i the thrid boke of kinges þ viii chaptre. And therfore leue frend sithen this maner of synne is so greuous/ so hydous and so abhomynable in goddes sight/ suffre it neuir to be do by none of your household/ for noo losse ne noo thyfte/ for no sekenesse/ for noo helthe/ for no welthe for no wo. For if ye do it your self/ or do it to be done/ or assēt to the doyng or suffre it to be done whanne ye

myght sette it/ ye been acursed & offende your god ful highly and fulle greuously for alle that do it or assente to the doynge/ and sette their feyth therin/ they forfete ayenst the firste commaundement ful greuously For in that they forsake god/ and make the feende their god/ and worshyppe him as god. And by what thing that they do their wychecraft/ be it fyre/ be it aire. or water/or erthe. or dede bones/ or any other thyng that is in their maluent and that they make simplitude to god. asmoche as in theym is. and worsship it as god And therfore god bade in the first comau̅dement. that man shulde nat make him liknesse that is in heuyn that is to saye/ neither in the firmament. ne in the fyre/ ne in the apre And so in that worde he forbedyth the iudicyal of astronomye. and pyromacie/ that is wychecrafte doone in the fyre/ and aeromancye that is wychecraft doon in the ayre Also he forbedyth men to make them lykenesse of any thynge that is i erth In that he forbedith geomancy that is wychecrafte done in the erthe. And also nygromācy that is wychecrafte done by dede bodies that been but erthe. and buryed in the erthe: Also

96

Precepte.

he forbedith men to make them symylitude of any thynge in the water vndre the erth. In whiche worde he forbedith ydromancy. that is wychecrafte done in the water He badde that men shuld worshyppe none suche thinges as god/ ne sette their trust ne her fayth therin/ For if they do they make suche thynges lyke god/ī asmoche as in them is. And nat oonly they make suche thinges lyke god in this maner/ But also they make the feendes lyke god/ whiche duellynge in the fyre. syme in the ayre/ syme in the water/ and some in the erth/ for to tempte manyk ynde/ and been besy nyght and daye to lese mānes soule and womanes.
Diues. Shewe me syme example of thies maner of wychecraftes. Pauper. I am besy for to distroye wychecraft and nat for to teche it. But wolde god that no man ne woman wyste what it is/ ne knewe thies ne none other/ for ther ben alle to many ȳ knowe these and many mo other to/ and practyse newe yere by yere/ at the feendes techynge/ I lyste moche of this londe is blent and shente with suche folye. For ouyt moche wychecraft regneth openly/ But moche more pryuely/ and namely amonges these

olde men and wymmen/ the whiche for age wolde fayne be holden wyse. And thanne begynne thy mooste to dote and to teche theire yonger/ many folyes and many nyce fantasies/ that been very wychecraftes. And therfore bothe olde and yonge shuld axe counseyl of wyse men of holy churche/ and wyt if suche thinges and doyinges as they teche. be lefulle or nat lefulle.

The xxxvii. chaptre

Diues. By comon sawes of clerkes god in the firste commaundement forbedyth thre principal synnes/ Pride that is vnderstonde by the lykenesse aboue in heuyn/ for there it begā. And the proude mā and womā wolde alway be aboue and worshypp his pryde as god For the proude man and woman/ wole haue for the their proude wylles ny se god wyl god And therfore Iob sayth that the proude feed is kynge of al children of pride And as seint poule saith/ proud anticryst shal haue him as god. a sytte in goddes temple as if he were god Also they sey that god forbade there the synne of coueityce/ that is vnderstonde by the synnes in erth/ for myscouetitse stondith moost in erthly thinge. And therfore seynt poule sayth. that auaryce is seruage of mawmettes of ydolatrie / For as saith seynt Ierome/the auerous man makith his money and his richesses his god Also they saye/ that by the same commaundment he forbade lichery and glotenye Whiche been vnderstonde by the lykenesse in the water vndre the erthe For as seynt poule saythe Lechoures and glutones make their wombe and ther body their god For their moste trauail and besynesse is to please. and serue. their wombe and their bely.

Pauper. In asmoche as euery synne is apenste the worshypp of god in somoche god in the firste commaundment forbedith al maner synne in generalle But as I sayde by the first commaundmēt he forbade in special mawmetry. ydolatrye wychecrafte & sorcery For afterwarde he yaue the iiii. maūdmēt specialy apenst pride aud vnbouūnesse. & the sevte. & the tenthe apenst lichery/ the viii and the nynthe apenst auarice & couetise.

The xxxviii. chaptre.

Diues. It is lefulle to vse lottes. Paup. Sūtyme to breke stryf in partynge & yeupynge of thynge that may natt wele be departed Or Whan men been in doute What is to do and mannys wytte fayleth. thanne is it leful to vse lottes ī thinges that been nat apenste the worshypp of god. soo that it be done with the reuerēce of god/ & holy prayer bifore/ as thapostles dyd in chesynge of seynt matthie. the appostle/ and eliezar in chesyng of a wyf to ysaac abrahames sone. gen. xxiiii. c. And therfore salomon saith Prouerbi. xvi c. that lottes ben put in preuy place/ and god tempzith them as he wole But to vse lottes without en nede: and only for vanytie. or for diuynacion/ settyng faith therin to wytt therby what shal fall/ is vnleful and repreuyd of god and holy churche And if mē set truste and feyth therin it is a greuous synne. Diues. Pleyng at the dyce stondeth in lotte and auenture of the dyce/ and yit y° game is lefulle Pauper. To vse that game for recreacion/ & only for pley it may be suffryde. soo that it be doon in maner honestly. and in place and tyme conuenyent/ and natt to moche in lesynge of tyme But for to vse it for to wynne therby. and putte thynges in auenture.

Precepte.

of dice, it is a fulle greate synne and euyl goten gode, that men gete therby. And therfore by the lawe if it were a man of holy chur che þ vsyd suche pley, he shulde be pryued of his benefice. if þ he hadde any. And if he hadde noo benefyce he shuld be vnabled, & disposed therto but if he wolde cease. And if it were a leude mā. he shuld be acursed. disti.xxxv. cās Et extra de Vita & honesta te clericorū. c°. clerici. And ther fore sayth the lawe. that no mā of holy churche shulde be att su che games.

The xxxix. chapter.

Dives. Sithen ther be soo many maners of wyche craftes þ they may nat be tolde. in specialle I pray the telle me in generalle. What is wychcraft Pauper. Euery craft that mā or woman vseth to knowe any thynge or to do any thyng that he may nat knowe ne do, by the wey of reson ne by the worchig of kynde. is wychecrafte. And though it be do by wey of kynd and the doer vse any charmes or nyce obseruaūces in the doynge wenynge that it myghte nat be done withouten that charme, &

suche obseruaunce or elles such charmes only to blynd þe peple. that they shuld trust in hym for his charmes, and nat I worchig of kynde It is wichecrafte a lif he say only his Paternoster. in the doyng for to be holde a char mer. and to do the peple trust in hym principally for charmes, al thoughe he say no charmes but worcheth only by kynde, yit he is a wytche & his doynge is wyt checrafte For by suche doynge. he blyndeth the peple and dissey ueth them, and doth theim trust I wychecraft, and so do worshyp to the feende and dispyte to god And what soeuir man or womā do by weye of kynde and reson. If he vse any craft of iapery and faiter for to blynde the people. for to do them leue that he were a wytche, and that he dyd it nat by weye of kynde, but by char mes and sorcery, he is a wytche in goddes sighte, and his doyng is wychcrafte For his crafte is to make men worshyp the feend in asmoche as he doth the peple truste in wichcraft, and so spede their gode in the feendes seruyce and to seke helpe of the feende. and forsake goddes helpe. And he that feyth hym selue to be holden a wytche and the de uylles seruaunte, thanne to be

The firste

holden goddes seruaunt / and se
upꝛ to take mēnys gode iŋ woꝛ
shyppynge of the feend thanne iŋ
woꝛshippnge of god And by the
cūnynge ⁊ grace that god hathe
pouen hi̅ / and by the mygħte.
and vertue that god hathe pouē
to thinges of kynde foꝛ helpe of
mannys kynde. falsely he enħā
cyth the feendes crafte iŋ distruc
tion of mankynde: Diues.
Tel some ensample. Pauper.
To hele mannes woūdes whŝle
they be fresshe and clene / blacke
wolle and oyle been ful medicy
nable withouten any charme as
experience shewith wele But
foꝛ asmoche as mē wene that it
were nought woꝛth withouten
the charme. and sett their feyth
pꝛincipaly iŋ the charme / therfo
re it is to them a wychecrafte.
But though a man iŋ the doing
say his paternoster. oꝛ some ho/
ly pꝛayer cleppynge the grace of
god iŋ his doynge it is no wyt
che crafte But it is wele doon

The xl. chaptre.

Diues. What if he say pa
ternost. oꝛ other holy woꝛ
des / oꝛ some holy pꝛayer pꝛyues
ly oꝛ aperte / foꝛ to do the people
wene that it is doone by weye of
miracle and foꝛ his payer ⁊ his
holynesse / Whanne he doth it by
reason and woꝛchyng of kynde
Paup. Than is it a ful greate
ypocrispe and ful greuouse syŋ
iŋ him that doth it on that ma
ner and foꝛ that end / But wyche
craft is it none Foꝛ it is no woꝛ
shypp to the feendes crafte / ne pe
peyle is stired therby to truste iŋ
the feende but rather iŋ god.
Diues. Is it any wychecrafte.
to charme edders oꝛ other bestes
and byꝛdes / wyth holy woꝛdes.
of holy writte oꝛ with any other
holy woꝛdes   Pauper. If
a man oꝛ womā take hede ī his
doynge only to the holy woꝛdes
and to the might of god / it is no
wychecrafte. But if they vse iŋ
their doynge any mysobseruāce
and sett moꝛe truste therin than
iŋ holy woꝛdes oꝛ iŋ god / thāne
as say clerkes it is wychecrafte.
And the effecte therof if it fal co
meth of the feende / and namely
iŋ adders and serpentes Foꝛ the
adder was the firste instrument
that the feende vsed foꝛ to dissey
ue mankynde / as we fynde Ge
nesis. iii. c. And yit by the adder
he doth men moste truste ī wyt
checrafte. Diues. Is it any pe/
rel to mā oꝛ womā to charge his
frede ī his dyīg to cōme ayē ⁊ tel

Precepte.

him ſoþ he ſaytþ Pauper. It is a ful grete perel. For as ſaitþ ſeynt poule. the feend ofte tyme makitþ him lyke an aungel of ligþte. But he may nat laſte in the beautie ne brigþtneſſe. And ſo ligþtly the feend migþt appere to him that were alyue in the lykneſſe of him that were dede. and telle hym leſynges. and in cas make him ſo aferyd that he ſhulde leſe his wytte. and falle I wanbileue. as felle to one witþ in a felwe yeres. And happely he ſhulde telle him that he were dānyd. thougþe it were nat ſo. Or telle him that he were in blyſſe. though he were in bytter peyne. and ſoo lete him of his almeſdede and from holy prayer and other gode dedes by whicþ nat only that ſoule ſhulde be holpen. But many other witþ him Alſo if he aperyd to him. or if he wede that he appered to him he ſhulde haue the leſſe mede for his byleue. thanne he hadde bifore For thanne were he cacþyd by experience to knowe that the ſoule lyuetþ after the body Alſo it is nat in the ſoules power to appere to man or woman after the deth of his body. ne man is nat able to ſe a ſoule. for it is inuiſible witþ oute ſpecial myracle of god. And ſo botþe he þ chargitþ hym

to come ayen/ and he þ botitþ to come ayen tempten god. And rigþt as god wol that euery mā and woman be ūcerteyn wþat tyme he ſhal dye/ for that alway he ſhuld be dredeful to do amys and beſy to do wele Rigþt ſo he wol that men be ūcerteyn of their fredes wþan they ben dede in wþat ſtate that they been/ for that they ſhulde alway be beſy to helpe ther ſoules witþ meſſes ſyngynge. almes doynge/ witþ bedys byddyng/ and other gode dedes nat only for help of þi but of other that haue lytel helpe or none Alſo for encreſyng of their owne mede For who ſo trauayletþ wel for a nother trauaylitþ beſte for him ſelf For as ſaytþe ſeynt poule. ther ſhal noo gode dede be unyoldē/ ne no wyckyd dede be unpunyſſhed. Diues. Thy ſkylle is gode. For if men wyſt þ their frendes were out of peyne they wold do rigþt nogþt for them And ſo they ſhulde leſe moche mede for that knowyng & ſoules leſe moche helpe And if men wyſt for certayn wþan thei ſhulde dye. they ſhuld be to bold to do amys in hope þ they ſhuld amende them in their dyynge

But yit nat witþſtondynge alle thy ſkylles/ ſomme clerkes ſayne that it is lefulle to men to

⁋The firste

charge theire frendes to come a¬
gen and shelwe them her state af
ter their dethe. For as they say it
is kyndely thynge for to desire
to knowe or to kune. For the
philosopher saith that euery mā
and womā by wey of kynde de¬
sireth to knowe and to kune.
Omnes holes natura scire desi¬
derant. Pauper. They say so¬
the/ and nat ayenst me. For it is
leful to euery man and woman
to desire to cūne and to knowe/
But it is nat leful for to desire
to knowe on that maner/ ne by
no mene vnleful nat by teching
of the feende/ ne by techynge of
them þ been dede.

⁋The xli. chaptre.

Diues. Howe is it that spi¬
rytes walke soo aboute.
Whanne men be dede. Pauper
Comonly suche spirites ben sen
des/ and go so aboute to sclaun
dre them that been dede/ & for to
bryng the people into erroure &
bacbityng and wicked demyng
that if ye peple demyd euyl and
spake euyl of them bifore theire
dethe/ to do them speke and de¬
me moche worse aftre their deth
& so to bryng the peple ful depe
in synne. And sūtyme they gone
ito ye bodies of theym þ ben dede
and buried/ and bere it about to

do them bisonp. But whanne
spirites goo on this maner. they
do moche harme and moche dis
ese. Natheles by the leue of god
the soules appere I what maner
god wole to them that ben alyue
sūtyme for to haue help/ sumty
me to shelwe that the soulis lyue
after the body to conferme them
that been feble in the feyth and
bileue nat sadly/ þ mannes soul
lyueth after his deth. But suche
spirytes do no harme but to tho
that wole natt leue theym that
they haue suche peyne/ or wole
nat redily helpe hem at their ap
pynge.

⁋The xlii. chapter.

Diues. Is it leful to trust
I these fastinges newe foūd.
to sle sodeyne dethe. Pauper.
It is a grete foly to trust therin
For as I sayde nowe late. god
wole that man & woman be vn
certeyne what tyme they shulde
dye/ and in what maner For
god wole that man and womā
be alway besy to sle synne/ and
to do wele for drede of deth and
alwaye redy what tyme god wo
le sende aftre theym. And
yf men were certayne/ by suche
fastynge that they shuld nat die
sodeynly but haue tyme of repē
taunce/ and to be shreuyne and
houselyde. they shulde be the

Precepte.

more rechelesse in their spuynge and the lesse tale peue for to doo amys in hope of amendemente in their dipng And therfore god grauntyth them nat the ende ne the effecte that they fast for For more sodepn deth vpste Ineuir that men hadde thanne I vpste theym haue that haue fastyd suche fastes vii. pere about/ ne more dispytefulle and shamefulle. in open punysshyng of their syn And was their neuir sdo moche sodepn deth so longe reignynge in this londe as hath be sithe suche fastynge beganne/ We may nat arte god ne putte him to no lawes And therfore we shulde putte alle oure lyf and our deth only in his vpste/ prapnge to hi of his grace that he wole ordeyn for vs bothe in lyf and deth/ as it is mooste to his worshyp and helpe of oure soule It is wele done to pray to god with fastyng and gode dedys that he saue vs from sodepne deth/ for alle holy churche prayeth soo But for to set feyth in suche nyce obseruaūces and wene to be syker of their dyynge for suche obseruaunces þ is nat lefulle/ for we may nat knowe the wyl of god in suche thinges wᵗ out special reuelaciō of god. We may praye and owe to praye But god shal graunt as him liketh/ and as he seeth it is mooste spedeful to vs and most to his worshyp And therfore salomon sapth. Nemo sit scrū amore an odio dignus sit Eccle. ix. c. No man he saith wote sykerly whether he is worthy hate or loue And yit we hope/ a owe alle to hope þ god wold loue vs and saue vs if we do our deuour Fastyng is gode if it be done in mesure a maner wᵗ iuste itē/ cion/ so that men sett no mysbyleue therin/ ne grounde them in no lesyngs ne in no nyce obseruaūces But in asmoche as they preferre in their fastynge dayes of their owne choyce bifore tho daies that been ordepned by holy churche to faste/ in somoche. they synne in presumption a do yudice to holy churche þ ordepned suche daies that been moste cōuenyēt to faste as wednesday fridaye and saturday. De cōse. distinc. iii. ieiunia a c. sabbato. Diues. I se no grounde ne reason in suche fastynge/ ne whye it shuld be more medeful to fast alle mondayes in the pere w̄ dan the feest of oure lady in lente sallyth on monday/ thanne to fast in worshyp of her wednesdaye. friday or saturday. For I leue sykerly that the mede of fastynge ne the vertue of fastyng is nat assigned ne lymyted by ye letters of the kalēder ne folowe nat the cours of the kalender, ne chāgith nat from one day to an other day. as if the lettres chaunge from one day to a nother And so as me thinketh suche fastyng is groundyd in some lesyng and faytre & in some mysbileue fulle nigh wicchecraft. Pauper. Me thynketh the same For alle if ye seest falle sumtyme on the monday, sumtyme on the tuesday. yit the dede in it self felle neither on the mōday ne on the tuesday But it fel on the friday For than the aungel gret oure lady & than she cōceyued goddes sone. lorde of blysse And thre & thritty yere. after the same tyme and the same day that is to say pon gode friday about mydday she sawe her dere sonne dyinge for mākynde vpon the rode tre. And so me thīketh that it is more plesaunt to god and to oure lady and more cōuenyent to faste the fryday in worshypp of criste, that dyed for vs al that day And also in worship of our lady that conceyued that day her dere sonne at the aūgelles gretyng than to fast either monday or tuesday And in as moche as they wene that suche faste shulde nat auayl theym to thende that they fast fore But if they chaungyd their fast yere by yere after the cours of the kalen

der. and that it muste be do vii. yere by yere, it is a nyce fantasy and mysbileue fulle nigh wicchecrafte For Cryste myght graūte them that boon as wele for fyue yere or for sype. or eight yere fastynge as for vii. yere. I found neuyr grounde wherof it came ne reason ne auctorite fynde I none Aye forth if thou wylte sū what elles.

The xliii. chapter.

Dives. Is it lefulle to sett any trust or any feyth on dremys Pauper. Ther been ii. maner causes of dremys. Done from inward, another from out warde Causes of dremes from in warde ben thre maner: Done is comon styrynge of mannes fā tasye. or womans in their slepe. and suche dremys ben but fanta sye & vanyte And therfore saith Salomon Vbi multa somnia: ibi multe vanitates. eccle. v. c. where been many dremys there ben many vanytyes, for on this maner one man shal haue moo dremys than sūme twenty other A nother cause from inwarde is disposicion of the body. For whanne men ben colde of kynd. they dreme of frostes and snow. And so by their dremys a wyse

seche may knowe in party dispo
sicion of her body/ be it to helthe
or to sekenes. The thridde cause
from inwarde is. disposicion of
the soule. For comonly men dre/
men of suche thinges as her soul
and their thought is moost occu
pied in whyle they waken/ either
by studye/ by loue/ or by hate/ by
wrathe/ by drede/ by sorowe/ by
care pride or couetise. Causes of
dremps from outwarde ben two
maner/ bodily and gostly. Bodi
ly is the disposicion of the ayre.
and of the place about him/ and
other thinges beside him. And
therfore in rayne wedyr men dre/
me of water and of fisshes. For
ofte mannys body chaungith af=
ter the disposicion of the ayre/ &
of his abidynge place. And for
these thre causes sayth the philo
sopher. De somno et vigilia.
That leches shuld take hede to
the dremps of them þ been seke.
to knowe therby how they been
disposed. Gostly causes from
outwarde of dremps been ii. ma
ners. The one cause is gode/ for
that is god by him self. Or elles
by aungelles/ and that on thre
maner. For some suche dreme by
ymaginacion onely/ as dyde the
kinge pharao and nabugodonosor. Some onely by vnderstodig
as dyd seynt poule and Balaam

Some dreme both by ymagina
cion and by vnderstondyng. as
dyd seynt John in apocalipso/ &
danyel in his prophecy. Whiche
sawe wounderful sightes by y-
maginacion and vnderstondig
what tho sightes betokenyde
But pharo and Nabugodono-
sor vnderstode nat the visiones
ne the dremes that they hadde
The other cause of dremes from
outewarde is nat gode as whan
it fallith by illusion of the feend
for tho principally serue to wytchecrafte. Sumtyme they come
of greate besynesse and trauayl.
that one hath whanne he is wakynge. And therfore Salomon
saith that after besynesse folow e
many dremps; for comonly mē
dreme of suche thinges. as they
been occupyed in whyle they w a
ke. Sultyme they come of ouir
done abstinence and of hungre.
Sultyme it cōmeth of excesse of
mete or drynke. Sumtyme of
myslikynge þ man hath whāne
he is wakynge. And in asmoche
as the effecte of thinges is tokē
of his causes/ as smoke is tokē
of the fyre. So suche dremps ben
tokenes of causes that they come of. And on this maner a wyse
man may telle by dremps causes of mennys dremps/ and soo
by causes tel other preuy thiges

The friste

that may falle therof. For oftyme one cause bryngeth forth dyuerse effectes. eche after other. Diues. Telle sume examples. Pauper. Experience shewyth that if a man trete moche wythe a woman and sette his hert moche on her by day. in the nyghte folowynge he dremyth of her some nyce dreme. By whiche dreme if he tolde it to sume wyse man. he wolde saye that he coupd moche that woman. and but he wt drewe hym from her cumpany/ it shulde turne hym to felony.
And so as saye clerkes in asmoche as dremys come by waye of kynde/ in so moche it is leful to telle what they signifie after the causes that they come of. Soo that in their tellinge and coniec tynge they passe nat the boūdes of kynde.   Also it is leful to telle thinges that been to come. by dremys that come by reuelacion of god/ if man and womā. haue grace to vnderstonde them as Joseph and danyel hadde. But for asmoche as dremys come on so dyuerse maners/ & it is ful hard to knowe. on what maner they come/ whether by god. or by kynde/ or by the feende/ or by any other weye. Therfore it is fulle perilous to set any feyth therin. as saythe seynt Gregoure

libro viii° moru̅. super illud Job Terrebis me p somnia. For sumtyme by dremes the feende. hoteth men grete prosperite and moche richesses/ to brynge them in pryde & hope of thinges that they shulde neuir haue Sumtyme by dremes he pretendith mo che aduersite and greate disease for to brynge sorʒe in sorowe & drede/ and greate heuynes/ and if he may to bryng them into dipepre. for nyce fantasies that he bryngeth hen in. And sumtyme for men sette feyth in suche dremys/ god suffreth suche myschaups falle theim as their dremys pretende in punysshyng of their synne/ for that they sette in dremys ayēst the lawe of god. But prosperite fallith them none for no suche drempnge.   Diues. Where fyndest thou that god for beddyth men to sett feyth in dremys.

The xliiii. chaptre.

Pauper. Leuiti. xix c. where god sayth thus. Non auguriabimini/ nec obseruabitis somnia. ye shal nat diuine/ ne make you wyse of thiges preuy by no wychecraft/ and ye shalle bayte after no dremys ne take hede therto/ ne set feith that

Precepte:

pnne. Also deutronomii. xviii. God forbedith alle maner wytchecraftes and charmes, and biddeth that no man shulde take hede to dremes And in the same boke viii. c. god sayth thus. If it be so saith he þ any man emõges you begyn to be a sothe sayer & a pphete and say that he had a dreme and a vision, and telle any wounder, whiche wounder and token fallith as he sayth, if he stire the to mawmetry or to any wytchecrafte, here nat the wordes of that prophete and of that dremer. For by him god assaieth you, that it may be openly knowen whether ye loue him wᵗ alle your herte and soule or nay And therfore god byddeth that suche dremers and prophetes shulde be slayn & though he wer thy owne broder by fader & by moder thou shuldest nat spare him in þᵗ caas. And therfore Salomon sayth that dremys haue brought moche folke in erroure and in foly. and they that truste therin falle to nought. Ecclesi. xxxiiii. c. For alle if dremys come oft tymes by wey of kynde as I said yit it is ful harde to knowe whã it cõmeth, by wey of kynd or by illusion of the feed And though they come by wey of kynde and though a mã knowe the causes

& kynd of dremes, yit it ful harde to telle sothly what shal fal therof. For only god knowyth þe for certayn thinges that been to come, and he may chauge and sett the worchynge of kynde And also though men knowe the causes of kynde that dremes come of, yit knowe they nat what settynges ben on other bihalue, by way of kynde. Diues. Tel some example. Pauper. Whanne smoke medlyd with fire cometh out of an house by the wyndow or by the couerys, men that seen it from ferre wole say that hous shalle goo on fyre. And yit ther may be so gode helpe nigh to queche the fyre, that, yᵉ hous shal take but lytel harme. And many a man by weye of kynde is disposed to dyuerse sekenesse. But yit he may so gouerne hym, and vse suche medicynes that he shalle let þ disposicion in kynde and nat haue suche seknesses

Diues. By the same skylle though a dreme come of goddes sonde to helpe of mannes soule. and in warnynge of myschefys to come, he shulde take noon hede therto. ne sett no feyth therin For he wote neuyr of whens it cometh: Pauper. Withouten reuelacõn of god he wote neuir of whens it cometh. And therfore

f ii

107

The friste

Whanne god sendyth suche dremps/ he shal shewe to him that drempthe this/ or to some other from whens it cumpth/ and what it betokeneth As he dyd to the kynge pharo by Joseph/ and to the kynge Nabugodonosor. by danyel.

The xV. chaptre.

Dives. If man or woman haue a dreme that styreth him to gode and to vertue/ and to flee synne. and to amende his lyf/ may he nat sett feyth therin. and do therafter. Pauper. Whether it cometh of god or of ye seed it is lefulle to him to sette fayth therin and to do therafter. For it styreth him to thyng that that he is bounde to withouten any dreme. And oft tyme bothe the feend and the feendes spyces techhe wele/ al yf they do euyl. But a man so drempnge muste be fulle ware/ that for suche dremps he take noon hede to other drempes that stire him to baynte or to curiouste for to knowe thynges that been to come/ or other thinges preupe/ or to mysdeme of his euen cristen/ or to hate or to mysloue/ or to baite after grete prosperite/ or to brede greate aduersite. or deth of frendes/ or losse of catel/ and suche other.

But in asmoche as they styre hy to god and to godenesse/ he may folowe his dremps and do after them wysely and warly/ for ofte the feende vnder coloure of holynesse discepueth bothe man and woman. Dives. Moche folke hadde leuyr dreme of the feende than of god or of his moder mary. for as they say whanne they mete of the feende. they fare wel in the day folowyng/ but whan they dreme of god or of oure lady they fare euyl afterwarde. Pauper. Suche folke fare the worse for their mysbileue & their nyce fantasy. and synne ful greuously. and euyl be disseyued by the gyle of the feend. For whan the feend seeth that a man shalle haue disease/ he maketh him on the night bifore to mete of god. and of oure lady/ & of other seyntes/ or of men of religion/ so to make hym to haue lesse deuocion to god and oure lady & other seintes/ and lesse affection to me of religion bicause of his disease that shal falle to him after that dreme And so by the bodily disease that he thynketh to brynge hym in/ he traueyleth to brynge hym into gostly disese and depe in synne And therfore whan me wole be foles. and sette feyth to suche dremps þ cometh so by gyle of the feende for asmoche as dis/

Precepte:

eafe fallyth to them onys or tuyes after suche dremys Therfore god suffreth the feende in punyſſhyng of their synne and of their myſbileue for to do them dreme ofte of suche maner/ and after to do them difefe as they bylene to haue And therfore Whanne men hadde suche dremys With difefe so folowyng and began to haue any fátaſy or feyth therin/ they ſhulde ſhryue them therof to ſome wyſe man and telle hym the feendes gyle/ and they ſhulde fare the better. Summe mete of god and oure lady and of holy men/ þ haue fare fulle wele afterward for they haue no suche fantaſy ne myſbileue in dremes And ſome fare ful euyl after for theire myſbyleue/ and ofte tyme they fare ful euyl whanne they mete neither of god ne of oure lady.

The ylvi. chaptre.

On the same maner. some man hadde leuyr to mete with a troude or a frogge in the way/ than wᵗ a knight or a squier/ or with any man of religion. or of holy churche/ for than they say and leue that they ſhal haue gold For sumtyme after the metyng of a frogge or a tode/ they haue reſcyued golde/ ɑ ſoo they falle in myſbileue and diſyyſyn their euen criſten For wele I wote that they reſſeyue golde of men or of wymmen but nat of froggene or of todes/ but it be of the deuel in lykneſſe of a frogge or a tode And they mete wᵗ many a foule frogge ɑ tode in the pere ɑ pit reſcepue they no gold for þ metyng And if they reſſeyued any golde. they ſhuld thanke god and their euen criſten/ nat the frogge ne yᵉ tode for they may nought yeue them   And theſe labourers deluers and dykers that mooſt mete with frogges and todes. been fulle pore comonly And but men paye them theire hyre they haue lytel or nought On this maner alſo ſome bileue þ if the kyte or the puttok fle ouir the way afore them that they ſhuld fare wel that daye/ for ſumtyme they haue fare wele after that they ſee the puttok ſo fleynge And ſoo they falle in wane byleue. ɑ thanke the puttok of their welfare and nat god But ſuche foles take none hede howe often men mete with the puttok ſo fleynge/ and yit they fare neuir the better. For ther is no folk that mete ſo ofte with the puttoke ſo fleynge as they þ begge theire mete from dore to dore

f iii

The xlvii. chaptre.

Dives. What sayst thou of theym that diuyne by the firste day of the yere. that is the first kalendes of Januarye. and by Cristmasse day What shal fal in the yere folowynge That if it falle on the sonday/ the wynter folowynge shalbe goode/ somer gode and drye. plentye of wyne Oyen and shepe shalle wex and multiplye/ Olde men and wymen shalle dye. and peas acorde shalbe made that yere.

Pauper. I say that it is open folye and wychecrafte/ and full bigge offence of the maiestye of god.   For he þ made al thynge and ruleth alle thyng is nat bounden ne arted to yᵉ cours ne salue of the kalender He nedith no kalender in his gouernaunce But he gouerneth and demyth this worlde by treuthe & equyte med syd with mercy/ and after þ men deserue he sendith them wo and welthe/ peas or warre/What day soeuir the kalendes of Januarye or Crystmasse falle on.   In the yere of oure lorde a thousande & foure hundryd/ the kalendes of Januarye fell on the thursdaye whan as they say shulde folowe plentye of alle gode and pees also But that yere folowyng grete hungre/ grete pestilence/ sodeyn deth. warre fell within the londe & wetre withoute/ drede sorowe & care/ & tribulacion in euery degree. The kalendes hath chaungyd sithen from day to day. and yᵉ yere is come ayē on the thursdaye/ But our disease chaungith nat but alway ito worse for our synne.   For oure synne alway moreth or encreasith and lessyth nat And on what daye euyr the kalendes of Januarye & Cristmasse day falle in one londe/the same daye it fallyth al aboute. And yit folowyth it nat therof þ it shulde be ouir al peas if it fal on the thursday or the sondaye. ne ouir all plentye/ ne ouir alle warre and hungre or pestilence. if it fel on the saturday. Dives. Summe diuyne by the thuldryng. & make theym wyse of al the yere cūmynge/ after the moneth þ it thundreth in. Pauper. And that also is an bigh folye & open wychecrafte For it is a kyndly thinge in somer tyme to thundre in may. apryl/ Juyn. iuly. auguste and septēbre But in other monethes þ been in wynter it is nat so kyndly to thuldre as than For whanne grete thūder I wynter fallith/ it is a pest kynde and token of the high offence of god and token of vengeaunce commynge: But if men amende hem

And so is euery thynge/ and namely wederynge that fallith apenst comon course of kynde. But for to diuyne therby in specyalle what shal falle either wel or wo, peas or warre, hungre or plentye/ helth or sekenesse, it is vnleful For only god knowith for certayne what is to come of suche thinges, and where ⁊ whan it shal falle. And god sitth nat the thundre as an horne to blow his counseyl aboute the worlde

The xlviii. chapter

Iues. It is a comon oppinion amonges gentiles. and others also/ that alle the yere folowith the disposicion of yͤ vii. daies in Crystemasse. So yͭ the firste moneth shalbe suche in wederyng as the firste day of the tuelue/ the secounde moneth as the secounde day/ ⁊ so forth vp ⁊ vp. Psuy. That oppinyon is false/ and open folye For it is a ful kyndely thynge to haue frost and snowe alle the tuelue daies. But it were apenst kynde to haue froste and snowe alle the yere folowynge. And sumtyme it falleth that it is ful reyny weder. al the vii. daies/ But it folowyth nat therof that it shulde rayne ⁊ be wete weder alle the yere after

It is fulle kyndely thynge that the sune shewe him nat thre dayes or iiii. to gider in cristenmasse. But it were moche apenst kynde if the sonne shewyd him nat thre monethes or iiii. to gyder namely in somer tyme And ofte it falsyth that in alle the tuelue daies it rayneth noo rayne/ But euery day sonne shyne. and fulle faire wedyr. but it folowyth nat ther of that it shulde be sonne shyne withouten rayne al the yere after/ for than beest and ma͠n shuld be in greate perel At the begynnyng of the worlde the feend hiȝte adam and eue/ yͭ they shuld be as goddes knowynge gode ⁊ wyckyde yͭ was to come/ if they wolde ete of the tree apenste goddes precept. ⁊ so he broughte them into care and sorowe/ ⁊ into her folye. And on the same maner these daies he bihoteth men to be as goddes knowynge wele and woo/ thatt is to come. by suche nyce fantasies yͭ he techith them tyl that he bryngeth them in wo and namely ⁊ glisshe naco͠n that moste takyth hede to his lore/ ⁊ moste taketh hede to wychcraft and to them that make them prophetes and make them wyse ī suche folyes apēst the lawe of god

The xlix. capter.

f iiii

The friste

Dives. Is it nat lefull to theym that can, to make metal golde or sylver/ and multiplye golde and silver from xx. pounde to xl. pounde/ & so forth

Pauper. If any man coude do it by weye of kynde/ it were leeful, and ful proufitable to this londe But wele I woote ther is no man that can do it: For if they coude they wolde first multiplye to theym self warde & make theym self riche And comonly alle that vse that crafte But if they haue ought elles for to take to, been ful pore and ful nedye. But whanne they may begyle any man of his gode, as they doo fulle ofte, and rene awaye with ocher mennys godes, and of the riche make ful pore men. They hoten them multiplication Butt they pleye alle with subtraction and bryng folke into greate pouertie Lytel nedyd oure kynge to charge the people with tayes and taliages/ if he hadde so moche folke in his Realme þ coude do that crafte, to make golde. & silver and so to multiply it But suche iapers and faytoures distroye moche golde and sylver in distruction of the Realme/ and blynde many a wyse man/ & begyle them of theyr gode. For the couetouse and the false accorde sone to gyder And for asmoche as whanne men haue ynough & been nat content therwith/ therfore god suffreth them to be begyled/ and so be sotted for couetise that they can nat ceafe tyl they be brought to nought or to ouir grete losse, for many a man hathe be vndone by this crafte And therfore this crafte is condempned & forfendyd as wyccecrafte By the lawe. xxvi. q. v. Epūs

The l. chaptre.

Dives. What sayst thou of them that wole natt haue men of holy churche, and namely men of religion with them on huntyng/ for their bileue is that they shulde spede the worse bycause of their cumpany.

Pauper. I pray to god euyl mote they spede, as ofte as they take any man of religion, or of holy churche to go or to ryde wt them on huntynge For suche hū tyng with horne and houndes. and grete noyse, is forfendyd to men of holy churche. Extra. li. iii. ti° Bt imo: ne clsci. c. i. et li. v. ti° xxiiii. De cle. venat. c i. & ii. & distin. xxxiiii. quoniam. And seynt austyn saith that tho men of holy church which haue likynge to se suche hutyng they shal see oure saujour and be ful sory. distinc. lxxv. vi. Dident.

Diues. What sayst thou of hem that whanne they go on huntyng or passe by the waye. if they mete with a man of holy churche or of religion, and namely with a frere, they wole leue him on their lefte honde. For by that they wene to spede the better, & the worst if they leue him on theire ryghte honde. Pauper. I say that suche been of false bileue and wycches peres And but they amend them god shalle putt them from his right honde. and put theym on his lefte honde with theym þ shalbe dāpned at the day of dome, and sende them into the pyt of helle without ende. I wold al suche were serued as one was fulle late. Diues. How was he seruyd. Pauper. Ther came a proude getteuer rydynge from london and mette with ii. freres walkynge on a dyches brynke. I a fote pathe to fle the foul way The getter came rydyng I grete haste crying with moche boste. On the lefthōde frere. on the left honde frere. The frere prayde him ful faire to ryde forth in his waye and kepe the horse waye. as they kept the fote waye He wolde nat, but algates he wold haue the freres on the lefthonde and precyd in with his horse bytwene the freres and the diche so nigh the diche, þ the frere shoof

bothe horse and man into a depe dyche And there laye bothe horse & man, tyl that other passynge folke drewe him oute Right so withouten doute but suche foles amonge hem and sette be suche nyce fantasies, god att the day of dome shal putt them on the left syde into the pytte of helle withouten ende, and sey to theym on this wyse For ye putt me on youre side so scornefully. therfore I put you nowe on my liftsonde with them that shal be dampned. And if they say Lord Whanne put we the on oure left honde scornefully or dispytously, He shal aunswere and say to them as he shal say to other. Quod vni ex minimis meis fecistis, michi fecistis. That ye dyde to one of the leest of myne ye dyd it to me And therfore we dyth nowe on the liftside into y fyre of helle, there to duelle with the feende and his aungelles wt outen ende.

The ii. chaptre.

Diues. Me lystithe nowe more to wepe thanne any more to speke. For I wende tyl nowe that englisshe nacion. had worshiped god passyng alle other naciones. But nowe I se.

The firste

it is nat so For moche of my na‑
cion is entrikcd and blent withe
suche fantasies/ many mo than
I can tel. And so they forfete hi‑
ghly ayenst the firste comaunde
ment þ ought mooste to be char‑
gyd For that techith vs how we
shulde worshypp oure god aboue
al thynge And ther is neither bi‑
shop ne prelate ne curate ne pre‑
choure. that wole speke ayenste
the vyces and erroures that ben
so high ayenst goddes worshyp
And so by mysuse and sleuth of
men of holy churche vice is take
for vertue/ and erroure for treuthe
the feend is worshypped and god
is dispysed Natheleße as men
say. god is in no londe soo wele
seruyd in holy churche/ ne so mo
che worshypped in holy churche.
as he is in this londe For so ma
ny fair churches ne so gode aray
in churches/ ne soo faire seruyce
as men saye is in no other londe
as is in this londe. Pauper.
As seynt Gregoure sayth in his
omely. god takith more hede to
a mannys herte than to his yift.
and more to his deuocion thane
to his dede He taketh saith he
no grete hede howe moche man
or woman yeueth or offreth in ho
ly church/ But he taketh hede of
howe moche deuocion & of what
herte he yeueth and offreth And
so a pore man or woman hath
some tyme more thanke/ for the
yifte of an halpeny/ thanne so
me riche man hath for twety shi
lynges If the makynge of chur
ches and the ournamentes/ and
the seruyce in this londe were do
ne pricipally for deuocion/ and
for the worship of god/ I trowe
this londe passide alle londes in
worshyppynge of god and holy
churche But I drede me that
men doo it more for pompe and
pride of this worlde to haue a na
me and worship therby in the cu
tree/ or for enuy that one towne
hath ayenst another/ nat for de‑
uocion/ but for the worship and
the name that they se them haue
by araye and ournamentes I ho
ly churche/ or elles by sligh coue
tyce of men of holy churche.
Diues. What fatasy hast thou
that men do it nat for deuocion
Pauper. For the people these
daies is fulle vndeuoute to god
and to holy churche. and they lo
ue but ful lytel mē of holy chur
che/ and they ben lothe to come
in holy churche. Whanne they be
bounde to come thider/ & fullo‑
the to here goddes seruyce Late
they come & sone they go aweye
If they been there a lytel whyle
theym thynketh fulle longe.
They haue leuir go to the tauer
ne than to holy church Leuyr to
here a songe of Robyn Hode. or

of some rybaudry. thanne to he/
re messe or matyns/or any other
of goddes seruyce. or any word
of god And sithen the peple hath
so lytel deuocion/ to god and to
holy churche/ I can nat se þ they
do suche coste in holy church for
deuocion. ne for the loue of god
¶ For they dispyse god day and
nyght wt their wycked swynge
and their wychyd thewys.

The lii. chaptre.

DIues. Me thynketh that
it were better to peue the
money to the poore folke to the
blynde and to the lame/ Whose
soules god bought so dere/ than
so to spende it in solemnyte and
prydr and makyng of hygh chur
ches/ in riche vestmentes/ in cu=
ryous wyndowes/ & grete belles
For god is nat holpen therby &
the pore myght be holpen therby
ful moche. Pauper. If it be
done for pryde. or nat with gode
mesure they lese moche mede If
they do it of deuocion with dis=
crecion. it is medeful For euery
man pore and riche after his po
wer is bounde to worshyp goddes
house. so þ god lorde of al be ho/
nestly and worshypfully serued
And therfore god bad in tholde
lawe þ his peple shulde make hi

a fulle costly tabernacle att his
owne deuyse And he badde Sa
lomon make him a ful costly te̅
ple. and yit without dout ther
was many a pore may that tym
and both blynde and lame amo̅
ges goddes peple Moyses Da
uyd Salomon. Ioas. Iosias. es
dras. Iudas machabeus &many
other bothe in the olde lawe and
in the newe ben prysed highly of
god for makynge and worshyp
pynge and mayntenyng of god
des house and his seruyce And
as we fynde in the gospel þ ther
was a pore wydowe that offrid
to amendynge of goddes teple.
but two mytes that been worth
a ferthynge And she was prysed
of Crist/ for her offryng passing
alle other that offryd than moch
more And we fynde Exodi.
xxx. c. That god badde that in
nombrynge of the people euery
ma̅ shulde pay to his tabernacle
half a sicle/ that was fyue pe̅s.
and that the riche shuld peue no
more as for thanne. ne the pore
no lesse In token that riche and
pore shulde be besy to worshyp.
& to meintene goddes house and
goddes seruyce. God bad that
bothe the riche & pore shulde pay
alyke/ in toke̅ that the pore ma̅
shulde holde hym self as moche
bou̅de to god as shulde the riche

The firste

and the gode as the wyckyde. The gode is bounde to god for he kept him oute of synne. The wyckyd is. for god keppth hym that he peryssh nat for his synne Also god hadde bothe ryche and pore. pape euen to his tabernacle/in token that they ben bothe bought with one pryce of cristes preciouse bloode/ and that they shulde bothe holde them self alyke bounden. and that they haue bothe alyke nede of suffrages & helpe of holy churche Also god hadde theym both yeue alyke. I token that he acceptith their yiftes both alyke/if their deuocion be alyke in their yeuyng that y[e] riche man shulde nat be proude of his grete yift and of his richesses/ ne the pore falle in dispeyre. for his smal yifte and for his pouertie Natheleffe Who so may best do moste is bounde to helpe goddes house What it nedith. & so it is ful nedeful to arape wel goddes house/ and mayntene & increase goddes seruyce And also it is nedeful to helpe the pore folke in their grete nede/ and sū tyme more medeful than is the other. And therfore secue freend thou muste take hede to the tyme and other circumstances. For in tyme of welthe of peas and of plente Whanne the pore hath enogh or lightly may

be holpen/thāne principally mē shulde trauayle to worship god des hous and to encrese & mayntene goddes seruyce. But in tyme of wo warre and hūger of pouerte and other tribulacion; thā shulde men principally trauayle besily to their euyn cristen/ and take hede that no mā ne womā perisshed for defaute. But by besy to helpe the nedy bothe by preupnge and lenynge In token of this We rede. ii: Regū Vii. & i° past. xVii. & xxii. c. That god wolde nat suffre the kynge dauyd to make his temple. nat wt stōding that he wolde ful fayne haue made it/ and brought and ordeyned ful moche thyng therto For in his tyme the lōde was in moche tribulacion by warre. within and without/ by hūger. moreyne/ by discension and debate of them selue But he sayde to dauid that Salomon his son shulde make him a temple/ For he sayde he shalle reigne in peas and rest/in somoche that he shal be clepyd kynge peasible/ for in his daies I shalle yeue pees and reste in the londe of israel And Dauid whan he was in peas & reste and had discoūfyte his enemyes/ thanne he beganne to ordeyne for goddes temple & wold haue made it God coude hym moche thanke for his gode wyll

Precepte.

But he wolde natt suffre hym to make it/ for he was nat in so go de reste. as he wende to haue ben in. For after that beganne greate warre apenst him/ as we fynde Secundo Regum vii. et viii. c. And therfore god sayde to him/ Thou shalte natt make to me any house/ For thou haste shed moche blode. and thou arte a man of blode shedynge Bifore me That is to say I haue ordey ned the for to fighte apenst myn enemyes. and to slee theym and so to make peas. And I haue ordeyned thy sonne aftre the to make me an house/ in peas and reste/ that I shalle set hym in by thy sightynge and thy doynge.

The liii. chaptre.

But it faryth these dayes. By moche folke as it dide by Judas the traytoure. We fynde in the gospel Jo. xii. c. y mary maudeleyn anoynted the blissfulle feet of oure lord Jhesu with a precious oynemiente nat for any greate nede that Cryste hadde therto/ But for loue & de uocion that she hadde to him. Judas bare heuy therof & grut ched and sayd. Why is this opne ment thus coste. It might haue been solde for thre hundryd pes. and be peuen to the pore folke. But as seint John sayth in that same place Judas saide nat tho wordes for the loue that he had to the pore folke/ But for he was a theif and robbyde Cryste and his disciples of money that was peuen them. And therfore he wolde that the opnement hadde be solde for thre hundryde pens. and pouen to Cryste whiche so upd wel pore folk/ that he my ghat haue myched the money a way/ for he bare the purce. And for that he hadde nat his purpo se of the thre hundryd pens/ ther fore he solde Cryste for thre hun dryd pens. that was thretty pla tes and peces of syluer. For eche one of tho thrytty was worth y. smalle pens. On the same maner/ these dayes sume folke gruche for deuociones and nede ful coste that men done in holy churche/ & say as Judas sayd/ y it were better to peue it to poore folke But many of tho peue ful lytel tale holwe euyl the pore pe ple fare/ for they do ful lytell to the pore folke or to holy church either. But by ypocrispe and sy milacion of almesdede/ they w' drawen mennys deuocion from god and holy churche/ and from pore folke also. And soo they robbe holy churche and the pore folke. For they done lytel

f 7

The firste

them self/ and lette other þ wold doo And if they do almes to the pore blynde and lame/ they doo it to haue a name/ and for to exclude or putte behynde greter almesses that they been bounden to as to worshyp holy churche. and in case gode mynysters & holy church/ and hem that trauayl holy in goddes seruyce. and studye in goddes lawe nyght & day and preche it to the peple & dede/ & worde/ and haue nede of bodily almesse/ of the whiche Cryste sayth in the gospelle. Luce. x. That suche werkemen and trauesoures ben worthy their mede And seynt poule sayth þ Cryste hath ordeyned theym that teche the gospelle & goddes lawe/ for to lyue by the gospel/ & by their prechynge/ nat as passyng beggers by the weye/ But honestly. & worshypfully as goddes knyghtes/ as seynt austyn sayth. super illud ßt. Producens fenū iumentis And therfore they that repreue nedefulle makynge of churches/ of bestmētes & bokes & nedefulle makynge of belles. and gruche ayenste the holy seruyce of god in holy churche/ ben foles & in Judas caas/ For they mayntene worldly worshyp. & lette goddes worshyp Natheles the waast cost of alle these thinges & other in holy churche done

for pryde and vayngloryе or envye of one parisshe ayenst another/ or for couetyce of the mynysters in the churche seculer or religious is gretly alway to be repreyd.

☙ The liiii. chaptre.

Jues. God byddyth in the gospel Mᵗ. xi. c. that whanne man or woman shulde praye he shulde go into his chābre/ and shytte the dore to hym. and so praye the fader of heuyn Paul. In tho wordes Cryste techyth vs nat oonly where we shulde praye/ but he techyth vs howe we shuld pray For the chābre that we shuld entre in is our herte/ for in our prayer we shuld gadre our inwyttes & oure thoughtes to gyddre in oure herte/ & sette oure herte only in god and take hede to oure prayer. The dore that we shulde shytte been oure v. wyttes outwarde to flee distraction. For thāne we shuld kepe wele ovre sight our heryng oure felynge/ oure tastynge and smellynge. that ther come noo distraction into oure herte by any of oure fyue wyttes.
And be badde alsoo in the same place/ that men in theire prayer shulde fle ypocrisye. and vayne glorie. And to flee alle this it is

Precepte.

fulle spedefulle to man and woman whanne they may nat goo to churche/ to go to their chambre/ and into their oratory. and saye there theire prayere and deuociones But if they dispyse goddes house & leue goddes seruyce for such pryue prayer/ they synne greuously/ and lese mede of their priuey prayer And therfore the kalwe bydopyth that they that haf pryue oratories or chapelles by leue of the busshop. to here in their masse and their seruyce/ that in the greate festes as Ester. Cristmasse/ epiphany/ ascencion/ penticoste/ seynt Johṅ Baptyst & other such/ they shuld go to churche. and no prest shuld thanne synge in suche oratories or chapelles withouten speciall leue of the busshop/ and if he did he shulde be put from his masse. De consecrac. distinc. i. si quis. extra. Bothe pryue prayer and open been gode if they be doone in due maner. and in due place. and in due tyme Prayer is gode in chambre and in oratory/ But it is better in holy churche wyth the comunyte/ whan tyme is of comon prayer/ and whanne men may wele attende therto wᵗ feruet charite Synguler prayer of one psone is gode in chambre/ & in oratorie and better in church. With euᵣ charite. But comon prayer of a comunpte i churche is better thanne a singuler prayer if euery partie of that comunpte be in charite For Criste sayth in the gospel/ that if ii. or thre be gadryd to gider in his name that is charite/ there is he in the myddes of theym/ that is to say in their hertes to helpe them in their prayer. And if ii. of you sayth he consent to gider by charite i her prayer/ what euyr they aye it shalbe doo to theym Mᵗ. ⁱ⁸viii. And therfore sayth seynt ambrose. sup istud ad Ro. v̄i. adiuuetis me in orationibus vestris. That whanne many smale been gadryd to gidre they ben fulle grete And it is nat possible that the prayers of moche folke in charite shulde nat spede. And therfore sayth the prophete Joel ii°.c. Halowe ye your fastynge. clepe ye cumpany to you/ gadre ye the peyple to gydre And whan ye be gadryd make ye you holy & clene of synne/ take ye the old folkis wᵗ you & gadre ye to gider the yong children souking al to prayer For right as a voice of a multitude is myghtier & ferther may be herde than the voyce of one psone alone/ so is the voyce & pyer of a multitude soner herd thã is the voyce of one psone al one & soner getith grace. & therfore the pphet saith Laudate d.o.

gentes/ et collaudate cum om̅s popu̅li. Alle foll;es p;yse ye the lo;de/ and alle peoples p;yse ye him to gydder And seynt Poule Ad colocenses iiii. c. Byddeth. b men shuld yeue them to p;ayers and wake in p;ayer and thāking es in that they shulde p;aye all to gidre. Diues. Moche peple. lye seke in their bedde/ and mo; che in p;yson/ many one on the see. and in other nedefulle occu; paciones/ and may nat come to churche/ and men duelle in ma; ny dyuerse londes. many thou; sā̅de myles atwynne/ how shuld they p;ay and p;yse god alle to gidre. Pauper. Al if they may nat come to gyder in one place/ ne in one churche/ yit they must cū̅me to gyder in charite/ that yᵉ multitude of cristen peple be of one herte and of one loue and of one feyth.

The lv chapter.

Diues we make many ga dryng̅es to gidre many ge neral p;cessiones and p;ayers in conion to p;ay for the pees/ and yit haue we noo pees/ But euery yere more warre thanne other &̅ euery yere spede worse thā̅ other Pauper. If men came to gidre and made their p;ayers in folw; nes/ clēnesse &̅ charite. god shuld

here them/ Fo; he sayth if ii. o; iii consent to gydre in charite what they axe to the worshyp of god. &̅ to helpe of their soules it shall be done to hem of my fader But oure p;ayers and p;ocessions be ayenst charite/ made with grete p;yde Fo; al yf men go on p;o; cession fo; the peas/ and synge &̅ say with their mouthe Da pacē domine. Lord yeue vs pees/ yit with hert men p;aye alle ayenst peas. Fo; they wolde noo peas haue/ ne desire peas/ But alway to haue werre and to shede cristē mennys blode Fo; nat withstō̅; dynge alle the myscheif that the peple is in bicause of werre/ and that we haue the worse on euery syde/ yit the peple sayth̅ that it is beter to haue werre than pees &̅ they haue leuyr to here of wer than of peas. And they say that they may natt lyue withouten werre And whanne god sent he̅ worshypfulle peas on euery side they dispysed pees/ and slewe he̅ that made peas fo; that they tra ueyled to make peas. And the peple had leuyr pay grete taxes fo; shedynge of mānes bloode/ thanne fo; to paye smalle taxes fo; to haue peas. And sithe they loue no peas/ ne desire peas and wole nat haue peas though god wolde yeue theym pees withou; ten doubte they p;ay nat fo; yᵉ peas for no man prayeth for a thynge that he wole nat haue And so in their prayers and pcessions they scorne god/ & more puoke him to vengeaunce thanne to mercy Also they make their prayer nat with lowlnes/ but w' grete pride/ for they wole nat be knowe of any myschepf. They holde them selue so stronge and so wyse that as them thynketh. they haue no nede of helpe. And therfore though god here vs nat in oure prayer/ ne helpe vs it is no wounder.   For with oure mouth we aye peas/ But w' oure hert we aye werre/ w' our mouth we say kyrieleyson.   Lorde. haue mercy on vs/ But with our herte we praye him to helpe vs. to sle our euen cristen that wold lyue in peas And so oure prayer is alle oute of charite/ and oure supynge is fulle synful. and ful highly ayenste the plesaunce of god.

☞ The lxi. chapter.

Dives. It is a comon prouerbe. that a shorte prayer thyrleth heuene. Oratio breuis penetrat celū. And therfore sayth Cryste in the gospell M'. vi. c. Orantes nolite multū loqui. Whanne ye praye sayth he. nyl ye speke moche. Pauper.

It is a comon prouerbe of trutes that sone be wery of prayers and haue more haste to tauerne thanne to holy churche and haue more spkynge in the worlde. than in god Natheles if it be wel vnderstonde/ the puerbe is soth gode and holy For euery thyng is cleppd shorte.Whan the endes been nigh to gyder. And the ferther that the endes of any thyng is atwynne/ the leger is the thig And so it sarith by prayer   For the one ende of our prayer is our herte/ and the other ende is god. And therfore sayth seynt austyn that prayer is a styenge vp of a mannys herte to god   And on this maner the nigher that a mānes herte is to god in his prayer. by loue and lownesse and deuocion and right intēcion/ the shorter is his prayer And this maner of prayer thirleth heuene/ for as holy wrytte sayth. the prayer of him that lowet him in his prayer. thirleth the skyes or the cloudes. For the more that man loweth him in his prayer.the more be nigh to god/ for than god of his mercy bowyth downe to him And therfore Crist saith b he that so lowyth him self in his pyer he shalbe highed vp to god. And therfore seynt James saith b god withondith the proude. & to the lowe and meke of herte he peuetħ grace And on this maner speke a man neuir so moche/ as longe as his hert is nygħ to god by loue and sobnesse/ and right intencion and deuocion/ so lōge his prayer is but shorte. though he speke neuir somoche with his mouthe And as long as he may contynue his prayer so in deuocion/ it is seful and medeful to speke in his prayer. But whāne his speche begynnyth to let him of his deuocion it is gode to cese of his vocal prayer/ that is ȝ his obne free wyl But if he be bou(n)den therto by a vowe or confession or by ordre/ or by office/ than he must saye his bedys that he is bounde to and do his dette And he must say distincly/ nat to perne ne to atrete. For if he say to perne he may lyghtly ouirskypp. And if he saye to atrete/ he may falle into grete distraction a lose moch tyme. and leue therby many gode dedys that he might elses do/ and brynge him self in so thynge of prayer and lettyng of deuocion of him self/ and of the people also/ that wolde here his prayer and his office.

The lvii. chaptre.

Dues. Why badde thanne Cryst that men shuld nat speke moche in their prayer.

Pauper. Cryst bad nat vtterly þt me shulde nat speke moche in their prayer/ But he bad that me shulde nat speke moche in their prayer as hethen men do. For they wene that god shulde nat here them But if they spake moche. Also he badde vs nat speke moche in oure prayer as ypocrites done. to be holden holy a soo gette mennys gode For as crist sayth ȝ the gospel. Luce xviii. c. Suche deuoute wydowes houses by feynynge of longe prayer For as the glose saith thet/ they praye lenger thanne other/ to be holden more religiouse and hoslyer thanne other. And therfore their prayer turneth into synne. Ȝ somoche that they may neither wele praye for themself ne for other. And for suche prayer they shal the more be dampned. as cryste sayth in the same place Mat. vii. c. This people worshyp me wᵗ their lyppes/ But her herte is ful ferre fro me For god is in heuene/ and their herte and thoughte al in erthe It is a comō prouerbe/ that who so spekyth vnwysely and beynely/ or in evyl maner/he spekyth to moche And therfore as longe as a man or woman prayeth wysely. deuoutly and with gode ītencion. so longe he spekyth nat to moch But if he praye vnwysely wyth

Precepte.

pryde and wycked intēcion/ he spekyth to moche though he spe ke neuir so lytle And therfore yͤ pharise spake to moche in his py er/ for he spake alle with pryde. And petit spake to moche/for he spake vnwysely/ a therfore crist repreuyd them bothe. Also they speke to moche in their prayer. that sett their hert and feyth mo re in sownynge and sayng of yͤ wordes. than they do in god. or in the thynge that they pray for and say ayen and ofte ayen We nynge that god herde them natt yl whanne by suche iteracions they been wery/ and leue many deuociones that they shuld saye

And therfore sayth the wyse man/ Non iteres verbū in ora tua. Eccle. vii. Sey no worde ayen in thy prayer For suche doubte is lettynge of deuocion. for suche speke ouir moche/ and make their prayer in wanbileue

For if mannes herte be to god ward. god herith his praier thōge or he speke it with his mouth. Diues. Sithen god is ouir all present/ why pray we more i ho ly churche than in other place. Pauper. For asmoche as he is ouir al/ therfore i euery place he owyth to be worshiped But for asmoch as we may nat worship him in due maner in euery place

Therfore is holy churche ordey ned that men shulde fulfyl there y they leue in other places. And therfore in euery salue god hath ordeyned certeyne places of pra yer where he wolde be worshiped in/ passynge other places/ and y for many styplles. Firste for co mon prayer and prisynge is mo re plesaunte as I saide firste Al so to fle errounes and ydolatrye For if eche man or womā drewe him alone alway in his prayer. the feende shulde diseyue hym. by illusions and by iapen/ as he dothe comonly them that fle cū pany. and loue to be moche so litary. Also for to exclude slouth in goddes serupce/ y man and woman shulde falle in For but they were boūde to come to gider in some certayne place. to worship her god and to here god des salue/ they wolde elles trou ant. and worshyp god i no place but ful selden And they wold ex cuse theym by vncūnyng if they dyd amys. Also holy churche is ordeyned for comon prayer and goddes serupce : that eche man a woman may bere wytnes of o ther at the day of dome/ ayenste the feend/ that he dyd in that as a cristen man oughte to doo and serupd his god. For as seynt poule sayth/ So must alle haue

g ii

wytnesse of oure feyth by dedys and tokens outwarde.

The lviii. chaptre

Dives. Wherto shulde we pray to god for any thyng for he is nat chaūgeable. And he may nought yeue vs but that he wyste were before the begynnig of the worlde that he shulde yeue vs Pauper. We pray nat for to chaūge his endles ordenaūce But for to gett by prayer that he ordeyned w'outen ende to graūte vs by prayer For sithe he is our lorde, and we may nought doone no thynge haue without hī. he wose that we pray to hym as to oure lorde, and in oure prayer knowlege hym oure lordeAnd he wose nat graūte vs many thīges that vs nedyth, but we pray hym therfore Diues. Why pray we to god with oure mouth, sith he knowyth alle oure thoughte, alle oure desire, al our wyl, and what vs nedyth. Paup. For as I sayde firste god wose that we knowlege hym for our lorde and knowlege oure nede þ we maye nat do, ne haue no thynge without hym. Whiche knowlegyng must be doone with the mouthe. For seynt poule sayth if a man, or womā wol be saued, he must haue right bileue in herte ward and knowlege it oute warde w' his mouth. Ro. x.c. Corde enim creditur ad iusticiam, ore autem confessio fit ad salutem. More ouer leue frende ye shalle vnder stonde, that ther is ii. maner of prayer, one is comon, another is singuler Comon prayer is the prayer of the ministres of hooly churche and of comon persones. in holy churche, whiche prayer, they make in the name of al the pepyle. And this maner of prayer must be done by mouth, that yͤ pepyle may knowe that they bye for them And therfore it is ordeyned by the lawe that suche prayer shuld be sayde, and sumtyme singe openly with highe voyce. that the people may here it But singuler prayer that is done but of one singuler persone, may be done with herte alone withouté voyce of the mouthe Natheleesse sumtyme it is gode to hym that prayeth to praye by mouth And that for many skylles, Firste to excite his herte to more deuociō by outwarde tokenes And therfore as longe as man or womā. is stired to deuocion by speche or vocal prayer. by knelynge, lou tynge fastynge, or any other oð seruaunce reasonable, so longe it is wele doone to vse it. in his

Precepte.

prayer/ But if he be lettyd therby from deuocion and/ falle therby in distraction/ it is better to leue it for a tyme than to vse it. For we fynde primo regū ii. c. That anne spake in herte to god with bytter terys/ and yitt ther herde no man her voice Also mē pray with the voice of the mouthe in yeldynge of dette. For man is bounden to serue god with euery might and vertue y god hath youen him/ w' hert worde werk with al his might with alle his wytte And therfore holy church syngith and saythe. Os lingua mens sensus vigor confessionē psonent. Mouth tunge wytte & mighte, make knowlechynge & praisynge to god. And on this maner bodys bidynge is partie of satisfaction for synne. Also men pray w' voyce of the mouþ for greate deuocion y is warde in herte Whiche brekith oute by speche of the mouthe/ as saythe Criste in the gospel. Luce vi. Ex habundancia cordis os loquitur. The mouthe sayth he spekith of suche thinges wherof is plentie in the herte. And therfore the prophete saith. Letatū est cor meū: et exultauit lingua mea. Myne herte sayth he was mery and glade ynwarde/ and anone my tunge made ioye oute

warde. Also men pray w' voyces in speche to the more confusion of the feende/ for he may nat knowe mēnys deuocion illward. But but by tokenes oute warde. And the more deuocion and soue that he seeth men to haue to god/ the more is his confusion & his peyne And therfore is he soo besy these daies to tempte men i holy church to pryde/ to couetise to sleuth/ glotony/ and lichery. to lett holy prayers in holy church/ Whiche is to him very confusion and sorowe And therfore sayth the prophete of him whan he herith holy prayers and seeth men deuoute. Peccator videb' et irascetur: dentib' suis fremit et tabescet. The synful wreche the feende of helle shalle se menys deuocion: and he shalbe sul wroth He shal crosche or gnaste with his teeth. and be sul euyl abasshed For the desires of deuyles and their disciples that wold let holy prayer shal perisshe and come to nought

The lix. chapter.

Ives. In the begynnyng of holy church and i the tyme of the apostles. Was no suche seruyce and solenyte in holy church as nowe is

g iii

The friste

Pauper. Than were but fewe cristen men/ₐ neither they mighte ne durste make suche solennpte for tyrauntrye of the hethen people. Their wylle was gode/ but they mighte nat/ but as they mighten they dyd worshyp to god. and encresyd goddes seruyce.

And therfore we rede I the lyf of seint clement that by his preching and teching within one yere wel made seuenty churches in oone lytel yle of Cersone. nat withstondyng that ther were ii. thousande of pore cristen men outlawyd and dampned to fulle hard trauayl/ and myght haue be releuyd fulle moche releuyd w' that that tho churches costyd.

Thanne holy churche was I his youthe and in his begynnynge. as sayth seynt Jerom ĩ prologo super actus aplõrũ. Nowe holy churche is weyyd. ₐ the feyth sprong and spredde and stabled in peas fro tyrauntes And therfore nowe we muste worshyppe oure god with alle oure myght. and oure cũnynge/ for we haue none excusation as they hadde.

And for to auoyde ydelnesse of prestys our faders bifore this tyme ordeyned the prayers in holy churche to be sayde after a certeyn fourme/ after the custome of diuerse cũtrees kepe theit our after the oures of the day/ as matynes at morowe and masse afterwarde. and euynsonge apeȝt euyn: so that god shulde be pryfed of the preestes alle tymes of the day. Diues. Me thynketh ẏ it were better to say goddes seruyce in holy churche withouten note thanne with note and hackynge of the syllabes. and wordes in oure prayer and prisynge as as we doo. For who shulde telle the kyng of Englond a tale or make his prayer to him and made soo many notes and hackynges in his tale/ he shulde haue lytel thanke. Pauper. The kyng of heuyn is aboue yͤ kyng of Englonde/ and otherwise we muste worshyppe hym thanne the kyng of englonde for he muste worshyp him with alle oure myght. and alle oure herte/ and al oure wytt/ as him that is maker ₐ lorde of alle thinge. And soo may we nat worshypp the kynge of englonde It nedyth nowe to speke to the kynge of englonde and to euery erthly man distinctly/ for they knowe nat mannys herte ne his wylle But god knowyth it long or we speke it with oure mouth And therfore whan we synge in our prayer with clenesse of lyf ₐ deuocion of hert we plese god in as moche as we wor

Precepte.

shipe hī wᵗ oure powre of voyce & tunge. For euery note so sunge to god in the churche or in other conuenient place for deuocion in our self, & to engendre deuocion in other is a praisyng to god. And therfore dauid saythe. Cantate exultate et psallite. Synge ye & make ye mery outwarde, and synge ye to god craftely. Jubilate deo omnis terra: seruite dño in leticia Introite in cōspectu eius in exultatōe Alle ye that duelle vpon the erth make ye hertly ioye to god. serue ye oure lorde in gladnes Entre ye in his sight with ioye and myrthe. For many sciplles leue frende, songe and melodye was ordeyned in holy churche. First to the more worshippyng of god. Also to the more excitatione of deuocion of the people. Also to putte away heuynesse and vnlustynesse, as saith seynt Bernard For many mā hay more liking more likyng to serue god ī gladnesse than in heuynesse And therfore goddes office shulde be said liuely, distinctly, deuoutly with gladnesse of herte. For if the office be sayde or sunge so hauely & dedely & so drawen alonge þ it so the both the synger or sayer & the herer, & bryngeth follre into heuynesse or distraction, it is euyl said or songe. For that maner of syngyng is settyng of moche godenesse, and cause of ydelshyp & of moche foly. for it maketh mē to withdrawe theym fro goddes house and from goddes seruyce. and so wante grace. De con. di. B. nō mediocriter. Also we syng in churche to cōfourme vs to seintes in heuen Whiche pryse god & serue god aluey wᵗ hygh voyce. and swete syngyng, as we fynd in the apocalipse. & many other places in holy wrytte And therfore dauid sayth. Cantate dño canticum nouum: laus eius in ecclesia sanctorū. Synge ye a newe songe to oure lorde. for suche is his prisynge in the church of al seintes And therfore songe in holy churche is gode Whanne it is sunge deuoutly in clenes of lyf, roundely nat settyng the deuout praier of the peple, as doth this curtiouse knackyng. sunge of the viciouse mynistres in the churche. & specially in grete and riche churches For it is ofte seen that the syngers in suche places. and other also ben fulle proude. glutones and lechoures also.

And the melody of suche men is no plesaunce to god, but harmeth themself and many other.

The lx. chaptre

Ⓓives. Why been nowe no martiris as were wont to be. Pauper. We haue these dayes martires alse to many in this londe. Diues. Howe soo. Pauper. For the mo martires. the more murdre and manslaughter and the more shedyng of Innocentes blode / the more Vengeaunce shal fal therfore. Diues. Moche sorre is slayne these daies / But that they shulde be martires I can nat say. Pauper. All that ben slayne for the treuth pacyently in charite ben martirs / in asmoche as they wytnessen the treuthe and stonde therwith Vnto their deth For martir in latyn is a wytnesse in englisshe It is no worshyp to any londe or nation to haue many martres of her slepynge / But it is an endles shame. And therfore the Jewes that slewe Cryste and his disciples. & prophetes & made martres withoute nombre / Ben in dispyte and repreef alse aboute the worlde. And therfore Criste saide to hem that alle the rightful blode whiche they hadde shedde from ye begynnynge of the Worlde shulde falle Vpon theym & harde Vengeaunce therfore shuld come to hem And the romaynes that slewe petyr and many martres in euery londe there they hadde lordshyp nowe they haue lost her lordshyp & Ben wretches of wreches / and Bothe the cite and the temple semyth acursed And now englissh nacion hath made many martires They spare neither their owne kyng ne their Busshopes / noo dignyte / noon order / no state ne degre / But indifferently slee as men Sheteth. and so Vengeaūce & Wreche folowith theym / and grace & worshyp hath forsaken them. Was it neuir worship to theim yt they slewe seynt Thomas. their Busshop and their fader. ne that they wolde by comon clamoure & comen assent haue slayne their owne kynge. Martyrdome is Worshipful theym that in charite suffre the deth / & to theim that holde with them in their treuthe. But it is shame and shenshyppe to theym that done them to deth Vnrightfully. And for asmoche as ye multitude of shrewdys is so greate / & falshode is so mightye yt the treuthe is ouirsette & Borne downe & true folke so martryde. We shuld wepe and nat joye for that we haue so many martires / & night and day cry mercy to sey wreche. If hethen peple or other nacions had made oure martirs We might reioyse Bo of our matris But in we haue slayne them oure self we ought be asshamd.

The lxi. chaptre

Precepte.

Jues. Sithe they be martirs why doth god no myracles nolle for them as he dyd for martirs/ and other seyntes i the begynnyng of holy churche. Paup. If a lorde haue but a felbe true seruauntes. he wole pryse them and magnifie them/ and do them worshyp. Bothe to holde theym stylle in hys seruice. and also to drawe other to his seruyce by ensample of them And the same dothe the maister in scole. to the children that lerne wele. And whane the moder hath but one childe she cherisethe it the more. and kepith him the more derely. Right so Criste in the begynnyng of holy churche hadde but felbe gode disciples or true seruātes/ and therfore he worshiped. and magnified theim with grete myracles to comforte them i the seyth/ and for to drawe other to the seyth. For but god hadde she wyd thanne grete miracles and many/ they þ were in the seythe. shulde haue forsaken the seythe and selbe wold haue come to þe seyth. And it farith by holy church ce ẻ by the seyth as it doth by a tree. Whan a tre is newly set mē water it and sett stakes and poles aboute to strenght it apenst the wyndes blastes/ for stormes shulde elles bryse it or breke it/ ẻ

felle it adowne. But whan it is wel rotyd ẻ comōly weyen than men cese of wateryng and take a way the stakes and the poles. Right so whan holy church and cristendome was in the begynnyng/ criste watryd holy church with greate pistes of grace/ ẻ of deuocion/ ẻ vnderset it wᵗ grete wounders and myracles/ whiche he shelwyd that tyme apenst the harde stormes of psecution that was that tyme apenst the seyth of holy churche. But nowe holy churche is spriuge and spred and the seith is stabled in mēnys hertes/ and therfore suche miracles cese. And if any suche myracles falle in any londe amonges cristen peple it is a token that sume of them be nat stable in the seith ẻ that god is nat al apaide with the people For seint poule saith þ tokenes and miracles ben nat pouen to folk of righte bileue. But to folk of false bileue And the mo myracles that men se/ þᵉ lesse mede they haue for her seith as seynt gregory sayth in his Omely And so multitude of martirs and of miracles proue natt godenesse of the peple that they been doone amonge. But rather they shelbe and preue the malice of the people.   Whanne god shuld distroy the kingdome

of israel and of iuda for ydola‑
try and other synne that nigh al
the peple was fallen in/ he sente
his famo⁹ pphetes as hely/ and
helisee. psaie. ieremye. danyel &
zechiel & other yit. pphetes whi‑
che taught the peple goddes law
& warnyd theym of mischeyf cũ‑
mynge but they wolde amende
theym And they cõfermyd theire
prophecy w' many greate mira‑
cles/ & yit the people was worse
than euir they were bifore At the
laste cryst came to preche and to
teche them and dyd many wou͂‑
ders/ and helyd alle maner seke
nesses & sent his apostles also a‑
monges theym/ whiche dyd ma
ny wounderful myracles. And
yit the people was thanne wors
thanne euir they were aforne In
somoche that they slewe nat on‑
ly the prophetis & the apostles &
cristes disciples/ but they slewe
criste himself goddes sone of he‑
uen. lorde of al thinge. Whiche
had done hem so moche worshipe
& done so many wonderful curtsees
amonges theym.

The lvii. chapter.

Diues. I trowe that if men
were nowe as holy as men
were thanne/ they shulde do my
racles nowe as they dyd thanne

Pauper Though they were as
holy or holier they shulde nat do
suche myracles For they be nat
nowe so nedefulle as they were
thanne/ ne it were nat pfitable
to the people. as I sayde righte
nowe And I hope that they ben
as holy that do no myracles as
many of theim þ done miracles.
For suche doynge of myracles.
stondith nat in the holynesse of
him that dothe the miracle/ But
it stondith in the clepynge. & the
vertue of goddes name to the p
fyrte of other/ and ofte to damp
natiõ of him that so clepith god
des name and doth the myracle
As saith the glose. sup' istud M'
Vii⁰ D͂ne nõne in nole tuo pphe
tauimus. Diues. It semyth
therby that shrewis and wycked
lyuers may do miracles Paup
Criste saith so himself M'. Vii.c
For as we rede there. at the doo
me many that shalbe dampned.
shal say to Criste O lorde we p
phecyed in thy name and castyd
out feendes and dyd many tok
nes and myracles in thy name.
But he shalle say ayen to them.

Wendyth hense fro me ye wor‑
chers of wychednesse. I knowe
you nat for none of myne. And
as sayth seynt Iohn Crisostom
in tractatu. Nemo seditur nisi
a semetipso.

Precepte.

That Judas the traitoure had powher of god for to do and dyde many greate miracles, yit is he dampned. Also doynge of miracles is no syker tokene of godenesse neither of the doer ne of peple there that they ben done. But only charitie and gode liuynge been syker token of godenesse. And therfore Criste taughte vs to knoll the gode prophetes from the wycked. nat by her miracles ne by their prophecy, But by her gode dedys and charite. Therby saith he men shal knowe that ye be my disciples if ye haue charite amōges you, nat by miracles ne by prophecy. For iudas dyde miracles, and cayphas and Balaam fulle cursed wreches. prophecyed fulle truly. And seynt Iohn Baptiste that was so holy dyd neuir suche miracles by his lyf. And therfore Cryste badde we shulde take hede to mennys dedys and knolle them by their frupt. Diues. Ipocrites and heretikes do ful many gode dedys and yit be they shrewys. Paup. Suche maner of folke haue ii. maner of dedys, one in priuey, another in apert or open.

Their dedis in apert be nat theirs. But they ben clothinges of shepe vnder whiche they hile theim or couer them as wolues to dissey-

ue gode shepe. And therfore crist byddith in the gospel yᵗ we shuld be ware of false prophetes. that ȳ come to vs in clothynge of shepe, for they ben inwarde wolues of rauey̅y. If their dedys be wycked, it is her owne clothing wherby they may be knowē. But her priuey werkes and their pryuey teching ben their owne frute whiche comōly ben ful wycked. And so by that that they do and teche priuely men may best knowe what they been. Diues. I may wele assent to thy speche for so many woundres haue fal in this londe within a felwe yeres in sunne mone and sterres, I fond I rede in the ayer that we rede I no boke yᵗ euir sel so many in so litel tyme. And as men sey ful wicked spuets do many miracles & prophecye, & yit we wante grace on euery syde, & the harde vengeance of god is vpon vs nighte & day, shewynge that god is greuously offedyd wᵗ vs. Pauper. As saith the glose. sup illud. ii. ad thessalo. ii. c. In signis & prodigiis mendacibus. For asmoche as the peple is oute of charite & wole nat knolle the treuth, But trust al in lesynges & in falshede. Therfore god suffreth false shrewys for to do woudres & miracles for to disceyue the peple. &

The firste

to holde them styl in her errour. I haue sayde as me thynketh say forth what thou wylte.

The lviii. chaptre

Diues. What seyst thou of them that wole no solempnyte haue in their buriynge. But be putt in erthe anon, and that þ shulde be spente aboute the buriyng they bydde that it shulde be youen to the pore for þe blynde and lame Pauper. Comonly in such priue buriynges ben ful smalle doles and lytel almes youen And in solemne buriynges. Been grete doles, and moche almesse youen, for moche pore people come thanne to seke almesse But whanne it is done priuely felwe wytte therof. and felwe come to aue almesse, for they wote nat whanne ne where ne whom they shulde aue it. And therfore I leue sikerly that summe fals executoures that wolde kepe alle to themself. Bigane firste this errour and this folye. Diues. And yit men holde it a grete pfection these daies. Pauper. Though men burie their frendes priuely. or auertly, it is no harme to the dede ne to the liuynge But if the worship of god be withdrawen. and the almesse of the pore nedy and the holy prayers and suffrages of holy churche/ Whiche ben ordeyned to be praied and done for the dede and the quicke that haue nede therof But it is a grete foly and also a grete synne to forsake solempne buriynges, þ be done principally for the worshyp of god and for the proufyt of the dede/ spendyng his godes to nedeful releuyng of holy churche/ and the pore nedye people þ been of no power to helpe theim self. for that is a custome of fals executoures that wolden make themself riche with dede menys godes/ and nat dele to the pore. after dedes wylle/ as nowe alle false executoures vse by custome. And so they that forsake worshipful buriynge as I haue rehersyd bifore sette the prisyng the worshippe/ and the sacrifice and offrynge that shulde be done to god. They do also dispyte to holy churche, in that that they forsake the prayer. and the suffrages of holy mynistres of holy churche. Also they offende all the soules of purgatory that shulde be releuyd by messes syngynge/ hooly prayer and suffrages of holy churche/ Whiche ben ordeynyde in buriynge to helpe

Precepte.

of alle cristen soules. And they please the feende that is besy night and day to lette goddes office, goddes worshyp and holy pier. Also they offende mankynde, and god that toke mankynde, of a woman, in asmoche as they putte their body in suche dispite and pryue it of the due worship. For the body of a gode man, or of a gode woman that is knytte to that precyouse soule þ Cryste bought so dere. With his precyous blode, with whiche soule it shal ryse apen at the dome, and lyue in blysse withouten ende, brighter than the sonne, it is of ful grete dignyte, al if it be here in grete mysschepf for a tyme for Adames synne. Mannys body is of ful grete dignyte in that, þ god toke oure body of a woman alone, and bicame man withouten parte of man, and bodily in oure kynde reigneth god and man aboue alle creatures. And therfore by wey of kynd and for worship of god that toke oure kynde, it oweth to be worshiped, namely in his deth, for than is no drede of pryde. And therfore sayth the wyse man. Eccle. vii. c. Mortuo non prohibeas graciam. Withdrawe nat thy grace, & thy mercy from the dede. That is to say withdrawe nat ne lette natt

the due seruyce and worshipfull cerymonies that longe to the body, ne the suffrages and prayers that longe to the soule as sayth, the the glose. And in a nother place he sayth thus. Sonne wepe thou on the dede man. With bytter teres and grete sorow, and after his state as righte is hyle his body, dispyse nat his buriynge. make mornynge one day or .ii. after his deserte. Eccle. xxxviii c. For by the lawe of kynde, by lawe writen, by lawe of grace & euery tyme worshipful sepulture after mennys power hathe be due dette to mannys body and womannes. In the lawe of kynde haue we exaumple of Abraham, Isaac and Jacob, and her wyues, whiche hadde ful costly buryinges. As we rede in holy wrytte. Gen. l. vi. c. And in the lawe wryten haue we exaumple, of Samuel, Dauid, salomyn, Iosaphat, ezechie, iosie, tobie, and of the machabeis, whose buryinges were costly and worshipful. In the lawe of grace that is in the new lawe haue we exaumple of oure lorde Ihesu Cryste, whiche nat withstondynge that he suffryde spytefulle deth for mankynde, pit he wolde haue, and hadde worshyppfulle and costly sepulture and buriynge.

The firste

As we fynde in the gospelle Jo. xix. c. Wherby as the glose saith there þe paue men exāple to kepe worshypful buriyng after þe custome of the cuntre And therfore þe cōmendyd mary mawdeleyn / þ she came bifore his dethe to anoynte his body so preciously and costly into the sepulture. And many seyntes were buryed worshipfully by the doynges of aūgelles / as seynt Clemēt. seint katheryne / seynt agace / and many other And seint poule the first hermete was buryed worshipfully and woūderly by worchinge of lyons / and of wylde bestes / & tokenyng that mannys body & womans owe to haue worshypful sepulture. For sithen aungelles and wylde bestes dyde suche worship to mannys body after his deth More more māk ynde shulde worshyp mannys body: after his deth / and doo worship to his owne kynde. And so men shulde releue pore folke in their myschefs / and specially in their dyynge by almes yeuyng Butte they shulde nat for that do any wronge by their lyuyng to their euen cristen for to make them riche to do morre almesse at their endyng. For as the lawe sayth. ther shulde no man be made riche with wronge and harme of ano

ther. Locupletari non debet aliquis cum alterius iuria Vel iactura. Extra de regulis iuris. li: bro vi.

The lxiiii. chaptre.

Dives. What sayst thou of them that holde markettes and feyres in holy churche & in sanctuary / Pauper. Bothe the byer and the seller and men of holy churche that mayntene hem or suffre them whanne they myght lett it ben acursed. For we fynde nat that euir Criste punisshed so hard any synne while he went here in erth / as he dyd byyng & sellynge in goddes house as we fynde Jo. ii. c. On a tyme he came into the temple of Jerusalem / and there he fonde mē biyng and sellyng oxen & shepe and doues to be offryd in the temple / and chaungers of money also to be offryd in the temple. He was hyghly offendyd / and made a scourge and bette them out of the temple / and saide to them on this wyse Myne house shuld be an house of prayer / and ye haue made it a dene of theuys. Bere ye out said he this marchaūdise Lede hēs these bestes & make ye nat my faders hous an house of

marchaundise and a dene of the⸗
ups. And as seynt Matheu tel⸗
leth & other gospellers/ he drewe
downe her bothes/ and ouirtur⸗
nyd theire stalles and their setis
and shedde their money. And as
seint marke sayth. He wolde nat
suffre no vessel that was nat lō⸗
gynge to the temple. to be borne
through the temple. And sithen.
Cryste wolde nat suffre thynge
be solde in the temple/ that was
only for the worship of god. and
help of the temple. Moche more
he wole nat suffre thynge to be
solde in the temple that longith
nat to the temple. But only to se⸗
culertie. Diues. Sithen god
was soo offendyde for that men
solde therin that was nedeful to
the temple. and for easement of
hem that came fro ferre cuntrees
what shuld he haue do/ if he had
founde them bivnge and selling
thynge of seculerte Or if he had
founde theym in bacbityng and
glotony/ dronkenshyp/ licherv/&
songe a specche of rybaudrye. as
mēvse these daies ī holy church.
Pauper. Seynt austyn sayth.
that as he trowyth he shulde haf
caste them to the pytte of helle.
Diues. Howe myghte Cryste y
was so pore a mā haue cast out
suche a multitude of people. It
is a wounder y they withstoden

him nat. Paup. For as the glo⸗
se sayth ther came suche a lighte
out of his face by wey of his god
hode as long as he wolde y they
were al aferid of the sight of his
face and fledde awaye. And for
the same sryplīy tyme of his pas
sio whā they came for to take hī
he sayde I am he y ye seke/ why
es they went bakwarde. and for
drede felle downe to grounde.
Diues. Why sayde he that they
made his hous a dene of theues
Paup. For who so is about to
begile any man or woman of his
gode/ he is a theef And in bying
and sellynge either of them is a⸗
bout to begile other/ and in that
they been theues. And for y they
doo it in goddes house & there ca
ste in their herte holve pryuelve &
how slighly they may begile her
euyn cristen/ therfore they make
goddes house a dene of theuys:

And comonly in suche fayres
and markettes where soo euir it
be holden/ ther ben many theues
nycchers and cutte purses.
Diues. And I drede me that
fulle often by suche fayres god⸗
des house is made a tauerne of
glutones/ and a bordelle of ly⸗
chours: For the marchaun⸗
tes and chapmen kepe there w&#xtsuperscript;t
theym their whyues & lēmannes.
bothe night and day. Pauper.

The firste

And if any man compne the flesshely with his wyf or his leman the churche and the church yerde also ben pollute And if it might be preuyd ther shulde no preeste synge ne say no messe therin/ ne body be buryed tyl it were recoū seiled ayen by the busshop. De con. di. i. Si motū. ꝭ c. significasti. Et io. in sūma sua. li° iiii. ti° CCxliii. Strū liceat/ Et durandus in sūma sua. li°. ii. p: t. di. viii. q̄ xxviii. Diues. And what if the prelates ꝭ the curates of the place take moneye of the chapmē for y° place y̆ they stode in by couenaunt made bifore/is it any symonye so to sel the londe of the seyntuary. Pauper. It is symonye ful grete for to selle any grounde in the sanctuary. for buryng. as the lawe shewith wele. viii. q̄. ii. q̄sta. ꝭ c° seqnti. Moche more to selle it or to sett it byte for marchaundyse And therfore suche marchaundyse in holy churche is forfendyd/ natt only by the gospelle/ but also by the comon lawe/ p vi: q̄. vii. Et hec diuinus/ For men of holy churche by suche symonye/ ꝭ takyng of thinges that they haue no right to/ ben bicome stronge theuys/ and make the chapmen theuys in that/ that they do hem occupye the place in sanctuarye

ayenst goddes wyl forde of the place And so they make goddes house a duellynge/ ꝭ a denne of theuys: Diues. Sithen men of holy churche do somoche dispite to god and holy church/ though they be ī dispite themself/it is no wounder Paup. That is soth For god sayth in holy wryt pri mo regū. ii. c/ Who so worshippeth me sayth he/ I shalle make him worshipful/ And they that dispyse me shalbe in dispyte. Diues. I thanke the with alle myn herte for that me thought sumtym no synne/nowe I kno we wele that it is a fulle greuo' dedly synne For the synnes and the erroures that we haue nowe spoken of/ ben openly ayenst y° worshpp of the high maiestye of god/ and ayenst the first cōmaū dement that moste oughte to be charged/ And thy sypples ben so grete and thy speche soo open/ ignoraunce myghte nat excuse me ne any wight elles that can reason And yit the peple by mys custome and ignoraunce of me of holy churche and of themself also by couetise and pryde of y° clergie is so blēt that they pbynk theym no synnes. And so we wander in synne blent with foly and wante grace. Pauper. Wykkyd custome aggregith syn

⁂The secounde precepte.

and nat excuseth synne. And therfore the lawe saith that euery wycked custome shulde be do away.

Here endith the firste pcepte. and begynneth the secounde precept. ⁂The firste chapter

DIues. I pray the enfourme me nowel yͤ secoũde gmaũdmẽt. Pauper. What doute haste thou therin Diues. In the secounde maundemente god byddeth that we shulde nat take his name i veyne. For who so dothe shalbe gilty ꝗ nat passe vnpunysshed. Pauper. In thre maners goddes name is taken i veyne. That is by mysspuyng. by mys speche/ ꝗ by mys heringe. Firste by mysspuyng/ for whan man or woman is cristned. theͤ he forsaketh the feende and alle his werkes and his lordshyppe. Whan his god fader and his god moder aunswere for him sayng. Abrenuncio. that is to say I forsake And there be knyttyth him to criste. ꝗ makith couenaunte with him to be his true seruaũte withouten ende And there be taketh the name of Cryste vpon him and bicometh cristen. For al

cristen people is named aft crpst and he is oure principal god fader. For cristen cũmyth of criste. and so alle cristen people bere yͤ name of criste vpon theim. And so in asmoche as we been cleppd cristẽ and goddes peple. in that we bere the name of god vpon. vs. And therfore sayth the prophete/ Tu in nobis es dñe et nomẽ sanctũ tuum inuocatum est super nos: ne dereliquas nos do mine deus nr̃. Jeremye xiiii. c. Lorde sayth he thou arte amonges vs/ as a lorde amonges his seruantes/ and thyn holy name is cleppd vpon vs/ lord our god forsake vs nat But if it be so. yͭ we lyue natt after oure name/ yͭ we haue taken of cryste ne lyue nat as cristen men ne as goddes seruauntes/ but forsake hym ꝗ turne ayen to the feende and lyue nat as cristen folk re/ But as iewys sarsyn or paynym/ or ellis worse. than take we goddes name in veyne. for oure name and oure lyf accordeth nat.

And as seynt poule sayth/ Wycked cristen folkre with their wycked dedys and their wycked lyuyng forsake god And therfore alle wych id lyuers and namely ypocrites that bere the name of holynesse and of cristes seruauntes. ꝗ whͪ they be yͤ feendes seruãtes/ they take goddes name in

h i

The seconde.

Beyne/ and do greate dispyte to goddes name And therfore crist saith to suche wycked cristen peple. Per vos tota die nomē meū Blaspsemat ī gētib⁹. psale lii c. Et ad Ro.ii: c. My name is dispised by you all day amonge other naciones or hethen men. For by the wycked lyuynge of cristē peple y name of crist is shamyd And therfore we say in oure prayer. Sanctificetur nomē tuū. Halowyd & worshippyd be thy name. That is to say graūt vs grace no thing to do/ ne wyl. ne to speke b/ wherby thy name shulde be vnworshyppde or shamyd in vs.

The seconde chapter

Also goddes name is take in veyne by mys speche/ & that in many wyse First by namynge of goddes name ī veyne tales tellynge/ in tapery ī scorne For in suche vanyte goddes name shulde nat be nampd. Diues. Telle sūme example Pauper. As if one sayde to the in scorne whanne he is wroth w' the/ god make the a gode man. And sūme say of a nother ī scorn that god hathe forsaken him/ &

tapers and disoutes comōly name goddes name ī veyne in this maner/ though they swere none othe. And al suche take goddes name in ydelshyp/ that teche any erroures or heresies apenst faith and apenst god/ or preche or teche the treuthe only for couetyse or for enuye/ or for vayne glory and nat for helth of mānys soule for worship of god And therfore the pphete saith thus. Peccatori autem dixit de⁹/ quare tu enarras iusticias meas: et assumis testamentum meum p os tuū. God sayde to the synful man/ why tellyst thou my rightfulnesses/ and takyst my testamēt ī my salv by thy mouth & so ofte nampst my name. For al tho that teche wele & speke wele and dose nat doo therafter: they take goddes name in veyne Also goddes name is takē ī veyne by cursyng & weryng/ as whan men or wymen in wrath or elles in nyce myrthe saye to a nother. god geue the mysschaūce/ god geue the euyl grace/ euyl deth Also it is taken in veyne oft tyme. By bowes makynge/ and that in dyuerse maner/ First if mā make any bowes to any creature. For bowes makynge is a dyuyne worshyp that owyth to be do only to god and to no creature.

And therfore the prophete saith. Vouete & reddite vnto deo vestro Make ye youre vowes to oure lorde god/ and yeldith theym to him. Also it is taken in veyne whanne folke kepe nat their vowes that been lefulle: But breke them retchessly/ or by freylte wᵗ outen nede & withouten auctorite. of their souerayne/ whiche haue power to dispēse with hem or chaunge their vowes. Also if men make vowes vnlefulle. agenst charite. & to do any thing agenst goddes lawe As if thou madest a vowe to sle thyn euyn cristen/ or ẏ thou shuldest neuyr do gode to pore men/ for parauēture sūme pore man hath aggreued the. Also whāne men make vowes vnwisely lightly wᵗoute aupsement and by comon custume of speche.

The .iii. chaptre

Dives. And suche vowes ben made these dayes ful many. For with moche folye be they ones spoken. they been noo more thought on. For they be so comon in theire mouthe.

Pauper. Therfore they synne ful greuously/ so takinge goddes name in veyne For ther shulde no vowe be made but for a thynge of charite/ and with a gode aupsement. ꟄWe fynde in holy wrytte Iudicum xi. c. that ther was a leder & a iuge of goddes peple/ whos name was Iept And whanne he shulde go to fight agenst goddes enemyes the sonne of amon/ he made his vowe to god that if he gaue him the victorye of his enemyes whā he came home agen what lyuig thing he mette first of his housholde in his cūmynge home/ he shulde sle it/ & offre it vp to god I sacrifice After this as god wold he hadde the maistree and came home with grete worship/ whan his doughter herde these tidynges she was full glade and toke her tymber in her honde and came in grete haste first of al the houshold daunsynge pleyinge & synginge agēst her fader for to welcome him home. Whanne Iept. sawe his doughter so cūmynge. agenst him he bithoughte him of his avowe and wexte ful sorye for he hadde no childe but her/ & he louyd her fulle moche Alas doughter/ allas sayde he. Whatt haste thou doone/ why cūmyste thou so sone agenst me. I haue openyd my mouthe to god. and made a vowe agenste the/ for I muste by my vowe sle the/ and offre the vp into sacrifice to god But the womā his doughter yt clene mayden was soo glade of goddes worship/ and of her fads worship/ and that goddes enmyes were so slayne/ that she made lytel sorowe or none for her deth and saide to her fader Iept. Sith thou haste made suche a vowe & god hath sent the victory of his enemyes/ fulfyl thy vowe. For I take the deth gladely. But I praye the of one boone or I dye Let me go with other maydens my pleyferes and mozne and bewayle my maydenhode amōge the hylles and the mountaynes. ii. monethes/ For it was that tyme repreef to a womā to dye wtouten issue of her body And Iept grauntyd her bone After ii. monethes. she came ayen to her fader Iepte/ and mekely suffryd ye deth for goddes sake and for the loue of her fader And thus seeue frende that womans deth which was clene maiden betoknyth cristes passion For right as she toke the deth wylfully for saluacion of goddes folke/ and distruction of goddes enemyes/ Soo criste clene mayden þ neuir was defouled with synne: and neuyr dyd amys. wylfully suffryde bitter deth for saluacion of alle mākynde and distruction of the feēdes power. Diues. Was nat his vowe lefulle. Pauper. It was nat lefulle For by his vowe if he hadde firste mette with a cat or an hounde cūmynge ayenst him he shulde haue made sacrifice to god therof/ which sacrifice shuld haue ben abhominacion to god for neither was able to be offred in sacrifice. And for asmoche as he made his vowe so vnwysely. god suffryd him to falle it to mischeyf to sle an inocēte his owne doughter ayenste goddes lawe. For god saith. Innocētē et iustū non occides. Thou shalte natt sle the innocent/ ne the rightfull manne woman And soo by his vowe so folily made/ he dyd ful greuous dedly synne. and forsetyd ful highly ayēst goddes law And therfore saith the master of the stories and Iosephus assoo that he was a foole in his vowe makyng and wycked/ and ouit done cruelly the fulfillynge. And therfore saith ye grete clerk ysodorus. in synonimis. li. ii. Et xxii. q. iiii. In malis pmissis rescinde fidem/ in turpi voto muta decretum/ quod icaute nouisti ne facias/ impia & pmissio. que scelere abimpletur. In wycked hestes kytte awaye feyth that is to say/ fulfylle noo wycked bihēestes/ kepe no faith to do amys. For in shrewyd bihestes it is bett to be holde fals thā true. For who so fulfilleth them is fals to god. In the bowe saith þ he is foule and vnlefulle chaūge thy dome/ and that that thou haste nat wisely auowyd doo it nat. For it is a wycked biheste þ is fulfilled & done with synne.

The iiii. chaptre

Dives. I assent/ say forth I pray the. Pauper. Also goddes name is taken veyne by blasphempe and spiteful speche of god/ as whan men grutch apenst goddes domes in seknes tribulacion and disease/ and sey that god is vnrightful and cruel or grutche apenste his mercy.

Whanne they may natt haue vengeaūce of their aduersaries. as they wolde haue/ & saye that god is to pacient and to mercyable. And they also that fal in wā hope/ and say that god wol nat foryeue theym their synne. And they also that presume to moche of goddes mercy; and wole nat amende theym/ for they say that god wole foryeue it them at the firste worde. Also sume saye that god slepith whanne he helpith theim nat as they wolde. Alle that speke thus or saye any other thing of god. that is apest

his worshhip and his godhode/ take goddes name in veyne by blasphemy. Also goddes name is taken amys and in veyne by mys speche of other swerynge. For who so wole lightly swere for a thynge of nought or of no charge/ or custumably or fallsly wytyng wele that he swerith false. or dispitously/ or dissepuably. or swerith any creature/ or by the any nyce othes/ or vnleful othes alle these take goddes name in veyne. For therwith noo man ne woman swere but for a treuthe of charge/ and whāne it nedith to swere to witnes of treuthe. And whanne a man shalle swere he shal swere by his god/ & by no creature. Dives. Moche folke is so brought in custume. of swering that vnneth they can speke thre wordes to gidder but they suere by god or by some creature/ or some grete or nyce othe Paup. As I saide bifore wyckid custume excuseth nat synne But accuseth and aggregith syn And therfore it is to drede þ they swere so custumably & so lightly þ they syn dedly swere they sothe swere they false And therfore salomon saith Iuracioni ne assuescas os tuū. &c. Ecclesi. xxiii. c. Lete nat thy mouthe saith he be vsed to swering/ for many harde happes & fallinges been in such

h iiii

swerynge And name nat to ofte saith he goddes name Wyth thy mouthe in swerynge/ ne be natt vsaunt in swerynge to medle the with seyntes names For if thou do thou shalt nat be clere of foly swerynge/ ne clere of synne For what man saith he swerith moche/ he shalbe fylled with synne. and shreudenesse/ and tribulatiō and disease shal nat passe fro hȳ & his housholde. For god saith þ who so taketh his name in veyne. he shalle nat passe vnpunyſshyd Suche swerynge and dispysyng of goddes name is so orryble a synne in goddes sight/ that as salomon saith in the same bo ke the xxiii. c. whan that men herde suche swerynge. the here of the hede shulde aryse for drede/ & they shuld stoppe their erys and nat here suche irreuerēce and disprise of goddes name. Loquelā multū iurās horripilationem capiti statuit/ et irreuerencia illius obturatio aurium.

The 9. chapter.

Iues. For the these dayes in iii. maners excuse hem of swerynge. Sūme saye þ they swere soo ofte for the loue þ they haue to god to haue hym ofte in mynde Sūme say why may nat I swere for I swere soth Sū me say but I swere ther wol no man leeue me Pauper. These been noo excusationes / But greuous accusacions & aggregyng of syn. For as for the first poynt it is fals For suche fals swerers loue nat their god/ for they kepe nat his cōmaundementes And they haue him ful lytel in mynd & swere many an horrible othe in baptie & shrewydnesse bicause of mys vse/ whāne they thynke nat of god And therfore that excusation is an open scorne/ and hygh blasphemye to god For if thy seruaunte had done a thyng that thou haddest forboden him the ofter that he dyd it the worse thou woldest be payed.

And if he scornyd the and sayde þ he did it for thy loue to haue ý in mynde/ thou woldest holde it a ful grete scorne/ & be moch the more offendyd with him/ namely if thou were his liege lord and his kynge Moch more than god þ is lorde & kyng of al thinges is offēdyd w't them/ þ so swere ayēst his forbode/ and excuse them so scornefully sayenge that they do it for to haue god in mynde And therfore is for to drede that they shalbe put oute of mynde from among goddes chosen For crist pleyneth hym of suche forre to his fader in heuene / ⁊ saith thus Dñi quē tu pcussisti psecuti sūt: et sup dolorē vulnerū meorū ad diderūt. Fader in heuene saith he for asmoche as these wycked swerers / haue pursued with their wyckyd tonges. hym that thou smytest ⁊ sendyst to suffre dethe for saluacion of mankynd / and putte newe sorowe aboue the so rowe and y⁺ bytter peynes of my woundes / that I suffryd for her synne and their sake / therfore fa der putte thou synne to synne. That is to saye. lette theym fal fro synne to synne / and let them nat entre into thy ryghtwysnesse for to be sauyd Put theym oute of the boke of lyf / from amonge them that shalbe in blysse with= outen ende Lete theym nat be writen with the ryghtwyse folke that shalbe saued These ben cry stes wordes pleynyng hym to the fader in heuen of suche foul swe rers. po. lxviii. Diues. It se myth herby that suche swerynge is fulle orrible synne and ful pe rilous. But what sayst thou of the secunde excusation. Paup. We ben bounde neuyr to lye. and no thynge say but sothe Nathe= lesse we ben nat bounde to say al the sothes / ne we owe nat to swe re for euery sothe / that we speke For as saith seynt Thomas. de

heritate theologie. Bothe he b for sū erith him aȝenst the treuth and he that swerith w⁺ the treuth without grete cause bothe they take goddes name i veyne For he that forswerith him wytyngly he nameth souerayn treuth ; and that is god and dispiseth it And he that swerith without grete cause takith his name i ydelshyp For he swerith without gode cause / and whan him nedith nat And so bothe lytel or nought set by goddes name / and so they ta ke it in veyne

The vi. chaptre.

Diues. In howe many ca ses is it lefulle to swere. Pauper. In vii. cases clerkes and lerude folke may swere leful ly Fyrste for to saue man or wo man from harme of his body. ⁊ ⁊ fro lesynge of his gode / whāne the treuthe may none otherwise be preuyd Also for confirmaciō of pees Also to kepe feith and treuthe amonges mankynde. Also for to kepe obedience. and ordinal subiection of the subget tes to their souerayues. Also for to saue fredome of holy churche Also for purgation and saluaci/ on of mannys name. and of his fame. Also for assoylynge from a

h iiii

The seconde.

curse Extra li° i° de elect. significasti And i every othe me must
haue thre thinges. Whiche been
treuthe dome and rightwysnes.
as saith the pphete ieremy iiii. c.
For who so shal swere he muste
haue treuthe in his conscience/ þ
he wote wele he swerith treuthe.
For if he be nat syker/ but only
wenyth to be syker. he shal nat
swere þ it is soo/ but that he wenyth that it is so as he sayth Also he must haue with him dome
that is a gode and a discrete auy
sement or he swere/ that he swere
nat but treuthe.   And for nede. that he to whome he swerith
wole nat elles bileue him i thig
of charge that is proufitable to
be bileupd but he swere. Also he
must haue rightwysnes/ that yͤ
thinge that he swerith for/ ⁊ the
maner of swerynge be rightful ho
nest ⁊ leful. Extra li° ii. de iure
iurando Et si ypo. Diues. I
wolde fayne fle suche othes/ but
as I saide firste. men wole nat
leue me but I swere. Pauper.
If it be a treuthe of charge right
pfitable to be leupd ⁊ men wolt
nat leue the for thy simple worde
thanne it is leful the to swere
as I haue saide. But if it be a
thinge of no charge ne nedefulle
swere thou nat. For if thou vse
the to swere comōly for a thyng
of nought/thou synest greuously

⁊ makest other of wanbileue/ þ
they shulde no more leue the for
thyne othe than they do withou
ten othe/ And wyse men wol the
lesse leue the for thyn othes For
comonly grete swerers and bsāt
swerers been fulle false. Diues.
Why so. Pauper. For in þ they
take goddes name so in veyne.
they ben false to god in their swe
rynge And sithen they been fals
to god in their swerpng/ they ye
ue lytel tale to be fals to man or
woman in their swerynge/ or to
begyle them with othes And ther
fore if thou wylt þ men leue the.
Vy ye. or nay. Vse the to speke
truly discretely ⁊ flee othes And
so worship goddes name. and be
true to god in bying and sellyng
in speche and in buyinge And
than men shulde leue the redily.
withouten any othe. Do so and
speke so that men may holde the
a trewe man And than men shal
leue the by ye ⁊ nay. Better thā
other with their greter othes.
And if thou be varyynge and vn
trusti in thy worde and in thy de
de/ men wole neither bileue the
by othe ne withouten othe.
Diues. Therfore sūme saye þ
cryste forbad al maner swerypng
whāne he saide in his gospel.
Ego autē dico vobis nō iurare
oīno Mͭ. v. c. I say to you þ ye
swere i no maner. Paup That

Precepte.

is nat y̆ englisshe of cristes word But this is the englisshe. I saye to you that ye swere nat i̇ euery maner/ that is to saye for euerye cause nat light lyne custumably Also he badde by tho wordes. þ men shulde nat swere by creatures/ as for wytnes/ neither by he uyn for it is goddes trone Ne by erthe. for it is the stole vnder his fete Ne by ierl̃m. for it is the cite of the grete kynge. Ne by thyne hede/ for thou mightest nat make one of thyn herys whyte ne blak Let your worde be yhe yhe. nap nap. M'B.c. Diues. Must we than say alwyes yhe. a thries nap Pauper That thou muste if thou wylt be true. For the same yhe þ thou sayst with thy mouth thou muste say it with thyn hert And y̆ same nap that thou saist with thy mouth. thou muste say it with thyn hert For thy mouth and thyne herte must accorde to gydder For if thou say yhe with thy mouthe. and nap with thyn herte/ thou art fals a dost ayenst cristes lore. Diues. yit Contra te Seynt James saith Ante olia fres mei nolite iurare. ɔc. Jacobi .v. c. Bifore al thinges my leue brethern/ wole ye nat swere. neither by heuyn ne by erthe. ne by any other othe/ wherby it semyth þ it is nat leful to swere. Pauper. Seynt James forst

dith Vanat Vtterly for to swere. But he byddeth that men shuld nat be in wyll to swere any othe for men shulde nat But for nede Diues. yit Contra te Crist byddeth in the gospel M'B.c. That our worde shuld be yhe yhe/ nap nap Quod autem his habundancius est/ a malo est. For What is more than this in spech it is of euyl. Wherby it semyth that if men say more than yhe. or nap by othes swerynge/ they do amys Pauper. Crist saide nat þ it was euyl to saye more than yhe or nap/ or to swere whan itt nedith But he saide it is of euyl that men swere a say more than yhe or nap For it cometh of wa/ byleue of him that wole nat leeue his euyn cristen/ But he swere Also it cũmpth of falshode of y̆ peple/ þ moche follre is so false. þ vnnethes men may leue theim Withoute oth or by othe Diues Where fyndest thou þ god badde me swere/ or that it is lefull for to swere. Pauper. In the gospel that thou allegist ayenst me M'B.c. Where crist saith thus. Reddes d̃no iuramenta tua. Thou shalt yeld to thy lord god thyn othes That is to say thou shalt swere by him a by none of ther a therfore he saith. deut. vi Thou shalt drede thy lord god a serue hĩ alon a swet by his name

The secounde

The vii. chapter.

Iues. Why forbidith crist men to swere by creatures Prauper. Ther is ii maner of swerynge. One is a takynge of wytnesse of thynge. that a man sweryth by/ and so it is nat lesul for to swere by any creatur For seynt poule saith. Holes ꝑ maior est suii iurant. ad hebre. vi. We swere saith he by their more/ þ is to say by him that is more of credence and of reuerēce than they been theim self But only god is more in dignitye and more in order of kynde than man. for he is both god and man And therfore he wole that we take in swerig no wytnesse but only of him/ for he is souerayne treuthe And therfor suche maner swerynge is a diuyne worship that longith only to god and to no creature For god wole that whāne men may haue no wytnesse of treuthe yat is nedefulle and profitable to be bisenyd/ þ they take him to wytnesse and swere by hym as by souerayne treuthe and by no creature For suche maner swerynge is a diuyne worship that longith to god ⁊ to no creature. As saith the glose M⁹ v. c. sup illud. Nō piurabis. And as austyne saith. I the same place/ who so swerith by any creatur/ he swerith by god þ made that creature And therfore crist bad. þ men shulde swere by no creatures. For if they doo lightly they falle in double syn. Bothe in ydolatrye and in piury. Firste in ydolatrye. for the worship þ longith only to god. they do it to creatures Also they falle ofte so in piury. For men drede lesse to lye and to forswere them whanne they swere by creatures than whanne they swere by god allone.

The viii. chaptre.

Another maner swerynge is by execration and imprecation/ that is whanne man or woman in his swerynge prayeth openly or priuely apenst hi self. or apenst any thinge that he louyth/ or any other thinge but it be as he saith. And th' sume mā sweryth by his hede/ sume man by his thedame For as seynt austyn saith/ he that swerith so he byndeth him self ⁊ leith his hede ⁊ his thedame/ in plegge to god. and prayeth to god that he lese his hede and his thedame. ⁊ nes vpr thryue but it be as he saithe. or but he do as he saith or hotith Sume swere by theire soule/ by their chaffare ⁊ by al the gode þ they haue/ and so bynde them to lese their soul/ their chaffare ⁊ al their gode. and bynde their soul to the fyre of helle withoutē ede But it be as they say.

Precepte.

Summe swere by faders soul and moders. and so asmoche as they may they bynd their faders soul and moders to þe peyn of helle withouten end/ but it be as they say/ or but they do as they hoten Summe in their swerynge praye openly ayenst themself/ as w hā they say so helpe me god. There they forsake the helpe of god but it be as they say Summe say elles the deuyl brenne me/ god gyue me elles myschaunce/ and suche other. And of this maner swerig is that solemne othe that mē make i dome & oute of dome/ Whā men say. so helpe me god at the holy dome/ or elles soo helpe me god and the holy dome. In this othe mē forsake þͤ helpe of god and of oure lady/ and of alle the cumpany of heuyn at the day of dome/ But it be so as they saye And ouir that if they swere fals. they clepe god to wytnesse. of a thynge that is false. and sayen that god whose name is treuthe beryth them wytnesse of a thing that is fals And so they lye on god and do him greate belonye. for he was neuir fals wytnesse. ne neuyr shalbe For he is souerayne treuth that nat dissepueth ne may nat be dissepued. And that shal these fals iurours fele at þͤ day of dome/ but they amēde them. Diues. Why ley men their honde on the boke whanne they shulde swere bifore a iuge. Pauper. For that men shulde charge their othe the more. For Whanne he seith his honde on yͤ boke. he forsaketh alle the feith of holy churche/ and alle the holy prayers writē in the boke. But it be as he sayth Also he forsaketh alle the ioyes of heuyn writen i the boke/ and byndeth him to alle the peynes wrytē in the boke/ but if it be as he sayth. And i that he leyth his honde on the boke in his swerynge/ he forsaketh alle the gode dedys that euyr he dyd or euyr shal do/ but it be sothe that he swerith For in holy wrytt by the hondes ben vnderstonde werkes And in þ he swerytß so with his mouthe. & kysseth the boke. he forsakith alle holy prayers and gode wordes that euyr he spake with his mouth/ or euyr shalle speke but if it be as he saith/ & but he swere sothe. And if he forswere him with his mouthe/ he maketh it vnable to rescepue the holy sacramēt of the auter/ that is crist him self souerayne treuthe/ vnder fourme of brede.

The ſeocunde

The ix. chapter.

Iues. What saiſt thou of theym that thoughe they ſwere ſothe/ pitt in ſligh wordes they diſſepue their euyn criſten whiche vnderſtond theym nat. Pauper. Suche be forſworne. For in ii. maners a man may be forſworne in ſwerynge ſoth. Firſt if he ſwere ſoth in gilous wordes and ſlighe for to begile his euyn criſten For as ſaithe. Iſodorus xxii. q̄. quinta. quacūqȝ. What crafte or ſlighte euir thou vſeſt in thy ſpeche and in thyne othes to diſſepue thyne euyn criſten/ god that knoweth thy thought and thy conſcience. takith it nat as you menyſt/ But as he vnderſtondeth it/ to whom thou ſwerpſt ſo in diſſepte. And as he ſaith thou doſt double ſyn ſo ſwerynge For bothe thou takeſt goddes name in veyne/ and alſo thou diſſepueſt thyne euyn criſten. Diues. Telle ſume example. Pauper. We fynde in the lyf of ſeynt Nicholas that a iewe lent a criſten man a greate ſume of gold vnto a certeyn day and toke no ſikernes of him But his feith/ and ſeynt Nicholas to borowe The day paſſide and yᵉ criſtē mā paied nat. Wherfore yᵉ iewe chalēged his gold of the criſten mā bifore a iuge/ for he ſaid falſly that he hadde payed hym. Whan the iuge ſhulde ſytt on the cauſe. the criſtē man bithoughte him of gile and feynyd him ſeke ⁊ came lenyng on a ſtaffe bifore the iuge/ in whiche ſtaffe he had putt al the golde yͭ he oughte to the iewe and more therto/ for yᵉ ſtaffe was holowe And whanne he ſhulde ley his honde on the boke/ he toke the iewe the ſtaffe in his honde/ prayng him to holde it while he made his othe The Iewe thought of no gyle/ But toke the ſtaffe to holde as he prayed himAnd than the falſe criſten man leyd his honde on the boke ⁊ made his othe on this manere. By god and ſeint Nicholas ⁊ ſo helpe me god at the holy doome I toke the al the money yͭ thou chalengiſt and more therto And he ſaide ſoth/ for he hadde taken it him that tyme in the ſtaffe. The iewe was wrothe ⁊ ſaid to him Now as wyſly as you haſt forſworne the by god ⁊ ſeynt nicholas. I pray god and ſeynt nicholas yͭ was thy borowe/ yͭ hard vēgeaūce come to yᵉ The criſten mā toke ayē his ſtaf of the iewe ⁊ went homwarde ayen lenyng on his ſtaffe Ther felle ſuchē an heuynes of ſlepe on him that he leyd hī downe i the way to ſlepe a lytel from the cite whet he had

Precepte.

made his othe/ and leyd the staf with the golde faste besides him Came a carte and wente vpon him/ and slewe him and brak his staffe. tyl the golde scateryd alle aboute Anoon the peple and the Iewe also ranne for to see. What was fallen. And whanne they sawe the staffe brokey/ and the golde so scateryd about they knewe howe gylefully he hadde sworne. and thankyd god. and seint Nicholas. that the treuthe was tryed and shewid The Iewe paue that golde to pore folke/ & bicame a cristen man. Diues. This ensample is open. Nowe I se that gyleful othes been ful perilous Say forthe I pray the Pauper. Also a man may be forsworne swerpng sothe vnwittingly and wenyth to swere fals to dissepue his euyn cristen As if I swore to a nother that it were nat day to dissepue him and sett him of his iourney/ wenyng my self that it were day/ al thoughe it were nat day but fer from day yit I were forsworne. As the lawe shewyth Wel. xxii. q. ii. c. i° Also if a man swere a treuthe wᵗ a blaspheme of goddes name. As if he swore by goddes bodye. herte/ iyen/ woundes/ or any su che other/ if he be custompd ther to/ he is forsworne. Whether it be

sothe or false that he suerpth.

℟he y. chapter.

W Herfore leue freend ye shal vnderstonde that in vi ma ners a man is forsworne First if he swere apenste his conscience. as whā he swerith false Wyttingly though he do it for drede Also if he swere a thinge vnleful and apenst charite/ as if he swere to sle a man or defoule a woman wᶜ his bodp/ or yᵗ he shalle neuir doo almesse to pore men/ ne come in his neighboures hous Also if mā do apenst his othe whiche is lee= ful alle though he do it for drede of deth/ if the othe turne to none euyl ende Also if he swere treuth for dissepte and gyle as I sayde nowe late Also if he swere vnwiselp/ as saith Durandus in sum ma sua. extra. de iureiurando c. sicut. & c. tua. And if he do it wᵗ aupsement or vsautlp/ it is dedelp synne. And he saith there that euery othe made vnwiselp is per iurye. Also if he compelle. a nother to swere wyttpng wele that he wole forswere him. As the lawe shewith Wele xxii. q. iiii Inter cetera. And seynt austyn also i a sermone that he maketh in the decollacion of seynt Johū Baptyste. Where he tellith.

That on a tyme a gode symple true man had lent a certeyn money to a false man, Whiche forsobe it, and saide that he sente hym none, Wherfore the true man puokyd hym to swere. Wytynge wele that he wolde forswere hym and so he dyd. and the true man loste his money And the nighte folowynge the true man thought that he stode bifore a grete iuge. Whiche said to hym on this Wyse Why didest thou that man swere sithen thou Wyste wele that he shuld forswere hym Lorde saide he for he denyed me my gode.

Thanne the iuge saide to hym. It had be better to the for to haue loste thy gode, thanne to stele his soule that god bought so dere With his precious blode. And anon he dyde hym bete harde and sore, in somoche that Whane he awoke his backe apperyd fulle of woundes and al forbeten ful blake and blo. But Whanne he repentyd hym and ayed mercye his synne was foryouen hym

The xi. chapter.

Dyues. It mighte welle be so, for bothe toke goddes name in veyne, and dyd dispise

therto, the swerer in that that he forswore hym wyllynge & wytynge, & he that made hym swere. For wyllyng and wyttynge he dyd he forswere hym, and dispise goddes name, and so he assetyd to piure And by the salve bothe he that doth the synne, and he that assentith therto been gilty of the synne and ben worthy the same peyn But I pray the what saist thou of theym that swere so dispitfully and horribly by goddes body, hert blode and suche other

Pauper. That maner swering is open blaspheme and grete dispyte to god And if a man or woman be vsaunt therto, swere he soth swere he fals. he synneth dedely. For nat only suche take goddes name in veyne But also in grete dispyte. And therfore it is forfendyd by the salve xxii. q. prima Si quis p capitulū. Ther shulde no man swere by the herte of cryste, ne by his hede, ne by no parte of criste, ne vse suche blaspheme ayenste god in any maner wyse. And if he dyd. But he wolde cease and amende hym if he were a man of holy churche he shulde be deposyde and degradyde. And if he were a selude mā he shulde be acursed and pursued by censure of holy churche. tyl he wolde amende him.

Precepte.

And by the lawe imperial as the glose saith there, suche foule sweters shulde be punysshed with ye bttereſt peyne and turmēt, saue dethe And therfore in almayne. suche ben punisshed shamefully in dyuerse cūtrees. And therfore in tho cuntrees ben vsed none othes, but it be bifore a iuge or elles for grete nede. Ther is theire speche as the gospel techith. ye ho and ney. that is ye and nay on englysshe. And they kepe more treuthe for ye ho and ney, thanne we do with alle the greate othes that we vse in this londe Of suche foule swerers spekith seynte poule sayng that asmoche as in theym is they doo goddes sonne ofte on the crosse, and haue butt a iape and scorne of his passion. Rursū crucifigentes sibimet ipſis filium dei & oſtentui. i. irriſioni habentes. ad hebr̄. vi. For they can nat speke to an vnskylful beeſt, but if they so rede criſt w' their othes, & day & nyght reteẃe criſt of his shameful dethe ye he suffride for their synne & her sake And there ye they oughte to take mooſte mater to loue hym and to worshyp him, they take mooſt occaſion of vnkyndneſse to diſpyse him. For ne hadde he dyed bytter dethe and shameful for oure gylte oure synne & oure sake, shulde we neuir elles haue sworne by goddes deth, & ne had he wepte salte terys with his eyn for oure gylt & nat for his owne shulde we neuir elles haue ſworne by goddes iyen And ne hadde he be ſtūge to the herte, & ſhedde his precious herte blode to waſshe vs from oure synnes, shulde we neuir elles haue sworne by goddes herte, ne by goddes blode. And ne had he ſuffryde the depe woundes & bytter peynes in his body & I his bones to saue vs from helle peyne, shuld we neuir elles haue sworne by his woundes, his body. ne his bones. ne his blode And so ayēſt the endleſſe loue ye he shewyd to vs we shewe hī grete vnkyndnes, & ayēſt the grete worſhip ye he did to vs & brought vs to endles worſhip, we do him outrageous velony. We fynde in the miracles of our lady that sum tym ther was a iuſtice rightful in dempnge, but ful gyltye in suche othes ſwerynge Sum, dele he was deuoute to oure lady. and grette her euery daye w' certeyne aves, wherfore our lady by nyght apperyd to him and shewyd him a childe alle blody. The iyen were putte oute of the hede, and henge downe by ye chekys, the herte was rente oute of the body, and henge a downe.

℧he secounde

by the side. and al the body was for torne and wrappyd in blode Thanne she saide to him/ thou arte a iustice peue me nowe a ryghtful dome: what is that man worthy that thus hath arayede my childe. The iustice aunswerpd and sayd He is worthy to be hangyd by the necke in the fyre of helle without ende Thane oure lady aunswerpd Forsothe. thou arte the same man/ For I hadde neuir childe but this allone. Whiche was borne of my body for saluacion of al mākynd.

And thou asmoche as in the is hast put oute his eyn/whā thou swore by goddes eyn/thou rentpst oute his hert. Whan thou swore by goddes herte. Thou haste alle to rent hym with thy foule othes. And therfore amend the or thou shalt haue the some dome that thou hast yough and hange by the neck ī the fyre of helle without ende.

℧he xii. chaptre

Dlues. What sayst thou of them þ swere by the cock for god/ sume by god. by pᵉ halidam. for god and the holy dome sume by saken/ for by oure lady sume by cockes bodye/ sume by their hode some by their tepat &

cap/ and many suche other nyce othes. nien Use nowe these dayes. Paup. If they swere any suche othes for to begile their upn cristen that understonde he nat/ they synne dedely and been forsworne And for to couple to gydder god and the holy dome swerpng in ernyst or in game/ it is a greuous synne. and dispyte and scorne to goddes name.

And if they swere suche othes nat for discepte. But for to fle greter othes: yit they synne ful greuously if they be vsaunt therto. For they do ayenst cristes sore. that byddeth Vs swere by no creature/ ne to swere but for greate nede and grete prosyst/ and elles nat/ but our worde shuld be yhe yhe. nay nay. And if a man be compellyd to swere he shal swere by his god. and by noone suche nyce othes. Moreouir leue frēd whāne þ man swerpth by his cap or by his hoode/ or by any suche other either he swerith so by wey of Wytnesse takynge or by wey of exectracion· If he swere so by wey of Wytnesse taking he doth hym self foul belony For he maketh his hode of more worshyp. and of more credence than hym self. For as seynt poule saytħ ther shuld no man swere for witnesse takynge/ but by his more.

Precepte.

¶ by his better And he offendith god ful highly / for the worship that longith only to god / he doth to his bode ¶ For why swerynge. as for wytnesse is a diuyne worship that longith only to god. And if he swere by bode by weye of execration. so þ he, mote lese his bode but he saye sothe / It is an oute scornfulle othe / for it is no greate losse a man to lese his bode to wynne an hūdryd pūde. Diues. And yit suche ben more true of their worde thanne other that swere greter othes. Paup. Sumtyme it is so ¶ For the feerde temptith them lesse. & to the lesse synne for to holde theym styll & the greter / and so drawe other to the same synne that they perceyue nat. ¶ For more syn it is to rubbe god of his worshyp. than to rob be a man of his catel But suche as swere by bode: do diuyne worshyp to boode / and take it from god and make other to do more worship to bode than to goddes holy name And oft suche so swetyng kepe treuthe.in smalle thinges and comon / to disceyue me in greter thinges of more charge And therfore I pray the vse nat suche nyce othes / Butt lette thy worde be. yee yee. nay nay. as crist byddeth it / so that it be said with sobwnesse & reuerence And if

it nede you to say more / say ye trusly / nay trusly / or sikerly or so thely / for that maner of speche is none othe ¶ For it is nought elles to say. But I say ye trusly, & nat falsly. I saye yhe sykerly, & nat disceyuably / and vse none othes But thou be compellyd by thy so uerayne / or for a thinge of that ge / & men shalle leue the it el by yhe ye yhe. and nay nay / without any more.

The viii. chaptre.

Diues. Is it nat more syn a mā to swere him by god than by his bode Pauper. It is more synne. ¶ For the holyer that the thynge is that man swerith by. the greater is the synne & the piurye / as sayth ye lawe And more syn it is a man to forswere him by god than by creatures / or by fals goddes or mawmettys. And though if you swere by any othe or by any creature / that is nat lefulle to swere by / thou syn nest greuously swere thou sothe swere thou false / But yit piury. by god is more synne thanne by creature. Diues. If a man swere by his bode / is he bounten to kepe his othe. Pauper. yhis if his othe be leful and spede fulle. or elles he doth synne to synne.

As the lawe saithe. xxii. q. i.

ii

The secounde.

Mouet te. Diues. Is it lefulle to a cristen man to take an othe of an hethen man that swerpthe by his false goddes. Pauper. Ÿe. if he may none other sykernesse haue of him. But it is nat lefulle to a cristen man to styrre him to swere so. Example of this haue we Gen. xxxi. Where Laban swoore to iacob by his false goddes Diues. Whãne seruauntes ben sworne to their lord that they shalbe true to him and warne him of his harmes, been they bounde to telle him al the myscheups falsededis. ¶ Bi sonpes. b been done to the lorde in housholde or out of boushold if they knowe them Paup. If the lord be felle cruel and baratous or suspecte apenste the psone. that is giltye I trowe the seruaunt by þ othe be nat boude to tel the lord therof, for to accuse the psoone. for so his othe is vnlefulle. For so in kepyng of his othe he shulde lede the lorde to greuous synne And therfore he shuld nat haue made that othe at the begynnynge, for it was semely þ more cheue disease might come therof if it were kepte. Natheselfe if that seruaũt that so swore knewe any wight beryng or takyng a way or wasting the lordes gode that he hath in keping, he owith

to warne the lorde therof, But if he may the more peasibly haue it apen, t saue the lordes pfytte And euery seruaunt is bounden to warne the lorde of the harme þ is done to the lord in his office for godes feithe and saluacion of his owne persone, if it maye nat elles peasibly be redressed And nentes other defautes þ touchen nat his office, if he may, pue them he is bounde to telle them to the lorde, if the lorde be pacient and skypsfull t nat to cruel If he may nat proue them he is nat bounde to telle them. As the lawe she wyth Wese xxx s. q. vi. Eps in synodo. et ii. q. i. Si peccauerit et q. vii. Plerisq3. Vi. q. ii. Si tm For if the seruaunt whanne he made that othe thought to bynd him to telle his lorde al the harmes þ he knewe, though he myghte nat preue it, his othe was nat lefulle t therfore it byndeth nat Euery seruaunt is bounde by his othe and by his feith to be true to his lorde t warne him of his harme t of his belonye in comon maner, But he is nat boude for to accuse in special, But if he may preue it, But it be ful pryuely to suche one that wole pfytte to the psone and nat harme him ne defame him, But only amede him For by accusyng in special

But if the pleynt may be preuyd falsith hate/ fightyng/ mā̄slauȝter diffamacion & grete disese.

The xiiii. chaptre.

Diues. Whāne a compnye or a college. swerpth for them and their successours to do or to kepe a certeyne thynge in tyme cūmyng/ if their successoures do it nat/ ne kepe nat theire couenaunt/ been nat their successoures forsworne. Pauper. Nay. For that othe byndeth the psones that swore and nat their successoures/ as for piurye Natheles the successoures ben boūden by gode feyth for to do & for to kepe. that their predecessours bounde theym to so swerynge/ if it were leful/ and haue the same proufytes therfore that their pdecessoures hadde Eytra e. Veritatis. et Rap. li. iº. ti. de piurio.

Item pone Diues. If a man make an othe to an other mā/ may nat that other mā that he makith it to vnbynde ħi from that othe/ & forgyue it him Pauper. If it be so that othe be made principally in fauoure of goddes worshyp/ pᵉ mā þ he made it to may natt assoyle him ne vnbynde him from þ othe ne none other may but by chauūgyng ito some thyng better. But nede or vnpower excuse him. If the othe be made principally in the fauoure of the man þ he swetith to/ that man may wele vnbynde him fro his othe And if he made that othe in fauoure of any other man/ only that other man may vnbynde him from þ othe. But ony condicion put in the oth lette it As I swore to the that I shuld yeue thy fader xx shelinges thou mightest nat vnbynde me fro þ othe But thy fader mighte wele vnbynd me therof Diues. Whether is a man harder boūde. By vowe or by othe Pauper. The vowe byndeth harder For oure vowe byndeth vs by oure feyth & the treuthe that we owe to god to paye to him oure biheftes Oure othes bynde vs principally to be true to oure euyn crysten for reuerence of goddes holy name. As saith iohōs in su. con. li. t. ti. ix. q̄. piiii. quero.

Diues. If a man or a woman haue do dedly synne/ of whiche he is shreuen and contrite/ may he swere sikerly þ he is nat gilty. of that synne/ for to auoyd sclā der of him self and of his fredes. and of other that wole nat leue him in that But he swere Paup For asmoche as he knowyth nat spherly that he is sufficiētly cōtrite/ he is natt syker Whether

l ii

155

his ſyn is foꝛyouen him oꝛ natt. And therfoꝛe he ſhuld foꝛ no miſchepf ſwere ſo foliſly Moche moꝛe he ſhuld nat ſwere it of his owne pꝛofer/ Whan him nedith nat to ſwere. In ſū. con. ti. ix. q̄ vii. qd de Spoꝛe. Extra li. V. de pur gatōne canonica. accepimus.

Diues. What if a mā oꝛ womā make ii. othes contraries maye nat be kepte bothe togidder.

Paup. The firſte ſhalbe kepte if it be lefulle. Hoſtienſis li. ii. Rubꝛica de iureiurādo. S. quot comites. v. Itm̄ si duo. But if a man make ii. vowes contrarie that may nat be kept/ the greter ſhalbe kepte if it be lefulle/ and foꝛ the other he ſhal do a ſyth by the dome of his pꝛlates Sū. con. ti. viii ͦ q̄. lxxxiii.

¶ The yv. chapter.

Diues. What is a Vowe pꝑ pirly? Paup. Vowe is bihotyng of ſūme gode thyng made to god with a aupſement. As saith Reymūde. Diues. Whan man oꝛ woman in anguyſſhe & diſeaſe makith a vowe to be holpen/ been they nat bounden to fulfylle that vowe though āguyſſh & diſeaſe catche. oꝛ ſtyrte theym therto Pauper. pʰis foꝛſothe if they thought on the cauſe why

they made it. & Were in puꝛpoſe. than to bynde theym if they had their deſire & helpe/ in that nede. ſo ꝑ by kepynge of their vowe. they ben better diſpoſed to kepe goddes cōmaūdemētes/ foꝛ therto ſhulde al comon vowes deſer ue And the Wyf that in peryl of childe beryng oꝛ of other ſekneſſe makith a vowe al if ſhe oughte none to make/ Withouten leue of her huſbonde/ yit ſhe owyth nat to do ayenſte ꝑ vowe by her owne dome/ ne Without dome of her ſouerayn/ if ſhe fele her hol pen by the vowe. Natheleſſe I trowe that her huſbōde may vnbynde her therfro/ and her conſeſ ſoure alſo/ by chaungynge into ſome other gode dede/ and name ly if yͤ keping of yͤ vowe ſhuld turne ito pludice of the huſbōde. oꝛ lettynge of the better dede. Foꝛ wyues owe nat to make gre te vowes that ſhulde be in diſeſe and pludice of their huſbonde Ne children within age. ſhulde make none a vowe/ Withouten aſſent of their fader oꝛ of their tutoure Ne the ſeruaūte ī pludice. oꝛ byndrynge of his loꝛde. oꝛ of his maiſter And if he do/ his loꝛde oꝛ maiſter may reuoke it/ and ſo may the fader the childꝛēs/ and yᵉ huſbonde the wyues Other vo wes that been no pꝛeiudice to yᵉ

Precepte.

husbõde/ the wyf may make as to say certeyne bedys But of no grete pilgramage/ ne of grete abstinence/ ne of continence/ ne to yeue grete almesse/ But if her husbonde be mys disposed ī his wittes/ or nat truly be of custome by reasone. For if her husbonde be vnpitous of nedy peple she may make a vowe to yef to porefolk to the plesaunce of god after her power sauynge their bothe astate Diues. Whethir is more medful to do a gode dede w^t a vowe or w^{t}ithoute a vowe. Pauper. With a vowe/ for vowe makīg is one of the hyghest worshyp þ man may do to god Quia est actus latrie. Also by vowe man sowyth hī mooste to god. and yeueth to god the mooste pyste þ he may yeue that is his free wyl. As he yeueth a greter gyfte that yeueth the tree with frupt/ thāne he that yeueth the frupt/ and reserueth to hym the tree Also by vowe manys wylle is more stabled in godenesse Natheleſſe for asmoch as man and womā ben fulle frayl & chaungeable/ therfore men shulde nat make vowes But selde and with a gode aduysemente For brekynge of vowes is greate disshonoure to god.

Diues. What if a man make a vowe only vnder condicion.

Pauper. If the condicion fall or be he is bounde/ elles nat. And if a man bynde hym by dyuerse causes/ if the one falle he is bounden though the other falle natt. As if I made a vowe. to goo to Seynt James in hope to fynde there my brother/ and also to haue redēpciō of my synnes/ though I wyste after certaynly that I shulde nat fynd my brother thet yit I were bounde to go thyder. for the other cause. Diues. For howe many causes is mā or wo/ man vnbounde from his vowe.

Pauper. For iiii. causes First if the principal causes of his vowe makynge fayle As if a man make a vowe to faste alle the sa kedayes to haue helth of his child if the child amende nat he is nat bounde therto. Also if it be made vndre condicion/ þat is nat ne fallith nat Also if he soue reyne vnbynde hym therof. Also by vnpower if may nat kepe it.

Diues. Thanne if a mayden make a vowe to lyue in maydē hode alle her her lyf/ if she be corrupte and lese her maydenhode. she is vnbounde from her vowe. for she may no lēger lyue ī may/ denhode Pauper. Al if she may no lenger lyue in maydenhode. yit she is bounde to ytynence al her lyf/ and to kepe her vowe in

l iii

asmoche as she may And so it is of other vowes þ men may natt alle do/ for they ben bounde to do that they may do. Moreouir ye shal vnderstonde þ sümé vowe is of nede/ as the vowe þ we make in baptym/ to forsake the fende/ and to kepe the feyth of holy churche. And other vowes of free wyl. as whanne man byndeth him frely to do a gode dede. Without whiche he may be saued as fastynge contynence pilgramage. Two thinges be nedeful in chagyng of vowe. Rightful cause. and autorite of the soueraynes In dispensacion of the vowe of abstinéce or such other must be taken hede to the richesses or the pouertie of the persone

For a pore man i caas owith to haue asmoche dispensacion. for a peny or for tight noughte. as a grete lorde for an hundryd marke Sume condiciones been vnderstonde in vowes though a man say them nat/ as I shalle do if I vue/ if god wole. Other condicions ben more special/ as I shal visyte seint thomas if I go into kent By both maner of these condicions if they fayl mã is excused of his vowe/ if it stõde ful in that condiciõ The husbonde may nat entre into religion/ but his wif make first vowe of ppetuel contynence Neither the wyfne the husbõde may make vowe of contynce withoute other assente Solempne vowe of continéce lettith matrymony doon. and for to be doone. If it be nat solène if the psone wedde the matrymony holdith.   He must yelde the dette of his body to his wyf/ but he may nat axe it of her Solempne vowe is made by takynge of holy ordre/ or by entre into religion Though a man or woman breke his fast bicaus of sehnes/ he brekith nat his abstinence.   Extra li° 3to de regulis iuris. quod non est licitum.

The xvi chapter.

Diues. What if a man or woman swere a thinge in hastinesse/ whiche other he wold nat haue sworne if he hadde auised him. Paup. If his othe be a meane to kepe the better goddes cõmaundement/ã to serue the by more spyalove the more god he is bounde to kepe his othe. and nat elles Diues. If childrê swere to do a thing seful whyle they be within age/ may their fader ã their moder reuoke that othe.

Pauper Fader and moder and his tutoure may reuoke the childes othes and their vowes/ also ne as they knowe therof And so may the husbonde of his wyf. ⁊ she is boūde to obey to his reuo=cacion But if he go forthe whan he wote therof ⁊ reuoke it natt. at the begynnynge afterwarde he may natt by the lawe reuoke it ne the fader the childes oth ne solwe. Diues. I suppose he re=uoke it afterwarde. Pauper. Bothe the wyf to the husbonde. ⁊ the childe to the fader while he is within age owyth to obey A=upse hym of the peryl that so re=uokith.

The xVii. chapter.

Diues. Whether is piurye more synne or manslau~ghter. Paup. Periury is more. For as saith seynt poule Ad he=breos Vi. c. Men shuld swere by their better and their greter and of euery contrauersye that is to say. of euery cause that is in de=bate to conferme the true party. the laste ende is an othe For eue=ry suche cause is termyned ⁊ en=dyd by an othe And sith it is so ꝑ the cause of manslaughter and of euery open synne touchynge mannys dome muste be termy=ned by an othe piurye muste be taken for a passynge synne and so it is. For who so forswerith hym wyttyngly he forsakith his god And therfore piury is grea=tyst syn of al synnes nexpt ydola

trye For it is ayenst the seconde cōmaūdemēt ⁊ imediate ayēst god ⁊ dispite ⁊ forsakīg of god But manslaughter is imediate ayenst mā And though many wt manslaughter greuyth god full highly pit he forsakith nat god ne dispiseth hi ne dishonoureth him so moche as he doth by piu=rye. And as the philosopher sayth. In principio metaphisice. Amō ges hethen men othe hath euir be worshipful For euery sect. ielwe saryn. paynym. fleeth to swere falsly by his goddes name as moste incouenient And if man=slaughter were more syn than p=iurye it were but a folye to trye the cause of manslaughter by a=ny oth For it is semely þ he that was nat aferide to do the greate synne of manslaughter shuld li=tel drede to forsete i the syn of p=iury if it were lesse And thus saiþ seint thomas in qde. de quoslibet ⁊ Jo l su. li. i. ti. q. xxiiii Siy. Diues. If alle men chargyd p=iury and fals othes as thou dost many may hadde ben hangyd ⁊ drawen and slayne in othir it ise þ pit spue and fare wele It is ful harde so lightly to sle a man wt a worde ll hanne his lyf may be sauedwith a worde For a man costith ful moche or he come to be a man Pauper. Therfore men shulde bisily fle piurye and

t iiii

The secounde.

falſe othes For ther is no thinge that cauſith ſo moche manſlaughter and ſhedynge of blode / as doth þe piury. Diues. Shelwe me that I pray the if thou can. Paup. Salamon ſaith Eccle. x°. c. The kyngdome is ſlyttyd and chaungyd fro nacion to nacion. for wronges. Unrightfulnes and deſpites done to goddes name in dyuerſe gyſes But piurye is cauſe of alle falſe domes & wronges / and of alle Unrightefulneſſe / cauſe of gyle and treaſſone / & of greate diſpites / þ been done to god and man For as I ſaide firſte euery cauſe muſte be endyd by wytneſſes or by queſtes / whiche been ſworne to ſaye treuthe / and alſo by a iuge whiche is ſworne to god. and to the kinge to deme rightful doome. And if they that ben chargyd to ſay the treuthe yeue noo tale to forſwere theym. and to lye / they ſhal diſceyue the iuge / and doo him yeue a falſe dome Suche piurers robbe men of their godes & diſherite moche folke They ſaue ſtronge theues / and ſlee true men Suche robbe folke of their gode name. ſuch ben fals to god to the kynge / to prelates of holy churche. Suche been cauſe that this londe is in poynte to be loſte & to be chaunged to a nother nacion & to a newe kynge And þ may

nat be withoute ſhedynge of moche blode and manſlaughtere. And ſoo periurye is cauſe of moche manſlaughter. Alſo piurye is cauſe why we haue ſo many theues & miſquellers in this londe For they hope alway to be ſaued by piurye and falſehede of queſtmongers / þ for ſpitelle gode woſe forſwere them. And therfore I hope of piury they ben ſo bolde in their ſynne / to robbe ſle. & brenne / for though they be take yit they hope to ſcape by piurye And if they were ſiker that ther wolde no man ne woman for ſwere bi to ſaue them / they wold neuir be ſo bolde to ſynne And al other ſhulde be the more aferyde to ſynne / if they wyſte wel that true dome ſhuld paſſe withoute piurye. Suche ſynful wretches as ſaith the pphete pſal̄. xxiii. haue put their hope al in leſiges & in piury / & by leſinges falſhede & piurye / they been maynteined. & nat chaſtiſed Alſo it is ſyn alſe ayenſt kynde to ſaue a theef I diſpyte of god / whoſe name they forſwere ayenſt his commaudmēt For he byddeth that ther ſhulde no man take his name in veyne Alſo he ſaith Non ſuscipies vocem mendacii nec iūges manū vt ꝑ impio dicas falſū teſtimoniū. Exodi xxiii. Thou ſhalt nat take the voyce of leſynges.

Precepte.

ne ioyne thyne ȝode in making of couenaunte to bere falſe wytnes for the wyckyd man to saue him. Maleficos nõ pacieris viuere. Exodi xxii. Thou ſhalte nat ſuffre wytches & open maleſactoures and felones lyue. But ſle theim in chaſtiſynge of other Sle one and ſaue many one. Alſo this is a ſyn al apeſt kynd and ouir grete folye, a man to ſle his owne ſoule wythouten ende to ſaue a theef that neuir wolde wayte him gode turne, but redy to robbe him & parauenture to ſle him whan he may A grete folye to offende god by piurye to pleſe a theef a mãqueller, that offendith god and alle the cuntre Su the been lyke the ielwes þ ſaupde Barraban the ſtronge theef & mã queller: & ſlewe ſwete iheſu ſoueraỹne treuth þ neuir dyd amys. And as holy doctoures ſay a mã ſhulde rather ſuffre the moſte diſpitoꝰ deth of body than he ſhuld forſwere hỹ or do any dedly ſyn. Moche more he ſhulde nat forſwere him ne do no dedly ſynne. to ſaue a theues lyf, that god & londes lawe cõmannde to ſle.

¶ It felle late in this londe that a Scott appelyd an engliſſhmã of hygh treſone, whãne he ſhuld fyghte bifore a iuge in their cauſe, the iuge as the maner is putt them bothe to their othe. Whãne the ſcotte ſhulde ſwere he ſaid to the iuge. Lorde I came nat hyder to ſwere I came to fyght. for my chalenge was to fyght, and therto I am redy, but ſwere wol I nat, for I made no chalenge to ſwere The iuge ſaide þ but if he wolde ſwere. that his appele was true, elles he ſhulde be taken as a coupete & a tayne traytoure, and be hangyd & drawen withoute fightynge And ſoo he was, for he wolde nat ſwere witynge wele that his appele was falſe, and made only for malice as he knowlechyd er he dyed. This man might haue ſworne. and happely haue hadde the better of his aduerſary and eſcapid the dethe. with worſhyp in this worlde But yit he had leuyr dye diſpitefully, thanne do diſpyte to goddes name, to ſwere falſly therby, and ſeuit to dye bodily. than to do that piurye to god. & ſle his owne ſoule. For he helde it as it is a greter ſynne thã mãſlaughter And though he wolde auẽge him on man for rancour of herte, yit on god he wold nat venge him by piurye. And ſoo god ſaued them both fro piury & mãſlaughter & gaue them grace to dye I charite, & do a ſeeth both to god and man.

161

The xviii. chaptre.

Diues. Sithen piury is so grete a syn, what peyne is ordeyned therto by the lawe.

Pauper. As the law saith xvii q̄. i. pdicedū. Asmoche penaūce shulde be enioyned for piury, as for manslaughter and auoutre. And they shuld neuir more be taken to swere or to bere wytnesse in any dome, but be forsaken in euery dome, as tayntefals, and alwey suspecte of falshede. And by londes lawe in many cuntreyes if they be taynt forswore bifore a iuge: they shuld be disheryted for euir. q̄ their house be drawen downe, their wodes hewyn downe, q̄ their trees also manes hight aboue the groūd. The stockes stode stylle to endeles repreof of theym q̄ of al their kynred.

For their is no synne so noyous to a reme q̄ to euery compnte as is piury. For bi is cause p yet may no syn be punyssshed, ne malefactoures ne felones chastised, nee wronges redressyd. Men of holy churche shulde be degraded, and selfe de forȝre accursed. xi. q̄. i. cōspirationū q̄c. cōiurationū. Alle other synners whāne they haue done penaunce for their synne q̄ been amendyd, ben by the lawe restored ayen to their fame, so p they may be wytnesses in dome.

q̄ their oth owyth to be resceiued But piures p ben taynt, shal neuir be restored to their fame: ne be taken for witnesse, ne his oth acceptyd in no dome. As saith Hostiensis. li. ii. Ru. de testibus S. de possit v. excipit. q̄. v. hoc ide Et extra li. ii. de testib⁹.c.ex pte, q̄ Bi q̄. i. quicumqȝ. And if he be taynt forsworne bifore a iuge, he is nat able to be any prelate either in holy churche, or in the laifee neither kynge ne busshop abbot ne prioure, prynce ne duke, or any chifteyne of worshyp

Diues. Why is piury so harde punysshed by the lawe. **Pauper.** For the synne is ouir greuous q̄ ouir moche hauntyd, and for it is moste openly ayenste the substaunce of treuthe and wytnesse and moste mayntenneth falshede and settith moste treuth and rightwysnesse. As saith the same clerke Hostiensis in the same place. Suche piurers may say that is writen. psalmo lix c. Concepimus et locuti sumus de corde p da mendacii q̄c. We haue cōcepued false contrypuynges, and we haue spoken of hert wordes of lesynge. And therfore rightful dome is turnyd bacwarde, and rightfulnesse stode from ferre.

He durste nat putte forthe his hede, and treuthe fel downe.

openly in the stretes He was bor ne dowñe openly, and noo man wolde helpe hi Up Equpte saith he ne euenhode in shiftyng. and in dempnge might nat entre, for treuthe is al forpeten And he fledde from wyched, was euery mannes prey. Diues. Nowe I se that piury is a fulle greuouse synne and fulle perilous to eue ry compnte, a cause of moch man slaughter, and shedyng of man nys blode a lesynge of realmes. For as I haue red, the Realme of englonde for piurie a fals hede was translated from Britons to saxones Afterwarde it was trans latyd for piurye from saxones, and englisshe men to the danys. Afterwarde whañe englisshe me hadde the kyngdome apey by p' deth of the danys, they kepte it But two kynges tymes, seynt ed warde and Haroldes, and anone it was translated apen for piu rye Unto the normaynes by wyl liam duke of normandy, which slowe up nigh al the cheualrye, of this londe, and chaungyd the lordship and the prelacy of this londe nigh alle Unto the frenche me And what mordre a shedyng of blode fele for these piurers in these thre tymes and chaungin ges is fulle harde to telle. And nowe alas newly in oure dayes we ben falle in piurye in the hy

ghest degre, nat one but nigh al And what blode hath be shedde sithe, Bicause of oure piurye, no tunge can telle And this londe by shedyng of blode is so feblys shed I euery state that we be nat of powēr withoute special mira cle of god lenger to withstonde. And so it is ful moche to drede þ this Realme in shorte tyme for oure piurye shalbe translatyd a pey to the Britones, or elles to su me other tunge. I pray the saye forthe what thou wylste

The xix. chaptre

Pauper. Ferthermore I saide þ goddes name is ta ken in veyne by myssweryng For if thou haue likyng to here grete othes of other men, or any mys swerynge, Or if thou wate nat veyne othes ne art nat mysplays ed whan thou herpst them, thou takest goddes name in veyne For thou doste no worship ther to: as thou oughtest to doo For as salomon saith a mannys here shulde ryse for fere, and he shuld stop his erys whan he herde god des name so dispised And if a man swere to the sadly I goddes name and aupsely, thou art bou de to lene hi for worship of god des holy name, But you haue y' more euidēce to y' ctrarie. And but thou accepte his othe a yeue credence therto But ye knowe ye contrarye/ elles thou takyst goddes name in veyn/ For thou doste no due worshyp therto/ but grete dispite/ in that that thou wylt nat leue so worshypfulle a wytnes as god is/ whome he takith to wytnesse so swerying For many a symple man wolde be mys payed if thou forsokest him for wytnesse of treuth Diues. If I fynde a man ofte false in his othes/ though I leue him nat I do god no dishonoure. Paup. That is soth/ for thou may wel wete that god souerayne treuth beryth him no wytnesse in his fals bode And therfore doo worshyp to his othe and to goddes name and repreue his falshode & dyspyte. that he dothe to goddes holy name Moreouir if thou here men swere or blasphe me goddes name/ or name goddes name in vanytie/ if thou haue lykynge theryn/ thou takist goddes name in veyne. And but thou snyb or rebue them if thou haue power ouir them/ & grucche ayen a their synful speche/ elles thou takyst goddes holy name in veyne. by beryng Also if thou haue likinge to here erroures ayenst the feith of holy churche to consent to hem or shrewyd tales/ or veyne tales medlyd with goddes name & vnhonest speche/ ayest the worshyp

ful name of criste and of cristendome/ whiche speche no gode cristen man ne woman owith to here/ thou takyst goddes name in veyne by hering For if thou loue wele thy god thou shuldest natt here pacientlp any speche ꝑ sowneth dishonoure to his holy name For if thou louedyst wele any man or woman/ thou wolde here no speche sownynge ayenst their name and worshyp ne that might be causes of their offense. or velonye.

¶ The xx. chaptre.

Also goddes name is takē in veyne by brekynge of couenaunte made in goddes name/ and cōfermyd by swerynge in goddes name. As whan peas and couenaunt is made bitwene kinges and realmes/ bytwene compnties/ and bitwene persones/ and bitwene compnte & psone/ & is confermyd by swerynge Than euery man & woman that knowith it shulde sle to forsete in worde or dede ayenst the couenaunte & the pease/ for reuerence of goddes holy name by whiche it was confermyd. And all tho that wyttyngly breken suche couenauntes/ or procuren by worde or dede or assenten therto. that suche couenaūt

Precepte.

shulde be broken/ if the couenāt be lefulˀ as if it be nat plesaunte they take goddes name in beyn And alle tho that knowe of the couenaūte and of the othe/ if by retchlesshede of speche or of dede ben cause of brekynge of peas & of suche couenaūtes Whether it touche theym or nat/ they take goddes holy name in beyne and do dispyte therto/ sithen the pees and the couenaūte was made ī goddes holy name/ and confermyd also. We rede also in holy wrytte/ Josue ix. chapter. That whanne Josue and goddes people bigāne to conquere the londe of bihefte/ the folke of gabaon in gyle sent messangers to iosue to make peas with Josue and with goddes people. The messangers in gyle dyd on olde clothes cloutyd/ olde shone patched and alle to torne They toke hored brede ī their scrippes. soure wyne in their boteles. and lodyd asses with old hored brede ī old sackes/ and came so to iosue/ and made a presaunt to hym of olde vitayles and said to hym Cyoure name springeth fer and wyde that ther may no kyng no nacion withstōde you Therfor we be come to you for saluaciō of oure lyues to make peas with you Thanne iosue and the peo-

ple saide to theym If ye dẅelˀ eˀ in the londe that god hath yeuen to vs/ we may no peas make it ī with you Thanne iosue ayed theym what they were and from whēs they came Sir saide they we ben thy seruauntes & came to the fro sulle serre cūtrees/ sente fro the lordes & the leders of oure londe to make peas with the Thou may see by oure araye þ we be come fro fer For whanne we come oute oure clothes and oure shone were newe/ they ben al to torne & alle to rente. Oure brede was newe baken/ nowe it is hooryde Oure boteles & oure wyne weren newe/ nowe oure boteles be nigh brusten/ and the wyne is soure. and oure vytayles and the hsauūt that we haue brought to the ben nigh lost for elde And thus they sped almoost euery worde & dis- cepued iosue/ for they duelte sy- tel ouir yx. myle thens Josue toke their presaunte/ and made peas with hem And he & alle the princes of goddes peple swoore to theym þ they shuld haue their lyues & their godes/ Within a fewe daies after Josue came to gabaon/ and began to fighte a- yenst the cite Anoon they came out & shelwyd her charter of pees

And how that Josue and the pryncer of goddes people. also

The secounde

hadde sworne to theym. to saue their lyues/ the people wolde haue slayne theym bicause of their gyle Thanne Iosue and the princes sayde to the people/ we may nat sle theym For we haue sworne to theym in the name of oure lorde And if we forswere us god shal take vengeaunce of us. Diues. I trowe ÿ clerkes these daies wolde say that they were nat bounde to kepe that othe/ sithen they gate that othe of them with so grete gyle. Pauper. If they auysed hem wele they wold say as Iosue saide For as I said firste. a man owyth to kepe his oth if it be lesul though he made it for drede of deth For euery oth lesul owyth to be kept though it be neuyr so moche ayenst herte. And that shewyth god wele aftyrwarde   For as we fynde the secounde boke of kynges xxi. c. Thre sudryd yere after. Saule kyng of goddes folk're slewe all the gabionytes ÿ he myght fynd to plese his peple/ whiche hatyd alway tho gabionytes for their gyle God was myspayed with ÿ dede/ & lete the kyng saul soone after be slayne in batayl/ & al his housebolde/ & moche of goddes peple After in tyme of Dauyd ÿ reignyd next after saul/ ther fel suche an hungre in the londe of israel thre yere to gidder ÿ moche of goddes people perisshed Dauyd asyd of god what was the cause of that hungre God sayde that the deth of the gabionytes whiche saul had slayn was cause therof. Dauyd sente after the gabyonites that were lefte. and sayde to them. I knowe wele ÿ for you this hungre and myscheif is fallen in my realme Axe ye amendes what ye wole & I shall do it Thanne they saide we axe neither golde. ne syluer/ ne noo mannys deth of israel But only vengeaunce on saule and his kynrede that so wyckydly oppssyd us and destroied us. we axe that euery man of his kynred be slayne. and that none be left of his kynrede. Dauyd myght nat graunte that axynge for thothe that he hadde made to Ionatas the sone of saul to saue his kynred Thanne they axed vii. men oonly of the kynred of saule. to hage hem on the gebettes ayenst the sonne/ and to sle theym dispitously in punysshyng of ÿe spite ÿ saul had do to goddes holy name/ in ÿ he dyd ayenst the solempne couenauntis ÿ his ÿdecessoures had made & cofermyd swerynge by goddes holy name For in that saul toke that othe & goddes holy name in veyne.   As sayth

Precepte.

the maister of the stories. Whan this was done the hungre ceased. and anone began reyne and plẽtye of corne and frupt. Diues. This example is ful gode and shewith wele that euery othe lefulle shulde be kepte And that euery man and woman shuld fle to do dishonoure or spite to goddes name Also it shewyth wele þ piurye and dispisyng of goddes holy name is cause of shedynge of blode / of hungre / and of myschepf / And that god wole nat suffre that his name be dyspised ne taken ĩ veyne Pauper Therfore god saith that euery man and woman that so takith his name in veyne. I shal do to the as thou haste hadde sweringe in disppte. and chargyste nat to breke couenaunt / therfore thou shalt bere thy synne & haue dyspite perfore Eze. pßi. c. Also he saith thus by the prophete If ye wole nat here ne sette in herte to yeue worshippe to my name / I shal sende in you hungre & nede and myschepf And I shal curse your blessynges / and take your myghte from you / that ye shalle nat withstonde. Malachie ii. c.

Here endith the seconde pcepte and begynneth the thridde

Dues. I thanke the moche. For nolve I knowe better thãne I dyd bifore / Holve the seconde commaundement shulde be kepte And what peril it is to take goddes name ĩ veyne. Nolve I pray the enfourme me in the thridde cõmaundmẽt. Pauper. In the thridde commaundement god byddeth that thou shuldest bithynke the. and haue wele in mynde to halolve thyn holiday. Sixe dales thou shalte worche and do alle thyne owne werkes. In the seupnthe day is the sabot / that is to saye. reste of thy lorde god In that daye thou shalte do noo seruyle werk / neither thou ne thy sonne thy doughter / ne thy seruaunte. man ne woman / ne thy beest / ne ne the straunger. that is within thy yate. Diues. Why badde god that the seupnth day shulde more be halolved thanne the syxte daye. Pauper. For as god sayth there In syxe dayes he made heuene and erth and see / and alle thynge that is therin. And in the seupnthe daye he restyd and ceasyd of his werkes And therfore he blessyd that day and halolvyde it / and ordeyned that in that day man and beeste shulde reste / And that man

The thridde

that day shulde specially thank god. For alle the creatures that he made bifore ī vi. dayes he made to helpe and serupce and solace of man Diues. Why saith holy wrytte that god restyd the seupnth daye. sithen he trauapled neuyr For as seint austyn saith he made alle thinges without trauapl/ ā as holy wrytt shewith Genesis primo. c. He saide butt this one shorte worde fiat. and badde that it shulde be done/ as non it was done as he wolde.

Pauper. Whanne holy wrytte saith that god rested the seupnth daye/ he understondeth therby ꝓ in the seupnthe daye he ceasyde to make new creatures For euery thinge was made bifore ī the vi. daies either in the thyng him self/ as aungel/ light sonne mone sterres; either in his kynde ā ī his simplitude/ as md best fysshe foule and grasse/ and tre/ either ī his causes/ as thynge gendryde of corruption/ and thyng made by crafte For god ī his godhede. was neuir in trauapl but alway in blissul reste withouten ende. And therfore holy wrytte sayth nat that he restyd after his werkne in his werke/ but þ he restyde from euery werke that he hadde made For he hadde no trauayle for any werke/ and he was natt

holpe by his werke/ for he made no thing for nede but al for loue Diues. pit contra te. Cryste saith in the gospel se Jo. Pater meus vsq; modo operat. et ego operor. My fader worcheth vnto this tyme/ and I worche also Therfore it semyth that god ceased nat the seupnth daye from euery werke Pauper. Two maner of werkis longe to god. creation and gouernaunce From the werk of creation he cesyd the seupnthe day/ and thāne principally beganne the werke of gouernaunce and of keppyng Whiche werke he contynueth and shalle contynue withouten ende. And of this werke of gouernaūce spekyth Cryste the wordes in the gospelle/ nat of the werke of creacion. Diues. Ben ther any mo skylles. Why god badde the vii. day be halowed Pauper. Sixe skilles ther been as sayen these clerkes. Firste for god the vii. day restyd/ that is to say/ he ceased fro creation of newe creatures Also in tokening that god in the vii. day delyuered the children of israel from the harde seruage of egipte/ and ledde theym through the rede see drye foote/ ī to the reste of the londe of bihest As we rede in holy wrytt Deut. v. c. Whiche deliueraunce was

Precepte.

token þ mankynde shuld throu/
ghe cristes passiō & by his blode
þ he shedde vpon the rode/ be de=
liuered out of the feendes serua/
ge/ and come to the endles reste
of the londe of lyf ☙ The iii. cause
is þ men shulde þ day principaly
yeue them to holy meditacione.
and to thanke god of al his 'gif=
tes & his beneficies/ and to lerne
goddes lawe and to pryse god
☙ The fourth cause was to be to=
ken that criste the vii day shuld
reste in his graue/ after þ he had
traueyled vi. daies to refourme
ayen mankynd that was lorne
through adams synne. ☙ The v.
cause was to be token þ vs must
alle cese from vices and the vii.
synnes/ if we wole be saued. As
the prophete saith. Quiescite a/
gere peruerse/ discite bene agere.
psa.i.c. Reste ye to do amys.
and lerne ye to do wele ☙ The vi.
cause is to betokene the endlesse
reste that we shal haue from syn
and peyne in heuyn blisse/ for ye
gode werkes that we do the vi.
daies of oure lyf/ that is to saye
al the daies of oure lyf/ & the vii.
ages of oure lyf. & for fulfillyng
the vi. dedys of mercy which cri
ste nameth in the gospel. For as
we rede in the apocalips pliii. c.
☙ The holy goste to whome this p
cepte is applied saith that nuɜ af

ter this lyf shulde rest from their
trauailes/ for their gode werkes
folowe them.

☙ The ii. chapter.

DIues. Sithen that god
badde the vii daye shulde
be halowed/why kepe we ye viii
daye. that is sundaye. and natt
the vii. daye.   Pauper.
God in the olde lawe gaue three
maner of preceptes for sūme wer
cerimonyal/ sūme iudicial/ and
sūme moral ☙ The cerimonialles
were but figure & shadowe of thī
ges that were to come And ther=
fore whan tho thinges were ful
fylled that the cerimonpasses be
tokenyd/ the cerymonials cesyd
& banisshed. alwaye/ as the sha=
dowe banysshet alway by lyght
of the sonne Judicial preceptes
were in punisshynge of synne/ &
iustisiynge/ of whiche sūme cea
sed/ sūme duelle yit stylle. Butt
moral preceptes þ teche vs to loue
oure god. & oure euyn cristen/ &
to flee synne/ & to loue vertues.
tho laste alway/as the p. cōmau
dementes & suche other. And for
asmoche as this precept is cerimo
nial in party as anentes the ty=
me/ and in party it is morall/ in
asmoche as it techith vs to wor/

h i

shyp oure god, and to reste from Vyces. Therfore in as moche as it is morall it is kepte. But in þt that it is cerymonyal, it is chaūgyd into suday as for the better. For that that it figured and betokned is fulfillid. That was ye reste of criste in the sepulcre i the vii day, after the grete trauayle that he hadde vi daies bifore in reformacion and redempcion of mankynde. Alle be we bounden to worship god nowe in ye newe lawe. But nat in that maner ne i that tyme that they were boūde in the olde lawe. Diues. Why is it more chaungyd in the sunday thanne into any other day.

Pauper. For the greate benifices ⁊ the grete worshipful woūders that god shewyd that daye to mankynde. For on the suday the worlde begāne, ⁊ lighte and aungelles kynde was made.

That daye god sente aungelles mete manna downe the the childrē of israel in deserte, and fedde them so .xl. yere. That daye god gaue moyses the lawe in moūte of synay. That day criste was borne of the mayden mary to saue mankynde. That day cryste rose from deth to lyf, yeuyng vs exaumple and hope. to ryse from dethe to lyf. That day the hooly goste lighted in cristes apostles.

and in his disciples. That daye god shal come to dome, as saith a grete clerke bochyng, sup deutronomii. And so that day was the firste day and shalbe the last day that neuir shalle haue ende. But it shalbe a daye of endlesse blisse to al þ shalbe saued. For right as cryste rose vp from deth to lyf on the sunday, and neuyr dyed after ne shal dye. So shall al we in the laste sonday þ shall be ye last day, ryse vp from deth to lyf and neuir dye after. But lyue in blisse withoutē ende, if we make here a gode ēde. This day is so worshipful that no bisshop may be sacryd but on the suday. As saith Reymūde li. t° ti. de feriis. And right as the saturday was halowed i the olde lawe for the reste þ god made in the satur day after the creacion ⁊ the werkes that he made in the vi. firste dayes, so holy chyrche through techyng of the holy goste hathe ordeyned the sunday, to be halowyd for the rest that mankynde shalle take after vi ages of this worlde on the sondaye, whiche reste and sabott shal neuir haue ende. Their sabott that was on the saturday turneth allway ayē to trauayl. But oure sabote that is in the suday at the laste shalle turne into endles rest ioy ⁊ blisse

Sabot in ebrewe is rest ⁊ englif
ſhe And euery day ĩ the woke is
cleppd ſabott ⁊ ferie þ is reſte in
engliſſhe For euery day we ben
boūde to ferie ⁊ to reſte from ſyn
Also al the woke is cleppd ſab=
bot as there. Jeiuno bis in ſab=
bato. And Mᵗ Vlᵗio. The ſun=
day is cleppd the firſte day of þe
ſabbottes/ as there. Vna ſabba
torū. And Mᵗ Vlᵗio. it is ſaide.
Prima ſabbti. For it is firſt nat
only ĩ ordre of daies/ but it is al
ſo firſte in dignite For the ſabot
⁊ the reſte in the ſolēpnyte of the
ſaturday of the old lawe is now
chaũgyd into the ſūday/ for ſyn
of the iewes which ſlewe cryſte
on gode friday/ ⁊ ſo putt oure la
dy ſeynt mary and al holy chur=
che in ſorowe ⁊ care ⁊ grete tra=
uaile bothe friday and ſaturday
while criſte lay ĩ his graue. But
for aſmoche as he roſe from deth
to lyf on the ſūday and apperyd
to his moder and to his diſciples
vii ſithes þ day/ ⁊ ſo on the ſun=
day begāne the firſte ioye blyſſe.
⁊ reſte of the newe lawe/ therfo
re by goddes rightful dome ye le
wys ſabot on the ſaturday/ tur=
nyd them to ſorowe ⁊ care ⁊ mo
the trauayſe. and oure ſunday
turnyd vs into grete reſte ⁊ ioye
and bliſſe And as the ſaturdaye
was halowed by the olde lawe.
for god graūted that daye firſte

reſt to mankynde after his dam
nacion to ppetuel trauayle for
adams ſynne/ ſo is nowe the ſū=
day halowyd/ for than criſte grā
typd firſte reſte ioye ⁊ bliſſe to mā
kynd in the newe lawe after his
paſſion ⁊ the ſaluacion of man=
kynde ⁊ the redempcion/ ⁊ ĩ nyd
the ſorowe that holy church had
on the ſaturday by malice of the
iewes; into reſte ⁊ bliſſe on the ſū
day And ſo it is fulfylled þ the p
phete Jeremye ſaide. xxxi. c.
Redemit dn̄s populum ſuum
God hath boughte ayen his pe=
ple with his pciouſe blode/ and
hath deliuered his peple oute of
the feendes powᵉʳ I ſhal ſay the
god turne their mournyng into
ioye/ I ſhal glade them of their
ſorowe and conforte them. And
by the pphete Oſee he ſaide þ he
ſhulde make the ioy of iewys ſa
botes/ ⁊ of al their ſolennyties.
and of al their feeſtes to ceſe bi=
cauſe of their ſynne Oſee.ii. c.

The iii. chapter

Alſo for halowyng in the
ſaturday was ceryemony
al For as we fynde ĩ diuerſe pla
ces of holy wryt. ⁊ namely Eze
chielis xx. c. Halowyng ĩ the ſa
turday was a ſpecial token po=
uen to þe iewys wherby they ſh=
ulde be knowen from other peo/

h ii

☞The thridde.

pse/ and so was circūcisioñ. and many other obseruaūcis and cerymonyes god paue theim to be knowen from other people And therfore right as the circumcisiō and other obseruaunces/ þ were bitaken them of god for token of distinction from other peple ceasyd in cristes passion/ so cesyd halowynge in the saturday in Crystes passion. For why. although it be a morall precepte to halowe the vii. day/ yit it is nat moralle ne byndeth us to halowe the vii day in the saturday And therfor we rede Exodi. xxxiiii.ᵗ xxxv ca. That whãne moyses hadde ben in the mounte of synay with god fourty daies and ꝑ nightes withouten mete or drynke/ and spoken with god and there takē the lawe of him in two tables of stone/ two stemps and bemes of light risen oute of his face/ as it had be t wo hornes so glysnyng ꝗ so bright/ that the people was adred of him ꝗ durste natt speke with him/ and therfore he putte a veyl bifore his face whãne he shuld speke to the peple/ and tel theym the lawes and the wyl of god And whãne he had so bydde his face wᵗ the veyl/ the first lawe that he paue them in goddes name was to halowe the saturday And he spake no worde than of

the other ix. preceptes/ But tosth forth other obseruaunces ꝗ cerymonyes whiche longed only to the iewys/ and were but figure, and shadowe of thiges to come. Whiche cesyd alle in cristes passion And soo he shewyd wele that halowyng in the saturday was cerimonyal/ ꝗ shulde cease with other cerymonies in cristes passion And therfore whanne he bad them halowe the satday/ he put the veyle bifore his face in token þ halowyng on the saturdaye. ꝗ other cerimonyes and lawes þat he paue them that tyme wer but a veyle hilynge gostly understōdyng/ under figures of thynges that were to come. And whanne tho thinges were fulfilled by the passion of cryste/ þ veyle ꝗ mystisede of figures shulde be done awaye and cese. And in token therof in tyme of cristes passion. the veyle of the iewys temple to rent and cleef in ii. parties that men mighte se al the priuey thinges that were in the temple/ whiche were bifore hyd fro the sighte of the people by that veyle Also the same texte of the cōmaundemente shewyth wele/ that halowynge in the saturday shulde be translatyd into the sunday/ that is clepyd the day of the sonne. For al though god cesyd in the

Precepte.

saturday from makinge of thinges of newe kynde/ yit in the saturday he made the saturday as he made eche day bifore in the same day   But in the sonnedaye next folowyng he made no new day in kynde/ for that was the firste day/ and so he restyd more in the sunday from worchynge. thanne he dyd in the saturdaye. Also after greate trauayl oll itħ to be more reste. But criste goddes sonne hadde more trauayle in recreacion & redēpcion of mākynde thanne he hadde to make al this worlde. For in makynge of alle the worlde he hadde noo trauayle/ as seynt austyn saith. But only he bad it shuld be done. and it was done anon. What he wolde. But in recreation & redēpcion of mankynde he trauepled so that he swat blode for anguisshe/ and dyed for trauayle & shed his herte blode/ and cesyd nat of trauayl tyl in the morowe tyde of the sonne day whanne he rose from deth to lyf to comforte alle mankynde þ wolde leue in hym. And he shewid openly than that he was and is lorde of al thing. And saide to his apostles. þ alle power in heuene and erthe was youen to hym in his manhode. And therfore the sūday is clepyd the lordes day. Dies dominic⁹.

And therfore sithen god wolde þ the saturday shulde be halowed in the olde lawe/ for god ceasyd thanne from creacion/ and so in maner beganne to rest/ morħ more he wose that the sonneday be halowyde in the newe lawe/ for god cesyd than from þe grete trauayl of our redempcion and our saluacion and recreacion.

¶The iiii chapter

Figure of this we haue also in holy wrytt. Leuitici xxiii°. Where we fynde that god badde the children of israel kepe pryncipally vii feestes in the yere of the whiche the laste was clepyd. Festum tabernaculorum. The feest of tabernacles He bad theym take bowes & braunches of palme trees and of other trees the fayrest that they might fynd and make hem tabernacles and logges & duelle therin vii. daies to gidder/ I mynde that god made theym to duelle ī tabernacles & logges pl. yere in desert & there he sauyd them & kepte them and he badde þ the firste day and the viii shulde be ful holy. By this feest of tabernacles þ came laste after þe other festes of the ieu̇ es ben vnderstonde the festes of þe newe lawe/ whiche came laste in the ende of the worlde. after the olde lawe. For alle the festes of the newe lawe been festes of tabernacles For whane god came to be man/ he made firste his tabernacle in the mayde mary whi the tabernacle was arayed. and bight with the fairest braunches and bowes of grace and vertues and of gode thewys. that might be foide in any creature/ for she passyd al creatures in grace and godenesse. Of this tabernacle spekith the prophete. Po. pviii. In sole posuit tabernaculū suū et ipse tanq̄ sponsus procedens de thalamo suo. He made his tabernacle in the sone/ that was our lady mayden and moder brighter thane the sonne. He came oute of her as an husbonde oute of his chābre Another tabernacle god made him in oure maho/ de and in oure kynde/ that was the blissful body. whiche he toke of the mayden mary For as the tabernacles wel made of the fairest braunches and bowes that might be founde/ so the body of cryste was made and gadryd to ayodder of the clenest droppes of bloode that were in oure lady. seynt mary clene mayden withouten spotte of synne In this tabernacle god was boorne of the mayden on Cristmasse day. In this tabernacle he was circumcided/ worshipped of thre kinges. and duellyd with vs i erth i our pilgramage xxxii. yere a more.

In this tabernacle he died for mankynde/ and rose from deth to lyf on Ester day/ and styed vp to heuyn on holy thursday. very god and very man/ and there syttth on his faders right honde a boue alle heuenes in this tabernacle lorde a kyng of al thinge. In this tabernacle he shal come ayen at the dome/ to deme the qc ke and the dede And alle the festes that we holde of any seynte. we halowe them and holde hem for the gode dedys that they dyd whyle they duellyd here in the tabernacle of their body/ I hope to come to endeles tabernacles ful of ioy and blysse withoute ende Of whiche tabernacle god spekith in the gospel whane he byd deth the riche men make poore men their frendes/ that they may receyue them into endles tabernacles/ of whiche spekith Dauid. Qm̄ dilecta tabernaculā tua dn̄e virtutū: cōcupiscit et deficit aīa mea in atria dn̄i. Lorde of vertues how louely and how lyhig been thy tabernacles/ My soule saith he despreth and longith. to entre into the halles of oure lord And for his desire is delayed/ he faileth and feynteth for sorowe. And so the solēnpte ƿ euir shalle laste. shalbe a solēnpte of taber=nacles/ Whāne We shal duelle iṅ endlesse tabernacles. With endes lesse reste ioye and blisse. There the firste day and the eight daye shalbe ful holy/ Which day is ye sonneday For that the firste day ҫ it is the .viii. day and shalbe ye laste day euir lastynge iṅ ioye ҫ blisse. And therfore in the feestes of the newe lawe that ben festes of the tabernacles is the sunday principaly halowed/ as god bad thāne For it was the firste daye and it is the .viii. daye/ ҫ shalbe the laste day euir lastynge ĩ ioye and blisse.

The .ii. chapter

Iues. Why bad god that We shulde thynke to ha=lowe Wele the holiday and the sa bot. Pauper. Ther is thre ma=ner of sabottes/ that is to say. of reste or of halowynge. Scilicet. pectoris temporis et eternitatis That is to say of reste of hert/ of tyme/ and of endelesse restynge. By reste of hert and of thought. men come to reste of tyme. And by reste of thought and of tyme. men come to endlesse reste. Soo Withouten reste. of herte and of thoughte/ may no man come to endelesse reste that the sabot and the holiday betokneth And ther fore god bad Vs that We shulde principaly trauayle to haue sa Bot ҫ reste of herte and of thouzt Withoute Whiche rest ҫ sabot We may nat Wele halowe any holy= day And therfore Cryste sayd iṅ the gospel. ƿ out of the hert Whā it is oute of reste/ come Wycked thoughtes māslaughters/ auou tryes/ lechery/ theftes/ false Wyt nesses/ dispyte of god. M᷈ᵗ.v.c. Whiche synnes distroye charitie. ҫ peas/ and been causes of moch Vnreste iṅ this Worlde/ and lette reste of tyme/ so that Vnnethes. may any tyme be reste And ther/ fore god saith. thynke that thou halowe Wele thyne holiday. Be thynke the if thou be iṅ charitie and reste of herte With god ҫ mā And if thou be styred ayeṅst thyn euyn cristen by Wrath hate or en uye. or haue any heuy hert ayeṅst thy brother/ go as god biddeth ĩ the gospel and be firste reconsey led to thy brother/ ҫ than come ҫ make thyn offryng of holy pray er of thankynge of prisyng/ and of thy giftes to god And Butt thou do so and putte aWay alle rancour and heuy hert/ elles thy halowynge and thy sabot is nat plesaunte to god Also Bithenke the if thou be in dedly synne, and repente the & be shreuen assoone as thou might in gode maner, & so offre vp thy self to god by charite, and by sorowe of hert & make thy self holy, and thāne arte thou able to halowe wele the holiday. For as longe as thou arte in dedly synne by wyl or by dede, so longe thou halowest nat thy haliday. For thou doste scruple werke of synne, and doist dispyte to the haliday. Whiche is ordeyned that men shulde thāne amēde them, and serue god more specially thanne in the woke daye. And as longe as man or womā is in dedly synne, he serueth the deuyl and nat god to plesaunce. Also god biddeth that mē shuld bethynke theim to halowe wele the haliday. For in the halidaye namely on the sōday men shuld drawe their wittes to gyddre frō the worlde and bethynke theym if they hadde oughte trespassed, that woke by rechelesbede or by couetise, or by lechery, or any other wyse, and aske god foryeuenesse. Also thynke on the goede & benefices that god hathe sente theym that woke, or euyr bifore, and thanke hym therof. Thank him of his endeles mercy, and his endelesse charite that he shewyd to mākynde. Thynk

how he made mā to his owne liknesse, to be apte and citezeyn of heuene. Thynke howe he made alle thynge for man. Thynke what blisse he hath ordeyned to man and woman if they do wel. What peyne if they doo euyl.

The vi. chaptre.
Therfore saith Origenes sup Leuiticum xxviii. c. On the sunday thou shuldest do no worldly thinges, but oonly yeue the to god and gostly thinges. Thanne saith he come to churche, sey thyne ere to goddes worde, thynke heuynly thinges thynke on the lyf that we hopen alle to haue in endlesse blisse. Thynke on the laste dome hou harde it shalbe and howe straite. Take thanne none hede to this worlde ne to thynges visible. But on the haliday haue thy gostely iye principally to thinges. that ben to come, and yit ben inuisible. He that thus dothe saith he. halowith wele his haliday. and he maketh ye sacrifice of ye sabott. And therfore the lawe saith thus. We haue ordeyned alle sundaies be kepte with all maner worship from euyn to euyn, and that mē absteyne bem from al maner vnseful werkes. that ther be no markette holden on the sonneday, ne plee, ne no

may dāpned to dethe/ ne to peyne. ne othe taken solemnely/ but it be for peas or for some greate nede. Extra li. ii. ti. de feriis. Omnes dies dominicos. The lawe saith that men shuld nought do on sunday/ but yeue theym to god, ne doo no seruyle werke. But that day shulde be occupied in prisynge & worshippynge of god and in goostly songes. De con. di. iii. Ieiunia Me shulde on the haliday serue god with hert mouth and werk. With herte. thynkynge as I haue saide/ with mouthe wele spekynge in prayer prisynge & worshippynge of god/ and gode iformacion of their euen cristen. In werke also of dedes of almesse. & peas makynge & accordynge of neighbours and suche other. But nowe alas is fulfilled that Ieremye saide. Trenor. i°. c. Viderunt eam hostes et deriserūt sabbata eius. The enemyes the feendes see mannys soule & womānes howe it was defouled with synne on the haliday, and scornyd his halidaies and his sabotes For ye haliday was ordeyned in confusion of the feende & worship of god/ & for saluacion of mannes soule/ But nowe it is turned to worship of manys soul to dispite & offēce of god. & I plesaunce of the fende. For in the sunday reigneth more secherpe glotony/ manslaughter/ robbery/ bacbityng/ piury/ & other synnes/ more than reynyd all the weke bifore And whan men come to churche/ they seeue bedys bydynge/ and spende their tyme in synful langynge. For there they caste gyle ayēst their euyn cristen There they holde their prypys of manye wronges. Whiche they thynke to do. And therfore god may say to theim y̆ he sayde to the iewys. It is writen saide he y̆ myn hous shalbe cleppyd an hous of prayer/ & ye haue made it a dene of theues/ & that ye cōtynue her gyle & falshede/ to robbe poure euyn cristen of his gode of his right & of his fame. And therfore he sayth by the pphete. Isaie i. c. My soule hatith your solēpnities & halidayes. They ben ful heuy to me/ I haue trauueil to suffre them But therfore sayth he/ whan ye shal lyfte vp poure hōdes to me I shal turne myn iyen alway fro you. And whan ye multiply poure prayer to me I shalle nat here you/ for poure hondes be fulle of blode & ye haue shedde and fulle of syn. And poure cūpanyes and poure gaderynges to gyder been fulle wycked. Iniqui sunt cetus &ti.

The vii. chapter.

Also leue frende god bade þat men shulde thynk to halowe wele the holyday For md and womā shuld so bethink them bifore þ the woke day and so ordeyne their occupacions/ þ they shulde nat nede to breke the holiday. For if a man nedith to breke the holiday/ and that nede come of his owne folye & of his misgouernaūce bifore/ he is nat excused by that nede. Moche lesse thanne is he excused if that nede come of purpose and of couetise. And therfore they þ wote nat go ne sende to market in the woke daye to bye their necessaries/ but abyde tyl on the sunday. for sparyng of tyme/ they be nat excused though tho thinges ben nedeful to them Men shulde studye and dispose hem as besily to serue god on the sunday. as they studie bifore to traueyl for them self on the woke day For god hath graunted vi. daies to man and woman for to traueyle for them self/ and the seuynth daye. he hath reseruyd to his seruyce ¶ We rede in holy Wryt Numeri. v. 8. c. That a man wente in the sabot day and gaderyd stychees He was taken and ledde to moises/ and he putt him in prison til he had an aunswere of god what he shulde do with him. God bad moyses þ he shulde be ledde oute of goddes castelles þ were clepid the duellinges and tētys of goddes folke/ and there al the peple shulde stone him to the deth And so he was slayne spitefully/ for he bithought him natt bifore to halowe the haliday/ for he might haue gadryd stychees in the day bifore And sith he was so spytfully slayne for gadering of stychees to make therwith his fyre þ was nedeful to him Moch more shulde they be punisshed that on the sūday gadre to gidre brōdes of synnes of couetyse. of lecherye pīury. and bacbityng/ to brenne with their soules in helle without ende but they amēde them. Diues. What clepith god seruyle werkes. Pauper. Euery dedly synne is seruyle werke. For as Criste saith in the gospel Who so doth synne he is seruaūt of synne and thral to the feende Qui facit peccatum seruꝰ ē pcti And suche seruile werke god forbedith euery day/ but mooste on the haliday For who so doth dedly synne on the haliday he doth double synne. For he doth þ syn and therto he brekith ye haliday ayenst goddes precepte Also seruyle werke is cleppyd euery bodily werk don pricipally for

tēporel sucre and worldly wyn/
nynge/ as biynge and sellynge.
eyynge solwynge/ molwynge/ re-
pyynge/ and al craftes of Worlde
ly wynnyng Also pledynge/ mo
tynge/ markettes fayres syttīg
of iustices and of iuges/ shedige
of blode and execution/ of punis
shynge by the lawe/ and alle the
werkes that shulde let mā from
goddes seruyce/ and dispose him
to couetise or to the feendes ser
uyce. Natheles if eryynge & solw
ynge repyng molwynge caryyng
and suche other nedeful werkes
be done purely for almesse/ and
only for heuynly mede/ and for
nede of them that they been to.
in light holidayes they been thā
noo scruple werkes/ ne the holy
day therby is nat broken Nathe
lesse in the sonnedaies and grete
festes suche werkes shulde natt
be done but ful grete nede com
pelle men therto

The p. chaptre.

Dues. Why bad god that
bothe man & beeste shulde
reste and halowe on the holiday
Pauper. For as salomō saith.
Sap. Bi. & pi. c. God loueth al
thinge that he made/ & hath cure
of alle thinges that he made.

And therfore he ordeyned reste ī
pe holidaies nat only for his ow
ne worship and for gostly helpe
of soule/But also for bodily help
bothe of man and beste But the
couetise of man were refreyned.
By reste on the holiday he shulde
neuir reste/ But with trauail
sle him self/his seruautis his sub
gettes/ and his bestes And ther
fore both to saue man and beest
and for grete pfyte of man/ god
bad reste on the holiday For bothe man and beste nedith rest aft
trauayle/ and shalle be the more
fresshe al the woke after to trauayle if they haue rest on the ho
lyday And therfore it fallith oft
that they which wole nat rest on
the sunday been made to reste
al ye woke aft/either for seknes
that they fal in by ouir trauayl.
or by seknes/ or by feblenes of
their seruautes/ and of their beef
tes/ or elles by deth. For often
they sle their bestes by ouir moche trauayle/ and contynuynge
of trauayl And therfore in the be
gynnynge of the worlde whāne
Adam synned in the syxte daye.
By etynge of apppl ayenst goddes forbode.   And that god
hadde dampnyd him and al his
to perpetuel trauayl for his syn
After this of his greate and
endelesse mercy he tempryd and

¶ The thridde.

slaḫpd his harde dome/ and ordepned reste bothe to man & best in the seuynth day And therfore saith holy wrytt Gen̄ ii. c. That god fulfillyde his werkes in the vii daye/ nat only for he maade than the vii day & cesyd of creacion/ but also principally for he shewyd thanne first mercy ayenst synne grauntynge and biddinge reste in the vii. day both to man & to beste whiche he dampned in the day bifore to ppetuel trauail for adams synne/ whiche mercy was fulfyllyng and pfection of al his werkes Quia miseratōes eius sup ola opa eius. For as dauyd saith goddes mercyes bē aboue al his werkes. And seynt James saith. Mercy enhaūsith rightful dome And But god had endyd his werkes in mercy in ye vii. day/ and slakyde his harde dome ayenste mankynde for Adams syn; elles his werkes had nat been complete ne parfyte/ in asmoche as the principal creature for whome he made al thinge was loste. For whāne the fynall cause of any werke faileth/ that werk is nat complete ne parfite. For this mercy that god shewyd to man whāne he ordeyned rest in the vii. day that was cleppyde sabott. figure of endlesse reste of mankynde Crist saith in the gospel. that the sabot was made for man/ nat mā for the sabbotte. Mar. ii. c. But synful man is so blent with couetise/ ꝑ he turneth his dampnation and his peyne into likynge/ and hath seuyt to trauayle to his vndoynge. and vnto his dampnacion/ than to reste to his saluation And hath leuit to folowe the harde sentēce of god to his punysshyng/ thāne to take his grace and his mercy to be esyd Suche ben lyke oules & backes/ whiche hate the day & loue the night/ lyke to the feendes of helle that neuir haue reste ne for malice wole seke reste.

¶ The ix. chapter.

D·Rouyr leeue frende we fynde iiii. maner of sabottes in holy wrytte One sabot of dayes that was the vii/ daye ordeyned of god for reste and ease. Bothe of man and of beest Alsoo we fynde a sabott of monethes. ordeyned also of god for rest bothe of mā and beest that was ye vii. moneth that man and beest shulde reste theym thanne. after the greate trauayl that they had in the ii. monethes bifore. Whiche was their herupste to gadre corne/ wyne and oyle and other frupt ¶ The seuynth moneth was

Precepte.

Septembre. for thanne in that hote cuntre herupst was al done Also we fynde a sabott of peres. that was the seupnthe pere For that pere the londe restyd that it might bere the better and the more plentuouslp after/ for that pere was no londe solwen Also we fynde a sabott of sabottes/ that was the fyfte pere ordepnede of god for rest of the londe/ of beest of man/ and namelp of theym þ were in trauaple of tribulacion. For thanne outlawed men mpght come apen home in suretie. Thanne bonde men were made free and dettes forpouen Than men rescepued apen their heritage Bp the sabott of daies/ is vnderstonde reste from vices in the lpf actpf/ that hach sire daies to worche Bp the sabbot of moneth es is vnderstonde reste. þ men haue in the lpf contemplatpf. both from vices and temptaciones For that moneth was moche holp/ but nat alle holp. Righte soo thep that haue the lpf contemplatpf thep haue more reste from vices and temptacions/ than thep that haue the lpf actpf/ but fulle reste haue thep nat in this world Bp the sabot of peres whanne the londe restpd the seupnth pere. is vnderstonde the reste. that oure soules shalle haue in blpsse/ whp

les the erthe of oure bodies shal reste in the graue Bp the sabotte of sabottes that was the fiftithe pere is vnderstonde the reste withouten ende/ that we shal haue in heupn/ whanne we shal wede apen bothe bodpe and soule/ to our heritage þ we loste through Adams spnne/ whanne al oure trauaple and tribulacion shalle cese and alle oure woo turne to wele bp vertue of cristes passion

The v. chaptre.

Iues. Sithen the sabott of daies was moste solepne I the old lawe/ for it was nat leful to go that day ouir a thousande paas/ ne to dight their mete/ and more ouir that day were offrpde two lambren passpng pe comon sacrifice that was doone euerp dape/ sithen thanne the solempnte of the sabbotes is translatpd in the newe lawe. into the sonne day/ whp is nat the sonne day as worshipfulle in the newe lawe. as was the sabotte in the olde lawe. For as that was clepp the sabott of oure lorde/ soo the sonne day is cleppd the dape of oure lorde passpnge other daies. And pitt we haue in pe pere manp daies more solempne

thanne the sunday. Pauper.
Alle the feestys of the newe lawe ben the daies and the sabotes of oure lorde For altho been of him self in him self/ or elles of him self in his seintes In the old lawe was no feeste of oure lorde But only the sabot/ whiche was halowed i mynde of the creacion of the worlde/ and i mynde that god the seuynth day cesed of creacion. And also than to thanke him for his endelesse godenesse ÿ he shewed to mankynde i his creacion/ whan he made al bodily & visible creatures to serue man/ & man to serue him here in grace and after in blisse withoutē ende Other festis of the olde lawe were but solēpnitees/ & myndes of auentures and prosperites. that felle to the iewys in tyme of the olde lawe And therfore the sabot amonges them was most solēpne. And amonges vs also the sūday is moste solempne and holy for the grete dedys & woūders that god dyd in the sunday But for asmoche as it commyth ofte we make it nat alway the solempne For it fallith the sūdayes in whiche god shewyd his wūders/ as Ester day and wytsonday/ to be more solempne: than other comon sundayes Other festes also as Cristmasse day/ and epiphanye daye/ in asmoche as they been oure lordes daies and come but ones in the yere Therfore we make more solennytee. in tho dayes/ than we do comonly on the sunday And so we do many other festes/ for al they be festes & dayes of oure lorde Natheles ther is no day so solempne in the self as the sundaye For that is alway solenyne/ for the woūders that god dyd therin. Other dayes ben sumtyme solēpne/ & sumtyme natt solempne. after that the festes fal therin by chaungyng of the yere So that other daies haue no solempnite of them self by custome ne by lawe/ but only by fallynge of festes as the yere chaungith The thursday was sumtyme as holy as sunday/ for criste that day styed vp to the heuyn. And thanne bigāne the pression that we vse on the sunday For thanne Crist went in procession with his disciples oute of Jerusalem into the mounte of Olyuete/ and ther styed vp in sighte of theym alle. And the crosse that is borne byfore vs in processione/ betokeneth ÿ Cryste dyed on the crosse.

And after roose from dethe to lyf. And on the holy thursday went bifore his disciples ledyng theym vnto the mount of oliuete But for as moche as many newe festes co∫men on/ and it was greuouse to kepe two daies solempne euery woke/ therfore the solennpte of thursdayes ceesed. and the pro∫cession in mynde of cristes ascension was translatyd into the sū∫day. Diues. Therfore me thyn∫keth that the sundaye shulde be the more solempne. Pauper. So it is/ and soo it ouзith to be moste halowyde thouзhe hooly chyrche do nat alway than most solempne. For that day is ordey∫ned for rest i the newe lawe both to man & to beest/ as the sabotte was ordeyned for rest in the old lawe.

The .xi. chaptre

Diues. Been we bounden by this precepte to kepe the holidayes that holy chyrch hath ordeyned in the newe lawe.
Paup. yhe forsothe. For alle thouзhe the precepte passyde in ꝑ. that it was cerimonyal as anen∫tes tyme/ yit it duellith in that it was & is moral/ and byndeth vs to se vices/ & serue our god one day more than another/ whiche day is the sonday i the new lawe by ordenaūce of god & holy chyr∫che For as the gospel saith. Mt. xii. c. Dns ē eni fili' hois & sab/

bati. The maydens sone crist ihesus is lorde of the sabot. And for asmoche as it was soo euyl kepte in the olde lawe/ & so mo∫che blode was shedde i the sabot & cryste him self suffryd so moch despyte on the sabote. Therfore he was myspayed & saide by the pphetes Jsaie.i. c. & osee ii. c.
That he shulde no lenger suffre their sabbottes/But as a lorde of the sabbottes he chaungyd that reste & solennpte of their sabbot∫tes ito the sunday/ for the scryp∫tures whiche J sayde bifore/ whych day al if it be the viii. day in the firste ordre of daies/ yit is but ye but the vii. day in obseruaūce of the pcepte For we haue nowe vi daies to worche in/ i token that god i vi daies made al ye worlde & the vii day we halowe as god badde vs/ in token ꝑ god the vii day cesed of creation & ordeyned reste in the silday As seynt poul in his ppstle/ Ad colocensis ii. c. saith openly that the sabott and other feestes of the olde lawe we∫re but shadowe and figure of the newe lawe And therfore after cri∫stes passion tho festes cesyd and noo man owith to kepe theym. And who so kepith them in that he forsaketh ꝑ Cryst was borne of ye mayden/ & dyede for man∫kynde. And seynte gregoure in

The thridde.

his pystle Ad Ro. saith That al that halowe the saturday/ for it was so holy in the olde lawe/ Ben antecristes disciples For āte crist shal do men halowe bothe sun͂day and saturday Sunday/ for to drawe cristen peple to his sect For he shal sayne him dede and to aryse ayen fro dethe to lyf on the sonday And the saturday to drawe the Iewes to his secte. De con. di. iii. Peruenit/

The vii. chapter.

Diues. Why wolde god make the worlde more in the nombre of vi. daies thanne in any other nombre of daies. Pauper. For as Salomon saith god made al thing in nombre weight and mesure He made no thinge to moche ne to lytel But he made euery thinge parfytely in his kynde/ and endyde al his werkes in pfytnesse. And for the nombre of vi. is the first nombre euyn that is pfyte/ therfore he made alle the worlde in nōbre of vi. daies Diues. How is the nombre of vi. more parfyte thāne another nōbre. Paup. For al his parties þ mete him if they be taken to gidder make euyn vi. As one ii. iii mahe euen vi. ã these thre nombres mete vi.

For sixe sithes one is vi. ã thries two is vi. and twies thre is vi. And this pfection is in no nombre within x. But in vi/ And fro ten. to an hundryd is none butt xxviii And from an hundryd to a thousande is but this euyn nōbre. foure hundryd lxxx/ xvi. The nexte is viii thousande an hundryd and xxviii. And thanne no mo suche butt one within an hundryd thousande And who so wole fynde that he muste study After an hundryd thousande be mo suche than al the clerkes vn dre sūne can telle/ mo thanne any herte may thynke or tūge tel and yit it is fulle harde to fynde one. And for that vi. is the furst parfite nombre in this maner. Therfore god wolde make this worlde in the nombre of vi. to ken that al his werkes were par fite And therfore saith holy writ Gen. ii. c. That heuyn and erth and al their araye were parfyte. And for the same skylle god ma de man the vi day as for a parfi te and a noble creature/ For the same skylle in the vi age of the worlde bicame man And on the vi day gode friday the vi/ oure of þe day i the vi age/ he bought ayen mankynde with his pcioꝰ blode in token that al his wer kes were parfyte. And that same

nombre of daies god hath graū/
tyd vs to worche in/ in token þ
alle oure werkes shulde be par=
fyte ᵹ gode/ and no thynge do a
mys/ that we shulde for no coue
tise do to moche/ne for no sleuth
do to lytel/ But alway holde vs ī
a meane and in euen hede For
god grauntyd vs no tyme to spȳ.
Therfore he whose alway þ we be
euen with god and with oure euē
cristen/as sype is alway euyn wt
his parties to giddre.

The viii. chapter.

Dives. Why bad god reste
on the seuynth day more
than a nother day. Pauper. In
token that as seuyn cumeth next
after the parfyte nombre of sixe
daies of worchynge/ so after par
fite werkes in this worlde shalle
folowe parfyte reste in the other
worlde Also he badde reste in ye
vii. day for that passith the par=
fyte nōbre in token that he whose
no thinge be done passinge pfec/
tion And therfore al synne is cō
pprehendyd in vii. dedly synnes.
For as vii. passith the parfite nō
bre of vi. so euery synne passith
perfection and is oute of pfectiō
of alle gode werkes Also god
badde reste on the vii. day/ for he
wole þ men reste them than both

gostly and bodily. Gostly from
besynesse ᵹ thought of the world
bodily. from bodyly trauayle.
For why vii. is made of foure ᵹ
thre· Foure betokneth bodily
thinges made of iiii. elimentes.
Thre betokneth mannes soule
made to the likenesse of the holy
trinite And therfore he bad reste
in the vii. day/ þ mē shulde than
reste bothe body ᵹ soule. Also
god badde reste in the vii day/ in
token/ þ after pfyte werkes shal
folowe endeles reste bothe of bo
dy ᵹ of soule For this nōbre vii.
in asmoche as alle tyme and all
duracion is cōpprendyd ī vii day
es. therfore it betokneth endles
lastyng And therfore reste on ye
vii. day bitokneth endelesse rest
Also frende god ordeyned reste ī
the vii day reste/ in token of vii.
blisses whiche we shal haue for
parfite werkes þ we do here ī vi.
daies and vi. ages of this of this
worlde For anētis the body we
shal haue foure blisses/ bright=
nesse and beaute without any
spotte For as Criste saith in the
gospel/men and wymen shal shi
ne ī heuen/ as bright as the sone
Also men shal haue there ī passi=
bilite and helth of body without
en al maner sekenes No thing
shalle dere them ne disease them.
Also they shal haue deliuer hede

The thridde.

of body and lightnesse withouten setting/for they shulde be as light as thought/ and in turnyng of any tye be whek they wol Also they shalle haue soteltie of body. Withouten any withstondynge/ for ther shal noo thynge withstonde hem But as ye sone passith the glasse without settig of the sonne/ soo shal they passe ouir walle and euery thinge. at their wyl withouten any disease or any settynge And anentes ye soule we shal haue the blissulle sight of goddes face. Brennynge loue to god/ and to our euyn crysten/ and alwaye haue him that we loue/ and what we desire. There alle oure loue shall be in iope/ withouten wo drede and sorowe In this worlde euery loue is medsyd with wo/ in tokene of these vii. blisses that we shal haue in endelesse reste for oure partyte werkes. Therfore god bad reste in the seuynthe day.

The xliiii. chaptre.

Diues. How longe owyth ye haliday to be kept and halowyd. Pauper. From euen to euen/ As saith Reymounde a the lawe also. Extra li. ii. ti. de feriis. c. Omes dies dnicos. And holy wrytt also and god hy self Leuitici xxiii. A vespa vsq ad vespam celebrabitis sabbata vestra. From euyn to euyn ye shal halowe your halidaies Natheles sum be gynne sonner to halow after that the feest is/ and after vse of the cuntre. Extra e. quoniam. But that men vse in saturdaies and vigilies to ryng holy at midday opessith nat me anon to halowe/ but warnyth the hem of the haliday folowynge. that they shulde thynke theron. and spede theym/ and so dispose hem and their occupacions that they might halowe in due tyme. Diues. Is it lesul for any caas in the sunday to gadre in corne, frupt or hay. Paup. Suche ne be it may be that it is excusable as if they may nat in other dayes gadre it in for enempes/ as in tyme of werre/ if they shulde gadre it they haue rightfulle cause to withstonde their aduersaries Also if corne or grasse be felde. & shulde be lorne but it were digge and gaderyd/ it is lesul in the ha lidaies to saue it and kepe it/ so that goddes seruyce be nat leste therfore But for to mowe/ or to repe carte or to sowe in the sunes day I holde it nat lesul but if ful greate nede. Principal festes shulde alway be halowyd/ butt right grete nede compellyd men

to worche/ so that grete nede ex/
cused hem For as the lawe saith
Extra li. B. De regulis iuris.
Nede makith leful that elles is
Vnleful by the lawe For nede
hath no lawe De con. di. i. sicut
et di. B. discipulos. Extra de
furtis. Si quis p necessitatem
Also it is lefulle to fisshe after þe
tyng on the sunday a other fisshe
also. that may nat be taken but
certeyn ceson of the yere/ for whi
che fisshe men muste go ferre on
the see and longe abide. Extra
de feriis. c. Licet. It is leful al
so to do rightful bateiles on the
sunday/ and in other halidayes.
for saluacion of the cõmyntie
It is leful thãne to saue that el
les shulde perisshe bothe mã and
beste frupt corne and other thin
ges alway with reuerẽce of god
and of the halyday. It is leful
thanne to leches to help the seke
folke It is leful to dyke walle.
defence townes castelles/ and to
araye men to bataple in the sone
day Whanne nede compellith/ ꝙ
peryl of enmyes Thus saith Jo.
in sũ. con. li. i. ti. vii. q̃. vii.
So that in al these and suche o=
ther/ nede and pite excuseth men
Cryste helpd men in the sabotte.
ꝙ repreuyd the Jewys that were
mispayed therwith/ and sayd to
them. Sithen a man takith his

circumcision in the sabotte Why
haue ye indignacion to me for J
haue made a mã a hole in the sa
bott/ Jo. vii. c. And in an other
place he saide to the Jewys/ who
is it of you that hath a shepe a it
falle in the diche in þe sabot/ b he
ne wole go and lyfte it vp oute
of the diche But for sothe man is
better thãne a shepe/ and therfor
saide he/ it is leful to do gode de/
des I the sabot and I the halyday.
Mt. vii. c. Another tyme crist
helpd a womã of an harde seke=
nesse that hadde holde her þ viii.
yere/ she wente stouping al dow
ne and might nat loke vpward
Thanne the maister of the lawe
and of the synagoge was wroth
and saide to the peple Ther ben
vi. daies to worche in/ come ye
thanne and be ye helpd/ and nat
in the sabott. Criste aunswerid
to him Jpocrite/ eche of you vn
tithe his oxe and his asse from þe
maunger or cracche in the sabott
q̃ ledith it to the water. Moche
more it is nedefulle to vnbynde
this doughter of Abraham I the
sabott from the harde bounde in
the whiche sathanas hadde hol=
den her bounden p viii. yere
And al tho ypocrites were assha
myd By these examples Cryste
shewyd that dedys of pitee and
of almesse/ and namely þ thinge

⁋The thridde.

and techynge/ by whiche mānes soule is losed out of the feendes bondes. Been medeful and nedeful in the haliday. And he excuseb dauyd by nede. that he ete of the holy looues of no selwyd man shulde haue eten of by the lawe. Also he excused his disciples þat they gnyddyd þe eerys ī þe feld in the sabotte/ and ete the corne. My' vii. c. For as he saith there. god loueth better mercy and pyte/ thanne any sacrifice.

⁋The pv. chaptre.

Natheleſſe. natt withstondynge alle/ this euery mā and womā shulde besily halowe þe halidaye/ and nat lightly for no smal nede breke the haliday. For god chargyd this cōmaundment ful highly/ whāne he said Thynke that thou halowe wele the haliday And in a nother place. Deu. v.c He saith loke þ you halowe wele the halidaye And ī any other place of holy wrytte he saith Loke ye kepe wele my sabott and my day/ for that is token bitwene me and you/ who so defouleth that day or doth any scruple werk in that day/ he shal dye. Exo. xxi. Leuitici. xvi. et xix. Itē iereme xvii. Ezechielis xx. a xxii. a xxiii. c. By ye

salue bokers/ tauerners/ ꝯ other vitailers may lefully dight ī the sunday vitayles to be solde ī the moneday/if they mighte nat dight them ī the daye bifore. to saue them and their vitailes/ soo þ it be done principally to goddes worship/ and for the comon profytte Also marchauntes þ leden their marchaundise in the sūday and other halidayes to feires in ferre cūtre by londe or by water ben excused if they may nat lede them in other daies. Also messangers/pilgrymes/ and wayfering men/ that may nat wele rest wᵗ outen grete harme ben excused. so that they do their deuer to þᵉ masse and matyns if they maye For longe abidinge ī a mannes iourney is costful and perilouſ Also they that lete to hire horſe ꝯ carte/ or shyp to pilgrymes. and to passinge folke in the sunday. to spede them in their iournaye. if they do it principaly for ease ꝯ spede of them that so hyre theim. they ben excused But if they do it principaly for lucre or for couetyse/ they be nat excused Also if men for hastineſſe do them shaue or do their horse sho in the sūday whanne they may nat wele abyde/ ne might nat wele doo it bifore/ they ben excused/ if nede compelle theym therto/ and nat couetise ne sleuth. Mylwardes crafte by wynde and water is leful in the sunday/ after custome in the cuntre/ for so it may be do with lytel trauayle. But for to do it with draught of beest in the sūday/ it is nat leful. for it may nat be done so without grete trauayl Thus saith Jo. in sū. con. li. i. ti. vii. De feriis et tabula iuris.

The xvi. chapter.

Diues. Is it nat leful me to begine grete iourneys in the sunedaie/ of longe pilgrymage or of fer passyng Paup. If they do it of custome or without nede/ they synne greuously al though they here their seruice er they wende/ and namely men of holy church. that shulde in halidayes moste occupye hem i god des seruice/ and deuocion and techynge of goddes lawe/ and yeue the peple gode example to halowe wele the halyday. Prechoures that trauayle from towne to towne in the sunday and greate festes to teche the peple goddes lawe ben excused & wynne moch mede But be they ware that Under colour of prechyng they rene nat to moche aboute in veyne in the sunday. Diues. Is it leful in grete halidayes to trauayle a boute makynge of holy churche as in cariage liftynge of stones. gadyng of stones & suche other. Pauper. As for a brayde it is leful/ but nat to do no longe trauayl ne ouir grete y shuld bryng men to werynesse to let them fro goddes seruyce For the halyday representith endlesse reste and halowynge withouten ende. And therfore J hold it unleful to make grete cariages in the sunday. or any principalle feste. for any churche makyng. Diues. Is it nat leful to helpe men of holy churche in the grete halidayes to housyng in cariage & other trauayle. Paup. If they be pore. it is leful as for a brayde to help theym in housynge But if they be riche ynough to pay therfore. in the werke day/ it is natt leful to trauayle for them in sunday and other grete festes. Diues. Is it lefulle to Vitaylers & other chapmē to ryde or go fro towne to towne in the sunday for to sel Vitayles or other thinges in the churche or in the church yerde or at the churche yate. Pauper. Nay forsothe For ther shuld no suche market be holden in ye sū day/ neither in seintuary/ ne out of seyntuarie. Extra de feriis. Omnes dies dominicos. And therfore bey market daies ordey

The thridde.

ned i other daies that men shuld than bye and selle/ and halowe i the sunday But it is leful to vp taisers to sel vptailes i their owne place/ so that they do it principaly for almesse of their euyn cristen/ and here their seruyce. A vp se hem that than bye. Diues. Is it leful to worche in the sunday Whanne euensonge is sayd and whanne me̅ haue herde goddes seruyce. Pauper. Nat But the greter nede compelle them to worche as I saide firste For elles ben men bounde̅ to halowe from euyn to euyn. And therfore wha̅ euensonge is done by nydouyt/ none in the sunday/ yit it is nat leful to worche And though the euensonge be sayde in the satur day by nydouirnone/ yit it is leful to worche tyl the sonne goo downe Natheles so lytel the werke may be p it is no synne to do it thanne. Diues. Howe shulde men knowe howe moche werke is leful to doo in the hali day/ & what nede excuseth man of trauelynge in the sunday/ & i̅ other grete festes/ for couetise and wanbileue p men truste nat to god/ But wene that god shuld fayle them/ put folk in drede of nede/ Whanne ther shulde elles be no drede of suche nede.

P.up. Therfore if they myght redily haue theire busshop/ they shulde axe him coūsepl/ or elles their curate/ or some other gode wise man And if the nede be grete and open/ their owne conscience olwith excuse them For they may thanne worche by auctorite of the lawe. And if a man or woma̅ axe counsepl in thinges of doute of him that be wenyth slyplfully shulde yeue gode coū sepl/ though the coūseplour fail in his counsepl yeuynge/ yit the axer is excused/ But he knoweth the coūsepl is nat gode. or elles dyd nat his deuer to knowe that And for he solwith hi to axe coū sepl and forsakith his owne wit and his owne wyl he gettith mo che nede.

The xviii. chaptre.

Diues. Whanne seruauntes trauayl in the sunday by compellyng of their soueray nes/ ben they excused bifore god by their maisters byddynge. Pauper. If they trauayl and do their maisters biddynge prin cipaly for drede & for obedience. that they owe to their soueray̅. and nat for couetise ne for none other euyl cause/ & the maner of trauayl be leful in the self/ than they been excused For as holy Wryt saith God loueth more obe dience than sacrifice. But ware þe souerayne þat cōpellith his seruaunte/ in the sunday or any grete feeste without grete nede. For to the souereynes is halow/yng of haliday principaly bodē for without their wylle her seruaunt ne their beste. shal do comōly no seruple werke Diues. Steracles pleyes and daunces. that are vsed in grete festes. and in sundayes/ are they nat leful. Paup. Miracles pleyes & dauces that ben done principaly for deuocion honestye and myrthe. to teche men to loue god the more. and for no ribaudrye/ ne medlyd with rebauldrye ne lesynges. ben leful/ so that the people be nat lettyd therby frō goddes seruyce/ ne fro goddes worde herig and that ther be no erroure medled in suche miracles and pleyes ayenst the feith of holy churche. ne ayenst gode lyuynge. Alle other ben forfēdyd both haliday and werkday. De con. di. iii. Irreligiosa Et extra li. iii. ti. i. cū decorē. Where the glose saith that for to reṗsente in pleyng at Cristmasse Heroude and þe thre kynges. and other processe of þe gospel bothe thāne and at ester. & in other tymes also/ it is leful. and cōmēdable. Diues. Than it semyth by thy speche þ in halidayes men may lefully maken myrthe. Pauper. God forbede elles for as I saide the haliday is ordeyned for reste and releuig bothe of body and of soule And therfore I salwe of kynde/ I salwe writen/ in salwe of grace/ & euyr frō the begynnyng of the worlde. the haliday hath ben solacyouse with onestie/ bothe for soule and body/ & for worship of god whos daye is that daye/ solacyouse in clothinge in mete and drinke/in occupacion/ honestie wᵗ myrthe makynge And therfore the prophete saith. Hec dies quem fecit dn̄s: exultemus et letemur in ea This is the day þ god made/make we now be mery & be we glade. Diues. Contra. Seynt austyn saith þ it wer lesse wycked to go at the plough and at the carte/ & carde and spynne in the sundaye than to lede daunces. Paup. Seynt austyn spekith of suche daunces and pleyes as was vsed in his tyme/ whan cristen peple was moche medlyd wᵗ hethē peple/ and by olde custome and example of hethen people vsed vnhonest daunces and pleyes that by olde tyme were ordeyned. to stire folk to lechery and to other synnes And so if daunsyng and pleynge nowe on the halidayes stire men & wymē to pryde to le/ chery glutonye and sleuthe/ to o uir longe wakynge on nightes. & to ydelship on the werk daies.

C iiii

The thridde.

and other synnes/ as it is ryght lykly they do in our daies than ben they vnleful both on the halyday and on the werke day And apenst al suche spake seynt Austyn But apenst honest daūces. and pleyes done ī due tyme and in gode maner ī the halyday. spake nat seint austyn. ¶Diues. Cōtra &c. We fynde in holy wryt ⁊ god badde his peple turmente their soules and yeue them to sorowe and mournynge in the halydaye. Dies expiationū erit celeberimus et vocabitur sctūs. affligetisq3 aīas vrās in eo Oīs aīa que afflicta nō fuerit die hoc: pibit de pplo suis. Leuitici. xxiii. ¶Thanne is semyth that god wole ⁊ men yeue hem rather to mournyng in the halyday thā to myrth or to welfare. ¶Paup. Salomō saith. Spes que differtur affligit aīam. Prouer. xiii. c ¶The hope the desire and the longynge ⁊ is delayed turmentith the soule. For the more that mā or woman longith after a thing the more it is disease/ tyl he hath his disese and his longyng. But nowe it so that the rest the mirth the ese and the welfare/ that god hath ordeyned in the halydayes. is tokē of endlesse reste ioye and myrthe and welfare in heuenes blisse that we hope to haue with

outē ende. For there men shalle halowe withouten ende/from al maner trauayle thought ⁊ care. And therfore as I saide first god wole that we thynke on the halyday of the reste ioye and blysse. ⁊ the halyday bitokneth. and haue it in thought/ in desire in lōging ⁊ hope to come therto And so turment oure soules by longynge. by sorowynge by longynge after the endelesse reste. And by sorowynge ⁊ for synne oure desire is so longe delayed In this maner god wole that euery mā and woman turmente his soule in halyday/ by loue longynge to god warde/ ⁊ by sorowynge for goddes offence Nat to shewe greate heuynesse outwarde/ and so doo bodily penaunce in any grete halyday Moreouir leue frende god badde nat that the iewys shulde turment their soules in euery halyday But only in one solempnite that was cleppyd the fest of clensynge ⁊ of forgeuenesse For that daye god forgaue the iewys the grete synne that they dyd whan they made them a calf of golde. and siluer/ and worshiped ⁊ calf as god/ and cleppyd it theire god nat withstondynge al the wonders that god hadde shewid hem a litel bifore/ledyng hem throu gh the rede see drye fote/ and brē chyd kyng pharo and al his oste and spake to them openly by voyce of aungelles, from aboue the mount of synay in thundre and lightnynge in fyre and smooke. and cloudes, ful grymme & voyces of trumpe and of clarion ful dredeful to here And for asmoch as that greuous synne was first forgouen them in that day, and they were furste that day maade clene from that grete synne, therfore god bad them halowe that day for ioy of forgyfnes. He bad them also that day turmet their soules for sorowe of þ greuouse synne, and for their vnkyndnes that they shulde haue mynde of their synnes & be asshamed therof And also haue in mynde goddes godenesse ayenst their shrewydnesse, and thanke him therof. This daye was the tenthe daye of Septembre.

The xviii. chaptre.

Diues. Where fyndst thou that god badde men mak mery & fare wele in the halidaye Pauper. In the same place of holy wrytte. Leuitici. xxiii. Where we fynde that god bad ye children of israel take braunches and bowes of palme trees & of yͤ fayrest trees þ they might fynde.

and make theym tabernacles, & duelle therin seuyn dayes to gider euery yere onys, & there make mery bifore theire lorde god. in the mynde þ god made theym to duelle in tabernacles I deserte xl. yere and there sauyd theym & kepte them fro wo And Esdras the prophete saide to goddes people This day is halowyd to our lorde god. wepe ye nat ne mourne ye nat, ete ye gode metes and fatt, and drynke ye gode drynkes, and ye that may, sende ye parte to them that may natt, ne haue no power wherof to dighte them mete or drynke. Be ye nat sory for it is goddes holy daye Gaudium eterni dñi est fortitudo vestra. The ioye of our lorde is youre strengith, that is to say, God is glade that ye be stronge glade and mery. Neempe viii.c. And therfore is fastynge forfendyd in the sunday. Di. xxx. Si quis tanqm &c. si quis prisbiter. Where fastynge is forfendyd in the sunday And also ther shulde no fastynge be vsed moche from Ester to pentecoste þ is wytsontide, for ioye of cristes resurrectiō & of oure saluacion. Di. lxxvi. Ieiunia. Et de cō. di. i. Ieiunt um. Diues. Where fyndest thou in holy wrytt þ daunces & songes ben leful and plesaunte to god.

Pauper. We fynde Exodi xv. That whan the children of israel were passyd the rede see drie fote / soo þ the water stode in either side of them right vp as a walle and god hadde drenchyd kynge pharo and al his oste / than moyses made a mery songe and pryspynge to god / Whiche songe begynneth thus in latyne. Cantemus dño gloriose: eni magnificatus est. Thanne mary the suster of aaron toke her tymber in her honde / & al wymen þ mighte toke her tymbers i her hondes. & wente daunsynge and syngyng the same songe pryspnge & worshippynge oure lorde god. ¶ We fynde also in the secounde boke of kinges in the vi. chapitre that whane dauyd shulde fetche goddes hutche into ierlm. Dauyd & al the people of israel went ther with & pleyed in al maner mynstralcye / songe and dauncyd and skypped for ioye. and so pryysed and worshiped god But michol saules doughter and Dauydes wyf scornyd dauyd for his dauncynge and for his skypppynge / & said. that it was nat semely to a king so skippe & dauce as a knaue. Bifore the people & bifore her maydens. Dauyd saide to her. I shal pley and daūce bifore my lorde god þ hath chosen me to be a kinge. & put thy fader & al thy

kyn from þe crown I shal pley bifore my lorde god / & put me in lower degre for his loue / and be lowe and meke in myn owne sight to plese god þ made me king And for þ mychol scornyd so dauyd for his skippynge & hisdaūsynge and his lownesse / therfore god made her barayne / þ she had neuir childe as saithe the boke there. ¶ Also god gladyd his peple þ was in care & moche tribulacion / & sayd. pitt shal maydēs make mery in songe and daūsynge / & olde folke to gider For I shal turne their care into ioye. & glade them & conforte them of their sorowe. Ieremye xxxi.c. Diues. It may wele be as thou saist For myrthe and gladnesse. confortethe men in goddes seruyce / and heuynesse dullithe and letithe al maner slypyng Pauper. Therfore dauyd saithe. Seruite dño in leticia. Serue þe oure lorde in myrthe & gladnesse But two thinges seue frende must be kepte in goddes seruyce. and in gode spuyng / sadnesse and gladnesse. Sadnesse in chere and in doynge. Gladnesse in hert thynkyng. Sadnesse withoute sorynesse of malice / of wrath hate / and of enuye. And gladnes withouten folye and ribaudrye. And therfore seue frende I praye you saddith wele / butt

Precepte.

sadditħ nat Be alwaye gladde.
But neuirmore mad By no folye
Alway sad / alway glade / so pat
poure gladenesse & pour sadnesse
Be alway medlyd witħ likynge
and loue of god / & wᵗ deuocion.

The xix chapter

Iues. Why been these iii.
preceptes cleppd þe scep
tes of þe firste table. Pauper.
For whanne god yaue moyses.
þe lawe in þe mounte of synay
he toke him þe x cōmaundemē
tes writen in ii. tables of stoone
In þe first table were writen þe
thre firste cōmaundmentes whi
che teche vs how we shulde wor
ship oure god. & loue him aboue
al thinge And therfore they ben
cleppd þe sceptes of þe firste ta
ble / botħ for wortħynes of them
self. and for they were writen in
þe firste table. In þe se
counde table were writen oþer
vii. cōmaūdementes / that teche
vs to loue our euēcristen as our
self / & ben cleppd þe sceptes. of
þe secounde table And so al þe
x. sceptes ben cōprehendyd and
closed in þe ii. sceptes of charite.
The firste precepte of charite is
this / þ thou shalt loue thy lorde
god witħ al thyn herte / witħ all
thy soule. witħ al thy mynde / wᵉ
al thy might. Whanne he saitħ

thou shalt loue thy god witħ al
thyne herte / he excludetħ al ma
ner of ydolatrie / that is for forsē
dyd by þe firste cōmaundmēte.
that no man set his herte / ne his
feytħ ne his truste in no creatuŕ
more than in god / ne ayenst god
des worshippe. For
who so louetħ wele a noþer / he
hatħe kyndly a trust and a feitħ
in him And after that he louetħ.
so he trustitħ And þat he trustiþ
moste / comōly he louetħ moste.
And therfore god badde þ thou
shuldest loue him witħ al thyne
herte / þ is to say wᵗ al thy feitħe
so that thou sett al thy feitħ and
thy truste in him bifore al oþer
as in him that is almightye and
may best helpe at nede And ther
fore the firste scepte of thies iii.
is applied principaly to þe sad al
mighty. Also god biddetħ þ thou
loue him witħ al thy soule / that
is to say as seint austyn saiþ wᵗ
al thy wyl. withoute cōtradicti
on / þ thy wyl be nat contarie to
his wylle. But alwey confourmed
to his wyl. And in that he byd
detħ þ thou take nat his name I
veyne But as thou haste taken
þe name of crist / & art cleppd cri
sten / soo confourme thy wylle.
thy lyf. & thy speche to the wylle
of Criste. þ thou wole no thyng
ne do no thynge. ne say no thig.
ayenste his wylle by thy wylle.

The thridde

& thy wyttynge/ ne make none othe ne vowe apenst his wyl. & his worship. And tho that thou haste made to his worship kepe them, and hope sikerly þ if thou fulfille goddes wyl here in erthe he shal fulfyl thy wyl in heuyn. And loke that thou spende alle thy lyf and thy beyng to his worship and in his loue And thanne louest thou him wᵗ al thy soule. in whiche principaly is thy lyf & thy beynge And therfore if thou spende nat thy lyf and thy beyng in his loue, thou louest him nat with al thy soule And therto thou takest his name in veyne. for his name is. Qui est. That is to say. He that is. For al thīg þ is takith his beyng of him And therfore if thou spende thy lyf & thy beyng in synne and vanitie. thou takyst his name of beynge in veyne Also loke that thou spende al thy wytte in his loue. þ thou study to knowe the treuþ þ is cristes name For he saithe Ego sum veritas. And so study to fle falshede & folye By help of criste goddes sonne þ is al witty And therfore the secoūde cōmaūdement is applied to the secoūde psone in trinyte/ þ is the sonne al wytty Also he biddeth þ thou loue him with al thy mynde, with outen forʒetynge of his benefices and of his giftes to the. & to

mankynde And in that he byddeth the kepe wele the halidaye. Whiche is ordeyned principally þ men shulde than withdrawe her thoughtes and their mynde. fro the worlde/ and thynke thanne on god and on heuynly thinges Than thynke on their owne vnkyndnesse and of goddes godenesse as I sayde firste And therfore he saith Memento. Thynk that thou halowe wele the haly day That is to say, loue god wᵗ al thy thought and with al thy mynde/ that thou be in wyl no thynge to thynke apenst his plesaunce/ and that thou haue sykyng to thynke of him by grace of the holy goste/ to whome the thridde cōmaundement is applied/ without whome as seynt poule saith. we may thynke no gode thought The firste precept is applied to the fader almighty þ may best helpe at nede. For malumettes and ydolatry may nat helpe The secounde precept is applied to the sonne al wytty. Whose name is treuthe and soueraync wisdome For he knowith al he may nat be dissepued And treuthe shulde natt be taken in veyne, but alwaye worshippde & wisely mayntened The thrid precept is applied to the holy gost whiche is clepid.paraclitus.þ is to saye comfortoure.

For the halidaye is ordeynyde to comforte bothe of soule and of body, to comforte a man and and beste. And the holy goste comfortith vs in sorowe and care, & he is bote of euery bale. He ye ueth reste after trauayl, he is solace in disease, and he abatith careful thoughtes, and prueth pees and reste in herte. And therfor the prophete saith to him Cogitacio hominis confitebitur tibi. et reliquie cogitationis diem festum agent tibi. Mānes thought shalbe aknowe to ye his mysche ues, and the remenauntes of his thoughtes shal make a haliday to the in the sunday and other festes. Secundū multitudinē dolorū meorū in corde meo: consolationes tue letificauerūt alam meam. Lorde saith he after ye multitude of sorowes in myne herte, so thy confortes haue gladyd my soule. For the holy goste biddeth that men reste from their trauayles here in the halidayes. and after in endlesse blisse.

The xx. chapter.

Also leue frende, as the gospel saithe Mar. xii c. ye shal loue god with al youre hert with al youre soule, with al youre mynde, with alle youre mighte. that is to say, as seint Bernarde saith, ye must loue him. dulciter. prudenter, fortiter. Swetely. Wisely, mightily. Swetely wip al youre herte, with alle youre soule, that ye haue likyng & him passinge al other. Wisely with al youre mynde & with al your thought, þ ye studye and be besy night & day to do his plesaunce. & to fle his offence. Also ye muste loue him mightily & stedfastly þ neither wele ne woo departe you, from his loue. And therfore seint poule saith þ no tribulacion hūger ne thruste, hete ne colde, syf ne dethe, ne no creature shuld departe vs from the charite in crist if we louyd him as we shulde loue. ye shal loue youre god with al youre hert, so that ye loue no thinge but for him & in him. ye shal loue him with al your soule so þ ye spende al poure wylle. & alle youre affection in his loue.

ye shal loue him with al your mynde, so that ye spēde al your thoughtes in his loue. ye shalle loue him with al youre mighte. so that ye spende al youre mightes in his loue, so that ye assente to no thing, ne thynke no thing ne do no thinge, apenst his plesaunce, ne þ shulde lett his loue. ne departe you from his loue. The firste cōmaundmēt techith vs to loue him mightily. The ii. techith vs to loue him wisely.

The thrid techith us to loue him swetely in ease and reste of herte By the firste cōmaundment god techith us feith and right bileue By the secoūde he techith us hope For as he saith by the prophete Ōsñ in me sperauit liberabo eū: protegam eum qm̄ cognouit nomen meū. For he hoppyd in me I shal deliuer him. and I shalle defende him for he hath knowē my name. Beatus vir cuius ē nom̄ dn̄i spes ei⁹: et non respexit in vanitates. et insanias falsas. Po. xxxix. Blessyd be that man whose hope is in the name of oure lorde/ and hath taken hede to no vanityes ne to no false wytnesses to forswere him/ and to take goddes name in veyne. For as seynt poule saith/ ther is no name in whiche we may be saupd/ but goddes name swete Jesus And therfore they that haue goddes name I worshippe/ may haue siker hope to be saupd And tho þ haue it in dispite owe to be in grete drede. By the thridde cōmaundement. god techith us charite For charite and gode loue is reste in every wo & trauayl For loue makith trauayl lighte and easy/ that shuld elles be ful diseasy. By the firste precepte of charite we be bounden to shewe loue to god in herte/ in worde/ in werke And therfore god biddeth that we shuld loue him with all our herte/ with al our soule and mynde/ þ is to say: wᵗ al our speche For speche outward is tokē of thoughtes ynwarde Also he biddeth us loue him with al our mightes/ that is to saye. wᵗ aloure werkes. And so the first pcept of the firste table techith us to loue god with alle oure herte The seconde techith us to loue hī wᵗ alle oure worde/ and shewe hym loue I speche For who so loueth wele a nother/ he wole speke gode and worship of him that he loueth/ and be glade to here of his gode name and speke him gode. & worship/ and sorye to here his name dispised and diffamed By ye thrid cōmaundmente we ben taught to shewe loue to god I dede/ þ is to leue oure owne occupacions on ye haliday & peue us principaly to serue god & to be occupied wᵗ hī/ & no thīg do but for his loue & to his worship/ or for grete nede of oure self For who so loueth wele a nother/ he wole sehe a tyme to speke wᵗ hī & dele wᵗ hī And therfore god biddeth us halowe wel the haliday & than attēde to hī & occupie us wᵗ hī as wᵗ oure dere loue/ þ made us of nought/ and bought us with his blode ful dere/ & saueth

Ꝫs/ and kepith Ꝫs/ and yeueth
Ꝫs al that we haue of any gode
and fyndeth Ꝫs alle that Ꝫs ne=
dith and moche more And if we
loue hym in this maner with all
oure myghtes and oure dedys/ ⁊
oure werkes/ and halowe thus
the halyday ⁊ the sabot ⁊ he hath
boden Ꝫs halowe/ He shulde ye=
ue Ꝫs a sabot and reste in heuen
blisse/ where as saith psalte the p=
phete. shalbe sabott of sabottes.
that is to say endlesse rest beton=
nyd by temporel rest in the haly=
daye. And moneth of moneth ⁊
is to say endlesse myrthe betoke
nyd and figured. By temporalle
myrthe in the halyday. psale lyo
xl. c. Amen.

Here endith the thridde precpte/⁊
begynneth the fourth. Ca. i.

Dues. As me thyn=
keth thou hast de=
clared the comaund
mentes of ye first ta=
ble ful wele and parfitly to ma=
nes soul Now I pray ye for god
des sake p fourme that thou hast
begune. and declare to me ye co=
maundementes of the secund ta
ble/ ⁊ I may the bett knowe god
des lawe/and the more plesaunt

ly serue my god/ in kepe me the
more peasible in charite wt myn
euencristen. For as I haue vn=
derstonde/ al the seuyn comaud
mentes of the secounde table be
knytte in the secounde precpte of
charite whiche biddeth Ꝫs loue
our euencriste as our self Paup.
Mankynde hath ii. begynnyn=
ges The firste begynnynge and
begynner is god. The secounde
begynnyng and begynner. is ye
fader and moder By the first co=
maundemēt of the first table we
be taught to worship god aboue
al thinges/ as hym that is begyn
nyng of Ꝫs and of al creatures.
By the firste comaundement of
the secounde table we be taught
to worship fader and moder yat
been oure begynnynge next af=
ter god And therfore he saith I ye
firste comaundement of the se=
counde table. Honora patrem
tuum et matrē tuā. That is to
saye/ worship thy fader and thy
modre. By the preceptes of
the firste table he taughte Ꝫs to
loue god aboue alle thinge.
By the preceptes of the secoūde
table. he techith Ꝫs to loue oure
euencristen as oure self. And
for asmoche as charite is moost
shewyd by worshippynge and hel
pynge of oure euencristen/ ther=
fore he begynneth by teching of

The fourthe

worſhip that owith to be doone to them that we owe by weye of charite moſte to worſhippe after god and mooſte to helpe that is fader and moder. And therfore he ſaith. Honora patrem tuũ et matrem tuam. Worſhip thou thy fader and thy moder. By which cõmaundement we ben boundẽ to helpe oure bodily fader ⁊ moder at nede and be to theym buxum and meke/ and ſe their diſpleſaunce. nat diſpiſe them/ nat agre hem vnſkilfully/nat banne ne warie them; ne harme theym ne ſcorne them for none age/ for none vnclenneſſe/ for no wantwytneſſe for that they ſay or do/ But ſupporte them ĩ their age and ſe bleneſſe/ as they ſupportyd vs ĩ oure youthe/ and holpe vs. and kepte vs ĩ oure febleneſſe/ whã we coude nat ne might nat help oure ſelf. ℂWe fynde Geneſis ix. c. That Noe had thre ſones. Sem Cham ⁊ Japhet. Whanne the floode was doon it happyd ꝑ their fader noe dranke ſo wyne. that he was drõke/ for he knewe nat the might of the wyne. For bifore the flode men dranke no wyne ne ete no fleſſhe. And whãne noe was thus drõke/ his myddel ſonne Cham fonde him liggynge bare/ ſo that he might ſe his preuy membris And anon

he laughed his fader to ſcorne/ ⁊ wolde nat hile his fad/ but wẽte. and told it to his brethern iapig and ſcornyng his fader But his brethern wolde nat ſe that vncſight/ but turned their face from their fader and caſt a cloth vpon him and hiled him oneſtly. Whã ne noe awoke. and wiſte whatt his myddel ſonne Cham hadde doon to him. He was wroth with him and curſed his Canaan and al that ſhulde come of him/ and made him thral ⁊ bonde to Sem and Japhet/ and to their childrẽ after them And thus for ſcornig and vnworſhip ꝑ that the ſonne dyd to the fader/ Began firſt bõdage and thraldom and was cõfermyd of god. Diues. Sithẽ Cham dyd the ſynne ⁊ nat chanaan Whiche was yit but a child Why curſed noe the childe chanaan. and nat cham the childrẽ fader. Pauper. Noe wolde natt curſe Cham in his perſoone/ for god hadde bleſſyd him in his perſone with his bretherne anoone after the flode And therfore he curſed his ſonne/ and him in his ſonne/ and puniſſhed him in his ſonne/ and alle that ſhuld come of him For it was goddes dome that right as he hadde do ſhame to his fader/ſo his children ſhuld be ſhame and ſhenſhip to hym

Precepte.

And as none hadde no loue of hi̇ so shulde he haue no loue of his children. Oiues. The scrypture is gode and rightful, saye for the Pauper. Therfore Salomon saith. Oculum qui subsannat patrē: et despicit partum matris sue, suffodient eū corui de torrē tibus ⁊ demones, prouer. xxx. c. The iye that scornyth his fader and dispiseth the birth of his moder, taunys of the brokes, that is to say, feendes of hel brokes shal delue oute and pyke oute ꝑ iye. And therfore he saith in an other place. Honora patrē tuū et gemitus matris tue ne obliuiscaris. Memento quīm nisi ꝑ illos non fuisses: et retribue illis quomodo illi tibi. Eccle. vii. c. Worship thou thy fader, and forgette nat ye siggynges of thy moder, ne what peyne she had whā she bare the of her body. Thynk that but by theym thou haddest nat been, and yelde them and do to theim as they dyd to the. And god bad him self in ye olde lawe ꝑ who so cursed or waried his fader or moder, he shuld be slayne. Leuitici. xx. c.

The ii. chapter

Oiues. Many children wolde ful fayn se their fader and their moder dede, ꝑ they mighte haue her heritage, ⁊ lyue at their owne gouernaunce. And ofte whāne they may natt haue it by their gode wyl ne by their dethe, they wole haue it by plee and by maistrye. Paup. Such children fulle late shalle thryue. and they shal haue ful lytel ioy and worship of her children, But moche shame and shenshyp. For as salomō saith, He that cursith his fader or his moder or disseith theym, his lanterne shalbe quenchyd i the myddes of derknesses. that is to say either he shal none eyre haue, or if he haue he shalle be without worship. For the heritage saith he to whiche childrē hasten fast in this maner, shalle want blessyng and grace of god in the laste ende. Prouer. xx. c. And in a nother place he saith. ꝑ he so withdrall it̄ any thyng from his fader and from his moder, and saith it is noo synne, he is as wychyd as a manqueller. Particeps homicidie ⁊. Prouer. xxviii. c. Also we fynde in the seconde boke of kynges xv. c. ꝑ absolon the sone of dauid wold haue put his fader dauid out of his kingdome, and he droue him oute of the cite of ierusm̄ bar̄ofote for he came so sodeynly on him that dauid was besy to fle. and

℣he fourthe.

saue his lyf Sone after absolon paue bataple to his fader in the felde. But as god wolde he was discounfited/ and moche of his folȝre slayne/ bothe by swerde. ⁊ by the wylde beestes.

¶ Thanne absolon fledde rydynge on his mule. dischevele. ⁊ is open heded And as he rode vnder an oke/his here that was ful longe and ful feyre smote vp amonges the bowes/ ⁊ there faste nyd so that ye mule passyd forth in his rene But absolon henge stylle by the here. tyl that Joab. that was cheeftepne and prynce of the oste of dauid came to him and smote him through the hert with thre sperys/and dyd stoone him ful vp to the deth/ that was the moste dispitouse dethe in the salve And soo absolon that was than ye fairest man lyuyg/for haste that he hadde to the eritage and dyd suche wrong to his fader/he loste bothe his heritage and his lyf Also adony his brother wold haue ben kynge whyle his fader dauid lyuyde/ and dauid pryued him of the kyngdome for euir. ⁊ made salomon kynge/ that was thane nat xi.yere olde And afterwarde adonye was slayne for he wolde haue ben kynge ayēst his faders ordenaūce Therfore god bad i the old lawe Deutro.xxi.c

¶ if ther were any vnbuxū child ⁊ wralwe ÿ wolde nat obey to his fader and moder/they shuld lede him to the rulers of the cite. and say to them in this wyse Oure sonne is stoute ⁊ proude/ he wol nat here oure techyng ne our biddyng/ But he peueth him to ryot glutonye and lechery/ ⁊ to grete festes and fare And god bad ÿ al the people of the cite or of ÿ towne. shulde sle that vnbuxū child with stones/in example of alle other For whanne yonge folȝre were rebelle to fader and moder and yeue them to suche ryot and welfare/ and ydelship/ But they be chastised ⁊ withstōde i the begynnyng/ they shal shēde the comyntee of the peple. by robbery. murdre ⁊ manslaughter/ by conſions ⁊ wicked cumpanyes and make rebellion ⁊ rysynge ayenst their souerayns/ and so be cause of destruction of the londe of the cite and of the compnte Also Mᵗ.yb.c. Criste in the gospel repreueth al tho that by ypocrisy. withdrawe nedful lyuyng from fader or moder/ vnder colour of goddes worship and holy chirch And he repreueth tho men of holy churche that so enfourme the children to say to their fader and moder. that they may nat worship god and holy churche for ye

202

coste ÿ they do to sustepne theim
self/ and so make fader and mo=
der to lyue in mysschepf/ ÿ mē of
holy churche may lyue in delice.

¶ The iii. chapter.

Ot only by the precept of
god ben we bounden and
taught to worshyp and help our
fader and oure moder/ But also
by example in kynde as tellithe
the maister of ꝓprities. That
whanne the storke that is clepyd
Ciconia. in latyn hath brought
forth her byddes to flyght/ both
the male and the female bē wor
en full feble for trauayle ÿ they
hadde in the bredyng and bryng
ynge forthe of their byddes/ and
so feble that they may natt wele
helpe theym self For bothe the
male and the female sytte by dy
uerse tymes on the eyren/ ¶ that
ge their trauayle in bredynge of
their byddes/ and in fetchyng of
mete and drynke for them self. ¶
for their byddes. And therfore
whanne the byddes been wore
and may fle/ they fetche mete to
their fader ¶ moder into the nest
as longe tyme as they trauailed
to bryng forth their byrdes/ tyl
they be releuyd and may trauayl
to helpe them self. Also he tel=
lith ÿ ther is a bydde that is cle=

pyd a pellicane. Pellicanus.
And ther is a greate enempte bi=
twene the pellican and the addre
The addre waiteth whanne the
pellican hath byddes/¶ whanne
she is out of the nest to gete me
te to her ¶ to her byddes. the ad=
der crepith vp into the neste and
steeth the byddes. Whanne the
pellican cometh ayen/ and fyn=
deth her byddes slayne on this
maner/ she mourneth thre day=
es aud thre nygtes for dethe of
her byddes. The thridde day she
settith her ayen ouir her byddes.
¶ with her bylle she smyteth her
selfe in the syde. and spryngithe
the blode on her byddes And by
the vertue of the bloode she ray/
seth them fro dethe to lyf. By the
bledyng she wexith so feble ÿ she
may nat trauayl to fede her self.

¶ Thanne some of her byddes
for loue and pitee put theym to
trauayle and fede their moder/ ¶
some yeue no tale of her but on=
ly fede theym self. Whanne the
moder is amendyd. and woxen
stronge/ tho byddes that helpyd
her she loueth and cherissheth.
And the other ÿ wolde nat helpe
her/ she betith and bylleth and ca
stith them oute of her cumpany.

¶ The iiii. chaptre.

m ii

☞The fourthe.

Diues. This precepte biddithe vs worshyp fader and moder/ꝑt we may do withouten ony coste and with litylʹ trauaile/For we may ryse a penys theym. knele to them and take ther blessing and speke to them with reuerēce and so kepe ye cōmaūdemēt/Paup ☞The cōmaundement bynde the vs not only to worshipe. fader ꞇ moder with such reuerēce doing But also to worship them wᵗ helpe at nede/Diues. Where findest thou that helpe at nede is cleped worship. Pauper In the firste pistle that seit poule wrote to ye Busshop tymothee. v. c. Where seit poule bad that he shuld worship verrey wideuis. That is to saye he shulde susteine them with godis of holy church And he clepith there Barrey wideuis. that had no good to be susteined withe of ther owne/And if that she hadde childrē or fader or moder or whe reof to liue. He bad that she shuld lerne to rewle hir housshold and helpe fader ꞇ moder as they hol pen her/And in the same chapter he biddeth that prestis and men of holy church that rewle welʹ her sugettis. shuld haue double wor ship of the peple. That is to say the glose that the people shulde obey to them ꞇ do them reuerēce and finde them alʹ that theym ne

de. and namely to them that tra uayle in prechinge and techinge of the gospelʹ Diues. It is ōly so ly. Whan folke for age and feble nesse maye not ne can not helpe them silf ne gouerne theym silfe thāne to be take to ther childrēs gouernaunce of the howshold.ꞇ putte them silf in keping of ther children and ther gouernaunce. Paup. More semely it is that they putte them in her childrens gouernaunce aud keping than i straungeris Namely if they ha ue founde them good and kinde to them bifore But for any trust in ther children I wold not coun seile them fully dyshyten them of her good/But alwey reserue the lorship to them silf. and ther children in daūgere/And therfor Salamon sayth/Audite me mag nati and omnes ppłi ꞇc. Eccłe. xxxiii. ye grete men and gouer nouris of holy churche and ye al people liste now to my sawe yeue to no man ne woman power vp on the by thy selfʹ Neithir to sone ne to doughtir ne to brother ne to frend yeue not alʹ ey to other mē thy good and thy catelʹ For hap pely it may repent the. and than shalt thou preye to haue helpe of thine owne good and thou shalt noon haue. Melius est vt filij tui te rogēt q̄te respicere in ma

204

Precepte.

nus filiorū tuorꝝ Eccl. xxxiii. c.
It is better sayth he that thi chyl
dren pray the and aye helpe of
the: than thou loke ito ye hādes
of thy children for helpe. I fynd
that an olde man bitoke to hys
sonne hys houshold and gaue hi
al that he hadd to kepe him wel
in his age. Firste he lay with his
sone in the chaumbre. at the last
he was put oute of the chaūbre
& layde him bisynde the spere at
ye haldore For he colyght a rol
gbide so: his sonne and his sones
wyf might no rest haue by hym
in the chaumbre. And whan he
lay so nigh the halle dore he had
moch colde and cleppd to hī hys
sonnes sonne a litel childe: and
badde him goo to hys fader: and
aye of him some cloth to kepe hī
with from colde. The childe ded
the erande: and the fader toke ye
childe an olde sacke. Haue sayd
he: and bidde hym lay this on hī
Nay fader sayde the childe. Butt
kytte it in too. and sende ye him
the halfe: and kepe ye to you ye
other halfe: tyl to the time whan
ye be olde that ye may thāne hil
you therwithe and kepe you fro
colde. Not longe syth thys caas
bifel in colchestre. There was an
olde man sumdel fettred: which
bitoke his sonne in his age al ye
housholde, and gaue him al that

he hadd for to kepe hī wel in his
age First he lay in chaumbre wi
the his sonne / after he was putt
aloone: in an oute chaumbre in
the perde: and was scruede sulle
eudl both at bedde and at boord
On a daye he prayde his sonnes
wyf to lene hym half a busshel to
mete by a certeyn thynge. Butt
he wold not tel hir what he shuld
mete. She toke hī half a busshel
hauyng greate wondre what he
shulde doo therwith. He wentte
into his chaumbre and shett the
dore to hym. He toke a selle pēs
and halfpens & ferthyngys / that
he hadde: and put them into the
crauises of the half busshel And
sone aft he toke hir a yen hir half
busshel. She loked besyly in the
halfe busshel: to knoll c what he
hadde mote therby. And thanne
she foonde that money hanging
in the crauises and cliftes of the
halfe busshel: and she wend that
he hadde mote money by the ves
sel: And went & she wide it to hir
husbond, and he wende the same
For his fader kept eū a gret hut
che besidis his bedde wel lockid
Right heup it was. But his sone
might not wete what was therin
But after this dede he hopit cē þ
ther hadd be therein moch mony
And in hope of that money he &
his wyf kepte well and onestly

M iii

205

hys fader in to hys dethe. Whāne he was dede: he brake vp the hutche for hete fonde he noṇ therto. And thanne fonde he iṇ þe hutche but erthe and stones and a bepl sṗynge ouer it With a fcr/ olwe theron in the wich was wreten in this maner / Whith this be til be they beten that her children her good shal ketṗn: and prue a/ way al ther thinge ã goon them self on beggṗnge.

Capitulū. 8.

Dues yet contra te. Crist sapth in the gospel. Qui non odit patrem suum et matrē suam: non potest meus esse discipulus. Luce. xiiii. c. He that hatith not his fader and his moder he may not be my disciple / But that we be bounde to hate we be not bounde to worship ne to helpe / Therfore thanne we be neyther bounde to worship fader ne moder: ne to helpe them at nede 'Pauper. Crist sayde tho wordes whanne nighe al the worlde was hethen and of falfe bileue: Whanne nighe al the faders and moders were in falfe bileue and in dedly synne. And therfore criste sapde tho words. Not that childrē shuld hate the psōs of yer faders ã moders But they shuld

hate their falfe bileue / and theyr wicked liuynge. and so vs muste al if we wyl be saued / We shul de loue euery man and woman and hate their synne / And in as moche as fader and moder with stonde vs in goddes weye: We sh ulde hate ther maleice and forsa ke ther wicked liuynge and sorowe godd and be besy to drawe fader and moder after vs in goddes weye by good techynge and ensaumple / Diues. yet contra te Crist sapth in the gospel. Veni seperare hominem aduers' patrem suum et aduersus matrem suam m'. x. c. Pauper. In goddes cause and in truth man and Woman owe the to forsake fader and moder if they wyl the stonde goddes cause / and holde a pens the truthe / And so Crist cam for to departe man and Woman fro ther fader and moder: that stode in falfe bileue a pens god / Criste cam not to put ful hate bitwene man and his fader and moder: But for to make man ã woman to forsake fader and moder for goddes sake: If they wyl let the from godde / And therfore he saṗ the in the same place. He that loueth fader and moder more than me he is not worthy to come to me / We shuld loue fader and moder and helpe them at nede / thou they be hethen and neuir so wicked but we shulde loue god more than them And if we may not please godd and theym also: we shulde offende thyem and please god: and alwey loue ther person and hate ther synne / And be bisy to amende them by good enformacyon with loue & softnes and reuerence. Diues. yet contra te Seint poule saith. Non debent filii parentibus thesaurizare sed parentes filiis. ii. ad cor. xiii°. c: Children owe not to tresoure ne to gadre to gidre to ther faders & moders: But faders and moders owe to tresure and gadre to ther children. Therfore thanne it semeth that children shulde not care for ther fader and moder: But fader and moder shulde care for ther children Pauper. Eche of them owe to care for other / But more the fader and moder for ye childe: thanne the childe for fader and moder Diues. why soo Paup. For the child is toward and by comon course of kynde is sempynge lenger to lyue thane his fader or moder / And his children shulde be his fadris children children and his moders / And so fadere and moder care not only for ther owne children: But also by wey of kynd: they care for yer children & children: & haue effectio moe to ther childre: than ther children for ther children / And more care for ther children: than ther children for them / And therfore right as the rote in the tree by wey of kynde peueth more moysture & vertue vp to the tree and to the crope / Thanne the tree or the crope peueth doune to the rote: soo by wey of kynde the fader and the moder moste be more besye to helpe ther children: and to ordeyne for theym. Thanne the children for fader & moder that sooner by wey of kind shuld dye / Netheles right as the crop refresshith the rote by moysture of dewe and of reyne and bisshadeth it fro the sonne: so ou the children refresshe ther fader & ther moder in ther nede: and kepe them from messhefe as moche as they may in good maner and kepe them wel and onestly. Not for to make them riche: ne norish them in delicitis.

The sixte chapter.

Diues. Whanne man or woman entreth into the religion: he is dede a penste the wordes: Therfore thanne it semeth that bi his religion he is vnbunde from this pecept / And he that is not bounde to helpe his fader

The fourthe.

or moder at nede / For whan he is professed in religion he maye not peue / For he þ nought haue nought may peue. Paup. Mã and woman by thys precepte is boūd to two thingis: to reuerēce fader and moder and to helpe thẽ at nede / As for the reuerence the religiouse is as moche boun/de or more as ye seculere in time and place whanne and where he may doo it. But as for ye secunde poynte that is to helppe theym at nede if hys fader & mo=der haue not wherby to lyue: ne be of power to gete ther liuynge onestly: the sonne owthe not to entre such religion: there he may not helpe thẽ for if he do he may be cause of ther deth: But if hys fader and moder haue enoughe to liue by: he may entre religion tho we fader and moder forbede it him: he shall not spare for lo=ue: prayer: for blessynge / ne for cursse. For as saint austen sayth in epłã ad letum. This precepte byndethe there that thynges of more charge & more profyte lett it not. Diues. yet contra te. If the religiouse kepe not this pre=cepte bicause of his religion: he dede a mysse in takynge of his religion Pauper. That is sothe. Diues. I suppose þ he se neuer aft his fader ne moder:ne do thẽ

no helpe ne reuerence: Howe he=peth he thanne thys precepte: Paup. Thow he se thẽ neuer af=ter: ne helpe theym at nede ne do to theym reuerence: if his wil be good to helpe them at nede: & to do them reuerence if he might co=me to them byn' silfe: or by mene psone: yet he kepe the scept / for thow this scepte byndeth alwey man and woman: yet it byndeth not for alweye. as say these cler=kes nat for eny tyme ne for eue=ry place :ne for euery cause. Butt only for suche cause: tyme & pla=ce whanne they may do it lesuł=ly / And thus bynde al preceptis affirmatiue / But preceptys ne=gatiue binde euery tyme and for euery tyme / Diues. What if fa=der and moder falle in mischeefe after þ ther sone is professed in re ligion: owe not her sonne to for=sake religion. and helpe his fa=der and moder in ther mischeefe. Pauper. Some clerkes seyth for as moch as he is dede a ÿenst the worlde by hys profession th=erfor he is dyscharged fro cure of fader and moder. as he is dyschar=gyd therof by bodely deth / And he owe not to goo oute of hys re ligion: But dwel styl vnder obe=dience of his prelate. Netheles he owe to do his deuor to helpe thẽ sauynge his obedience and ones tee of his religion. In sit.cō.li°. iiii°.ti°.xxxiiii.q.CC.xlix. Diues. As I sayde firste. He þ nought haue nought may yeue. but the religiouse maketh so his profession þ he may no thing haue in propre / Hou shuld he than helpe either fader or moder: or o/ ny other of his kyn Pauper. If he be a religious mendinaūt : he may begge for his fader and moder as he doth for him silfe : and so releue and helpe them by mennys almes./ And if he do so : With oute doute god shall sende hym enoughe by cause of his charyte And he shal fare the bettre for th/ em bothe in body and soule./ And if he be a religious possessionere endewyd by temporall godes he may releue them in the same maner. Or elles by almes of the house. Which is endewed principelly to helpe the nidy. and namely fader and moder / For seint poule sayth that who so haue not cure of hys next: he is wors than iew sarsepy or paynym.

The seuenthe chapter.

Diues. As thei say the godes of holy churche maye not be aliened: ne youen in God to the vse of seculeris. Pauper. for bede elles / For all that holy church hathe. it is youen to holy churche. or ellis purchasyd by substance of temporel lordes to helpe cristen people in nusche/ ese / And therfore holy churchys goodes ben cleped the goodes of the pore and of the nedy. p vi. q. i. decime et c°. qui°. Diues. The se religiouse possessioners endew ed in so grete richesshys: saye that they be the goodes of the house: And therfore noon of them may yeue ony thing of the goodes wi oute comon assent of the couent And leue of ther souerayne / And so me thinketh that it is full harde to ony religious possessionere to helpe ether fader or moder by goodes of hys house / For the re/ ligiouse may scarsely help them sylfe by goodes of hys house :' he shal ful euyl or may releue fader or moder by goodes of his house For redely he shall fynde bothe hys prelate and his couent ayēs hym: alegginge dilapidacion & wast and pouertie and greate ne de withe oute nede / For yet ther is no house that wyl saye þ they

The fourthe

haue enoughe. ℘auper. A forȝ lordſhip is thanne the lordſhipp of religeouſe that may nat in ſo greate richeſſys paſſynge dukes eerlis barons. releue the myſſhef of theyr owne fader and moder. But ſo help they ſhewe wel that al ther beſineſſe is to ſpare to purchaſe to begge of lordes and ladies. and of other men londes & rentys gold and ſiluer. Not for help of the pore: But for to mayntteyn ther pride and ther luſt fare Saynt Benett e ofte wythe goode conſience gaue to the couentys gode to folke i miſchefe For we rede p°. li°. dialogor. That there was a good ſimple man diſeſid for he ought a man twelue ſhillinges: and he had not where with to paye / He cam to ſeint benet and prayd him of help Seīt Benet ſayde that he hadde noght thanne wher with to helpe hym. But come a pen ſayde he to me: after too dayes: and thāne I ſhal helpe the if I may / Seint Benet for petie that he hdde on that man praide to god for help / And ſodynly he foond ligging threttene ſhyllinges on the hutche of the couent that was full of whete. whiche money ſeint benet toke & gaue to that ſory man / and bad him paye twelue ſhillinges for his det / And twelue pens of

he bad him kepe for his liuynge And withe oute doute if ſeint benette hadde hadde ſo moche money of the couent: he ſhulde haue do the ſame with the couents money with out aſſent of the couent / For we fynde in the ſame boke that there was a grete hungre in that cuntre þ ſeint benette dwelled in / And whanne he ſaw folke at myſſheſe: he gaue away nigh al the godes of the couent ſo that there was no thing left in the couent wherby to liue but a litel oyle in a glaſſe / Ther cam a man to hym whos name was agapitus: And prayde him for goddes ſake to ȝeue him a lytyl oyle / Seint Benet bad the monk that hadde the oyle in keppynge deliuer that oyl to that nedi mā The monke for negardſhip and for that it was the couentys gode wolde not delyuer it to the nedy man / For if he gaue that away ther ſhuld noon leeue to þe couentt / Seint benet was myſpayde: and badde another monke take the veſſel of glas withe the oyle and caſte it oute at the windowe: for þ the monke was ſo vnobediēt for the oyle / whan it was caſte oute: it felle doune more than an hundred foote on cragges and ſtones For the hou-*ſe ſtoode vpon*

Precepte.

any oygꝪ oyl/ꝯ neyther ye glas bra
ke ne the oyle ſpylt .Thānne ſt
benet bad the monkes take it as
it was/and yeue it to ye nede ma
And thanne bifore al the mon=
kes he vndernamte the celerer of
hys pryde and of his wanebileue
Thanne ſaint benett wyth hys
bretheren prayde to godd that he
wold ſende them ſome oyle wher
by to leue/And anon a tūne that
laye there beſyde voyde ſodenly
was ſo ful of oyle that it ranne o
uer in the flore/We reden alſo in
the lyf of ſaint gregory that the
re cam a man ꝯ ayide ſaint gre=
gory almes for goddis ſake. For
he hadde loſt al hys good on the
ſee: and onnetꝪ he eſcaped wyth
lif Saint gregori that was than
but abbot: bad his almener ye=
ue hym ſixe pens / And he did ſo
The ſame day he cam ayen: and
ayide almeſſe: and hadde as mo
che/ He cam ayen the thyrde day
and aleggide greate pouertye: ꝑ
he hadde loſt moche goode: and
gate but litel a pen Seint grego
ry bad hys pcuratour ꝯ rewler of
the couentis goodes that he ſhuld
yeue hym his almiſſe / He anſwer
de and ſayde that there was non
thinge lefte: but a diſſhe of ſiluer
in which his moder was wonte
to ſende hym mete/ Saynt gre=
gory bad hym yeue the poreman

that diſſhe/And ſo he dede This
pore man was goddes aungel: I
ye ſekenes of a pore man/ꝯ for
thys almeſſe god made ſeint gre
gy afterward pope of Rome / we
fynde alſo ī the lyf of ſaint fraū=
ces That he had hys brethren ta
ke the clothes of our ladies auſt.
ꝯ yeue thē to ye pore folk. Biii.c.
Diues. the religeouſe ſaye that
the godes of the couent ben alle
theyre goodes in comon . And
therfore may non of theym yeue
oute a wey wythoute aſſente of
them al: For by comon rewle of
the lawe: that toucheth al moſte
be approued of al / Quod omēs
tangit: as hominibꝰ approbari
debet. And by another rewle, the
re may noo man yeue any other
right: but ſuch right as he hathe
hym ſelf / Nemo poteſt plus iu=
ris transferre in alium qm̄ ſibi cō
petere dinoſcitur / And therfore
ſith no perſone of the couent ha=
th any right in godis of the couē
tys: therfore non of them maye
yeue any almes of the couentys
godes ne non other goode with
oute aſſent of them all: or of the
more parte / For what thinge is
any monches of the couent: it is
the couentis/And what ſo he get
teth. it is the couentys. Quia de
quid adquiritur monacho: ad
quiritur monaſterio. Pauper.

☞The fourthe

Bi such ipocrise vnder the color of poute they mainteyn ther pride & ther auarice:& occuppe gretter lordshippis than do many dukes erlis and Barons to grete hindrynge of the londe and gret disease of the pore people / For þ god ordeined to be comon to helpe at nede all men at nede: they say that it is thers and no mānis els / So that foure men of religion in one house myghte spende xx. thousend marke bi ther wil & by ther comon opinyon / al that good shuld neythir turne to help of the lond ne of the pore people But all to helpe the pore couent
Diues. Say to my shillys.
Paup. Thy shillys be not worthe / For the godes of religiouse shulde be more comō than other mennes godis: to helpe the lond and the pore peple / And therfore sayth ye law: þ comō spī is nedeful to al men / & namely to them that wyl folowe the lif of cristes disciples / For as the eyre: or the light of the sonne may not be departed: ne appropryd to one place more thā to a nother / So saith he shulde al these worldly godes be comon in nede. vii.q̄.i. dilectissimis / And therfore they þ haue most nede: haue moste right to godes of the the religeouse And the lordship is no more appropryd

to the religiouse than to the seculers / For bothe seculers and regulers shulde be holpen therby But dispensinge gouernaunce: And keppynge of the goodys of holy churche: is appryd to the religeouse and to other men of holy churche / And therfore sayth holy writt that in the begynnyng of holy churcħ al thinges were comon to the multitude of al cristē people nat only to the apostlys: But to al cristen people. Actuum. quartum. capitulm̄.&.vii.q̄.i. dilectissimis. And therfore if religeouse mispēde the godes that be taken to them.& help not the nedy peple: they do cristē peple grete wronge For they withhold them her right: and make ppre to them þ owthe be comon to al It is a shame and an ouer greate abusion: þ a man of religion shal ride with his tenth sūme or with his twenty sūme on an hors of ten pounde in a sadel al gold bigon And for pouertye that he byndeth him to in his pfession as they saye he maye not peue an halfpeny for goddys loue ne helpe his fader and moder at nede withouten askyng leeue of hys souereyn / Sytħ god that is souereyn of al bad them helpe fader & moder at nede / For goddis biddlg̃ is most to charge And

212

Precepte.

seint peter saytħ/ Obedire opor/
tet domino magis ħ hominibus
Men muste obeye to god more
than to man/ And therfore god
may saye to such folke of religi=
on that Witholden almesse from
fader & moder & from the pore pe
ple to make her house a her couét
riche.p' he sayde to the maisters
of the lawe and to the pharisées
that were men of religion that ti
me Quare transgredimini man
datum dei ppt tradicionem Bes/
tram/ whý breke ye goddes com=
maundement for youre statutys
and poure fore m'. p B.ir.c. Di=
ues. It is long sith I harde the
speke of this matter. passe forth
& speke more to purpos. Paup.
Also we be bounde to Worshipe
fader and moder/ nat only in re=
uerence doing and helping at ne
de But also in obeying to her bid
dyng and her fore/ For salomon
saytħ/ Audi patrem tuum qui ge
nuit te/et ne cōtēpnas cum senu=
uerit mat tua. p b. rriii.c. here
thy fader that the begat & dispise
not whanne thy moder is olde.
That is to saye/ For any age di
spice hir nat/ But be low and me=
ke to hir and set hir teching i hert
Judicium patris audite filii di=
lecti.&c. Eccl. iii.c. ye dere chil=
dren here ye the dome of your fa
der: and do ye so that ye be saued
he that worshipetħ his moder: he

maketħ hi a tresoure in ye w or=
de compnge/ he that worship
tħ his fader: he shal haue ioye of
hys children/ And he shal be hard
of god in hys prayer: and he shal
liue the lenger good lyf/ And he
that obeitħ to his fader: he shal
refressħ his moder/ he that drede
god: he worshipe fader & mader
And he shal serue hi that bigate
hi as his lorde i worde & in dede
and in al paciéce worship thy fa
der saytħ he: that goddes blessíg
mai com to ye The fadirs blessíg
saytħ he maketħ ħ stable & seker
ye housis of her children: and the
modris curs distroitħ her housis
doñe to grounde he is ful of wic
kide fame that: forsaketħ hys
fadris obedience/ And he is a cur
sed of god p' angretħ his moder
& wyl not do hir biddíg/ As these
ben salomonis wordis eccle.iii.c
And therfore god bad that chil=
dren vnburum to fader and mo
der shuld be stoned to detħ deut.
rri. we reden ieremie rrrv.c.
That ionadab bad his children
that they shuld neuer drike wyn
ne make house ne sowe londe ne
set vine/ And for that they kepte
her fadris bidding: god seyde to
them by the pphete ieremye/ For
that ye haue obeide to the precpt
of ionadab your fader and kept
al his cōmaundemētis: therfore
ye kired of ionadab shal not fail

his cōmaundemētes. Therfore the kynrede of Jonadab shalle nat fayle/ But al daies that kynred shalbe in my sight/ & I shalle haue iye to them and helpe them But the wicked people of iuda. and of ierlm that wold nat obey to my cōmaundmentes I shalle distroye. Therfore seint poule saith Filii obedite parentibꝰ Be stris. &c. Ye children saith he obeye ye to your faders & moders for that is rightful thinge. Worshyp ye fader and moder for this is the first cōmaundment and be heste/ that ye may be wele in lyupynge longe vpon erthe And ye faders saith he prouoke ye natt. ne styre ye nat youre children to wrathe Vnskylfully/ but norysheth them in gode lore and Vndernampynge of oure lorde god. Ad ephe. vi. c. Criste goddes sonne god and lorde of al thing Bicame subgett to mary his moder (& to ioseph his keper/ peuyng vs al ensample to obeye and to be buxum & meke to fader & moder And salomon saith. Audi fili mi disciplinam patris tui. My dere sone here ye lore of thy fader/ & forsake nat the the lawe of thy moder/ & thāne thou shalt haue grace and worshyppe. Prouer. i. c. And as he saith in a nother place. He is a fole & scor=

neth his faders lore. And he that kepith his faders vndernampyng shalbe the more wise and the more slye. Prouer. xv. c. Also be muste worship fader and moder with gode lyuynge For as salomon saith. Dolor patris filius stultꝰ. The childe fole is sorowe and shame of his fader. Confusio patris de filio indisciplinato Of the sone euil taught cūmeth shame and shenship of the fader. and his doughter fole & euyl taughte shal lese his worship/ & the wyse doughter shalbe gode heritage to her husbōde to saue him. And the doughter that shendith her husbonde is in grete despyte and shame of her fader. that bigat her Eccle. xxii. c. The wise sone gladith his fader The sone b is a fole in lyupynge is his moders sorowe Prouer. x. c. Ira patris filius stultꝰ: et dolor mrīs q̄ genuit est. puer. xvii. c. The fole childe is wrathe & tene of his fader/ and sorowe of his moder. that bigatte him.

The v. chapter.

And therfore salomō saith. Virga et correptio tribuunt sapiam/ puer aūt qui dimittitur voluntati sue confūdit matrē suā. puer. xxix. c. That is to say The yerde vndernympyng yeuen wytte and wysdome to

Precepte.

the childe/ and that childe þ is setē haue his wylle iṅ his pouthe ſhendith his moder & al his kynrede. Example we haue iṅ the firſt boke of kinges. of Hely that was highest buſſhop and preeſt. of goddes salue/ and of his sonnes ophny and phynees. That for their fader Indirnam theym nat ne chaſtiſed hem of their wicked tacches/ for the children ſyn and for his myſ ſufferaūce. god toke from him his dignyte. & frō al his kynrede for euyr/ & ſlewe his children and nigh al his kynrede in Batayl. And ſo the wyched tacches of his childrē Unworſhippd him and alſe his kynrede for euir/ & brought them to endeleſſe ſhame And his myſ ſufferāce was cauſe of their deth and of his ſhenſhip and ſhame to al her kynrede. The synne of his children was pride letchery luſty fare and glutonye/ and ſleuth & recchleſneſſe iṅ goddes ſeruyce and iṅ goddes salue And therfore go de frendes & gode childrē I pray you alle that ye be buxū & meke to fader and moder/ & worſhipe them nat only with reuerence doyng iṅ dede and ſpeche/ But principaly with poure gode ſpuyng. & poure gode beryṅge. For that is the moſt worſhip that ye may do to them/ and the moſte beloṅ

nye if ye do amyſs And do ye ſo þ poure faders and moders & pour kynred may haue ioye of you/ & than ſhal ye haue ioye of poure children. For the wiſe man saith Qui honorat prēm ſuū iocūdabitur iṅ filiis ſuis Eccle. iii. c. Heb worſhipeth his fader ſhalle haue ioye of his children. And who ſo worſhipeth nat his fader & moder iṅ this maner/ but doth them wrath and tene by his miſſpuyn ge and euyl tacches/ he is a curſyd of god Maledictus qui nō honorat patrē ſuū et matrē ſuā. Deutro. xxvii. c. Acurſyd be that childe saith he that worſhipeth nat his fader and moder with his gode ſpuynge/ But Unworſhipeth them with his myſſpuynge. For al the myſcheups of the childe turne to biſonpe & ſhame of fader & moder. And al the godeneſſe and al the gode beryṅg of the childe/ turne to grete worſhip of fader and moder/ and of al the kynrede A grete worſhip. is to fader and moder whāne mē bleſſe them and pryſe theym for godeneſſe of their children & ſup. Bleſſyd be ye fader that the child begatt/ & bleſſyd be the moder þ him bare Therfore saith the wyſeman that god worſhyppeth the fader iṅ his children. Whanne he ſeeth theym gode children.

215

The fourthe

Eccle. iii. c. It is grete vilonye to fader and moder whanne men curse them and depraue theym for wyckednesse of their childre And therfore the wise man saithe. Non iocunderis in filiis impiis Haue thou no ioye ne lykyng in thy children if they be shrewys & drede nat god It is better sayth he to haue one gode childe, than a thousande children shrewys, & better to dye withoute, thane to leue after them shrewyd childre. Eccle. xvi. c. For as he sayth e. Sapie. iiii. c. Alle the children þ come of wycked folke shalle be wytnesses of wyckednesse ayenst their fader and moder/ whanne they shalbe chalengyde of theire wyckydnesse at the dome For the fader and the moder shal all sweren thane for their owne wyckednesse, and for their children wyckednesse But the wise man saith, if thou haue children tech theym wele, and bowe them and make them souple and meke in their poushe. If thou haue dou/ ghters kepe wele their bodies & honestly, But shewe them no gla de chere, Be nat to homely wisse them Eccle. vii. c. While a tree is a smalle spryng e it may be bo wyd as men wole haue it But whanne it is ful woxen, it wole nat be bowyd So may the child

in the pougshe w't a sytel twygge be chastised and made lowe and meke But whan he is woxen & royd in pride and mysuse of sp upnge, it is ful harde to lowe hit or to amende him. And therfore the wise man sayth. Qui parcit virge odit filiu: et qui diligit il lu instater erudit Prouer. viii. c. He that sparith the yerde hatith his sonne, and he that loueth his sonne techith him and chastiseth him bisily. Example we haue in kynde of the egle. Which of al foules may se ferthest, and is mi ghtiest in sight, in somoche that he may se & loke ayenst the sone Whanne it shyneth moste bright without blempisshyng of the iye. And whanne she hath briddes & they be ful woxen, she doth hem loke ayenst the sonne And tho loke wele ayenst the sonne With oute blempisshynge of iye, them she loueth and cherissheth. And them that wole nat ne may nat loke ayenst the sone, or blemiss their iye in lokynge ayenst the sone, she betith them and bytteth them. And but if they amende them, she castith them out of the neste, and putteth theim oute of her cumpany as for noon of her briddes. Thus shulde faders and moders teche their children, to haue their iye vp to god, that

Precepte.

to sonne of rightwisnesse: & take hede to goddes lawe by example of tobie: Whiche sayde to his sonne / Al the dayes of thy lyf haue thou god in mynde: & Be ware that thou assentte to no synne ne leue not goddys comaundement. Tobie. iiii. c. And therfor salomon sayth. Eccle. vi. That the wicked man that loketh not vp to the sunne of rightwisnesse is so blent with derkenesse of sinne / that he woot not what is gode: ne what is wicked / And therfore sayth he in the next chapter wisdom with richessis is more profitable than with oute richessys: & it profith moste to them that se the sunne. that is to say to them that haue iye to the sune of right wisnesse. that is god / For as salmon sayth. Oculi sapientis in capite eius. Eccle. ii°. The iyen of the wise man be alwey in hys hede. That is to say in crist that is hede of holy churche and of al thingis / And dauid sayth. Sic oculi seruorum in manibus dno tum suorum et sicut oculi ancille in manibus domine sue: ita oculi nostri ad dominum deū nostrum donec misereatur nostri. As the seruantys haue ther iyen to the handes of ther lorde: and as the mayde in chaumbre hath hyr iyen to the handys of hyr la-

dy: So muste we haue oure iyen vp to oure lorde god til he vs haue mercy on vs.

The eleuenth chapter

DIues. Reson peueth that men shuld teche ther children goddes lawe: & gode the wis / and for to take hede to god þ made vs al of nought / and bought vs so dere. But now men saye that there shulde no lewed folke entirmete them of goddes lawe: ne of the gospel: ne of holy writ: nether to kun it ne to teche it. Pauper. This is a foule errour and ful perilous to mannys soule / For euery man & woman is bounde aftir his degre to do his besines to knowe goddis lawe that he is bounde to kepe. And faders and modrs godfadrs and godmodres be bounde to teche ther children goddes lawe or elles do them be taught / And therfore god sayth. Erunt vba hec. &c. These wordes þ I bid ye thys daye shulde be in thy herte. Thou shalt tell them and teche them to thy children / Thou shalt thenk theron sittige i thy house amougys thy folke: And whan thou goest by the way. Whan thou goest to slepe. & whan thou a risest thou shalt bynde them as a

n i

The fourthe.

token in thy hande in thy dede: ⁊ thy werke they shulde be alwey styrring byfore the yzen of thyn herte / Thou shalt wryte theym in thy thresseolde and in thy dorys of thyn house that is to saye Whanne thou comest in: and wh̄anne thou goest oute. I thi begin nynge and ī the ending of euery dede alwey loke þ thou ne noon of thyne forfette a pens goddes lawe by cause of the. Deuto. vi. c. And in another place of the same boke he sayth thus / Thou shalt teche my wordis to thy children: to thy folke. and to thy kinnesmen. Deuto. iiii. c. And saint austen sayth that ech man in his owne honshold shuld do the office of the busshoppe in techynge: and correctinge of comon thyn/ges. And therfore sayth the lawe That the office of techinge and chastisinge longeth not only to the busshop: But to euery gouernoure after his maner / ⁊ his degree. To the pore man gouning hys pore housolde / To the riche man gouernig his folke / To ye husbondman gouernynge hys wyf. To the fader and mo der gouerninge ther children To the iustice gouernynge hys cuntre. To the kynge gouernynge hys people. piii. q. iiii. duo. q q. S. no putes. And oon neighbore shulde teche another / For saint Peter sayth. Euery ntan mineſtre on to other the grace that he hath taken of god .i. petri ii°. c. Diues. My fader and moder be dede: And therfore I lete me dischargid of this commaundement. Pauper. Thow they be dede: yet art thou bounde to doo them worship and to helpe ther soules with holy prayers and almesse dedys if thou mygh̄teste Also thou art bounde to worsship them with thy good lyuinge: as I sayde firste / For the wisman sayth That he that techeth well hys childe: he shal be praysed and worsshiped in hys childe amongis hys kynred he shal haue ioy and worsship in hys childe / The fader of the well taught childe in some maner is dede: ⁊ I some maner is not dede. For he lefte hys chylde lyke after hym / For all if the fader dye bodely: yet he lyue and is worsshipped in the goodnesse of his children / Est mortuus et quasi non ē mortuᵘ. Eccl. xxx. c. And in the wichyd lyuig of the childe: the fader is vnworsshiped and dede. Whyle he goth̄ vpon erth̄ / Also by thys cōmaū/dement we be bound to worship god fader and godmoder.

The xii. chapter.

Precepte.

Also to worſhip god: that is fader of al thynge that is cleped fader of mercyes: and god of al conforte. Pater miſƿ. et deus tocius conſolacionis. He is oure fader for he made us of nought. he bought us wyth his blod he findeth us al that us nedeth and moch more: he ſaueth us. he kepeth us. he ledeth us he fedeth us: he medeth us. He is our fader by grace / For by his grace he hath made us eyrys of heuen bliſſe. Was there neuer fader ſo tendre ouer his childe: as god is tendre ouer us / He is to us bothe fader and moder / And therfore we be bounde to loue hym. and to worſhip him aboue al thīge. as I ſayde in the firſte commaundement: But he maye ſay to us as that he ſayde to the unkynde Iewis / Filius honorat patrem: et ſeruus dominum ſuum timebit. etc. The ſonne ſayth he by wey of kynde worſhipith his fader / and the ſeruant ſhal drede his lorde. Syth thanne I am fader of al. Where is my worſhip And ſyth I am lorde of al Where is my drede: Neyther ye worſhyp me as a fader: ne drede me as a lorde Malach. i. c. Nunqd non eſt pater un⁹ omniū Beſtrū Nunquid non deus unius creauit uos: Haue ye not ſayth he al oon fader. & oon god made you all / Why thanne ſayth he deſpiſe ye ech man other. That is hys brother by pryde and ouerledige and brekynge the cōmaūdemēt of poure formfadris: Malach. ii. c. Alſo for tendre loue the hath to mākynd: he cleptȝ hymſylfe oure moder ſuyng to ſinful ſoule: Weneſt thou ſayth he: that ye moder may foryete hir yong childe that ſhe bare of hir body: and haue no reuthe ne pyte theron: And thou ſhe foryete hir childe & haue no pyte theron: yet I ſhal not foryete the to ſſhe we the mercy. pſa. plix°. c. And therfore he ſayth. Ego mater pulcre dileccionis &c. I am moder of fayre loue. of loue drede. of knowynge of holy hope. In me is al maner grace of truthe & of lyf / In me is al hope of lyfe of uertu of mercy al of al maner goodneſſe Eccle. xxiiii. c. And thus by this precepte we be bounde to loue our god and worſhip him aboue al thynge as oure principal fader & moder / And that principaly for the mercy and pety that he ſheweth to mankinde i his gouernaunce & keping By the firſt cōmaūdement we be boande to worſhyp him aboue al thing for he is endles might as god & beginner and ſhaper of alle thynge.

n ii

The xlii. chapter

Also we be bounde by this cōmaudemēt to worshyp oure gostly fader that hath cure of oure soule: as pope .and oure busshop oure prelate. oure pson. oure vecary. oure curate. our cōfessoure. And oure moder that bo muste worshipe is holy churche. Of this maner fader and moder sayth salomon / Audi fili mi disciplinam patris tui: et ne dimittas legē matris tue. Mi dere son sayth he here the lore of thy gostly fader: and forsake not the law of thy moder holy church. pū.i.c. Of these maner faders speketh also holy wryt / Lorde saythe he here byfore thou madest chosyn faders. and madest them ful holy. ii°. macha..i.c. Prelates of holy churche be cleped faders / For ther offyce is to gendre folke in right byleue: and to norishe thē in good thewys: and vertuous liuynge. And therfore saint poule sayth / Per euangeliū ego vos genui. By this gospel I begate you in crist / Such faders be worthy double worship: as saith poule saythe / For they be worthy to be reuerenced of ther subgettis: ⁊ to haue ther liuynge / Therfore they owe to haue tithes and offeringys of ther chyldren: that be

The fourthe.

ũnder cure / For as saint poule sayth in the same place / The werkeman that wel traueileth is worthy hys mede. i. tymo.v.c. But now god may say. Regnauerunt sz nōn ex me. Prelatys haue reygned in holy churche: not of me ne by my plesaunce I made them not I chase thē not And therfore saint poule saythe that thow men haue ten thoused maisters yet they haue but selde faders. For prelatis for the most part seke not ther own pfyt thā profyt of mannys soule. Omnes que sua sunt querūt nō que Jesu cristi / Such prelates and curatis be not faders of the peple: but wolues of raupn that deuoure goddes peple. Sicut escā panis Of such prelatis ⁊ curatis speketh ysaie the prophete. Ipi pastores ignorauerūt itelligēciam. ⁊c. Such shepeherdis prelates and curates knowe not goddis lawe ne the ũnderstondyng of goddes lawe / Al they bowed awey from goddes wey ito ther own wey of false consience from the higheste to the lowest. ysaie. lvi.r. And for that sayde he. that the shepeherdis prelates and curates of holy churche dede soo folyly: ⁊ wyll not seke by oure lord god to plese hym and to serue hym / Therfore they haue lost ũnderstōdig

Precepte.

and wit to teche the people/ And so al ther flocke is disperplid by eresie debate diuisyon & discencion Jeremie.x.c. Who sayth god by toke the shepherdes & prelates þ thus disparplen and alforrende þe flocke of my pasture or ceselwe þt is cristen people.Ieremie.xxiii.c. And therfore saint gregori in his omelie.omē.xVii. De signauit dominus. Maketh his mone & sayth thus Praye ye to god that he wyl send trewe werkemen into his corn. That is to say amōgis his people/ For ther is moch corn and moch people to be taught/ But selwe werkemen of prechours to teche them and to tyll mannys soule. For thowe there be folke to hyre/ There be selwe to sepe or to teche/ We se wel sayth he that the world is ful of prestes/ But ful lytel ony of theym worchethe in goddes corn/ For we take sayth he the offyce of presthode: but we fulfyl not to do the werke of the offyce.

The xliii. chapter.

Also by this precept we be bounde to worshyp oure elder.that be oure faders in age And therfore god sayth. Coram cano capite consurge.&c. Ryse vp sayth he byfore the whyt hered man: and worship you the p sone of old man or woman: and drede thy lorde god/ That is to say For drede of god worshyppe thou thyn elders: and despyse thē not for no age for no febilnesse .leuitici.xix.c. And therfore saint poule bad the Busshop tymothie that he shulde not vndernyme hys eldre ne olde folke to sharpely ne to proudly: But prai them as faders to amende them. yonge men as bretheren. olde women as moders. yonge wemen as systers in al maner chastytye t.adtimo.iiii.c. Diues. Oft tyme olde folke be more shrewd ys than other and be ful harde to amende thei be so roted i sine And therfore as me thinketh them nedeth to be harde vndernoman & sharply/ For god saithe.þ þe chil de of an hundered yere shall dye and the synner of an hundred ye re shal be cursed.psa.xlB. Pauper. Some olde folke be vertuouse and not customable to sine Suche owe to be worshipped: & if thei do some tyme amisse: for that þ they be not customable to synne/ therfore ther prelatio shulde the more spare them and mor worshipfully speke to them Som olde folke be customable to sine and wyl not amende them: and such be worthy no worshyp: as god sheweth wel by the wordys of ysaie. And therfore saint
n iii

The fourthe.

gregori sayth that the olde man sose shuld be harde vnder nomā

The ix. chapter.

Diues. Thy answer is skilful: say forth I praye the Pauper. Also by thys precepte we be bounde to worshyppe oure kynge. oure sege. oure souereins alle / For al tho that haue gouernaunce of vs or of the comontie o we by ther office and ther dignite : to be faders of the comontie & of ther sugettys / And be besy to saue ther sugetty s : as the fader hys chyldren / And therfore naaman prynce of syrye was cleped fader of hys seruantys. iiii. k̄. v. c. And iob sayde. Pater erā pauperum. I was fader of the pore and ye cause that I knew not I traced it and sought it vp be sylylob. xxix. c.. And therfore saynt poule byddeth the pepłe do worshyp and obey to ther souereyns. And he sayth thus. Serui obedite dn̄is vestris carnalibz. ye seruantes obey ye to your flesshy lordes with drede and trimelyng in simplenesse of poure herte : as to crist / Serue ye thē not only at ye ive to plese them: But as crystys seruantis : do ye the wyll of god of hert wyth gode wil seruynge them of oure lorde god. Not as men. That is to saye : serue ye them truly for ye drede of god and for the loue of god And then ke ye that the scrupte that ye do to them : ye do it to god. And he principaly shall yeld you poure mede / For wete ye well sayth he that euery goode dede that man or woman doth : be he free be he bond : he shal take his mede therfore of oure lorde god / And ye lordes & souereins sayth he do ye the same to poure seruantis : and foryeue them your thretnynges and thenke ye and wete ye it wel ꝑ god i heuin is god both of you and of poure seruantys. and soo ye and they haue bothe oon lord oon god that accept no man for hys persone. But yelde eche man and woman after he deseruth. Ad eph. vi°. c. Diues. By these wordes it semeth that seruantys for her true seruice : shal haue mo ch mede. Pauper. That is soth For he that doth goddes byddig god shal yeld him hys mede / And it is goddes biddynge and goddes wyl : that they serue truly & solwly ther souereyns / And therfore sayth the glose: That sythe crist biddethe the seruantes serue truly : if they serue truly : they serue not only ma ne woma but principaly they serue criste / Diues. Why byddeth the apostle that the seruantes shuld obeye and serue to flesshy and carnal lordes Pauper. For the glose sayth: Them most by goddes lawe obeye not

222

Precepte.

only to good lordes: but also to shrewys. Therfore saynt Peter sayth Subiecti estote oĩm hunane creature ꝑpter dm̄ ꝛc. Be ye sugettis sayth he to euery man & woman that is poure souereyn not for them sylfe: but for god. Be ye sugettis to kynges to dukes & to temporal lordes & them ye that odg hathe ordeyned them to veniaunce of wicked doers & to preysinge of good folke. For thus is the wyl of god that with youre good dedys and poure mene seruice ye stoppe & make styll the vnkunnynge of the vnwise folke. Serue ye as fre men: that is to saye: not only for drede of man: but for drede and loue of god as goddes seruantes. Drede ye god. and worshyp ye youre kynge. And ye seruantes be ye sugettis and meke in al drede to poure lordes that is to saye not only in scruple drede. But also in loue drede for goddes sake. Be ye sugettis for goddes sake: not only to gode lordis and weltreued: but also to shrewys and tyrauntis. Non tantū bonis & modestis sƺ etiã discolis. For than ne is man and woman worthy thanke of god. whanne for consciens and goddes sake he suffereth paciently disese wythe oute sylt. If ye be beten and boteted for youre synne and poure trespase: ye be worthy no thank neyther of god ne of man. But if ye do wel. and with that suffre paciently disese vngyltly than be ye worthy moche mede of god And for to do thꝰ criste paue you ensaumple. whanne he suffred paciently bitter deth wythout gilt that ye shulde folowe hys steppes and paciently suffre woo wi th oute gylt. These be the wordes of saint peter in hys first pistle. ii°. c. Here to accordeth the saynt poule in his pystle. Ad rosinos. viii°. c. where he sayth thus Euery soule. that is to say. euery man and woman moste be suget and meke to the power aboue theym and to hys souereyns. For there is no power ne lordshyppe but of god and of goddes ordinaunce: And therfore sayth he .whoo so wythstondeth the lorshyp and the power of his souereyn: he wythstondeth goddes ordinaūce and getthe him dampnacion wytheoute end. For why sayth he prin ces & lordes be ordeyned of god to drede of wycked werke: not to drede of gode werke. wolt th ou not drede the power of thy so uereyn? Do wel and thou shalt haue preysing of him. For if he be a gode lorde: he shall loue the the better. And if he be a shrewe thou shalt haue the more preisig of god & thou doest wel vnder a

n iiii

The fourthe.

Wyched souereyn as saythe the glose/Thy kyng thy lord is goddes ministre ordeyned of god to thy good If thou do amys drede thou For he beryth not the swerd without cause For he is goddes mynistre: to venge the wrath of god in hym that doth amys And therfore sayth he. Be ye sugettys and meke to your souereyns as to the nedful ordinaunce of god not only for to fle wrath of your souereyns: but also for conscies And therfore ye yeue tributes to poure princes and lordes: for they be goddes mynestres and serue therfore in defendyng and gouernaunce of the people/And as the glose sayth. in that ye yeuen them tribute ye serue god: for they be goddes mynistres.

The xxi. chapter

Iues. Whanne saint poule sayde tho wordes: emp oures kynges and nyghe al prynces and temporal lordes vp on erth were hethen and of false byleue: hou myght they be goddes mynystres or goddes seruantys?
Paul. Euery creature is suget and seruant to god: or wyth hys wylle: or wythe oute hys wyl. And therfore saynt austen vp$ psalme. Exoudi deus oracionem meam. sayth thus Wene ye not god suffereth wicked for he to be in thys worlde with oute cause? For euery wicked man sayth he eyther god suffereth hym to lyue for to amende him. or elles that good men maye be amended by hym. and wynne mede by him in that that they suffre hys malyce pacyently: and trauayle for to amende him/The malyce of shrewys is purgatorie to gode folke and shrewys be goddes scourge: to chastyse goddes children which he had ordeyned to the kyngdome of heuen. and to punysshe and purge the synnes of theim god loueth. and also to punyssh other shrewys/And therfore god sayde to the synful iewys For ye wil not here my wordes ne kepe my lawys: Therfore I shal send aft my seruant nabugodonosor kynge of babylonye: and bryng him $ al his peple vpon this lon de: and distroy this londe bi cau se of synne. Jerele. xxv.c. Thys nabugodonosor kynge of babylonye was an hethen man a sy shrewe and had noo loue to god ne knewe hym for hys god/He was a wicked tyraunt $ destroied goddes lawe and goddes peple and goddes temple in ierslm. And yet god clepeth hym his ser uant/For he was goddes yerde

Precepte.

to chastise shrewys and to punisshe the synnes of goddes people And as ye se that whanne the fader hath beten his childe with a perde he castith the perde into ye fire: right so whan god hath chastysed and scourged his chyldren by wycked men and by wycked tyrauntes that be goddes perde. but if the tirauntes amend them he shal cast them into the fyre of helle with outz end / And therfor he sayth. De assur virga furoris mei et Baculus ipse &c. Woo be to the people of assur and to hys kynge: for they be the perde and the staf of my wrath:

I shalle sende theym a yens the false peple And ayenste the peple to wich I am wroth I shal byd him distroy the peple: robbe thē. & sle them / But he weneth not so But he witethe it al to hys owne myght. & he doth of malyce & I bid hi do my rightfulnes ysa.x.c

The xviii. chapter.

Diues. Syth it is so that al lordship and power & etc cometh of god: me merueleth moche why god yeueth wycked men such power in thys worlde? Pauper. The power cometh of god: But the malyce & wickednesse & wycked couetise cometh of man. Diues. God knowith ther maleice and what they wyll

do. Why yeueth he than such lordship and power to shrewis Pauper. For comon synne of the peple / For synful people rebel and false is worthy to haue no good lord merciable ne benygne But for to haue cruel lordes false tyrauntes lyke the peple / And therfore Iob sayth. Regnare facit ypocritam ppter pctā ppli. God maketh an ypocrite a ruched lyuer to regne for synne of people. Iob. xxxiiii°.c. And therfore sayth the holy wryt that god yaue hys people a kynge in hys wrat such as shulde disese them. Ose. viii. Dabo eis regem in furore meo. Diues. The phylosofre sayth the iiii°: ethi. that the wicked man is worthy no worship: and only ye goode man is worthy worshyp / For as he sayth there / worship is mede of vertue / And so he that is not vertuous and vicious as sy rautys be: is worthy no worship Pauper þ is soth Diues. Why byddeth than god & peter & poul as thou hast sayd þ mē shuld do worship & obey not only to ye goode lordes But also to the wycked Paup. As I sayd the first We shulde obey & do worshyp to them not for themsilfe But for god and for power þ god hath youen theym And for that they represent god des psone in erthe we shulde worshype theym not ther owne per sonnes But for the dignitie y god hath youen them and made thiʒ oure souereins And they be gode and vertuous we shuld do them worship and obeye to them not only for her dignite: But for ther vertu and oure owne pfyt / And therfore saint poule sayth. Obedite prepositis vris. &c. ad hebr. ʒiii. c. Obey ye to youre prelatis and souereyns and be ye meke & suget to them: For why sayth he they be ful besy and traueil to saue youre soulis. as thei that shulde yeue ansvvere for your soulys at the dome. Diues. Many of them care ful lytel for mannys soule / They care more to get money and mannys good / And many of them be ful febyl lyuers. Pauper. Whanne they be suche take no ensaumple of ther wycked lyuyng. do not as they doo. But as thei sey whanne they teech wel. and reuerence theim for ther dignite and for ther ordre. for so bedeth criste in the gospel. Diues. I suppose that thei neyther do wel ne teche wel: for many of them be ful lewed / Pauper. yet as longe as they be thy souereyns or thy curates thou shalt obey to them in al thing resonable and leful that longeth to her office. and do them worshyp for ther dignite. not for ther persone

But for god. Whos persone they present in messis singing in shreftis hering and in other sacramentis yeuyng and in gouernynge.

The ɣviii. chapter.

Diues. I suppose that my lege lorde the king bydde me do a thynge. and my mayster or my souereyn bydde me do the contrary or if my curate byd me do athing, cōtrary to my bisshopis bydding to whom shal I obey Pauper. In that cas tou shalt obey to thy kyng that is thy souereyn. and thy maystyrs souereyn also. and thou shalt obey to thy busshop that is thy curatys prelate and thyn also. if the kynges bidding and the busshoppys be not ayens goddes worshyppe And if thy kyng thy pope: or thy busshope: or any other souereyn byd the do any thynge that thou knowist wel that it is ayēs god des worshyp and ayens hys law thou shalt not obey to thē i but to god y is ther souereyn: a thin also. And therfore sayth saint peter to the ie wis Obedire oportet mage deo qm hoīb3 It bihoueth to obey to god more thā to men: If it be rightful to het you rather thā: god: deme ye. and ye lawe saythe that if oni souereyn bid his suget ony thing that is contrary to god: the suget shal not obeye ne do ony thing vnrightful and vnonest: ne that shuld harme ye comontye for hys biddinde if he knowe wel that the biddinge be not leful.i.q̄.iii.nō semp. ⁂Diues. I suppose that the sugette be in dout whether it be goddes lawe or nay. Paup. Than shal he obey to hys souereyn: and he is excused, but if it be in such thinge þ he is bounde to knowe a to hun. As if he byd him ony thing þ is openly ayens goddes cōmaunde-ment or ayens the seyth or ayens goddes lawe or lawe of holy church, that he is bound to knowe thanne shal not he obeye in ony wyse to hys bdidige. ⁂Diues. Is the suget boūde to obey to his souereyn in al thing leful. Paup. Seruage and subiection came amongys mankynge for pryde and other synne. But as sayth a greate clerke. seneca .li°.iii°. de Beneficiis. This seruage wentt not into al men ne in al wemen: but the better parti of man and woman that is the soule is oute takyn from such seruage a only mānis body and womās is bou-de to seruage of tēnporall lordes and of ther souereyn. a man nys soule and womans is fre so

that he maye haue hys thought hys loue.his wyl inward as him selue. with oute leue of his souereyn, And therby he offedeth not hys souereyn ne pleseth · but only god þ knoweth suerly mannys herte, but only in the dedis of ye body the suget is bounde to obei hys souereyn. ⁂Diues. In which dedys? Paup. In suche as lon ge to rewle and gouernaūce and in such thinges as he hath made hym suget into hys souereyn: in such the suget owthe to obeye to hys souereyn, as knyght in ar-mes is bound to obeye hys cheftetyn a hys leder in thynges that longe to armes. The bond man to hys lorde I doing seruyle wor-kes in dutie of his bondage: the sonne to his fader: in thing that longeth to good norture a rewle of his housholde: the wif to hir hus-bōd: I thing þ loge to matrimony a social liuing, not in werkes of vilepy seruage. And if the wif o-bey more than she is bounde to. and do more dedis of lownesse I plesaunce of hir hussonde than she is bounde to: she is more to prayse. and the more he owth to loue hir a haue hir in worship as his ownefleshe, and if she do it for goddes sake: god shal be hir mede tholwe hir husbound be ful vnkinde. But in thinges that

𝕮𝖍𝖊 fourthe

longe to the kyng of mannis body: man ne woman is not suget to hys lorde ne to hys souereyn temporal. But only to god/For al men in thinges that longe to kynde of body be euen: as substaunce of the body: in bringing forth of children/And therfore the seruaunt may wedde withoute leue of his lorde. and the sonne withoute leue of his fader/ And the seruant may kepe hym chast withoute leue of his lorde and a pens hys byddynge. and the son a pens the byddyng of hys fader and wedde a pens his byddynge and if him like. Netheles it is gode that yonge folke in such thinges folow the counseile of fader and moder and of ther frendes: But if ther counseile be to let them from god/For this shal also husbond and wif as a pens syn gof ther body be euen and eche of them hath power ouer others body.

The pix. chapter.

Diues. Is the people bounde to obey to the Pope to ther busshop to ther curate in all thingis what they wyl byd them do? Pauper. In al thinge that longeth to keping of feyth and of goddes lawe: and fleing from sicns to which thingis they both be them in ther baptem: they be bound to obey/ And in al thingis of the which the gouernance longeth to men of holy church by comon lawe grounded in goddes lawe to gouern the people not in other thinges that long not too men of holy churche: ne in ther preceptis not grounded in goddes lawe/ And i the same maner clerkes be bound to obey to ther prelates in thinyes that long to ther offyce grounded in goddes lawe & religious to ther prelates i thinges that long to keppng of religion/ Diues. I suppose lordship or prelaci be occupped Unrightfully by might and falsnesse. By symonye gyle and tresse ther sugettis bounde for to obey to them? Paup. If they obey to them in thingis lefulitis medeful/ Netheles some clerkis sai that such cas men be not bound to obey: But for to fle slauder and the more defese. Petrus in scrip. sup ii. sent. d. Bt.a smi. confes.li° iii.ti°. pppliii.q.B. But for as moche as god geueth oft tymes the realmes and the lordshipis of this worlde: and prelacye also not by mannys lawe ne mannys dome. But by his owne presup dome and he is soueray might lorde of lordes & kig of kigges therfor it is most sure to obei

228

Precepte.

to such lordes and souereyns as longe as god suffrith them. For god peueth lordshipp and prelacie in thys worlde: bothe to good & wycked. And therfore as we fynde in danielys prophicie: god made nabugodonosor the wycked tyraunt kynge and lorde of the greate part of thys worlde. And after for hys pryde he toke hys kyngdome fro him: and made hi in wyt lyke a beste. that he wend to haue be a beste halfe vpon halfe oye. and so he went on all foure and fedde him amongis bestes i the forest seuen monethis tyl he knew þ god was prycypal lorde of euery kigdome & þ he peueth kigdom lordshyp to whom þ he wyl danielys. iiii°. c. And therfor god sayde to sedechye that was kyng of goddes peple: and to other kynges in the cuntre besyde I made erth man and beste vpon erth in my greate might: and I haue youen the lordshyp to hī that me lyketh. And I haue youen al these londes & kingdoms here a boute to nabugodonosor my seruant kyng of babylony: & al nacyons chulen serue hī & his sone & his sones sone. & what nacion or kingdome wil not serue him ne obey him: I shal distroy þ nacion by swerd hūgre & moreyn & whoso wyl serue hī & obey to hī

I shal late him dwel styll in hys owne londe. And therfore serue ye him mekely & obey ye to hym & ye shal liue & fare wel. ieremie. xxvii. c. And crist in the gospel sayde. Reddite que sunt cesaris cesari: et que sunt dei deo. yelde ye to the empour of Rome: that is the emperours and yelde ye to god that is goddes. And yet the empoure of rome had no right to ye lordshyp that he occupied: but onli bi the peft of god & by swerd.

Diues. I suppose that the busshop byd a prest curs a man which man the prest holdeth vngilti and the multitude of the people also. Pauper. Eyther the busshop biddeth the brest denounce him a cursed. or he bideth him a curse hym. If he byd the preste denounce him acursed in the busshoppis name. if he may not wel put it of. But he shal by wey of charite excuse that man & as moch as he knowth him vngilty. And also excuse the busshop: saying that he is mys enformed: & if he had konwe the trewth: he wol be not haue cursed him. And he shal counsel that man to suffre it so wly for helpe of his soule. And he shal enfourme the busshop as sone as he may of that mannys vngyltynes. But if the busshop byd the preste acurse hī the prest

moste take hede whether his vngilty pede is opēly knowen or is ī
doute: or it is certeyn but not o-
penly knowen / If his vngylty
ede be openly knowen: the prest
shal alegge to ye busshop that he
is vngilty and proue it by wytnesse And if he faile ī his profe he
shal obey to the busshoppis byddynge thow he knowe that the
man is vngilty / And if he maye
preue hym vngilty: he shall not
curse him. thow the busshop byd
him neuer so ferlly If it be ī dout
whether he is gilty or nay: Than
the prest shal obey to the busshop
pys byddynge.   Sm̄.gf.li.ti.
xxiii. q̄.Bi.Quid si episcopus.

The xx. chapter.

Diues. Whan the officerys
of the kynge knowe well
that a man or woman is dampned to the dethe vngylsly: shall
they obey to the iuge that bydde
them sle man or woman withou
te gylt? Pauper. If the officer
be seker þ he is vngilty: he shall
not sle him: But he shal obeye to
god that biddeth him sle no man
ne woman vngilty/ But if he be
ī doute whether he is gilty or vn
gilty: thanne he shal obey to the
iuge q̄ do his biddind / And he is
excused by his obediens. Kap.lī.

ti.ix.de iuramento q̄ periurio.C.
viiii.quid de iudice. Netheles ye
sugettis moste beware in suche
doutis. þ they p̄sume not to mo-
reȝ of ther owne wyt/ For fuloft
a man Weneth to knoW a thing
q̄ be in certeyn of his knowinge
and yet he is deseyued:q̄ it is not
as he weneth/ And it is fulpere-
lous to the suget to repugne the
dome of his souereyn: q̄ to reshue
ye wit q̄ the setēce of many wyse
men / And therfore I counsele
the sugettis q̄ the offpiceris ī such
thinges to stond to ye consiens q̄
the ordinance of ther souereyns
q̄ obey with he soroWe of herte ha
uing pety of mānis deth q̄ of his
disese q̄ no lyking in cruelte And
therfore god bad in holy writ: þ
men shuld folow the sentence of
ther iugis q̄ do ther bydding And
Who so Wolde not obey them. he
shuld be slayn. deut°. xBi°. c.
The kynges iustice represent the
the kynges persone in ful hygge
degree / And therfore men moste
be more adred to withstond hys
sentence and hys dome / For his
dome is cleped goddes dome: q̄
as salomon sayth / Sicut diuisi-
ones aquaꝝ ita cor eius in ma-
nu dn̄i. q̄c. As the watris saith he
may lightly be depted q̄ draWen
in diuerse perties: so is the herte
of the king q̄ of iuges: q̄ rewlers

in the bonde of oure lorde / be sh
aseclyne it whederhe wyl / For
the dome that semethe vnryght/
ful to mannys wyt: is rightfull
in goddes sight / And thowe the
dome be rightful in goddis sight
and thowe the man be worthi to
dye. if ye iuge wene that it be vn
rightful (a he peueth the sentence
wenyng se herly / that it be vn=
rightful: he senneth dedly. thow
his sentence be rightful / For as
saint poule sayth All that is not
done of feyth and of good consi
ence it is synne / If the man be
gilty: the law and his mysdedis
slee hym / If he be vngyltly slay
ne by fals dome of the iuge or by
a false queste or by them þ myse
enformed the queste they slee him
& not the officerys. But if he do it
wetyngly ayens the worship of
god: whanne the falshede of the
dome is openly knowen. or if he
do it withe lyeng in crueltye.
Diues. Is the religious man or
woman bounde to obey hys pre
late: whanne he byddeth hym to
ony thing ayens his rewle. Pau
per. In al thynge that longeth
to very obseruance of hys rewle
or is nedeful to good & trewe ke
pynge of the rewle: he is bound
to obeye. But he haue resonable
excusacion / In other thynges
that be ypertinent to the rewle &

to hys profession. or contrarie to
the rewle: he is not bound to o=
bey / For if he were bounde to al
such byndyngis: his veer of no=
uycete shulde serue of nought.
For hys prelate might so agreg/
ge the hardnes of lyuynge in reli
gion in doubble more than he ma
de hys profession to. and bynde
hym to more penaunce without
comparison than euer he thou=
ght to bynde hym to: and vnty
l another maner lyuyng. that he
made neuer hys profession to: ne
knowe in the yere of hys assaye &
hys nouycery / And by the lawe
euery vowe is sette in some cer=
teyn / But if the religious were
bounde to obey in al thynge: his
profession were al vncertein and
vnassayed in his nouycery / Ne
theles it is a greate perfection to
obey in alle thyngys lesful after þ
man or woman may do sauyng
hys rewle and goddes worshyp
And if hys prelate byd hym doo
ony thynge ayens hys rewle: he
most take hede whether hys pre/
late may dispens with þ point of
rewle or nay / If he knowe well
he may dispes with þ: he owth to
obey his biddig. But if he know
wel þ he may not dispens with þ
poynt of the rewle: he shal not obei
to him l that: & he shal also obey
if he be in doute whether he may

¶ The fourthe

dispense or not ¶ Diues. Tel me some exaumple ¶ Paup. In fastynge in walkynge: in silence kepinge/ & in diuerse obseruāce of religion: the prelate may dispense as I cas he owth to dispens apens his sugettis wyl: whan he seeth that his sugett may not kepe suche poyntis of his rewle without te vndoinge of him silfe or without bindering of other thingis that be more to goddes worship And oft tymes the sugettis wyl do more than they may do: and put them to more than they mai perfourme/ And than ther prelate as a good fader owlthe to take hede therto: and for saluacōn of hys suget dispēce with hym & put hil discrete goūnāce for saluacion of the persone. and for ye worship of god/ And the sugette owth to obey his biddyng & stōd to hys ordinaunce: With good conciens/ In some thynges the prelate may not dispence: as in the principal poītis of euery religion. that is to syue in obeidence: in pouerte and & chastite/ And many other thingis ben exempt by lawis of religion in which re prelate may not dispence/ And therfore if the prelate byd the sugetdo ony thȳge that is apens ye thre principal poīntis of his rewle or apens such thingis I which

he may not dispence: hys suget owth not to obey hys biddynge

¶ The xxi. chapter.

Diues. If the Busshop byd a clerke yeue hys boke to his nece or neuewe or resigne his church/ & his benefice that ye busshope may yeue it to hys nece or neuewe: or to some of his kyn: is that clerke bound to obey ye byddynge of the Busshop: ¶ Pauper. Nay forsoth/ For it longeth not to the Busshop to bidde such thinges / Netheles if the clerke haue gode bokes and is vnable to profite in boke / and the Busshop bid de him lene the boke to a nother clerke that is able to profyte in boke and to helpe holy churche: he is bound to obeye / If he gate tho bokes of holy churche godis or by cause of holy churche: as if it were poupy or biquethid til to profit of holy churche: But if ye bokes be puerly his owne: he is not bound to obey that biddyng ¶ Diues. What if the hussbond bid hys wyfe breke a vowe that she hath made to god: as of fastyng of pilgrimage. continence. woshward goyng and such other: Is she bound to obey his byddynge ¶ Paup. ye forsothe/ And but she obey the hys bidynge in that cas

Precepte.

ſhe ſpynneth/And if ſhe do his bid
dyng only for obedience: ſhe wꝑ
neth moche mede. for in that ſhe
obeyth to god Which biddeth hyr
obey to hyr huſbond/And ſo in þ
ſhe doth the wil of god: thowe þ
ſhe be ſory that ſhe may not per
fourme hyr vowe ꝓpiii.q.v.no
ſuit More ouer leue frēd ye ſhal
vnderſtonde that as ſayth ſaynt
Bernard l'epła ade moch. Sume
thinges be puerly good of the ſil
fe: and to ſuche we be bound by
goddes lawe. as ten cōmaūdmē
tys/Sume be ful wicked of the
ſiſf/and tho we be bounde to ſle
by goddes lawe wythouten any
byddyng of any ſouereyn vnder
god/And therfore in ſuch thyn
ges ſtondeth not properly the v
tue ne mede of obedience to man
or woman/Other thinges there
be that maye be goode and they
may be wicked. and wel do and
euyl do. and ī ſuch thinges ſton
deth ꝓperly obedience: þ men
owe to ther ſouereyns: For in ſu
ch we ſhulde ſtonde to ther wyll
and to ther wyt more than to ou
re owne/For in ſuch ſtondeth ꝓ
perly the vertue of obedience: þ
we owe to man for goddes ſake
And the harder that the precepte
be: if it ſtond with reſon: the mo
re medeful is the obedience / For
the more þ man or woman forſa
keth his owne wyl for goddes ſa

ke the more is his lowneſſe. and
the more is his mede.

The .xvii. chapter.

Also leue frend by thys cō
maundement we be bound
to worſhip alle that be in hygher
ſtate ⁊ dignite than we be / For
al ſuch be cleped our fadirs ī wor
ſhip Patres honore/And therfor
ī holy wryt al men of worſhip be
cleped ſenes et ſeniores. that is
ſenyours in frenche/And in fren
che tung meye of worſhyppe and
lordes be cleped ſenyours. ⁊ pe
ris that is faders ī engliſhe/For
they be faders in worſhyp ⁊ ow
en to be worſhypped as faders by
thys cōmaundement For comō
ly in men of worſhyppee is and
owth to be ſadneſſe of wytt and
wyſdome as in men of age/For
in them is the age of ryth. Wiſ
dome: Thow they haue no gre
ate age of perys/ And therfor
ſayth ſalomon. Senectus Vene
rabilis eſt non diuturna neq̄ an
norum numero cōputata. The
age of worſhip ſtondith not l̄ lon
ge lyuyng ne in noumbre of pe
rys: But it ſtondeth in wytte and
wyſdome/For the wittys of the
wyſman ben old and ſadde: and
a clene life is cleped age of elde.
Sapie.iiiiº. c. And therfore god
byddeth in old lawe. Honora ꝑ
ſonam ſenis et time dominum
of

The fyfte

deum tuum). Leuitici .xix. Wor/
shyp thou the persone of an olde
man & drede thy lorde god/ And
in the newe lawe he sayth thus.
Deum timete regem honorifica
te/ Drede ye god and Worshyp ye
poure kynge .i. petri iio.c. That
is to saye for drede of god Wor/
shyp thou thyn elder and for dre/
de of god Worshyp thou thy kyng
and thy soureyn and all that be
in hygher degre than thou art.
For syth god hath put them I de/
gre of Worshyp: thou moste for
drede of god Worshyp them/ And
But thou Worshyp them: elles th/
ou offendeste god/ And therfore
saint peter sayth/ Omnes hono/
rate. Worshyp ye al men and Wo/
men after ther state and ther dig/
nite And saint poul biddeth that
al thinge shulde be do onestly & l
ordre. Omia honeste et secdm or/
dinem fiant .i. ad cor. xiiii.

The xxiii. chapter

Also leue frende by this co
maundement we be bond
to Worshyp holy aungels & sain=
tes in heuen: for they be oure fa/
ders in age in Worshyp in cure & l
heppynge of Us/ For they songen
after Us that ther noumbre and
ther cumpany that was lessed by
the pryde of lucifer myght be re=
stored ayen by saluacion of Us.
And therfore nyght and day thei
prayen for Us to god for helpe &

grace nedful to Us. Of these fa=
ders speketh saint poule in hys
pistle: and sayth thus I knele &
praye for you nyght and day ye
fader of oure lorde Jesu criste of
Whom is named al maner of fa=
derhede in heuen and in erth Ex
quo omis paternitas nominat
celo et in terra. ad eph. iiio.c. For
as the glose sayth ther disposici=
on the aungels be oure faders in
heuen ordeyned for Us and in er
the platis be oure faders hauing
cure & heppynge of Us/ And so bo
th prelatis in erthe and aungels
in heuen ben oure faders/ And
therfore as saye al these clerkes
Ech man and Woman hath two
aungels assignyd to hym of god
oon another of the fende/ For ye
fende sathanas at goddes suffe=
raunce assigneth to him a wicked
aungel to tempte him and to le=
se him/ But god of his goodnes
assigneth him a good aungel to
saue hym and to kepe hym/ Of
which good aungel criste sayth
in the gospel. that they se alwey
the face of the fader in heuen: for
they be alwey in his presence &
speke for Us and praye for Us.
And therfore sayth saynt ierom
Up on the same worde of criste y
aungels bere oure prayer & oure
good dedis into heuen and kepe
and defend Us ayens the malice
and the sleyght of the fende And

therfore the aungel raphael whāne he had led the sone of tobie in
to ser cuntre and sauid him from
many perelys and brought hym
ayen in greate welth: he sayde to
thobie /whanne thou prey'dyste
with bytter teeris and beryedeste
the dede bodeis & lestest thi mete
& haddeste dede bodyes by daye
in thyn house and beryeiste them
by nyght for goddes sake ayens
the wyl of the wicked king sena-
cherib: Thanne offered I thy pier to oure lorde god. tobie. iiii°. c.
Also we rede i the fourth boke of
kynges the vi. chapter. That ye
propheete helesye was sodenly
by nyght byseged in the cetye of
dothaym with the ost of the kynge of sirie. In the morowe the seruaunt of helisee sawe the oste a-
boute the cety and he was ful sory: and sayde to his mayster helisee Alas alas alas what shal we
do: we be so byseged wyth oure
enemyes that we may nat escape
Than helise sayd to hī Drede ye
not For we haue more folke with vs thanne they haue with thē
Thanne helisee prayde to god ỹ
he wold open the iyen of that seruant : that he myght se what helpe helisee had with him / And a-
non he sawe the hilles aboute helise ful of hors and charettys brē
nyng as fyer and a greate peple
arayed to bateil that was the ost

of aungeles sent of god in to he-
pyng of helpse through whoos helpe the prophete helise sedde al ye
oste that byseged him into the cety of samarie amongys alle ther
enemys / For they were so blent
that they wyst not whether they
went / They come to take helise
and helisee toke them wyth helpe of aungelos: and dyd w ith thē
what he wolde / And therfore dauid sayth. Monte in circuitu ei'
et dn̄s in circuitu ppli sui. The
hyllys: that is to say aungelos be
aboute the gode man and the gode woman to kepe thē / and god
is aboute his peple to saue them
And therfor saint Cecile sayd to
hir husbonde Valerian / I haue
goddes aungel that louethe me
ful wel and kepeth my body with greate cherte that no man shal defoule me / And if thou w pst
by foule loue defoule me: he shal
sle the / And if thou loue me with
clene loue and wil kepe my mai-
denhode hool and clene. he shall
loue the as wel as me / And w hā-
ne thou art cristened: thou shalt
se him / Anon hir husbond Valerian by hir counsel went and w as
cristened of the busshop saint Vr-
ban. And when he w as cristened
he cam ayen & fond saynt cecily
prayig i closet: & the aungel stōdig
bisidys hir with wingis & fethers
ful bright and his face shon and
o ii

The fyfte

glymered as the flame of fyre He hade in eyther hande a garlonde made of rosys and lelyes ful fayre and fresſh and ful swete i smellyng/ He yaue vnto saynt cecile one another to Valerian and bad them kepe them in clennes both of body & of soule/ For why sayd he. I haue brought them oute of paradise/ And ye ſhal knowe by this token/ For they ſhal alwey be grene and fresſhe and neyther welke ne fade: ne lese ther swete sauore: and no man ne woman may se them: But they that loue clennesse and chastyte: as ye do We rede also in the lyfe of saynt agnes / Whane ſhe was but thretene yere of age: suffered deth for the loue of god: and for the loue of chastite. for ſhe wolde not aſsent to be wedded to the grete lordes sone of rome: for he was hethen/ And also for ſhe wolde kepe hir maydenhode to crist/ ſhe was made naked and led to the bordel house: to be defouled of synful wretches/ But sodenly hir here wex so moche: that it hilled and hidde al hir body/ And whanne ſhe came to the bordell house hir good aungel was redy: and brought hir a clothe as whyte as snowe ful mete to hir body: and bylapped hir with so grete lyght that there might no man loke vp/

on hir: ne no man durst entre ye place/ Thanne the lordis sonne as fole hardy ran into that light for to defoule hir/ And anon the fende whom he wolde haue serued him: ſlough him/ But saynt agnes with hir prayer to god and help of hir gode aungel reysed him from deth to life. to ſhame and ſhenſhip of al hethen peple/ For anon he went oute of that house and cried openly that there was no god but crist: and despised hir mawmetys and ther falſbyleue Also Whanne saynt agace was beryed hir aungel in the liknesse of a yonge man clothed in cloth of silke with an hundred yonge men al clothed in whyte: that were aungels also or els holy soulys: came to the beryjng and layde a stone of marble vpon hir graue with a writyng of grete comfort to al the contre: & went not thens tyl al the beryjnge was do and neuer after was se any of al that cumpany/ Also the good aūgel brake the whelis that ſhulde haue slayne saint kateryne And whāne ſhe was dede for goddes sake the aūgels toke hir body & bare it i the erth into ye moūte of synai and there beryed it worſhipfully/ And therfore leue frend I pray you y ye haue saintes in heuen and holi aūgels i reuerence

Precepte.

and deuocion: for they be to vs fader and moder as I sayde first worship ye oure ladi moder and mayde aboue al: nexte after god and thanne other sayntes bothe man and woman and holy aungels as god yeuethe you grace. worship ye theym: not as god but as oure tuters defondours & kepers and oure leders and gouernours vnder god and men is betwene vs and god that is fader of al and souereyn iuge to que me him & to praye for vs to gete vs grace to do wel & forpeuenes of oure mysdede And therfore dauid sayth Pro hac. id est p missione pcct orabit ad te oīs scīs in tempore oportuno / Euery saint shal pray to the lorde in byhoful tyme for mercy and forpeuenesse of sinne / And leue frend by ye hertely to youre aungel as to hym y is next you and hath moste cure of you and is moste besy to saue you vnder god And if ye wyl folowe his gouernaunce and trust h him i al goodnes & w' reuerēce & clēnes by ye hi faithfully pleine you to hi & speke ye to hi homely to be youre helpe as he is youre tuter and keper assigned of god and say ye oft 'that holy prayer / Angele qui meus es &c.

The xxiiii. chapter
Diues. Thy speche plesete me wel and thy wordis be goode and deuoute: But I pray the say forthe of thys cōmaundement if thou can more. Paup. Also by this cōmasldement men of holy churche be bound to worship ther patrones / For the patrone of the churche is fader of ye churche and of the benefice l that that he begynnethe it of nought y vi. q. vii.. pia in glosa. Diues. For which thingys is a man cleped patron. Pauper. For thre thinges / For fundacion that is peuyng of ground: for the firste dotacion: and for makyng of ye firste churche. Patronum faciūt dos edificacio fundus. Diues. What worship owe men of holy churche to do to ther patrones: & what right longeth to ye patron Pauper. It longeth to him for to present a persone able and yeue the churche and the benefice by wey of almes to whom he thenketh able by assent of ye busshop Also it longeth to hi to maintey ye churche and to kepe it fro dilapidacion and from destruccōn & from al maner wrongys as a gode fader & a gode tutoure & as a true aduohet to kepe & defēd the churche and the mynystrys of the churche from al wrongis and diselys by on hys power. And if he fynde person vicher or curate or ony other clerhe or prelate mysusynge the benefice l which heis

o iii

patroun: he owthe to amende them in fayre maner if he maye And if he may not he o wth to tel the busshop therof: or summe of his officeris. to whom longethe the correction of such defautys: And if the busshop do not his deuoure ne his officeris: he shal tel it to the archebusshop And but he do hys deuour he shal tel it to pe kynge: x Bi. q. Bii. filijs And therfore men of holy churche that be auaūced by ther patrouns most nedely do ther patrons worshyp and haue theym in reuerence by weye of kyndnesse: and for nede of helpe to be maynteined in ther right / And also for drede of ther offens / For if they misbere them ther patrons may depryue them of ther Benefice by assent of the Busshop: and in case opens the Busshoppis wyl / Also it longeth to men of holy churh to sustepne ther patrons & ther chidren whanne they falle to nede / And if they be taken prisoners to help to pai ther raunsome. p Bi. q. Bii. q cūq3 Ep. li. iii. de iure patronat. c. nobis fuit Et pii. q. i. aplicos &c. sacrorum . et ibidem q. ii. aureū. And it longethe to men of holy churh to do ther patrones worshhip l sittinge in goinge: and put them by fore in sitting in goinge p Bi. q. Bii. pia mentis / And it congeth to pe patron to haue pe principal place and sytt principaly l hys church . Tabula iuris : dicci one patronat & And for worship of the patron: & his ese the preste may singe two messys l one day Extra. li. iii. de celebracōe missay cōsuluisti And whan the patron presenteth a persone to the busshop : whiche persone he wyl auaunce: the busshop is bonde to resepue that persone : But if he be proued & know for a wicked man and vnable p Bi. q. Bii. monasterij / Also the patron may in hys fundacion byfore the halowyng of the church reserue to him a certeyn rente by yere by assent of pe busshop to resepue it of the churche. Ep. de iure pat. t. plea. Et hostiensis l sm sua li. ij. e. ti. Also if a plate be chosin in a church collegiat: as in an abbey pory chauntry: he shal by the lawe be presented to the patron: or that he be confermed and if he be vnable: he may & owth to withstond the confirmacion. Ep. de iure patronatus . c. nobis fuit p Bi. q. Bii. filijs. Also he maye in hys fundacion of the church collegiat reserue to him to be in the ellection of the plate of the church with assent of the busshop or of the pope by the same lawe : But he moste she we that writen v hane he wil vse it / Hostiensis li. iii. Ru. de iure parōat / Et tabula

Precepte.

iuris diccione pronat⁹ Et extra de iuro patronato nobis suit in glosa Diues. Patrons synd ful oft ther auaices ful vnkynde to them and ful prowde/ And therfore many a patroun maye saye Filios exaltaui et enutriui: ipsi autē spreuerunt me. psalie.i°.c°: I haue auaunsed chyldren and brought them vp of nought and they haue despiced me. Paup. Suche vnkind men of holy church but thei amēd thē thei shal haue goddes curse: that he paue to al suche in the same chapter. Ve genti peccatrici pplō graui iniqtate: semini neqm filiis sceleratis/ Woo be to the synful people heuy through wickednes. to ye wicked sede. to the vnkynd synful children. Diues. If a church be destroied: and a man do it make ayen of his cost: shal that man be cleped patroun of the churche Pauper. ye thowe he do make it ayen of the same mater that it was made of byfore/ And the patron that was byfore patron only by makynge of the churche or peuyng of the grounde leseth his right of the patronage But if he were patron bi botacōn he leseth not hys right of patronage. In tabula iuris patronatus. If the patron vary in his representacion presenting first one and sythe another: it stondeth in the dome

and the wyl of the busshop to resepue whichh he wyl/ Thou e the patron of laise present a persone vnable: he leseth not his right of representacion ne owth to lese it But if a college present a persone vnable: in that he leseth the hys right of presentacion for that tyme/ And if a clarke present a persone vnable he is worthy to lese his right of presentacion for þ tyme. Extra de eleccione. cū l cūctis/ The patron of ye laise mai abyde but foure monethis of his presentacion/ The college and the clerke patron mai abyde six monethis: and if they passe ther tyme by retcheleshede or by brynge: the busshop shal ordeyn for þ churche and benefice/ No man owthe to present himsilfe/ The patron maye lesully present his sonne: hys neuewe. and ony of his kyn: if they be able & power: And if a patron be pore and nedi the busshop may yeue hym that benefice in whiche he is patron: and he may take it of his peste: so that peste come only of the busshoppes free wyl: With oute ony pcuringe of hymyslfe: Hostiensis li°. iiii° de iure patronatus.

The xxv. chapter.

Diues. I thāk ye for thou hast told me more of thys comaūdemēt than euer I harde bifore/ But yet me merueleth
o iiii

moch why þ god biddeth not mē do almesdede to straūgerys & to other folke at nede I noṅ of a spetē cōmaundementys / For but men be bounde therto by goddes cōmaūdemēt: I holde it no dedly synne to leue it: Ne men shuld not be dampned for they dede it not Paup. By thys cōmaūdement pryncypaly we be bounde to helpe alle nedy folke vp oṅ oure power / For by thys precepte we be bound to shewe pety to al mē Diues. Contra God speketh in this cōmaūdmēt only of worshyp þ longeth to fader & moder Pauper. That worshyp stondeth þe in two thyngys: I affection of herte thenhlge: & in dede doynge. By affectōn of herte we shulde loue al men & wemē w' drede to offēd them Vnskilfuly. By dede doing we shuld do al men reuerence aft ther degre: & helpe theym in nede as we wolde be holpe oure silfe: And therfore saint peter biddeth vs worshyp al men / And saynt poul biddeth þ ech man & womā shuld put other bifore I worshyp for ech man owth to holde wyth other his fader I sū degre.

The xxvi. chapter:

Diues. Why so? Pauper. For ech man passith other I some degre of worshyp, & in that he is his fader / Or in beynge or I wisdome: or I goodnes / In beinge we haue many faders, for sūme be faders of oure first belg as oure bodely faders & moders: þ vs bigate / Sūme be faders in welbeyng: and that in two maners: for sūme gostly sūme bodely / In welbeing gostly: be oure faders prelates of holy church and al that haue cure of oure soulys. In welbeinge bodely be oure faders al that haue cure and gouernaūce of oure body and of oure liuing in thys worlde as kinges princes: lordes and suche other: Also al that be elder in age & had ther beinge byfore vs: be oure faders / Faders in wisdome be prechours techers: men of lawe clerkys and men of age: whyche by long experiēce knowe more thā ther yonger / Faders in goodnes be al holy men: and al that passe vs in goodnes / And for that ech man owth to deme other: better than himsilfe: therfore eche man owe to worshyp other as fader in goodnes: But if open malyce make hym lyke a beste and noman. And therfore saynt poule sayth Supiores sibi iuicē arbitrantes Euery man and woman deme other his souereyn in goodnesse. Ad phīlip.ii°.c. / For as the glose sayth there: Thowe we seme so uttern to other by some goodnes and dignyte that is in vs openly knowen: yet ther mai be ful goodnesse preuely in a nother of lower degre: in which goodnes he is oure souereyn in goddes syght./ Diues. Why is this comaundement youen with a biheste of helth and welfare more than any of the other comaudemētis/ For he sayth thus: worshyp thy fader & moder: that thou may lyue long vpon erthe & fare wel in the lond that thy lorde god shal yeue the. Deut°. ͛v.c. Pauper. For sythe god hoteth so grete mede for heping of this precept: that is moste natural: and wherto man & woman is moste enclined bi wey of kynde: he shewth wel that men shuld haue moch mede for kepig of other preceptis that be not so natural. And by the mede assygned for kepig: god shewth wel what peine man & woman shal haue for the brekyng: þ is to saye shortly/ se vpon erth. & euyl fare: Both here and in lond of deth: and after lese the lond of life without end and wende to the londe of woo & of derkenes/ Terrā miserie et tenebrarū. And for that this precepte is principal of the secunde table and in maner includeth al six folowing. therfore to this comaudement he knitteth the mede for the keping of al: and payne for brekig of al. For after he hoteth many diuerse medys to theym þ kepe hys hestys: & many myscheues to them that breke the/ And al they be cōphended i thys short biheste knit to this cōmaudemēt For the biheste is moste couenient to this cōmaudemēt/ For as saint Poule sayth: ruth pety and almesdede is good for al thigys and hath hys mede both in thys worlde & also i the tother world that is comyng Diues. Shewe me that. Paup. For it is good reson that they lyue long: which maynteyn wel theym that be begynnynge of ther lyfe: that is fader and moder/ For whanne the rote of the tre faylleth by defaute of the tre aboue thanne ye tre shal sone fayle and sere vp. And it is not worthy that he liue log ne fare wel that worshipeth not them ne helpe them: By whō he lyueth: and hath his lyfe and hys welfare/ And he that worshipeth not the begynning of his his beynge: is worthi sone to lese hys beinge/ And he that helpeth other with hys good to lyue longe good life: is worthy to haue good and good lyfe.

The xxvii. chapter

Also leue frend ye shal vnderstonde ȳ god sayth these wordys not only to euery persone by hymsilfe: But he sayd thē to al the peple ⁊ to euery people as to one psone not onli for worshiping of ther fleshly fader and moder: But also for worshiping of ther souereins ī ther degre as I sayd bifore. For why as longe as any peple is bugū ⁊ meke to ther souereyns:⁊ wyl folowe her gode gouernaunce. and worship men after ther degre:⁊ euery mā be payde wᵗ his owne degre ⁊ do the dute of his degre: so longe the peple is able to kepe ȳ lond that god hath youen them to — for god be spte. But whanne they wyl rebelle ayens ther souereins and wyl not stond to ther ordinaūce But euery man wyl be hys owne man: and folowe hys owne fantasies: despice hys souereis ther dome ⁊ gouernaūce: ne yeue no tale of goddis lawe ne of londis lawe ne of holy chyrchys law: ne haue men of vrtue ⁊ of dignyte ī worship: But for pryde haue thē in despite and be Bestᵗ to worship thēsilfe ī hindering of other that peple is able to the swerde: ⁊ as ble to lese his londe. For as ye se at the ipe ī tyme of tēpest: thogh the bowys of the tre bete thēsilfe togyder ⁊ altobrest ⁊ fall doune as long as ye rote of ȳ tre kepeth hym fast iȳ hys place and ryseth not: so long ye tre shal not fal But whā the rote beginne to rise oute of his place: anon the tre begyn to fal. Right thus it faretħ by ye peple of a lond. Thogħ tempest of pride of couetise: of enuie: of lecȝery fal sūtime ī the croppe of the tre: þ is to say amongis lordes ⁊ souereins ⁊ the grete mē. if the pore peple þ is rote of the tre ⁊ of al the comonte kepe thē styl ī sowdnes:⁊ do meke ly ther dwte to god kepīge hys cōmaūdemē tys ⁊ the good preceptys of ther souereins: so longe is hope þ ye peple shall fare wel after þ tēpeste ⁊ not be destroied. But if they ryse ayens god by customable ded ly synnes: ⁊ ayens ther worldly souereins:⁊ wil entermete them of euery cause of that londe ⁊ of holy chṙurch:⁊ termine euy cause by ther wyt Body ⁊ crop of ȳ tree shal falle. For it is not possyble that the rote shuld be so bigge as the crop of the tre: But the tre fell Neþ the fote shuld be aboue the hede: But the body fel se Diues. This is ful soth we se it at ye iye For pyde ⁊ rebellion of ye pore peple is cause of destruccōn of this lōd. For sytħe they aresen ayens ther souereis: was there neū stabilite ī this lōd: But alwey sytħe ye tre of ye peple of this lōd ⁊ the realme: hatħe stond iȳ fallynge

The fyfte

Pauper. Unbuxumnesse & pride was principal cause of lesing of londys and of realmys / And principaly the cause of saluacion of realmes londys and comontees is obedience and buxilnesse: þe/ the man in his degre obey to his souereyn & worshyp hi as fader/ & therfore leue frende I pray you for goddes sake that ye worshyp al youre faders and moders: in ther degre: as I haue sayde And haue ye old folke & feble I worshyp: Whyle ye be in yonge age: & worshyp ye the age that ye draw to and haue no scorne of the old folke for feblenes and unclenes that ye se them in / But thenk ye that suche shall ye be if ye abyde ther age: feble unsoure and loth to the syght / For suche as ye be nowe: such were they sumtime It fareth bi age of man and woman as it doth by a precyous stone þ is clepyd crisolitus / Thys stone as sayth the mayster of kindes i the begynnyng of the day it shyneth bright as any gold / But as the day passeth so passeth his bryghtnesse / And the nyer euen the more it fadeth: so that bi euen it is lyke a clot of erth / Thus it fareth by man and woman in this world / For in ther youthe and i ther begynnynge they be fayre: rede and rody and fresshe as rose in may: ful lusty to the iye But as youthe passeth so passeth ther bewte / And as they olde: so they fade: tyl at the laste the daye of ther lyfe cometh to an ende / And than be theye but a clott of erthe ful unsoure & gastly to the sight Here endeth the fourthe precept & here begynneth the fift precept.

The firste chapter.

Diues. As me thenketh: thou haste enformed me well in these .iiii. comaundementis Nowe I praye the for charyte þ thou wolt enfourme me: in the fifte Paup. The fift comaundement is this Non occides that is to say. Thou shalt nou slee In whych precept god forbedeth us al maner manslaughter unleful both bodely and gostly / He biddeth us þ we slee no man ne woman unryghtfully ayens the lawe. neyther with herte consentig to his deth: neyther by wrathe & hate For as sayth saynt Iohn Qui odit frem suu homicida est / He þ hateth his brother is a manslear: For of wrath & hate cometh manslaughter / Also bi this preept he forbyddeth beting fightyng and maynig þ sonyng banisshig out / lawinge / For these & such other be a maner of dethe & despose to dethward / & therfore it shuld not be do to man ne to woma withoute

The fyfte

grete gylt/Also he forbiddeth ꝑ we sle no man ne woman with oure tunge: by syndering and procuringe hys deth: ne fauoure peupnge: ne false witnesse beringe: ne lesynges makynge: ne by diffamyng ne backityng for backyters and wycked spekers. be manquellers. And therfore salomon sayth: that moche folke hath falle by the swerde: but not so many as haue be slayn by the tunge. Ecclĩ. xxviii°. c. And therfore he sayth puer. xviii°. c. That lyfe & deth bel ꝑe hondis of ꝑe tũg for by hondis I holy writ ĩs ūnderstond myght and power And therfore dauid saith Lingua eorũ gladius acutus. The tunge of the iewis and of other wicked spekers: is a sharpe swerde. For the iewys slowe criste with ther tunges. not with ther hondes/for they procured his deth by false witnesse: and by exctig of the people/ But paynyms slowe him with ther hondys and dyd him on the cros/ And yet as sayth saint austen the iewys were more gilty of cristys deth than pylate that dampned hym to the deth: or the knyghtys that dyde sl on the crosf for with her tunges the iewis slowe him: and were cause of hys deth/And therfore sayth the lawe. that he that sleeth hys brother with his hond and he that hateth hys brother and he ꝑ backyteth his brother. al thre be manslecro. De pe.di.i. homicidiaꝝ. The backyter sleeth thre at onys/He sleth himsilf by his owñ malice. and him that hereth him: and him that hath lykyng in hys false tales and hym that he backyteth/ for he maketh him to lese his good name: and perauenture his lyf/He maketh him also to lese charyte: whã he knoweth his wekid spech ꝑ he hath sayde byhind hym And so by lesinge of charite he leseth god that is hys lyfe of hys soule And therfore the wys man liche neth the backiter to the adder ꝑ byteth and styngeth in slynesse Eccle. x°. A shrewyd adder is the backiter that sleth thre with oon breth/Therfore salomon sayth Kepe ye you from backytyng of the partid tũge For wekid word sayd in preuy: shal nott passe in vayn and wyth oute woo/for the money sayth he that lyth sleth soule. Sap̃/i. c.

The seconde chapter.

D Iues. Is flaterynge ony gostli mãslaughter Pauper. In so moche as it sleth the soule bothe of him that flatereth & of him that is flatered: I so moch it is gostly manslaughter.
Diues. Is euery flaterynge

Precepte.

goſtly many ſlaugḣtyr and dedly ſynne? Pauṗ. Nay. For flate/ринg is a ſpecḣe of veyn prayſiġ ſayde to man or woman with intencion to pleſe them / And that maye be do in three maners: as prayſing man or woman I good ueſſe and in good that he hathe. Or els prayſinge them in good/ neſſe and good þ they haue not. Or els praiſing them in threw ib neſſe and falſneſſe: of ẇḣich ma ner flatering ſpekeṫh dauid and ſaytḣ. Qſt laudatur peccator in deſideriis anime ſue et iniquus benedicetur / Forſotḣ ſaytḣ ḣe ye ſynner is praiſid in beſiris of his ſoule: and ye wicked man is bleſ ſed of folys / For ẇhanne threw/ lis haue fortḣ ther wyl in ſḣreẇed neſſe: thanne the worlḋ praiſetḣ them and worſḣyp theym / The firſte maner of prayſynge if it be do only to pleſe man & not god: It is ſynne. and in cas dedly ſyn/ ne / And therfor ſaint poule ſaitḣ that if ḣe wolḋ only pleſe man & not god: ḣe were not criſtys ſer- uaunt / But it be do to pleſe god and for a good ende it is cōmen/ dable and medful / For in good ſoḣe vertue þ is praiſed wepetḣ Virt' laudatur creſcit / Butt this maner prayſinge is no flatering The ſecunde maner of prayſing if it be do for god and for a good ende it is ſufferable: & in cas cō/ mendable and medeful / But if ḣe do wetingly: only to pleſe mā and not god. it is dedly ſynne. The thyrd maner of prayſynge if it be do wyllynge and wetyng it is dedly ſinne And therfore da uid ſayde. Oleum peccatoris non l pinguet caput meū.   Lord god ſaytḣ. lete not the oyle of ye ſynner make fatte my hede & oi ſay. late my herte neuer haue no lykynge ne ioye in falſe flaterly For as ſaint auſten ſaitḣ ye tūg of ye flaterer do moreḣarme þan the ſwerde of the enmye purſuig Therfore ſalomon ſaytḣ: it is better to be vndernomen of the wyſe man: than be deceyued by flaterly of folis. eccle. vii°. This ſynne of flateringe is ſo grete & greuous þ if any'mā of holi chur ch were cuſtomable therin: ḣe ſḣ uld be degraded / Alſo if ḣe were a traytour or a teller of ſḣriſte. diſtincc. xlvi. clericus / God pe- uetḣ curs to al falſe flaterers ſay inge in this wyſe. Ve qui conſu unt puluillos ſub omniū cubito manus et faciunt ceruicalia ſub capite vniuerſe etatis ad capient dū alas. Wo be to them þ ſowe ſmalcſofte pelowis vnder euery elbowe. and make pelowis vn- der the hede of euery age to take the ſowlys of my people / They qchened ſoulys þ were not quik but depe in dedly ſynne: and ſo

245

¶ The fyrste

defouled me by fore my people. For by cause of ther flaterynge they youen no tale of me: ne dreded me: ne worshyp me / For an handful of barly sayth he & for a gobet of brede they slowe soulis that were not dede: and they quikened soulys that lyued not makynge lesynges to my peple that loued lesyngys / And they conforted synners in ther synne and in ther falsnesse: and dysconforted good folke in ther goodnes and in ther truth. Eze. xiii°. c.

¶ The thirde chapter.

Dives. This vice of flaterynge regneth ful moch in this lond for the peple is so blent with flaterynge and lesynges: þ they se not the mischef þ thei be in And therfore they lyue forth in pride and not lowe them to god ne pray to god for helpe as they shuld do: if they knewe ther mischefuousnesse that they be in.

Pauper. Therfore god sayth Popule meus qꝰ te beatum dicūt ipsi te decipiunt et viam gressuū tuorum dissipant / My people they that se that thou art blessed & in welth: thei dissceyue the & distroy the wey of thy goinge: that thou might not forth ne haue no spede in thi werkys for defaute of grace. psa. iii°. c. Dives. What is vnderstonde by the pillouis þ god speketh of a yens flaterers

Pauper. As saint gregory sayth. moraliu. xviii°. c. sup illud. iob. xviii° Donec deficiam nō recedam &c. He that preyseth man or woman in hys wicked werke he leyth hys pyllowe vnder hys elbowe / And he that gladdeth þe herte of the synner in hys synne he leyth a pelowe vnder his hede For by the hede is vnderstonde the herte / For why by such flaterynge they reste softly and slepe in ther synne and dye gostly wythoute payne and perseyue not her owne deth /   And therfore salomon sayth. that he that iustifith the wicked man and dampneth the rightful man: both thei be abhominable to god puer. xviii°. c. Therfore god lychenneth flaterers to them that playstren & paten wallis and wowys with out For thinge that is foule thei make it to seme fayre and make folke to haue lyking i ther synnes. Therfore god sayth that the sinner maketh the wal of synne bytwene hym and god. But flaterers playsteren and paynten the wal of synne. Eze. xiii°. c. Also flaterers be lichened to an adder that is cleped dipsa which as the master of kindes sayth. li° xviii° he is so litel þ thow a man trede theron he mai not se it But hys venī is so violent that it sleeth

a man or he fele it & he deth with
oute payne / Right so flateringe
semeth but a smal synne and yet
it is ful venemous and sleth ma
nys soule or he fele it / And with
oute payne bringeth him to end
les payne / Flaterers be lykened
to an adder that is cleped tyrus.
Whiche is leest of al edders: and
yet his venym is not curable as
sayth the maykster of kynd in the
same place / Right so flaterynge
semeth but a ful lytyl synne and
yet it is so venemous that it wyl
not be lightly helpd / For whan
man or woman hath lykinge in
flateringe and reulethe hys lyfe
after flateryng tunge: it is ful
harde to that man or woman to
be saued / For as longe as men
prepsen him in his synne: so lon
ge he is bolde in hys synne / And
if men begynne to lacke him: he
falleth into soro we and dispey=
re / Therfore saint iames sayth
that the tunge is but alityl mem
bre: and reyseth vp grate desese
it is a wichid thing that hath no
rest ful of dedly venym. iac. iii. c.
And the prophete dauid saythe.
Acuerunt linguas suas sicut ser
pentes: Benenum aspidum sub
labiis eorum / They haue shar=
ped ther tungys as addris: the ve
nym of addrys is vnder the lyp=
pes of flaterers and wiched spe=
kers / And if a man do his dedys

only for to be preysed & flatered
of the people: flaterynge is hys
mede / And whanne flaterynge
ceseth and the wynde turneth: a
peny him he hath no lenger lykig
in good dedys / and so as the gos
pel sayth. for that he seketh that
ke in preysinge only of man for
hys good dedys and not of god:
therfore al suche be lykened to
the fyue maydens folys þ wolde
mete with ther husbond criste ie=
su at the dome with lampis with
outen oyle / That is to say with
good dedis with oute goslti mer
the and ioye and conscience For
they hadde no ioy in ther goode
dedys: But in preysing and flate
ringe of the people / And therfor
criste sayth in the gospel they ha=
ue take ther mede in this worlde
and at the dome they shalbe shet
oute of heuen blisse from endles
mede bothe flaterers and they þ
haue lykynge in flaterynge and
do ther dedys only for flateryng
and preysing of the people / But
the fiue wys maydens as sayth
the gospel hadden oyle i ther lam
pis that is to say gostly ioy and
lyhlg i ther good dedys And ther
fore they shal be recepued of ther
husbod crist into the blesse wyth
outen ende / And as saint austen
saith in hys sermon bi oyle is vn
derstonde both gostly prayspng
¶ and worldly prayspnge

The fyfte

and myrthe. Gostly prepsyng & gostly myrthes is cleped the oile of the holy gooste/ But worldly prepsing and worldly merthe is cleped the oyle of synners/ And therfore he saythe that slaterers selle oyle to the maydens folye that is to saye to synners as ofte as they flater theym and preyse them in ther foly and in ther pryde for to haue mete or drinke or money or worshyp. or any temporal lucre. & so bringe the in errour & foly & plese & praise theim in ther synne/ But as dauid sayth. Deus dissipauit ossa eorum qui hominibus placent. God hath dystroyed and shal distrope ye bonys of them that plese men in dyspite of god and dissepue men and Wemen by slateringe/ Wyched tunges do moch harme and sle many soules But the slaterig tunge is worste of al/ And therfore the wyse man sayth. Susurro et bilignis erit maledictus a deo Ecle. xxViii. The musterer and the double tungedman shal be accursed of god. For he troubleth moche folke that haue pes. The thyrde tunge sayth he hath stired and moued moch peple oute of pees & disparplid theym fro nacion into nacion.

The fourthe chapter.

Iues: What is susurro. It is cleped a musterer. Paup. It is a preuey rowner: that pryuely telleth false tales amongis the people for to make discencion and debate amongis the people: and telle tales preuely why che he dare not tel openly ne may not avowe them/ Of whych folk saint poule saythe Susurrones detractores deo odibiles. Ad ro.i.c. Such musterers and bacbyters god hateth them/ For susurro is a preuy bacbiter & a preup lyer that maketh debate amonges frendes/ And as the wyse man sayth. God hateth altho sowen discord amongis brethrene and frendes. puer. Vi. c. And as he sayth in another place. suche preuy musterers defoule the soule. and thei shalbe hated of al Bothe of god & of al the courte of heuen Eccle. xxt. And therfore god sayth. Non eris susurro nec criminator in populis. Thou shalt be no musterer amōgis the people to lette loue and pees: ne thou shalt be no tale teller ne blaabbe to defame man or Woman fallly or any synne that is preui Leuitici. xix. c. Soche preuy musterers and Bacbyters make discencion and heuinesse in euery comonte. in euery houshold in euery cumpany/ And therfore

Precepte.

whanne they be knowe for suche they shulde be put oute of cumpany: or elles chastised / For the wyse man sayth whanne the wode is withdrawe: the fyre abateth and is quenched. Right so sayth he withdrawe suche preuy mustres and bacbiters: and put them oute of cumpany: and chidinge and debate shal cese.   Prouer. xxvi.c. Diues. what is bilignis that thou clepest a double tunged man. Pauper. Bilguis and ye double tunged man is he that say the one with hys mouwthe: and thenketh another in hys herte: & he that spheketh good byfore a man: and bihynde hym he speketh him euyl: he that sayth a trueth the one tyme: and another tyme he forsaketh it he that is vnstable in speche: and nowe sayth the one and nowe another / Of suche god speketh and sayth. Do bilygue detestor. prouerbior. viii.c. I hate and loth the mouth þ is double tunged. Diues. what clepeth the wyse man the thyrd tunge that doth so moche woo. Pauper. The thirde tunge is þe flaterynge tunge: whyche is the worste of all / For euery flaterer that flatereth man or woman in his synne: he is a flaterer he is a bacbiter: he is double tunged: & so he may be cleped in lateyn tri-

linguis: that is treble tunged in englisshe / The flaterer blyndeth so folke that he flatereth: that they take no hede to theym sylfe ne to god: ne knowe not the silfe and waxe so proude þ they yeue no tale of ther euencrysten / Also the flaterer lacketh and bacbiteth altho that he heteth: & hom he flatereth so to plese him: and flatereth another mannys name to enhaunse his name: and so maketh discorde and discencion. Also flaterers be double tunged. For as lyghtly as they preysen man or woman: as lyghtly they wyl lache theym. if they fayle of ther purpose & haue noo suche by ther flaterige as they wend haue had. For comonly greate preysers be greate lachers: and as moche as they preyse man or woman oute of mesure by flaterynge: as moch they will lache him or another by bacbytinge. Therfore seneca sayth: Lauda parce vitupa percius. Preyse scarsely. but lache more scarsely / For these shyp̄sis salomon sayth: that the thyrde tunge hathe stired moche ito pride: and so made them falle I shame and shenshyp and dysperpled the fro nacion to nacion. It hath destried walled townes: & dosue by the housis of grete lordis. It hathe hyt a weye the myght and

The fyfte.

the vertue of peple that were ful strong and made them feble For flaterers make townes nacions and lordes bolde to begynne wertys: plees and debate: by whych they come to nought/ For they be so blent by flatering and ouerprepsynge: that they knowe not themsylfe: But wene to ouersede as men tyl at the last they be destroied themsilfe/ Also as the wyse man seyth: the thirde tunge hath caste stronge wemen: that is to saye good wemen spher and vertuouse oute of ther vertue: & priued them and put them from ther trauaples/ For whäne a gode woman hath traueyled moch of hir lyfe to plese god & to haue a gode name: cometh a false flaterer in gyse and with flatering wordes & fayre bihestis of matrimony: or of richessys bryngeth hyr to synne & doth hir to lese hir good name and bryngeth hyr to shame and velenny/ And therfore seyth the wyse man in the same place. Eccle. xxviii. c. that who so taketh hede to the flaterynge tunge: that is the thirde tung: to haue lyhinge therin: he shal neuer haue reste/ And he shal haue no frende in whom he may reste ne trust/ For flaterers be no true frendys: But alle blinde so men þ thei mai not knowe ther frendis

ne take hede to the speche of ther fredys that wold say them the soth & warne theym of ther harme.

The fift chapter.

Iues. That many a gode woman is deceyued: and destroyed by flatering: men knowe wel/ But that flatering destroyed cetyes: lordes houses nacions and desperpsed them from nacion to nacion I se not: But I praye the telle some exaumple: Paup. As we fynde i the fourteth boke of kynges and the boke of ieremye/ For the chyldren of israel wolde not here the wordys of ieremye and of other true prophetys: ne do therafter: But had lykinge in flateringe of false prophetis which bihight them welth and prospite for to plese the peple: therfore was the cetye of ierusalem destroied and nigh alle cetyes and castellys of the londe The kynge sedechie was take & his children slayn byfore hym: & after his iyen were put oute/ All the lordis and the gentilis of the londe eyther they were slayn: or elles ledde prysoners into babysopne/ The peple was slayn with hungur moreyn & swerde And al tho that were left a lyue after

Præcepte.

that the cetye of ierusalem was taken were desparpled in diuers nacions: and slayn in diuers maner: for they trusted alwey in flaterynge of false prophetys: and slowe ieremye and other good prophetys that sayde them the truth and wold haue saued them And I dare say that flateringe of false prophetis and precþours: and of other spekers that blynde the people with plesaunt lesīges: ne wyl not vndo to them ther wickednesse: is principal cause of destruccion of many realmys and londes people: and cetyes into thys day: as we might se at ye if flateringe and lesīges blent be not Diues. Men preech these dayes ful welle apens synne. Pauper Sūme do so: But apens the grete synne that al the lond is entriked in ꝙ al cristendome knowth ꝙ is open cause of oure myschefe apens that no may precheth but nigh al be aboute to maken it. Diues. Which sīne is that Pauper. Ofte haue I tolde the: But thou beleuest me not / Go ouer the se: and there men shal tel it ye if thou aye / we fynde i the thyrd boke of kynges: that the kynge of israel whos name was achab was styred to besege the cetye of ramath gilaad ꝙ so begine werr apens the kynge of sirie/ This a

chab sent after foure hūdred false flatering prophetys of his londe Whych were wont to plese hym ꝙ to flatere him: ꝙ ayed them counseyle and holv he shulde spede: They flatered hym al and badde him go and fight: and sayd that he shuld spede right wel and take the ceti and destroie al the lōd of sirie / Thanne at the counseyl of iosephat the king of iuda that was come to helpe hym: he sent for mychee goddes prophete to knowe what he wolde saie / And as he came towardys the kynge the massēgere sayde to michee ye prophete Al other prophetys wi. the one mouth tel oure lorde the kynge good tidynges and say þ he shal spede right wel. I praye the saye as theye saye / Thanne the prophete answered what my lorde god sayth he to me: that shal I speke to oure lorde the kynge And whanne he cam vp fore the kyng he said to ye king achab. I sawe bi visōn al the peple of israel desppled i the hillys ꝙ scatered aboute as shepe wythoute a shepeherd Anon the king was wrath and saide that he tolde him neuer good ne welthe / Thanne the prophete sayde / Here the worde of god. I sawe oure lorde god sittynge on hys sete: and al the oste of heuen stondynge bisydys him

p ii

251

The fyfte.

on the ryght syde and on the lifte syde / Thanne sayde oure lorde god: who shal deseyue achab kynge of israel to do him go & fyghte in ramoth galaad and fal i fight. Anon a wicked sprite stode fore the: and sayde I shal desseyue hi. Than oure lorde ayed him hou he shuld disseue him. I shal seide he go oute and be a spryte lyer in the mouth of al his false prophetys. Thanne oure lorde god seyde Thou shalt deseyue hym and thou shalt haue the maistri of hi. Go forthe and do as thou haste sayde / Thanne the kynge was more wroth: and comaunded hi to presone / The kynge lefte the counseile of the prophete michee and folowed the counseile of his false prophetis: and went to batteile and was slayne: and his peple discoumfyt. Diues. Dauid speketh moch in hys boke of the gylous tunge: that is cleped in laten. lingua dolosa. Pauper. The gylous tung is the flaterig tunge / For comonly euery gyle in spech is medled with flaterige In gilous spech be two thingys sleyght and flateringe. And therfore gilous spech is lykened to an anglyng of fysshe / For in the anglyng be two thinges: the hoke & the mete on the hoke / The hoke is the sleyght in spech: the

mete on the hoke is flaterynge þ drawith many woma on to the deuelys hoke. Thus adam and eue were desseiued with ye fendes speche: for sslyly he ayed Eue. by god bad that they shulde not ete of euery tre i paradise / And wha he sawe hir unstable and doutig he put therto the mete of flaterig and sayde: that they shulde not dye but be as goddes kunnynge good and wycked. And so by flateringe the fende loste alle mankynde / Figure hereof we haue i ye secud boke of kiges xx c. whe re we fid b ioab gitiously scough the noble prince amasam wyth a knyfe craftely made syghtlye to go oute of the sheth / And wha he shulde stele hym wyth the knife he toke hi by the chyn and sayde to to him heyle my brother And for hys flaterynge and fayre wordis: amasa tok no hede to the knyfe / And in the same maner whanne iudas betraide crist he sayde in flaterynge and gyle Aue rabi Heile thou master.

The sixte chapter.

Diues. Thou hast wel declared the myschefe of flateringe tunges Say forth what thou wylt. Pauper. Also god forbedeth vs by thys commaundement that we slee no man: ne woman by oure dede: him a mys doynge or him hurtinge / And so by this commaundement he forbiddeth vs wrathe: and wretche chydynge. despisynge: smitynge scornynge: and al suche meanes and motyues to manslaughter. Diues. As thou wel saidest god forbyddeth not al maner manslaughter: But only manslaughter vnrightful and ayēs the law For god bad that men shuld not suffre wycked doers lyue in dysese of the people. Maleficos non pacieris viuere. exo. xxii And also he bad that we shulde slee noo man ne woman rightful and vngilty. Innocentem et iustum nō occides. exo. xxiii. c. Therfore I prai the telme in howe many maners a man is slayn vnrightfully. Pauper. On thre maners First if he be slayn without gilt Also if he be slayn with oute ordre and processe of lawe / Also if he be slayn without lawful iustyce ordeined of hys liege lord to whom god hath youen lyfe & lyme and the swerde to punysh therwyth: as saint poule she weth wel in hys pystle: Ad romanos. xiii. c. Also if he be slayn by enmite hate and crueltye: for to haue vengeaunce: not for saluacion

of the truthe and of the people.
℟ The seuenth chapter.

Dives. Thy speche is shilful say forth Pauper. Also if ony man or woman dye for defaute of helpe: Thanne alle ẏ shulde haue holpe them and might haue holpe them and wyste therof and wolde not helpe them be gylty of manslaughter / And therfore sayth the salt e. Pasce fame morientem, si non pascis occidis. dist. lxxxvi. pasce. That is to say Fede hym that is i poin te to dye for hungre / If thou wil not fede hym whanne thou myght: thou sleeste hym. Moch more thanne they be manslеers that by extorcioun: raueyne and oulledinge by might fraude and gyle robbe men of ther gode: or wyth holde men of ther good wherby they shulde lyue: and brynge them so in thought: sorowe and care and so haste ther deth. Therfore god saythe that such maner folke as tyrauntes extorcioners and false men deuoure his peple as the mete of brede / Deuorant plebem meam sicut escam panis And therfore he forbiddeth them and saythe to theym / Lystne ye princes & lordes: and lede rs of the people to you it longeth to knowe ryghtfulle dome to deme

The fyfte.

What is good and What is Wycked: What is truthe and What is false. But te nowe ye hate good thinge and loue Wycked thinge and lothe goodnesse: And loue shreweddnesse. By Violence and myght ye bilde men, and take ther synnes from them and take ther flesshe from the boonys: These ete the flesshe of my peple and bylde awey ther shinnis fro aboue them & breke ther bonys Mycheee.iii°.c°. And so al suche be man slears in goddes syght. For they haste mannys deth by mysshefe: and sorowe and cares that they brynge them in. Diues What is Vnderstonde here by the shine flesse and boonys Paup. Thre thinges be nedeful to euy man and woman lyuynge by lyfelode: and helpe of frendes in feblenes & disseaseBy the shine & byleth and clothe the flessh is Vnderstonde: clothinge: housyng armure: by Whyche man is hiled and defended fro tempestis: cold and hete and enemies and many deselys. By flessh is Vnderstond mete and drinke: Wherby the flesshe is norisshed. By the bonys & here by the flesse and strenthe the flesshe ben Vnderstonde manys frendys: Whych helpe hym at nede: and bere hym Vp and strenth hym in feblenesse and disese But these tyrautys and extercioners and false folke take aweye the shine of the pore folke. For thei robbe them of ther housinge and of ther clothig And thei ete awey ther flesshe: for they take aweye ther lyflode: Wherby ther flesshe shulde be susteyned. For they pille them so and make them so pore: that they haue neyther house ne home: ne clothinge to ther body: ne mete ne drynke to lyue by Also they breke ther bonys: For thei pursue ther frendes & wolde helpe them: and put them i such drede that theye dare not helpe them and ofte bete them and breke ther bonys and mayme them Ensaumple of thys we haue i the thyrde boke of kiges: Where we fynde that there was a true man dwellynge besidys the paleys of achab that was kynge of israel: and the pore man was cleped na both. And for he wolde not selle hys gardeyn to the kynge at hys Wyl: the kynge was wroth. And by false donne and false witnesse he dyd him be stoned to deth and so by fraude and manslaughter he escheted to hi the pore manis gardeyn. Wherfore the kyng after warde was slayne. And the quene iesabel for she assented: and halpe to the deth of the true man: and was slayne also. And houndys ete hyr flesshe: and hyr boonys and lycked Vp hir blode

Precepte.

in vengeaunce of tħe detħe of na
botħ. Tħe kynge was slayne in
werre. Hys wyfe Iesabel was cast oute of hir soler wyndowe and trode to detħe wytħe fete of horsys. And otħer two kynges of hir alyaunce: and nigħe alle ħyr kynred was slayne afterwarde in vengeaunce of tħe detħe of nabotħ. Achab ħadde sixty sones and ten spupynge after ħys detħe and tħey were byħeded in vengeaunce of tħe detħ of nabotħ. iiii°. regum. ỹ. c°:

Tħe eygħt chapter.

Also tħey be gylty of manslaugħter: tħat defraude seruauntes of tħer ħyre. Tħerfor tħe wyse man saytħe: Tħat ħe tħat taketħe awaye from tħe seruaunte ħys brede and ħis lyflode: tħat ħatħe gote in swynche: and swete: is as wycked as ħe þ sleetħe ħys neygħbore. And ħe tħat sħedetħe mannis blode and ħe tħat dotħe fraude to tħe ħyred man be bretħern: tħat is to saye tħey be lyke in synne: and wortħy in lyke payne. Qui effundit sanguinem et qui fraudem facit mercenario sunt fratres. Ecclesiastici. xxxiiii°. And tħerfore

saynt James saytħe tħus to tħe false rycħe couetouse men. Se þe ħou tħe ħire of poure werke men & laborers tħat ħaue reped poure feldys is defrauded by you: and not payde crietħe to god for vengeaunce. And tħe cry of tħeym is entred in to tħe erys of tħe lordis of ostys. Jacobi. quinto capitulo. And tħe wyse man saytħe tħat who so offeretħe sacrifyce of tħe pore mannys good: is lyke ħim tħat sleetħe tħe sonne in tħe sigħt of ħys fader. And ħe tħat defraudetħe tħe pore man of ħys good is a manslleer. Homo sanguinis est. Ecclesiastici. xxxiiii°. Diues. Tħys poynte of manslaugħter toucħetħ mocħe men of ħoly churche. For as tħe lawe saytħe: Tħe tytħes of ħoly churche be tributes of tħem tħat be in nede: To releue tħeim in tħer nede. And alle tħat men of ħoly churcħe ħaue: It is tħe pore mennys goodys. And tħer ħousys sħulde be comon to alle men at nede. Tħey sħulde be besy to resceue pylgrymps: and kepe hospitalite after tħer power. xbi. q. i. decime. etc. qui quicquid. Wherfore me tħenketħe: if ony pore folke perissħ by tħer defaute & for tħat tħey wolde not ħelpe tħem: tħey be gylt of manslaugħter. Pauper. Tħat is sotħe. And tħerfore

piiii

The fyfte.

criste sayde thries to saint petyr. Pasce / That is to saye fede my lambys and my shepe that be yo soulys that criste boughte wyth hys blode / For prelatys and curatys of holy churche moste fede ther sugettys by goode ensaumple peuynge: and by helpe at nede / And therfore criste sayde thries to saint peter: fede my lambis But the thyrde tyme he sayde: fede my shepe / For as long as thei be lambis they peue neyther milke ne wolse. But whanne these be wayen shepe they . peue bothe milke & wolse And so criste in his wordys badde that prelatis and curatys of holy churche shuld haue double cure of the pore peple: to fede theym goostly and also bodely: Wyth the bodely helpe at nede But they be not bounde to fede the ryche folke: But goostly: & the that haue noo nede: Wyth the holy churchys goodys / And of the pore folke peue they no tale: But to pylle them: and haue of them: & gette of theym What they maye by ipocrisie: by fraude: by drede and biolence / And therfore god Vndernymethe theym by the prophete ezechiel: and sayth thus to theym / De pastoris⁹ israel Woo be to the shypherdis of israel: that is to saye to the prelatys and curatis of holi church: Which shuld be she pesherdys of goddys shepe:

and of the soulis that criste boughte so dere: Woo be to the shepeherdys: ffor they fede them sylfe and of the pore people peue they no tale / ye ete sayth he the mith and clothed you withe the wolle And that was fatt ye slowe to fede welyoure wombe: But ye sede not my flocke of my people: that was feble: ye helpped it not ne conforted not : And that was sore & syk ye heled it not. And that was broke: ye boūd it not apen that was cast a wepe and forðr ueu: ye fetched it not apen: ne sede be it a pen / That was perysshed ye soght it not: But withe feernes and hardnesse and by power wytheoute petye ye commaunded to theym many grete thynges and greuous and reygned amongys theym as emperours / And so my shepe be scatered / For there is no shepeherde: that peuethe ony tale of them . Ezechielis. xxxiiiº. And in another place he sayethe thus / Woo be to the shepherdys that thus descaterne: and sorrende the flocke of my leswe: and of my pasture. Jeremie. xxiiiº. cº. And therfore god acceptethe not ye prater of such mē of holy churche: For they be wyth oute charite and ful of crueltye in pyllinge of the pore people / And therfore he saythe to theym . Cum extenderitis manus vestras &c. Whan

256

Precepte.

ye shal lyfte vp youre hondys to me: I shal turne my yien alwey fro you: and whanne ye shuld multi-plye prayers to me: I shal not here you: ffor youre hondys be ful of blode. psa.i.c. Vpon whyche wordys thus sayth the grete clerk/ he groshed. dicto xxiii°. An vn-iuste scheder of mannis blode ha the blody hondys: ffor blode she-de oute is in the hondys of hym that is ye shreder oute. as the effeccion of the werke is in the cause: For the hond of the sheder is cause of blode shed/ So thanne syth bodely fode: is cause of blode of mannys body by whych hys lyfe transitorye is sustepned: he that wythdraweth sustynaunce fro the poore in myssese: he wyth-draweth from the poore man hys blode: wherby hys lyfe shulde be sustepned/ And therfore god say the that the blode of the poore fol-he lain the hondys of thepm: in whos hodys ye thigis be wythhold vniustly/ By whyche thyngis or by the pryse of thoo nedy folke shulde be sustepned/ Also all tho that wythholde poore men ther go-de eyther by violence or by frau-de or thefte or ony deseyte bi whi the goode the poore folke shulde lyue: they haue ther bodyes defou-led wyth the blode of poore folke. And in that that they fare delycatly wyth poore mannys goode they ete and drynke the blode of the poore folke/ And ther clothig is defouled wyth the blode of pore folke/ And if they housen & byd-den wyth the poore mannys gode they grounde ther housyng in ye blode of poore men.

The nynthe chapter.

Also euery man & woman and namely men of holy churche that drawe folke to syn-ne by mys ensynge or by wyc-ked ensaumple: or by false lore: theye be gylty of manslaughter gostly/ And therfore saint grego-ri saythe in hys omelie: that men of holy church be gylty of as ma-ny dethys: as they drawe soulis to bedly synne by ther wicked ex-aumple: and ther wycked siuige And therfore cryste byddeth in the gospel: that there shulde noo man sklaundre the sellyd simple folke/ For who so doth it: it we-re better to hym that he were cast in the se wyth a mylstone abou-te hys necke/ wyth word as saith ye glose is specialy sayde for me of holy church/ And therfore sait poule saith to al crysten peple: & namely to prestys & clerkis. Ne ponatis offendiculū frīb' Vel scā-dalū: b is to say as sayth ye glose Do no thīg b mai be cause of fal

The fyrste

tyge & perisshyng of youre brethern ne cause of sorowe and heuines Ad rom. viiii°. & therfore the lawe byddeth that whanne busshops & ther officerys go aboute for to visite: That they shulde do no tyrauntrye: In takynge of ther costys but visyte with charite: & solvnes without pompe of grete araye and of grete mayne besi to amende the defaultys: and to preche goddes worde and to winne mānis soule. not to robbe the folke of ther good but take ther costys in esy maner. So that thei sclaudre not ther brethern ne ther sugettys: ne be not greuouse to them: x.q.iii. cauend./ Alle men and namely men of holy church moste besely fle sclaundre. & they yeue no man ne woman occasyon of slaundre ne of synne: but ofte tyme lyfe the harder and abstayne them fro mani thinges leful to fle sclaudre/ For as saythe saint Ierom: super mycheam All that yeue occasion of sclaudre be gylty of al tho that perisshe by & sclaudre. i.q.i. hii. quosquilq3 Et nota pro Vitando scandalo in rebus licitis. ad rō.viii. et p.ad cor Viii° For these causys god saith to men of holy church by the prophet osee/ ye be made snare to mē lokyng a fer: and as a net sprede abrede on the hylle of thabor: &

ye haue bowed down sacrifices to the depnes: that is to say yt ye ought to be ware lohers to worche wel: and warne men of peret of synne: be made a snare and a net in holy church: that is the hyl of thabor: to take folke in synne and drawe them to foly/ And so ye haue slain soulis & bowed the doun into the depnesse of dampcion and so made sacrifice to the deuel of the soulys that god to ke you to kepe. Osee. 8°.c. Also men of holy church sle ther sugettys goostly that mys eggyng mis counseyle: and mys enformacyon bringe them in dedly synne: & in eresie or elles sette them fro good dedys that thei wolde do & so slayn good purpose and good wyl that man or woman is in: & in maner sleyn ther sayth Werbi they shulde lyue. For the pphete sayth/ Iustus ex fide viuit. The rightful man lyueth by seyth. And saint James saith that saythe wythoute good werkes of charite is but dede/ And also prayer wythoute deuocion is but ded as sey these clerkes. Diues. Thanynge alle the prayers that men make: be but dede. For comonly in oure prayere we be destracte and thenk on other thinges And it is not possible to be alwey to thenke on what we saye.

258

For there is nothynge so chaunge
able as thought / & how we then
on that we sey. yit it is not in ou
re powder without special gyfte
of god to haue deuocioun therin
Pauper. Take it not so straite
For it is understonde thus Prey
ere withoute deuocion is butte
dede: that is to say prayer ma=
de apens deuocioun is but dede.
Diues. Howe a pens deuocion
Pauper. As whanne men prey
apens the saluacion of oure sou
lys or other soules: & not for the
worship of god but for ipocrisi or
els for worldly lucre Or whan mē
preye apens charite: as for to ha/
ue vengeance of ther enemyes: or
for ony thyng apens goddis wor
shyp: and in ther prayer submytt
not ther wyl to the wylle of god
Euery prayere that is made to
the worshypp of god by weye of
charite and for a good end with the
purpose to plese god: that prayer
is made with deuocion: thow we
be that preyeth be distracte: and
thenketh not on his wordys: &
perauenture understondeth them
not: ne hath but lytel lihing ther
in / Netheleſſe man and woman
oweth to do ther deuoure: to the/
be on god / and of that that he set
the in his prayere.

¶ The tenthe chapter.

Diues. Thy speche please
me: seye forthe what thou
wylte Pauper. As I seide first
al that lette man or woman of
ther good dedys: and good pur=
pose and tyse them to synne and
foly and bryng them in erroure
or eresie by mys techyng be ma=
sters and spynnys of the synde.
Whyche as criste sayth in the gos
pel is a manqueller from the be=
ginige of the world For throug
hys mys counseyle: and hys so=
dinge: he slough al mankynde
bothe gostli and bodely at the be
gynnynge of the worlde. Also he
slough hymsilfe throughe pride
and many thousandys aungels
that assentyd to hym / And yet he
sesethe not to sle mannys soule:
by false suggestiouns and temp/
taciouns: and that by hymsilfe &
whanne men se hym not / And su
tyme visibily in the lickeness of
sum visible creature: as so he tep/
ted criste: eue and saint martyn:
mani other / Sumtyme he temp/
tethe and sleth mannis soule bi
hys cymes that be wicked men &
wymen: Also men of holy chur=
che sle men and wymen gostli of
goddes word and of gode techīg
For as crist sayth Nō ĺsolo pane
Biuit homo: sz in omni verbo ꝗ

℈he fyfte

procedit de ore dei. m⁺. iiii°. c°. Man lyueth not only in bodeli brede: but moche more he lyueth in euery worde that cometh of goddes mouthe: that is to saye i the wordys of the trewe prechour For euery tru̅e prechoure sentte of god is cleped goddes mouthe And therfore god saythe to the p̅phete/ Si seperaueris preciosum a vili quasi os meum eris. Jere. x̊s°./ If thou departe precious thinge from thinge that is foule and of no pryse: thou shalt be as my mouthe/ For it longeth to ye prechoure of goddis worde to co̅me̅nde vertuis and despise vices to chese truthe and lette falshede to commende heuen blysse: and goostly thinges and repreue pom̅pe and pryde of thys worlde and fleshly thinges/ And thāne is ye prechoure as goddes mouth and speketh wyth goddes mouthe: and bys worde is goddes worde by the whyche man and woman lyueth goostly: and escapeth endles deth. And therfore dauid sayth Misit verbum suum et sana uit eos: et eripuit eos de interi ticionibus eorum/ God hath sent hys worde and hathe heled hys people from goostly sekenes: and delyuered them from ther diynge whanne they shulde haue dyed: through synne and helle payne

And therfore he sayth in the gospel. that who so kepeth hys worde: he shal not ataste the deth wi the oute ende. Sythe that god des worde is lyfe and saluacion of mānys soule: alle tho that let goddes worde: and lette them haue auctorite of god and by order take to preche and teche that they maye not preche and teche goddys worde ne goddes salue: they be mansleers goostli and gilty of as many soules as perisshe and dye goostly by such lettynge of goddes worde: and namely these proude couetouse prelatys and curates that neyther kunne teche ne wyl teche: ne suffre other that kūne and wil and haue auctoryte to teche of god and of the busshop that peueth theym ther orders: but lette theym for drede that they shulde haue the lesse of ther sugettis or els the lesse be set by: or elles that ther synnes shul de be knowe by prechyng of goddes worde/   And therfore leuer they haue to lese the soulys that criste so dere bought thā to here ther owne synnes openly repreued generaly among other mānys synys As saint austen sai th goddis worde owth to be wor shipped as moch as cristys body And as moch synne doth he that letteth goddes word & despiseth

Precepte.

goddis worde or taketh it retchelesly as he that despiseth goddis body: or through hys neccligens leteth it falle to the ground .i.q. i.int rogo boe / There the glose shewethe: that it is more profitable to here goddes worde in prechynge: than to here ony messe: And rather a man shulde forbere hys messe than hys sermoun. For by prechynge folke be styrede to contricion and to forsake synne and the fende and to loue god: & godenes & be illumined to know ther god and vertues from vices truthe from falshede: and to forsake errours and eresies / By the messe be they not so / But if they come to messe in synne: they goo awey in synne: and shrewis they come: and shrewys they wende. And also the vertue of the messe stondethe pryncypaly in true byleue of the messe: and specialy of criste that is there sacred i the ost But that may man lerne by prechinge of goddes worde: and not by hering of mes / And I so moch seryuge of goddes worde: trwly preched is better than heringe of messe / Netheleſſe the messe profiteth them that be in grace to gete ye more grace and forȝeuenes of venyal synne: and encreſſing of mede: and leſſynge the payne of purgatory. And the preſt mai

be so good that his prayer for reuerence of the sacrament shal gete grace of amendement of hym that he preyeth for both be gode But goddes worde owth to be more charged and more despred than heringe of messe. For whanne the people diſſpiseth goddes worde / & loth goddes worde / that is gostly fode to man: that pepse is but ded in goddes syght: and nyghe to the pathys of hell. And therfore dauid saith: Omnem escam abhominata est anima eorum: et appinquauerūt vsq; ad portas mortis. Ther soulis haue lothid al gostly mete: that is to saye al trwe preching & teching of goddis worde and so they be nyghed to the pathys of dethe.

The eleuenth chapter.

Also tho prelates and curatys be gylty of maſſlaughter gostly: that knowe ther sugettys in dedly synne: and wyl not snybbe them ne speke ayens ther synne. di. plii. ephe sseis: And therfore god sayth to euery curate & prelate of holy churche and to p/ chours of goddes worde / I haue made the a bailwaite to the peple of israel: that is to saye to crissten peple & thou shalt here the worde of my mouth & tel it the impna/

The fyfte

me And if I saye to the synfulh he shal dye and thou telle it him not: ne speke not to hym that he may amende him and turne him fro his wicked wey and syse that synful wretche for thy defaute shal dye in his synne: And I shal seke the blood and the deth of hī of thin hond: and thou shalt answere for hys deth. Ezegie. iii°c. Also they be called mē sleers: ꝑ de fraude and take alwey holy chur che goodes .vii. q. ii. qui ꝑbi: q: q abstulerit / Also that preeste is a man sleer gostly that denieth the sacrament of penaunce to man or woman in his laste ende and wyl not assoyle theym whanne they repent them: and aye absolucion / For so they put folke in despeire ayens ye goodnesse and mercy of god that is endles: and alwey redy to al that seke mercy as long as the soule and ye body be knyt to gedre: Exaumple of the thefe that henge on the right syde of crist: the which for payne knowleched his synne and ayed grace and gate the blysse of paradyse: whanne he sayde lorde have thou minde of me whan thou comest into thy kingdome / And a non criste rightful iuge that best knewe his herte sayd to him: I sey ye for sothe: thys daye thou shalt be wythe me in paradise.

xx Bi. q. Bi. si presbit. q c° agnouimus / Where the lawe sayth that they that be so harde vp on men in ther dying: do not els but put deth to deth Deth of soule to be the of body Oiues. Moch folk presume so moch on the merci of god: that they yeue no tale to lyue in ther synne moche of al ther life in hope to haue mercy in last ende. Paul. And yet if they aye mercy in due maner: they shal haue mercy: as the lawe sayth wel in the same place: and holy writ in many places / For god sayth by the prophete. Ezechielis xxviii.c° That in what oure the sinner sighith for his sinne and aye mercy I shal forȝeue him his sinne and forȝete his synne Nethles I dare not hote suche folke ꝑ they shulde haue grace stede and tyme to aye mercy as the nedeth to aye For comonly such maner folke be desseyued by soden deth or elles in ther dyinge they lese ther bedys and ther wyttys: and begynne to raue. Or elles they haue so moch payne in ther body and so moch besynesse withe the world. that they thenke neyther of god ne of thē silfe / And as seith saint austen in his sermone de innocentibus Justo dei iudicio agitur Et moriens obliuiscatur sui: q dū viueret oblit⁹ est. It is

Precepte.

goddis rightful dome þ he forye/ te hymsilfe in his dyinge that haþ forȝeten god in hys lyuynge. As fel in englond besides oxen=ford/ There was a tyraunt in þe cūtre that dredde not god ne had pytye of man/ Ofte men preched hym: & conseyled hym to gode He had despite of ther wordes: And sayde that if he myght haue thre wordes byfore his dying: he shulde be saued as wel as the beste man lyuynge/ At the laste it by=fel that he rode by the weye to be on a queste byfore a iustice/ And he bygan to slepe: hys hors stom blid: & he fel doune & brake hys necke/ And in his fallyng he say=de with greate herte. Dre Daun=te a deblis. that is to say in en=glisshe: Nowe forth to the deuyl And so he had thre wordis to his dampnacion: not to his saluaci=on/ Therfore the Wisman saytħ De ppiciatu peto̅ noli esse sine metu/ Be not wythoute drede of forȝeuenesse of thy synnes: ne put synne to synne: ne sele not þ the mercy of god is grete: he shal haue mercy on the multytude of thy synnes/ For mercy & wrathe also hastli come fro him nighe to mankynd/ But his wrath loke=th to sinners that wyl not amēd theym: and hys mercy to theym that wyl amend them Ne terdas

conuerti ad dominum &c. Ther/ fore lette not to turne the to god and delaye not from day to day For if thou do: hys wrathe shal come sodenly and destroye the. Eccl.5°.c. For suche folke that be so bolde in ther synne in hope of the merci of god & do the worð by cause of his godnes: they scorne god and seke vēgeaunce: and no mercy/ They take hede to his mercy: and not to hys rightful= nesse. Dauid saythe. Vniuerse vie domini misericordia et veri= tas. Al the weyes of god and al his domes be mercy and teruthe: If thou seke mercy it were ayēs hys rightfulnesse but he shewed mercy: and but thou seke mercy rightfulnesse moste dampne the Seke mercy: and mercy and his rightfulnesseWyl saue ye: if thou seke it in due maner.

The vii. chapter.

Dives. These wordes be gode and confortable and resonable: Say forth what thou wylt Pauper. Also he is a man/ sleer gostly: that maketħe ony man or woman to forswere thē For he sleth hys owne soule and he soule þ he doth soo forswere hym. xxii. questione. 5. ille Al

The fyfte

so men sle theymsilffe as ofte as they assent to wicked thoughtis in herte: & turne them aweye fro god in whom is al oure lyfe And therfore salomon sayth. Auertis paruulor interficiet eos. pu.i°. that the turnig away of the lytel children sle them / For they that sone be ouer come in temptacion and sone assent to the fend: be lykened to yonge children that be feynt and feble to withstond ony thinge / Of such children god saith that y child of an hundred yere shalbe acursed of god isa. lx° c. Also they sle ther soules that gedre foule lustys & vnlesul desires in ther herte and wyl not redely put them oute Therfore ye wyse man sayth. Desideria occidunt pigrū. puer. xxi. c. Wicked desiris sle theym that is slowe to put them oute / And therfore dauid sayth Beatus qui tenebit et allidet peruulos suos ad petram Blessid be he that shal holde him with god and smyte doune hys smale yonge thoughtys and desirys to the stone: that is cryste. Blessed is he that a non as he begynneth to haue suche wycked thoughtys / anon beginne to thynke on cristis passion: and of goddes lawe as sayth saint ierom in hys pystle. Ad paulam et eustochium Diues. It foloweth

of thy wordys that Who so doth ony dedly synne: he is a manssleer: And so euery synne is forbode by this precepte. Non occides Thou shalt not slee / Why haue than god ten preceptis. syth they be al cōprehendid in one Paup. For dulnes of manys wyt: it neweth to yeue mo than one to declare manys synne: that he may knowe Whanne he synneth: and solue he may fle syne Al the lawe and al the prophycie as criste seith in the gospel hangeth in two preceptys of charite Which teche be to loue oure god aboue al thinge: and oure euencristen as oure silfe / But yet god wold declare tho two preceptys by ten preceptis that man & woman shuld the better knowe them and preseshin: & the more sle his offes Diues. Why declared he then more by ten preceptis than by twelue or by nyne / For he myght haue youen many mo: Whanne he yaue but ten / Pauper to yeue of don many was not prophitable ne to yeue oudon felwe / And therfore god yaue hys heestys in the noumbre of ten / for as ten is noumbre perfyte: and contepneth al noumbrys: so goddes lawe is parfyte: and al is compreshended in ten hestys that be so knytte togedre and of so greate accord tha

Precepte.

who so trespaseth in one he tres∕
paseth in alle/And therfore sai∕
the saint James in hys pystle:þ
tholw a man kepe al the lawe:⁊
he offende in one:he is gilty in al
For why sayth he:god that bad
the do no lecherye: He badde the
not stee/And therfore sayth he:
Thowe thou do no lecherye and
thou stele:thou brekest the lawe.
Jacobi.i°.c°. For as sayth saint
austen.in li.10 de decem cordis.
Alle the ten comaundementys be
conteyned in the two preceptys
of charitye:And the two precep∕
tys of charitie be conteyned and
knyt in thys one precepte of kin
de.Quod tibi non vis fieri:alte∕
ri ne facias. tobie.iiii°. That
that thou wylte not be do to the
do it not to another:And soo as
saynt austen sayth there:Al the
lawe is conteyned I thys one pre
cepte of kynde.That thou wylt
not be do to the:do it thou not to
non other/And so nedys he that
offendeth in one: offendeth in
al/And therfore dauid and saint
austen also clepe goddes lawe a
sawtree and an harpe of ten cor∕
dys/And therfore dauid byddes
the us preyse god in the harpe:⁊
in the sawtre of ten cordys:that
is to saye in good kepinge of the
ten comaundementys/Confite∕
mini domino in cithara in psal∕
terio decem cordarū psallite illi

And if it be so: that one corde in
the sawtree or in the harpe be bro
ke:or oute of tune of a corde wᵗ
other cordys:al the songe that is
pleyde therin shalbe vnlikynge
to al that here it and not plesaūt
As telleth the mayster of kynde
Lt°.xviii°. That thowe the har/
pe be wel stringed wyth stringis
made of a shepe: and ther be one
stringge that is made of a wolfe
sette in the harpe:it shal make al
other at discorde: So that
they shulde not a corde whyle it
is there And it shal frete at wo al
the other cordys/Ryght so tholw
a man or a woman kepe wel all
the comaundementys as to ma∕
nys syght: if he breke one: he is
gylty of alle in goddes syght: as
saint James sayth and hys lyfe
whyle he is suche is not plesaūt
to god/And the songe of his har
pe: that is his spupyng and his cō
uersacioun is at discorde wyth e
god and al the courte of heuen
⁊/as the wolfe is alwey contra∕
rius and enmie to the shepe:so is
he at discorde and enmye to god
bys shepe that be al tho þ be I wei
of saluacyoun:And as longe as
thou kepeste w̄ el the ten hestys I
lowenesse:so long the stringes of
thyn harpe be in good acorde as
the stryngges that be made of a
shepe/But if thou folow the ma
ners of the wolfe.and breke ont
q i

265

ℭhe fyfte.

of goddes cōmaundementys by gyle: by rauyne. By malyce and falſe couetyſe: by falſe cōtriulge Thānne thou makeſt l thyn harpe a ſtringe of the Wolfe: Whych ſhal ſhend the harpe of thy ſuulg and deſtroy it: But thou doo it awey by ſoroWe of herte: ſhrift of mouthe & amendys makyng.

ℭhe viii. chapter.

Dues. I wolde ſe more opēnli thou be that ſyneth in one ſynneth al ten cōmaūdemētis Pauper. If thou treſpaſe in manſlaughter: thou treſpaſyſte ayens alle ten heeſtys/ For thou Vn worſhipeſt thy god: in ỹ that thou brecheſt hys cōmaūdemēt: and ſo defouleſt hys image Alſo thou takeſt in veyne hys name: that is criſte and criſtē For thou doyſt not as acriſtē man ſhuld do/ Alſo thou halowpſt not from ſynne as god bad the by the thirtd cōmaundement/ Alſo thou deſpiſeſt ...d not worſhipeſt fader and moder that be god and holy church: and thi bodely fader and moder/ For thy Wycked tacchys be ſhame and ſhenſhip to thy fader and moder/ Alſo thou doeſte lecherye in that ỹ thou loueſt thi Wycked Wyl and thi malyce more than god/ And for to haue thy Wycked Wyl perfourmed: thou forſakeſt god and takyſt thi ſoule to the fende/ For What thinge man loueth mor than god: With that thinge he dothe goſtly lechery and fornicacion and auoutre Alſo thou beryſt falſe Witneſſe & ſpeſt many leſingys to mayntein thy ſynne: or elſes to hyde it: Alſo thou ſteleſt thi ſoul & his ſoul Whom thou ſleeſte fro god: that bought hi ſo dere alſo Whā thou ſleeſt: thou doſte ayēſt the ynnth the tenthe cōmaundement/ For euery manſlaughter is do for couetyſe of vengeaunce: or for couetyſe of erthely good. or for couetyſe of fleſſhely luſt: as of mēnys Wyues: or of ther children or of ther ſeruantys: or for couetiſe of Worſhyp: ſo that if thou ſlee: thou forfetiſt ayens al ten commaundemētis/ And ſo it may be ſheWid of ech of al ten. that he ỹ brecheth one: brecheth al: and he ỹ is gylty l one dedly ſinne: is gilty l of vii. a i alle ỹ cōmaūdemētis And in token of thys ſaint Iohn ſalwe a Woman ſityng on aredde beſt ful of names of blaſphemie Which beſte had ſeuen hedis & ẋ hornys. Apoc°. ẋvii°. By thys Woman is Vnderſtonde pryde. & banyte of this Worlde/ By the red beſt that ſhe ſate on is Vnderſtond the fende & dedly ſyne that is ful of blaſphemie ayens god: This beſte had ſeuen hedys and ten hornys: That is to ſai ſeuen dedly ſynnes and breking of the ten cōmaundementys: in token that what man or woman falle/ the to oni dedly sine opēli: he falle th̄i al seuē preuest i goddis sight. And whanne he breketh one cōmaundement: he breketh̄e alle. And therfore sayth saint James þ he that offendeth in one offen/ deth̄e i al ꝯ is gylty of al. iac. ii. c°.

The xiiii. chapter.

DIues what longeth to ye precepte of kynde þ saynt austen speketh of: to the loue of god or to the preceptys of the firste table. For we may do to god neyther good ne euyl. Pauper. soth it is þ we mai not do to god neyther gode ne euyl. And yet as saynt austen sayth in the same boke. De dece cordis. Thys precepte of kynde byddeth vs to loue oure god and serue him wel & trwly: and kepe alle hys heestys. For why al we be goddys seruā/ tys. And if thou haddist a seruāt sayth saint austen: thou woldest that thy seruaunt serued the wel and trwly. I pray the thāne sayth he serue thou wel & trwly thy god: that is thy lorde and his for/ de: Thou woldeste that thy ser/ uant were trwe to ye and not fal se be thou not fals to god. Thou woldest no mā shuld defoule thy wyfe: defoule thou not thi soule

that is goddys spouse. ne noy o/ ther soule: Thou woldeste that no mā shuld destroi thi house: ne defoule it: defoule thou not than goddes temple: that is euery cle/ ne cristen soule. Defoule it not by lecherye ne by no dedly synne. For saint poule sayth: that who so defouleth goddes temple: god shal destroy him. Thou woldest thy seruant kept wel thy cōmaū/ dementys: and dyd not aȝens thy byddynge. kepe than thou god/ des cōmaundentys: and do not ayens hys byddyngys. Thou woldest that no man despise thy image paynted on a borde: de/ spyse thou not goddes image by ony dedly synne. For syth thou may not please god in sinne and shrewednesse: therfore thou offē dest thy god in thi synne and thy corrupcion: and doest wrong to hi thi sylfe. Thou doest wrōg to his grace: to his gyft: thou mai: not do wrong to thy brother but thou do wronge to god: þ is thi lorde and his also. And therfore saythe saint iohn i his pistle that who so saythe þ he loueth god: & he hate his brother: he is a lyer. i. io. iiii°. For in that he doth wrō/ ge principaly to god: and to hys brother also. And therfore god sayth. Quicūqȝ effuderit huma gum sanguinem: effundetur sā: nuinis eius. geñ. ix. He that shed

q ii

267

The fyfte.

deth oute mannys blode wrōg/fully: hys bloode shalbe shedde: For whi saythe he: man is made to the lykenes of god And so mā slaughtyr is open wronge do to god i p that his seruaūt is so slai= in: and his image dispysed: and distroyde. Therfore god sayd to the first manslcer that was caim Which sloughe hys brother abel falsely for enuy of his owne go/denesse: What hast thou do caim The voyse of the bloode of abel thy brother crieth to me fro erth and ayeth vēgeaūce of the/ And therfore thou shalt be cursed vp/on erthe: Whyche hathe opened his mouth & hath takē the blode of thy brother abel of thyn hōd Thou shal traueil in tylth of ye lōde: & it shal yeue the no frute: Thou shalt be wanderinge and flemed vpon erthe. geñ. iiii°. And the same vēgeaunce comōli so lowth murdre: For murdre mai not be hydde: But nyght and dai it ayethe vengeaunce/ The mur dre shal myshappe in his doinge and be vnstable and wandering and odious in his lyuing/ This synne of manslaughtir is so gre/uous in goddes sight That he cōmaunded in the olde law that if ony man bi lyinge in a wayte or by preuy aspyinge: or by pur pose kylled ony man: and after

fled to goddes auter for socoute he shulde be take all aye thens & be slayne for that deth. exo. xxi°. c°. And therfor saint Iohn sayth i the boke of goddys preuitees p̄ he that sleeth shalbe slayne: Apoc: xiii°: For as criste saythe in the gospel. that same mesure p men mete to other: shalbe moten aye to them / And therfore in tyme of hys passion he seide to peter put vp thy swerde For eche man that vsethe swerde to shedde mannis blode wythoute lawful power graunted of god: shal peryssh by the swerde: that is to sai bi swerd of bodely vengeaunce : Or by the swerd of goddes mouth: whiche is ful sharpe on euery side vnysshinge bothe body and soule: Apoc. i°: c°. For comonly he that vsethe the swerde: or ony wepen to slee ony man or woman he sle ethe firste himsilfe by the swerde of hys owne malyce But trespa sours that wil not be amended in other maner. may by iuste do me be slayne by them that bere the swerde of temporal punysshyng as saint poule sayth. Ad romanos xiii°.

The vj. chapter.

Iues. It semeth to moch folke that god forbedeth

By hys precepte al maner sleynge bothe of man and of beste / For he saybe generaly. Non occides Thou shalt not sle. Paup. By thys worde occides I latyn he specifieth a shelweth he þ he forbyddeth sleynge of man: and not of beste. For occisio in latyne is in englissh manslaughter quasi hominum cesio And therfore the p pre englisshe is thys. Non occides Thou shalt not slee no man Diues. Whanne god sayd the sixt heeste: that non mechaberis. þis to saye thou shalt do no lecherye he forbyddeth al maner of lecherye. And whanne he sayde the seuen heestys: Non furtum facies þis thou shalt not stele: he forbiddeth al maner theft both of mā and of beste and of al other thīges / And by the same skil me thynketh whanne he badde Us not sle: he forbadde Us al maner sleynge: Pauper. It is not the same skil ne lyke that shyl. For as I sayd firste by pperte of the same worde Occides: He forbiddeth only manslaughter. God graunted man power to slee bestes and lyue therby. gen̄.ix.c. But he graunted hym neuer to do lechery wythe ony creature: ne take ony thynge by wey of stelthe: or of false couetise Diues. Contra te we fynde that Balaam rode on hys asse to curse goddis peple ayens goddys wylle. An aungel stode in a right streyght Wepe ayens him The asse sawe the aungel and fledde asyde for drede of þe aūgels swerd a bare Balaam apens the walle: and brosyde hys foote Balaam sawe not the aungel / And therfore he was wrothe wyth the asse and smote him ful harde thāne the asse throughe the might of god Vndernam Balaad: hys master and sayd to hī: What haue I do ayens the: why betest thou me? Thanne Balaam sayde: For thou haste wel deserued it: wolde god I hadde a swerd to slee the: Thanne the asse saide ayen: Haue I not alwey be thy beste on whiche thou hast be wont alwey to ryde. Seye whanne I dyd euer the suche disese into this day / And anon god opened the iyen of Balaam: a thā he saw þe aūgel stōdig aȝēs hī wt his swerd drawne And the aungel sayde to Balaam / why haste thou so bete thyn asse / For butte thyn asse hadde goon oute of the wey a youen me place I shulde a haue slayn the: and þe asse shuld lyued. Numeri.xxii°. Syth thā it is so that Balaam was blamed for he bette hys asse not withstōding that he hurt him: moch mo to he shulde haue be blamed if he

hadde slayne him And so it seme/
the that it is not leful to slee any
beste Pauper. It is grauntid to
man to sle bestys whāne it is p̄-
fitable to him for mete or clothi-
ge: or to auoyde noyaunce of ye
bestys: whyche be noyouse to man
And therfore god sayde to noe/ &
to hys children/ Also fysshes i the
see be take to poure power: and
to youre hondes: and al thinge þ
stryretħe and lyueth vpon erthe:
beste and bridde shalbe to you in
mete I haue take them al to you
as grene erbys: oute taken that
ye shalle not ete flesshe withe the
blode: Gen. ix c: And in another
place he sayth thus: If the lyke
to ete flesshe: sle and ete after the
grace and the gyfte that god hathe youen the: so that thou ete it
withe oute bloode. Deut°. xii°.
And so grauntid god to man for to
slee bestes flesshe and foule to his
profite: But not to sle thē for cru-
elstye: ne for sylynge in vanyte
and shrewidnesse / And therfore
whanne he forbadde man to ete
flesshe with the blode: he forbad
him to slee bestes by wey of cru-
elstye: or for sylynge i the shrew-
ednes/ And therfore he sayd Ete
ye no flesshe with the blode: that
is to saye: with crueltye / For I
shalle seke the bloode of youre
soulys of the honde of al bestys:
that is to saye I shal take venge

aunce for alle the bestys that ye
slayne only for crueltye of soule
and syyhynge i shrewidnes. Gen.
ix. c. For god that made al hath
cure of al. And he shal take vengeaūce of al that mysuse his creature / And therfore salomon saythe that he shal arme creaturys to
vengeaūce of hys enemyes Ar-
mabit creaturam in vlcionem i-
micorū. sap. v°. c°. And therfore
men shuld haue rueth on bestys
of brydays and not harme them
withoute cause in takȳg rewarde
þ they be goddes creaturys/ And
therfor they that for cruelte and
vanyte heded bestes and turmēt
bestys or foule more thā it is spedefull to mannys lyuynge: they
synne in cas ful greuously.

¶The xvi. chapter.

Dyues. As thou saydest byfore by this comaūdemēt
is forbode al wrongful massau-
ghter / Tel me in what case it is
leful to sle any man Paup. Sutyme manslaughter is do by hate and enuye: as whāne a man
is slayne maliciously of hys enmye. Sutyme it is do for wicked
couetyse to haue a mannys gode: Sutyme it is doo by ordre of
obedience and processe of lawe:
as whā a mā is slayne by aqust
& by sentence of a iuge ordynarye
Sutyme māslaughter is do for
nede & for helpe of the comontye

Precepte.

a for þe saluacion of þem þat be vngylty / As whãne þe knyght fightethe in his right / (for ye ryght sleethe hys aduersary. To sle any man into ye first manere þat is to saye / for hate wrath & enmyte: or for false couetyse: is alwey vnleful. But for to slee a man þe third maner and þe forthe / þat is to saye by processe of lawe withe a lawful iuge / or by lawe of armes by þe hondys of knyghtys or of men of armes rewled by law of god it is leful: whã me be gilty / & therfor saint austẽ saythe li°.i° de libro arbiterio If it be so that the knyght sle his aduersary in rightful bateyle: or ye iuge and hys officerys sle hym þ is worthy to dye / me thenketh þei synne not / But lene frende thre thinges be nedeful / so that manslaughter shuld be leful and rightful / Firste that the cause be rightful ordre & processe of lawe and þ iustice haue lawful power to slee / and that he þ shalbe slayn be conuicte of hys trespase / Also the intencion of the iuge / and of the pursuers and of the officerys be rightful: that they slee him in saluacioun of the right / And for saluauacõn and ensaumple of other / not for likig of vengeance ne of crueltye: not hauig lykig I his peyne: so þ the cause be right-

ful and the ordre and processe: & the entencion be rightful: Justa causa .iustus ordo .iustus alm⁹. Diues. Cõtra te. yet the gospel sayth / Quod de⁹ coniuxit hõ nõ seperet .m .ix. There shulde no man departe thinge that god hath the knyt to gydre. But god hath knytte the soule and the body to gidre therfor thãne it is not leful to any man for to departe ye soule from the body: neyther to slee man ne woman Paup. Whãne the man that is gilty is slayn rightfully by the law: man sleethe him not / But as goddes mynysters and goddes offcers / for the lawe of god & god hisilffe sle him & that that god cõmaudeth suche to be slayne / God is pricipal iuge of hys dethe / and man is but goddes officer to do his bydding And therfore sayth the lawe that thei that sle men rightfully be not clepyd mansleers for why sayth he the lawe sleeth thẽ not the. xxiii. q.v. si holcidiũ & l qdiB⁹ sc.

The xvii. chapter.

Dives. Sythe it is so that trespasors lawfully may be slayne by the byddyng of god why maye not prelatys of holy churche and mynystrys of ye auter sle suche trespasours / ne sit in the dome of manys deth: ne yeue

The fyfte.

the sentence/ne yeue assistence to the domesmā sythē ī thē old lawe prestes and mynystres of ye auter myght lawfully sle trespasors as we fynd in many places of holy wryt Exo. xxxii. de seruitis et numeri. xxii. de phinees. i. regum xv. de samuele q̄ īterfecit agag. Et iii°. regū xviii°. de helia q̄ īterfecit sacerdotes Baal. Paup. As ye law sepṫḣ. xxiii. q̄: viii. occidit Moche thyng was lefull ī ye old lawe: that is not leful in the new lawe In the olde lawe the swerd was grauted to prestes & minystres of goddes auter In the new lawe god forbiddeth thyem the swerde/ whanne he seyde to peter in tyme of hys passion/ anon as he hadde betaken hym power to make the sacrament of the auter Conuerte gladiū tuū in vagina &c. Turne thy swerde ito the she the For he that smith with swer/ de/ shal perisshe with the swerde. In such wordys god forbiddeth the swerd to al the mynystres of goddes auter/ as the lawe sayth xxviii. q̄. viii. de epīstīs. cū alīīs capīīs sequenetib; Diues. Why forbadde he them the swerde. Pauper. For god wolde that men of holy churche shuld be mē of pees of mercy and of pyty/ And ther/ fore he sayde to theym/ Discite a me quia mitis sum & humilis cor-

de. Lerne ye of me: for I am softe and meke of herte. mᵗ. xi°. c°: He badde them not lern to pley with the swerde/ ne with the staffe: ne lerne to fyght and shote. to sle ther enemyes: But he badde them lerne to be softe and meke of herte and to lyue in pacience as lambys amōgys wolues And he bad them loue ther enemyes: and do gode to them that hate them. mᵗ. v°. c. He badde them shewe pacience/ pees and pyty/ not only in worde wyl and dede: But he bad them absteyne them from al to- kenes of ynpacience of ynpees: and of crueltye And for that shed- dynge of blode and manslaugh- ter is ofte token of ynpacience & ynpees of wrathe and of cruelte in them that slen and disposythe them to crueltye/ Therfore criste forbadde the swerd to al the my- nystres of the auter. Diues. Tel me some other skyl. Paup. Another skyl is thys For the sa- crament of the auter that the py- stes make by the vertue of cristes worde is a sacrament of charitie and of oneshed/ For it represents the oneshede that is bytwene crist and holy churche: And also it re- presenteth the oneshed of the sou- le with the body/ For as the sou- le quykeneth the body/ so cryste by the sacrament of the auter &c-

272

Precepte.

heneth holy church a manis soul Also it representyth the onehede of the godhede with our manhed i crist a therfore holy church sayth thus. Nam sic' ala racionalis et caro vnus est homo: ita deᵘ et homo vnus est ȝpc Ryȝht as rosonable soule and the flesshe is one man: so god and the man is one criste, and one criste is both god and man And therfore he that destroyeth the onehede of the soul with the body and departeth the atwey by manslaughter he shewth not in himsilfe ne in his dede: the sacrament of onehede of crist with holy church and of the godhede with the manhede in criste. Butte he doth apens that sacrament by speracion and diuision. that he maketh i manslaughter: and shedding of blode And therfore he is irreguler: and vnable to make the sacrament of ye auter And for the same skyl if a ma haue wedded two wyues and so deperted his flesshe in diuers wymen, he is irreguler. and vnable to the auter And therfor not only prestys: But dekones and subdekenes in that they be assent to the preste in makynge of the sacrament must be witout such departing that is contrary to the sacrament of endles charitie and of onehede bytwene god and holy church and bytwene al goode cristē peple þ is i charite for al they be one a com to gidre i this sacrament · For this skyl it is not leful to men of holy church to shed mannys blode: ne to sle: ne to mayme The newe testament is a lawe of loue And therfor criste wold þ ye mynystres of the auter i the new testament that shulde mynystre the sacrament of hys endles loue and of his endles mercy to mankynde, that they shewe loue mercy: and petye: and noo tokēn of crueltye The olde testamēt was a lawe of drede and duresse: and nigħe al the sacrifices that the prestes made was don with sheddig of blod not only in figure of cristys passion: But also i tokēn þ he that synned was worthy too be slayne as the beste that was slayne That was offeridde for hys synne, And therfore the swerde was graunted too prestes And the mynesterys of the olde lawe to punysshe rebelles: whanne it nedeth And moche of ther office was to shedde blod And so by ther offyce they were disposed to crueltye: In so moche that they were notte aferede too slee goddes sonne ther lorde ther souereyne: and ther god, And for that preestys of the olde lawe be cruel tye slowe criste god a lord of alle

273

The fyfte

Therfore sheddyng of blode & man/slaughter is forbode to preestys & the newe lawe/and maketh them vnable to the auter: that shedde mennys blode or helpe therto.

The .viii. chapter.

Sheddynge of blode in men of holy churche is so abhomynable & orrible i goddes sight: y if any clerk dye i batayl & fightyg or i pleies of hethē men of whi che foloueth sheddinge of blode: and dethe/as in pleyinge at the swerde and bokeler/at the staffe two bondis swerde hurlebat in turmentys: in iustys: for that clerke holy churche shal make no solempne messe ne solempne prayere for him but he shuld be beried witheoute solempneyte of holy churche. xviii. q. viii. q cūq3 clericus And if a man in hys woodnes: & ranynge sle man and woman or childe: though his woodnes passed yet he is irreguler and vnable to goddes auter v.q.i. si quis insaniens/Netheleesse if he be preest or that case fall bym whāne his woodnes is passed and be in hope of sehet beīthe he may sey his messe Also if a man smyte child: man or woman by wey of chastisyg & he dye of that stroke: he is irregu

ler. xv. q. i. Si quis non iratus & extra. li. v. de homicidiis. c. psbīterū. Also if he be in doute whether he dye of ye stroke he shal abstepne hym from goddes auter. Extra. e. ad audientiam/Also if a preste or clerke or any man see the thefe that robbeth the churche he is irreguler. Extra. e. significasti/Also if clerkes fight ayens sarasynes and ayens hethen men if they sle any man wome or child they be irreguler & if they be i doute whether thei slough or nai thei shulde abstepne them from the auter/Extra. e. peticio. Also ye iuge. the aduocate. the accessoure. the officere. the witnesse by whyche man or woman is slayn and the writer. and he that sayth the sentence or redeth in dome ye examinacion of the cause: or wryteth ye enditement or other settris by whiche man or womā is slayne/he is irreguler. though ye cause and the dome be righfful Rap. li°. ii. ti. i. If a man be dryuen by nede to sle man or woman/ if he fled in that nede by hys owne defaute and fledde not that nede: whanne he myght haue fledde: he is ful irreguler. But if it were such nede that he might not fle & ye nede cam not by his defaute holy churche suffereth him in the Cordys that he hath takeen to

Precepte.

mynystre therl butte he shal take non hygher ordre. If any man slee manne woman or childe casuely and by nyfsse happe whether hys ocupacioun was lesful or not lesful: if he dydde not hys besynesse to slee manslaughte he is ful irreguler But if his ocupacion were lesful & he dydde his besynes to slee mãslaughter thow he salbe not byfore al chaunsis þ myght falle: he is not irreguler. Rap.li°.ii°.ti°:i°. With him that sleeth man woman or childe wilfully wyth hond or with tung is no dispensacioun. Jtm̃. If a man smyte a woman with child whã the childe is quyche or poyson hir with venym: if the childe be ded borne: or els born oute of tyme and dye by that poysoun or by þ stroke: he is irreguler: But if the childe were not quyche: he is not irreguler But he shal be punyssh ed by the lawe of holy church: as a manqueller. And so shal ye mã that yeueth venym or any drinke or any other thing to let woman that she may not cõseyue ne bryge forth children. And if the woman wylfully take suche drynkps: or do any mys crafte to let hirsylfe or any other from berige of children: she is amansleer. If many men fyght togedre:& one or mo be slayn & it is not knowē en by whom of that company al that smeten or came for to se: or for to sygt although they smeten not be mansleers.

And al that came to helpe mansleers thowgh they sloghe not:ne hadde wyl to sle: butt come only to conforte and to helpe of ye sleer and al that were on þe wrõg syde: be irreguler. If mã or womã dye by defaute of the leche: & by hys vnkunnynge:and my nyce dyeynē: ye leche is irregulerAnd therfore it is forbode men of holy churche to yeue any persons drynkps or to brinne men by surgery or to kytte them/ For ofte dethe or mayme cometh therof. Also they mayme themsilfe wythoute nedful cause:or be mayned by other men:or by ther owne foly al if they dydde theim gelde to be chaste and soo plese god: they be irreguler For there shuld no mã serue at goddis autð had any greate foule mayme / If a man with drawe him that wold saue a man fro dethe: & if he wyl not himsilfe saue fro ye deth if he may and namely if it longe to hȳ of office: he is irreguler/ Hec Rap.li°.ii°.ti.i°. If any clerke be re any wood or fire or any mater to the brennynge of any eretyke if he be dede therby: or hys dethe hasted therby he is irreguler.

though the pope or the busshoppe yeue pardon to al that helpen to the deth of that eretike. In scī. conf. li°.ii°.ti. q̄.xxv. quid de iꝑ. If a preste sende a yonge chylde to water his hors: though he bidde hym beware of ye water: and the childe by hys sendynge drenche the preste is irreguler: for he put so the childe in auenture. Ibide q̄.xxvii. quid de presbitero. Et hoſt°.li.v.Ru. de holcidio quid de presbitero Diues And what if the preste sende oute his child on his erande barelegged and barefote and euyl clothed in froste and snowe: if the childe dye for colde or take such seknes by that colde that he die therof: is not the preste irreguler Pauper. yis forsoth For he ought to do his diligence to saue ꝑ childe: and to fle that parel in whiche he might lightly falle in that wedr. Diues. And what if any prelate sende oute wetyngly his suget barelegged ℸ barefoote in suche weder: ℸ euyl clothed: if he dye by ꝑ colde that he taketh so by hys sendīg: is ꝑ not ꝑ preſt irreguler Diues. In that that he sleeth hym so by colde: he is irreguler: ℸ mānquellʳ.

The xix. chapter.

Diues..Seye forthe what thou wylt.

Paup. Prelates of holy chirch may not fight ne sle and yit they may styre men of armes and the people to fight for the feyth and for the truthe of goddes lawe: ℸ of holy churche: and though men be slayne therby: they be not irre guler: as the lawe shewth wel. xxiii. q̄. viii. igitur cū aliis c°. If thou go by weye wyt hym ꝑ gothe to slee any man: though thou counseile hym to cese of hs purpose: and wylt not cese ℸ thou goo forth with hym to defende hl: ℸ he sle: thou arte irreguler as seyth. Hoſt. li°. v. Ru. de holcidio q̄. quid si quis. If a clerke pleyn hym to the iustice on hl ꝑ robbed hym of his gode only to haue a⁊ his good and not to pursue hys deth though ye iustice sle ye thef the clerke is not irreguler Ex.c. postulasti ꝛc. tua nos. S. ad vl timū. If a clerke help to take a thefe or to binde hym to lede hī to the iustice: or write only lettre to take ony man: if the thefe be slayne or that man slayn) ye cler ke is irreguler: Netheles he may elepe to bold ye thefe tyl he haue his good or holde hym hīsilfe: ℸ if he crye holde the thefe or crye the ues theues: if it were semely to hl that manslaughter shuld folow therof: he is irreguler: if any mā be slayn therby. But if

Precepte.

he hope therbi onli to haue apeyꝛ his gode without manslaughter he is not irregular: tholwe manslaughter folowed therof / Clerkys may bere wepeyꝛ & hane thei passe by perelouse placys to a sesse theues: But theye owe not to smyte: If a clerke lene ony man bolwe arblast oꝛ oni other wepeyꝛ to seyght wythe: if any man be slayne therwith oꝛ maymed that clerke is irregular If a clerk erre in answeringe and by hys mysse answere folowe manslaughter: if the clerke be holde alwyse man he is irreguler / And tholwe he be but simple lettred and he erre so I suche thinges that he owethe to knowe: and manslaughter come of his mys answere: he is irregular / As if a clerk dsey that it is lessful to sle a thefe: and to sle lecherous: oꝛ to ryse ayens ther souereyns oꝛ sle them: if men folowe his counseile and sle: he is irregular: If a clerke byd men stoppe the theues mouth that he cri not so to lede him the moꝛe stilly and the moꝛe seherly to his iuge: if he be slayne: the clerke is irreguler If men pursue a thefe oꝛ ony other man to take hym: and they aye a clerke if he salwe ony suche if he teche them: oꝛ wysse theym wetinge oꝛ supposinge that thei seke hi foꝛ to desease hi: if b. man

be slayne: the clerke is irreguler: But if he haue no fantasye why they seke him but good: he is not irreguler / Tholwe a man sle not ne peue counseile to sle: if he suffre wetingly ony thynge wherof it is semely to come manslaughter: if ther come therof manslaughter: he is irreguler / Also if he counseile men to take a castel to caste engyne to a towne: oꝛ to a castel: oꝛ to shote into house walled town: oꝛ castel that men were walled theri: if ani man be slain ther by: he is irreguler / If ony man counseile a nother man to goo & sle and be slaine himsilfe: he that paue that counseyle: is irreguler Tholwe pꝛest oꝛ clerke counseile men to seyght foꝛ saluacioun of the cuntre and of the seyth so that he bydde them not sle. he is not irregnler tholw thei sle tholw he bid them put himsilfe to the deth foꝛ saluacion of the cuntre & foꝛ the truthe If oni man wolde sle his enempes. And a nother man counseile him not sle: and he byꝛon that he trust & abydeth and is slaine. he that paue him that coūseyle: is irreguler / But he were in hope to haue saued hys lyfe & that he might haue saued his life oꝛ by poweꝛ oꝛ by frenshyppe: & in truste therof byd sl abyde tha is he not irregular But if he

presumed to moche on hinself:
or was retcheles in kepinge: or
gylous: thane is he irreguler. If
ony man in nede sle his aduersa/
ry to saue his owne life: if he mai
not elles wel saue hym silfe: He
synneth not: so that his nede co/
me not by his foly. For if his fo/
ly brought him in that nede: He
synneth and is irregulat. Hec I
sm. cōfessor. li°. ii°. ti°. t°.

The xx. chapter.

DIues. Me merueleth mo/
che lr hy sheddinge of blo
de and the swerde is soo straytly
forbode to men of holy churche.
For as we rede i the gospel Crist
badde his desiples selle ther clo
thys and bye them swerdys: whā
he sayde. Qui non habet vēdat
tunicam suam: et emat gladiū.
Luc. xvii°. He that hath no swerde sylle hys cote and bye hym a
swerde. Pauper. Crist sayde tho
wordis not to al his apostlis but
to iudas ye traitoure not biddig
him bye him a swerd: But so shew
inge and saiynge by fore the wic
hed wyl and the wicked purpose y iudas was i to begge asu red
to come for to betray criste: and
to take him: that whāne the iew
ys came wyt the sw erdis & staues
to take hym as the gospel saithe

he shulde haue his swarde redye
to defende himsilfe. if ony of cris
tys discyples wolde smyte hym.
And therfore criste sayde not tho
wordys in the plurel nōbre: as
to many: But in the singuler: as
to one iudas alone / For he only
was in purpose to betray hym:
to begge hym a swerde for drede
of knockys / And by tho wordis
criste bad him not begge a swerd
But bi tho wordys he vndernam
him of his malyce: in such maner
that onli iudas shuld vnderstōd
it: and non other of the apostlys
For criste wold not puplissh eyther discure hī to the apostlis but
only vndernam hym in such speche: that only iudas shulde wite
that crpste knewe hys wycked
purpose and wold not discure hī
And so he shewed goodnes ayēs
his malyce to stere hym to repens
taunce. Diues. Why answerde
thanne the apostles and sayd.
Domine ecce duo gladii hic Lor
de lo two swerdys here redy And
oure lorde sayde: Satis est: It
suffisethe: it is inoughe. Pau.
For as I sayde: The apostles
vnderstode not why ne to whom
criste sayde tho wordis And ther
fore they wende as moche folke
wenethe yet that criste hadde bo
de theym haue boughte swerdys
to fyght / And therfore they

Precepts.

answerde in that maner: and by gunne to speke of swerdis and of fightinge/ And thanne crist was displesyd wyth ther spech & bad the be stylle of such spech Satis est. It is inough: it suffiseth ye haue spoken i this maner speche Now nomore of this mater And therfore as luke saythe in the same place: they cesed of ther spech anon and went with crist ito the mounte of oliuete/ On the same maner god sayd to moyses wha he prayde hym that he might entre the londe of byheste. Sufficit tibi. It is inoughe to the þ thou haste sayde. speke nomore to me of thys mater. Deut°.iii°.c°. Also god sayde to the aungel that slowe the peple: Sufficit cōtine manum tuam. It is inough Withold thy honde/ And criste sayd to hys dysciplys in tyme of hys passion Whanne he fond hym slepynge. Sufficit. It is inoughe that ye haue slept nowe: awake ye/ And as he made an end of her slepinge   By thys worde sufficit:it suffisethe: so he made an ende of ther vnkunnyng speche Whanne they begūne to speke of swerdys by thys worde. Satis e It is inoughe: that is to saye: ye haue spoke inoughe in this mat nomore hereof . For they wyste not what crist ment nomore tha they wyste what criste ment wha

he sayde to iudas. Quod facis fac cecius. That thou doiste to it anon. In suche wordys criste vndernam iudas of his euyl pur pose þ he shuld an:20 hl/ And yet it is a custum with moch folke þ Whanne theye here ther children or seruantys speke vnwysly to put them to silence and do theym be stylle wyth the same worde: and say: sone it is inoughe thou hast sayde inoughe. Diues. And many clerkys say: that whanne the apostlys sayde lo here two swerdys: and criste sayd ayen Satis est It inoughe. In tho wordys crist graunted men of holy chur che tho swerdys: bothe goostly swerde and bodely swerde Pauper. Theye erre as the apostlys did For thei vnderstode not whi ne to whom criste saide tho wordys / For criste graunted neuyr too clerkys the bodely swerde to shedde blode: But he forbad it to them in the same tyme whanne he vndernam peter smiting with the swerde and bad hym put vp hys swerde into the shethe/ For whi sayth he:who that smytethe wythe swerde: He shall perysshe witthe the swerde/ And so alle the processe of the gospel if men vn derstond it wel: sheweth þ cryste hathe forbode men of holy chur ch the bodeli sword/ & therfore as saith saint ambrose ther armuer

279

The fyfte

and ther fyghtinge shuld be bytter teerys and holy prayers. Diues. Pet contra te Criste sayth in the gospel, Non veni pacem mittere sz gladium. I cam not saith he to sende pees in erthe: but the swarde. m'.y.c°. Pauper. By the swerde I that place is vnderstod the swarde of goddys worde: as saythe the glose. By such swarde man is departed from synne and from wycked cumpanye: as the gospel shewethe wel there. And by thys swerde synne is slayn in mannys soule. Diues. Sythe god forbad men of holy churche the swerde and she doyng of blod and manslaughter: why slow saynt peter ananyam and saphariam: hys wyfe for hyr false couetouse and for hyr lesynges. auctuū. 8°. Pauper. As the lawe sayth xxiii.q.viii. petr⁹. He slowe them not wyth the material swerde: but only by power that god yaue hȳ to do myraclys, wyth hys prayers be reysed a woman from deth to lyfe: whos name was thabita auctuum.ix.c. And wyth the wordys of hys blamynge he toke hir lyfe from ananye and safira, he prayde not for hyr deth: but only vnder name them for ther synne and a non they fel doun dede by the vertue of the swerde of goddys worde that peter spake, and the holy gooste by peter. For as sayyt poule saythe, the swerd of goddes worde ful ofte departeth the soule from the body And therfore the worde and the cursynge and vndernymynge of holy men and of men of holy churche: is moche for to drede, or elles by sufferaunce of god: anon as saynt petyr vndernam them: for theire pented them not: the fende sathanas toke power ouer them: And slowe theim bodely: as he slowe theym fyrste goostly by the syne of false couetyse.

The xxi. chapter.

Diues. Is it leful in ony cas to sle ony man or woman vngylty? Pauper. In no case as the lawe saythe openly. xx.q.8. si non. Diues. I suppose that ye queste dampneth a man that ye iustice knoweth vngylty: shal not the iustice yeue the sentence and dampne hym: sythe the queste saythe that he is gylty. Pauper. God forbede. For thanne fallethe the iustice in manslaughter For he maye by no lawe sle hym that he knoweth vngilty xxiii. q.8. si non. Diues. What shal he do thanne? Pauper. If he haue no iuge aboue hym: he shal

Precepte.

saue hī by his playn power. And if he haue a iuge aboue hym, he shal sed the man to hym & tel hym al the case þ he may of his playn power deliuer hym and saue hym from the deth. or elles seke sum other weye for to saue him. But he shall not yeue the sentence of hys deth. Pylat trauaylsed ful besyly to saue criste from deth: for that he wyste him ungylty moch more a cristen iuge owethꝫ to trauayle to saue the innocentys lyf whom crist boughtꝫ with his blode, and flee false sentence. Pylat myght and ought by lawe haue saued criste. But for to plese the peple, and for dred þ they shulde haue accused hym to the emperoure he folowed ther wylle and put criste to the deth, and therfor afterwarde he was dāpned. For the false queste pilate wolde not haue dampned hym in that that he wyste him ungylty: But only for drede and to plese the people: he dampnede him. And sythe he theyn lawe sleethꝫ no man ungilly: moche more cristen lawe shal sle no man ungylty. But the iuge shal do al hys besynesse to flee shedding of blode withoute gylt Therfore he is made iuge to defcase the truthe to saue the ungilty: and to punyssh the gylty and to lette malyce, foly and falshed

of the questys & of the false wytnesse. Therfore god sethꝫ thus to euery iuge: thou shalt not take the voyce of lesyges: ne thou shlat not ioy ne thyn hond to sey false wytnes for the wycked mā that is, to saye, thou shalt make no couenaunt to saye false wytnesse ne assent therto. Thou shat not folowe the peples wyl: to do any euyl thinge or any falsnesse in dome. Thou shalt not assent to the sentence of many to go aweye from the truth. Exo.xxiii. c. Therfor the lawe biddeth that the iustice be not to light ne to redy to leue: ne to redy to take vengeaunce. Di.lxxx vi.si quid Et q̄.j̄.vi.iiii.quāuis Et p vi.j̄. viii si quid. The ende of euery dome shalbe iusticia. That is rightwisnesse in englisshe. And rightwisnesse is a vertue: and a stedfaste wyl alwey to yelde euery man & woman his right. Extra de b. significatione c°. for. in glosa. And therfore whanne the iustice doth wronge in his sentence yeupnge. that is no rightful dome for it endeth not in rightwysnes But more wrong may he not do to man or woman. thanne robbe him of his lyfe and slee him with oute gylt. Therfor thanne wꝫ hat iuge sleeth man or woman ungilty wytingly he is no iuge: But

ri

The fyfte.

he is a tyraunt: and doth apens al salwes Whyche be ordeyned to do right to euery man to punissh the gilty and to saue the vngilty And therfore seyth the lawe that he is no iuge if rightwysnesse be not in him. Non est iudex si non est in eo iusticia xxiii.q̄.ii.iustū.

The xxii. chapter.

Iues. It is lefulle to any man or woman in any case to slee themsylfe. Paup. In no case. and that for many shyllyps Fyrste for by wey of kynde euery man loueth himsilf and is besy to saue himsilfe and to withstōd al thinge that wold distroy him And therfore it is synne apens al kynde man or woman to slee him silfe / Also it is apens charite ffor eche man is bounde to loue him silfe and his euencristen as hi silf Also he doth wrōg to ye comonte of mankynd / For as the phi losofre sayth. B°:ethicor Eue ry man is aparte of the comonte as euery menbre is aparte of the body. Also for mannys lyfe is an high gyfte of god youen to man to serue god / And only god may take it away whanne he wyl. And therfore he that sleeth hym silfe: he synneth apens hys god: in that that he sleeth his seruant

apens his wyl / For though god yeue a man auctorite to slee ano ther mā for his misdede: yet god yeueth no man auctoritye to slee hymsilfe. And therfore sayth the lawe .xxiii.q̄.B. non licet. That no man ne woman shulde slee hi silfe: neyther to slee nyscheeffes of this world.ne to slee other mē nys synne: ne for sorowe of hys owne synne that he hath don: ne for to go the soner to heuen / For if he slee himsylfe as sayth there the lawe: he goth to endles mis cheeffe. And he falleth in ouer greuous synne / And I that he sle eth hymsilfe falleth in wanehop e.and doth dispyte to the mercy of god as iudas dydde For after his deth he may not amend hym of that greuous sine of mās slau ghter And by that manslaughter he leseth hys lyfe in thys world and his lyfe in heuen blysse: and goth to the deth in helle wyth oute end. And therfore ther shuld no woman slee hir silfe to saue hir chastitie that she be not defouled For if she be defouled by violen ce apens hir wyl: she synneth not For as saint lucie seyde to the ty raunt pascbasius ye body is not defouled but by assent of the sou le. But the synne is I him that so defouleth hyr / And lesse synne it is to fal in lecherie / than man or woman to sle hīmsilfe: for there is no helpe after/ Ne ther shulde no man ne woman slee hīmsilfe ne mayme hīmsilfe for dred that he shuld sent to gsynne: But trust in god that may kepe hym from consentynge: and sette occaciōs of synne And though mā or womā be constreyned to synne for drede of deth: Better it is ꝗ a seyrer that a nother sle hȳm: thā he sle hīmsilfe for that is dampned in euerī lawe Diues. Contra te. Sampson ꝗ dyuersother slough themsilfe as we rede in holy writ Pauper. As seyth saynt austen de ciuitate dei. They slough thē silfe by the preuy counseyle of ye holy gooste: that wolde by ther deth do myracles /As whā sāpson toke the twoo pylerys of the paynymis temple whych bare vp al the temple and shook them to gidre With his armes tylle they brosten ꝗ the temple fell doune ꝗ slough many thousandys of the hethey people that was gadrede to wondre on sampson in dispyt of god of heuen Whos seruaunt sampson was.

The xxiii. chapter.

Diues. Whether is it more synne to slee the rightfulman or a wycked man? Paup. It is more synne to sle the right

fulman/ for in that the sleer noyeth most hī whom he ought more to loue Also for he doeth wronge to hym that haue not deserued it and more ayens rightwisnesse Also for he pryueth and robbeth the comontye of manhode of a greate iewel/ For euery gode mā and gode woman is alwesse to ye comontye of mankynd/ Also for he doth more dispyte to god: for to al good criste seyth. Qui vos spernit. me spernit Who despisith you despisith me. Diues. Contra If a good man be slayne: he shal sone go to heuen/Butte the wicked manne if he be slayn vnwarly: he shal goo too helle/And lesse synne it is: to send be sleig a man to heuen: than to hel Pauper. Saynt poul seyth .i. ad cor iii°. that euery mā ꝗ woman shal thake his owne mede: after that his traueyle is Therfore the gode man so slayn shal go to heuen for his good dedys: notte for the malyce of the sleer/And the wicked man so slayne: shalle goo to helle for his owne wicked dedys not for the wycked dedys of the sleer/ And the sleer shal go to hel both for the sleynge of the good and of the wicked/ But he shal be depper in helle for sleyng of the good than of the wycked: For he shewethe more malyce ꝗ

The sixte.

more aggreuethe god and al the courte of heuen in sleynge of the good than of the wicked And he shal answere for al the good dedys that the good man shuld haue do: if he had lyued lenger And he shal be punysshed: for the sleinge of the wicked man: for that he sleeth hym ayens goddes law and setteth hym that he may haue no tyme to amende hym Diues. Is it leful to any man to sle his wyfe: if he take hir I auoutre Pauper. To sle hir by lawe cyuyle there lawis ordeyne man & woman that don auoutrye to be slayne: It is leful so that he doo it only for loue of right wysnesse and of clennesse: not for hate ne for to be auenged on hir.

And sette hym wel charge his conscience: if he be ought gylty I the same: eyther I wyl or in dede and take hede to his owne freelte and thenke that the law is as wel ordeyned to punyssh hym if he do anyys as to punyssh the woman But any man to sle hys wyfe by his owne auctorite or doo hir be slayne withoute lawful iuge: it is not leful by alle goddes lawe. And though any londys law ye= ue men leue to slee ther wyues in any case: holy churche shalle punysshe theym and enioyne them ful harde penaunce as for man=
slaught. Diues. Whether is more synne a man to slee his wyfe or to slee hys fader or moder. Pauper. Bothe be greuous synnes: & moche ayens kynde / For the man and hys wyfe be one flesshe and one blode / And he oweth as sayth the saynt Poule loue his wyfe as hys owne body / And therfore he to sle hir ayens kynde / Butt yet it is more synne: and more ayens kynd to sle fader and moder: for of them man hath his begynnig his flesshe & blode / And also if he sle any of the he forsetteth openly ayens the comaundementys of god the fourthe and the fifte. For in that he vnworshyppeth ouer moche his fader and hys moder: and falleth I cruel manslaughter and therfore it is more synne to slee fader and moder: than to slee his wyfe: as sayth the lawe in sm. cōfessor. li°. liiii°. ti°. ix. q. y.

The xxiiii. chapter.

Diues. Sythe god byddethe that no man shulde slee vnrightfully: Why suffereth god soo moche werre be in erthe: & so many bateylles. Pau. For moch folke is worthy to die and wyl not stonde to the lawe of pees/ Therfore god hath ordeyned

Precepte.

and cōmaūded the lawe of swer/ de and of cheualrye to brynge thē to pees with the swerde that wyl not obeye to the pees by lawe of charitye and reson. ¶Diues. Thā it semeth that men of armes mayste men lefully that wyl not obey to the pees and too goddes wyl ¶Pauper: That is soth For Abraam. moyses. iosue. dauid. iosie macchabeis and many other were men of armes and slowghe moche folke. And yit god repreued them not but he badde them sle and halpe them in ther sleyng and in ther fyghtyng. ¶Diues. I may wel assent that bateyle is leful: if it be ryghtfull. For god is cleped. Dominus exercituum & domin⁹ sabaoth. That is to sey lorde god of ostys ¶Paup. Thre thynges be nedful: that bateyle be ryghtful. Justa causa: iustus animus: et auctoritas legitum principis a ryghtful cause. a ryghtful intencion and auctorite of a lawful prynce/ Fyrste it is nedful that ye cause be ryghtful that they fyght only for the right: and to mayntene right and for saluacion of the comontye: and of them that be vngilty and wold haue pees/ For as seyth synt austen. the ende of bateyle shulde be pees. xxiii. q. i. nolite. Also ther in tencion most be ryghtful that thei fight not for pryde to gete theim

a name. ne for no false couetyse to gete worldly good: ne for noo malyce for to be vengede: ne for no cruelte and lykynge to shed blode: For if ther intencioun be wycked: thoughe ther cause be true: they synne in manslaughter. And for ther wycked intencion god suffereth men to be ouercome in a ryghtful cause / Also it most be do by auctorite of a lawfull prynce: that is prynce made by comon custom: or by comon lawe: or by comon assent of the comontye: or by comon lawful election: For though a person ga dre to hym rebellys ayens hys lege lordes wyl: although the rebellis make hym ther hed and her prynce: they may not by his auctorite do ryghtful bateyle But al though auctorite of a prince lawful be nedful to ryghtful bateyle that is solemply don by mannis lawe: yit a ryghtful cause at nede man may by lawe of kynd wt oute auctorite of any prynce fight and defende hymsilfe: and hys godis ayens wycked folke. For it is the lawe of kynd euery man to saue himsilfe and putte awey force wt force. and myght wt myght Licitū ē vim vi repellere. Soo þ his purpos be not to slene ne to rebel ayens his souereyn ne ayens the lawe: But only in truth to saue hym and his fro wicked doers

r iiii

The fifte.

Netheles clerkes shuld not fight for no worldly goodis / but they may in case with fightynge and smitynge defende ther owne persone apens clerke and lewed mā And so may the lewed man defende hīmsilfe with smitynge apens the clerke that seketh to smyte hī if he may not els sekerly saue hīsilfe / And if he may sekerly saue hīmsilfe: eyther by flight: eyther by shettyng of dore or of gate or any other weye: he owthe to saue hīmsilfe and not smyte a clerke: But wysely saue them both. But alwey be he ware: that his flight be not cause of his deth And syth that the lewed man oweth to fle the clerke if he may in seker maner to saue thē both Moch more the clerke that shulde shewe pacience and fle sheddynge of blode: By hys ordre oweth to fle a lewed man / if he may to saue hīmsylfe sekerly and to saue theym bothe.

If the sugettys be in doute whether the cause that they fyght for be true / they be excused by the precepte of ther prynce for vertue of obedyence: so that the subgettys haue no cause to misdeme of her prynce by his comon lyuyng But that they suppose that he ī al his lyuyng be rewled by reson ā godes law But if they be seker that the cause is false / they be not excused ne owe not to fight / Or els

if the prynce be man oute of godde gouernaunce as frentyke / or brayneles. or els that he be in hys lyuyng openly rebellyng apens god: thanne the peple oweth not to obey to his biddyng whāne he byddeth them fyght: But if they knowe sekerly that his cause be trewe / But thāne they most obey the prynce of heuen that biddeth them sle no man ne woman vngylty / Sowdeours & other knyghtys and men of armes & other frendes of the prynce not subget to hīm by obedience / if they fight for hīm in a cause that is doute they be nott excused from dedly syne and māslaughter. In sti. confesso. li°. li°. ti. β° q̄. ‖ β. q̄. ‖ βt.

Thus leue frende haue I declared you the fifte heeste that byddeth you and vs al / not sle / And therfore leue frende al if youre persone be not able to fight ne to sle plt I pray you that ye be ware ye assent to no mannys deth neyther byfore ne after: But ye were syker that they were gylty and worthy to dye / For the lawe seythe / that bothe they that don the mysdede / and they that assente therto / But worthy euen payne. A gētes & cōsencietes pari pena puniātur. Iustifye ye no man nys deth / Butt ye knowe well the cause of his dethe / For I am syker þ god dampneth moch mans ſlaughter that ye and other iuſti/ſye. and the dome of god ſhal fal that he ſeyde to ſaynt peter / He ӊ ſmyteth withe the ſwerde / ſhal peryſſhe with the ſwerde./And he that robbeth ſhalbe robbed. De q̃ pdaris nonne predaberis. pſa. xxviii°. Al day ye may ſee what vẽgeance falleth for ſhedinge of mannys blode euery yere more & more / Other nacions ſle vs in euery ſyde and robbe vs / and we haue lytel ſpede or non But only to ſle oure owne nacion / Therfore be ye ware of goddes ſwerd: and of mannys ſwerde alſo / and iuſtiſye ye not ӊ god dampneth̃e Here endeth the fifte precepte:¶ bygynneth the ſyxte precepte.

¶Iues. Thy couſeyle of gode God ſend vs pees: and kepe vs fro the ſwerde. Nowe I pray the declare me the ſixt cõmaũdemẽt. Pauper. The ſixt cõmaundement is thys. Nõ mechaberis That is to ſey i engliſſhe Thou ſhalt do no lecherie: ne medle with no thyng fleſſhly but only withe thy lawful wyfe. As ſeyth the gloſe / And ſo by thys precept he forbyddeth al ſpyces of lecherie Diues. How many ſpyces be ther of lecherye. Pauper. Nyne And theſe be they . Fornicacion and lecherie wyth comon

wymen . auoutry defoulynge of mayden hode . defoultg of chaſtite auoued to god defoulyng of them that be nigh of kyn / of aſenitye . or of goſſypprede . and ſodomye that is myſuſe of mãnys body or womans in lecherye ayens kynde. and polucion of mannys body or womans : by ther owne ſtyrynge and by themſylfe whyche is a ful orrible ſynne / And alſo ſynful medlynge to gedre bytwene huſbond and wyfe / Fornicacio . meretriciũ . adulteriũ Stupri̇. ſacrilegiũ. Ice ſtus. peſtm ſodomiticũ Volũtaria l ſe polluc̃io q̃ p ſe puocat . et libidinoſue: coitus cõiugalis. Diues. In hou many weyis may ye huſbõd ſynne medlynge with his wyfe? Paup. In eyght weyis Firſt if he medle withe hir only to fulſyl his luſtys and his lecherye takyng no hede to god ne to ye oneſtie of matrimonye / Alſo if he paſſe meſure in his doyng / Alſo if he medle with hir in tymes whyche holy churche cõuſeyleth men to cõtinẽce / as in holy tymes and in time of lente in tyme of faſtynge and of other prayer : whych tymes he may medle with hyt ſo hodely ayens reuerence of the tyme / and of god ӊ he ſhal ſynne dedly / For peter and poul techi that wedded folke ſhuld in holy tyme / and in tyme of preyr abſteyne them fro

r iiii

The sixte.

suche lustys that ther prayer may ye more gracously be herd of god and ther herte the more pouen to godd / For suche luste as for the tyme draweth the manys hert and Womannys moch fro god: and maketh them ful flesshly and ye les goostly / Therfore as we rede Gen̄. vii°. in the tyme of the flo/de in noes tyme for the herde tri=bulacion and dred that they wer in al that yere: noe and his thre. sonnes kept them chaste and lay by themsilfe and ther wyues by theym sylfe. so that by holy prey=er and contynence they myght the soner be delyuered of that perel & myschefe that they were in / Also if he medled with his wyfe I holy place without nede / For I tyme of werre though he medle wyth his wyfe in church: if he dare not ly out ye church for dred of en/nemyes he is excused: & the church is not polute / or elles it were polute. And also if he medle with his wyfe whanne she is grete with child nygh the tyme of ber=the. For thanne lyghtly he myght sle the child. Also if they medle to gydre with euyl condicion / Also if he medle with his wife wetyg=ly I hir comon seke enes at his owne proffre. But if husbond & wife medle to gedre flesshly without these defautis only to bryng for/

the a beyne too the herte. And he th children to goddes seruyce els to fle fornicacion and lechery on other halfe: or to yelde the det of ther body ech to other thāne they synne not / But thanne as sayth saynt poule ther wedlok is worshipful / and ther bed wyth oute spot of blame.
Honorabile connubiū I olbus & thorus īmaculat⁰. Ad hebre. viii. c°. Vpon which worde sayth the greate clerke haymo and the glose also. b it is a worshipful wed=lok whāne man weddeth his wi=fe lawfully to bryng forth chyl=dren to goddes seruice: & absteyneth hym fro his wyfe in dwe tymes. And thanne is ther bed wyth oute spot of blame: whanne he medle with his wif lawfully and for a good end kepe mesure and maner: thanne ryse they vp oute of bed with oute spott of blame.

The secunde chapte.

Matrymony was ordeyned of god for ii. causes Firste prynycypaly into office / to bryng forth children to goddes seruice. Also into remedie to fle fornica=cion and lecherye / For the fyrste cause it was ordeyned I paradise byfore adams synne. For the ii. cause it was ordeyned oute of p abiſe after adams ſynne / Thre goode thynges be pryncipaly in matrimonye / The firſte is ſeyth that eche of them kepe truly hys body to other: and medle fleſſhly wyth non other / The ſecunde is bryngynge forth and noryſſhynge of children to the worſſhip of god and to goddes ſeruice. For elles it were better that they were vnborne. The thyrd is the ſacrament which may not be vndo: but only by deth / And therfore the ordre of wedlok is fulworſſhipful / for it repreſenteth the gret ſacrament of vnyte & of endles loue bytwene ye godhed & ye manhede of criſte berry god & berry man & bitwene criſt and holy churche. and bytwene criſt and criſtē ſoule / And the ſeythful loue that oweth to be bytwene huſbōd & wyfe bytokeneth the loue and the ſeyth that oweth to be bitwene criſt & criſtē ſoule: and bytwene criſt and holy church / For the huſbond ſhulde loue his wyfe wyth true loue / And therfore whāne he weddeth hir: he ſetteth a rynge on hir fynger / which rynge is token of true loue that oweth to be bytwene them. For they moſte loue them to gedre hertely / And therfore it is ſette in the forthe fynger / For as clerkes ſey fro that fynger goeueth hir but one rynge i token that they ſhulde loue theym ſyngulerly to gedre. For as a pens compnyge of ther body / the huſbond ſhulde loue his wyfe & non other / and the wyfe hir huſbond and non other / The rlg is roūde aboute and hath non ende in token that ther loue ſhulde be endles: and no thynge depart theim but deth alone / Alſo the rynge is made of golde or of ſyluer in token that as gold and ſyluer pas al other metals in value and clēneſſe: ſo ſhulde ther loue paſſe al other loues. And the huſbond loue his wife paſſyng al other wymen: And the wyfe loue hir huſbond paſſynge al other men And as gold and ſyluer paſſe al other metals in clēnnes / ſo ſhulde ther loue al be ſet ī clēnes & not comō to gedre / But for bryngyng forth of children or to flee fornicacion or to yelde the dette of ther bodyes Thys loue bitokeneth the loue that we owe to god that is oure gooſtly huſbonde too whoom we be all weddedde in oure baptē / For we ſhulde loue him hertely wyth al oure herte ſyngulerly wythe al oure ſoule laſting ly wythe al oure mynde myghtely wythe al oure myghtys / And therfore he ſaythe. Deut 10. vi°. Thou ſhalte loue thy lorde god with al thy hert wᵗ al thy ſoulʷ

The sixte

al thy mynde with al thy might. The husbōd betokeneth crist ye wyf betokeneth holy church and cristē soul which is goddes spouse & oweth to be suget to cryst: as wyfe to husbond. The ornamētes longe pryncipaly to a wyfe. A rynge on hir synger a broch on hir brest: & a garlond on hir hede. The rige betokeneth the true loue as I haue seyd. The broch bytokeneth clennesse in herte & chastite that she oweth to haue. The garlonde bytokeneth gladnesse. and the dignitye of the sacramēt of wedlok. For the husbond bytokeneth crist: and the wyfe holy church. Which is cleped quene: & goddes spouse. And therfore seynt poule sayth thus. Viri diligite vxores vestras. ye men loue ye youre wyues as crist loued holy church, and put himsilfe to the deth for holy church. So shulde men do if it neded for ther wyues as sayth the glose. Men sayth he owe to loue ther wyues: as ther owne bodyes. He that loueth his wyfe: he loueth himsilfe. Syth thanne thys sacrament of wedlok is so greate and so worshypful in crist and holy church therfore euery man loue his wyfe as himsilfe. And the wyfe loue hyr husbond and drede him. Wymen saith he most be suget to ther husbondys as to ther lorde. For man is hede of woman: as criste is hede of holy churche. And as al holy church is suget to crist: so most wymē be sugettis to ther husbōdys. These be the wordys of seynt poule. Ad eph. quinto.

The thirde. chapter.

Syth that the ordre of wedlok is so greate & so worshipful in criste & holy church as saynt poul saith without doute they ꝑ breche it or misuse it in lust and sylyng of the flesshe and so solue only ther lust as bestes and refreyne not themsilfe by reson & by goddes lawe, they synne ful greuously. Therfore we fynd in holy wrytte. tobie. vi°.c°. That there was a woman that hyght sara and she was wedded to vii. husbondys: and a deuel ꝑ hyght asmodeus slough them alech after other the firste night or ꝑ they medled with hyr. For they wedded hir more for brenyng luste of ye flessh, than for any true cause of matrymonye. After the aungel raphael cam to yonge Tobie & seid to hi ꝑ he shuld wedde sara. Thā yong tobie seyde to the aūgel I haue hard he seyde ꝑ ye deuel hath power oū almen ꝑ wed hir, and slethe them. Thā the aū-

Precepte.

gef fepde to hī / I ſhal tel ȝe ouer whiche men the fend hath power ouer them that ſo take wedloke that they putte god from theym: ⁊ fro ther mynde ⁊ ȝeue tente to fleſſhely luſtys / as hors and mu- le that haue no vnderſtondynge ouer them the deuel hath power butte thou ſhalt not take hir in ſuche maner: But three nyghtys ye ſhal kepe you chaſt / and ȝeue you to holy prayere: and thanne thou ſhalt take thy wyfe wythe the dred of god pryncypaly to brīg forthe chyldren to the worſhip of god / Sythe thāne the deuyl ha- the ſuch power ouer them that ſo mifuſe ther wyues and the ordre of wedlok / Moche more power hathe he ouer them that breke þe ordre of wedlok ⁊ take other thā ther wyues / Therfore god bad in the olde law. Deut°. xxii. that if any mā medyl with another mā nis wyf / they ſhal be ſlayn both ye mā ⁊ the womā. And the wyſe man ſeyth / that he that dothe a- uoutrye for myſchefe of herte / he ſhal leſe hys ſoule: ⁊ he gadereth ſhame and ſhenſhyp to hīmſylfe. ⁊ hys ſhame ſhal neū be do awey Prou. vi°. And there he ſayth þ althougghe theft be greuous ſyn ne / yit I regard of auoutrye it is but a ſmal ſynne / And ſo ſaith ye greate clerke Bede / and the gloſe

alſo. Many myſcheues falle to them that lyue ī auoutrie moch ſi- keneſſe : moch myſhappe loſſe of good: wanpſſhyng of cateyl / and lytel foyſon therin : ſodeyne po- uert euyl name and moch ſhame greate hurte / and ofte maymīge and myſcheuous deth / as dethe in preſoun and hangynge / and ofte ſodeyn dethe / and inſtruction of eyrys and of ther eryṫage /

And therfore the wyſe man ſeyth Filii adulterorʒ. ⁊c. The chyldren of theym that lyue in auoutrye: ſhal ſone be at ende / and the iſſue and the ſede that cometh of the wicked bed ſhalbe diſtroyed and though they liue longe they ſhal not be ſette vp and ther laſte age ſhalbe wythoute worſhyp. Na- ciones iniqʒ dies ſunt conſumma- cionis They that be mſborne moſte comonly they haue har- de ende. Sap. iii°. c°. And as he ſeyth in the next chapter folow- ynge / Children borne in auoutre ſhal ȝeue non deperoyps : ne ſette no ſtable gronude butt they ſhal alwey be in tempeſte of tribula cion / Ther brauncheys ſhal bre- ke / and ther rotys be plucked vp The frute of theym ſhalle be vn propfytable / and they ſhalle be ful bytter ⁊ euyl mete ⁊ able to ri- ght nought. Sapientie. iii°. c°. In token ⁊ cōfirmacion of thys

The sixte

We fynde in the lawe: ꝑ the holy Boniface the thyrde whych was a metter wrote to the kynge of englond in this maner As it is tolde openly by the cuntres. and spyrydyd to vs that be ĩ fraunce and ytalie: and hethen men repreue vs therof: that englyssh peple despise the lawes of wedlok and peue theim to auoutrye and lecherie as dyd the folke of sodõ. Butte wyte it wel: if it be soo as men sey of them / the people that shal be borne of such lecherie and spouse brech shal be vngentil pepel and represe to al ther kynred They shalbe wode in lecherie / ⁊ al wey the people shalle come to wors and wors / and at the laste be vnable to bateile. Vnstable in seyth and withoute worshyp and not loued of god ne of man: as it falleth be to many other nasions: ffor they wolde not knowe gods des lawe   Distinc°. lxi. si gens anglorum. Dives. It semeth be ꝑ the pphicie of that ———— is nowe fulfilled / For what auoutre hath the reyned in thys londe many perys: it is no coũceyl ⁊ namely amõgys these lordis which haue nowe brought this londe in bitter bales / Sũme of them be slayne: ⁊ sũme of theim yit lyue ĩ moche woo Goddes law is forgete and forbade that men shuld not kus

ne it ne haue it in ther moder tũge The people is vnworthy and in despyte to al crystendome. for ther falshede and ther false bylevupnge: and soo wood in lechery that the brother is not ashamede to holde openly hys owne sustre. They be harlottis in lyvyng vnstable in seyth: vnable to batey le: ouercõme nyghe ouer al hated of god and of man withoute grace and spede nygh in al ther doig Pauper. Exaumple to thys we fynde in the secunde boke of kyngys. pii°. c°. Where we fynd ꝑ whãne dauid had don auoutre wyth barsabee the wife of the noble knyght vrie: and after that trecherously slayne that knight god sentte the pphete nathan to dauid: and repreued hym of hys synne and seyde: that swerd and debate shulde neuer passe fro his houshold e. and fro his kyrede I shal sayth e god reyse my scheffer and disease ayens ye of thyn owne menye: and take thy wyues and peue them alle to thy neyte. and he shal openly ly by thy wif Thou doiste it preuely. I shalle punyshe the openly. And so it befel/for absolon hys owne sonne droffe hym oute of hys owne kyngedome ⁊ lay by hys wyfe: in the syght of al the people And ꝑ was there neuer after

Precepte.

stabilyte in hys kyngdom, And yit the auoutrye of dauid was more punysshed: For the chylde that was bygoten i auoutry dyed sone after for the synne of the fader and moder. And afterward aaman dauidis sone lay by thamar his owne suster. And therfor absolō hir brother sloughe aamā his brother in trecherie. And alle these myscheues fel for dauid is synne wyth Bersabee. We fynde also in holy wrytte. Iudicū yy c. that for defoulyng of one manys wyfe were slayn sixty thousande and fyue thousande. It is a comon prouerbe in latein. De Bile fundamentū fallit opus: A feble grounde disseyueth ye werke. For whanne the grounde is feble and false: the werke that is sette theron shal sone fayle. But the grounde and the bygynnyng of euery peple is lawful wedloh and lawful generacion in matremony. And if that fayle the peple shalbe vnstable and vnthrifty, and that god shewethe wel in the begynnyng of the worle. For whanne mē wedded vnlawfulli and brake the boondys: and the lawes of wedloh whych god ordened at the begynnynge. thāne god sent the gret flod & destroied almankynde: saue noe and hys wyfe & his iii. sones & ther wiues

The fourth chapter.

Paup. Whanne pase god lawes of matrimony and what lawes paue he: Pauper. Whanne god had made adam, he put a grete slepe in adam: and in his slepe he toke oute one of hys ribbys: and fylled vp ye place w^t flessh. And of that ribbe he made eue & broughte hir to adam. Thā adam awoke and as god inspyred hym: he tolde ye lawes of wedloh and sayde thus. Thys bone is nowe of my boonys: and thys flesshe of my flesshe. For thys thynge man shall forsake fader and moder: and take hym to hys wyfe. And they shal be two i one flessh. Gen. ii°. In whych wordys: Whanne he sayde that man for hys wyfe shulde forsake fadir and moder: and take hym to his wyfe: he shewed ye sacramēt of trewe loue and vnyte that oweth to be bitwene husbond & wyfe. And by the same wordys he shewed what feyth oweth to be bitwene theym. For he shalle take hym to his wyfe and medel w^t the hir and with non other. and she wyth hym and with non other. And in that he sayde that they shulde be two in one flesshe: he shewid that they shulde medle to gedre prynceypaly too brynge

¶ For the chyldren to

The ſixte

goddes worſhip / For I ther child huſbond and wiſe ben one fleſſh and one blode / Alſo i that he ſeyde that the huſbonde ſhuld cleue to his wyfe: he forbiddeth fornicacion and auoutre / And that he ſeyde in ye ſynguler noumbre to his wyfe and not too his wyues: he forbiddeth bigamie that a mā ſhuld not haue two wyues to gedre ne one woman two huſbōdis to gidre / And in that he ſeyd that they ſhulde be two in one fleſſhe. he forbad ſodompe / And alſo by the ſame wordys he ſheweth þ eche of theim hathe power ouer others body and non of them may conteyne: but by aſſent of theim both. Diues. Why made god woman more of the ribbe of adā than of another boon. Pauper: For the ribbe is nexte the hert in tokē that god made hir to be mānys ſelowe i loue and his helper. And as the ribbe is nexte the herte of al boues: ſo ſhulde the wyfe be next in loue of al wymen: ⁊ of al men / God made not woman of the fote to be mannys thral ne he made hir not of the hede: to be his mayſter: but of hys ſyde and of his ribbe to be his feolowe i loue and helper at nede / But whā eue ſynned: thanne was woman made ſuget to man: that the wyfe ſhulde be reuled by hir huſbōd and drede him and ſerue hym as

ſelowe in loue and helper at nede ⁊ as nexte ſolace i ſorow: not as thral and bond in bilein ſeruage For the huſbonde owth to haue his wyfe i renerēce and worſhyp in þ they be bothe one fleſſh ⁊ one blod. Diues. Why made not god woman by hirſilfe of the erthe as he dyd adam. Pauper. For to encreaſe ther loue to gedre: And alſo to yeue womā mater of ſownneſſe) Firſte for encreſſyng of loue. ffor in that woman is part of mānys body: man moſt loue hir as his owne fleſſh and blod. And alſo ſhe muſt loue man as hir begynnynge: and as hir fleſſh and hir blode / Alſo ſhe oweth to take grete mtaer of ſownneſſe: and thē/ke þ mā is hir perfection: and hyr begynnyge and haue man in reuerence as hir perfection: as hyr pryncipal: as her begynnyg and hir firſte in ordre of kynde / God made al mankynd of one for he wolde that al mankynde ſhulde be I one charite as they cam al of one. The fifte chaptor.

Diues. Whether is auoutre gretter ſynne in the man or in the woman. Pauper. Comonly it is more ſynne i the mā For the higher degre ye harder is ye fal ⁊ ſinne more greuous Alſo mā is mot mighty by wey of kide to withſtōd ⁊ hath more ſkyl ⁊ reſon wherby he may withſtōd

Precepte.

and be ware of the fyndes gyle. And in that he is made maister & gouernoure of woman to gouerne hir in vertue: and kepe hir fro vices/ If he falle in vices and in auoutre more than woman he is moch to blame and worthy to be repreued shamefully/ Therfore saynt austen .in li°. de decem cor bis: Vnder nymeth husbodis that falli auoutre and septh to ech of them in thys maner/God septhe to pe thou shalt do no lechery þ is to sey: thou shalt medle with no woman: butte wythe thy wyfe/ Thou avist this of thy wife that she medle with non but with the And therfore thou oughtist to be by for thy wyfe in vertu thou fallest doste vnder ye fith of lechery Thou wylt that thy wife be oūcomer of lechery & haue the maystry of the fend/ and thou wylt be ouercome as a colwerde & sy dost in lecherye/ And not wythstondynge that thou arte bede of thy wyfe yet thy wife go bifore ye to god and thou that art bed of thy wif goeste backward to hel/ Ma septh he is beed of woman/ And therfore in what housholde the woman liueth better than ye mā in that houshold e bangeth the bed dounwarde for sith man is bed of womā: he oweth to lyue better than womā: & go by for his wyfe in al gode bedys: þ she may

sue hir husbond and folow hir he de the bede of ech houssholde: is the husbond: and the wyfe is the body By course of kynd theder þ the bedde ledethe: thyder shulde the body folowe/ Why wolde thanne the bede þ is the husbond go to lecherye: and be wyl not þ his body hys wyfe folowe/ Why wold the man go thyder wheder he wyl not þ his wyfe folowe: & a sytyf after in the same boke sait austen sayth thus/ Daye by day playntes be made of mannys lecherye. altogh ther wyues dare not playn the of ther husbondys Lechery of mē is so bold & so customable/ þ it is take nowe for a lawt so moch þ mē tel her wyues þ lecheri & auoutry is lesful to mē But not to wymē: thus seith salt austē. Diues. And sumtyme it is wist & hard þ wyues be take sylyg wᵗ her seruātis & brought to court bifore ye iuge: with moch shame But þ any husbōd is so brought to court bifor ye iuge for he saye wᵗ his wymē: it is seldō sen ꝑau per. & yet as septh salt austē i þe same boke: it is as gret sine i þe husbōd as i ye wyfe & sūdel more But forsoth saith he it is not the trueth of god But ye shrewdnesse of mā þ maketh mā les gilty thā womā i the same sine Mē be not so oft take i auoutry ne punyssh bedd for auoutrye as wymen be

295

not for they be les gylty: But for
þ thy be more gylty & more migh
ty & more slygh to maynten ther
sine, & nygh eche of them confor
teth other in his synne. Men be
witnessys iugis and doers to pu
nysshe auoutrie in woman, And
for they be ouerdone gylty in a-
uoutre. Therfore they trauayle
nygh al with one assent to main
tayne ther lecherye. In woman
is seldom se a voutre: And ther
fore it is ful sclaunderous whāne it falleth and harde punysshed But in men it is so comon þ
there is vnnethys ony sclaunder
therof whymen dare not speke a-
yens the lecherie of men: and mē
wyl not speke to repreue the lecherye of man, for they be so moche gylty. Synne that seldome
falleth is moost sclaunderous.
and yete in case lesse greuous.
And synne that ofte falleth, and
is mooste in vse, is leeste sclaunderous, and yet it is mooste greuous. For the more customable
and the more blode that men be I
synne and the lesse drede & shame
that men haue to synne itthe more greuous is ther synne. Therfore saynt austen i the same place speketh more of this mater a-
yens the lecherye of men and seythe thus. Parauenture thy wyfe
heretthe in churche by prechynge

that it is nott lesful to the to take
any other but thy wyfe. She co-
metthe home and grutcheth ayēs
thy lecherye and seythe to the: þ
thou doeste thynge that is notte
lesful. For why we be both criste
The chastite that thou axiste of
of me. yelde thou me, I owe too
the seythe: and thou owiste seith
to me: and both we owe seyth to
criste. Though thou dissepue me
thou dissepueste not god: whos
sernantes we be bothe. Thou dis
sepueste not him that bough vs
bothe for he knoweth al. But
weneste thou seyth saynt austen
that the man wylbe heled and a-
mend with hir wordes.
Nay nay seythe he, but anon he
shal be wroth and he shalbe wor
de bothe withe hys wyfe, & wyth
the prechoure and curse the tyme
that his wyfe cam to the churche
to here the truthe. These be the
wordis of seynt austen in the same boke And yet after i the same
boke he seyth thus. Parauēture
thou lechoure wolt excuse the &
sey, I take noon other mannys
wyfe. But I take myne owne
seruaunt, wylt thou seythe he:þ
thy wyfe sey to the, I take noon
other husbond I take butte my
seruaunt. God forbede that thy
wyfe shulde sey so to the. Better
it is that she haue sorowe of the

synne: than folowe the or take ensaumple of the / Thy wyfe is chaste & an holy woman and a true cristen woman: She hath sorowe of thy lecherye: not for the flesshe but for charite / And thy wyfe wolde that thou doeste not amys: not for that she dothe not amys / But for it is not spedefull to ye / For if she kept hir chast & did not lecherye onely for þ thou shuldeste doo no lecherye / if thou doest lecherye: she shulde do lecherye But for that the gode womā kepeth chastitye: not only for þe septh þ she oweth to the / Butt also for the seythe that she oweth to criste / For though the man do amys / yit the woman yeuethe hir chaste to god. Therfore saythe saynt austē in ye same place Crist speketh in the hertys of gode wymen wythin in ther soule: there ther husbond hereth it not / for he is not worthy to here it / and confortethe his doughter withe suche maner wordys / Thou art euyl deseased wyth the wrongys of thy husbonde: What hath he do to the I pray ye haue pacience be sory of hys mysdede: But folowe hym not to do amys &. But he must folowe the in goodnesse / For I that that he dothe amys lete him nott be thy hede to lede the: Butte lete thy god be thy hede / For if thou folowe hym as a hede in his shrewednesse / Both hede and body shal fal doune into helle And therfore myght nott the bodye that is the Wife folow the wycked hede But myght she holde hyr to the hede of holy churche that is criste / To him the wyfe oweth hir chaste to hym pryncipaly she most do it or slip: for he is pryncipal husbōde Be hir husbond present be he absentte / the goode womoan shall altvey kepe hir chaste / For criste hir husbond to whom pryncypaly she owethe hir chaste. is neuer absente / Chaunge youre lyfe ye men letcherous: saythe saynt austen there / And fro thens for war de be ye chaste / Ne seye ye notte that ye maye not kepe you chast For it is shame to sey þ mā maye not do: that a woman dothe: ne be so chaste as a woman is / The Woman by ryght hath as freel a flesshe as the man / And Woman was firste deseyued of the adder. youre chast wyues shewe to you that ye may be chaste if ye wyl. Theyse be the wordys of saynte austen.

The sixte. chapter.

Iues. Wymen maye better be chaste than men for theye haue moche kepynge by-

The sixte.

on them / The lawe byddeth them too chastyte. Ther husbondys be besy too kepe them and harde lawes be ordeyned to punysshe them: if they do amys Pauper. To thys answereth saynt austen in the same boke: & sayth thus / Moche kepyng maketh the woman chaaste: and man bode shulde make man chaaste. To wooman is ordeyned moch kepyng. for she is more freel. Woman is ashamed for hir husbond to do amys / Butte thou art not ashamedde for criste to do any. Thou art more fre than the woman / For thou art strenger: and lightlier thou myghteste overcome the flessh and the send if thou wylt / Therfore god hath byhaten the to the. Butte one womā is moche kepynge of hir husbōd dredful lawes good norture greate shamefastnesse. and god pryncipal / and thou man haste only god aboue the / Thy wyfe fleeth the lecherye for drede and shame of the for drede of the lawe: ffor good norture and pryncipaly for god / Butte for al these thou kepeste not the chaaste / ne thou leueste not thy lecherie neyther for dred of god ne for goddes law ne for shame of the worlde: ne for shame of thy wyfe: to whō thou arte bounde to be trewe. ne thou

wylt leeue it for ne good norture But lyue as an harlotte and vse harlottys maners / Thou artte not ashamed of thy synne sayth saynt austen / For so many men falle therin. The shrewdnesse of man is nowe so greate that men be more ashameedde of chastyte than of lecherye / Manquellers theues: plurerio: falsewytnessis rauenourys and false men be as abominable and hated amongys the people / But who so wylt lye by hys woman and be a bold lechoure / he that is loued he is preised / And al the woundes of hys soule turne into game / And if any man be so herdy to sey that he is chaaste and trew to hys wyfe and if it be knowe that he be such he is ashamed to come amongys men that be not lyke him in maner / For they shulde iape & scorne him and seye that he is no mā For mannys shrewidnes is now so greate: that there is noo man holde a man: But he be ouercōme wyt the lecherie / And he that ouercometh lecherye and kepeth hī chaaste he is holde no man.
These be the wordes of saynt austen in a boke de decem cordis Diues. Me merueleth moche that saynt austen: and you also accuse mā so moch of lecherye: & put more defaut in man than in

woman· Pauper. Crist dyd the same/we rede in the gospel. Jo. viii°. that on a tyme whanne criste satte in the temple of Jerusalem techynge the people his lawes/Thanne the scribis: and the men of lawe: and the pharesyis broughte a woman newly taken in avoutrye: and sette hir byfore criste/and seyde to hym al in gyle. Maystre thys wooman right nowe was take i avoutrye/The lawe of moyses byddeth be stoned al suche/Butte what sayeste thou therto. Al this they seyde in gyle. For hadde he bode the stoned hir: he hadde seyde apens hys owne prechynge/For hys prechinge and techynge was ful of mercy and pety/And if he had seyde that she shulde not have be stoned thanne hadde he sayde apens moyses lawe and thane wolde they haue stooned hym/And therfore he seyde neyther the one ne the other. But he stouped doune: and wrote wyth hys fynger in the erthe/And whanne he had wreten a whyle he set hi vprighte ayen and sayde to them/whyche of you be withoute synne: he caste on hir firste the stone/And after he stouped doune and wroote in erthe/And whanne the accusers of the wooman herde theyse wordes of criste and se hys wrytynge/they were asshamed: and went oute eche after other/and the eldeste went oute firste/and non of them lefte there/For as seye these clerkes: eche of them sawe in that wrytynge alle the euil synnes that he hade doon of lecherye of spousebreche or of a= dy other synne/And eche of them wende that al other aboute had seen hys synne/And so for drede and for shame they went out for they sawe wel that they were more gyltye in lecherye than the woman and more worthy to be stoned/But criste of hys goodnesse wroughte so/that eche of them sawe there his owne synne: and non other mannys: soo peuynge vs ensaumple to hyde other menys synne: and not defame oure euen cristen: whyle ther synne is preuye/And whanne they were doon oute for drede and shaame Thanne saide crist to the woman where be they that accused the. No man hathe dampned the Lord sayth she that is soth no man hathe dampned me: Thanne criste sayde to hir/Ne I shal not dampne the/Go and be in wyl no more to synne Diues. By the lawe she was worthy to be dede/why wolde thanne criste that paue ye the lawe saue hir Pauper. although she were worthye to dye

The sixte.

pit hir accusers and the people that brought hir theder were not worthy to dampne hir/ne to put suche hir to deth/for they were more gyltye than the woman / And therfore seyth the gloose in that place /Though the lawe bid that he slayne that be gyltye: yitt the lawe wyl not that they shulde be slayne by them that be gyltye in the same synne / Butte he that is vngyltye in the same synne shal punysshe him that is giltye / And therfore seyth the glose: that they so accused the woman: by right of lawe / or they moste haue lete hir go or ellis be stoned with hir for they were more giltye in that synne than the wooman / And so by the lawe cryste delyuered hyr rightfully: and saued hir mercia bly / Therfore seyth the lawe of holy church: that tho that be gyltye in any grete synne shuld not be take for accusers ne witnessis in dome: no manqueller no theues: ne wicked iogulors robbers of churchis: rauenours: ne open lechours. ne they that be in auoutrye. ne they that poysone folke. ne periurers. ne false witnesses ne they that are counseyl of witches / All these and suche other be vnable for to accuse in dome: or to bere witnesse in dome: Butt if it be for to accuse them that be ther

felowys: and helpers i ther synne iii.q.v.cõstituim⁹. Et vi.q.i.q crimen/And saynt ambrose seythe: that only he is worthy to be domesman and dampne the errours of a nother that hath nought in himsylfe that is dampnable .sup Bti Imaculati. Et iii.q. vii.iudicet. And therfore the lawe putteth many a case in which ye husbond may not accuse his wife of lecherye. Firste if he be gyltye in the same. xxxii.q. nichil liquus Also if he pute hir occasion to do fornycacion by withholdyng of det of his body xxxii.q. vii. Si tu Also if she be defouled by strenth and grete violence ayens hir wil xxxii.q.v. Ita ue. also if she wened hir husbond be ded. xxxiiii. q.i. si y bellica. And if she be wedded to a nother wenyng that hir husbond be ded whane he comes the doomesshe moste forsake the secunde husbond and go ayen to the firste: and but she forsake the secunde anon as she knoweth hir firste husbond is a spye. elles she falleth in auoutrye: and hir firste husbond maye accuse hir & forsake hir / Also if she be desceyued and meble with another wenynge that it were hir husbonde xxxiiii.q.ii. in sectum/ Also if he knowe hir lecherie and suffereth hir in hir synne. and meblessh w⁺

300

Precepte.

hir after that he knoweth hir syn or foryeueth it hir: & reconseyle hir to hym / thanne may he notte accuse hir xxvii.q.i. Si quis vx/orem. Also if hir husbonde putte hir to do amys. Extra li°.iiii°. ti.xiiii° discrecione/ Also if any he-then man forsake his hethen wi-fe and she be wedded to anoother hethen man, & after they be bothe turned to cristen feyth/ thanne is he bound to take hir ayen/ butt she fell any other fornicacion/ Not withstondynge that she be kno-wen fleshlly of the secud husbond Extra li°.iiii°. de diuorciis .c°. gaudemus. S.si g°.

The seuenth chapter.

Diues. Is a man bound to forsake his wyfe: whanne she falleth in fornicacion Pau-per. Either ye fornicacon is pryuy or it is open / If it be pryuy: and may not be preued / he shal notte forsake hir openly/ ne he is notte bound to forsake hir pryuely/ as anentys the bed/ If hyr fornica-cion be open: eyther there is hope of amendement: or there is noon hope of amendement/ If she wil amende hir / and there be gode ho-pe of amendement/ he may leful-ly kepe hir stylle/ If there be non

hope of amēdemēt: he oweth not to kepe hir styl / For if he do:it se meth that he consenth to hir syn-ne. Sm. con.li°.iiii°.ti°.xxii.q. Si.quero. Diues. May a mā by his owne auctoritye forsake his wyfe /if she falle in fornicacioun Pauper As anentys hir bed: he may forsake hir by his owne auc toritye But not anentis dwelling to gydre wythoute auctoritye of holy church And if he forsake hir company as anentis dwellynge wythout auctorite of holy chur-ch : he shalbe compelled to dwelle wyth hir / Butt he may anon pre-ue hir fornicacion/ If a mā med/ le wyth his wyfe after that ꝑ he knoweth hir fornicacion: he is ir-reguler / though he be compelled therto by holy church. Sm. con. li°.iiii°.ti°. xxii.q. Stil. St̃ū Sir. If the husbond be deperted from his wyfe by auctoritye of holy churche: He may if he wylfe entre into religion wythoute hyr leeue / Butte whether he entre or nay: he is bound to contynence al hir lyfe/ and he may non othir wyfe haue as long as she lyueth for only deth deꝑteth the bond of wedlok Diues. Contra If a man wedde a woman he may en tre ito religion or he medle wythe hir: & she may take another hus-bond and yit neyther of theim is

The sixte.

deed. Pauper. There is bodely deth and goostly deth: that is entre into religion/ For thanne man or woman dyeth ayens the worlde/ If he medle wyth hir bodely: only bodely deth may depert them as ayens the bonde of wedloch. But or that he medle wythe hyr bodely: goostly deth that is entre ito religion may depart them For tyll whanne they medle togydre bodely: the bonde of ther wedloh is but goostly/And therfore goostly deth brekethe that boonde/ And for as moche feue frend as the husbonde is as wele bounde to kepe feythe to his wiue/ as the wyfe to the husbonde. therfore if the husbond trespasse and falle in fornicacion: she hathe as greate accion ayens hym as he shulde haue ayens his wyf if she dyde amys. Quia quo ad fidem matrimonii iudicatur ad paria.

The eight chapter.

Dives. I maye wele assent that auoutrye be a ful greuous synne bothe in man and in woman/ But that simple fornicacion bytwene syngle man and syngle woman shulde be deedly synne/ I may not assentt therto And comon oppynyon it is: that it is no dedly synne. Pauper. Euery synne þ excludeth the man or woman oute of heuen is dedly synne/ But simple fornicacion excludeth man and woman out of heuen But they amende theim here/ therfore thanne symple fornicacion is dedly synne Diues. Where fyndeste thou that simple fornicacion excludeth man and woman oute of heuen Pauper. In the pystle of saynt poul where he seyth: that no fornicaries ne they that do auoutrye. ne sodomitis. ne theeues. ne malwnetreyps ne glotons. ne wycked spekers. ne they that spue by raupn/ shall haue the kyngdome of heuen. i. ad cor. vi. And in the chapter next bifore. he byddeth that men shulde not medle wyth such fornicaries and with suche wycked lyuers not ete wyth them ne drinke wyth them: for they be acursid of god and of al the company of heuen/ And in anotther pystle saith poule sayth thus. Wyte ye it wel and vnderstond ye it that no fornicarie: ne vncleene man of hys body: ne fals couetous man shal haue eritage in the kyngedome of criste and of god/ And therfor seyth he/ Late ye no fornicacon ne vnclennesse ne auarice be named in you: ne filth ne foly speche ne harlottre: But al maner oneste

Precepte.

as it bicometh sayntis. Ad ephe. 8°. And in another place he sayth that god shalle deme fornicaries and them that do auoutrye. Ad hebre. xiii°. That is to seye as seyth the glose / God shal dampne them withoute ende / although they wene not so But sith that god peueth no tale of flesshly synne / And therfore saīt John sayth in the boke of goddes preuitees to fornicaries: and manquellers liers and periuteris and such other cursed folke: ther part shalbe i ye pit wellyng and brennynge with fier and brymstone. Whych is the secunde deth of hell Apo. xxi°. c°. And the wyse man biddeth that thou shalt not peue thy soule too fornicaries in any thyng that thou lese not the and thy soule and thyn eritage in heuen / And euery woman fornicatrye shal be troden vnder foot of the fendis as drit ye wey Eccle. ix. c. Diues. Contra Al the ꝑcep/tys of the secunde table be pouen of god to lette wrongys that men shulde elles do to ther euen cristē But whāne a sēgle mā medleth with a sengle woman: he doth no man ne woman any wronge For eyther of them is in his own power Pauper. Though ech of theym be in hys owne power, yit ech of them doth other gret wrōg For ech of theym slecth other by dedly synne: and ech of them sleeth himsylfe: and ech of them doth wrong to god: in that they do ayens hys forbode: and slee the soules that he bought soo dere: And both they do wronge to ther euen cristē: in that they peue the wicked ensaumple and mater of sclaundre Diues. pit Contra te God seyth to euery man and woman Crescite et multiplicamini. Wexe ye and be ye multiplyed. Therfore thanne if a syngle mā medle with a syngle woman to brynge forth chyldren: it semeth to me no synne. Pauper. God sayde notte tho wordes to euery man and woman / Butte only to them that were wedded to gidre by goddes lawe: that as they were wedded to gydre to bryng forth chyldren: so god badde theym brynge forth chyldren: God sayde not tho wordys to sengle folke but to adam and eue his wife And vn to Noe and hys wyfe / and to hys sonnes: and ther wyues / And therfore Tobie sayde to hys sōne / Attendite tibi fili mi ab omni fornicacōne. &cetera My sōne kepe the fro al maner fornicacioun: ne medle with non wooman: but only wyth thy wife. Tobie. quarto. capitulo. And saynt poule sayth Mortificate

The sixte.

membra vestra que sunt super terram. Slee ye youre synful membrys that be open ettße / Slee ye fornicacion. Unclennesse. lecherye / These be the membrys that be byddeth vs sle. not the pypes of oure body / as the glose saythe And the glose saythe also / That euery lyinge with a woman oute of lawful wedlok is cleped fornicacion. and forbode as dedly synne / And therfore god badd in the olde lawe: that if the preestes doughtir were take in fornicacion: she shulde be brent. Leuytici xxi°.c° And if any other mannys doughtir: fel into fornicacion in hir faders house or she were wedded / she shulde be stoned to deth. Deu. xxii.c That therfore god wold ꝑ his moder marie shuld be wedded or be were conseyued of hyr. For if she hadde be founde with childe oute of wedlok: the iewys shulde haue stoned hir withoute mercy / And if it were leful to syngle man and syngle woman to medle to gydre & gendre: god had n.ade matrymony in vayne and there wolde no man knytte hym vndepartably to any wooman if he myght withoute synne medle with what wooman he wolde Therfore crist in the gospel dampneth the symple fornicacion and al maner lecherye: and saythe that

Who so loketh on any woman: in wyl to medle with hir oute of matrymonye: he doth lecherye a yens goddes commaundement and synneth dedly / Math. v°. c°. And therfore as I seyde firste generacion: and bryngynge forthe of chyldren is graunted only to theym that be wedded too gydre lawfully.

The nynth chapter.

DIues. Be al wedded folk bounde by thys precept of god Crescite et multiplicamini: to do ther diligence to bygget chyldren: Pauper. Byfore mankyd was multiplyed: wedded folke were bounde to do ther deligence to bryng forth children / Butte nowe that mankynde is multiplyed ; the precept byndeth them not so moch to generacion / But they be fre to continece and kepe them chast: if they be both of one assent therto / For many shyllys god ordeyned that man and woman shulde nott medle to gydre but they were wedded to gydre. For by auoutrye and fornicacion falleth ful oft that ye brother lyeth by hys suster and the fader by his doughter / And manye an vnlawfulle wedlok is made by

Precepte.

cause of anoutrie / And he ꝑ dotħ auoutrye he is a these and robbe the man or woman of his bodye ꝑ is better tħā any worldly catel For the wyues bodye is the husbondis body: and his body is hir body / For neyther of theim hatħ power of his owne body: to yeue it to any other by flesshly luste And he that dotħ fornicacion he robbetħ crist of his right botħ bodely and goostlye / And therfore saynt poule saytħ. that the lechoure taketħ the membre of criste ⁊ maketħ it ye membre of ye strūpet With whom he medletħ. i. ad cor. ui° Also by auoutrye be made false eyris: and true eirys truly bigote put oute of ther eritage Also by auoutrye goddes lawe ꝑ he made so solempnely in the begynnynge of the worlde fyrste of al lawes: is broken / And therfor he that breketħ it: is an opē traitoure / To this accordetħ ye wordes of the wyse man: Where he seytħ that the woman whicħ forsaketħ hir husbonde / and take another: and maketħ eritage of another matrimony dotħ many synnes First she is misbileuynge to goddis lawe / and brekethe goddes lawe. Also she trespasetħ ayens hir husbond / Also she dotħ fornicacion in auoutry / and maketħ childrē to hir of another mā

But hir sones shal yeue no rotis and ther braunches shal yeue no frute She shal leeue ther mynde in cursynge and hir shame shalle neū be do away. Eccle.xx.iii.c. And therfor seitħ ye glose ꝑ auoutry is as dānable in the man as i the woman / And therfore in the same chapter he repreuetħ auoutrie ⁊ fornicacōn i mā ful highly

The tentħ chapter.

Dīues. Reson ⁊ holy wryt drpuetħ me to graunte: ꝑ botħ auoutrye ⁊ symple fornicacōn be ful greuous sinne but more greuous is auoutrye: And sayne I wold kepe me fro botħe synnes But wymen be ye sendis snare. and so tempte me to lecherye. that it is ful harde too me to kepe me / Adam sonpsonem petrum dauid ⁊ Salomonem Femina decepit: qs modo tutꝰ erit. Womā deseyued adam. sampson petir. dauid ⁊ salomō / Who may thāne be syker fro womās gyle: Pauꝑ Many a man hatħ be deseyued by wycked wymen: more by his owne folyythan be dissepte of wymen But many more wymen haue be beseyued by malice of mē: thā euer were mē deseyued by malyce of wymen / And therfore the wooman lechoure is cleped ye snare of ye fēd ꝑ hūtitħ after mannys soule. For the

The sixte

wyse man seyth. Inueni ama/
riorem morte mulierem ꝗ c. I ha
ue foũde womã more bitter than
deth / Such is the snare of the hũ
ter: hir herte is a net and hir han̄
dys be harde boondys / He that
pleseth god shal escape hir: Butte
the synful mā shalbe take of hyr
Eccle.vii°.c. But men be cleped
not only the snare of the sed but
also they be cleped hys net spred
abrode on the hyll of thabor for
to take many at oones Osee v°.
Mannys malyce is cleped a net
spred a brode on an highe hyl for
it is open and bodely don: notte
in a selue: But in many / And ther
fore whãne holy wryt speketh̄e
of the malyce of men: he speketh
in the plurel noumbre as to ma/
nye / But whanne he repreueth
the malece of woman he speketh
in the synguler noumbre: as to
selue: in token that there be more
shrewes of men than of wymen:
and comonly more malyce ĩ mē
than in wymen: although sũme
woman be ful malicious. Figh̄
tyng robberye. manslaughter o
pen lecherie. glotenye. gyle fals
nesse piuri tratoury. falsse contri
uynge. and suche other orryble
synnes: reigne more in man thā
in woman / This false excusa/
cion that excuse so ther synne by
the malyce of wymen: bygānne

first in adam and lost adam and
al mankynde: For synfullye he
excused his synne by womã whā
god vndernam him of his synne
and put woman in defaute, Also
he put god in defaute that made
woman and answerd ful proud
ly: as men do these dayes ꝗ sayd
to god / The woman ꝑ thou paue
to me to be my felow gaue me of
the tree and I ete therof / As who
seyth, Haddeste thou not youen
hir to be my felow I shuld not ha
ue synned / And so notwithstan̄
dynge that he was more ĩ defaut
than the womã: yit he wold not
knoulege any defaute. Butte he
put woman and god principaly
that made woman in defaute.
Diues Hou was adam more in
defaute than woman. Pauper.
For to him principaly god paue
the precepte that he shuld not ete
of that tre: and eue knewe it not
but by adam / Woman was tēp
ted by the fende wonderfully in
the adder whyche wentt that ty
me ryght vp: And hadde a face
lyke a wooman. As sayht Be
de and the mayster of stories.
And she was dysseyued wyth his
fayre byheestes and his falsse sly
speche For he bygat hir that they
shulde notte dye: But be as god
des kunnynge goode and euyl:
Adam hadde noo temptacioun

Precepte.

from outward but a simple worde of his wyfe that profered hym ye apple / For we fynde not that she sayde to hyl any deseiuable worde And therfore syth man was forbode of goddes mouthe: and she not but by man. and man hadde lesse temptacion than wooman. and therto in no thyng wold accuse hymsilfe: ne yelde hym gylty But put defaute al in wooman & in god therfore he synned more than woman: For woman yeldyt ayltye. But she aysed no mercy She made no such excusacion But in grete perty yelded hir gyltye. in that she seyd: the adder hath deseyued me / For in that she knowlegyd that she was deseyued she knowlegide that she had do amys and vnwysely & other wys than she oughte haue do / And for that woman lowede hir and knowlegide hir vnwisdom and hir foly: therfore god put in woman that tyme an hope of oure saluacion Whanne he sayd to ye adder I shal put enmitye bitwene the and woman : end bitwene thy sede and hir sede: and she shal breche thyn heed that was the sede whiche was heed and leder of the adder that tyme / The sede of the fende be wicked werkes and wycked folke: to whom god seyde in the gospel / Vos ex patre diabolo estis. Jo.viii. ye be of the fader the fende / The seede of the woman goostly be hir goode dedys / With whiche the fende and ye fendys tymes haue greate enuye And comonly wymen more orribilitie of synne than do men And by our lady blessed mote she be: the fendys power is destroyde / Also the sede of woman is criste borne of the maid marie withoute parte of man / And so there was neuer man properly sede of womā but crist alone / & alwway is enmitye bytwene criste & the fende and hys seede / For as saynt poule sayth criste & Belial. light and derkenesse may not acorde / For thys shil saynt poule sayth. that adam was not deseyued in the first priuaricacōn: But woman was deseyued. i. ad thi°. ii And therfore as seyth the glose Whane god vnder nam adam he sayde not that the wooman had deseyued me: as the woman seyd the adder hath deseyued me. Butt he sayde the woman paue me of the tree. & I haue eten / And also as the glose sayth there / add was so wise he might not bileue ye sendys tales ne be deseyued i þ maner / as ye womā was And for ye womā was not so wise as adam was therfor she bileued ye sedis tales & so was deseyued / And ye

The sixte

wyser that adam was: the more was his synne whāne he fel But although adam was not deseyued fro outwarde by another: he was deseyued fro inwarde by hi=selfe by preuy pryde as saith saīt austen .de ci.si°.yiiii. c°.yiii. Where he sayth that adam and e= ue bygūne firste to be wyched in=warde: by whych preuy wyched=nesse they fel in open vnobedien=ce/ For as he saythe there Pryde is begynnynge of euery synne. Inicium omis peccati superbia Eccle.y°. And as salomon saith Contricionem precedit superbia: ante ruinam exaltatur spc. pū. p Bi°: Byfore brekynge and bri=sure goth pryde. and byfore open fallynge the spryte of a man and a woman is enhaunsyd by pryde And therfore sayth saynt austen in the same chapter that bothe a=dam and eue were wyched: and deseyued by pryde: and wel sette of them silfe byfore they ete of ye tree/ For preuy fallynge inwarde went byfore/ open fallyng out=warde by inobedience: and so a=dam was deseyued and fel by pri=de or eue yaue him the apple and eue was deseyued by pryde or ye serpent deseyued hir. For as sey=the saynt austen BBi.sm. they co=ueted more excellence and hygh=er degre than god ordeyned them

to/ They both synned greuous=ly: but adam more greuously as I said first And therfor saīt poul sayth/ not al men dyed through the synne of eue but through the synne of adam Ne god sayd not to adam: Cursed be the erthe in e=ues synne ne he seyde: Cursed be the erthe in youre synne/ But to adam alone he sayde. Cursed be the erthe in thy werke and in thy synne /And therfore sayth saynt ambrose .sup lucam. That eue synned more by freelte / and vn=stablete and chaungeabletie than by shrewednesse. Mobilitate ma=gis animi ꝙ suitate peccauit: Crist bycam not womā: But man to saue mankynde/ That as mā kynde was loste by man: so mā kynd shuld be saued by mā /And therfore in manshede he wold die for mankynde: for mansed had loste mankynde. And also he by=cam man and not woman to sa=ue the ordre of kynde. And forth womās synne was lesse greuous than adās synne: and lesse dered mankynde .and womā was les infect ī the first priuaricacōn thā was man: therfore god toke hys māshed only of womā wythout part of man /And so īh he bycam mā: he did gret worshyp to man. But īh he toke his māshede only of womā wīthoute part of man he dyd greate worſhypp to womā for only of woomans kyn: he made medycyne to the ſyne of a/dam: and to hele mankynde of the hard ſikenes of adams synne

The eleueth chapter·

Dives. Thy wordys be wonderful/ But yt I can not anſape the for drede of oure lady moder and maide that ga te grace to mankynde and is oure helpe in euery nede/ But yit I ſeye as I ſeyde firſte woman diſ=ſeyued ſampſon ¶ was ſo ſtrong Pauper. woman diſſeyued him not til he had diſſeyued himſilfe. by lecherie and miſgouernaunce of himſilfe/ Firſte he wedded an hethen womā ayēs goddes law. and ayens the wylle of his fader and moder: for luſte and myſto=re that he hade to hir/ After that he lay by a comon woman: that was hethen/ And after that he to ke another hethen woman to his concubyne that highte daliba whi the ful diſſeyued hym ¶ broughte him to his deth/ He was falſe to god/ and wymen were falſe to hī wymen ſey that he was byſotted vpon them. and therfore they tre ted him as a ſot/ He diſſeyued hī ſilfe ¶ did ful vnwyſly: whāne he

ſuffered a woman to bynde hym amongys his enemyes and told an hethen woman his counſeyle and in what thyng hys enemyes myghte mooſte dere him/ And alle thoughe god turned hys foly de=dys to the worſhip of god and of goddes lawe: yit ſampſon was nott excuſed therby for he dydde myche amys and moche folye/Alſo dauid was deceyued by hys mys luſt: and his lecherye. not by the woman Berſabee as thou ſeydeſt in thy Beero/ For thus we rede in holy wryt in the ſecunde boke of kynges. xi ca°. That on a tyme whanne kyng dauid roos from his ſlepe after mydday ¶ romed in his ſoler of his paleyſe: he ſaw a fayre woman waſſh hir in hir ſoler. he knewe not the woman ne the woman thoughte nott on him ne knewe not of his wicked wyl as the boke ſheweth there A non he ſentt after thys wooman and whanne ſhe cam to hym: he lay by hir: and bygate hir wyth a childe/ and non as he knew that ſhe was with child. to hide his ſy ne he ſet after hir huſbond vrie. ¶ ſhuld come home ¶ medle w' hys wife ¶ ye child ſhuld be named to hī and not to dauid/ And for ye godeknyght wolde not come ho me at his wife. ne uſe luſte of his body whylys goddes ooſte lay i

The sixte

the feelde in seege of a citye that hight rabath: dauid sente him a peny with letters of hys dethe to ioab the prynce of the ooste, and traytourly dyd hī sle. Here mightest thou se that dauid was ouercome with lecherie and deceyued by the fende, or the woman cam to hym. For as criste sayth in the gospel. For who so loketh on a woman in wyl to do amys wyth hir: anon he hath do lecherie and forsetteth apens this cōmaundement Non mecchaberis. Dauid loked on that woman in wil to do lecherie: whanne the woman thought non euyl, he sent after hir as after his lege woman, and she wyste not why. And whanne she cam to hym as to hir kyng he lay by hir synfully. for it was ful harde to hir to lette hym. Also peter forsoke cryste in tyme of hys passion and ran alwey fro cryste. or any wooman spake to hym b tyme & so he deceyued himsilfe: & the woman deceyued hym notte. She dyd hir offyce, For she was vsshere and keper at the dore, as sayth the glose and saint gregori and she seyde to him that he was one of cristys disciplis as she seyde soth. For she was bounde that she shulde lete non of cristys disciplis entre. And and at the first worde he forsoke criste and sayd that he knewe him not. And not only woman dyd saynt peter for sake criste in this maner, but mē sayde to hym the same wordis & for drede he forsoke crist soneast and suore that he knew him not. And therfor if it be repreue to womā þ womā made saint peter forsake criste: as moch repreese it is to men and moch more. For alsethough he forsoke criste at þe womans word yit he swore not therfore ne forswore him til men seyde to hym the same wordys. Mt xxvi.c.ᵒ & mi.xiiii.c.ᵒ. Also salomō disceyued himsilfe or any womā disceyued hym. For he toke to hī many hethen women of false bileue to haue his luste, he sought them: they sought nott hym, He wyste wel that it was apens goddes law a kyng to haue so many wyues & concubines as he hadde. For god bad þ kynges of hys peple shulde nott haue many wyues, ne multiplye theym manye horsys in greuaunce of the peple ne multiplie to hym greate weightys of golde and syluer in dysease of the people: as holy wryt shewethe wel. Deutronomio xvii.ᵒ capitulo. Also it was forbode to him and to al other so to cumpanye wyth hethen wymen And apens alle thys dyde Salomon in hygghe offence of god.

Precepte.

Salomon sought the cūpany of hethen wymen. The wimen wer stable in ther false bylecue. He was vnstable in his right bileue and folowed hir false bylecue: & forsoke goddes lawe in greate pyte, and worshiped false goddes Lecherye ouercam hym longe or many of the wymen knew him And so be men right these dayes. ouercome wyth lecherye wythoute womannis cumpanye and wythoute doyng of wymen. For as criste sayth in the gospel who so loketh on a woman in wyl to do amys wythe hir, thoughe she thenketh not on him: be doth lecherie. And if he hādle hir or smel hir or speke to hir or go to hir: or sehe by wilys, or by slepgstyps to haue bys luste of hir, thoughe the woman consente not to hym & thoughe he be letted of his wycked wyl: yet he is gyltye in lecherye, and doth apens this camail dement of god. Non me haberis. Men lechours gon and ryde fro towne to towne to gete wymen: after ther lust. They seke the wymen: and not the wymen theym. They caste many wyles to gete womans assent I spyne. Men comonly be worcħers and bygyłers of lecherye and thāne whether ye woman assent or not assente: yit the man is gyltye. And for oft ty

me it falleth that whanne men wende be seker of the woomans assent thanne the wooman wyl not assent for drede of god and if she assented byfore and hight the man to folowe his lust and after repenteth hir and withdraweth hir from his wycked cumpanye thānne shal the lechours may diſ= fame al wimen and sey that they be false and desepuable. For such lechours speke moste bylenye of wymen: for they may not haue ther foule luste of them at wil and for they maye notte defoule them wyth ther bodyes: they defoule them wyth ther tūges: and speke of them fuleupl and defame them falsely: and procure to theym the harme that they may. Exaumple we haue in the boke of Danyel. xiii°.c°. of the goode woman susanne and of two falſ olde prestis that were iugys and gouernourys of the people for þ pere. Whycħe by one assent way= ted to haue thys woman aloone in hir gardeyne, whāne she shuld go to waſshe hyr: as the maner was thanne. And for she wolde not assent to ther wickednes but cryed after helpe: anon they cried apens hir. And whanne men come: they sayde that they fonde hir lignge wythe a ponge man.

℄ And soo falsely dampnedde

The sixte

hir to dethe: for they mighte nott do ther foule luste with hir/ But at the prayer of susane god sente daniel hys prophet and toke the and conuecte them in ther falsehede and stoughe theym and saued susanne/ We fynde also in ye secunde boke of kynges. xiii. capi. That amon the sonne of dauid feyned hym sehe and prayde hys fader dauid y thamer hys suster mighte come and kepe hym And whane she was come he spake to hir for to lygh by hir: butte she wold not assét/ And thane he opyssed hir: and so defouled hys owne suster/ And anon he hated hir more than euer he loued hyr. Bifore/ Bicause that she wold not assent to hym/ And spitfully put hir oute of his chaumbre and did shete the dore after hir/ For thys dede amon was slayne sone after of his brother absolon.

The vii. chapter.

Diues. And yit many a Woman wyl assent to luste of flesshe ful lightly if it be profryd. Pauper. That is sothe/ But wymen be not so redy to assente as men be to profre it And he that profereth it and biginneth: he assétteth firste and is more in defaute Diues. Thou excusefte moche wymen: and acusefte men Pauper. I accuse no good man: butt lecherous men: ne I excuse noo wicked woman but gode wymen that be falsly defamed of lechery not only in ther persones/ But in ther kynde generaly/ For the proude malice of man defameth Vnskilfully the kynde of woma And as adam dyd put hys synne on womon and wolde not excuse his owne malice to get mercy. Diues. Salomon speketh moche euyl of wymen. Pauper. And salomon speketh moche gode of wymen/ For he sayde Mulier timens dm̄: ipsa laudabitur. The woma that dredith god she shal be preysed. Salomon repreueth wycked wymen: and praysethe good wymen/ and he repreueth wycked men and preisethe good men Diues. Salomo seythe. Ostio malacia nequicia mulieris. Breuis est ostiū malicia super maliciam mulieris Ecclesiastici xxv°. The wyckednesse of woma is al malyce//And euery malyce is short aboue ye malyce of woman. Pauper. Soth it is whanne wemen yeue theym to shrewidnes: they be ful malicouse. And whanne they yeue thē to goodnesse: they be ful gode. y therfore the wyse man i the next chapter. folowig praysith wimē

Precepte.

fulmoch and saithe. that blessed is that man that hath a gode woman to hys wyfe/ hys yeris shal be doubled. he shal end hys yeris in pees/ A good woman is a gode part: in a good part of them that drede god/ And she shall be youen to a man for hys gode dedys/ The grace of the besy woman shal lyke hir husbond/ and make his bones fatte/ Hir disciplyne and hir norture. is the gifte of god And the holy woman and chaaste is grace vpon grace And as the sonne shynynge lightneth the world in ye heyght of ye day so ye bewtie of a goode wooman is in confort and aray of hir husbonde/ And as golden peleris set on splū basys so be siker feete on the solys of the stable wooman. And endles groundes on a seker stone: be goddes cōmaūdemētis in the herte of an holy woman. Fundamenta eterna super petrā solidam: mandata dei in corde mulieris sancte. Eccle:xxvi.cᵒ. Diues. Salomon saythe Vinū et mulieres apostatare faciūt sapientes Eccle.xix°. Wyne and wymmen make wyse men to dote. and forsake goddis lawe and do amys Paup. And yit ther is no defaute in the wyne: ne oft tyme in the woman/ But defaute is in hym that vnwysely vse the wyn

and vnwysely vseth the woman & other goddes creaturys/ Thoghe thou drynke wyne tyll thou artte drunken and fallest in lecherye by thy glotenye: the wyne is not to blame: but thou þ canst not or wylt not mesure thyselfe: And thoughe thou loke on a woman & art caught I hir bewtye: & assenteste to do amys: the womā I case is not to blame: ne hir bewtye nott to lacke that god hathe youen hir But thou art to blame that no better kepeste thyn hert from wyched thoughtys/ But te there thou shuldeste preyse god: thou thenkeste euyl: and misusseste goddes fayre creature in offence of god there thou shuldeste preyse hym: And if thou felest ye tempted by the syght of woman: kepe thy syght better/ And if hir daly̅aunce stire the to lecherye: fle hir companye/ For a yens lecherye flegth is best fight/ Thou art fre to goo awey fro hir: no thyng bydeth ye to do lecherye but thy lechours herte.

The viii. chapter.

Diues. Womans aray styreth morhe folke to lecherye. Pauper. Although i case ye aray and the atyre is not to blame nomore than is hir bewte: yit by comon cours of kynde bothe man and woman seke to be onestly arayed after ther estat and after ther degre: and after the custom of the cuntre that they dwelle in not to tempt folke to lecherie: ne for pryde ne for non other synne But for onestie of mankynd and to the worshyp of god: to whos lykenesse man and woman is made / And he is oure brother: and this is the custome of good folk But if they do it for pryde / or to tempte folke to lecherye or for any other synne or þ they toke on the atyre þ is not accordynge to them if it be to costful or to straunge in shap. or to wyde or to syde not tewled by reson: they synne ful greuously in the syght of god / And namely tho men that cloth theym so short: that man & wooman may se the fourme of the shap of ther pryuy membres whiche be shameful to shewe and the syght is grete cause of temptacyon and of wicked thoughtis Saynt poule byddeth that wymen shulde atyre theym in onest araye with shamefastnesse: and sobrenesse. not in broydynge of ther heere: not in golde and syluer ne in perrie ne in ouerdon clothe. i: ad thī iii°. And the same seyth the saynt peter in his fyrste pistle iii°. c°. Where he bydderh that men shulde haue ther wyues in worshyp and kepe them onestly. Diues. Wymen these dayes araye theym ful moch ayenst the techynge of Peter and Poule / and therfore I drede me: that they synne ful greuously pauper. Peter & Poule forbyd not vtterly suche a raye / But they forbydde wymen suche araye to vse in pryde: or to prouoke folke to lecherie and to vse such araye passyng ther estate / or for an euyl ende / For we fynde that saynt cecilie and many other holy wymen went arayed in clothys of golde and in riche perrie & wered the hayre vnder þ solempne atyre / And Peter and Poule sayde tho wordys pryncipaly for tyme of prayer. as for lent: ymbre dayes gangedayes. frydays: Vigilies / and in tyme of general precession made for nede In such tyme namely man and woman shulde leeue al tokens and signes of pryde in aray / For as the glose sayth: ther proude clothynge getteth no goode of god: and maketh folke to dempamps: namely if it passe mesure and good maner / The pryncipal entencyon of saint poule there he sayth tho wordys: is to enfourme men and wymen in prayer

Præcepte.

For whom they shuld pray why and how, and where they shal py as sayth the glose. And be enformeth them to prey in lownesse: without pompe of clothyng & of grete araye. For I am syker: that the foule stynkyng pompe and pryde of araye that is nowe used in thys londe in al thre partyes of the churche, that is to sey in the seudorys and in clergie & in comoners wyl not be vnuenged. But if it be sone amended: by verry renpentaunce and forsakynge of thys synne. For fro the hyghest vnto the lowest in euery staate and in euery degree and nygh bond in euery persone: is now aray passyng to mannys body and womans apeys al reson and the lawe of god. Diues. Syth it is soo that man is more prynciplal in ordre of kynde than is woman, and more stable and myghty and of hygher discrecion by cours of kinde than is woman and shulde as thou haste wel seyde be more vertuous and stable in goodnesse than woman: how may it be that wymen kepe theyr oft more chaste, and be more stable in goodnesse than man. For we se that whanne men take theym to be ankeris and reclusys. With inne fewe yerys comonly eyther they falle in reufys, or trespes or

they breke out for womãs loue, or for itkyede of ther lyfe, or by som gile of ye send. But of wimẽ ancris so inclusid is seldome herde any of these defautys. But hoolely they begine and hoolely they ende. Pauper. Man by wey of kynde is more stable than is woman and of more discrecion. But by grace wymen be oft more stable in goodnes than be men and haue better discrecion & goodnes than many a man. Diues. Why so Pauper. For men truste to moch in themsilfe and truste not in god as they aught to do: wymen knowinge ther freelte trust not in themsilfe. But only in god and comend them more too god than do men ofte tyme. And the wyse man seith Inicium sapiencie timor domini. pū.iy.cº:pſ.no. The drede of the lorde is begynnynge of wysdome. For who so dredeth god with loue drede as the good childe the fader: that loue drede shall teche hym what is plesaunt to god: and what may displese him. And it shall make hym besy to do hys plesaunce, & to lef hys offence. And comonly whãne men bicome ancrys they do it more for ye world than for god. They do it for ipocrisie: to haue a name of holines & of wysdome, or for couetise to get gode

tii

The sixte.

or be oute of obedience: and at ther owne wyl. to ete and to drinke: wake and slepe whanne thē sypketh. and to doo as theym lyketh them therof: ne wyte whether they do well or euyl: or whether they praye or not prate And comonly men auctrys haue more dalyaunce wyth the worlde both wyth men and wymen: thā euer hadde they or they were an erys. And though they were selde foolys byfore: thāne men holde theym wyse. and aye of them doubtys of conscience and of thynges that be too come. of whyche thynges they kun noo skyl And yit what they seye. the peple taketh be it for gospel. and soo they deceyue many a man and many a wooman. And syth they groūde theym alle in pryde in ypocrisye and in couetyse: and truste in themsylfe more than in god therfore he suffereth the fende haue power ouer theym. and desease theym and brynge theym to wicked ende. But wymen take oft that state for no such ende: butt only for god. And they seynge ther owne freelte cōmende theim to god. And therfor god kepeth theym so: that the fende may not deceyue theym in suche maner: ne dissceyue theym. We rede I holy

wryt. Gest. gli°. q. pp. c°. That whanne abraham cam in to strāge londys he badde hys wyfe saray that she shuld not be aknow that she was hys wyfe: but seye that she was hys suster. For she was so fayre a wooman. that he wyste wel that men shuld couete hir for hir belwetye. And if they wende that she were hys wyfe: they shulde slee hym: To haue hir at wyl. For auoutrye was harder punysshed than manslaughter. And therfor to saue hys lyfe abraham sayde: and badde hyr seye that she was his suster. For as seyth doctor de lyra abraham wyste wel that she was a goode wooman: and had suche an angel to kepe hir that no mā shuld haue power to defoule hir / and so it byfel. For anon she was take and led to the kynge of egipt & kept there ye in kynges courte longe tyme: And abraham fared wel by cause of hir. But god set suche sykenasse to the kyng and to hys wyues and to hys concubynes. and to alle hys houshold that thay hadde no myght ne the kynge too defoule hir. Thanne the kynge axed hys preestes: and maysters of the lawe. Why deseseth he vnto hym: and to hys houssholde. And they by reuelacion of god. saide. that it was for

Precepte.

þe pilgrymes wyfe/And thāne þe kynge lette hym goo wyth worshyp/We rede also that abra ham hadde two sonnes. ysmael. of agar his seruant. and ysaac of sara hys wyfe/Abraham loued wel ysmael/for he was the elder son On a tyme sara saw ysmael pleye wyth hir sonne ysaac: nott goodly: she was mispayde: and sayde to abraham: that he shuld putte ysmael & hys moder agar oute of housholde: For ysmael sayde she shulde haue noo parte of eritage wyth my sonne isaac Abraham bare ful heuy of theise wordes: for he loued moche ys mael/Thanne god sayde to A= braham Thake it nott so harde ne so sharpely that sara sayde to the of thy chylde: and of thy ser= uant agar/But in alle thynge that sara saythe too the: here hyr voyce. and do therafter.   And thanne abraham putt them ou= te housholde: Full moche ayens herte/And so nott withstōding that abraham was so nygh god that he was cleped goddes frende/yit as for thanne hys wyfe knewe more of goddis wyl than dyd he/Also we rede of Isaac and rebecca his wife that they hadde two sonnes borne at onnes Which were Esau and Ja= cob ysaac loued better Esau thā

Jacob/But Rebecca loued bett Jacob thā esau: and so did god And by techyng of the holy gost she begyled ysaac and esau also: and dyd ysaac yeue hys pryncy= pal blessynge to Jacob: there he wolde haue youen it to Esau: & al was goddys dede and so con= fermed by god/that whāne ysa ac wyste of gyle: yit he durst not withdrawe hys blessynge For he sawe wel that it was goddes wil and goddes doynge And therfor he sayde to esau weppnge for he was so begyled/Benedixi ei: et erit benedictus I haue blessed yt and he shalbe blessed.

The yiiii. chapter.

Dives. I assent wele that by grace a woman may be as stable in chastitye: in good nesse as a man And without gra ce neyther man ne woman may kepe hym chaste/For the flesshe bothe of man and woman is ful freel and fulredy to falle/   And therfore I pray the tech me some remedie ayens the temptacōn of of lecherye. Pauper. One reme dye is resonable abstynece from mete and drynke. and for to flee deynte metys and deynte drynk= kes. and to flee glotony as most bygynnynge & mene to lecherye.

ciii

The sixte.

And therfore glotenye is forbode by thys cõmaundement as mene and wey to lecherye/Another remedye is harde lignge watche: and trauayle. that the body haue not to moche ese. But be wel ocupped / For the wyse man sayth that idylshyp hathe taughte moche malyce / Multam enim maliciam docuit ociositas: Therfore sayth he. Ryght as to the asse longeth the fedynge/ perde and birdeyn so to the seruaunt þ is to seye to the flesshe that shuld be sugett and seruant to the soule. longeth drede and chastisyng and werke of good ocupacioun Eccle. xxxiii°. And god sayth þ pryde and plentye of brede: and welfare and plentye of rychessys and idelshyppe. were cause of the wyckednesse of Sodomites: & of there lecherye. and for they loued not pore folke. Ezechi. xvi. c°. And therfore almesdede is a grete remedye ayens lecherye to gete grace of chastytie. so that it be youen to the pore nedye: that is in myschesse. and to such that haue not byhynd to get ther lyuelode by trauayle of ther body and if they begge they do it without auarice: with mekenesse. & clennesse of lyuynge: to such bid deth criste do almesse seyinge. Date elimosinam: et ecce omnia munda sunt vobis. Luce:

yeue ye almes. and so al thyges be clene to you: if ye wyl amed you/& another remedye is a man to haue mynde of his dethe: and thenke hou he shal wende hense. wyth bitter payne. and thãne al hys luste shal turne into wo and sorwe and thenke. that by mã or woman neuer so fayre: soo welfarynge. so hole: so lusty: so slypinge to the iye. so myghty so witty. so grete of lynage. so ryche so grete of name. or of lordshyp. Eyther by man eyther woman. be euer so plesaũte: shal die: and turne to erthe and aisshis & wormes mete And if he smel now neuer so swete: he shal stih thã ful sowre. Therfore the wyse man sayth. In omnibus opibus tuis memorare nouissima tua & letẽ num non peccabis Eccle. vii° c. In al these werkes thenk on thy last thynges: and thou shalt not do no synne without ende: we rede that in englonde was a big that had a concubyne. whos name was rose / And for hyr grete bewte he cleped hir rose amõde Rosa mundi / that is to saye/rose of the worlde / For him thought that she passed al wymen i bewtye / It bifel that she died & was buried whyle the kynge was absent / And whanne he cam ayen for grete loue: that he had to hyr he wolde se the body in the graue

Precepte.

And whanne the graue was opened there sate an orrible tode vpon hir breste bytwene hir teetys: and a foule adder bigirt hir body aboute in the midle / And she sta̅de so that the kyng ne non other myght stonde to se that orryble sight / Thanne the kynge dyde shette apen the graue / and dyde wryte these two veersis vpon ye graue Hic iacet in tu̅ba rosa mu̅di non rosa munda. Non redolet sz olet quod redolere solet That is thus to sey i englissh / Here lyeth in graue rose of the worlde but not clene rose / She smelleth not swete but stynketh ful foule that su̅tyme smelled ful swete And another remedye apens lecherye is that a man and woma̅ kepe wel ther fyne wyttes that a man kepe wel his bodys and his body from nyys touchynge. hys eerys fro misherynge . that he he: re noo tales of lecherye / ne foule spech / For saynt poule saythe. Corru̅piunt bonos mores collo quia praua . i. ad cor. xv°. Wyc: hed spech destroyeth chastyte & good thewys / Also he most kepe wel hys sight . takynge exau̅ple of Job whic̅h made a couenant with his iyen . that he shulde not thenke on a mayde to haue mys thyng i the thought And ye pphe̅ te Ieremye sayde þ hys iye had

robbed his soule in the woma̅ of his cetye trenox. iii° . For the ise ku̅pilys the prophete sayde : that deth is entred by oure wi̅ndouys that is to saye / by oure spuc we̅ tys whych be wyndouys , and wi kettys to the soule. Ieremye ix° c° . And another remedye is a mi̅d to kepe wele hys herte from idel thoughtys / and from wycked thynges. For as criste saythe in the gospel . oute of the hert co̅ wycked thoughtys : ma̅slaught , auoutrye fornicacion . theft iui̅s wytnesse . blasphempe . My xv° . And therfore seyth the wysman ; Omni custodia serua cor tuum . pu̅ : iiii° : c° . With al kepyng kepe wel thyn herte / For of the herte cometh lyffe and deth / The mayster of kyndys . li° . xviii . Seyth þ there is a best þ is clepyd tapus . þ is a broh or a bawsyn i glyssh / And there is a greate en̅ enmytye bytwene the fox and hi̅ The fox is besy to put the baw syn oute of hys denne / And for he may notte do it by myght : he doth it by sleyght / He waytethe whane ye baust is gon out of his denne tan̅ he goth and pisseth & maketh foule the bawsonys den And for the bawsym hath stench and vnclennesse : whanne he co̅ meth and fyndeth hys denne so stenkyng and so defouled he for

319

soke hys denne and seketh hym another. And thanne the foxe entreth: and there he bringeth forth a shrewed brode. By the ball that hateth stenche and Unclenesse is understond cryste Jesus borne of the mayde floure of clennesse. By the foxe is understond the fende Which is aboute nyght and daye to put crist oute of his denne: that is mannis soule and womans. For mannys soule is goddes denne, goddes teple, goddes house. goddes dwellig place And for the fende may nott putt hym oute by myght, he putteth hym oute by sleyght. He maketh the foule i mannys soul and womans. He putteth in ther soulys foule stynkyng thoughtys of lecherye. firste smale and aft gretter. And anon as man or woman begynneth to have suche thoughtys: anon ther soule bygynneth to stenke in goddes sight & if they assēt to ye thoughtys to do thē in dede. or for to delyte theym therin. Thanne ther soulys stinke so foule in goddis sight that he forsaketh tho soulys and wendeth oute, and than the feende entreth. And there he bryngeth forth synne after synne. tyll at the laste he bryngeth theym from shame to shame: to wycked deth and to wicked end

Therfore saynte Austen in hys sermon byddeth vs that we shul be traueyle that oure god fynde no thynge in his temple. that is to sey in oure soulys that maye offende the iyen of his maiestye. But mote the dwellynge of oure herte be voyded of vyces. and fylled wyth vertues. shett to the fende and open to cryste.

The xv. chapter.

Another remedye ayens ye temptacion of lecherye is deuocion and mynde of crystys passion. For as sayth saynt gregori, there is non so harde temptacion. but that man shuld ouercome esily enough. if he thought enteerly on crystys passion. We fynde in gestys that on a tyme a greate kynges son loued wele a pore woman. For thoughe she were pore, yit she was fayre and plesaunt in beryng. The kynges sonne tooke hir to hys paramoure and wedded hir. Wherfor his fader & nigh all his kyn was myspayde. For them thought he was moch disperacid by hir. Wherefore he seyng that his kynred bare so heuy of his mariage he wente into fer londes & gaue hym to armes. & what he myght

Precepte.

wynne with his swerde he sent it home to hys wyfe: sauynge hys worship and his spuynge / In euery iourney he had the better of his enemies & so his name bigan to spzynge fer and wyde. At the last he cā I so hard feight al though he hadde the maystry yit he was so wounded. that nedys he muste dye / Thanne he sente home his sharte ful of woundys: & of holys: and alforbledde to his wife with a lettre under his seale sayinge in this wyse / Cerne cicatrices: Vectis Vestigia pugne. Quesiui ppzio sāguine ǣquid habes. Byhold my woundys & haue theym in thy thought / For alle the goodis that be thyne with my blode I haue theym bought And whanne this woman sawe this sharte. and redde the lettre she fel doune I swowne And whā she was releued she heng vp this shettel a preuy place of hir chambre. and whanne euer any man cam to hir to speke of weddynge or of fleshly luste: she wente ito hir chaumbre and loked on hys sharte. and cam oute ayen styffe and stedfast in hir husbondis loue that was ded: and denyed togeder ayenge. seiyng in this maner / While I haue his blode I my mynde / That was to me so gode and kynde / Shal I neū hus bonde take / But hym that dyed

for my sake. And thus she kept hir in clennesse and chastilye all hir lyfe for loue of hir husbonde. that dyed for hir loue By thys pore woman that was soo fayre is vnderstonde mannys soule & womans which is made too the lykenes of god / But it was made ful pore through the synne of adam / By the kynges sone is vnderstonde criste goddes sone whi che loued so moch mannys soul that as sayth sayt Poule he auentissed himsilfe and disparisched himsilfe into the likenes of a seruant: and maried to him oute kynde and mannis soule and lyued here two and thritty wyn ter and more in moch wo to wynne the loue of mankys soul and faught ayens the feude. the fles she and the worlde that be alwey besy to lese mannys soule. And alwey he hadde the maystry: by might of the godhed / But on go de fridaye he cam in so fel a fight with that tyraunt ye fend of hel & though he had the maistry: yit he was so for wounded. & By wey of mahod Whiche he toke of the mayde nedely he must dye / And thā he sent home a lettre of loue to his spouse mānys soul seiyng as the knyght sayde. Cerne citatrices &c. Beholde my woundys and hane them I thy thought. For al ye godis & be thine wᵗ my

The sixte

blode I haue them bought / For why al the ioye and blis that we shulde haue in heuen and all the grace and goodnesse that we haue here in erth. al haue we by ver tue of cristis passion. For but he wold haue died for oure sake els shulde we haue layne in hel payne withoute ende / By this shirte ful of woundys and so blody I vnderstōd his blessful body For as manis body is clad i his shert so the godhed was clothed in the blessful body of criste / Whiche body was al blody and so ful of woū dys: p as sayth the prophete Isa ie .i. c. Fro the sole of the fote to ye top of the hede there was noo hole place in his body / Therfore lue frende I pray you hange ye this shertte in a preuye place of youre chaumbre: that is to saye Sette ye crystys passion enterly in youre herte: and whonne the fende: the worlde. or the flesshe. or any wycked man or woman. Bygynneth to tempte you to syn ne: anon wende ye to youre hert & loke ye on thys shert / Thenke hou that blessful body was born of the mayde marye wythoute synne and sorowe and neuer did amys / Thenke hou it was for rent and fortorne / Byspeted for oure synne and oure sake: & not for his owne gylt / and if ye doo

so and thenke enteerly on cristis passioon / ye shal lightly ouercō euery temptacion. and haue the better pacience in tribulacion. Wherfor an holy man sayth thus Reminiscens sacrati sanguinis. quem effudit amator hominis / effundendo lacrimas: Non est locus ingratitudinis. Vbi tor tante dulcedinis attigit alas &c. Whanne I thenke on cristis blo de / that he shed vpon the rode I fele terys smert. What man may be vnkynde That cristis blode hath in mynd. enteerly I his hert Swete Iesu crystÿ What is thy gylt That thou thus for me arte spylt. scoure of vnlothfulnes. I am a these and thou diest. I am gyltye and thou obeyste al le my wickednes why pauest thou so moch for thy ñ What winest thou wyth thy thyne harde payne: ryche in blysse aboue: Loue thyn herte so depe hath sought That peyne of deth letteth ne nought to wine mannys loue Another remedye ayens lecherie is redynge and da liaunce of holy writ and of holy mennys lyues / And therfore seit Ierom sayth ad rusticum mona chum Ama scienciam scriptura rum & carnis vicia non amabis Loue kunnynge of holy wrytte and of goddes lawe: And thou shalt notte

Precepte.

loue vices of the flessh. And ther for god sayth/ Nō videbit me homo et vinet. Exo.xxxiii. Ther shal no man se me by deuocion and lyue flesshely/ For no thynge sleeth so moch the lust of the flesshe as deuocion/and the lyke of god/and studye in goddes lawe/And another remedy is to thenke on hel peyne/For as seyth saynte Thomas de veritate theologie In hel shalbe ouerdon hete of fyre and gnastyng of teeth for cold and for payne derkenes and smoke and bitter weppyng. withoute ende/Rorynge and be lewyng of foule fendes. weplyng and weylynge sobbynge a sigh= pyng of synful soules/ and ende les repreue of ther synnes endles drede. endles thirst stenche/syght thundre and worme of consciēce boondys. presoun. drede. shame wantyng of the blissful sight of goddes face/and woo withoute any hope of any welthe: There men shal seke deth and not fynd it/and wisshe that they hade neuer be borne/ And as saint Bernard in his meditacions seyth/ there shal be harde weppyng & grogyng of teeth rorynge of seendys: and hidous thunder There ther sight shalbe foule. wormys todys ad= ders: and orryble faces of the fē= des and misshape thynges. there

wycked wormes shal gnawe the herte rotys. there shalbe sorowe and sighynge: and orrible drede There synful wrecchys shal br͞en ne in the fyre without ende/ In ther body they shalbe turmēted by fyre and in ther soule by wor mie of conscience: There shalbe deth without deth For alwey they shalbe in dying and lyuer payne and may not die/ Butt al= wey lyue in dyinge/ Ther smel= lynge shalbe fylled wyth orrible stenche. for there shalbe no hope But whanne they be in these pay nes ten hūdred yere: yit ther pay ne is newe al to begynne And therfore if loue of god: ne mede of heuen styreth vs not to fle lechery and al other synnes/ lette vs fle lecherie and all other synnes for drede of endles payne.

The xvi. chapter.

And another remedye ayēs lecherie is to thenke of ye harde vengeaunces ye god hath take for lecherie first take hede what vēgeaūce god hath take for symple fornicacion we finde in holy wryt Gen. xxxiiii. that dyna ye doughter of Jacob wēt fro home to se ye wymen of that cuntre: and to se ther atyre Than sychem the sone of emor: prynce ye cuntre wēt & defouled this dyna by might And not withstōdyng

The sixte

his besines for to haue weded hir / yit he was slayne for his lecherie and his fader. and al the men of that cetye. and that cetie destroyed / we rede also i holy writ Numeri xxv°. For that the children of israel dyd lecherie with the wimen of moab. god was offended And bad mooses take the pryncces of his peple and hang theym vp on iebetys / for they were asentynge to the synne. and bad euery man sle his neyghbore that was gyltye in that synne / For by lecherye they fel into idolatrye And so for ȝ lecherye were slayn i tyme foure ⁊ twenty thousand ¶Thanne phynees the sonne of eleazar saw one of the children of israel lye by one of þe wymen: ⁊ to venge hys synne he toke hys swerde and roof them both togydre into the erthe: throughe ther preuy membrys / And god was so moche pleased with hys dede that he graunted to hym: and to his children after him the dignytye of preesthode wythoute end ¶For but he had do that dede god shulde elles haue destroyede the peple / Also for auoutrye and vnlawful wedloh alle mankynde was destroyde in tyme of noeis flode safe eight soulys. Gen. vi. And for defoulynge of one man nys wife were slayne sixty thousand and fyue thousand and all a cuntrye: and a greate cetye destroyed at the byddynge of god. Judiciū. xix°. ⁊ xx°. Also dauid for auoutrye was dreuen out of of hys kyngdome. and he and al his houssholde and al his kynred were afterward ful hard punysshed for his lecherye. ii°. Re. xi. ⁊ xii° c°. And by the olde law both man and woman shuld be slayne: if they were take in auoutrye / we rede that Judas the sonne of iacob had thre sonnes by one wooman her. onan: and selam / But her that was the eldest sone was a shrewe and mysused hys owne wyfe / Wherfore god was wroth with hym and slough hym with soden deth / for he vsed hys wyfes luste and wold not bygete chyldren of hir / But dyd so þ she shuld not conseyue. Gn. xxxviii°. Also for lecherye: seuen husbondis of sara that was after the wyfe of yonge tobie were slayne of þe fende for ther foule luste. Tobie vi° Also for lecherie of the þ be of kynred ⁊ of affenitye: god hath take hard wrath. as whā Iamā lay by his suster thamer. he was slayne of his brother absolon: ⁊ Loth þ brother of Abraham by drūkenship: lay by his own two doughters ⁊ bigat of thē ii. chyldrē moab ⁊ amon which childrē

Precepte.

and the peple that cam of theym were alweye enemyes to goddes folke and acursed of god Also Jacob cursed his sone Ruben for he lay with one of his wyues Also for the foule synne of sodomye: fyue fayre cytees Sodom & Gomorre and other thre cytees. were destroyde I tyme of abraham For god rayned vpon them fyre and brymstone from aboue And the erthe shoke so and tremblyde that they sonke doūe ito hel house. Lond man. and chyld .and best and al that they had There was no thyng saued butt Loth & hys two doughters. His wife mighte haue be saued. But for that she loked ayen to þe cetie ayens þe aūgels byddyng / Whāne she harde the rewful crie of them that perished therfore she turnid ito a salt stone For þe aūgel bad the streit so that they shuld not loke ayen And al that cūtre which was byfore likened to paradise for fayrenesse and plentye of the cuntrye: turned into a foule stynkige podel: that lasteth into this day: & is cleped the dedde see / For there may no thīg lyue therin for filth and stench in vēgeaunce of that stynkynge lecherie. Gen. pij°.

Diues. Me merueleth moche þ god toke so general wreth to slee man and woman and chyld / For I am sphēr. ther were many chyldren ful yonge and vngiltie in þ synne / Also we fynde notte that wymen were thanne gylstye in þ synne / The boke sayth that alle the peple of men fro the child male to þe old cam to do that synne But of wymē speketh he not that any cam therto Paup Though women vse notte that synne .yit they were gylsty in that that they forsoke not ther husbondys þ were gylstye / For sodemye is moost sufficiēt cause of dyuorce bytwene husbond & wife Whāne it is openly vsed / And sythe they wold not forsake ther husbondys in þ orryble synne: in maner they assented to ther synne: & so ryghtfully they perished I synne wyth them. Of the chyldren vngiltye the mayster of stories saith. that god slough theym for ther beste. For if they had lyued forth into nighty age they shulde haue folowed the lecherye of ther faders and so it was better to theym to die or they were gylstye: than to haue lyued lenger and died gylstye and go to helle without ende

The xvii. chapter.

Diues. Fel there any vengeūce for lecherye of men of holy churche? Pauper. we fynd I the secunde boke of kyn-

The sixte

ges ii.c°. that there was a dekē i the olde lawe: Whos name was Oza And whanne he touched ye hutche eyther arke of god to holde it vp whannd it shulde els haue falle: his right arme serid and dryed sodenly: and anon he died For as seyth the maystter of stories. þ night he had delyd wythe his wyfe Syth thanne the dekē of ye old law was so sterd punysshed for he touched goddes hutch þelles shuld haue sal for he meddled that nyght with his wyfe moche more preestys and dekens of the newe lawe be worthy moche woo: if they psume to touch goddes body or to mynestre at god/ desauter. Whanne they haue comoned de wythe other mennes wyues: or wythe ther concubynes. And therfore the lawe byddeth streitly that there shulde no man ne woman here masse of ye preste whiche that he knoweth sikerly that he holdeth acōcubyne or is an open lechoure & notorye Distinc.xxxii.nullus &c. þt hec. And in the same law it is forboden in payne of cursinge that any preste lechoure: shulde saye any masse. or any deken lechoure rede any gospel. or any subdeken rede any pystle in the office of holy churche/ And in another place the law biddethe þ suche notorye

lechourys shulde haue no offyce in holy church ne benifice. and if they had but if they wold amēde them. they shuld be pryued both of offyce and of Benefice Distc. xxviii. decreuimus/ And if any man of holy church haunted moche the place and the cumpanye of suspecte wymen. But he wold cese He shuld be deposed Destc. lxxxi. clericus/ And there shuld no straunge wymen dwell with men of holy church: But ther modris beldames auntes and godmoders and brothers doughter. or susteris doughter. Ibm c°.cū omnibus And if there might any euyl suspecōn be of ther dwellig togydre or for youth. or for they be suspecte in other byhalue. that thay shulde not dwelle with them in housholde. But in some other place. Ex. de cōhtacōne cōscorā mꝛsterū.i°.c°. Diues. Though a preste be a shrewe. the sacramētys that he mynystreth be not ye worse/ For the goodnesse of the preste amendethe nott the sacrament. Ne hys wyckednesse appeyrethe theym not as the lawe shewethe well in the same place. Obi supra pꝛimo capitulo. Pestra. Why forbiddethe thanne the lawe men to here massys of synful preestys lecchourys.

326

Precepte.

Pauper. Not for defaute of þe sacrament. For the secrament is not the worsse for the malyce of the preeste. But therfor this lawe forbiddeth men to here ther masses and ther offyce: that they might be so ashamed of ther synne and the soner amende them. Diues. Whan is a man of holy chur che cleped i the lawe an open no torye lechoure. Pauper. Whan the dede sheweth so the silfe that it may not be denyed ne excused or whanne he is aknow it bifore a iuge or conuycte therof byfore hys iuge Extra e.c°. Be stra. & c°/ quesitum. Whane it is thus noto rye and open: there shuld no ma ne wooman here ther masse ne ther offyce wetyngly. Suche cler kes lechours. Be he preeste. be he busshop. be he dekyn or subdekyn he shulde lese his degre and not abyde in the chaunsel amonge o ther clerkes in tyme of office & he shuld haue no pte of ye godes of holy churche. Distc. lxxxi. si qs ĉ altis capitulis sequentibus And therfore saynt Gregori bid deth in the name of god: by the auctorite of saynt Peter that no preeste lechoure. ne dekyn ne sub dekene lechoure shulde entre ho ly churche tyl that they wolde a mende them. And no ma ne wo man sayth he: be so hardy to here

ther office. For why he sayth ther blessynge turneth into cursynge & ther prayer into synne. For god sayth to them. I shal curse your blessynges. And altho sayth he that wyl not obeye to thys holy precepte. they fal i synne of ydo latrye. Distincc. lxxxii. si qs sunt Therfore god seyth to. Vyched men of holy church: Butt ye wyl here me and sett youre hertys to worshyp my name: elles I shall sende to you my scheef and curse youre blessynges. Malachie ii. c.

The xviii. chapter.

Diues. Whether is lecherye more synne in wedded fol ke: or i mē of holy church. Pau per. In lecherye be many degre es. as I seyd byfore. For auou trye is more synne than is sym ple fornicacion. But in ceste bis lecherye with theim that be nigh of kyn: is more than auoutrye: And sacrilege that is lecherye in theym that haue auoued chasti tie as in men of holy church and in men of religion also: is more than auoutrye. Hec siti. consn̄. iii°. ti°. xxxiiii°. q. CLi. quero. Where he saith that sacrilege and bregynge of the volde of chasty tye: is more than auoutrye. And

℧he sixte

a therfor ye lawe saith ỹ fastīg fro the higher chastite ỹ is vowed to god is more and worse thã avou trye/ For sythe god is offended whanne the wyfe kepethe notte seythe to hir bodely husbond: or the husbonde kepeth nott seythe to his wyfe: moche more is god offended if seythe of chastitye is not kepte to hym whiche was profered to hym frely: not ayed nedely. And the more frely it was made withoute compellyng.the more synne is the brekynge. xxvii.q.i. Nupciarū in fine .c. &c°.impudicas. & c.sciś. Also the lawe sayth that the synne that is don īmediatly ayens god is more synne than ye synne that is do prīcipaly ayens man/ And therfore seyth he: sacrilege is more synne than any fornicacōn or avoutrie.ꝑVii.q̃.iiii.sunt q̃.Oiues.Contra te.The lawe sayth that avoutrie is mooste of al synnes.ppli.q̃.Vii.quid in omnibˀ Pauper.The glose answereth therto and seyth .that it is amaner of speche to do wlate avoutre and shewynge that avoutrye is ful greuous/ But he sayth there that manslaughter and incest:& sacrilege by brekyng of the vow of chastitye is more greuous. And also it may be take for gostly avoutrye:that is whāne a crīsten soule forsaketh the seythe of holy churche that he reseyued iɳ his baptem:and forsaketh crist to whom he wedded hym.& turneth to the fende and to false byleue/ And euery dedly synne is goostly avoutrye. Diues.I am answerd seye forthe what thou wylt. Paup.Also lecherie is more synne ī men of holy church thã iɳ wedded folke: bycause of thy persone/ For men of holy church may better withstonde the fleshly temptacion/than wedded mē For they owe to passe the people iɳ kunnynge and vertue/ And therfore god seyth in the gospel: that the seruante knowynge the wyl of his lorde and not doynge hys.wylshalbe harde punysshed. Also for his vnkyndnesse. For why ỹ the gretter his benefyce is & the more that hys dignytye is ye more is he boūde to god and the more is his synne if he be vnkyɳd And therfore holy wrytt saythe. Potentes potent tormenta paciētur/They that be mygħty iɳ thys worlde by welth and worshyp that god sendeth them: shal suffre myghtely turmentys/If they be vnkynde Also for the synne repugneth more to his person Both for his digite & for ye vow of chastite ỹ he made ī takyng of holy ordre.

also his synne is more greuous
for it is more sclaunderous. and
noyous to the peple. for his wic=
ked ensaumple. And therfor saĩt
gregory sayth. that they shal an
swere for as many soulys as pe/
risshe by ther wycked ensaumple
For whanne the hede and the le/
der falleth: the body lyghtly shal
falle / And more discomfort it is
to an oste if they se ther chefteyn
flee and turne the backe. thanne
though they see twenty other sĩ
ple men turne the backe and flee
and more conforte to the enem=
es And so it is of mē of holy chur
che that shulde be leders of crist
people For they turne the backe
to god & fle oute of goddes ooste
as ofte as they falle in dedly syn
ne / Also it is more greuous ĩ mē
of holy churche / For they maye
better flee lecchery than men of
the worlde / For it nedeth not thē
not moch dele wyth wymen : ne
wyth the worlde. ne it longeth
not to theym. But it longeth to
theym to fle the cumpanye of wi
men and euery occason of synne
Dide in sm̃. conf. li°. iii°. ti. xxx=
iiii.q̃.LCii. For these shyplys
clerkes sey that ye studious thē/
kynge of lechery defouleth as
moch a clerke as doth ye dede of
uoutrye of the lewed man:
Tantum coinquinat clericum

studiosa cōcupiscēcia quātũ laĩ
cũ ad ustii culpa. sicut dt̃ in trac
tatu Qui bene presunt.

¶ The xix. chapter:

Qjues. Why be men irregu
ler for bigamye: Pauper
For many causys. Firste for dig
nyte and onestie of holy ordre: &
of the sacramentys of holy chur/
che / Also to shewe token and ex/
aumple of contynence & of chas
tyte Destinc: xxxii. posuisti.
For he that shal prech continēce
and chastyte: moste shewe con=
tinence and chastyte in hĩmsilfe
Also for ther is not ful sacramēt
of matrimonye And he that shal
mynystre the sacramentys of ho=
ly churche. moste haue no defau
te in any sacramente / wherfore
thou shalt vnderstondde as that
I seyde firste. the sacramente of
matrymonye bytokeneth the
vnite and the knot bitwene crist
and holy church. as bitwene one
husbonde and one wife mayden
wythoute spotte. as sayth saynt
poule. and that is bytokened by
the cōiunction and the knyttige
togidre bodely of husbonde and
wyfe in matrymonye. Also that
bodely knyttynge to gedre ĩ ma/
trymonye bitoenheth the vnyte
and ye knot bitwene the godhed

The syxte.

and the man bed in the chambre of the mayde marie Whiche knot and Vnitie and matrimonye by/ganne in time of patriarkis and prophetys. and it Was made sy/ker and stable in the tyme of grace in the Birthe of crist and in hys passion. But it shal be ful ended and made perfite in heuen Blisse And therfore sayth saint Austen in questio lb3 oroſii. that as god made Woman of the rib of adam sleppnge and of his syde. so out of the syde of crist slepyng Vpon the crosse. ran Bloode and Water. Which be the sacramentis of our redempcion. By Which sacramē/tys holy churche is fourmed: and Wedded to criste as eue to adam Also matrimonie bytokeneth þe Vnytye and the knotte bytwene criste and cristen soule. and that prpncipaly for the goostly knot that is bitwene the husbond and Wyfe I assent of ther Willys. For as moche thanne as he that is in Bygamie is not only one husbōd to one clene Wyfe. as crist is one husbonde too one holy churche mayden. Or the Wife is not on/ly Wife bodely to one husbonde. But the husbonde hathe deperted his flessh in two Wiues. or þe Wy/se departed hir flessh in two men therfore there is defaute in þ sa/crament of matrimonye / For it

signifieth not pfitly the Vnyte bitwene crist and holy churche. And in many maner may falleth in Bigamye and so in irregularitye First if he haue two Wyues law/fully one after a nother & knowe the theym flesshly. Also if he ha/ue two togydre or mo. as one by the lawe openly and by dome of holy churche, and another by lawe of conscience, and knowe theim flesshly. Also if he haue two on þ maner one after another & know ethe theym flesshly. Also if he ha/ue Wedded a Wedolwe corrupte Also if he Wed any Woman cor/rupte of another man. Where he knoweth hir corrupt or knowes the it not. Also if he knew flessh/ly his owne Wyf after that she is knowne of a nother / Whether he knoweth it or knoweth it notte Also if any man of holy churche or pfes in religion Wedde a wo/man and medle Wyth hir: be she mayde or corrupte. he is irregu/ler. Versus. Si ducas ibu cant. Vel quam corrupit alter. Vnā post aliam binas q; simul tua coniuy. Cognita si fuerit bi gamie lege teneris. Et si possici/tam Violasti Virginitatem. In al these casys man is irregu ler. Diues. Though the man be not mayde Whanne he Weddeth a mayde: is he not irreguler. for

Præcepte.

his own corrupcōn whṗ is he tha irreguler for corrupcōn of ye woman / For it semeth that his owne corrupcion shulde rather make him irreguler: Than the corrupcōn of the woman. Pauper. In the coniunction of criste to holy church is vnyte and oneshed in bothe parties And therfor if eyther man or woman in matrimonie hath departed his flessh byfore: there is a defaute in that matrimonye. as anentis that sacrament / For ther matrymonye bytokeneth not perfytly the matrimonye bytwene criste and holy church. But more onehed and clennesse is nedful in the womā than in the man, For in the man it is nedful that he haue wedded no woman byfore flesshly butte one. But it nedeth not that he be a mayde: But if the woman it is nedful that she be not corrupt byfore of any other man. Diues. By what skille: Pauper. For the corrupcion byfore matrimonye causeth not irregularitye in him that is corrupt: But it causeth the irregularitie in the other that is knyt to him / For that dede of corrupcion falleth not thanne on him that dyd the dede / But on him that is knitte to him in matrymonye / And therfore right as the man is not irreguler for he is corrupt himsilf whanne he wedded: But for he weddeth a womā corrupt right so if womā were able to holy ordre: she shuld be irreguler / not for that she is corrupt: But for that she knytteth hyr to man corrupt: But she hade be corrupt byfore in other matrimonye / Another skylle maye be thys / For the knott and vnitye made bytwene criste & holy church: and bitwene the godhed and the manhed: it is one and onys made for euer / Therfore it is bytokened by the bodely knytlyge togedre of the first matrimonye But whanne man passeth to the secund wife and weddeth also bodely: or if she be corrupte: Thanne goth he from vnitye to pluralite / Therfore the secūd matrimonye may not figure perfytly the coniunction of criste to holy church: ne of the godhed to the manhed: Which coniunction is one: and but onys don for eū. and not chaungeable / For there the thyng tokened is but one: ye thynge tokenynge that thynge moste be one / And the thig tokened & ye thyng tokenig ẏ thynge most be lyke / Also more clennesse is nedful to the woman to saue the sacrament of matrymonye: thā i the man: for ye womā bitokeneth holy churche wedded to criste: Which as saynt poul saith most be clene mayde with oute

B ii

The sixte.

spot / Also the woman bitokeneth the manhed of criste that he toke of the mayde marie withoute part of man / Also the womā bitokeneth cristē soul whiche most be withoute corrupcōn of synne if it shal be cristys spouse / For these supplyes: to saue the sacrament of matrimonye: ye womā most be mayden / Diues. I suppose a man had defouled a mayden: and after that he wedded hir is he irreguler for he weddeth ye woman so corrupte / Pauper. Sūme clerkes saye yea and sūme nay / But most comon openyon is that he is not irregnler: for he departed not his flesshe ito another wyfe. so that the mayden be not defouled of anotherDiues. Saynt poule sayth / Oportet ys biterū esse vnius vxoris virum. p. ad thi.iii.c. It bihoueth a prest to be husbonde of one wyfe / And so it semeth that euery preste moste haue a wyfe. or elles he maye be no preste: and so there shulde no preste dwelle mayden. Pauper. The wordes of saynt poule be thus vnderstond: that there may no man be preste that hathe had two wiues bodely for thanne is he bigamus. Diues. What if a man wene to wedde a mayd and he fynd hir corrupte. Paup. He is irreguler. And if he wed a may-

de and she medle after with any other man. and hir husbōd medle with hir after that she is knowen of another. thoughe the husbond wite it not: yit he is irreguler / And if a man accuse his wif of auoutrie & he medle withe hyr after: that by his owne ayīng or by his wyues ayynge: he is irreguler: be she gilty. Be she not gilty / And by comō openiō though she be compelled by holy churche to yelde to hir hir dette of his body. if he yeld it: he is irreguler If a man wedde a mayden: and she dye a mayden: and after that he wedde another mayden & know hir flesshly: or if he know ye first and not the secunde: in thys case he is not irreguler For he deptethnot his flessh into two wyues ne his wyfe into two men. And if he wedde a wedow mayd: he is not irreguler / If a man hath made a contract with a woman: & after weddethe another and knowe the hir flesshely if he know nott the firste flesshly: he is not irreguler / But if he be compelled by holy churche to go ayen to the firste anon as he yeldeth hir the det of his body he is irreguler / If a mā haue two wyues byfore his baptem: or one bifore: and another after bodely: he is irreguler: He is bigamus shal haue no lope of

Precepte.

any preuilege that longeth to ye clergie: and be subget to other seculer iuges/ as other lewed men. And vpon peyne of cursynge. he shal bere no tonsure: ne vse clothyng that longeth to clergye. In sm.conf.li°iiij°.ti° de bigamē

The xx.chapter:

W Hanne wymen be deliud of ther children they may entre holy churche to thank ther god what tyme they wil or may the lawe letteth them not/ And by the same skil men of holy churche may sige bifore thē in ther oratorie aud oneste place: if thay haue leue. Extra li bro iiij°. ti°. de purgacione post pertum And therfore they that clepe theym be/ they wymen for the tyme þ they slye in be folys: and synne in case full greuously. Diues. May a man yeue his wyf leue to medle w' another man: or the wyfe yeue the husbond leue to medle w' another woman Pauper. Nay For neyther may yeue other leue to do dedely synne ayens the precepte of god. Non mechaberis. Ne the Pope himsilf may yeue theym leue. Diues. Contra. We rede.Gen̄.xvi°. That Sara the wyfe of Abraham gaue abraham leue too medle wyth he Agar hir seruant to gete on hir a childe & so he dyd: for he bigate on hir ysmael Paup. To this clerkes sey that Abraham was excused. For it was the maner amonges the good peple of god that tyme that if the wyfe were bareyne: by ther bothe assent the husbond might take hī a secūdarie wife: not for luste / but only to multyplye goddes peple / And so Abraham by assent of hys wyfe and by the preuy leue of god: nott for luste but for to haue a child to goddes worshyp toke Agar to his wyfe And so she was his secūdarie wife: and sara the chefe wyfe / And so also had Jacob foure wyues lefully not for luste / But for to multiplye goddes peple / and for token of thīges that were to come / And þ was do by auctoritye of dispensacion of god: whych is aboue al lawes / But though god dispensed wyth abraham & Sara to do in that maner: or wt Jacob to haue many wyues to gedre: for figure and skillis that god knewe: yit men may not take nowe this tyme example ther of to do the same / For the skillis aforsayde be fulfylled And the lawe sayth: Priuilegium paucorum non facit legem communē.

v iii

The sixte.

xxv.q.i.cº. Vsciōppe sinenī. The preuylege of a selue maketh no comon lawe. And therfore Isaac the sonne of Abraham had neuer but one wyfe that was Rebecca of which he bygate but two children: at one tyme as sayth saynt Austen. And he medled neuer wt other woman for desyre of chyldren, ne for lust of his flessh. And so by his continence he shewethe þ his faders doyng was but a special preuylege graūted of god to hym: and therfore in that he toke non ensample therof. For that Abraham dyd: he dyd it by special despensacion of god: and i figure of thynges to come. For by his seruant Agar: and his sonne ysmael: is vnderstonde the olde testament and the iewes and all that lyuen after the flessh and in dedly synne. By Sara & hir sonne Isaac is vnderstonde ye new testament. and folke of the new lawe that is cristen people. that lyuen gostly oute of dedly synne. And that Abraham at the biddīg of god droue oute eyther put out of housholde his seruant and his chi... Whanne Sara had borne hir sonne ysaac. Bytokeneth þ in tyme of grace whanne the newe testament that is the newe lawe and cristen people bygāne: that the olde lawe shulde be putte a=

wey. and the iewes put from ye houshold of heuē: But they wold be conuerted. And also that alle that lyuen after the flesshe and in dedly synne: shalbe putte oute of goddes houshold. But they amēde theym.

The xxi. chapter.

Dyues. I haue ofte harde saye that fendes in mannys lykenesse haue leyne by wymen and made theym wyth chylde. And that is wonderful to me For the fynde is but a sprite and hath neyther flesshe ne boone: ne any thynge of mankynde wherby he shulde gendre with womā Pauper. The fende by sufferaunce of god may sadde the eyre and make hym a body of the eyre: in what lykenesse god suffereth hym in so moch that as saith saynt Poule: he transfygureth hymselfe into an auugel of lyght Moch more than he may transfigure hym into lykenesse of mā or womā by sufferaunce of god. for mannys synne and womās. And the fendes þ tempt folk to lecherie be moste besy to appere in mannys likenes & womās to do lecherie wt folk & so brīge thē to lecherye. And in speche of folke: they be cleped elues. But in latyne whā they appeir in mannis

Precepte.

ſphenes: they be cleped Incubi. And whāne they appier in ſpheneſſe of wymē: they be cleped ſuccubi. And for they haue no matyne ſede of themiſilfe to gedre: therfore they gendre and take the ſuperſluyte of the mater and ſeede of man that paſſeth from maſtepynge and other tymes. and wᵗ that mater they medle with wymen. Alſo they gader matyr and ſeede of Wooman.   And with that medle with man in wo mans ſphenes. And of ſuch medlynge as god ſuffereth comon ſūtyme good children: ſūtyme wicked: ſumtyme wele ſhapen. ſum tyme euyl ſhapen. Butte nedys one moſte be man or womā For ſende with ſend may not gendre Suche ſendys be moſte beſy to ſſende wymen And therfore it is perelous to wymen that deſpreyn moch mannys cumpanye. to be ouermoche ſolitarie withoute oueſt cumpanye. And ſuche foule ſpritis do ther lecherie in this maner: not only with man and womā: but alſo with vnreſonable beſtes: and appere to them in ſyp knesſſe of beſtes: as a Bole to ky ne: and as a ram to ſhepe. And ſo by ſendes doyng come many of theyſe myſſhape thynges that be borne both of wymen and of beſtes: as a calf with an adders tayle: a childe with an adders hede. a child born of a ſhepe with wolle in the necke. Al theſe haue fall in oure dayes.

The xxiii. chapter.

Iues. It may be wele as thou ſayſte. But I praye the telle me what is goſtly foruycacion: goſtly auoutrye and micherpe: Pauper. Alle thre be take for one: and pryncypaly it is cleped ydolatrye. Whanne man or woman withdraweth hys loue and his truſte fro god and ſetteth it more in creature than in god and the worſhip that longeth to godhed doth it to creature thankynge creature of the benefices that only god may do. And ſo the worſhip that longeth only to god they yeue it too creature: ſtocke or ſtone man or woman: or to ymagys made witbe mannys hondys that neyther may ſe here: ne helpe at nede:

Whanne man or woman is criſtened: his ſoule is wedded to criſte by right byleue and trew loue and charitye that he hoteth there to gog to kepe his heſtys and to forſake the fende. But aft whā he forſaketh god and goddes heſtes and turneth hym to the fende by his owne ſyndiges of mis luſtes ⁊ leueth ye loue of criſt for ye loue of any creature that he doth

Ɓ iiii

The sixte.

goostly lechery with the fend And therfore sayth Dauid: that they haue do fornicacion in ther own fyndynges/ And on thys maner al flesshly thoughtis and of mis luste and vnrightful doyng and vnleful couetyse in that it with drawe the loue of man or of wo man fro god: it is cleped goostly fornicacion and auoutrye / And thus euery dedly synne is cleped goostly auoutrye and goostly for nicacion: But principaly ydola tre & forsakyng of the feyth Also false prechyng / and fals exposi cion of holy Wryt: is cleped spiri tuel fornicacōn As they that pre che principaly to please the pe ple and to gete a name or to get temporal good / Of such sayth saynt Poule: that they put god des worde in auoutrye: Adultes rātes Verbum dei. ii. ad. cor' iiii°. For there they shuld vse it to the worshyp of god/ and to the pro fyt of mannys soule: they vse it to ther owne worship and to ther owne worldly profyt and to ple saunce of the fende and harm of mannys soule / Also fals couety se is cleped goostly fornicacion.
Therfore saynt James sayth to false couetyse men: Adulterii nescitis quia amicicia huius mū di inimica est deo. Jacobi iiii°. ye auoutereys & lechouris wyt

ye not that fredship of this wor lde is enemye to god / Therfore the Boke of goddes preuytees co uetyse and pompe of thys world and couetous and proud people is cleped the cetye of Babilonye that is to say the cetie of shesshyp And it is likened to a comon wo man w' which liges prynces lor des. marchauntys and alle coue touse folke haue do goostly leche rye: and it is cleped moder of for nicacions and of abominacōns For as saynt Poule sayth: coue tyse is rote of alle wickednesse And therfore god byddeth there that his peple shuld go out of ye cetye of Babilonye that is to sey forsake synful cumpanye: and forsake luste of the flessh & pom pe and couetyse of thys world maketh men to forsake god and do goostly lecherye with the fende Wende ye oute saith god fro this wicked Babilonye: and forsake this wchild comū womā of lust & of false couetyse: that deseyueth alle this worlde/ For in one day shal come al hir destruccōn/ And that shalbe endles deth: wepyng and hungre without end:& there shal be brennynge fyre & smoke without end and that al þ haue do goostly lechery & liued ī delicys & fals couetise / shal wepe & say ve ve:alas alas.apo c.p viii. & p viii.

Precepte.

The xxiii. chapter.

Dives. Although thy speche be skylful: yit in one thyng clerkes holde ayens the in that that thou seist that the synne of Adam was mare than the synne of Eue. And they argue thus ayens the / God rightfully iuge punyshed eue harder for hyr sinne: than he dyd adã for his sinne But y͏̓ shuld not god haue do: But for hir sinne was mor greuous thã the synne of adam / therfore than the synne of eue was more greuous than the synne of adam.

Pauper. Thys argumente is grounded in two false maxymis First that euery punishyng and vengeaunce assigned of god for mannys synne and womans is assigned after y͏̓ the synne is mor or lesse / And this maxime a grosse lie is fals / Wherfor thou shalt vnderstond that god punisshe some synnes in this worlde: and some in the other worlde: sũme bothe here and there In the other worlde he punysheth euery synne after y͏̓ it is more greuous / or lesse greuous / But in this worlde he doth not alwey so / But oft i this worlde he punysseth the les synne harder: than he doth the more synne / Therfore in the old lawe auoutre was punysshed as hard or harder than manslaughter: & pit mãslaughter is more greuous synne than auoutrie And god to he more temporal vengeaunce in this worlde for lecherie. than euer he dyd for ydolatrie. And yit ydolatrie is gretter synne than lecherie: for it is imediat ayens god & ayens the first precept of the first table / And manslaughter is harder punysshed in thys worlde thã periurie / And yit periurie is gretter synne: as I sayde in the secũde cõmaundement / And synnes in symple pore folk be harder punisshed in this worlde / than synnes of the gret mẽ / If a pore mã stele an horse: he shal be hanged But if a lorde by rauepy and extorsions robbe a man of al that he hath: he shal not be hanged ne lityl or nought punisshed in this worlde / Dauid did auoutre and manslaughter for which synnes he was worthi to be slayne by comon lawe of god / & yit god wold not haue him slain But if a pore man had do tho synnes he shulde haue be slayne / A symple mã went & gadered stychis i the sabot: & god bad moyses stone him to deth. Salomon Jeroboã achaz did gret ydolatrie and drough mech of ye peple to idolatre & yit were they no slayne: therfor the smaler synnes god punisheth i this world that ye soules

v

The sixte

punysshith i this worlde ɫ ye soulis of the synners maye be saued if they cun take it i pacience And comonly he punisshith harder pore folke in this worlde / than he do riche folke: as by comon lawe / For the synne of greate men: as in ye same spyce of synne is more greuous: than is the synne of ye pore man / And therfore god reseruethe the greuous synnes and ye synnes of greate folke to punisshe them in the other worlde: or in helle or in purgatorye / There may no temporal payne be full punysshynge for dedly synne saue contricion alone / And therfor god punisseth no alwey folke in this worlde after the quantite of ther synne: But as he seth it most nedful and spedful to the people and to hys worshyppe / For only god knoweth the greuoushed of dedly synne / For oft that that semeth moost greuous in mannys sight: is lesse greuous in goddes sight: and apenward. Therfore god mesureth not alwey peyne: after the quantite of the synne. But ofte he punyssheth in thys worlde them that be lesse gyltye as moche as theym that be more gyltye / As in tyme of the flode of Noe: and in the perisshyng of sodom and gomorre: and many other tymes he punisshed wymen children and bestis that were not gyltye in the synnes : for whyche that vengaunce fel / And ofte he sendeth siknes and dysese to gode men / in punysshynge of ther synnes in thys worlde. and suffereth shrewes to haue ther wyll: & lytyl or nought punysseth them thys worlde / And as the spon is chastised by beting of the whelp so ofte tyme god punisseth and chastiseth ful hard in this worlde them that be lesse gyltye: to warne them that be more gyltye that they shulde amende them / Therfore crist said to the iewes: Wene ye ɫ tho men which pylat slough for ther rebellion were gretter sinners than other folke of the cuntre / Nay forsoth / But I saye to you forsoth: But ye amend you: ye shal perissh alle / And wyne ye saythe crist that the eightene men vpon which fel the tour of syloa in Jerlm and slough them wene ye that they passed in synne alle the men of Jerusalem / Naye forsoth But I say to you: But ye amend you: ye shal perisshe alle to gydre. Luce. xiii°. And so the punysshyng of tho men soo slayne was a warning to them that were more synfulle that they shulde amande theym / And so thou myghteste wele see that thy Chyrche is nought worthy: god

Precepte.

punysshed eue harder i this worlde than he dyd adam: therfor hir synne was more than the synne of Adam.

The xxiiii. chapter:

Also the seconde mayyme and ground iwhych thou sayst þ god punysshed eue harder than add: may skylfullye be denyed. For in punysshig of adam god gaue his curse and sayde. Cursed be the erth in thy werke i in thy synne/ He sayd not cursed be the erth in thy werke of eue ne he sayd not cursed be the erth in youre werke: as for comon synne of them bothe: But he sayd only to adam/ Cursed be theerth in thy wrke/ In punysshynge also of the serpent he gaue hys curs: i sayd, Thou shalt be cursed amõges al thynge lyuynge vpon erthe/ Also god cursed caym whan he punysshed hym for sleynge of hys brother Abel/ But whanne god punysshed woman/ he gaue not hys curse/ And we rede not þ euer god gaue hys cursse to any woman openly i special/ Ne god repreued not eue so moche: as he dyd adam/ And so the gret repefe a blamig a the curs that god gaue in punysshyng of adam more than he dyd in punisshing of eue shewynge welþ the synne of add

was more greuous than was ye synne of eue/ and that there was more obstynacye in adam than was eue/ For cursyng is not pouer of god ne of holy church but for obstinacie/ As I sayde fyrste adam answerde full obstynatly/ God blamed adam pryncypaly for brekynge of hys cõmaundement and sayde to hym that brekyng of his cõmaundemẽt was cause of his nakednesse a of hys sodeyn myschefe: and not wyth stondynge the techynge and the styrynge of god: he wolde not be aknowe of his senne: But put his synne on god: and excused hym by eue: and so put synne to synne in excusacion of his synne.

Whanne god punysshed adam he cursed the erth for his synne whi the curse turned to woo and trauelye of hym a of all mankynde which we may not fle/ And therfore he sayd to adam. thou shalt ete of the erth in trauaile a sorow alle the dayes of thy lyfe/ I shal brig the forth breris and thornes and thou shalt ete erbis of the erthe/ Also in punysshige of adam god gaue the setence of deth vpon hi a al mãkide for his synne: a therfor god sayd to adam thou shalt ete thi bred i swlk a siuet of thy face til thou torne ayen into the erthe   For erthe thou arte ☙: and into erthe ayen thou

339

The sixte

shalt wende / Syth thanne god for synne of adam, gaue soo greuously hys curse: and blamed so harde adam of his synne: and for his synne dampned hym and all mankynde: and punisshed al erthely creaturis for his sine & dampned him and al mankynd to perpetuel traueyle Whanne he sayde. thou shalt ete thy mete with traueyle and sorowe al the daies of thy lyfe / And also for the synne of adam he gaue sentēce of deth: to him and to al mankynd that is moste of al peynes: it foloweth that god punysshed harder adam for his synne: than he dyde eue for hir synne / For w by in punisshyng of eue god repreued hir not so moch as he did adam And he gaue thanne no curse ne peyn perpetuel safe subiection: I shal sayde god multiplie thy myscheues and thy consepupngys: and in sorow thou shalt bere thy children: & thou shalt be vnder power of man: And he shal be thy lord God seyde not to woman: I shal multiplie thy thy myscheues all dayes of thy lyfe / For she maye kepe hir chaste if she wyl and fle mischefe and peyne of chyldren bythe / And that god made woman subget to man for the synne of eue: is was no newe thyng to woman For as sayth salt aus

ten sup gest. li° xi°. c° xliiii. Womā was subget to man bifore by ordre of kynde: But that subiectiō was only by loue and charytye But for hyr synne she was made subget: not only by loue: But also by nede and bondage of onest seruyse werke to obeye to man & be vnder his gouernaunce / Byfore hir synne she was subgett to man only by loue / But after hir sinne she was mad subget to mā not only bi loue but by drede and by nede For she most drede man & she hath nede of his helpe / For that was the pryde of adam and of eue: that they desired to haue no soueraigne ne gouernour but god alone as clerkis sey And therfore the send in ople byhight thē y they desired saiyng to eue if ye ete of ye tree y god hathe forbode you: ye shal be as goddes knowynge good and euyl: that is to saye: ye shal nede no soueraigne ne gouūoure to teech you ne to gouerne you but god / And for y they desyred it lightly they leuyd it / For as sayth the mayst of storyes: Thynge that is desired: lyghtly it is beleued And therfore god rightful iuge punisshed theym bothe in subiection of drede and of nede: and of harde seruage He made woman sub

(get to man / and aftwarde

Precepte.

he made man subget and thralle to woman: for the synne of adam as sayth saynt Austen Sup.gen.b. sup. nior thā eu he made womā subget to man. for the synne of eue: as sayth saynt Austen. sup. gen.b.s. For though woman be in thraldome to temporal lordis as be men. that is not for the synne of eue: But pricipaly for þe sinne of adam / The subieccōn that womā is put ī for the synne of eue: is the subieccion that the wif owethe to hir husbond / And alle the souerayngtie and lordshyp þ any man hath here in this worlde eyther ouer man or woman: it is medled with moch woo and gret sorowe and care / For euery soueraigne in thys worlde moste care for his subgettys: if he be wyse. And in higher degre that he be of lordshyp and of dignitye: in the higher degre is he of perel of drede of sorowe and care in punishing of adams synne: And so bothe lordship in this worlde: & subieccion be punished of adams synne / And if subgettis can haue pacience with ther degre. they be in more siþernes both of body and of soule, and in more gladnes of hert thā be the souereignes / And so punysshed god adam as moch in maner: in that he made hī lorde and gouernour of woman as

he punysshed eue: Whane he made hir subget to adam / For in þ god bonde man to haue cure of wooman & hyr mischeefe to saue hir and to kepe hir: that was by comon soo feynte: soo feble and freel: and so mischeuous by cause of hir synne.

The xyb.chapter.

Dyues. yet clerkys argue ayens the and sey that woman synned more greuously thā adam: for she put hirsilfe ī synne and hir husbond adam / Butte adam put only himsilfe in synne. Pauper. This skill is nought For as I said first adā was shēt withe preuy pryde and welth of himsilfe and felle into synne or eue profered hym the apple / Also saith saint Austē de ci.dī.l.xiiiiº cº.xiº. Adam wyste wele that it was a greuous synne / But eue was soo desepued that she wend that it had be no synne / And therfore the synne that she dyd by ignorance and desepte of the fende excuseth not: ne lessethe nott the synne of Adam that he dyd wytyngly and wyttyngly. Adā was hir souerayne and shulde haue gouerned them bothe: and not obeied to þe voice of his wif as

The sixte

the voyce of god that forbad hī the tree Exāple if a symple mā be vnkunnyng and by desept of sum shrew do a foly wenyng not to do amys: and he come to his prelate or his busshop and coūseyle him to do the same: and his prelate or his busshop do the same wetynge wel that he doth amys: and that it is a greuous sīne: euery man wyl deme that ye busshop and his prelate synneth more greuously than the symple mā that wend not to do amysse And thus nigh al circumstaūcys that agreggen any synne agregged the synne of adam more than the synne of eue / For he was soueraigne and perfit more in kynde wyser and myghtier to witstonde the fendes sodynge / And with lesse temptacion fel in synne and brake goddes cōmaūdemente wytyngly / But eue by desepte of the adder synned by ignorance. as sayth saynt austē. ŧ. sup̄ ꝑlo. a sidor' de sū. Bono li°. ii°. Eue yelde hir coulpable. adam did not so. Eue wend not haue synned. adam wetyngly sīned in hope of forpeuenesse: As sayth saynt austen: & the mayst of sentence li°. ii°. d. xxii. And so adam synned in hope and p̄sūpcion ayens the holy gooste: and thys is a fulle greuous synne as crist shewth ī ye gospel Mᵗ. xii°

Quicūqȝ dixerit verbū cōtra spiritum sc̄m non remittetur ei. &c̄. Where the glose sayth that they that synne by ignorance may lightly haue forpeuenesse. But he doth it wetyngly ayens the maiestie of god ayens his conscience: he is worthy no forpeuenesse Also adam was more obstynat than eue was. Diues. Shewe me that Pauper. For god blamed hym firste of al: and declared to him his synne: aud god abode of punysshyng tyl he hadde vndernome eue: and after eue ye fende ī the adder: and fyrst he punisshed ye adder & thā eue had shuld haue beware & ayed mercy And so god blamed him first and punisshed him last: so peuyng hī respite of repentaūce: But for al this adam repented hym none wolde aye mercy ne knowe hī First god punisshed him fro set in the adder in that he cursed the adder that was his suget & made the adder enmye to hys wife and to hir sede: that is to seye to the children that she shuld gett of adam /& so god made the adder ꝑ was bifore suget & meke to him rebel & enemye to his loue & was his wife & to al þ shulde come of the two / yit and stode abstinat. Thā god punisshed eue his wife his loue his help: & so punisshed him in Eue / For if he loued hys

Precepte.

so moch as clerkes sey. it shulde haue be to him ful greate payne to se his wyfe his loue so punisshed / For as clerkes sepe. the grete loue that he hadde to eue: made him to breke the cōmaundemēt of god / And yit these dayes it is ful greate payne to kynde folke trewe in loue to se ther loue: and ther frendis in sorow and desese. Also god punysshed adam & eue. In that he punisshed hir with mischeues of sykenesse. freeltie and feblenesse / For in so moche god toke from him his help that was woman made to be mannis helpe / But the more feble that god made hyr for synne: the lesse she might helpe man / Also god punisshed theym bothe anon as Adam ete of the tre: and made thē so naked and so vnoneste & they were ashamed of themsilfe Whi the peyne fel not too adam ne to eue tyl adam hadde ete of the apple / And not withstondyng alle thys: yit adam stode obstynat & ayed no mercy ne knowlege dno synne And thanne god rightful iuge punysshed him ful herde / Bothe in thys worlde and in the other worlde and punisshed al mankynd for his synne as sayth saynte Poule and saynte Austē and other doctouris / God punysshed adam and mankynd

ful harde for his synne: Whanne he toke moche of his lordshyp as wey from hym: and made nighe al creaturis rebelle to hym: and brought hym so lowe in ordre of kynd that though by wey of kinde man byfore adams synne passed woman in vertue and perfection of kynde Nowe after adās synne woman ofte tyme passeth many men in uertue and discrecion: and in other gyftis both of kynde and of grace / And byfore the synne of adam: man was so souereyne to woman: that woman shulde not haue be hys souereyne / But nowe for adamis synne of tymeman is suget to woman as to hys lady by bondage and thraldome: by harde seruage by nede: and drede: and owethe more seruage and subiection to woman for adamys synne: than doth woman to man for ye synne of eue / For god made womā for the synne of eue only subgett to hir husbond in seruice of onest werke as felawe notte as chorle in belenye werke of worbly bondage. Also man for the synne of adam is ordeyned too many more perelys bothe on lond and on water & too werre / and too wo. and besynesse of thys worlde and to moche traueyle: and
 Cmanye perelys

v i

more than wooman is ordeyned to Diues. Wondre I haue that any clerke shulde hold ayens the in thys mater of adam is synne. Pauper. Clerkes speke ofte by opynyon in thys matere & other maters also. and not alwey affermye that they sey to the vttermost but put it in the doome of other clerkes. if they kun saye better. And so do I at this tyme / if any clerke can say more skilfully. Here endeth the sixte precepte and bygynneth the seuenth precepte.

The firste chapter.

Diues. I thanke the for thou haste wel declared to me the sixte precepte. Now I by the ensourme thou me & the seue= the shrest Pauper. The seuenth precepte is this. Non furtum facies That is to sey Thou shalt do no thefte. neyther in wyl: ne i dede as saith the glose And so by this precept is forbode al maner mys takynge and al maner false witholdynge and withdrawyng of other mennys good ayēs ther wyl. and al the menys that lede to thefte be also forbode by thys precepte as false weightys. false mesurys. false othes / gylous spe

che. gyle in crafte. and gyle i cha= farye false werkmanship & feint laboure in laborerys that taken greate hire and do lytel therfore. Also rauerpus extorcions. false witholdynge of det and of men= nys hires. and false witholdyng of mannys right and womans. and settynge of ther right. Al the se be forbode by this precept And so by thys precepte is forbode al maner thefte both bodely & gost= ly Diues. What is bodely thefte Pauper. As sayth the Repmūde. li.ii.ti. de furtis Bodely theft is a gylous and vnleful tretyng and bsynge of another mannys good mouable ayens the wyl of the lord that oweth the thyng to gette the thyng in the silfe to his auauntage. or to haue the vse of the thyng for a tyme or for to by de it for alway and denye ye pos session: though he thenke to ma ke restitucion / And thus sum is open theft / and sū is preuy theft Open theft is whanne the thefe is taken with hys pelfere or con= uicte by trewe wytnesse of thefte and such thefte is punyshede by lōdes law and by holy churches lawe / Sum is do so preuely that the theefe may not be take ther= with ne conuict / And suche may not be punisshede openly by nō lawe but only preuely by law of

conscience in the dome of his cō/
fessoure Which is bounde to coū/
seyle and to saue his name & hys
fame/ And as the law says
the: euery vnleful vsyng and ta
kyng of other mannys good me
uable or not meuable.is theft.
q.iiii.q.v.penale & xxvii.q.iiii..
meretrices. For as the lawe seith
there.god that forbyddeth theft.
forbyddeth rauyne/

The secund chapter.

Also leue frende ye shal vn
derstond that as holy writ
wytnesseth.there is theft and rob
brye of mannys name and wo
mans and yt is cleped Bacbitinge
and defampnge through Whiche
man and woman leseth hys go
de name/ And therfore the wyse
man sayth/ Ne appelleris susurro in vita tua.Eccl.v°.Be thou
not cleped a musterer: ne preuy
bacbyter in thy lyfe. Be thou not
take false in thy tunge & thou be
not shent for to that thefe & stele/
the a mannys good name /is ordey
ned moche shame and moche
payne and ful Wicked dampna
cion is to the double tunged mā
and womā and to musterys and
preuy bacbiters is hate & enmite

and desppte.Eccle.v°.c°. For
thys maner of theft is ful greate
and greuous. For as Salomon
sayth Melius est nomen bonum
qm diuicie multe.et super aurū &
argentum gracia bona/ A good
name is better than many riches
es.and good grace of good loue
passeth gold and sylu'er pū.xxii.
c°. For the beste iuel and most ri
chesshes that man or womā may
haue vpon erth.is to haue a gode name and loue and. grace a-
mongys his neyghbors and in
the cuntre/ And therfore bacbyte
lesyngmongeris and Wicked spe
kers that robbe man or woman
of ther good name and bring thā
in wycked name and fame: they
be ye worst theues vpon the erth
and they may nott be assoyled of
thys thefte: But they do ther de
uore vpon ther power: to restore
man or woman ther gode name
and fame: that they haue wyckedly robbed theym of/ And ther
fore sayth the law that they that
wyth bacbytyng destroye the go
de name and the goode lyfe:and
the good thewys of other folk be
worse theues than be they: that
robbe men of ther godys: and of
ther catel.vi.q.i.deciores/ And in
the nex chapter .the lawe saythe:
that bacbityng is a ful gret wic
kednesse. For who so bacbyteth

At

The seuenth.

hys brother he is a mansleer and there shal no such these ne mansleer haue part i(n) the kyngdome of heue(n)/ And therfore the law sayth in another place that it p(ro)fyteeth not as anentys mede i(n) heuen a ma(n) to fast or pray or do other godes dedis of religion but his thou ghtys be withdrawe fro wicked/nesse and his tunge fro bacbitl(n)g De condici.D.nichil enim p(ro)dest ͱ not only he is giltie i(n) bacbitl(n)ge that speketh euyl of his eue(n) criste(n)/ But also tho that gladly here suche wicked spec(he) and shrewed tales of ther euen cristen. Bi.q.i. c(u)m merito.pxi.q.iiii. no(n) solu(m). And therfore the wyse man sayth/put away fro the the wicked mouthe and put away ser fro the lyppys bacbyty(n)ge.pu.iiii. Hegge thyn eerys with thornes .and here not the wycked tunge .and make dores to thy mouth : and lockys to thyn eerys. Eccle.xxviii. The(n) ke ͳ he wyl speke of the as euyl bihy(n)d the: as he doth of another bihy(n)de hym/ The(n)ke what woo and myschefe cometh of bacbytynge and wycked tunges : and shewe him no gode chere : But sh(r)ewe him by thy countinance and thy chere ͳ hys spec(he) pleseth the not / And anon he shal cese / and be asshamed of hys malyce/ For the wyse man sayth Right as the northe wynde destroieth and scatereth the rayne and the cloudys soo the scup face of the herer destroyeth the tung bacbity(n)g .pu. xxv°. The children of israel bacbited goddes doy(n)g / and lacked the londe of byheste /Whane they shuld haue entred/ ͱ god was offended with them /and bad them wend ayen bacward into desert and there he held the fourty yere tyl they were dede euerychone: ͱ cam oute of egipte: saue two me(n) Josue and Calephs For they two spake good of the lond of byhest and held with god / And soo the children of the peple that ca(m) oute of egipt entred the lond of biheste and not the faders: saue Josue ͱ Calephs/ And that for ther bacbity(n)ge. Numeri.xiiii. Also marie the sustre of Moyses bacbyted hir brother moyses and spakeuil of hl ͱ anon she was a foul lepre ͱ might notte be heled til moises prayd to god for hir. num i.xii.c.

The third chapter.

Also there is theft of wordys / Of which theste god speketh by the prophet Jeremie xxiii°.c°. Where god vndernim(m)es the false p(ro)phetis and fals p(ro)phou(r)ys: Which stale alwey his wordis fro the peple and told not the truthe as god bad them : Butte only sayde such thynges ͳ shal please

Precepte.

the peple and so deseyued the people with lesynges and with false myracles. as men do these dayis feynyng myracles of ymagis as men do these daies to mayntey͡n ydolatrie for lucre of offerynge & false myracles of wicked spuers and sey that god dothe myracles for them: and so blynd the peple in falsnesse. And so they yeue the worshyp of myracles doynge to ymagis that man hath made: & to wicked spuers goddes enemyes. Whiche miraclis only god may do & so robbe god of his worship And in that they withdraw goddes worde. and the trewethe the goddes lawe that longeth to mē of holy church to tech. and to the peple to cun and to knowe. And so they deseyue the peple in that they be theues of goddes worde and shalbe punisshed ful hard of god for such theft of goddes worde. For god sayth to euery prelate curate and prechoure + Specula torē dedi te domui israel & cetera I haue made thee a daywayte to the houshold of israel and to my peple. & thou shalt here my worde of my mouth. and shew it and tel it in my name to them. If I sey to the wycked man þ he shall dye for his Wickednesse. And thou tellest him not butt ypdeste my word. and spekest not to hī

that he may turne hi͡m from hys wickednes and leue it: that wicked man shal dye I his Wickednes and I shal seke the blod and the deth of him of thyn hond. that is to say thou shalt answere for his deth. Ezech.iii°.c°. Also they be theues of goddes wordes that þ the goddes wordes to ther oll ne wordly auantage: not to þe worshyp of god. ne to profyt of mannys soule. Also they be theues of goddes wordis that eleggen goddes wordes and holy writ falsly to mayntey͡n errours and eresies or synne or shrewdnesse.

The fourth chapter.

ALso there is a theft of wordly good. Of suche theste Job sayth Agrū nō suū demetūt They repe other mennys feldys & make vintage of ther mennys wynes. & take mennys clothyge fro them: and late them naked I the colde wynter. and robbe morderles childrē & pore widowis by myght and spoyle and robbe the pore peple. The these saythe. he riseth vp in the morwe & sleth the nedy and the pore. and by nyght he steleth as a mycher. Sz deus iustū abire nō patit. Job xxiiii.c. Diues. Hou many spices be of theft: Pauper. Full many. For sum tyme a thing is stolne pueyly

A ii

☞The seuenth.

without wetyng of the lorde or of the keper and ayens ther wyll ⁊ it is cleped mycherie. Sumtyme it is do openly by might and vi olence wetyng the lord ⁊ the ke per ayens ther wyll. and that is pprirly rapina rauepn. Sumtyme it is do wetyng the lord or the ke per and aparte ayens the wyll. But not all ayens ther wyl. vn der certeyn condicion of wynnige not lefull in the taker. and thane it is cleped vſura. gouel or vſure in englyſſh. Alſo al maner vn rightful occupying of any thige lordſhip or any other auert thys world: is cleped theft. And ther fore ſaynt auſten ſaith thus. The thyng that man or woman hath by the lawe: that is his by ye law and non other mannys. And ma hath by ye law that he hath right ſully. and he hath that rightfully that he hath wele. And therfore ſayth he. euery thyng that is miſ had is other mennys. and euery man hath he his goode amys that vſeth his gode amys. In epſa ad macedoniū. Alſo withholdyng of almes from the pore nedy folke is theft in goodes ryght. For the couetous rich men withdraw fro the pore folk that longeth to thē and miſpende the pore mennys good wherby they ſhulde be ſuſ teyned. And therfore the wis mā

ſayth. Sone defraude thou not the almes of the pore man/ne tur ne not alwey thin iyen fro the po re. ne deſpyſe not the hūgry ſou le. ne tene ne angre thou not the pore in his miſcheffe/Torment thou not the hert of the nedy: ne delay thou not the yift from him that is in anguyſſh/Caſt not a wey the preyer of him that is deſ ſeſed: ne turue thou not thy face awey fro the helpleſe for wrath ne yeue thou not him that ayeth the goode non occaſion to curſe the by hynde the/For if the pore man curſe the ī bytternes of ſou le: hys prayer ſhalbe harde/For he that made hym ſhal here hym And therfore make the pleſaunt in ſpeche to the congregacion of pore folk/and bowe thyn erre to the pore without heuyneſſe: and yelde thy dette and anſwere peſa ble thynges and mekeneſſe: nott to arunt them ne rebuke them ne chyde theym but only thou haue the more open cauſe. Eccle. iiii°. Therfore ſaynt Poule ſayth: þ god loueth a gladde yeuer.

Diues. By the lawe of kynde ⁊ by goddes lawe. al thynge is co mon/And therfore ſayth the law pii. q. i. dileċtiſſimis Right as the eyre ne the lyght of ye ſone may not be departed by lordeſhyppyn ne apropryd more to one perſone

348

Precepte.

than to another: ne to one colle∣ge more than to another: no mo∣re shuld other thynges that be po∣uen comonly to helpe of mãkid. be departed by lordshippis: ne a∣propred more to one thã to ano∣ther. But al thynges shuld be co∣mon / And therfore we rede Actu∣um iiii°. that in the begynnynge of holy church alle thynges were comon to the multitude of cristẽ peple / And apens lawe of kynde is no despensacion. Deſtlc.viii. H.i°. Why bad god thãne þ men shuld not stele. spth al thynge is comen to gode mẽ Pauper. By goddes law: al thyng is comon to gode men / For as sapthe sait austen Omla sũt iustorum / Alle thynges be the rightful mennys But as the law sayth. vii.q.i: di∣lectissimis Douision a pperte of lordship is made amonges man kynde by wyckednesse of fals co∣uetyse. Both of riche and of pore. For the rich drawe to themsylfe. that longeth to other For why al that the rich man hath passynge his oneste liuyng after the degre of his despensacõn. it is other me∣nys and no hys / And he shal pe∣ueful harde rekenyng therof at the day of dome Whãne god shal sey to hym / Redde racionem villica∣tionis tue / yeld acõute of thy ba∣lye / For rich men and lordes in

thys worlde be goddes balyfes and goddes reues to ordeyn for the pore folk and to susten them And therfore sayth saynt Poule Habentes alimẽta a quib⁹ tega∣mur: hiis contẽti sim⁹. If we ha∣ue nedfully felode and hillge: be we payd therwithe. and couette we nomore Also pore folk be not payde with sufficiẽt lyuyng but couete more than theym nedethe And for couetyse: more thã for nede take thynges apen the lor∣des wyl. in hynderig of hym and of other that be more nedy. and shuld be holpe therby / And ther∣fore god forbad al maner thefte that mẽ shulde take no thige for anymis couetise ayẽs the lordes wyl.

℧he fift chapter.

Diues. Spth alle thyng is comon by goddes lawe: a by lawe of kynde: hou maye any mã be lord of any thig. more thã another man Pauper. There is lordship of kynde. a there is lord ship of this world groubed only i couetyse. a there is lordeshyp of despensacõn and of gouernãuce and so Ioseth the sonne of iacob was cleped lord of eqipt. Gen. pl8.c. The first lordship is comõ to euery gode man and woman. For kynd made alle men euene

Aiii

The seuenth.

in lordshyp, And in token therof both lord and seruant fre & bondriche and pore: come Into this worlde naked and powre: and wendhens naked and pore. Nought they bring with them. But we pigh sobbyng and sorow. And bere no thyng with them: but ther dedys gode or wycked. The lordshyp of thys worlde is sufferable and worshipful, for as saynt Poule saythe, Omnis potestas a deo est. Every power and lordshyp in this worlde cometh of god. And therfore he biddeth that every man & woman shuld be subget and meke to the lordshyp aboue them. For though the couetise and wycked nesse that lordes and ryche men ground theym in be of themsylf, yit the lordshyp & power is of goddes gyft: as sayth saint Austen, & therfore it moste be worshypped. The lordshyp that is only of dispensacion compted by a souereygne is medful, worshypful & comendable. Also ther is thre maner of ppertes & ppirshed. One is that kynd yeueth, as man to spe. And every man hath hys owne hert, his owne sowle & hys owne wyl, for to do wel or euyl and this ppertie is nedful. Another ppirtie there is, that cometh only of couetyse, by whiche couetise folk say, this is myne & thys

is thyne. And so they propren to themsilfe by couetise: that is comon by kynd, And thys ppirtye so groūded in couetise is dāpnable and synful. The thirde is dispensacion. For one man hathe moch thyng in hys dispensacion & gouernaūce: that another man hathe nought to do of. And thys dispensacion cometh sumtyme of goddes gyft, as whanne he sent one man more riches I this worlde than another. Sumtyme it cometh by ordinaunce and gifte of lordes and of souereigns here in erth: As whane lordes & prelatis cōmptte to ther subgetys gouernaunce of ther godys of ther places and benefices. And thys dispensacion if it be wel do it is ful medful: Diues. But as saynte Poul saith, it is a question, who is found trewe amonge suche dispensouris, for nigh alle seke ther owne profit. But not the worshyp of Jesu crist Pauper. Many be ful false. And yit sythe dispensacion of worldly goodys is so cōmptted to theym, in that they haue lordshyp of ther propre dispensacion ordeyned of god: and be cleped propre lordes of ther propre dispensacōn, not for ther false couetise, ne for no propre hede that they chalenge by false couetyse, for I that be they no lordes but tyrauntys and raupnourys. And so though they haue propre lordship of dispēsacōn of worldly goodis more than the pore people: they haue yit no more lordship by wey of kynd than the pore man / ne non other lordship than the pore man. But only of dispēsacion / And so thoughe the riche folk haue more lordship of propre despensacion thāne the pore yit the lordship of kynd i nedful thynges stondeth styl comon to riche and pore / But for synne it is not so fre. as it was byfore the synne of adam. For god wyl not that the pore folk take any thig without leue of the propre dispēsatour that is clepid lord therof & therfore god sayd. Non furtū facies. Thou shalt do no theft / þ is to say. thou shalt nought tak without thy lordes leue / Diues. this is wonderful to me that the pore man is as grett a lorde by wey of kynde as the rich and yit may he nought take without his leue Pauper. It is more wondre þ the good pore man is lord of alle thynge nedful to him by weye of kynde. and the synful riche man is lord of rightnought by wey of kynde. for he is goddes traytour And yit god wylle that the pore take rightnought of the goodes þ the riche man hath in his dispen/

sacion without leue: Diues. that is to me more wonderful tel me thou this may bee: Pauper. Thou mightst se at iȝe the kynge beyre aparāt & other beyris of grete lordshippes: not withstondyng that they be heyrys and for des of all: yit shal they not entre the office of ther officers / ne take any thyng apēs: ne bere apēs without leue And if they do: they shal be hard undernome: and in case bete of ther master and of ther tutoure / For fredam in youthe is cause of pride and of many other vices / Right so god seynge that mankynde which is lorde of a ertheły godys and ordeyned to regne in heuen blysse: If he had hys fredam in vse of ertheły thynges he shuld falle in pride and many vices as adam did while he was fre / Therfore he hath put mākid and namely the pore people under the gouernaunce of the ryche folke / and of ther lordes which be ther tutourys & dispensatourys of godys of this world to saluacion of the pore people / And therfore saynt Poule saythe: Quanto tempore heres peruul' est nichil defert a seruo cū sit dō/ minus omnium. sed sub tutoribus et auctoribus est usq3 ad p̄finitum tempus a patre. ad gal. iiii°. As longe as the heyre is yōg

A iiii

The seuenth.

ponge and sykes. ther is no diffe¬
rence bitwene him; & a seruaunte
sithe ther is a lorde of alle/But he
is vnder tutour and gouernoure
vnto a certeyn tyme ordeyned of
the fader And therfore sith the ri¬
che forre ben tutours & dispensa¬
tours of these worldly godes or¬
deyned of god to saluacion of ye
pore peple/ god wole þ nomā ta¬
ke of the godes þ been comittyd
to them withoutē their wyll and
their leue. And if any man take
therof ayēst their wylle & ayenst
goddes ordenaūce/ he doth theft
ayēst this precepte. Nō furtū faci¬
es. Thou shalt do no theft.

The vi. chapter.

Diues. Is it lefulle in any
cas to stele. and take any
thinge ayenst the lordes wylle
Pauper Stelth sothnesse comō
ly theft & robbery/ and sumtyme
sothnesse pryue takyng without
wittyng of the lorde. And soo it
may be done in iiii. cases withs¬
oute synne For nede. for almes.
for right/ for happe of fyndinge.
First for nede & mischeif/ for if a
ny man or woman for myscheif
of hungre/ or of thrist/ or of cold.
or of any other mischeif. whiche
mischeif he may nat flee. to saue
his lif but he take thinges ayēst
the lordes wylle. If he take any

thinge so in pel of deth/or in gre¬
te mischif/ nede excuseth him fro
synne/ & fro theft. if he do it only
for nede & nat for couetise. And
he oweth to enfourme his cōsci¬
ence & thynke þ if the lorde of the
thinge knewe his myscheife. he
shulde nat be myspaied. & thāne
dothe he no theft/ for in the caste
nede al thing is comē Also for ye
lorde is bounde to helpe him at þ
nede. & also for nede hay no lawe
Exāple we haue in the gospel
wher we fynde þ the disciples of
Criste for hūgre toke erys in the
felde & gnyddyd theym/ & ete the
corne for hungre The pharises
were asclaundryd therof & saide
to Crist þ his disciples dyd thing
þ was nat leful. And thāne criste
excused them for nede of hungre
& saide that they were vngiltie
& inocentes in that. And he putte
them example of dauid. that ete
for nede of the holy loues in god¬
des tabernacle/ whiche loues on¬
ly prestes shulde ete by the lawe.
Mt. xii. c. For it is a generalle
rule in the lawe/ that nede hathe
no lawe. Diues. Is þ man þ so
takith for nede boūde to restitu¬
cion Paup. Nape. And yit for
more sikernesse. & to putt him in
drede of stelth/ his cōfessour shal
yeue him sundele penaūce for yt
doynge. Also by weye of almesse

Precepte.

þe wyf may take of her lordes gode in whiche she hath dispēsacion/ as in mete drynk & clothes & yeue almesse mesurable to the nedy/ & thynke yt her husbonde shulde be pleasyd with her gifte. if he sawe þ mischeif of þe pore. & if he sūtpm̄ forbede his wyf/ to do almesse/ she shal nat fulcease from almesse discretly doon. For husbondes make ofte suche inibicions to their wyues to tempe ther yeupng nat fully to let hem

And if she seeþ her husbonde be selaundryd & wrothe with her peupng. though his wrathe be vnskilful. she must tēpre the more her yeupng But whāne she may wele sūwhat yeue for them both with gode cōscience. Natheleffe if she se him greatly agreupd for her peupnge/ and he forbede vtterly her to yeue almesse/ thanne it is gode that she obey to his biddynge & be sory þ she may nat yeue/ and be allway in wyl to yeue if she durst. & so wynne her mede by wylle alone/ as she dyd bifore by wyl and dede. Diues. If ye wif haue gode in ppre by her self Bona paternalia. may she natt yeue therof withoute her husbōdes wylle. Paup. She may ye ue. & she is bounde to yeue/ & he oweth nat to lette her. Diues. I suppose. þ þe husbonde forbede his wyf vtterly to doo almesse of his gode & she se a mā or a womā in vtt mischeif/ may she nat thā yeue them almesse & helpe theym. Paup. in þ nede she is boūde to yeue & she shal yeue/ & thynke þt if her husbonde sawe þat nede he shulde nat be mispaped. ℂ We rede in the firste boke of kinges. xxv. c. þ ther was a greate vpgarde & an angry shrewe. whose name was nabal. He had a gode womā wise and faire to his wyf whose name was abigail. That tyme dauid fledde the psecucion of kynge saul. & lyued in deserte wt vi. hundryd men with him as outlawes. And for mischeif he sente x. men to this riche nabal. prayinge him of sūme almesse in mete and drynk But this nabal dispised dauid & his messangers. & cleppd them theues & outlawes and flempd men/ and wolde noo gode yeue hem/ nat withstōding that they had sauyd his goode/ & his bestes/ al the tyme that they were in deserte. Whanne dauid herde these tidinges he was wroth and came with iiii. hundryd mē. to sle nabal/ and alle that lōged to him. It hapnyd that a seruāt of nabal tolde his wyf abigail. howe dauid hadde sent messangers to Nabal: and howe he had despysed theym.

The seuenth

Anon Abigail without lettyng of Nabal charged Assis with brede and wyne with soden flessh of fyue shepe. figges & with reisens and other vitaylles grete plentye and sent to Dauid by hir seruauntis: and she folowed after: and happened to mete Dauid in hys comynge. Thanne Dauid repreued hir husbonde Nabol of hys vnkyndnesse: and seyde he shuld sle him, & al that longed to hym. Thanne the good woman Abigail felle doune to grounde and worshipped Dauid. and prayde him of audience. Thane she ayed mercy for hir husbonde Nabol and excused hirsilf. that she wyst not of his massegers whane they were there and prayde Dauid þ he shuld not so venge himsilfe & taught him moch goodnes. and proficeid to him moch welth and prayde that he wolde accepte hir presaunt. and so he did. Thane Dauid sayde to hir. Blessed be oure lorde god that sent the this day to me, and blessed be thy speche. and blessed be thou that this day hast letted me fro sheddyng of blode to venge my silfe. And thanne Dauid turned ayen into desert. & she cam home ayen and fond hir husbond nabal at soper sotely. But that nyght she spak nought too hym of that mater.

for he was ful drunken. But in the morowe whanne he was sobre: she tolde hym what she had do to saue his lyfe. And anon his herte died for sorow, and he wex heuy as a stone, and with in ten daies he died wicked deth. & than Dauid wedded his wife Abigal Also if man or woman stele awey mannys swerd whanne he is wood to lette hym of manslaughter of himsilfe: or of other: he dothe no theft ne synne. Also by cause of rightwisnesse man maye take aweye other mennys goodys ayens ther wyl. as in rightful bateyle: soo that they that feyght rightsully ayens the vnrightful take ther goodys not for couetise: But for rightsulnesse to shewe þ they haue ocupied tho goodys wrongfully. But if they take ther goodys for euyl couetyse: they do rauyne. thoughe the dede be rightful in the sylfe.

The seuenth precept.

Dives. If a thynge be loste and he that fyndeth it kepe it sylfe: is it theste.
Pauper. He þ findeth it: is bounde to restitucion: if he may wete to whoom it longeth. And

Precepte.

therfore he shal do men to wyte of the fyndynge by open speck in towne strete and in chvrche / that he that oweth it may chalenge it And if noo man chalenge it: he ſode it may by auctorite of albis confessoure kepe it stylle if he be pore and nedy and pray for him that aught it or elles yeue it to other nedy that they may pray for hym p aught it: ꝙ so make restitucion Therfore saynt Austen sayth in omelia. if thou hast foūd any thynge / and not made restitucion: that thyng thou hast stolen / For he sayth god taketh more hede to ye hert than to the ɡōde And therfore theft is doon in as smale thynge: as in a grete For god chargeth not the thyng that is stolne: But the wicked wyl of the steler as sayth saīt austē ꝙ saīt gregori / And therfor if children l ther yongthe stele pynnes or apples or any other smale thynges anon as it is pseyued / they shuld be hard chastised in ye begynnig For the phylosofre sayth Princi plis obsta Withstond the begynnynge of vices and of micherye. For Whāne childrē in yonge bygynne to haue lykynge in mycherie / though the thyng be smal I valu: ther synne is not the lesse ne the synne of them that suffre thē. Therfor it is goddes dome ꝧ

When they be not chastysed l ther yongth for such mycherie afterward they stele gretter thynges: and be hanged. to shame ꝯ shenshyp of al ther kyn / And therfore as Boicius de disciplina scolariū telleth Whāne a mannys sone of Rome shuld be hanged: he pyed hys fader to kys him And he bote of his faders nose. seying to hī Thenke wel fader on this toke: and chastice better thy chyldren. For haddest thou chastysed me wel in myy outh I shuld not haue be hanged / Therfor the wyse man sayth / Qui parcit virge odit filiū suū ꝛc. He that spariethe the yerd: hateth hys sone. And he loueth his sone that chastiseth yt and techeth him besely. pñ. viii. We rede that on ꝯ tyme a poūre mā was tēpted to ete good flesshꝫ But he durst not stele for drede of hangīge. On a day he met wyth the fend and he bad ꝙ stele a goose and ete enough at onis And he did so / And sone after he stale an ox and was take ꝯ led to the galowes And thanne the fend mete with him ꝯ sayd to him Wheder a wey Thāne the thefe sayd to the fend: woo worth the wicked wyght: for thou hast brought me to this end / Thāne sayde the fende blame me not / for thou myghtest se by ye byl that it was no good

¶The seuenth

¶The eight chapter.

Dives. I suppose a man haue borowed a thyng, & he that lent it him taketh it awey fro him duely ayens his wyl, & a yens the couenaūt of the lenyng. do that man theft. so takynge a yen his owne gode: Pauper. He doth theft for it is not for þ time fully hys owne goode. as sayth Raynuld li°.ii°.ti. de furtis/ And if lord or lady: or any other man by take his seruaūt or his officer any thynge to kepe. and he take it awey fro him without his wetyng: for fals couetyse or for malice to endaūgere the seruaūt. he doth theft / For though the thinge be his own: yit it is not frely hys own: as long as the seruaunt by his assent hath keping and dispēsacion therof. Dives. I suppose a man weneth to take hys owne gode whan he taketh anoter mānys gode ayens his wyl/ or if he take his owne goode vnlefully. Wenyng þ it were leful so to take it doth he any theft in this case: Pauper. Nay. For all though in case he do vnlefully: yit i thys case he doth no theft ne dedly synne: And yit he is boūd to restitucion / Theft icludeth alwey gyle & falsnes without which is no theft: And if a man take of another mannys gode withoute hys

wittyng if he haue a iust cause to wene þ he shuld not be mispayd though he wist it thā doth he no theft ne sinne / & if he take another mānis gode wenīg that it be not his wyl though it be his wyl he take it: yit he doth thefte & dedly synne in goddes sight: But he is not boūd to restitucōn whāne he knoweth þ it is the lordis wil: ne the lorde may not aye restitucōn syth it was his wel / If a man or womā by mis egglg take awey another mannys seruant he doth theft / If a man selle or bye man or woman that is fre. or peueth him or taketh him of gift ayens his wyl/ he doth thift: as sayth Raynuld. Obi sup. If a man or womā be take presoner i time of rightful batayl he is not fre And therfor his master may yeue him or sell hi by lawe of armes: Butte ware him of law of conscience: & of charitie. Dives. If a man haue hired or borowed an hors or any other thing into a certeyn place and for a certeyn tyme: and he pas that place or his tyme ayēs hys wil that owethe that thynge doth he theft: Pauper. If he do so of purpos and for couetyse or sum euyl cause / he dothe thefte But if there falle a sodeyne case whāne he cometh to that place

¶That he hyred it to and

Precepte.

he knew not of that case Whānne he hyred that thyng / and hī most nedis pfourme that case: or elles falle in grt harme: thānne he may take that fors or other thing ferther and lenger without: theft so that he may truly paie for that þ he passeth in the first couenaunt Diues. And What if a man lene awey another mannys good without assent of hym: Which good he lent him to his vse. Paup. he doth theft: But he haue iust cause to wene that the lord of ye thīge shal not be misspayd / For in þ lening he vseth another mannis gode apens his wil for sucre and wynnyng of frendshyp / And if a man lene another any thyng vpon a Wed.   And he vse þ Wed without leue of hym that oweth it: he doth theft / but it be for saluacōn of ye thīge For if he vse it for sparig of his own gode for sucre or for fals couetise apens his wyl that oweth it. he doth thefte as sayth the same clerk If at thīg stolne perissh . though the theefe haue no profyte therby: yit is he boūde to restitucōn . and he most peld as gode or better thā it was whā he toke it And he is boūd to mah restitucōn Both of ye thīg & of the pfyt that cam therof to hī And for ye pfyt that shuld haue come therof to the lord in the tyme that ocupied it apens his wil

And if he haue amēded the thing that he stale / he may nott aye asyen ne without his expēsīs / And he shal make restitucion after þ the thyng was worth whānne he stale it or better If the thefe pfte the lord in couenable tyme & place the stolen thīge : and the lorde wyl not receyue it : if the thynge after that by mishap perisshe : the lorde hath non accion apens the thefe for the lettige of restitucōn ne for the pfyte that might haue come therof after that he pfered it to him: But for the tyme byfore If a mā haue stolen a thīg he is bound not only to restitucion of the thynge: But also of the value of the vse. Diues. If a man or Woman bye in open markette a thyng stolen : wening that it were not stolen : Whanne he knoweth the soth . may he aye the pryse of that thyng of him þ oweth it : or withdraw it : til he haue payed hī as moch as he payd therfor Paup. Reymūd & other clerkes sey nay. And therfore be ware another tyme / both for losse of his and also for suspeccion of theft. for lightly for beggīge of stolen thīg he might be take as a these / Netheless be my rightfully aye hys payment of hym that sold it to hym Whanne he hath restored it to the lorde of that thynge / & if he spēt any thyng in amēdemēt

The seuenth

of that thyng whyle it was in his
kepyng: he may with good fay/
th aye that of him that owth the
thyng without restoryng of the
prophet that he had of that thig:
bifore he wyst that it was stolen
But whāne he knoweth that it
is stolen. ⁋ other mennys kepth
it styll for couetise or any other
vnlefull cause: he is boūd to resti
tucōn fro þ time as long as he ke
peth it of the pfyt to the lord: If
the thing perissh whyle he kepe it
not knowyng that it was stolen
by good feyth: he is bound to restitucion. And if he solde it away
or paue it or he knew of the stel
the he is not bound to restitucōn
of the thing. But of the pfyt. if he
be amēdyd therby and this is go
de lawe of cōscience. If a man ste
le fro a rich negard or any vsurer.
any thyng to do almes: he doth
theft. Quia nō sunt faciēda ma
la vt veniāt bona. xxxii.q.iiii. sic
non sunt. For as saynt Austen.
sayth. alle though he peue in almes all that he hath take in stelth
he is not excused of thefte. for he
putteth synne to synne. First he
steleth. and in þ peueth it away
he maketh he himsylfe vnable: to
make restituicōn. And though a
man purchase moch good falsly
and do almesse of þ misgote gode. he is not excused of rauayne.

The nynth chapter.

Dives. May not cristē mē
stele yong childrē of Iewes
& of hethen peple. & baptise them
ayens the wyl of ther fader and
moder. Pauper Nay. And that
for thre thinges. Fyrst to fle peryl
of the feyth. For whāne they come to age they myght lightly be
peruerted fro the feythe. By mys
eggyng of the fader and moder.
Also by rightful lawe of kynde
the childe is vnder cure of the fa
der and his moder and of his fredes tyl he come to yeris of discrecion. But whanne they be in age
of discrecion, they may be cristened ayens the wyll of ther fader
and moder: but nott ayens ther
owne wyll. Also it was neuer the
maner of holy church to cristene
yonge children of hethen people:
ayens the wyll of ther fader and
moder. And if it myght haue be
don lefully saynt Siluestre and
saynt Ambrose & other holy men
of holy church shulde haue gette
that leue of cristen pryncys that
were lordes that tyme: bothe of
cristen and hethen people. But
they ayed neuer that leue: ne did
it by ther owne auctorite: as sey
the saynt Thomas In quadam
Cqueſtione de quolibʒ

Precepte.

q ſm̄. cōf. li°. i°. ti. iiii. Dtrū pueri.
Diues. If a woman ſtele any thyng or ſhe be wedded. may ſhe make reſtitucōn after that ſhe is wedded without any leue of hir huſbond: Pauper. If ſhe haue ſtole thyng: ſhe is bond to make reſtitucyon therof / though hyr huſbond apenſay it: For hir huſ/bond hath no right in that thing And if the thynge ſtolen be waſted: ſhe is bounde to make reſtitucion if ſhe may of hir owne traueyle and of hir owne wynnige But of hir huſbondys godys: ne of other godys in comon ſhe may not wele make reſtitucion with oute his leue: But if he were conſentynge to the theſte / and if the huſbond ſtele any thynge: if the wife conſent therto or haue part therof in eſtge and drynkyng or any other uſe: be it with hir wyll be it ayens hir wyl. ſhe may preuely make reſtitucōn of ther comon godys / For in that ſhe doth no gyle ne theft to hir huſbonde. But ſhe doth that he aught to do But if he forbid hir vtterly to make reſtitucion: and ſhe be not cōſentyng to the theft it is ſiker that to hir to obey and make no reſtitucion ayens his wyl / a though ſhe dyd / it were no dedly ſynne. And if ſhe ſtele any thyng: a hir huſbond be cōſentyng therto: or

wetingly taketh part of ye theft ſhe may make reſtitucion puely of ther comon godys: if ſhe maye not do it of hir own laboure. Hec ſm̄. confeſ. li. ii°. ti°. Vi°. qd de illa
Diues. If a man haue ſate hys houſe or place to ferme for a certē tyme may he in any caſe put the fermore out within that tyme.
Pauper. In many caſe he may put him out: Firſt if the place be nedful to his owne dwellīge. for his other place that he dwelled ī: whanne he ſete that to hyre is periſhed by fire or by miſhap: or take fro him: and he hath nō other to dwelle in. But if he had non o ther whāne he ſete him to hyre: he may not put him out for that nede / For he might aupſed hȳ whā he ſete it ſo to hyre / Alſo if the houſe haue nede of amendemēt. Which bygāne after that he ſe te it him to hire / But in theſe two caſis he moſte aleſſe the hire that the fermoure ſhulde pape for the time þ hath dwelled therin Alſo if the fermonte myſuſe the houſe and the place / as if he kepe ſwy/ne in houſe of oneſtye: or waſte the place / And in theyſe caſys he may do hȳ pay ful paimēt for ye tyme that he hathe ocupied it: a make amendys for ſuch harmes And if he fayle gretly of his pay/
℄ment at hys terme: and

⁋The seuenth

bꝛeketh couenauntꝭ made by﹅
twene theym / Also if by his folẏ
and bẏ ſaute he bꝛynge the loꝛd
oute of tilthe / Also if the loꝛde of
the houſe oꝛ place / falle iṅ greate
harme ⁊ enmpte by defaute of ꝑe
fermoure Alſo if the fermoure be
ꝑe open theues oꝛ open lechoutꝭ
oꝛ other malefaſouris in his hou
ſes: oꝛ bẏs reſepuourẏs: of ſuche
wicked folke: thanne maẏe the
loꝛde ſkilfullẏ put bẏṁ oute.
Sṁ.cōſ.li.ii.ti.Bſto .in quiꞵus

⁋The tenth chapter.

Diues. If a mā bẏ gẏle do
another mā ſel a thing y⸍ he
thought not to ſel oꝛ doo hẏm ſel
it foꝛ leſſe than he thought haue
ſolde it: Doth that man
anẏ ſynne / As theſe men that tel
folke that there is moch coꝛne ⁊
moch ſalt compnge newlẏ fṛom
byonde the ſee . ⁊ ſo make men
to ſel greate chepe ther coꝛṅ and
ſalt y they haue: that theẏ maẏe
theẏmſẏlfe afterwarde ſylle ther
coꝛne and thez ſalt the deter And
as chapmen that come home bẏ
tẏmes byfoꝛe other: tel that ther
felowes be take of enemẏes and
that lẏtẏl moꝛe chaffer ſhal come
And ſo bẏ leſẏngeſ they ſell ther
good moꝛe dere than theẏ ſhuld

elleſ ſelle Pauper. They ſynne
greuouſlẏ. and iṅ maner theẏ do
theft / Netheles the contract that
men make with theym iṅ byig
and ſellẏnge moſte ſtonde: but
if it be ouerdoṅ outrage and opē
falſhede / Butt he moſte doo pe
naunce foꝛ his leſynges and bẏ
gẏle Diues. Is it leſful to ſel a
thẏnge foꝛ moꝛe than it is woꝛth
Pauper. If the ſeller ſelle anẏ
thẏng foꝛ moꝛe than it is woꝛth
to be gẏle the bẏer.he doth greate
ſynne and theft / But if he do no
gile ḭ his ſellẏng than he maẏ ſel
it after that theẏ accoꝛd / Foꝛ al
though it be not ſo moche woꝛ
the to another mā as he ſelleth it
foꝛ: ẏit ḭ caſe it is ſo moch woꝛth
to hi y begerth it. ⁊ he that ſelleth
it maẏ not foꝛgo it foꝛ leſſe pꝛice
without greate damage / Andḭ
thẏs caſe one thinge maẏ be ſolḍ
foꝛ moꝛ thā it is woꝛth ḭ ẏe ſilf bẏ
comō eſtẏmacōṅ But if ye ſeller
maẏ foꝛgo it w̉out damage ſo ḇ
he haue the valeu bẏ comoṅ eſtḭ
macioṅ he is bounde too ſelle it
foꝛ the comoṅ vſe . and nomoꝛe
take therfoꝛe / And if the ſeller be
moche harmed bẏ the ſellẏng: ⁊
the bẏer moch amēded bẏ the bẏ
ẏnge: he owethe bẏ good conſcḭ
ence if he maẏ do ſum reward to
the ſeller. al though londẏs lalbe
compel hẏm not therto / And th

same oꝼ with the seller to the byer. if the seller be moche amendyd by that sellyng/ and the bier moche apeyred Diues. It is harde to knowe what is the righte value. of a thynge Pauper The righte value and the iust price of thing is after þ the comō market gothe that tyme And soo a thing is as moche worthe as it may be solde to. by comon market. Tāti valet quanti vendi potest. Hec ſm con. li. ii. ti. viii. ꝗ. i. et ꝗ. ix. If a man or womā selle a thing for gode and he knowe a default therin by whiche defaute the bier is disceiued/ he doth gile a theſte Also and if the bier begile soo the seller. And therfore god seyde to the false iewys. Argentū tuū verſũ ē in scoriam/ et vinū tuū miſꝛ west aqua Thy siluer is turned into drosse of siluer and into fals metal/ and thy wyne is medlyde with water. psa. t° And therfor they that begile for þe with false money wyttyngly/ do grete syn. and perilous theft Also if he selle wyttyngly by fals measure/ and by false weightes And therfore god saith thou shalt nat haue dyuerse weightes more and lesse/ to bye by the more/ and selle by the lesse. Ne thou shalt nat haue a more busshel and a lesse busshell. ne none other fals diuerse mesuꝛ

But thou shalt haue iuste weizt and true and euen busshel ꝙ true. that thou may lyue longe in the londe that god shalle yeue the God hatith that man that doth suche gyle/ and he hatith al maner of vnrightfulnesse. Deutro. xxv. Also if man or woman sell sethe thing for an þose thing wittyngly to begile the bier/ he doth theft/ and is bounde to restituciō. And though he knowe nacht default/ whan he selleth it/ whan he knowith þat default he is boūden to make sūme recōpēsacion. as saith the same clerk in the same boke and place. ꝗ. vi. Also if the seller sel a better thynge than he wenyth to selle in grete dama ge of him self/ as if he selle golde for latō. or if he sel a gode thing for a smalle price/ wenyng that it were litel worth if he be moche harmyd therby/ the bier is bounde to restitucion or recompēsacion. Diues. Is the seller holden to tel the bier the defautes of a thīg that he selleth Pauper. If the defautes be preuy and pisous/ he is holden to telle them to the bier and selle that thing better chepe. For if he sel an haltyng hors for a swyft hors/ and a rupnoꝰ hous for a stronge hous/ it is pisouse and harme. to the bier/ and he is bounde to restitucion But if the

Di

The seuenth.

defaute be open/ and thoughe it may nat serue ye seller it may serue the byer/ thanne it nedith nat the seller to tell the defautes but he is boūde to selle it for the lesse prise. Diues. May a man selle a thing a derrer thāne he bought it. to Pauper. Elles mighte no man lyue by his marchaūdise ne by his craft He must take vp his costes and susteyne him and his by measure and Worship god and holy churche/ and helpe the pore nedy after his estate And for this ende it is leful and nedeful to the chapmā & to the Werkman to selle thynge derrer thāne he bought it. to And therfore seit Poule saith. that no man is holden to trauayle on his owne costes for the compnute/ neither in knighthode ne in chapmanhode ne in Werkmanship. And they þ with false othes/ and lesynges/ & slye speche begile folke in byeng and sellynge/ synne greuously. & be holden to restitucion/ if they begile so folke wyttyngnly. Diues. If ii. psones betake the thridde psone a thing to kepe by couenaunt that he shal nat deliuer it but to them bothe to gider. is he bounde to kepe couenaunt Paup. yhe forsothe. Diues. And what if he deliuer it to oone of them in absence of the other/ &

withouten his wyttyng Paup. He dothe amys/ and yit neither of hem hath lauful accion ayest him for to compelle him to yelde it. For he that resceyued it apen hath none accion to hym/ for he toke it him apen. And the other. hath none accion ayest him/ for he is nat bounde to him withouten the other that made the couenant with him/ and hath resceyued it apen. Thus saith Hostiē, sis in sū. li. iii. Rubrica de deposito. S. cui detur. v. si vero.

The xi. chapter.

Diues. May nat a mā do almesse of euyl gote gode Paup. Salomon saith. Immolantis ex iniquo: oblacio est maculata. The offrynge of him þ offeth of euyl gote gode/ is spottyd and foule in goddes sighte And he that offeth sacrifice of ye pore mannes gode/ is lyke him. that sleeth the sonne in the sight of his fader. And god that is highest approueth nat the yiftes of the wicked mē/ne takith hede to their offrynge. Ecclē. xxiiii. And therfore Salomon saithe Honora deum de tua substācia. Worship thy lord god with thyne owne gode/ nat of other mennes

Precepte.

gode Prouerb. iii. And Tobie saide. Ex substancia tua fac elemosinā. Of thyn owne gode do almesse. Tobie iiii. c. Diues. Contra. God biddeth in the gospel that men shulde make theim frendes in the blisse of heuyne of richesses of wickednesse/ Facite Bobis amicos de māmona iniqtatis. Therfore it semyth pat it is leful to do almes of euyl goten godes Pauper. In thre maners a thing may be euyl goten/ For sūtyme it is so mys goten þt it must be yolden ayen to him pt owyth it/ as in thefte/ rauepne/ t Bsurie if he may be founde. And so of mys goten gode men shuld do none almesse/ But yelde it ayē Also a thing is mys goten whan bothe þe peuyng and takyng of the thyng is ayenst goddes lawe/ t both the peuer and the taker lese their right/ as in symonye. And therfore neither they may do þe saide almesse of that gode so mys goten. Also a thynge is mys goten/ whanne the dede and the crafte that it is goten by is so vnleful that the taker may kepe it stylle lefully/ But the peuer may nat aye it ayen/ as thinge goten by licherye and by synful iapery of irregulers of mynstralles wit ches/ and suche other. Which maner wynnyng is clepid foule wl-

nyng. that is Turpe lucrū in latyne. And of suche euyl goten gode they may do none almesse. But they shulde make no open offrynge at the auter ne sacrifice of so mys goten gode. And therfore god saith. Non offeres mercedē pstibuli in domo dni dei tui quia abōminatio ē apud deum Thou shalt nat offre þe mede of the woman a comen lechoure in the house. of thy lorde god/ for it is abōminacion to god. Deutro. xxiii. And officers of kinges princes lordes and ladies of bisshoppes and prelates/ þ take yiftes of men by comyn custome or by pfte/ that they shuld mayntene them. and peue them fauour in their causes/ they may doo almes of godes so gotē/ al though it be ful ofte euyl goten. piiii. q. B. non sane. For to suche Cryste bad that they shulde make them frendes in heuene/ of richesses of wyckednesse/ that is to say of richesses so mys goten For he that taketh it hath noo righte therto. Diues. Why praysed Crist in þe gospel the false bayly that so for yaue men their dett/ in fraude of his lorde/ to haue thanke of them and helpe at nede. For he foryaue one the halfdele his dett/ Another the fifte parte of his dette. Paup. Crist prised nat the fals

B ii

The seuenth.

Lasarus. Butt Cryste saith that his lorde praised him nat, for his fraude but for his sllghte that he dyd in helpe of him self ne Criste tellith nat that parable in the gospel, that men shulde take example of his fraude. to helpe theym self by fraude of robbere of other mennys gode, But to recheue to make theyn frendes by dedes of mercy and of almesse, and foryeue other men their dettes as they wole that god foryeue them ther dettes and make them fredes, in heuene W'richesses of this World Diues. Why cleppd Crist richesses of this World richesses of Wickednesse Paup. For they been to moche folke occasion of moche Wyckednesse. and moche disease of hate, Wrath, enuye, of debate of plee and of grete discension And it is ful harde to gete them or to kepe them Without synne. and grete disease And therfore seint Poule saythe that they pat couepte to be riche in this World. fal in the feendes snare. And the Wiseman saith if thou be riche in this Worlde, thou shalt nat be Vngiltie ne cleen from synne. Also leue frende ye shal Vnderstonde. that Wyckednesse in holy Wrytte is taken nat only for synne, But also for peyne and disease & myshcups of this Worlde And so go

des of this World been cleppd richesses of Wyckednesse, that is to say of peyne. and disease. and of mischeif For they Bringe men in to peyne trauayle and moche disease, for men haue moch trauail in gettynge, moche drede in kepynge, and moche sorowe in the lesyng. Diues diuicias non congregat absq3 labore. Non tenet absq3 metu, nec deserit absq3 dolor They Bote sikernesse and bryng folke into grete perel, grete drede and in grete enempte They Bote a man to haue his lust & slypyng and Bryngen him in endlesse hungre For as salomon saith the couetouse man hath neuir ynough Auarus non impletur pecunia. But alway couetith more & more Also they Biheteth a man ease grett and Bring him in moche trauaill. for nigh alle the trauayle of this Worlde is to gete gode. Another stylle ther is Why they been cleppd richesses of Wickednesse For the lawe saith. p.q.i. dilectissimis By wey of kynde alle men Ben euyn in lordeshippe and richesses. But By Wyckednesse of false couetise in the people men Ben Vneuel riches For sume haue moche, some litel, sume Ben riche sume Ben pore, and god hath youen more richesse to one man in dispensacion and gouernaunce, thanne to

364

many other. And ÿ is to refreyne the wyckednesse o false couetise in the peple And for wyckednes is cause that oone man is richer thanne a nother/ therfore they be clepyd richesses of wyckednesse. For ne hadde be the wyckednes of Adames synne/ and of fals couetise of mannes herte/ elles alle men shulde haue been euynly riche. But nowe they ben vneuyn in richesse for synne and shrewidnesse/ and therfore godes of this worlde ben clepyd richesses of vneuenes and of wyckednesse. iniquitatis id est non equitatis. And therfore alle the richesses ÿᵗ one man hath passinge another. it is richesses of vneuenesse. For in þat he is vneuyn with his euē cristen. therfore they ben cleppyd richesses of vneuynnesse. Therfore god biddeth the riche men ÿᵗ been but his Baillies and his Reues in this worlde make frendes of the pore folke/ bothe by peulg and foryeuynge/ as that baillie dyd/ and be nat to harde to their subgettes but merciable and foryeue hem their dettes which they owe to god & to them For god is so greate a lorde and so riche þ ther may no man do him fraude. of his gode ne hyndre ne lese hys lordshippe.

The pli. chapter.

Diues. In the fift precept thou seidest that riche mē. that wole nat help the pore folk ben mansleers. Here thou seest ÿᵗ they be theupo, and so it semyth that they do ayēst bothe preceptes. Pauper. In that the pore man may die for the riche mā wᵗ holdith his gode from hym/ in ÿᵗ the riche man is a mansleer/ and dothe ayenst this precepte Non occides. thou shalt nat slee And in that he witholdith his goode. from the pore man in his nede he is a theef and dothe ayenst this precepte Non furtum facies Thou shalt do no thefte. For al that ÿe richeman hath passynge his neduful lyuyng. after the state of his dispensacion/ it is the pore mannes And therfore saith seint Ambrose. that it is no lesse synne. to the riche man for to denye the pore man helpe at nede whanne he may helpe him of his abūdāce. thanne it is to robbe a mā of his goode. The brede saith he ÿᵗ thou witholdest in superfluytee. is the pore folkes that haue hūgre And the waste clothynge þat thou shittest vp in superfluytie. is the pore wydowes. And þe moneye that thou hydest in the

The seuenth.

erthe in waste is the raunsome of the prisoners and of mischeuo[us] folke/ for to deliuer them out of prisone and oute of bondes/ and helpe them oute of woo. And therfore saithe he/ wylte thou itt wel. that of asmany godes thou arte theif and rauenoure as thou mightest peue to helpe of the pore folke if thou peue them nat. Noo man shulde saye any thing his owne that is compne to alle. Diues. J assent wele to thy wordes that riche men shulde peue almesse of their haboundaunce saupynge the state of their dispensacion, a his fulle harde to do For moche thing is nedeful to the riche man more thanne to the pore. Bicause of his state. of dispensacion. For moo thinges ben nedefulle to a kinge thanne to an erle. and moo to an Erle thanne to a simple knighte. and so it is of other staates. To kinges princes and lordes it is nedful to haue treasoure to wage men of armes in defence of the Realme/ & to wage their officers in gonernaūce of the Realme and of ther lordshyp. And therfore an Emperour saide. Qui omnibus preest: omnibus indiget. He that is Lorde by dispensacion of alle thinge in this worlde/ hath nede of alle thinge. And so the more

lordshyp in this worlde/ the more nede. Pauper. Therfore of suche thinges so nedful to man after the state of his dispensacion. he is nat bonde to peue the pore. but in greate nede. But of other superfluyte that is nat nedefulle to him in that degre/ he is bonde to peue For alway the compn profyte owith to be chargyd more. thanne the profytte of one psone Diues. Jt semyth by thy wordes that men of holy churche whiche spende the godes of holy chirche in wicked vse/ as in pompe. pride/ glutony/ lechery/ and in other vanities be theues/ for they witholde pore mēnys gode/ and spende it mysuse apēst the wylle of god and of pore folke. Paup. That is sothe/ for seint Jerome saith that al that clerkes haue of holy churche godes/it is the pore mennys/ and for helpe of the pore folke principaly holy churche is edowyd. To them that haue the beneficees and ye godes of holy churche/ it longith principaly to peue almesse and to haue cure of the pore people. Therfore seint Bernard/ in epistola ad eugeniū/ saith thus. the nakyd crie and the hungre pleyne them and say. ye bisshopes what doth gold in your bridles/ it may nat putt away cold ne hugre fro ye bridle

It is oure that ye so spende I pō=
pe and Vanytie. ye take it from
us cruelly/ and spende it veynes=
ly. And in a nother pistle that he
wrote to a chanon he saide thus.
If thou serue wele goddes auter
it is grauntyd to the to liue by ye
auter/ nat to bye their bridelles.
siluerid or ouirgilt For what
thou kepist for thy self of the au
ter passinge thyn honest nedeful
lyuynge/ it is rauepne/ it is theft
it is sacrilege. Therfore these
men of holy churche that boocle
ther shone with boocles of siluer
and vse greate siluer harneys in
their girdylles and knyues/ and
men of religion/ monkes and cha
nones/ and suche other. that vse
grete ouches of siluer and golde.
on their copes to fastne their ho=
des ayenst the wynde/ and ryde.
on high horse with sadles harnei
sed with gold and siluer more po
poussly thanne lordes/ be stroge
theupō and do grete sacrilege so
spedyng the godes of holy chur=
che in vanite and pride/ in luste
of the flesshe/ by whiche gode the
pore folke shulde lyue. A lady
of a thousande marke by yere cā
pynne her hode ayenst the wynd
with a smalle pynne of laton pit
for a peny. But a monke that is
bounden to pouertie by his pro=
fession wole haue an ouche/ or a

broche of golde and siluer in va=
lue of a noble or moche more.
Diues Be nat suche men of holy
churche so mispendyng the pore
mennys godes bounde to restitu
tion. Paup. If they haue wher
of to make restitucion/ they ben
holden to restitucion/ as saithe
Dockynge super. Deutro. v. c.
Quia non dimittitur peccatum
donec restituatur ablatum.
And therfore seint Austyne. In
epistola ad Macedonium. saith
thus. If a nother mannes gode
be nat yoldē ayen whāne it may
be yolden/ he that stale it doth no
verrey penaunce but he feyneth
penaunce For if he do verrey pe=
naunce he must do restitucion to
his power. Diues. And what
saist thou of tho clerkes that spē
de holy churche goodes. on their
kynnesmen and wymen. and o=
per riche folk for to be mayntened
and for to haue a name and for
to be worshiped in this worlde.
Pauper If they yeue their kyn
nesmyn and their frendes to rele
ue theym of their nede/ it is wele
done. and the ordre of charite ay
ith it. But if they yeue the godes
of holy churche to make them ri
che and grete in this worlde. of ye
pore mennys gode/ it is rauepne
theft and sacrilege. Also to
yeue riche folke measurablye to

Bliii

The seuenth.

mayntene them ryghtfully in ho‑
ly churche/ it is wele doon But
to yeue them holy churche godes
to be worshipid and to haue a na
me of pompe it is euyl doon/ and
it is sacrilege & thefte so to spend
the godes of holy chirch that ben
the pore mennys godes. Diues.
What sayste thou of theym that
spende the godes of holy church.
in their owne nedefulle vse/ and
doo nat their duite ne serue natt
therfore.   Pauper. The same
Clerke Dockynge in the same
place saith/ that they ben theues
For the godes of holy churche/ &
the Benefices ben youen to them.
that they shulde trauayl and ser‑
ue holy churche in techynge pre‑
chynge and sacramentes yeuige
and in besy gouernaunce.   And
but they do so. they be natt wor‑
thy to haue Offices of holy chur‑
che ne to yeue vp holy church go‑
des. And therfore Seint Poule.
saith. Qui non laborat. non māducet. He that trauapleth natt
shuld nat ete. And if þ they take
holy churche godes/ and trauayl
nat therfore as they ben bounde
they ben theuys. For if a labou‑
rer toke money to trauayle in ye
felde. and he trauayled nat ther‑
fore/ But he yaue it ayen he shuld
be holden a theef.   And therfore
seint Poule saide. Qui episcopa

tum desiderat/ bonum opus de‑
siderat. He þ desireth a Busshop‑
rike/ he desireth a gode werke.
Prima ad Thimo. teercio For
as saith the glose/ in that that he
desireth a Busshoprike/ he desirey
a werke nat a dignitie. He desy‑
reth trauayle/ nat ease and reste.
nat to weye into pride/ but for
to come from pride to more low‑
nesse/ to be seruaunt and mini‑
ster of alle his subgettes of which
he hath cure/ or elles they be nat
worthy to lyue vp the godes of
holy churche   For the benefices
of holy churche be nat youen hē
for to go pley theym/ but for to
trauayle aboute their cure.
Diues. They haue their Vikers
and their parisshe preestis vndre
them. Pauper. The vyker and
the parisshe preest shal aunswere
for that they they resceiue and ye
persone for that/ þ he rescepueth.
And he that more rescepueth mo
re is bounde. And the benefices of
holy church be nat youen to clerk‑
kes that they shulde betake to o‑
ther men the cure/ but for they
shulde haue principal cure them
self. For elles the sely wyd man.
Woman might haue the benefi‑
ces of holy churche/ as saithe the
same Clerke. And he saith that
persones which absent them fro
their churches only for ese or for

Precepte.

courtife. or for lufte of their flef=
fhe. and so spende the goodes of
holy churche/ they been theues
Nathelesse as he saith they may
absente them from ther churches
for a tyme by leue of their soue=
raignes that may yeue theym leue for sunne gode cause/ as for ler
nynge or for helpe of their chur=
ches. Also they that rescepue the
benefices of holy churche and be
vnable in that tyme whane they
rescepue them to serue holy chur/
che/ or to haue cure of that bene
fice/ they ben theups. But whan
they falle in age and in feblenes
after that they haue truly trauel
led/ or after that ye bnfice is po=
uer them they may lefully lyue
by their benefices But if they haue sufficient patrimony to be su
stepned with. Also they that appro
pre to them godes of holy church
betheups & do sacrilege as saith
the same Clerke dockyng, in the
same place For clerkes in theire
begynnynge saie. Domin⁹ pars
hereditatis mee Oure lorde god
is part of myne heritage For as
saith seint Jerom. ad nepociani
he must be pte of god. and haue
god to his part/ and so haue him
in his lyupynge/ that he haue god
with him and that god haue him
And sithen he saith god is my pt.
he owpth no thinge to haue butt

oure lorde god. And if he haue
golde siluer/ possessions and su=
che other richesses/ oure lorde dis
depneth to be his part with these
parties And if I be parte of oure
lorde/ I take no part ne worlde
lynesse amōges other folkes But
lyue by the tithes and am sustey
ned by seruice of the auter that I
serue. And so Ishalle be paied
with mete/ and drynke/ and clo-
thes/ & so folowe naked of worl
ly gode him that hangyd nakyd
for me on the rode. vii q̄ i. cleric⁹.
And therfore he biddeth that pat
euery clerke shulde take hede to
his name What it signifieth/ and
trauayle to be suche as his name
signifieth. Quia cleros greci dī
sors latine. For clerk in greke
and in latyne. is lott and part in
englisshe For euery Clerk shuld
be the lotte and the parte of oure
lorde god/ and in that they been
ordepned to goddes seruice pas=
synge the comen people Ther
fore they been cleppde Clerkes.
Clerici. that is to saye/ chosen by
lotte.　　For they been kin=
ges/ and gouernoures of hooly
churche. And in token therof
they bere the crowne on their he=
de by shaupnge a waye of theire
heere. For the shaupnge away
of their here. signifieth & betoke/
neth doing away of tēpal godes

and wilful pouert. By yͭ hicħ they been kinges in heuene. Ibidem. capitulo. duo. And therfore saith the salue there. Capitulo Res ec clesie. That thinges of holy churche ben nat hadde as propre But as come, and owe to be spet in the vse that they be pouen to. For alle that thou Clerke haste, more thanne sufficeth the to thy nedeful spupnge, But thou preue it and spende it in gode vse thou witholdest violently as a theef. Distinctione. ꝑlvii. Sicut. And if clerkes haue patrimony, sufficiently of their owne to lyue by, if they waste the godes of holy churche that been ordepnede for pore folke. they do theft and sacrilege. xvi. q̄. i. in fi.

The xliii. chapter.

Diues. What is propirly sacrilege. Paup. Sacrilegium est sacre rei violatio, vel eiusdem vsurpatio. Vnde sacrilegium quasi sacrilediū id est sacrū ledens. Sacrilege is defouling of holy thing, or mysusyng and mys takynge of holy thinge. Diues. In how many maners is sacrilege done. Paup. Sūtyme sacrilegie is done for the persone that is dispised and mysbosden As whanne clerke or religiouse is beten or smyten in despit Sumtyme sacrilege is doon because of the place as Whan chirche or churcheyerde is pollute by blode shedyng, or any holy place is reupd of his fredom. Also sacrilege is done bicause of thing pat is stolen or mysused, and that in thre maners. Or for that holy thinge is taken out of holy place, or thinge nat holy oute of holy place, or holy thinge out of na holy place. xvii. q̄. quarta. q̄sdus. Diues thā it sempth yͭ they pat witholde ther tithes fro god and holy churche, doo theft Pauper So saith the salue. xvi. q̄. vii. decimas. For the tithes of holy churche been the auowes of cristen people, raunsome of synnes, and patrimonie, helpe and heritage of the pore people, and tributes of the nedy soules. xvi. q̄. i. quia iuxta. et .c. decime. Where the salue saith that tithes be dett to god. And alle that witholden them falsly, they doo sacrilege, ⁊ robbe the pore folke of their godes And he that witholdith hys tithes, wrongefully shalle aunswere at ye dome for asmany soules as perisshe for hungre and mischeife. in that parisshe.

Precepte.

where he duellith. And he þ wole nat pay his tithes shal myspede and his goode. shalle banyshe/ and he shalle haue sekenesse. and sodeyne pouert. Ibidem. c. Reuertimini. And if he pay his tithis truly he shal haue helth of Bo by/ and the more plentie of gode and grace of god/ & forpeuenesse of synne/ and the kingdom of heuyn. As saith the lawe, ibidm c°. decime. Et Raymundus in sūma sua li. i. titulo de decimis. And therfore the lawe saith there that god ayleth nat the tithes for pfite ne for nede but for worshyp þat we shuld knowlege him/ our lorde and ȝeuer of al gode he ap ith of Bo the tenthe part for oure pfit nat for his pfit It is a synne to paie late/ but moche more syn is neuir to pay idm ȝ. c. Diues. Of what thinges is a man bounde to tithe Pauper. Of corne in herupst/ of wyne in wedage/ of frupt. of bestial/ of gardeyn/ of perde/ of medowe/ of venery/ of spues/ of fisshing. of wyndmyl. and of watermylle/ ꝑ Bi ꝗ. Bii. Quicūqʒ et c° sequenti. Extra. li. iii. ti. ꝑꝑꝑ° pastoralis. And as Raymonde saith Tithes owe to be pouen of al the frutes of ye erthe Of apples of tree/ of erbes of pastures/ of bestes/ of wolle. of mylk/ of hey/ of fisshinge/ of fermes/ of mylles/ of bathes/ of fullynge places/ of mynes of silueꝛ & of other metal/ of ȝretis of stone/ of marchaundise of crafte and of other goodes and also of tynne li° t°. ti° vii. And as saith hostiensis libro iii. eodē titulo Of euery thing riȝtfully goten a man shulde tithe and of his seruyce and of his knyȝhteshippe.
Diues. Moche thinge is wele geten and with lytel auätage of them þat gete it. and oft with grete losse/ and therfore me thynketh it is unskilful that a man shulde tithe his chaffare and his crafte or his seruyce or his trauayle there his wynnig is lytel or nouȝte. Pauper. Ther been ii. maner tithes. Sūme come of therth/ as corne wyn bestiale that is broughte forth by the londe And suche tithes ben cleppd prediales in latyne Sūme tithes come onlye of the partsone/ as by marchaundise. and werkmasshippe/ and suche tithes ben cleppd parsonales in latyne.

And in suche tithes that been parsonales/ and comen of marchaundise. Or of crafte/ or of suche. other trauayle/ a man shal accompte his expenses/ and loke whether he is encreasyd/ or natt. And tithe his wynnynge and his free encreases.

The seuenth

in payng of tithes prediales þat come of þe londe/ he shal nat acounte expēses but frely pay þe tithe neither worste ne beste. But as they cūme to honde without chois Extra li.iii.e.ti.pa storalis. et c. cū homines. Natheleſſe if a man for deuocion yeue þe best to god/ it is prisable and Wele doon. Diues. Shulde mē tithe al thing þ newyth. Paup. Thinges þþey tayed in þe lawe men shulde tithe/ nat al thynge þat newith/ for moche thynge newith þat is natt profitable. And though it be profitable. yitt it is nat worshipful as houndes. and cattes. Diues. I suppose a man cūme by fre yift or by succeſſion and by heritage to gret lordship and moche ricchesses/or take frely grete yiftes/ is he bounden to yeue þe tenth part of that eritage or of tho yiftes to holy church. Paup. Nay. for so al poſceſſions and lordshippes shulde falle to hooly churche. Extra e. pastoralis in glosa. And if a riche man paue a pore mā y pēs to bye him wᵗ a clothe. or to pay his dettes/or els to his lyuynge. he shulde paie þe tithe to þe pst and þat were ayenst reason. For if al free yiftes shulde be tithed. holy churche shulde be to riche. & þe people to pore   For soo he

might aye þe tenthe part nyghe of euery testamament

The y iiii chapter.

Diues. To what churche shal man paie his tithes. Pauper. Tithes personales as of marchaundise & of crafte man shal pay to his parisshe churche. there he duellith and takith his sacramentes/ and herith his seruice. But tithes prediales shuld be paied to þe church/ to whiche maner and the londe longith to. But custome be in þe contrarie. as saith silma conf. Tithes prediales shulde be youen/ anon in þe begynnyng/ But tithes psonelles may abyde til þe ende of þe yere for þe more auantage. of þe churche. Diues. Howe shulde the tithes be spent Paup The tithes and the godes of holy churche shulde be departed in foure partes/ after that the parties haf nede and be worthy One to the busshop if him nede Another to þe ministres of þe churche. The thridde to pore folke The iiii. to amendmēt and making of the churche if it nede. vii. q. iiii. quatuor. Where the glose concludith and saith þat clerkes shulde be compellyd to reparacion

Precepte.

of the churche and nat the selue people ꝟ. q̄. i. decernim⁹. But as saith Guydo in rosario in ꝟ men must take hede to custome of ꝑe cuntre and what the part is that longith to the churche Diues. J suppose ꝟ the curate of the chirch waste the godes of holy churche. in synne and lechery/ and be an open theef or an open lechour or mansleer/ so that his mislyupng. is sclaunderous & notorie. shuld men pay their tithes to such wicked lyuers Paup. Hostiensis saith that if the prest or curate or curate of the churcḥ mispende holy churche godes. or be a notorie lechoure/ the selue man is natt bounde to peue hym his tithes But he shal peue them to his soueraigne nexte aboue hym which is bounde to spende them in profytte of the churcḥ/ or of the pore parisshyns Diues. The lawe is ayenst hym Extra li. iiii. ti. de decimis c. tua nos. Where the lawe saith that for wychednesse of the mynystres of holy churche. men shuld nat withdrawe their tithes from them Pauper. Hostiensis aunswereth therto and saith ꝟ as longe as their synne is pryue. men shulde nat withdrawe their tithes And so meneth that lawe. But whanne their synne is open. and notorie thanne men shulde.

nat paie to them but to ther soueraigne Thus saith Hostiensis in sū. sua. li. iii. Rubrica de decimis .S. et quare in fine And he alledgith many lawes for hym and many lawes ben for hym that he aledgith nat For the grete Clerk Gracian⁹ in the decrees ꝟ is cheif booke of lawe canon saithe ꝟ the clerke notarie lechour shulde haue no part in the goodes of holy churche. distinct. lxxxi. Si quis amodo cū aliis capl̃is sequentibus And ther saith the glose that to whome it is forboden to doo office in holy churche/ to hym is forboden and interdiit his benefice But as the lawe saith there. To al suche notorie lechoures. prestes dekenes subdekenes ben forboden the offices of holy chirche ꝑat they shulde do no offices in holy churche/ and the people is forboden to here their office. Therfore than their benefice. is forbode ꝯe til they amēde hem lxviii. Si qui sunt prisbiteri Upon whiche lawe saith Gwydo in rosario. That if prestes be founde suche open lechoures and malefactoures/ their subgettes maye of their owne auctorite put them from their office. And nat abide sentence ne doome of their souereyn/ al though the bisshop wer fauourable to suffre suche.

The seuenth

wycked lyuers / For why saith he suche been suspended by the pope and by the lawe. Diues. This sentence is wonderfulle and nat plesaunte to men of holy church and yit as me thenkith it is skilful For if any man ought me dett and paied it to myne enemye / to strength him in his malice ayens me wyttyng wele that he shulde robbe me therof ⁊ nat paie it me. he dyd moche ayenst me and robbed me cruelly of my gode. And so as me thynkith do they þ paie tithes and ducties that longe to god and holy church and to pore folke / and paye theym. to suche wycked lyuers and open enemyes to god / for they been loste for euir Or if he kept them stille / or paied them to his souerayne. as Hostiensis saith / than were they sauf and holy churche ⁊ the pore people might be holpen therby

Pauper. It is leful so to kepe them and nat ayenst the lawe / yt they aledge ayens Hostiesis and ayenst other clerkes ⁊ ayenst the comon lawe / for þ lawe acordeth with al other clerkes if it be wele vnderstonde. For these been the wordes of the lawe. Preceptu neqͥcie clericorum nequiunt eas. q. decimas nisi quibus de ma dato diuino debētur suo arbitrio errogare Extra libro iii. de deci mis / c. tua nobis. That is to saye in englisshe Lewde men may nat vnder colour of wyckednes of clerkes yeue by their owne dome the tithes butt to theym that they been dette to / by the comaudement of god. For it is nat leful to yeue away a nother mannes gode withouten the wylle of the lorde of the goode as saith þe lawe there. These wordes be nat ayenst Hostiense / for Hostiense. spekith of clerkes open lichours and open wycked lyuers.

This lawe spekith of clerkes whos synne is preuy and of them that been defamed falsly by malice of the people / and he biddeth there that they shulde be yeuon them ayen Also this lawe saithe that it shulde natt be youen but to them that it longith to by the commaundement of god But by the the commaundemente of god they longe nat to suche wycked lyuers. Therfore they shuld nat be youen to them. Also though the lewde man witholde his tithes and his ducties fro suche wycked men in holy churche and paie them to his souerayne or elles kepith them stylle for spyte of holy churche. in that he yeueth them nat away butt kepith thē sauf to pfit of holy chi che And that lawe men alledg

apens hostiesi. s. tua nobis/ spe=
keth ayenst the lewde men. that
peue alwey tithes of holy church.
& dispende them as them liketh.
and peue them alway to whom þ
they wole/ and this is nat lefulle
wtoutē autorite of busshopes.
If the busshop or any hous of re
ligion resceiue so many tithes in
a parisshe by olde custome/ that
the curat of the churche may nat
lyue honestly by his bñfice/ than
a certeyne porcion of the tithes.
may be youen to that curate. for
to lyue by. nat wthstondyng ye
olde custome Extra li.iii. de pre
bendis/ c. extirpande/ Where the
lawe saith/ þ he that hath cure of
a parisshe shulde serue it him self
and nat by a nother/ But nede of
other cure compelle him therto

The viii chapter.

Diues. Shal holy church
aye tithes psonales of Je=
wys that duelle amonges cristē
people Pauper. Nay. For they
be nat of holy churche/ and they
take natt sacramentes of hooly
churche ne seruyce of the curate.
If a man gylously selle a porci=
on of corne or it be tithed/ bothe
the byer and the seller ben bound

to tithe it The seller for his gyle.
and for he hathe the value of the
tithe. And he þ bieth it is bolden
for that corne passith to him. wt
charge of the tithe. And so hooly
churche may aye ye tithe of whe/
ther of them that he wole But if
he gete it of the one of theym/ he
may nat aye it of the other But
if the byer thought no gyle in his
byynge if he paied the tithe after
þ he bought it/ the seller is boun=
de to make him restitucion. And
if the byer and the seller wist wel
yat it was nat tithed/ them must
bothe do penaunce as for thefte.
And if the byer paie the tithe/ the
seller is bounde to restitucion But
the byer bought it to suche a pris
þ he may yit wele saue his owne
If the corn be stole or it be tithed
and the lorde of the corne wel to
slowe in the tithing & tithed natt
after the custom of the place But
delayed it/ holy church may aye
of him the tithe of the corn so sto
len But if it be taken away with
in the tyme of due tithynge he is
nat bounde to restitucion of the
tithes. Hec Raymundus li° i° de
decimis. Diues Is a mā boūde
by the precepte of god to paie al
his tithes bothe predialce and p
sonales. Paup. As Innocent
the pope the thridde. Extra e. in
aliquibus. and Reymonde also

The seuenth

say Al the tithes must be payed that ben tayed by goddes lawe. Leuitici vltimo. And al other ti thes bothe pdiales and psonales after custome of the cuntre long approued For consuetude or cu stome in lawe positif that is ma nes lawe. is expositour and ter mynour of the lawe. Consuetus do approbata est optima legum interpres. extra. li. c. tt. iiii. cu di lectus Et consuetudo est altera lex. But ther may no consuetu de or custome be kept apēst god des lawe/ ne apenst lawe of kide Diues. Why badde god that mē shulde paie more the .x. part thā a nother part. Pauper For x is nombre so parfyte that it conteyneth al nombre For al nombres after x. ben made of ten and nō bres within x. And nyne is nom bre vnparfite/ and alle nombres within x ben vnpfite in regarde. of .x./ And therfore god bad that men shulde yeue him. the tenthe part/ and kepe to them self nyne partes/ in token that al oure par feccion cūmeth of god and to hī it must be arretted by pzisynge & thankyng/ and al oure impfecci on cūmeth of oure self And ther fore we withholde nyne partes to oure self/ and yeue to god the. x. parte/ so knowlecchyng that alle oure pfeccion and godenesse cū

meth of him/ and al oure impfec cion cūmeth of our self And in to ken that he is our lorde and lord of al/ and al pat we haue cūmey from him/ as al oure nōbres ben contepned in x/ and come of x.

The xvi chapter

Diues. Is symonye any spice of theft Pauper. It is theft and sacrilege in that y a man stelith and occupieth vnri ghtful thinge that is nat his Of suche theues spekith Crist in the gospel. Qui non intrat p ostiū in ouile/ sed ascendit aliūde/ sie fur est et latro. Jo. x. c. He pat entrith natt in the folde of hooly churche by the dore that is Crist. and takith nat his benefice frely by weye of almesse for cristes sa ke but by symonye/ he is a theif. & a mycher And al that so cūme. into the benefices of holy church by symonie/ they ben mychers/ & theues Diues. What is symony Paup. Symonye. is a studiou couetise and wylle. to bye or sel. thinge spirituel/ or thing anney ed or knytt to spiritual thynge. For as the philosophre saith nat only he that stelith priuelyy is a mycher But also he that wole stele priuely/ is a mycher & a theif

Precepte.

But here thou shalt vnderstonde that sūme thīges be forbode. for they be symonyent as bieng and sellyng of the sacramentes of holy churche/ in whiche wylle alone withouten dede makith a mā giltie in symony Sūme thinges ben symonient only for they ben forboden by holy churche. As if a clerke resigne his churche in couenaunt that it shalbe youen to his neuewe or to sūme of his kyn suche wylle without dede maketh nat a man symonient ne giltie in symonye as anentes holy churche/ But if it be done only for profytt of the psone and nat for profytt of holy churche. He is giltie bifore god And if he resigne it frely in couenaunt and in wyl that it shalbe youen to hym that is more able to profyte to mannes soule thāne he is him self/ in that resignyng he doth no symonye. Diues. Wherof came the name of symonye Paup. Of symon magus a grete wytche For he proferyd to seint Petir a grete sūme of money to haue grace of the holy goste to make men hole of seknesses/ and to do wondres and to make the holy goste to light in men and wymen/ as seint petyr dyd But seint Petir forsoke his money and saide to hym. Thy money be stylle with the in

pdicion and perisshing of dampnacion/ for thou wenyst to gete ye yift of god wᵗ it actuū iiii And therfore alle that bye any thinge spirituel or any thinge knytt to spirituel thinge/ ben cleppd propirly symonietes And they that selle it ben cleppd giezites Giezite in latyne For Giezi the seruāt of Helisee the prophete toke mede of the grete lorde Naman for that god hadde made him hoole. of his lepre/ by the prophete Helisee that was his maister And so he selde falsly the yifte of god. in asmoche as was in him/ ayēst the wyl of god and of the pphete Helisee. And therfore he was a lepre and al his kynne after hym. iiiiº Regū 5. Natheleesse comonly bothe bier and seller of spirituel thinge ben cleppd symonietes For symon magᵘˢ dyd that was in him to bye the grace of the holy goste/ and was in purpos and wylle to selle it forth to other for money and for yiftes Diues. In howe many maneres is symonie doon. Pauper In thre maners as thing spirituel is bought and solde by thre maner yiftes For sūtyme it is bought by yifte of honde/ sūtyme by yift of seruyce/ sumtyme by yift of tūge/ yift of the hōde is cleppd money and other richesses/ yift of seruyce. is

℃ i.

377

The seuenth.

cleppyd their seruyce pouen nat I due maner/ne rightfully to haue a thing spirituel/ yift of tunge is fauoure flateryng and prayer yt men make them self or by other. So to haue spirituel thinges Also in rescepuyng of holy ordre is do symonye/ sumtyme only on his side that makith ordres As whā sūme frend of him that shalbe ordred yeueth the bisshop sūme yift Withoute the wityng of him yat shalbe ordred Sumtyme it is do only on his side that shalle be ordred/ as if he yeue any yiftes to a ny of the bisshopes officers to speke for him that he may be ordred and of whiche yift the busshoppe knowyth nat Sumtyme it is do of bothe the parties/as whan the one yeueth and the other takith. Sumtyme it is done and yift in neither ptie/ as if a frende of him that shalbe ordred yeue or bote a ny thing to the bisshopes officers to help him in that cause/ and nether he ne the bisshop knowith of tho yiftes. And in these maners may also be done symonye. in yeupnge of Benefices of holy churche. If any may yeue any yift for me or pray for me that I may be ordryd or resceyue Benefice if I assey and assent natt therto his yifte/ ne his biheest/ne his prayer/ lettith me nat fro myne

ordres ne fro my Benefice/ But if I assent therto bifore or after paying the money that he behigghte. I falle in symonye. And thouggh it be neuer so preuy I must resigne/ And if myn enemy yeue or bihete yiftes for my pmocion I wil so to let me by symone/ and it be nat myn assente/ his dede lettith me nat Extra li. 20 iiii. de symonia c. sicut tuis litteris. If any frende yeue any yift me vnwytyng for my pmocion/ and after that I wyste therof or I were cleppyd of the busshop to my pmocion. and I wyst it wele þ I shuld nat be clepid But for þ yift I shuld nat resceyue that pmocion. Hec sū. conf. li. i. ti. i.

The xviii chapter

Iues. May no thinge be poue lefully for thing spūel. Pauper. yhis. For both yift of honde of tonge and of seruice. may be poue for spirituel thinge Yift of honde may be poue for spuel thing in v. cases as saithe Reymunde. First if it be pouen frely for deuocion and for reuerence of the sacrament & of spūel thing withoute any couenāt. or any ayīg of the taker. But for to yeue any thing by wey of couenaunt or bying/ or sellyng/ or of chaungyng it is nat leful And if it be dout whether the yift be pouen by couenaunt or by eupten/tencion/ men muste take hede. to the state of the peuer/ & of the taker whether the riche peue the pore/ or the pore to the riche. or tyche to riche Also to the quātite of the thiste/whether it be of greate price or of lytel price. Also to the tyme of the peuyng/whether I tyme of nede or iny other tyme And so by these circumstaunces deme in whᵗ maner it was pouen The secoūde cas is/whanne men peue frely to any man of holy church. any thing for spūal dedis as for certeyn seiyng and syngynge to whiche he is nat boūde. The iii. case is whanne it is youē to clerkes for spūal dedes to the whiche they bē boūde of office For ther is no man boūde to trauayle for noughte/ ne the curate serue the churche for nought/ ne the pchor to trauayle for nought And therfore seint poule saith that they pᵗ serue the auter shal lyue by thauter. And so god hath ordeyned yᵗ they þ pche the gospel. shal lyue by the gospel. Prima ad cor̄ ix. Natheleste the more frely that a man pchith the more is his mede And though he axe nat ye peple is boūde to peue him frely/ As saith seint austyn sup illud Producēs fenū iumentis. The iiii. cas is to haue lyf without ende

& for yeuenes of synne Therfor Daniel saide to the kynge Nabugodonosor Pctā tua elimosinis redime Dan̄ iiii. Bye ayen thy synnes with almesse/nat yat we may bye heuene/ ne foryeuenesse of synne/ But by almesse doyng we may deserue to haue foryeuenesse of syn/ & heuene blysse and so bying is taken for deseruynge. The fift cause is whāne a man for to haue peas byeth away the wronge that ht suffryth in spūel right whāne he is spher. & his cause is rightful. Extra de symonia c. Dilecto filio

The xViii. chapter.

D Iues. What peyne is or deyned ayēst symonye.
Pauper If a clerke be a symonient in takyng of his ordre/ he is suspendyd of his ordre both as nentis him self and anētes other so þ he may nat do execucion of his ordre And whether his symonie be pryue or apert he is suspē dyde. And if he be coūicte bifore his iuge/ shalbe deposed. & Unableed to euy worship & lese ye money þ he paied therfore And he yᵗ ordryd him wyttyngly by symonie/ or paue him bnfice by simonie or he thᵗ resceueth any bnfice by symonye/ or is meane therto though their syn be pryuy/ yitt they be suspendyde. as anentes

The seuenth.

them self. And if it be open, they ben suspēdyd both anētes theim self and anētis other And he þ taketh his benefice wᵗ symonye, he must resigne & make restitucion of al the profyt þ he hath take therof, & for the profyt þ might haue be taken therof for his tyme. For it is a general rule in the lawe that who so occupieth any thing withoutē rightful title, he is bounde to restitucion of al the harmes & of al profyt camē therof, or miȝt haue come therof for þ tyme, sauyng his expensis þ he spent i profyt & saluacion of þ thyng. And both clerke & selwyd man þ doth symonye, he is acursed in þ dede. And if it may be preuyd, þ selwde man shulde accursed openly i holy churche. Prima q̄. i. repiūtur.

Diues. If the officer of the busshop axe of custome any yiftes i makinge of ordres, in sacryng of busshopes, in blessynge of abbottes, if they þ shulde be ordryd or blissed or sacryd, yeue them suche yiftes, for custome that they allege, is it symonye. Pauy.

If he yeue it principaly for such custome & for their axing it is symony But if he yeue it frely, nat for ther axing ne for custome ne by couenaunt, it is no symonye But most siker it is that he yeue none thanne ne for thanne, for it is syke symony. And seint Poul biddeth þ men shuld abstayne them from euery wycked liknesse Also they that yeue or take any thige by wey of custome or of couenāt for blessyng of weddynges, for sepultures, for diriges, for creame or oile, or for any sacramente in whiche is youen grace he doith symony. If any curate or parisshe preest for yiftes, for prayer, for loue, for fredship, bide a ope syn of his parisshyn obstinate in syn or recounseile him that wole nat amēde him, or for hate & enemyte wole nat recounsey him that wole amende him, or for hate or loue or yift or prayer putteth any man or womā from the sacramentes of holy churche, he doth symony. If a preest be bounden of office to say a messe, or dirige, & such other prayers & he axe money therfore, he doth symonye. But if he be nat bounde therto of office, and he hath nat his nedesful lyuyng he may take money for his trauayle and lett his trauayle to hyre by daies and yeres as annuelers done, as saith Reymunde. Et extra ne prāti. Dices suas & cᵒ Vltimo. But if he haue sufficient lyuyng and he be nat bounde to say that messe or dirige, thanne he shalle say it frely, or elles nat say it For elles it se-

meth that he doth it principally
for couetise. If a preſt haue said
a maſſe if he say a nother maſſe
that day for money or for to ha=
ue thanke of the worlð/ he doth
symone. De con. di. i. ſufficit.

The xix. chapter

Dues. If religiouse or se/
culer clerkes in auaunce=
ment of their kynnesmen make
couenaūt to gidðre and say/ Aſ=
sent thou to auaunſynge of my
newewe and I ſhal aſſēt the aua
sying of thy newewe Or elles one
saith that aſlonge as I lyue ſhal
ther no grace of any auaūſemēt
paſſe while I may lette it/ but I
haue this grace for him þat I ȳ
for. do these any symonye.

Pauper It is symonye. For
the lawe saith. Abſit omīs pactō
ceſſet omis conuentio.t. q. ii. qſt
pio. In spiritual thinges euery
couenaunt ſhulde be awaye/eue
ry conuencion cease. If the cu=
rate wole nat burye the dede bo=
dy/ ne ſuffce it to be buried/ but ī
couenaunt that he ſhal haue his
bedde or his beſt clothe/ or sūme
other thing he doth symone. alle
though it be cuſtome to paye. þᵉ
he ayith. And therfore he ſhulde

frely burye the dede and bleſſe the
that been nedy/ and so abſteyne
him fro euery spice of symonye.
and afterward compelle them to
pay and kepe gode cuſtomes/ if
that they might wele do it for po
uert. Eytra e. ad apoſtolicam
If a preeſt wole nat baptiſe but
he haue money therfore he doth
symonie. And rather the selwyd
man or womā ſhulde baptiſe the
childe/ thanne peue money ther=
fore And if he wet of age þ ſhuld
be baptiſed. and there were noo
man ne woman butt the preeſte.
though he were in peryl of dethe
he ſhulde rather die without bap
tyme of water/ thanne he ſhulde
be baptiſed by symonye. For in
that case the baptym of the holy
gooſt ſuffiſeth to him Euery mā
and woman may baptiſe for ne=
de. If any patrone peue a be/
nefice in couenaunt that he that
receyueyth it ſhal helpe him tē=
porally and his also/ it is symo=
nye Eytra e. nemo. And if he
peue it to sūme of his kynne soo
to magnifye him self/ and to be
the more mighty worldly by aua
sying of his kynrede/ it is symone
And if a patrone ſelle a patrona
ge by the self/or ſelle the maner þ
is annexed therto/ the more dere
for the patronage/ he doth symo
nye As saith Petrus tarentinus

C iii.

The seuenth.

sup quartum) sent. distinct xxv. And therfore he saith that chopp̄yng of churches without auctorite of the bisshop/ is symony. And he saith there also that right of patronage may natt be solde. But it passith forthe with byinge of the londe that it longith to.

If precchours or pardonpstris or other folke that goo for almesse, pray the parisshe preest or the curate to pcure them sume gode in their parisshe in couenaunt þ the preest or the curat shal haue a certeyn part therof/ it is symony as anentis the preest/ for both do sy symony/ and also they do sacrilege & theft/ in that þ they defraude men of their gode/ and put it nat in the almesse that they peue it to and both the preste and the pardoniste be bounde to restitucion.

The xx. chapter.

If a man or woman peue money to be resceiued ito house of religion/ and so in religion in couenaunt þ he or she shall peue a certeyn money to þe hous it is symonie though it be comen custome so to peue Natheleesse if he be resceyued frely as the salue wose/ he doth no symonie. Extra e. sicut p certo et c. in tantum c° veniens. c°. audiuimus c. Jacobus. Natheleesse if the house be pore & ouircharged wᵗʰ p sone so cladde/ they may afterward pray the fredes of that psone/ of sume almesse in releuynge of the hous and of that charge. If a man or a woman peue money to prestes riche or pore/ for trental/ for ānuel/ for perday/ or for to say messe of the holy goost or other masses or to peue money to clerkes/ for sayinge of psalters or of diriges. or to pore men in couenaunte of certein prayers/ with intencion so to bye their prayers he doth symonye. scōm glosam Wilh't et habetur in sū. con.li. t.ti.i.q xlii. And yit as he saith there/ it is lefulle to take and to peue money and other temporel thinges/ for suche spirituel thing/ and for þ er by wey of deuocion and of fre pift/ so to eycite deuocion and loue of psones the more to pray for them. And in this maner men may peue to colleges certein money to kepe their pereday/ nat by wey of couenaunt of byinge/ and of sellynge/ but so to stirre theim frely to graunt them their ayng by wey of more charite and mot deuocion. For suche spirituel thing may nat be solde And therfore men shuld peue their goode frely to men of holy churche by wey of almesse/ and they shulde take it frely by wey of almesse And the peuer w' his pifte of cha rite may aye certein prayers. of them that he peueth to/ & if they grauntyd him they ben bounden to kepe their graunt Therfore saith seint Austyne that the apo/ stelys to he frely their liuynge of them that they prechyd frely to. And as grete synne it is the preest to sel his prayer/ as the prechour to selle his prechynge. Criste badde i the gospel that me shuld make them frendes of the riches/ ses of this worlde pat they might resceyue them into endlesse taber nacles that is to say pat they mi/ ght so pray for hem & they might be resceyued into blisse And thus muste alle men of holy churche. take their lyuyng if they wol be clene oute of symony. For they may nat sell ther office that they do in holy churche/ ne their pray er/ But by fre yiftes take their suf ficient lyuelode Extra ne prati. Vices suas. c° qm enormis. Diues Contra. It is ordeyned by constitucion synodalle what money a parissh preest and what an annueler shuld take Paup. That is natt for his office but it is done to lett the false couetise. of men of holy churche/ to putte

in certein hou moche is sufficiet: to their lyuyng that they shulde no more aye. ne men no more ye ue theym. But if it be nat suffici ent/ they may take more by leue of their prelates And that tax inge is natt ordeigned by the pe/ uer of the money/ But by the pre lates of holy churche bothe anen tis symonye and ayenst falfe co/ netyce of their clerkes.

The xxi. chapter

Diues. It semeth by thy wordes/ that they & synge the golden trentalle. go fulnigh symonye For they make woun derful couenaunte. of their syng yng. Pauper Leue frende thou shalt vnderstond that couenant makynge maketh ofte symonye that shulde elles make no symo nye/ As if the peuer aye what it is worthe to synge many messys and the preest answereth twenty shillynges. or ten shillynges/ or a noble.   Or if the peuer seye. say what wylt thou take to syn ge it. and the preest answere and sey no lesse than twenty shillyn ges. or ten shyllynges. and thus bargeyne and broke. aboute the syngynge of the messe. that may

The seuenth.

nat be solde ne boughte, as men do in bipnge and sellynge of any horse, thanne they falle bothe in cursed symonp. Also if the peuer say to the preest in his bargapnynge, that he shal synge for certeyne soules and for no moo and he bihotith him soo, thanne ben they bothe accursed for that foule symonye. And also for it is apenst charite, for the preeste is bounden to synge for alle cristen. And for the mo he prayeth in special by weye of charite, the more he plesith god. and the more ben tho soules holpen, for whiche he takith his sellarie. And in that he byndeth him to say special messes in certeyne tyme, he muste in cas leue the messe of the daye that he is bounden to. if he be a curate a so doth symonpe. as saith Raymounde, and other clerkes. ☞ Also he doth in that apenst the ordenaunce of holy churche. Extra lib.10 tercio de celebratione missarum. c. secudo Where it is bode that ther shuld no man leue masse of the day for other specialle messes, As of the Trinitie oure lady, or other nat for it is euyl to here or to say such specialle messes. But for it is euyl to leue messes of the day for suche special messes, as saith the glose. Neuirtheelesse if a man wole here suche special messe in reuerence of the Trinite or of our lady, it is wele done, so that he leue nat messe of the daye for such messes. Diues. Thanne me thynketh that curates, that been bounden to say messe of the day, to the parissh, or I cas messe of Requiem, may nat wele syng suche golden trentalles. Paup. That is sothe, ne no preest that hath sufficiet lyupnge by other salarie. And therfore it is forbode the synodales of englonde, þ any persone or Vyker shuld make couenaunt with his parisshe preest, that he shulde besides his salarie, take annuel or trentalle or any such other, that they clepe vantages. Inhibemus districtius. But they shal yeue to their parisshe preest sufficient salarie. Wherby they may lyue without suche false couetise. And in the constitucion of Lambeth the seconde chapter, it is bode that no preest shalle bynde him to su the special messes, by the which they myghte be lettyd, that they mighte natt serue the churche of laufulle seruyce. of the daye, as they be bounde. Diues. Sithen than it is so that messe of the day is as gode as suche speciall messes, and that it is as gode or better to here and to say messe of the

Precepte.

daye as suche special messes/ me thynketh that by suche maner syngynge of golden trentales/ soules been moche discevued.

Pauper. That is sothe For tho thritty messes that they aye/ as they say muste be in doynge al a yere nereßande/ there they might haue thritty messes as helpyly to the soule oute of peyne/ it is by thritty daies. For in suche syngyng is done moche symony. moche ypocrisie and moche folie. For sume prestes faitoures telle the people that butt the messes be saide in thre daies principally of tho feestes/ that is to saye in the festis and in two daies next folowynge/ elles the soules be nat holpen by tho messes. And so if the preest felle selfe tho thre dayes so that he might nat synge/ although he had sung alle thother messes/ that trental mighte nat be done that yere by their oppinion. And soo in cas he shulde happen to be in syngyng of one trental x. yere/ or twenty yere; there as he might every yere synge his annuel. Also if oure ladies day in lente falle on gode friday he may nat thanne synge tho iii. messes. Also same prestys bißißßte to faste brede. and water/ and to were the heire every day whanne they shal synge. any of tho masses for tho soules And so them must fast brede and water/ and were the heire on Cristmasse day Ester day/ and nigh alle the high feestis of the yere.

Also they say that they muste haue a specialle Orison/ that is nat of the missalle/ ne approved of holy churche/ butt ofte reprevyd. or elles as they say the messes ben litel or nought to profyt of the soules. And thus by faitrie and ypocrisie many foole prestys bißißßt more and bynde theym to more for x. shillinges. thanne a gode preest wolde doo. for x. marke. Diues. And they say that Seynt Gregorye. ordeyned that maner of syngyng to haue his modre oute of purgatorie. And therfore they clepe it. seynt Gregories trental. Paup. They lye on seynt Grigory For his modre was a ful holy woman as we fynde in his lyf. And we fynde nat that seint gregory dyd any preeste synge in that maner. for any soule But we fynd lib̃ro iiii. dialogorũ That whan seint gregory knewe by revelacion v' one of his monkes was in harde peyn of purgatorie for he hadde been a proprietarie vnto the tyme of his dyinge/ seint Gregory

hadde one of his monkes which he leet a gode man syng for him thritty messes day by day And in the thritty daye‘ the dede monke. apperyd to the same monke and thankyd him/ for vnto this tym saide he I haue be in harde peyn But nowe I am deliueryd.
And seynt Gregory tellith alsoo libro quarto dialogorum. that a soule apperyd to a preest and pyed him that he wold haue mynde of him in his messe. And he songe for him seuene daies by and by. and so the soule was deliuered For better it is to deliuer a soule oute of peyne within vii. daies. or xxx. thanne so to let him languore in peyne al ye yere whanne he might be holpen within thritty daies And so wolde euery man. and woman that is in bodily disease and in prison. And he were no gode frende that lete his fredespue in prison al a yere/ whanne he might haue hym oute within vii. daies or within xxx. daies.

The xvii. chapter.

Diues. And so it may be yt the feend sonde by the golden trental so to languore soules in their peyne/ there they shulde the soner be deliuered. Pauper Therfore seint Gregory. iiii°. et quarto dialogor. shewith by many an example that it is beste to synge for the soules day by daye if the preeste be wele disposed to synge so. And he shewith there letyng of any day syngynge. is grete disese to the soules o/ for thei desire ful moche to be deliueryd. oute of their peyne But the people by faitre of couetous clerkes is so blent. that they haue leuyr. to yeue xx. shelinges to languore the soules in peyne al a yere/ than to yeue xx. shillinges or x. to haue them oute within a monethe. or moch lesse tym But leue frede better it wer to yeue xx. shilliges to helpe them in haaste with the worship of god and of holy churche. than for to yeue xx. shillinges late to helpe theym and that with offence of god. and piudice of holy church And better it is to haue four score messes/ sunge togidre day by day for twenty shillinges thane to haue thritty messes songe in the long yere for xx. shillinges For why ye may for twety shillinges do synge a quarter of an annuel and do the soules haue part nat only of thritty messes/ But of asmany messes as be pens I xx. shilgis For though ye yeue a thousande pounde for a

Precepte.

nesse. the preest may nat appro/
pre that messe to any soule/ Butt
only praye for him after yᵉ he is
bounden/ & he must put his prai
er in the wylle of god/ and in his
presaunce/ for in cas the soule yᵗ
he praieth fore is dampned And
parauenture a pore mā. that no
preest thinketh on in special/ yat
die din more charite than he that
the preest praieth fore in special.
shal rather be holpē by the messe
of the preest thanne he for whom
he prayeth in special. More
ouir leue frende vnderstōde that
praier is a grete gracious gift of
god. For as say the clerkes holy
praier is a styīng vp of mannes
herte and womannes to god.
Oratio est ascensus mentis ī de
um. And that may no man ha
ue withouten special gift of god
For Criste saith in the gospel/ yᵗ
ther cūmeth no man to him/ But
ye fader of heuene drawe him by
inwarde gostely mocion that is
inwarde deuocion/ And with=
outen this inwarde deuocion py
er of mouth is right noght worth
And therfore it is gode sumtyme
to yeue almesse to a gode preeste
whiche hath neede of almesse to
meue him to pray for you yat ye
may haue the grace of god & swe
tenesse in him by the praier of the
yste and your almesse. Natheles

ye shall nat yeue him almesse to
cōstreyne him to certeyn prayer.
after your deuise so to set him of
his deuocōn. Ne ye shal nat ye=
ue him almesse with intēcion to
set him to pray for whom that he
wole after that his deuocion is &
after yᵗ god yeueth hī grace. For
alway the prest must be more fre
to pray thāne ye may be to yeue.
ne ye may nat with your yift cō=
streyne him ne lett him to praye
for whom that he wole praye.
For al though the preest be ar=
tyde by the lawe of his takynge
ther may though noo lawe arte
him of his praier but that he shal
alway be fre to praye for whom
that he wole/ and as his deuoci=
on is for al cristen/ and for the cō
uersion of al hethen folke. And
therfore leue frende ye shal yeue
freely to the preest what you ly=
keth so to excite his deuocion to
pray for you and the more to ha
ue you in loue and mynde in his
prayers/ nat to lese his charite to
pray for other. For the mo that
he praieth fore by wey of charite
the more profite it is to you and
to your freendes soules. that he
syngith fore.

☞The xyliii. chapter.

Dives. thy speche semethe to me ful reasonable But I pray the if religiouse/ or seculer clerkes selle any grounde of scitarie in church or churchyerde to buriynge of dede bodies/ is it symonye Pauper. Neither the office of buriyng ne the grounde of sanctuarie may be solde to buriyng Withoute symony Tercia q. ii. a c. postqm̄/ et in sūma cōf. li. i. ti. v̇ vi. q. prima. Moch more thanne it is symonie to sel the grounde of sanctuarie in church or in church yerde to chapmen to sell on their bothes and their stalles for to make goddes house an house of marchandise/ and a den of theups ayenst the lore of crist.

And if the colleges or curates. selle the rynginge of their belles at buriynges or at diriges/ soo þ they wole nat suffre their belles. be ronge But they haue a certein money therfore/ it is symonye/ & to selle the office of ryngynge is symony. Natheless the ryngers may take for their trauayle And he that hath thoffice of ryngyng frely yeuen to him may let that office to hire Withouten symony In sūma. conf. li. iᵒ tiᵒ. i. Dives. It semyth by thy speche that clerkes charged sutymes moche the vyce of symony Pauper It muste be chargyde. for it is a

synne þ god punyssheth ful hard For as Ierom Austyn a Gregory say/ symonye of the preestes of the olde lawe was one of the principal causes. Why god distroyed the cite and the temple of ierusalē/ and the kingdome of iewes Diues Is it symonye if colleges of religious or of seculers abbot or priour selle oute of their hous ſyuerunſe Paup. Many clerkes sey that it is no symony/ but it is a ful vnsiker marchaundise And I dare say that it it sacrilege and theft ful nyghe symonye. For why the godes of holy churche so wele endowed ben youen to helpe of the pore & to kepe hospitalite nat to selle them apeyn to riche men to mayntene them I vn lust and in Bodily ease But that the clerkes that serue the church shall lyue therby/ and to spende the remenant in hospitalite/ and in almesse to the pore people.

And so the godes of that colleges been nat here But as dispensoures. For they been the pore menys to whom and for whom tho were yeuen And By suche symonyes/ the colleges be brought to pouertie/ and the pore and the seke that shulde be holpen there By/ been fraudyd/ and robbyd of their ryghte And persones been made riche/ and the comynutee ouīr poꝛe ⁊ charite is exiled oute of the cōgregacion. For whanne the money is paied the religious that solde the spuersunes desire the deth of the bier. And comōly suche spuersunes ben solde in hope that the byer shal sone dye/ oꝛ in hope þ in his endynge he shall yeue to them al his gode oꝛ moꝛe therof passynge his couenāt And so sellyng of suche spuersunes is ferre from charite. and de/ pe groundid in false couetise ⁊ it is þift and sacrilege in that þthei so mynystre the godes of the poꝛe follꝛe and selle theym alweye/ By which godes the poꝛe folk shuld be holpen/ and so bothe the byer. and the seller do sacrilege. For these sylles and many moo sel/ lyng and biyng of suche spuersū nes ben vtterly foꝛboden. By the lawes of holy churche. in cōstitu tionibus octo bon. c°. bolentes.

¶ The xviii. chapter.

Diues. Is vsurie ⁊ gonel. any spice of thest paup. In cas it is ful greate thefte. Diues. What is ꝓpirly vsurye. Paup. Vsure is a wynnyng ay ed by couenaunt of lenyng. and foꝛ lenyng/ as saith Raymunde li°/ ii. e. ti. And it is done mooste comonly in thinges of nombꝛee.

of weight ⁊ of mesure/ as in mo ney þ is tolde/ oꝛ metall oꝛ other thinge that is weyed/ oꝛ in coꝛne oyle wyne/ þ is mesured. Diues Howe many spices ben they of vsury. Pauper Raymounde saith that ther ben ii. spices of v sure/one is spitel and rightful of which Crist spekith in the gos pel Luce xix. Quare non dedis sti pecuniā meā ad mensam). ⁊c. Why yaue thou natt my money to the boꝛde/ þ is to say my grace ⁊ my yiftes to ꝓfyt of other men By open cōmunicacion. And soo spirituel vsure is cleppd multi plicacion of the yiftes of god/ ⁊ of the graces that god hath youē to man oꝛ womā nat to byde the But to compne them foꝛth to pꝛo fytt of other And so with the gra ce and the yift that god hath yo uen to man foꝛ a litel trauayle. to wynne an hundꝛyd folde me de in heuene. Another vsurie is bodily vsure and vnrightful. that cūmeth of false couetise by couenaunt of lenyng. For if wynnyng come frely to the lener foꝛ his lenyng withouten coue/ naunt/ so that his intencion wer nat coꝛrupt in his lenyng/ but þ he lente pꝛincipaly foꝛ charite/ ⁊ nat pꝛincipaly foꝛ woꝛldly wyn nyng/ it is none vsure although he hope to haue and so haue auā tage by his lenyng But if he set principaly in hope of worldly wynnyng Whether he lent it with couenaunt or without couenaunt of wynnynge for his fals couetous intencion he doth vsure / & is an vsurer Therfore Crist saip in the gospel. Date mutuū nihil inde spantes. Luce vi. Cpeue ye your sone hopyng no wynnyng therof that is to say / as saith the glose Do ye it principaly for god. and nat for man / But hope ye principaly to haue your mede of god þ biddith you lene And thanne whether the borower pay or nat pay god shal yelde you your mede. Diues. May the lener axe no thig of the borower for his lenynge. Paup. No money ne thinge that may be measured by money / neither mete ne drynke. ne cloth / ne gift of bonde of tūge ne of seruyce. But other thingꝭ may nat be mesured by moneye. he may axe / as loue and charite. gode wylle and gode frenship for his lenyng Diues. Why is vsurie holden so grete a synne.

Pauper. For the vsurer sellith to gidre the thing that he lenyth and the vse of the thing And therfore vsure cūmyth of the selling of the vse. The vsurer sellith the thinge that he lenyth in that vat he takith more out for the vse. of the thinge. Wherfore thou shalt vnderstonde that many thīges ther be that may nat be vsed withouten waste and distructiō. of the thinge / as mete and drink and suche other; and in suche the vse may nat be departed from ye thing. But nedes he that grauntith the thinge / grauntith the vse of the thing / and they may natt be solde a sundre. And in suche thinges / if the seller take for the vse he sellith that thinge twyes. and sellith thinge that noughte is. For the vse of that thinge is fulle waste therof. and for suche sellynge of the vse it is cleppd vsurp. For the vsurer sellith the thinge in it self and the vse ouit. Sūme thīges ther be I which the vse is nat full distruccion of the thinge / as vse of an house is the duelling or occupacion therof & I suche the lordship of the thinge may be grauntid withoutē the vse & the vse without the lordship. And so a mā may take his hous & he settith to hire axe to hī & out take for the vse of the hous But as the philosoph. saith v°. iii. politicor. the vse of money is chaūging of one for a nother to helpe and ese of the compnute which chaungyng is destruccion of the money and wastynge in maner. In that he that chaungith it

Precepts.

for other thing so spent it alway. And therfore it is vnleful. for to take any thing for the vse þ olvt to be comen to al/ as it is ordeyned to help and ease of al   And therfore it suffiseth þ the lener take ayen the eupne value/ & if he take more ouir for the vse he doþ vsure/ and he is bounde to restitucion Diues Contra. God paf leue to the Iewes to take vsure of other nacions.   Paup. That was to fle the more euyl/ for els they wolde haue taken vsurie of their brethern for couetise/ and þ god forbade them & grauntyd to them to take vsure of other nacions aboute them & amonge them bothe to spare their owne nacion and also to gete so ayen in ptie þ longid to them by the graunt of god For al þ londe theraboute enhabite with the hithen peple conggyd to the Iewes by the graunte of god/ & wrongfully the hethen peple witheolde moche londe fro them.

The xxv. chapter.

If lordes of mylnes. lene money to bakers/ or to other folke in couenaunte.þ they shal nat grynde but at their myles they do vsurie & so lete theim that they may nat grynde freely where they wole. And if they be harmed therby/ the leners be bouden to make restitucion. But if they be nat harmed therby. they be nat bounde to restitucion but for that they let them of their fredome/ sumdele they ben bounde. And the same is of chapmē. that selle to creaūce to let the bier frō other chapmen/ or bicause of her lenyng selle to theym more dere. thanne to other. Suche sellers ben bounde to restitucion/ in þt the bier be harmed and hyndrid. If the lener or ony other mā wol nat yeue to his dettour lenger tyme of paiement whanne he may nat kepe his day assigned/ but he haue sūme yifte/ thoughe he aye no yift opēly he doth vsure And if a chapmen selle the more dere. for the lenyng of his price thāne he shulde selle if he paied anoon he doth vsure. and he is bounden to restitucion Extra li. e. ti. cō siluit   If the borower vpon vsure faile of his day of payment. he that is his borowe may paye that money with the vsure to ye lenner. & do his dettour for who me he is borowe pay to him aȝē. that money with the vsure. For it is to the borowe none vsure.   For he wynneth nought therby/ but so fleeth myscheyf.

that shulde elles falle to him) If a man be cōpelled to borowe money with vsure for safshede of his dettoure that wose nat paie him at his terme that false dettour is bouden to make restitucion nat ōly of his det/but also of ye vsū yat he was compelled to pay for his falsshede/ or elles deliuer him out of daunger if it be pit to pay Extra libro tercio de fideiussori bus. c. puenit. et c. cōstitutus. If a man or a woman lene ꝑ.shellinges at Ester or in other tyme. to resceyue asmany busshellis of whete at migghelmesse/(the whete be better for that tyme thanne is the money; ꝙ it be in doute skilfully whether the whete shalle be more worthe or lesse. in tyme of paymēt it is noon vsure. But if it were semly that it shuld be more worth in tyme of paymēt and he lent the money in hope of yat lucre he dyd vsure. Extra e. titulo nauiganti. et in suma conf. li bro ii. titulo Bii. If the seller selle a thing for the more price bicause that he abideth of his pay. he doth vsure And if the bier bye a thing for lesse than it is worthe for ꝑ he paieth bifore or the thing bought may be taken to him/ he dothe vsurie. ibide in suma cōf. If a man lene siluer or wyne to haue ayen the same quātite I cer

teyn tyme/ only in hope that the same quātite shalbe more worth in tyme of paymēt/ he doth vsu̅ And if the dettour wole pay hun his det bifore that tyme to fle his owne harme/ and he wole nat take it of him to the tyme assigned of the payᵗ so to wynne by his lenyng/ he doth vsurie. If a man lene money to resceyue a certein tyme corne wyne or other thing therfore/ he shal take asmoch as cūmeth therto in tyme of payᵗ & no more If a man lene money to resceyue other maner money. therfore I certeyn tyme to wynne therby ꝙ so to charge his dettour he doth vsurie. If a man selle a thynge for certein price. as the market gothe in tyme of the selling in couenaūt that if it be better worth bifore eller that he shal pay so moche more/ and though it be lesse/ worthe he shalle paye noo lesse. he doth vsurie. If the byer bye bors or other bestes for lesse price than they be worth in tyme of biyng. to resceyue theim after in certeyn tyme of feire/ it is vsure/ but he wene sikerly/ that it shulde be thanne only so moch worth or lesse worth. But if he wene that they shulde be that tyme more worthe it is vsure.

The xxvi. chapter.

Precepte.

If a man let his horse, his oxe or cowe to hire, in couenaunt that if the best die or appeyre, he that hireth it shal stond to half losse and to half wynyng if it amende. He doth Vsurie For it is nat semely that he shulde haue as moche profyt by the amendment of the beest as he shuld haue harme by the deth. Natheless though he that lettith it to hyre, make suche couenaut with him, that hireth it to do him be the more besy to saue the beste. He doth no synne, if his purpos be nat to take though the beest perisshe without his defaute. But if he do it for gyle or couetise, he doth Vsurie. And therfore it is goode to fle suche couenauntes. For all though his intencion be gode yit the maner of the couenaunte semith wycked and sclaundrouse, to folk that knowe nat his intencion. Natheless he that hyreth a thinge may lefully take to hym, the pel and the mischeif of y^t thig that he hireth if he wole. If a man betake his beest to a poore ma to hire or to kepe in couenat. Vtterly that if it dye it shal die to the pore man and lyue to hym for, for he wole haue as gode therfor it is wycked Vsurie. Suche Vsurers ben the feendes charmoures for to suche folke their shepe, ne their bestes shal neuir die.

If men in tyme of plentie bye in corne or other nedefull thinges. principaly to selle theym forthe. more dere in tym of derth and of nede, it is synne. But if it be doo principally for comyn profytt, & for saluacion of the cuntre, it is medeful For Joseph gouernour of egipt dyd so to saue the people in tyme of hungre. Gen. xlvii
Also a man may do so for his owne profit to fle mischeif comyng by wey of puidence, and though he selle forth in tyme of neede, to help of other as the market goth he dothe no synne in that. But if he witholde it and wole nat selle forth in tyme of nede thinge y^t he hath passig his spuyg, But kepith stylle in hope of more derth, he synneth greuously And therfore salomon saith. Qui abscondit frumentū male diceturin populis. Bndictio dñi sup caput Bendenciū puerbi. xi. He that hideth whete in tyme of hungre shall be accursyd amonges the people And the blessyng of god vpon ye hede of them that selle forth. Also it may be don by comon right of marchandise, they to wynne therby ther true liuyng, soo that they cause no derth by ther bying And namely they may bie so feefully y^t haue nat wherby to lyue.

D i.

The seuenth.

But suche marchaundise But if they do it only of auarice/ and to compelle men to bye men at ther likyng/ and as dere as they wole thāne they synne greuously and namely couetouse clerkes/ that haue enough elles Wherby to lyue For to clerkes it is nat grauntyd suche marchaundise. If a clerke bye a beest or other thyng and by his husbondry or by craft leful to him it be amēdyd or put in better degre thānne it was bifore he may selle it forth lefully. for more thānne he bought it to. For such doyng is cleppd propirly craft. and nat marchaundise. xviiii. q̄. iii. canonū glosa. et de con. di. B. nunq̄. If a man lene olde corne to haue therfore newe corne at herupste/ and wole nat take olde corn for old corne. as good for as gode. Whānne the Borower may pay it he doth Vsurie as saith Raymond Et sūma conf. Bbi supra But if it be done principaly to saue his owne gode. that elles shulde perisshe/ or principaly for help of his neighbour he doth none Vsurie By goddes lawe al Vsurie is dampned. By empoures lawe & by mannes lawe sumtyme it is suffryd nat for vat it is gode ne leful But for to sle the more euyl. for ofte men shulde perissh. But they might borowe vpon Vsurie. For elles the couetous riche men. Wole nat lene to the nedeful/ and so the lawe of man rightfully suffrith it for a gode ende But the couetouse mā doth it vnrightfully & for a wyched ende. And therfore holy chur che dampneth them that lene vpon Vsury but nat in them that borowe for nede/ or for a goode cāe vpon Vsurie Whēne he may nat elles Borowe But if they borowe for a wyched cause/ as for pley at the dyce/ or to spende it in glotonp lecherie or pride/ or in other Wycked vse/ they synne greuously And though it be leful to Borowe for a gode ende vpon Vsurie/ yit it is nat leful to lene vpon Vsurie/ ne to counsepl any to Borowe vpon Vsurie. As it is lefulle to a cristen man to take an hethen man b swerith by his fals god And yit it is nat leful to the cristen mā for to axe of him that othe/ ne to styre him therto. For Why othe and swerynge is a diuine. Worshhip that longith only to verrey god Also notaries b make instrumentes vpon couenaūtes of Vsurie ben forsworne. For whanne they be made notaries. they make an othe that they shal neuir make instrumentes vpon couenaunt of Vsurie And so if they make any suche instrumēt

Precepte.

they been forsworne/ & they may neuir after bere wytnesse in any cause ne make instrumēt in any cause For they ben made therby of wycked name. and vnable to euery office worshipfulle/ in the lawe and to euery dignite And if any plate vnder wrytt to such co uenaunt or sette his seale therto. Wyttyngly/ is gilty of vsurye. though he haue no wynyng ther by. Hec in suma conf.

The xxvii. chapter

Diues. What peyne is or deyned in the lawe for vsu ters Pauper. Alle vsurers by the lawe ben bounden to restitu cion And if they been open vsu rers/they ben accursed by the la we in thre thinges For they shuld nat be houseled. ne holy churche shal nat take ther offryng ne res ceyue them to cristē buriyng But they amēde thē bifore their deth. And what preest elles taketh her offryng & burieth them/ he shalle make restitucion of þ he taketh to the busshop in help of the pore folke And he is worthy to be sus pendid of his office & of his messe Extra e. ti. quia in omnibus. If the vsurer may nat make res

titucion/ he muste aye forȝeue nesse of hem that he is dettour to if he wole be saued And nat only ye vsurer/But also his heir is bou den to restitucion/and he may be compelled by the lawe to restitu cion. Extra e. ti. su nos And if other men be bounden to him for vsurp he may no restitucion aye til he haue made restitucion to o/ ther that he is bounde to for vsu rie Extra e. ti. quia frusta.

Diues. Wherby shulde men knowe an open vsurer Pauper If he kepe open stacion or open shoppe to lene or to chaunge for vsurie. Or if he knowlege it bi fore a iuge in dome/or be cōuicte by wytnesse/ or if he bere the na me of an vsurer with dedys open ly don accordyng to that name.

If a clerke be an vsurer/ or an heir to an vsurer But he wole ma ke restitucion he shalbe suspen dyd And but he wole amende bi he shalbe deposed. And if he be so icorrigible that his busshop may nat amēde/ him he shalbe chasti sed by seculer bode. Extra libro secundo titulo de iudiciis. capi tulo cū non ab homine. The clerke shal make restitucion of his owne gode if he haue wherof and nat of godes of holy churche But if he haue ought spēt of such vsurie to profyt of holy churche

D ii.

The seuenth.

If a prelate resceyue offrynge of the vsurer / summe clerkes say that he shalle take it ayen to the vsurer in repreef of his synne. Summe saye that he shalle take it to the busshop which shal take it ayen to the vsurer. And if that vsurer may nat be founden the busshop shalle yeue it to the pore folke.

If the borower swere that he shal pay the vsurer & nat aye it ayen. he must paye it to saue his othe. and he shalle nat aye it ayen.

But he may make denunciacion to prelates of holy churche. of that vsurie. that the vsurer may be compellyd by lawes of holy churche to amende him / and soo to make restitucion. And if he swere that he shalle neuir bewrey him to holy churche. of that vsurye / he is nat bounden to that othe. For it is ayenst the saluacion of his euyne cristen. and ayenst the precepte of god.

¶ If the vsurer bye an horse or londe withouten money of his vsurer / and yeue it to a nother / he that resceyueth that yifte is bounden to make restitucion. if he wyst that it was so bought and youen. Extra. e. cum tu.

Seruauntes and labourers / that serue vsurers in honeste thinges. may lefully take their hire of the. Butt if they serue theim in thynges nat nedefulle ne leeful. they may nat take their hyre of the vsurer. If the seruaunte borowe money vpon vsurie / withouten biddyng of his maister / though he borowe it for the nedys of hys maister / or any man borowe money vpon vsurie for the nedis of a nother withouten his bidding. he that so boroweth. is bounden to restitucion / if the vsurer wold lene withouten vsure freely. He that conselith it nat to lene but vpon vsure is bonde to restitucion / for he settith the proufytte of his nighboure. If a Iewe lene to a cristen man vpon vsury / he synneth And he may be compelled by prelates and by lordes to make restitucion. Extra e. post miserabile. And it is nat lefulle to any cristen man or woman to take vsurye. of any man cristen or hethen.

No lorde / no college / no man shuld suffre vsurers duelle i their lordshippe. ne lete theym to hyre to duelle in / But within thre monethes that they knowe of theire vsurye. they shulde putte theym oute / and neuir resceyue suche vsurers more after. And if busshoppe / or archebusshop doo the contrarie they been suspendyde. And they that been of lesse degre. been accursed if they doo the contrarie / and colleges and compns tes falle into interdit And if they stonde stylle in their malice/ one moneth alle their londes ben interdited And lewde people that suffre suche vsurers to duelle in their lordship. or in their houses. shulde be compellyd by censure of holy churche to putt them out scdm grego. decimu/ et consilium lugdunense ti. de vsuris c°. Vsurarum. Hec in summa conf. li. secundo. li. ti. e. Also if a ma selle a thing for moche lesse thanne it is worth in couenaunt to haue it ayen what tyme that he wole pay the price that it is worth/ it is vsurie For the byer gettith ayen al that he paied and as moche therto As if a man selle a thyng for ten shelinges that is wele worth xx. shelynges/ he shal haue it ayen. for so the byer wynneth by vsure ten shelinges ouir that he payed furste.

The xxviii chapter

But suche slightes and many other that been nat written here/ the false vsurers cursed of god begyle and robbe the pore people ayenst the precept of god there he saith thus. If thou lene. to my pore peple/ thou shalt nat therfore my bede him ne trauayle him the more therfor/ ne ouirpsse him with vsurie. Exodi xxii. If thy brother saith he be nedye. pore or feble. take none vsure of him/ take no more. thanne thou haue drede thy god that thy pore brother may lyue with the/ Thou shalt nat lene thy money to vsurie/ ne aye of him ouir habundauce. Take no more than thou lentyst Thus saith god Leuitici xxv. Non senerabis fatri tuo ꝛc. Thou shalt lene to thy brother by vsurie neither money ne corne ne any other thing But lene it to him withouten vsurie. that thy lorde god may blesse the in euery werk that thou hast don Deutro. xxiii For who so leneth to his euen cristen withoutꝭ vsurie he shalle spede the better. And they that lene with vsure. shalle spede the worse. And in what londe vsurie is vsed openly that londe shal mysfare Therfore dauid saith/ that wychednesse hath besegyd that cite a ꝫ compnte by day a by night aboue the walles and trauayle and vnright a mosche wronge is in b cite. a gyle. a vsure faileth nat from the stretis of b cite. Die ac nocte circumdabit ea sup muros ei' iniquitas. ꝛc. For suche vsurie a gyle and false othes in byyng a sellyng/ the prophete zacharie saith p be salue a boke fleyng in the eyre b was xx

The seuenth.

cubites longe & v. in brede. And he ayed the aungel of god what it might be, & the aungel saide to him, it is the curse of god þ goth to the houses of theuys, & to men nys houses that forsuere theym by the name of god. zacharie v°. And therfore salomon saith that who so gadreth tresoures with a lyyng tunge, he is veyne and vnpfyted, and he shal stumble to the snares of deth. Raueyners and robbries of wicked men shal drawe theym downe to helle. for they wolde do no rightful dome Prouer. xxi. To suche god peueth his curse. Woo he saith be to you that ioyne house to house, & couple felde to felde, and saye of right that is wronge, & of wrõge þ is right, and put light into derknesse, and derknesse into light, byt ter into swete, and swete into bit tre. psa v. c. For these false men of salue and sligh couetouse folk be a mannys cause euir so goode but they haue moneye to stonde with him they shalle saye that is a wycked cause. And be it euir so clere in right, they shal seye. it is ful derke, they can se none helpe therin. And be it neuir so derke yͤ nõ can se right therin, for money they shal say that it is clere e nough. And be it euir so siker, or esy to pursue & swete l ye siff they

shal say it is a bytter cause & vnsauery to dele w', but they haue money, & be it euir so pitous and bytter for money they shal say þ it is siker enough. He that robbeth his euyn cristen of any gode he doth ayenst thre lawes. First ayenst the lawe of kynde þ saith thus That thou hatist to be don to the, do thou it nat to a noiþer. Also he doth ayenst lawe writen. Nõ furtũ facies. þ biddith Thou shalt do no theft. Also he doth ayenst the lawe of grace For charite is principal beest of the lawe of grace biddeth þ men shulde yeue to other of their gode & nat take from them wrongfully. We fynde in holy wrytt Josue vi. et vii. cap. þ for achor stal golde siluer & cloth ayenst the heest of god, he and his wyf, his children, and al his bestes were stooned to the deth first, and afterward brente. With al the other god that he had, and xxxvi men slayne with enemyes for the theft of Achor, that so stalle ayenst goddes bihceste. And god saide that til whan his pefte was punysshed, the people shulde neuir haue spede in batail ne in other iourney. Diues. It is thanne lytel woundre that our folk spede euil these daies in werk vpon their enemyes. for they go more to robbe & to pile thanne to sight for any right Pauper For that synne and many other, they spede ful euyl / For they be soo blent with synne that the light of grace by which they shuld be wissed in ther dedys is hid a wey fro theym, and so they wandre forth amonge ther enemyes as blynd bestes. and for they seen no myscheif til they falle therin / For as the wyse man seith / Obcecauit eos malicia eorum. sap. ii° Ther malice hath made theym blynde Telleth a greate clerke. Solin' de mirabilibus mūdi that in the londe of ferdynye is a welle of ye which welle if a trewe man drinke, his sight shal amende / But if a these drynke therof, though his sight be bifore euer so clere. he shal wex blynd / By this welle I vnderstonde plentie of worldly goodis and of richesses that god sendeth amonges mākinde which e, goodys and richessis comen of the erth and newen yere by yete, as water in the welle. and alle trewe folk that drynken of thys welle, that is to seye, that comen trewly to ther good and richessis of this worlde and spenden them wele to the worship of god. and pfite of ther euen cristen: they haue more light of grace to se what is to doo / and what may please god / And they that falsely come

to godes of this world by pist. By gyle. and by sure and by fals othea they wexen blynd. for they lese the light of grace and be blent w' ther malice / Therfore seint Ambrose sup lucam septē. that in the richessis is no blame. But the blame and the defaute is in theym y cāy nat wel vse ther richessio/ And as richessis saith he is lettig of vertue to shrewis. so it is help of vertue to gode folke that can and been in wille to vse wele her richessys. Diues. I drede me that nigh alle oure nacion hathe so drunken of this welle of fardynye, that they been gostly blynd For if I take hede what theft of symonye regneth in the clergye. what theft of vsure regneth principaly amonge marchautes and rich folke / what theft of rauepne and extorsion regnethe amonge the lordes. and grate men. what mycherie and robbere among the pore comons that be alwey inclined to sle and to robbe. me thynkethe that moch of oure nacion is gyltie in theft (ouerdon moch blent with fals couetise / Paup. Therfore god seyth thus / A minimo vsq; ad maximum omnes sequūtur auariciā / A pphā vsq; ad sacerdotem cūcti faciunt mēdacium. et ideo corruent. Fro ye lest to the most al they folowen

D iiii

The seuenth.

auarice and false couetise from the prophete to the preest al they make lesynges and doo gile and falsehede. And therfore they shalle falle. And I shalle yeue their wymmen to straungers and their londes and their feeldes to other heires Iere.viii. And by the prophete psaie god vnder namyth the gouernours of the people bothe in temperaltie and in spiritualtie. and saith thus. Principes tui infideles socii furum & c. Thy princes been false. and felowys of theues. Alle they louen yiftis and folowe meedys & peldrynge ayen. For they demed not after the right. But after that men might paye.psa.i°. Si videbas furem currebas cum eo et cum adulteris porcionem et cetera. If thou seye a these thou ran with him to helpe him.as false iuges in temporalte don these daies. And with lechouris and auoutreris. thou puttedist thy part as iugis in spiritualte don these dayes.

☞Here endeth the seuenth precepte or commaundemente. And begynneth the eight precept or commaundement.

Iues. It is ful moche to drede that gile. and falshede shal vndo this londe as thou sayst but god of his mercy, he do bote I thanke the with al myne hert, for thou haste wele enfourmyd me in kepinge of the seueth commaundement. Now I pray the for charite that thou wylt enfourme me in the eight commaundement. Pauper. The eight commaundement is this. Non loqueris contra proximū tuū falsū testimonium. That is to saye. Thou shalt speke no false wytnesse ayenst thy neighboure. In wordes as saith seint Austyne. & seynt Thomas de Veritate theologie libro quinto. God forbedeth alle maner lesynges and hydyng of treuthe whanne it shuld be saide. For as the lawe saithe. Qui tacet consentire videtur. He that is styl and wole nat say the treuthe whanne he shuld say it semyth, that he consentith to falsenesse And so by his stylnesse he witnessith with falsenesse ayenst treuth, and ayenst his neighbour and synneth dedly with his tung for that he wole nat vse it to witnesse the truthe whanne he shuld And therfore saith seint austyne. that bothe he that hideth the treuthe and he that lieth ayēst the treuth been giltie aȝenſt this precepte.

For why he that is ſtylle wole nat porſye to his euencriſten, and he that lieth deſireth to harme his euen criſten. In Epiſtola ad caſulanum. For man and woman is bounden by this precepte nat to harme his neighbour with his tunge And therfore Iohn Criſoſtome ſaith that nat only he is a traytoure to the treuthe, that lyeth aȝenſt the treuthe, But alſo he that ſaith nat frely the treuth. Þ he oweth to ſay, or nat frely defendith the treuth which he oweth to mayntene and defende And ſo altho that by ſtylneſſe enforce theym nat to knowe the treuthe. that they knowe and wole natt be a knowe in due tyme, they be lyers and falſe wytneſſes Natheleſſe leue frende ye ſhal vnderſtōd that ther is thre maner of ſtylnes One is anentis god, another anentis oure euen criſten The iii. anentis oure ſelf. The firſte is wycked whanne we ceaſe from due pryſyng of god, and thankig for his beneficee. The ſeconde is wycked whanne we ceſe from due maner of techynge and vndernymyng of oure euen criſten. The third is wicked in two maners, Firſte if a man or woman for drede or ſhame, or for pryde wil nat ſeye thyng that he ſhuld

ſey to pleyne him of his miſcheif and to ſeke help of ſoul by ſhrift or good counſeile, or of body by other help and by good counſeile But gnawynge and fretyng him ſilfe inward and wil not pleyne him outward to them that wolde conforte him, and ſpeketh ſo moche inward without confort tyl he falleth in wanehope, and ſhendeth hym ſilfe by angre ⁊ inward ſorowe Therfore ſaith ſeynt Gregory li°. viii. moraliū That moche follie whanne they haue wronge ſufferen moche the more diſeſe inward, for they wille not ſpeke it outward, For why ſaith he If they ſayde peaſebly ther diſeſe outward with ther tunge ſorowe and deſeaſe ſhuld paſſe out of ther herte, and oute of ther cōſcience. Si illatas inquit moleſtias lingua tranquiſſe diceret: a conſciencia dolor emanaret Sumtyme men be ſtille in deſceit of other, that they may the more bodely accuſe other.

The ſecunde chapter

Diues. Hou many maner been there of leſynges. Paup..Seint auſten li° de mē dacō putteth viii mañ of leſīges

The eight.

Whiche ben comprehendyd in thre. Quia omne mendacium vel est pniciosū. Vel officiosū. Vel iocosum. For euery lesynge or it is suche þ it doth harme. and than it is cleped in latyne pniciosū. that is to sey Wycked in englisshe. Or it is suche that it doth good and none harme. and that is cleped i latyn officiosū. that is profitable in englissh. Or it is suche that it doth neyther good ne harme. and that is cleped in latyne Jocosū that is Sourdefull englyssh: as whan men make lesynges only to make follie mery. The firste maner that is cleped pniciosū and Wycked is alwey dedly synne. But the two other maner of lesynges ben venial synne to the comon people. But to men of holy chirche and to religeouse and to alle that shulde be follie of psection. they ben dedly synne if they ben done by auysement, or by custome as saith seint Austyn. The first maner of lesinges is done in 9. maners. First if any man sey preche or teche any thing ayenst the feith of holy chirche. The ii. is. Whanne the lesyng harmeth sume & psiteth to none, as lesynges of bacbiting & fals wytnesse of sey þ compy salue punysshet þ. The thridde is þ so psitith to one þ it harmeth to a nother, as false wytnesse in cause of dett or of heritage or of suche other. The iiii. is whanne the lesynge is maade withoutē psyte, and withouten cause. saue only for likyng to lie and to discepue, and for custome of lesinges. The fift is whan the lesynge is made only for to plese as flateringe Alle these maner of lesynges ben forboden by this comaundment to alle maner folk. as dedly synne. The lesynge of flatering may be done in thre maner, or prisynge a man in thyng. that he hath more than he is worthy to be prised, or prisyng him i thing that he hath nat, or prising him and flateryng him i his syn. and shrewdnesse and in his foly And this maner of flatering if it be done wyttyngly, it is dedly synne. The secoūde maner of lesyng that is cleppyd Officiosū and proufitable, it is done in iii. maners. First for saluacion of catel that shulde elles be loste wyckedly by theues if they wiste where it were. Also for saluacion of man or of woman innocent. that is souȝt of his ennemyes. Also to saue man or woman fro synne. As if a syngle woman say that she is a wyf, soo to kepe her clene from theym that wolde be foule her. Suche maner of lesynges þ soo auayle & psyte and also lesynges bourdful been venial synnes to the compny peo ple. But to men of pfection, they ben dedly synne, namely lesyn ges bourdful whan they been in vse custumable. For it fallith nat to men of holy chursche. and of religion to be iapers ne spers. But it fallith to them principal ly to fle ydel wordes For Criste saith in the gospel, that men shall yeue aunswere at the dome for e uery ydel worde that they saye. But suche lesynges bourdful in men of pfection turne lightly to lesynges pnicious and wycked. For they do harme to theim that here them, in that þ they be asclā drid of their sanyte and of their lesynges For them thinketh and sothe it is, that men of holy chur che & of pfection shulde nat be ia pers ne disours ne liers ne beyne But sadde in chere in word & dede Therfore the maister of senten ces. li. iii. distinct xxxviii. saith openly that such maner lesynges. been venial synnes to them that be of vnpfyte state, & dedly syn nes to them þ be of pfite stat And seint Austyn libro contra menda ciū saith þ treuth shuld nat be cor rupte for any tempal pfyt. And no man ne woman shalbe led to enlesse belthe with help of lesyn ges, for euery lesyng & falshede.

is ayenst crist. that is souereyne treuthe And seint Gregory libro xviii. moraliū. saith thus. Os quod mentitur occidit alam.
The mouth that lyeth sleeth the soule And the pphete saith Lord thou shalt lese al þ speke lesiges And therfore saith he mē of pfec cion must wt al besynesse fle lee synges, in somoche þ for saluaci on of any mannys lif they shuld nat lye to helpe a nothers body & harmig of their owne soule. And therfore god saith Nō mencient & nō decipiet vnusq̄sq3 pximum suū Leuitici xix. Lie ye nat & no man disceyue his neighboure.

¶The iii. chapter.

Iues contra. We rede in holy wryt Exodi. i°. that pharo assigned to the wymen of israel two mydwyues Sephora and phua. & badde them slee alle the children males & kepe the wy mē But they for the drede of god and for pite dyd nat so but saued bothe male and female and with a lesyng excused them to the kig and saide that wymmen of israel colde better helpe themsilf than wymmen of egipte & had children or they come to them, And as holy writ saith there / therfore god gaue them house and londe.

The eight.

Pauper Nat for the lesyng but for they dredde god, and for the drede of god they sauyd the children. Therfore god gaue them house and londe, & nat for the lesynge and so saith holy wrpt. Natheleſſe summe clerkes sey þ for her lesynge god chaungid the endles mede þ they had elles be worthy. into temporel mede of hous and londe. Diues. yit Contra te. We finde in the gospel that after þat criste was risen from deth to lyfne went with it. of his disciples. cleophas & another in the liknes of a pilgryme & spake with them of his deth & of his passion. Butt they knewe him nat And at euen whanne they came to the castell. of emaus, ne feyned him to goo ferther And yit at their prayer he went in with them But feyning as seint austyn saith is a maner of lesyng, therfore nat euery maner of lesyng is synne. Pauper. It semyd to their sight that crist hadde feyned, nat by fals seynyng inwarde I dede as he shewyd outward for he was fer fro ther feith And therfore he shewyd him outwarde as a straunger and a pylgryme passing for they knewe hym nat ne beleupd nat I him stedfastly Also by that doyng he shewyd that he shulde passe forth bodily out of this worlde, and wende aboue alle heuenes.

Diues. We fynde gen. xxvii° that Jacob in in disceit of his fader þ was blind and in fraude of his brother Esau said to Isaac his father to haue his blisſig J am esau. thy first sonne, & that was false And yit god approuyd his dede Therfor thanne it semeth that euery lesinge is synne. Pauper That Jacob dyd was figure and prophicie of thinge that shulde falle, And for that prophicie is doy I dede, therfore it was no lesing For though he were not his first sonne in berthe. yit he was his first sone I dignitie by ordenaunce of god, that ordeyned that the peple cumyng of Jacob. shulde be soueraigne. to the people cumpng of esau. And that the grete bihest of cristes birth made to Abraham and Isaac shulde be fulfilled I iacob and nat in Esau. as their fader wende that it shulde haue be.

¶ And so though Esau. were the firste sonne, and principalle to Isaac, by the dome of Isaac yitte was Jacob his firste sonne, and his principalle sonne by the dome of god. And thoughe he were nat Esau. bodily in persone yit he was Esau in dignite.

Diues. Contra His fader Isaac seyde that he came gylefully. and tooke his bleſſynge.

Precepte.

Paup. Isaac said as he wende but nat as it was. For he knewe nat thane the wyll of god in þat doynge. For it was noo gyle ne falsenesse in Jacob. For it was nat the dede ne the speche of Jacob, but it was the dede, and the speche of the holy gost þ wrouȝt in him and spake in him.   And therfore Criste saide to his disciples.   It ben nat ye that speke but the holy goost of your fader in heuene spekiþ in you. And so he spake in Jacob. and Rebecca. his moder that counseiled him so to gete his faders blissynge.

The iiii. chapter.

Dines Seint Austyn saiþ that lesynge and lyynge is nat only in feyned speche but also in feyned dedes.   Pauper Seynt austyn saith nat that all feyned dedes ben lesynges & syn. But he saith that al feyned speche in falshede is lesyng and synne. For man hath more fre myȝte to gouerne his speche thanne for to gouerne his dedys, for alwaye a man may speke as he wole, butt he may nat alway do as he wole. And the philosophre saith. p° pp armynias, þt speche is token of thouȝtes in the hert. For it is ordeyned þ man by his speche shuld shewe thing to be or nat to be, as he feliþ and thynkeþ in his hert. And therfore Crist said in the gospel. Sit sermo vester est & non non. Be your speche yhe yhe. nay. nay. That as it is in the hert soo it be in the mouthe. þt þe of the mouthe be þe of the herte.

And nay of the mouthe be nay of the hert, so þ the mouthe & the hert must alway accorde. For as saith seint austyn In libro contra mendacium. The mouth beriþ wytnesse to the hert And therfor if man or woman say otherwise thanne it is, in his hert, he beriþ fals wytnesse aȝest his hert & aȝenst him self. & doth aȝest the precept of god þ biddeth him say no fals witnesse aȝest his niȝbour ne aȝest his neȝte. þ is his owne hert and his soule Another skyll is this for dede is nat ordeyned, principally to be wytnesse to the thouȝt of mannes herte. But it is ordeined to the profit of the doer and to the proufytte of his neyȝbboure & to the worship of god. And therfore. whanne feynyng in dede is profitable to the doer. and to his euyn cristen and to þe worship of god, it is leful and in case fulle medeful. And therfore dauid whan he was amoges his enemyes in perel of of deþe, me defully feyned him to be woode. so to saue his lyf to the worship

The eight.

of god and the profyt of his naciõ and of his frendes and of his enemyes. that shulde elles haue fallen in manslaughter. Primo regũ xvi. But spech is ordeyned of god principally for to be true. Wytnesse of thought in hert. And therfore who so saith other wise. thanne it is in his hert and in his conscience he synneth, for he mis useth his speche ayenst the ordre of kynd ordeyned of god. Diues Sithe feynyng of dede is nat al way synne/ as feynyng of spech telle me whanne it is synne. and whãne nat. Pauper Feynyng in dede is done sũtyme by slight. for a gode ende As we rede in the fourth boke of kinges. iiii. Reg. x°. that Jeū. the kinge of israel. dyd clepe to giddre al the prestes of the false mawmet Baal. into a certein day/ as though he wolde haue made a grete solempnytie. and worship to Baal/ & dyd cloth alle the false preestes in one certein clothe that he gaue theym/ & by the clothyng men shuld knowe them from other. And whanne they were al gadryd to gidore in their temple to worshyp Baal/ the king Jeū badde. men of armes go and sle them alle/ and so they dyd. Also Josue leder of goddes people feyned slight. to disceyue goddes enemyes/ Josue. viii. c.

Suche feynyng so that it be doo withouten lesyng of the mouthe is lesul and in cas medeful/ Also ther is feynyng for gode teching And so Crist feyned him to go ferther to stirre his disciples to hospitalite. Also ther is feynynge of significacion/ and so Jacob. as by mannes dome feyned him to be esau But in goddes doome it was no feynyng of falshede/ but figure shewyd by holy goste that spake in him and wrought I him Also ther is feynyng of falsenesse and of doublenes for to disceiue. and suche is in ypocrites. & false folke And al suche feynynge/ is lesyng and forboden of god. By this precepte.

The ix. chapter.

Diues. Is it any synne to bileue thinge that is false. Paup. Ther is falshede of the sayer/ and falshede of the thyng that is saide Falshede of the sayer sumtyme is vnycious and wicked/ and to bileue lightly. suche falshede/ itt is dedely synne and dampnable. Sumtyme falshede of the sayer is profitable as touchig worldly thig. & nat noyous as to the world. & sũtyme it is neither pfitable ne noy' to the world as lesiges made only. for

406

borde þ harmeth no man worldly ne profiteth And to bileue tho ij. maner of falshedes it is venial synne Also ther is reprouable falshede of thing that is sayd And either that thing longith to the nedefulnesse of oure saluacion as be articles of the faith and to bileue suche falshede, it is dedly synne, or it longith nat to the nedefulnes of our saluacion and to bileue suche falshede lightly it is benial synne, or elles no syn as saith Dockyng sup Deutronomiū Natheleffe ther shuld no wyseman be to hasty to bileue thinges of charge that sounde either grete prosperite or grete aduersite: For the wiseman saith Qui cito credit leuis est corde. He that sone bileupth is light of hert and vnstable Ecclesiastici xix. And therfore saith he bileue nat euery worde that men telle the. ibidem The fole simple man saith he byleueth euery worde but the wyseman takith hede to his paas, and gothe ne bileueth nat chaungeably after mennys speche ne after lesynges but after the lawe of god that is nat chaūgeable Prouer. piiii. & eccle. pppiii. Diues. Sithen it is so þ a man may syn berpng false wytnesse of him self whether synneth he more prisyng him self falsly or lachig him self

falssly Paup. Bothe ben solp. & in cas grete syn For caton saith. Nō te collaudes nec te culpaueris ipe. Prise thou nat thy selue, ne lache thou nat thy self. And salomon saith Laudet te alien⁹. et non os tuū. Extraueus et nō labia tua. Let another mā prise the & nat thyne owne mouthe, a straūgers & nat thy lippes. puer. xxvii And therfore by comyn opinion of clerkes, it is more syn a mā to prise him self falsely by auantement than it is to lache hi self falsly For audtmēt cometh of pride þ is worst of al synnes But lackyng of him self may come of lownesse medefully For euery mā of hi self is more to lack than to prise. And therfore saithe the prophete Omnis homo mendax Every mā & womā of hi self is fals and a lyer. And salomon saith þ no mā wote whether he is worthy loue or hate of god And so do mā wote what he is worthe i goddes sight And asmoch as he is worth in goddes sight so moch he is worthe & nomore Therfore saith aristotle iiii. ethecor. piiii c þ the auaūter of him self is worse than the lacher of him self Jactator vitupabilior est q vituparor. Et idem dicit Ricardus de media villa sup sentencias li. iii. di. xxviii. questione quarta.

407

The eight.

Diues. Whiche ben cleppyd by the lawe false wytnesses. Paup. They that ben broughte to bere wytnesse and ben sworne to saye the soth/ and do ayenst their oth. sayng fals or hidyng the treuthe and thing that shuld be saide/ or transpose thinges that shulde be saide. Or a man say thing for certein that he is nat siker of though it be treuth that he saith. And also he is false wytnesse that swerith a treuth with sligh spech for discept. Suche maner folk seynt Austyn likneth to Judas. And moche folk saith he these dayes dispise the dede of Judas/ & pitt they doo the same that he dyd or elles worse. For why saith he. Altho that for mede bere false wytnesse/ they selle Criste that is souerayne treuthe for mede. Et est sup illud My'. Quid vultis mihi dare et ego eū vobis tradam. But such fals witnesses be wors thanne was Judas. For he solde crist for thritty pens. But many false wytnesse selle Crist for moche lesse/ and sumtym for noght only to shewe malice or to be byyd. Judas made restitucion of the money that he toke to bitray crist and wolde nat reioise it. But false witnesses these daies make no restitucion/ but spue by suche false synful lucre. Judas biles

uyd nat that Crist shulde rise fro deth to lyf. and deme the quycke and the dede. But we beleue þat he rose from deth to lyf and shall come to deme al mankynde Very god and very man. And therfore cristen men false wytnesses been more to blame thanne was Judas.

The vi. chapter.

Diues. May al maner mē bere wytnesse in doome. Pauper. Nay. for bonde seruātes shulde bere no wytnesse i cau ses of their lordes/ neither ayēste them ne with them/ but in asmoche as the cause touchith other of his seuauntes iiii. q. iii. Scrimi nali. v. Itē serui. Ne wymmen shulde bere no wytnesse of preef in causes of felonie/ but in matri monie and in causes of purgaci on of wymens euyl name. they may bere wytnesse of preef. And wymen may accuse in causes of felonie. Also no yonge folk with in viii. yere/ ne foles ne beggers ne ful pore folk/ ne hethen men. ne cristen men openly loosed of falshede/ or onys teynt false and forsworne. ne open wycked lyuers and of euyl name/ none of these is able to bere wytnesse/ in

Precepte.

domte bifore a iuge. v' Condicō seruꝰ etas discretō fama Et for tuna fides in testibus ista reqre.

By false wytnesses the iewes slewe seint Steuyn, and by fals wytnesses they slewe Criste, and by false wytnesse the true man na Bothe, and by false wytnes they wolde haue slayne the holy woo/man Susanne. But god saupde her and brought the false wytnes ses to the same dethe. ꝑ she shulde haue hadde, if her witnesse hadde been true, and that was the lawe that tyme, and yit it is in manye londes. And if they disherite any man or woman, or do him lese a ny thinge by false wytnesse, they ben bounden to restitucion Also Bacbiters forfete ayenst this pre/cept, whiche by malice bacbyten them that ben gode, and by lesin ges diffame theym Also slaters ꝑ falsly prise them that be wyched so to fauour them in their synne. And so bothe the bacbiter bacby/ting the gode man, and the flate ter prisynge the wyched man ha/ue goddes curse, that he yeueth to alle suche, thus sayinge. Ve qui dicūt bonū malū, et malū bo nū. Wo be to al them that say the gode wyched, and wyched gode psa. 8. c°. And namely they that ben nygh to lordes and to greate men and been their gouernoures

or ther counseilours or cōfessours and to please them, and to flater theim be it neuir so false, and ta ke none hede to god ne to treuth. But only to plese, and say nay or yhe, nat after the treuthe is, but after the lorde wole haue it, and so harden him and blynde him in his folie. Such flaterers be lyke to a beest that is cleppyd camelio. Whiche best changith his coloure after the thinges that be besides him, nowe white, nowe blacke, nowe rede, nowe grene, nowe blewe nowe yalowe, Right so suche fla terers chaunge their speche, after that they hope best to please ther lordes. and other men For nowe they speke gode of a man, whyle the lorde is his frende And if he falle enemy to hym, anone they speke him harme and belonye so to plese the lorde and other alsoo that ben that mannes enemyes. In presēce of his fredes they spe ke a man gode, though they wo le him no goode and in presence of his enemyes they speke him e= uyl And as the fane of the steple. turneth after the wynde. so turne flaterers and bacbiters their spe= che, as companye spekith that they ben in The mosel and the face. of the camelion is lyke a swyne. and an ape. For euery flaterer is a bacbiter And as a swyne hap

E i

The eight

moore spikynge to sye in a foule slough thanne in a faire grene/ & with a rotynge of his snoute desouleth the place ther he gooth. so hath the bacbiter.moore likyng to speke of other mennys defautes and of their vnhonesties and synne thane to speke of their godenesse and honestie/ and vpsy speche. Wrotyng vpon their defautes to appere & defoule their gode name And in that he is a flaterer he is lyke the ape/ that what he seith other men do he wole do the same. For flaterers ruse their tunge nat after the treuthe. But after the plesaunce and speche of other men. But this beest Camelion though it be faire whyle it is alyue yit assone as it is dede it is ful foule as saith the maister of kid Right so suche flaterers and fair spekers that speke wele and doo ful euyl although they seme fair and worshipful in this worlde. In the other world after their deth they shalbe ful foule and fendes felowes in helle peyne/ But they amende them/ And al that speke wele and do nat therafter forfete ayenst this precept For they denye by their dedes the treuthe that thei say with their mouthe. Of suche. seint poul saith hw' their mouth they knowlege them self to knowe god. But with ther dedes they

denye it. Confitentur se nosse deum/ factis autē negant. Tite. p̃o And therfore god warneth solue of suche false wytnesses that speken the treuthe with their mouth and denye it I dede. and saith thꝰ Omnia quecunq; dixerint nobis facite: scdm vero opa eorū nolite facere. M̃' xxiii. Alle thinge that they bydde you do/ do ye it. But do ye nat after their wicked werkes.

The vii chapter

ALso these men of lawe that for mede mayntene falshede ayenst the treuthe. or for mede byde the treuth that they shulde maynten/ or for mede withdrawe them to suffre or lett falshede haue his forth. they forfet ayenst this precepte whiche forbedith al maner falshede. I rede on a tyme there were ii. men of lawe dwellyng in one towne The one at euyn came home from the assise. and the other axed him what he hadde wonne that day And he saide py marke. and that he had right moche trauayle therfore. yhe sayde the other/ and I haue wonne as moche and more/ to be at home. and nat to trauayl. Suche men of lawe and baretres of

Precepte.

lawe that haue no science, may wele say þ is wryten in the boke of psal̄ the prophete Concipim⁹ et locuti sum⁹ de corde verba mē dacii. &c. We haue conceyued. By study and by gode informaci on knowyng of the treuthe, and of our owne herte, and of our cō truyng we haue spoken wordes of lesynge and of falsshede And therfore rightful dome is turned bacwarde. and rightfulnesse sto de from ferre and myght nat nygh treuthe selfe downe in the strete. and equite myght natt entre, the treuth is al forpeten And he that went away fro wycked thinge, & wold haue lyued in pees & treuth he was open pray to false men Qui recessit a malo prede patuit psu. lix. But wolde god that they wolde amende theym. and say that is writen the same chapter. Lorde god oure synnes been multiplyed bifore the, and oure synnes aunswere to vs for oure grete synnes been with vs and accuse vs. We knowe oure wyknesses. for we haue synnyd and lyed falsly ayenst oure lord god. we turnyd vs away and wolde nat go after oure god, to folowe him in treuth, But spake ayenste him falsshede. and passing of god des lawe for to endanger the simple folk. Also prechoures of goddes worde that preche moore for wynnyng of worldly gode than for wynnynge of mannys soule. & seke more their owne worshyp. thanne goddes worship in their preching and preche nat the treuthe, ne wole say men their sothes in repuynge of their synnes. they been false witnesses and do ayenst this precepte. For if they hyde treuthe in fauour of synners and wole nat preche ayenst their vy ces. Or if they preche falsshede and erroure to shewe their wyt by curiousl of spech, or preche high materes nat profitable to the people nat helply to mannys soule. alle suche prechoures ben clepyd false wytnesses. Also they that preche so harde ayenst the mercy of god, that they bringe folke in wanhope. And also they that preche so moche of the mercy of god and so lytel of his right wysnesse that they make folke to bolde in synne, suche prechoures ben fals wytnesses of crist For al his mercy is medlyd with rightwysnesse and al his rightwisnesse is medlyd with mercy. Therfore dauid saith Vniuerse vie dn̄i mīa et veritas. Alle the wayes and the domes of our lorde god been mercy and treuthe. Deus iustus et misericors. God is rightful and he is merciable. to alle that wole

The eight

amende them). Alle prechours of goddes worde shulde be wytnes ses of Criste. that is soueraigne treuthe. And therfore Crist saide to his disciples. Eritis michi testes in ierusalem &c. ye shalbe wytnesses to me in Jherusalem. and in al iurye and in samarye. and in euery londe to the last end of the erthe. Actuum primo cº. And therfore prechoures shulde auyse them wel that they prechid no falshede ne say no thinge for certayne that is in doute to them and that they hide nat the treuth that shuld be saide, and that ther lyf and their techyng accorde wt the techyng and the lyf of Cryste For if they teche otherwise thane Criste taught, and lyue natt as cryst lyued they ben false wytnes ses to crist Cryst taught chastite. a comendyd pouert and lownesse And therfore if the prechoure of goddes worde be a lechoure and a carnal man proude of hert and couetouse. he is nat true wytnes of Criste And if he repreue in his dedys pouert and chastite. a saye that criste was nat pore for man nys sake, he spyth vpon Criste a he is to him ouirdone false wytnesse. For Crist saide that foxes hadde their dennys, and the briddes her nestes. But the maydens sonne hadde nat where he might

reste his hede. M' viii. c. And seint Poule saide that Crist bica me may nedy for vs & this world to make vs riche w' his myscheif Propter nos egenus factus est: cum esset diues: Vt illius inopia diuites essetis. ii. cor. viii.

The viii chapter.

Also alle ministres of holy churche, and namely men of religion. shulde be wytnesses of Cryst to edificacion of the peo ple and of their neighbours, that ben al men and wymen And ther fore men of holy churche ben be tokyned by galaad that is to say an hope of wytnesse For al their lyuyng in hert in worde in weth. and in clothinge shulde bere wyt nesse to crist. Diues. How shuld men of holy churche bere wytnes in clothing to Crist Paup. For in clothing they shuld shewe sad nesse honestie a lownesse, as nigh folowers of Criste, and wytnes ses that taught sadnesse ayenst va nitie, honestie ayenst glotonye a lechery, lownesse ayenst pryde, a pouert ayenst couetise And ther fore the outclothing of men of ho ly churche, and namely of men of religion shulde nat be to strayte ne to short. to shewe. the shap of their body. for pryde and vanite and to tempte wymmen/ ne to precious ayenst pouerte/ ne ouirdo ne feble ayenst their degree. and honestie of holy churche/ ne to syde ne wyde ayenst measure.

Diues. Of this mater thou spake bifore. I couepte no more to here therof. For as thou sothely saidest men of holy churche & namely men of religion passe in grete array and pompe/ temporal lordes. Paup. Also as oft as the prest syngith his messe he representith the psone of Crist yt dyed for us alle vpon the cree. And by his clothyng and by his messe syngyng he berith wytnesse of Cristis passion. and shewyth that al that he doth in seyng of his messe/ he doth it in mynd of cristes passion and if he haue no mynd of cristes passion after that his clothyng shewyth that he shulde be/ he is a fals wytnesse in discepte of his neighbore Therfore seint Gregorye saith that no man doth more harme in hooly churche/ thanne he that hath a name and ordre of holynesse and lyueth wyckedly.

Nemo amplius nocet in eccl̄ia. q̄ qui puerse agens nomē et ordinē sanctitatis habet. Diues. What betokneth the clothing of of the prest at messe. Paup.

The amyt on his hede/ at the begynnyng betokneth the cloth þt cristes face was hyled with in tyme of his passion/ whanne the iewys hyled his face and boffyde him/ and badde him arede whoo smote him The longe aube betokneth the white cloth that Erolde cladde with crist in scorne as he hadde ben a fole. The fanō the stole and the girdel/ betoken the boondes. whiche Criste was bonden with/ as a theef/ in tyme of his passion. The fanon betokneth bondes of his hondes. The stole ye rope þ he was led wt to his deth. The girdel the bondes þat he was bounde with to the pyler and to the crosse. The chesible betokneth the clothe of purpure in whiche the knightes clothed him in scorne. and knelyd to him and saide in scorne Hayle thou king of iewys The busshop passynge other prestys hath a mytre and a crosse. The mytre on his hede betokneth the crowne of thornes. þ crist bare on his hede for mannes sake. And therfore the mytre ha/ the two sharpe hornes. in token of the sharpe thornes. The two tunges þ hange downe on ye mytre betokē the strempys of bloode þ ranne downe fro cristes hede by prychyng of the crowne of thornes. The crose that the busshop

The eight

beritħ in his honde betokneth ye rede spere that the knyghtes turmentours put in the honde of crist in scorne for a ceptre And the archebusshoppes crosse betokneth the crosse that crist died vpon for vs alle The busshoppes gloues at messe in his hondes betoken ye naples in cristes hondes, and the sandalies on his feet at messe betoken the naples in cristen feet If it be so than vmē of holy churche hauyng thies tokenys of cristes passion in their messe sayng haue no deuocion in cristes passion ne mynde of his passion they bere false wytnes For it is nat wt them inwarde as the tokenes shewen outwarde Also the amyt betokeneth the basinet of helth þ is hope of the lyf that is to come, & forsakyng of erthly thinges. The longe albe betokneth chastite of body and soule The gyrdel fanon and stole, betoken the comaundementes and the counseylles of crist in the gospel by ye whiche mē of religion & of holy churche ben bounden passyngloter to serue god The chesible betokneth the holy clothe of Criste without seme also wōne in one whiche betokneth parfyt charite The mytre on the busshopes hede wt the hornes betokneth cunnyng of two testamentes olde &

newe whiche cūnyng he owyth to haue and to teche with two. tunges, with tūge of dede, & with tūge of speche & shewe them both in dede by gode example peupnge, & in speche wel techyng, & þ betokenyth the ii. tūges hangyng behynde on the mytre. And the same betoken the ii. tunges hangynge behynde on the aube on the prestes shulder. For euery preest shulde cūne goddes lawe & preche it with tunge of dede & gode example, & with tunge of speche These ii. tunges hange higher on the busshop than on the symple prest in token þ the busshop is more highly bounde to the tūges of gode ensample and gode techyng than the symple preest. Diues. It is a comon sawe that tho ii. tunges on the preestes shulder betoken this londe hath ben twes renegat and puertys. Pauper. That is false. For sithe this londe toke first the feith, the peple was neuir renegat But the peple of this londe was slayne nigh al vp for ye faith til ther was no cristē man to duelle therin, but only hethen peple þ had slayne cristen people, & by the swerde kept this londe they wāne of criste people Therfore Bede de officio diuino saith þ it betokneth ii tūges þ mē of holy church owe to haue as I haue

414

Precepte.

ſaide And therfore they ben clee
pyd tuges. Also the pſtes crow
ne betokneth the crowne of thor
nes on criſtes hede and the digni
tie of the preſthode. And his ſha
uyng as ſaith the ſalue/ betoke
neth pouert i ſoule/ and forſakig
of worldly godes.

DJues. What   The iy. c.
Betokneth the buſſhoppes croſſe.
in maner of ſpnyng. Paup. As
ſaith a grete clerke Bede. li. i. de
diuino officio. The buſſhop cro
ce is cleppyd a ſhepherdes ſtaff. to
to ſtirre the buſſhop to ſowneſſe.
and to thinke on the cure and on
the beſineſſe and the charge that
he taketh vpon hym Whanne he
is made buſſhop He berith no cep
tre of worldly dignyte to ſtire hi
to pride/ ne berith no ſwerde that
is token of crueſte/ but he beryth
a ſhepherdes ſtaf/ nat to ſle/ ne to
ſmyte/ but for to ſaue his ſhepe.ſ
ben his ſubgettes ſpiritualy/ Whi
the ſtaffe aboue is crokyd in ma
ner of an hoke/ to drawe ayen y
wold nat come/ or elles go alwey
For the buſſhop ſhulde principa
ly trauayle to drawe ſynful men
and wymen with fairneſſe by go
ode wordes. and by gode enſam
ple to the mercy of god/ and natt
to be ferce ne felle to the ſynfulle.
And therfore as Bede ſaith abo
ue on the hoke of the croſſe is wri

ten thus aboute. Cum iratus fu
eris miſericordaberis. Whanne
thou ſhalt be wrothe thou ſhalte
thynke on mercy. In the rounde
knott bynneth the hoke is writen
homo. that is to ſay a man/ to do
the buſſhop thynke that he is but
a man as another is/ and natt be
proude of his dignite. Bynneth
beſide the pyke of ſpon iowriten
parce. that is to ſay ſpare. For he
muſt ſpare his ſubgettes a ſhelle
grace to the as he wole haue gra
ce of god And in token therof the
pyke of the croſſe ſhulde nat bee
ſharpe but blunt For the doome
of the buſſhoppe ſhulde nat be to
ſharpe/ but alway medſyd with
mercy The ſtaffe of the croſſe is
right and nat wronge. in token.
that the buſſhop ſhulde deme ry
ghtfully and gouerne his ſubget
tes in right and equite. and doo
no man wronge Vnde Verſus.
Contra p primũ/ medio rege.
parce p pmũ By theſe tokenes
outwarde buſſhopes and preſtes
wytneſſe them ſelf to be ſuche in
warde as the tokenes ſhewe but
if they be nat ſuche. they be falſe
wytneſſes to criſte and to criſtes
lore in damage of their eupn cri
ſten/ for by ypocriſy they diſceiue
the people Forſothe it is a leſing
any mã knowlege him ſelf a buſ
ſhop preeſt/ or clerke/ or man of
religion. and worche contrarye

Eiiii.

The eight

thynges to his ordre. and apeyns the tokenes that he bereth of holynesse / It is a lesynge any man or woman to saye hym cristen. ⁊ do not ne lyue noe therafter. as a cristen man or woman. But peraucnture wors than iewe. sarasyne or panyme / Therfore sayth seynt Iohn in his pistle / þ who soo saithe that he knoweth god and kepeth not his comaundementis. he is a lier / there is no seith in him. i. Iohannis secudo And he þ saith þ he loueth god ⁊ hate his brother. he is a lier. Io. iiii°. And so euery wicked lyuer is a lier And therfore saynt Ambrose sayth in this maner / Bretherne flee ye lesynges / For alle that louen lesynges. ben the children of the fynde / For as criste sayth in the gospel. alle such haue the fende to ther fader / Whych hath euer be a lier and fader of lesynges: and neuer stode in treuth But with a lesyng lees alle mankynde as criste himsilfe saith i pe gospel. io. viii. And yit into this day vnnethis he bryngeth any man woman to synne But with lesynges And so with lesinges he sleeth mannys soule and womās ⁊ euer hathe be a cruel manslȝer and a false lier: as criste saith i þe same gospel Oines. Telle me I praye the ; thou Wyttnessis shuld

haue them i dome for to be trewe witnessis / Pauper The witnessis ol dome and the iuge also shuld be indifferent to both perties and saye the treuth for both perties. And the iuge may not by the lawe take mede to deme treuly / ne the witnesse may nat by the lawe take mede to bere trewe witnesse. Moch more than ye witnesse oweth to take no mede to bere false witnese. ne the iuge to yeue vnrightful dome. viiii. q. b Nō sane Netheles the witnesse may lesully take his costis of hym þ bringe the hym to witnesse / And if a man see that his neighbore shuld fall in his truth and lese his right for defaut of witnesse / if he know ye treuth and may bere witnesse in the cause. But he bere witnesse ⁊ saie ye treuth for saluacōn of his neighbore. elles he synneth greuously though he be nat brought to bere witnesse. And in that case men of holy church may ⁊ owen to bere witnesse: so that it be not i cause of blode ne of greuous syn And if a man take meede for his witnesse. he is boūd to restitucōn

⁂ The tenth chapter.

Iues to whom shal he make restitucion: Pauper. If he toke mede to bere fals wit nesse. though he bere treue wytnesse. or no witnesse / he shal make restitucōn. nat to him that paue it. For he is not worthy to haue it apen. syth he gaue it for falsehed and for synne. But he shal make restitucion to hī apēs whō he toke it to do him wrong / And in the same maner shal make restitucion if he toke mede notte to bere witnesse. But for to be stylle. and nat saye the treuth And if ye witnes take mede to say the treuthe/he shalle make restitucion to him that gaue it to him in help of his right / For it was leful to him so to geue. But it was nat lefulle to the witnesse so to take / And if it be in doubte for what ende the gifte was youen: thanne he shal make restitucion and geue it ye pore forthe by the doome of holy church / Hec Reymundus li.ii.ti. de testibus. ¶Diues. hou many witnessis be nedful in doome.

¶Pauper. After that the cause is: so most be, the noūbre of witnessis / And after the persone or the persones been apens whom the witnessis been brought / For a yens busshopis and preestis. and apens men of holy church & apēs persones of temporalle dignitye most be brought more witnessis and of more worship. than apēs symple forke: ¶Diues why so

Paup. For there shulde no man be in dignitye neyther speiritual ne temporal: But treue folke. to whos treuth mē shuld geue more credēce. thā to specȝ of sylle folk which knowen not welle what is treuth. ne what is false. What is pfitable to the comonte. ne what is nopous. and ofte ful litil dredyng god / Also psones in dignitie in that they be souerainges & iuges and gouernouris of the peple. for ther rightful domes: and sumtyme for vnrightful geten thē moch hate of the people. and oft withoute gilte and for ther good dede. and so they haue many aduersaries / For it is not I ye power of the gouernoure to please al But nedis either he most offende god. or elles men that dreden not god/And therfore the iuge shalle not lightly leeue a fewe witnessis apens such psones / Also if psone of dignite might lightly be dāpned by the symple forke. the peple shulde be to bolde apens ther souераignes and litil set by them And so dignitye both spiritual & temporal shuld be in despite and come to nought / And therfore sūtyme it is better to suffre a shrewed prelate or a curat and a shrewed man to regne: thanne lightly att the requeste of the people to despose hī. But his syn be wel opē

The eight.

and be ſclaunderouſe & noyo⁹
 Diues. Is ther any caas in whiche it is leful to ſtonde to one wytneſſe Pauper. iy that is no preiudice to a noþer/ it is lefulle to ſtonde to one wytneſſe As if it be in doute whether a child be criſtenyd/ or a churche halowyd. or an auter/ or veſtment halowyd. Alſo by aſſente of bothe ptes mē may ſtōde to the wytneſſe of one Alſo men may ſtonde to the wytneſſe of the preeſt ſeyng that his pariſſhyn is amēdyd if the ſynne be nat open. Vt dicit hoſtienſis. in ſūma li. ii. Rubrica de teſtib⁹. S. quotus eſt numerus Alſo the wytneſſe ſhal ſay for certeynte y^t he knowyth for certeyne/ and ſey in doute thinge that is to hym in doute. Diues. Ofte a man wenyth to be ſyker of thinge and he is diſcepued Paup. If he do his deuer to knowe the treuth/ thouȝ he be diſcepued ſo ſayng ayenſte treuth/ he ſynneth nat dedly For it is nat his wylle to bere falſ witneſſe.

The xi. chapter.

Diues. Is a man bounde to kepe counſeyl of thing that he knowith by priue telling Paup. That a man knowyth only by ſhrift he is bounde to kepe pryue & no wytneſſe bere therof For he knowith it only as goddes pryue miniſter. But if he knewe it nat only by ſhrifte. but by other weye thanne by his telling that is ſtreyyn to him therof/ if it be ſuche that it be greate harme of the comynte/ or of any pſone/ thanne he is bounde to tel it oute for ſaluacion of his euen criſten/ ſayinge aſmoche as. he may the pſone that tolde it hym. ſo that he be ware of more harme by his telling If it be ſuche that it be nat to harme of the comente ne to greate harme of any pſone if he haue bōde him to counſeyl he ſhal nat be it a knowe for no biddynge of his ſoueraigne For it is a ſalue of kynde to kepe cōſeyle that man knowith by counſeyl/ if the kepyng of counſeil be nat ayenſt charite For ayēſt charite may no man be bounden neither by bihees^t. ne by othe. And for to diſcoure counſeyle that is tolde him for counſeyl Whanne he may lefully kepe it counſeyle it is a falſhede. And therfore the wyſe man ſaith/ that who ſo diſcuret the priueties of his frende he leſith faith Eccleſiaſtici. vicesimo ſeptimo. For that is the manere of falſe freendes that whāne they turne to enemynte.

Precepte.

than to telle the priuetyes of ther frendes to shende them/ as saithe the Wyse man/ Ecclesiastici ṽiͦ. Wytnesses must accorde ī the thīge and iṇ the psone the place ꞇ iṇ the degre/ and iṇ the tyme. If one wytnesse stonde ayēst many wytnesses/ his wytnesse is nouȝt but he be write with them iṇ any instrument. If the wytnesses contrarie amonges themself/ the iuge shalle deeme aftere the more partie/ butt the lesse partye passe the other partie iṇ worship. and dignitye/ and iṇ gode name Or elles if their witnesse be more semely to the treuthe/ and yᵗ they preue better their wordes thanne the other ptie/ but that must stōd iṇ discrecion of the iuge. They that shal atteynt other witnesses must be mo iṇ nōbre and of mot worship and of better name than the other were. If wytnesses ben euen iṇ bothe pties iṇ nombre/ ꞇ iṇ dignitie/ the iuge shal deliuer him that stondeth for giltye/ for mercy must be principal vertue. iṇ the iuge And therfore saith selt James that mercy enhaūsith the dome. Hec iṇ sū. conf. li. ii. ti. de testibus. Also ther is wytnesse of dede ꞇ by dede withoutē wytnes of worde/ as whāne the dede shewith the self distinct ꝓ̄ Viii pri usq̄. Ther may no man be iuge.

and wytnesse and accuser to gyd der iṇ the same cause, but iṇ cas. the iuge may be wytnesse of treu/ the to excuse iiii. q̄. iiii. Nullus. Inqua. Iṇ euery dome muste be foure maner psones/ a iuge/ accu ser/ defēdour and wytnesse ibidē Iṇ cause of felony of a grete syn shulde no man be wytnesse ayēst the gilty. that had borne wytnes ayenst him bifore iṇ any doome. for it is a token of enemyte. iiii q̄ iii. testes. § Item iṇ criminali. The wytnesses shuld be worship ful true and sadde. ibidem Such folke shulde be wytnesses iṇ do me that knowe best the treuthe. xxxv q̄. vi. §. i. By wytnes of one shalle no man ne woman. be dampned/ butt his trespasse be so open that the dede shewith the self. iii. q̄ iii. testes. Et deutro xix. et numeri xxxv. Noman is sufficiente wytnesse iṇ his owne cause. v̄. questione tercia. sane in fine Item quarta questione tercia. testes. §. Item iṇ crimi nali. Post me. Euery man may be wytnesse iṇ dome ayēst hym self but nat for him self quarta q̄. secunda §. i. The defendoure may forsake wytnesses that ben his enemyes. quarta. questione. tercia Testes. Noo man may be compelled by the lawe to bere wytnesse. ayēste his owne

⊤ħe eight.

kynnesman/ ne apēst any of his nigh aspauce. ibidm. An heretike and an hethen man may bet witnesse apenst another heritik and apenste another hethen man. in helpe of a cristen man But apēst a cristen man shulde they bere no wytnesse. xxiiii qōne i. mirātur.

⊤ħe vii. chapter.

He þ is vnable to be a prste shulde bere no wytnesse a penst a preest in cause of felonye and of grete synne. ii. q̄. vii. ipī. apsī. He that berith false wytnes forsaketh crist souerayne treuth xi. q̄ iii. abiit. If prestes or dekenes be taken with false wytnesse beryng/ they shulde be thre yere suspendyd from their office. and do harde penaunce. B. q̄. vi. quis in si. Euery false wytnes shuld do vii. yere penāce. xxii. q̄. v. si q̄s de. And by the same. he is vnable to euery office and lauful dede of any worship. worthye to lese his godes and to be beten and harde chasticed and punysshed/ ꝛ the same peyne is he worthy that brynȝ gith men wytingly to bere false wytnesse. xxii. q̄ v. si q̄s se. And as the same saith there he shulde fast of dayes ī brede ⁊ water/ and vii. yere folowyng do harde penaunce/ ⁊ neuir after he without penaūce of sorowe and contricion for his synne And al þ were as sentyng to false wytnesse and to piury/ shuld do the same penaūce ibidem. The wordes of wytnes shulde be taken to the best vnderstondyng and moost benigne. Extra libro ii. ti. de testibus. c°. cum tu. The wytnesse that apē saith him self is of no credence. Extra li. ii. ti. de pbationibꝰ c°. Licet. Men shulde stonde to the furste speche that man or woman saith in his cause if he varie another tyme. e. ti. p tuas If the wytnesse by distraction say amys, it is leful to him anon to amende his speche. But if he abyde wt an ynteruaī/ though he chauge his worde and amend it/ he shal nat be accept ne herde Extra. li. ii. ti. de testibus cogendis. c° pterea wytnesse in dome shulde natt be herde apenst him that is absente. But he were obstynate and wold nat come Extra de testibus c. ti. He þat saith first the treuth must be taken for one wytnes. e. ti. in omni. If a man haue sworne to the partie nat to bere wytnesse of the treuth/ with the other ptie. his othe is vnlefulle. And therfore nat withstondynge his othe he may bere wytnesse of the treuthe. e. Intimauit.

Precepte.

No man shal bere wytnesse to a nother in his cause if he haue the same cause, or any lyke that, to spede for hym self For suche a persone is suspect that he wolde doo fauoure to a nother mannes case to haue hym fauourable to hym in his cause. e. ti. personas. No man vpon wytnesse shalbe resceyued in dome i preiudice of a nother, But if he swere though the wytnesse be a man of religion. e. ti. nuper. The honestie and the worshippe of the wytnesses is more to charge than the multitude. e. ti. infra For to discusse irregularite of by gamye, both lewde man & lewde woman, may be taken for wytnesse. e. ti. cam is. Seke folke & pore folk may nat be compellid to come bifore the iuge, & to bere wytnesse But the iuge may sede to them wyse men to wyt of them the treuth. e. ti. si qui. Euery man and womā shulde hate false wytnesse, for god hatith fals wytnes as saith Salomon Deus odit testem fallacem Prouer. vi. And euery lyer is a false wytnesse and ful of gyle And the sodeyne wytnesse disposeth and ordeyneth a tunge of lyīg For he that is redy to bere wytnesse bifore he be aupsed, he disposeth hi to lye Prouerbi. vii. But as Salomō saith The false wytnesse shalle nat be

vnpunyshed, and he þat spekith lesynges shal perisshe. Prouer. xix. Ferthermore leue frende, ye shalle vnderstonde that ther ben thre maner of wytnesses.

The viii. chapter.

Ther is a wytnesse aboue vs that knoweth alle and may nat be disceiued, that is god that seeth al, and he shalle at the day of dome be to vs bothe iuge and wytnesse. Ego sum iudex et testis. I am iuge and wytnesse. saith oure lorde god. Ieremye xxix And Job saide. In heuene is my wytnesse, and he þ knowith al my counseil. is aboue in high And ther is a wytnesse within vs that is oure conscience. For as seint poule saith. oure ioy is wytnesse of oure conscience And ther is a wytnesse withouten vs, and þ is our nighbour & all creatures that shal bere wytnesse ayenst vs at the dome bifore the high iuge. But we amende vs by tyme and deme wele oure self For moyses saide. Testem inuoco celum & terrā. I clepe heuene and erth to witnesse, that if ye make to you any lykenesse, or ymage to worship it & breke goddes lawe, ye shal sone perisshe. Deutro. quarto. And in an other place he saith thꝰ.

421

The eight.

I clepe heuyn and erthe to wytnesse that I haue sett bifore you lyf and dethe/ gode and euyl blessyng and curse. And therfore chese the lif that ye may lyue and a loue your lorde, god and obeye to his voyce and cleue to him by feith and loue. for he is your lyf: and lengith of youre daies. And if your hert be turned away from him and ye wole nathere his law es but worshippe false goddes. I say to you bifore that ye shall sone perisshe. Deutro. xxx°. And therfor sene frend if we wol be spilt er at the last dome/ and come sikerly bifore oure souerayne iuge that knowith al/ Us muste deme wele our self in this world. For seint poule saith That if we demyd wele our self/ and discussed wele oure lyf/ we shulde natt be dampnyd. Prima ad Cor xi° Dines. Howe shulde we deme our self. Pauper As the glose saith there. Thou shalt be thyne owne domesman Thy sete shal be thyne herte/ and sett thy selue gilty bifore thy self domesman. Thy thought and thy cõscience. shulde thy two wytnesses/ for to accuse the. Thy turmentoures shulde be drede and sorowe/ that in maner shulde shewe thy blode by weppyng of salt terys Whanne by wytnesse of thyne owne conscience and of thy thought/ thou haste demyd thy self giltye/ and nat worthye to come to goddes borde ne to heuene blisse. And there saith the glose that seknesse feblenesse/ and sodeyne dethe fal comonly/ aftre Ester amonges the people/ for men in Estre receyue vnworthily goddes flesshe and his blode. Ideo multi in firmi et ibecilles et dormiũt mul ti.s. per mortem. prima ad cor. xi. Butt for euery man is fauourable to hym self. and to his owne cause. therfore thou shalte haue with the two. assessoures by whose counseile thou shalt deme thy self/ and tho shall be treuthe. and reasone. Take with the treuthe that thou make no false excusacion of thy synne. Ne lye thou nat for to excuse thy self ne for to accuse thy self falsly. ne to greuously. but as thyne other as sessoure reasone wole accorde. And if tho ii. wytnesses that is to say/ thy thought and thy conscience suffise nat to bere wytnesse ne to ful enfourme the of thy syn ful lyf. Take to the. the thridde wytnesse that is thy feyth. And so lete thy doome stonde in wytnesse of two or thre. And feith saythe thus. Fides sine operi bus mortua est. Feyth withouten gode werkes is dede. For al thoughe you beleue as a cristē man. But thou lyue as a cristen man / elles thou art dede in soule and worthy to die withoutē end Feith that faileth in worde. and thought is dede and helpith natt to blisse. And anon conscience & mynde shal accorde to hym / and say thus. He that vsith amysse his free wyl that he die it is skyl withouten remedie sauyng goddes mercy. And take hede ÿ thy clergie may nat saue the. For ho ly wrytt and clergie say. Anima peccatoris morietur. The soule of the synner shal dye. Also thy clergie may nat saue the. if thou be in dedly synne. For thou arte bigamus. & twyes weddyd. First to crist i thy baptym. and after to the feende by assent to syn. And so thou art wydowe. fro crist wedded to another widowe that is ye feend forsaken of god for his pry de. to whom he was weddyd att the begynnyng of the worlde. Ne trust thou nat in thy bonte. on a gode cuntre. For if the quest co myn of the v. commaundementes whiche thou hast broken / and of the ii. preceptes of charite ayenst whiche thou hast offendyd / and of the vii. articles of the faith a yenst which thou hast eryd / and of the vii. dedes of mercy. which thou hast natt fulfilled / & of thy

v. wyttes which thou hast mys spendyd / and the foure cardynal vertues ayenst whiche thou hast trespassed / this solempne queest of yt true wytnesses shal dam ne the as a man queller of thyne owne soule. And as a thecf tray toure thou hast robbed thyn ow ne lorde of his goode. For robbe ry is cleppyd alle maner mystrea tynge of a nother mannes gode. ayenst his wylle. And thou haste robbyd Cryst of that preci ouse soule. that he bought with his dere blode / and mysused and myspent his creatures. ayēst his wylle. For as saith seint Gre gory in his Omelie. alle thinge that we tak of god to vse of gode spuynge / we turne it into vse of wycked spuynge. Quicquid ad vsum recipimus bite: in vsū conuertimus culpe. For the helthe of body that god sent vs. we spende it in synne and in wyc kednesse. faire wedyr in beyne oc cupacion of pride & of couetyse. peas / in beyne sikernesse / plētee of vitailes / in glutony and lece ry. And so this solempne quest of fourty wolde dampne the for gil tie. Therfore ther is none other remedy but truly deme thy self & yeld ye gilty & tak the to the mrcy of god & punysshe thy self by dre de and sorowe of hert & putt the

The eight.

in the dome of goddes iuge / that is thy confessoure / & make amendes after his dome and by his assent. For god apenst whom thou hast so highly offēdid wole stōde to his rightful dome / and accept such satiffaccion as he assigneth the by the lawe of god to doo / if thou do it with gode wylle.

The viiii. chapter.

Thus deeme thou thy self / and thanne shalt thou bee syker at the dredeful dome whā criste our brother very god / and very man / shal come doune to deme the quycke and the dede. And as saith seint poule / he shal come downe with the voyce of a trūpe that is to saye. With the voyce of aungelles and of archaungelles whiche shal crie and say Surgite mortui venite ad iudicium. Rise ye up that ben dede / and come ye to the dome. And anone in the twynklyng of an iye we shal al awake of the longe slepe and ryse up and come to the dome pope and prynce / kinge and caiser. lorde and lady free and bonde riche and pore. greate and smalle. al they shalle awake and rise up body and soule. a pen knytte togidre. That voice shalbe so hydous so dredeful and sterne that heuene and erth shal begynne to quake. The stones shal ryue / & al the dede aryse from deth to lyf eche man and womā to aūswere for him self / no man ye atturney. Nowe oure iuge Crist is a lomb merciful and meke / than he shall be as a spon dredful and sterne. And the spon with his crye abasheth al other beestes & maketh them to stonde stylle saue his owne whelpes / whiche with his crye he reyseth fro deth to lyf / soo the voice of Crist at the day of dome shal arere vs al from deth. to lyf whiche voyce shalbe ful dredful to them that lyue beestly / and take none hede to god ne to his lawe. Them it shal arrest and make them stonde stylle. as prisoners. on the erth and abyde their iuge. For they shal so be chargyd with synne / that they shal nat wende up apenst Crist. as the gode shal wende up and mete with Cryste. For to them that ben goddis children that voice shalbe ful swete. and ful likyng to here and make them so light that they shal wēd up & mete with criste in the ayre. as saith seint poule. To his children Crist shal say venite. &c. Come ye my faders blessyd children & take ye the kingedome of

Precepte.

heuen that was ordeined to you before the begynnyng of þe worlde. But to these bestial follze. ⁊ wycked lyuers to the proude to the couetouse. to the enuiouse/ ⁊ to lechouris. glotons. and to ve̅geable folke. his voice shalbe ful dredful and ful bitter whanne he shal saye to them Discedite a me maledicti etc. Wende ye hens fro me ye cursed wretches into the fier of helle withouten ende. there to dwelle with the fende and hys aungelis And so he shal send the̅ to sory place and to sory cu̅pany withoute any remedie/ Was ther neuer thunderblast so dredful as his voice thanne shalbe to theim that shal be dampned/ And was there neuer songe so mery. ne melodye so likyng as his voice shal be thanne to al that shalbe saued. And therfore deme welle thy silfe here: that thou be not dampned there. Stond here to the lawe of ye greate queste of treue witnesses. wich I haue nempned to the and demeth isylfe therafter/ And be treue domesman of thi sylfe or els thou shalt haue the same jst. apens the at the dredful dome. And therto alle aungelis and archaungelis and al the seyntes in heuen and alle creaturis shal tha bere witnesse apens the and aye vegeaunce on the/ Thanne

as sayth John crisostom super illud. Plangent se omnes tribus terre et c. The aungelis shal bryng forth the crosse. the spere. the nayles. the scourges. and the garlo̅d of thornes with which criste suffered his passion. Thanne shal crist sit on high to deme þe qcke ⁊ the dede/ he shal departe the gode from the wycked and sette the gode on the right syde. the wycked on the liftesyde/ He shal turne hi̅ to the wicked on the liftsyde and shewe theym the crosse. the spere the nayles. the scourges and the garlond of thornes and his wou̅ des alle fresshe which he suffered for alle ma̅kynde. and saye to the wicked on this wyse/ Ecce miseri et ingrati quanta p̅ vobis sustinui ppter vos homo factus sum ꝗc. Se ye vnkynde cursed wretches what I suffered for your sake. For wha̅ I was god ⁊ kynge of kynges and lord of lordes and neuer had wyst of woo. for poure sake I bicam man for youre sake I suffered to be beten and bounde. be spateled and despised be nailed to the crosse crowned with thornes. stongen to the harte with a spere. and was slayne dispitous deth as ye maye see to bye you from endles deth.

Where is the rau̅som of my blode where be the soules þ I bought

f i

The eight

so dere: Where is the seruice that ye shulde haue don to me: Where is the loue that ye shuld haue shewed to me: I loued you aboue alle creaturis/ I loued you more than I dyd myn owne worshyp For why. for youre loue I putte mysylfe to sorowe and care. And ye loued more a lytel mucke and a lytyl luste of the flesshe. than ye dyd me or my ryghtfulnesse: and lytyl for nought wolde do for my loue. For whan I was hungry ye wolde not fede me/ whan I hadde thurst. ye gaue me no drynk Whan I was naked/ ye hylde me nat/ whan I sought myne harborowe: ye rescepued me nott Whan I was seke and in pryson: ye visited me not/ And therfore wende ye hens from me into the fier of helle without end there to dwelle with the fende and hys aungelis/ O. sayth seynt Gregori thou synful wretche what shalt thou do. fle may thou not. ne hyde the may thou not. and if thou apere as nedys thou moste thou art but shent/ for yet thou shalt haue al thyng ayens the/ Aboue ye thou shalt haue the dredfulle domesman redy to dampne the On the ryght syde thou shalt haue the wicked werkes to accuse the On the lyft side the foule fendes redy to drawe the to helle/ Bynethe the

thou shalt haue ye endles depnes redy to swolow the in/ Without the thou shalt haue al the worlde on fier redy to brenne the/ Within the thou shalt haue thyn own conscience worst of al/ gnawyng the and fretynge the withouten ende Thanne as sayth the wyse man Alle creaturis shal feyght ayens vs/ Sap 5°. Thanne as sayth the greate clerke/ Crisostomus. heuē erth water sōne mone nyght and day & al ye world shal stond ayens vs in witnesse of oure synnes And though al thing wer stil oure thoughtis and oure conscieuce/ and oure werkes/ shal accuse vs and stonde witnessis ayens vs/ Therfore seynt austen in his omelie sup illud Estote misericordes sayth thus Brethern take ye hede to the mercy of god: and to the harde dome of god: Nowe is tyme of mercy. after it shal be tyme of dome Nowe god clepeth ayen that been turned aweye fro him: and foryeueth thē ther synnes that turne ayen to him: and he is ful pacient and abideth of wrech that men shulde turne thē to him and be saued. And anon as sinners turne them ayen to god he foryeueth the synnes that been passed & bysetith iopes to comig Now god stireth and monestith thē that been slaw to gode dedis

he confortith them that been dis/
easyd, he techith them that be stu
diouse, and helpith them þ fighte
aȝest vices He forsaketh no ma
ne womā that trauepleth to doo
wele if they clepe to him He pe
ueth to vs that we shulde peue a
pey to him to please him Whāne
we haue offendyd him For we
haue nat ȝou̅ him ne wherwith
to queme him, butt that we take
of him The tyme of mercy is ful
grete. I pray you bretherne alle
lete ye natt this tyme passe you.
But take ye it while ye may After
this tym shal cūme tym of dome
Whanne men shal doo harde pe
naunce withouten frupte, for itt
shal nat helpe them Thāne syn
ners that had their welth in this
worlde shal sigh and say w̅ grete
sorowe Quid nobis profuit sup/
bia &c. What hath profited to vs
pride, what hath nowe holpē vs
oure pompe: oure boost, oure ri=
chesses: Al thies ben passed alway
right as a shadowe. These been
the wordes of seint austyn.

The yv chapter.

Whāne they that shalbe dā/
ned shal say a salwe of sor
rowe þ neuir shal haue ende. De
fecit gaudiū cordis nr̅i. Versus ē
i luctū chorus nr̅. cecidit coro=
na capitis nostri, ve nobis quia
peccauimus. The ioye of oure
hert is done and past alway, to so
rowe & care is turned oure ȝlepe.
the garlonde of oure hede is falle
to grounde, that euir we dyd sy̅
Welalway the stounde. Trenor.
quarto. Therfore leue frende ta/
ke we to vs the tyme of mercy &
amende we vs while we may for
elles we shal nat whāne we wold
And the lēger þ god suffrith folk
to reigne in their synne, & the mo
re pacience þ he hath with them
the harder he shal smyte them But
they amende them. And therfore
the doome of god is lykned. to a
bowe For the bowe is made of ii.
thinges Of a wronge tre. and a
right strynge So the dome of
god is made of ii. maner folke
Of them þ ben wronge through
synne, and lyue wronfully, and
do moche wronge, & of them þ be
right & rightful in lyuynge The
archer shetig in this bowe is crist
And the more þ ye bowe is drawe
abak, the harder it smyteth whā
the archer lousith. So the lenger
þ Crist abideth, & so draweth his
dome abake, the harder he shalle
smyte but folk amende them
And as the archer in his shetinge
taketh the wronge tre in his lifte
honde, and the righte strynge in
his right hōde and drawith them

The eight

acwynne, so Crist at the doome. shal sett the wrong spuers on his left sode. the rightful spuers on his right honde, & sette the arowe in his bowe, that shalbe the dredful sentence of his dome, & drawe the rightful from the wronge, the gode from the wycked. Whanne he shal say to the rightful. Come ye with me vp into heuene blisse. Withouten ende, and to the wrong spuers he shal say. Wende ye hens fro me downe into helle peyn. Wt outen ende. Of this bowe the prophete saith Arcum suũ tetendit & parauit illũ. God hath bent his bowe, and made it redye, and he hath arrayed or made redy therin tacle of dethe. and hathe maade his arowes hote with brennynge thinges For they that ben brente with synne shal brenne with the fyre of helle withouten ende. Of this bowe dauid also saith Dedisti metuẽtibus te significationẽ: Vt fugiant a facie arcus. Lord thou hast yeuen a tokenynge to them that drede the, to fle alway from the face of the bowe.

The xBi. chapter.

Dues. What tokenes ben tho Paup. Ther is dome in special, and dome in generall. b shalle be in the laste day of this worlde Dome in special. ech mã hath anone as he dyeth And therfore crist saith. Nunc iudiciũ est mundi.   Nowe is dome of the worlde, for anon as thou art dede, thou shalt be dempd either to heuene or to helle, or to purgatorye. Of this dome speketh Salomon. Memor esto iudicii mei Haue mynde of my dome, for suche shalbe thy dome, yisterday it felle to me, to morowe it shal fal to the Bifore this dome goo many tokenes of warnynge to synful wretches, as age, seknesse, febleness, daselyng of sight, blindenesse, defnesse, tynyngyng or tryuelyng of skynne, fadynge of coloure, faylyng of mynde, losse of catel, of fredes by deth & other Diues. Whanne shal that day of general dome falle Pauper. as Criste saith in the gospel ther is none aungel, ne saint in heuene that wote whanne it shal fall But sodeynly & vnwarly it shal falle, and come as a theif, and as deth doth to many a man y wole nat be ware by tokenes bifore.

No more shal men thanne blent with synne be ware of the last dome ne of the first. that shalbe deth no more thanne the men wolde be ware by the prechinge of Noe to fle the flode that brenchid al saue Biii. soules.   Diues. Sithen rche man and woman is dempd anon as he is dede / wherof shall serue the general doome.

Pauper. That al men bethen and cristen may se the rightfulle donne of god / nat only in them self but in al other / that bethe men may se and knowe their false bileue for whiche they been dampnyd And cristen men se and knowe their vnkyndnesse / and howe rightfully they and alle other be dampned that die in dedly synne

The xviii chapter.

Mannes dome is puerted by iiii. thinges as saith the lawe xi.-q. iiii. Quatuor. By drede By couetise of giftes / by hate / By lowe But crist he is almighty / he dredith no man He is lorde of al he nedith no mede ne giftes. He hatith no gode man ne woman. and therfore he shal dampne no gode man ne gode woman He coueth al maner right / and therfore he shal do no wronge. He knowith al / and therfor ther shal no fals witnes ne slight of mē of lawe disceyue him. Euery man shal be ther a true wytnesse of his owne dome / for his owne conscience shal saue him or dampne hī

And therfore leue freende be ye a true wytnesse of your self in this worlde to saue your self here in tyme of grace / and thanne shal ye be a true wytnesse to youre selfe. to saue youre self. in tyme of the dome. False wytnesses in this worlde haste their rightful doome of dampnacioun in the other worlde. For they been false witnesses to them selfe / & to the other also. As saith seynt Johṅ with the gilden mouthe. super Matheum opere imperfecto Omelia vi. Ther is no man able to be a true wytnesse to another man but he be firste a true wytnesse. to hym selfe in his owne dome.

At the doome god shalle axe of vs reknynge and aunswerynge / of the benefices. that we haue taken of him / he shalle axe them ayen / in nombre in weight and measure. He shalle axe of vs how ofte we haue resceiued of his giftes. howe moch we haue resceyued & how we haue spent them And the lettres and the tayles of oure conscience. shal aunswet and say that we haue resceyued goodes of kynde / that is to say of body and of soule / Also godes of fortune that ben temporal godes and temporal richesses and godes of grace that ben vertues and cunynge. Thanne the

F iiii.

429

soueraygne iuge shalle axe of vs aunswere of his benefices in the plurel nombre saynge. Esurinui ꝛc. I hadde hungre and ye gaue me no mete I hadde thriste and ye gaue me no drynk I was nakyd and ye clothed me nat. I sought my herborowe and ye refceyued me nat. I was seke and in pryfone and ye visited me nat ne comforted me nat And sithen the dome shalbe so harde to them pat helpe nat their euencristen ii the their gode at nede/ moche moore streit it shalbe to them that robbe their euencristen/ as to theuys pt soure extorcioners and maquerels lecchoures and to al wicked doers Thanne men shal geue an swere of euery ydel worde þ they speke/ as crist saith in the gospel And as seynt Bernarde saith the riche man shal geue aunswere of euery threde in his clothe/ of euery crumme of brede ẏ his brede siꝛep of euery droppe of drynke of his batel and in his tūne ẝ in his ves sel Also Criste shalle axe rekniġ by hole mesure. For as Criste saith in the gospel. men shal thē reken and yeld to the left ferthiġ without forgeuenesse And sū the measure as men mete here to other shalbe moten agen to them mercy for mercy/ harde for harde Also god shal thanne axe of vs reknyng in weight of strayt dome for al oure dedes shal there be weyed by the dome of god and of oure owne conscience/ and after that they wey they shalbe rewardyd/ the gode in blisse the wicked in peyne Thanne the honde of god shal write in the conscience of euery mā and womā that shal be dampnyd these thre wordes. Mane techel phares. Whiche iii. wordes he wrote on the the walle of the kinges hall Balthasar. to his dampnacion Danielis v°.c. Whiche vision apperyd to the kiġ in tyme of the greate feest that he made in dispyte of god/ and made men drynke in the vessels of goddes temple/ Whiche vessels wer halowed to god. For Mane is to say in englisshe. God hath nombred thy kingdome and dayes of thy reigne and made an ēde therof. Techel. is to saye/ thou art weyed in a balaunce/ ẝ thou wepest to lytel. Phares. is to say thy kyngdome is departed from the For after the dome the synful man may no lēger loke after the kingdome of heuene Whiche was ordeyned to him if he wold haue deferuyd it But thanne he shalbe departyd fro that kingdome pat he hath loste by his folye. and go to pryson of hell without ende Whiche he hath deseruyd For thā

Precept.

Criste shal say to every man and woman Tolle quod tuu est et vade. Take that is thyne. and that thou haste deserued and goo thy wey to heuene if thou haue do wele/ or to helle if thou haue do amys and nat amendyd the. Thanne al wycked cristen men shalbe demed and dampnyd/But hethen men shalbe dampned and nat demyd For as Criste saith in the gospel He that bileueth natt in Criste nowe/ he is demyd Summe shalbe demyd and sauyde/as gode cristen men comyn lyuers. And summe shal be saued and nat demyd/ as men of pfection/ For they shal deme other as crist sayd in the gospel Vos qui reliquistis omnia. &c. ye that haue forsake al worldly godes for my sake/ & folowed me in pouertie and in pfection/ ye shal sytt on xii. setys demyng the xii. kynredes of israel. that is to say/ all that shal be demyd.

The xviii. chapter.

Diues. It is dredeful thing to thynke on this dome. Pauper. It shalbe more dredeful to here it and to se it/ & moost for to fele it. and namely to riche folke that haue rescepued many godes of god that spendyd them ne dispensed them to his worshyp And seynt gregory in his omelye saith/ the more the yiftes of god come to a ma̅/ the more weye reknyngꝭ & aunswere of the yiftes. Therfore seint James spekith in this maner to pou riche men Agite nunc diuites &c. Nowe ye riche men do ye so that ye may saue your self/ wepe ye and wayle ye for your myschaunce that shall falle to you but ye amende you. Youre richesses ben roten/ your clothes be mothe eten/ your gold and siluer is rustyd and the ruste therof shalbe wytnesse ayenst you at the dome. and ete your flesshe as fier. For ye kepte your goode so harde from the pore folke/ therfore ye haue tresouryd wrath and wreche to you in the laste dayes. Jacobi 5. Diues. Wele is hym that is wele dede Paup. And wele is him that wele lyueth For as seint Austyn saith He that lyueth wel may nat euyl die Therfore as I saide first Deme wele to thy self/ and of thy self For as Salomon saith The true wytnesse deliuereth soules of wo bothe I his owne and in many other Prouerbi. xiiii. And as the ppete saith Seke ye vp oure lorde god with almesse dede. Whyle he may be fou̅de. clepe ye him whyle he is nigh. Nowe he is high now he crepith vs to his mercy Nowe he may be soilde benigne and bonour to alle. But after the dome and after oure deth he shalbe fel and fiers to vs. But we amende vs. Thanne shalle we fynde no mercy but that we deserue by our lyf And therfore leue frende doo ye as seint Poule saith Dum tempus habemus operemur bonum. ad omnes. Whyle we haue tyme worche we gode to al. And the wise man saith what gode thynne honde may do do it besily whyle thou might. For ther shalbe noo worching reason ne cunynge ne wysdome. after thy dethe to wyn the mede Ecclesiastes iy. Therfore Crist saith in the gospel that ther shal cume a nighte whanne no man shal worche to wynne his mede The day is oure lyf the nyght is our deth. for be we dede we may no more worche to wynne mede. ne to amende vs.

¶Here endith the viii. precepte. And begynneth the nynthe.

Dues. God sende vs grace to doo as thou sayst. I thanke the for this informacion. for I hope it shal do profyt Now I pray the that thou wylt enfourm me in the ix. commaundemente. Paup. The nynthe precepte is this Non concupisces domū proximi tui. Exodi. xx. Thou shalte nat coueite thy nighboures gode with wronge house ne londe In the viii. preceptes bifore god forbediht all wycked werkes. In these ii. last he forbediht al wycked wylles and consent to synne For of wycked wyl cumeth yuel dede And therfore Criste saith in the gospel that oute of the herte cometh al maner synne. for without wylle and assēt of the hert is no synne done. De corde exiunt cogitaciones male/homicidia adulteria fornicaciones/furta falsa testimonia/blasphemie. M'. xv. Therfore seint Poule. saith that couetise is rote of alle euyl. And therfore god forbediht al wycked couetise. bothe of the worlde and of the flesshe Couetise of the worlde is cleppyd couetise of the iye. I other mēnes gode Couetise of the flesshe is cleppde wylle to lechery and to glutony. And righte as a wycked wede is clene clensyd oute of a londe whā the rote is drawen away/ and til whanne the rote is drawē vp the londe is nat clene clensyd ne wel wedyd/ and bodily seknes is nat

Precepte.

wele cured ne helpyd tyl the roote of the sekneſ be thus diſtroyed Right ſo mannys ſoule and wo/mans may nat be clene cleſyd of ſynne. ne goddes lawe may natt be kepte/ til couetiſe of the herte whiche is rote of al maner ſynne and of all goſtly ſekeneſſe be dra wen oute of the londe of mannes hert/ and diſtroyed. And therfore whanne god hadde youen viii.p ceptes by whiche men ſhulde flee al wycked werkes/ he put therto other ii.preceptes apenſt falſe co uetiſe/ byddinge that men ſhulde put wycked couetiſe oute of hert For falſe couetiſe is principall fetter of keppyng of goddes lawe and rote of al wickednesse Ther fore in this cōmaundement god forbedith principaly falſe worldly couetiſe. and ſpecially of thin ges nat mouable by them ſelf whā he byddeth that thou ſhalt nat co uepte thy nighboures gode with wronge houſe ne londe. In the ſeupnth pcept god forbedeth the dede of al wrōgful takyng whā he biddeth the nat ſtele In this heeſt he forbedeth al maner wrō geful deſire and mys couetiſe of any mannys goode/ of houſe/ of londe/ of golde/of ſiluer/ of cloth of corne and of all ſuch other thi ges that may nat ſtire themſelf.

This precept is principaly a
yens falſe purchaſoures/ that for falſe couetiſe ben beſy to begyle. and with falſhed to robbe men of houſe/ and of londe & put theyn oute of their heritage. To ſuche falſe purchaſoures god peueth his curſe and ſaith thus. Ve qui cogitatis lutile et operamini ma lum iŋ cubilibus Veſtris. &c.
Woo be to you that thynke un p fitable thinge/ and worche wyc ked thinge in poure beddes of the morowe whanne pe may nat ſle/ pe For thāne they caſte gyle and falſhede apenſt their euencriſten. They haue couetyd other mens nys feeldes ſaith he/ and by myȝt take them away from them/ and robbe them of their houſes/ & fal ſly chalenge the mā and his hous and his heritage For ofte they chalenge men for bonde/ and ſo entre into their houſe and londe. and haue alle their heritage with goddes curſe. Michee.ii. Alſo god peueth them his curſe by the prophete pſale ther he ſaith thus Ve qui coniungitis domum do= mui. et agrum agro copulatio &c

Wo be to pou that falſly iop= ne houſe to houſe/ & couple felde to felde/ to the ende of the place ꝑ pe may ſay/all this is myne and noo man hath ought within me.

Wene pe ſaith god that pe alo= ne ſhal duelle upon erthe.

This false couetise saith he sow neth in myn erys And therfore many a fair house and grete shal be forsaken/ and no man ne wo/ man duelle therin. psa. b. And thus the wise man saith Non at tingas terminos paruulorum &c Touche nat the boundes of the smal pore folke. to reue them of their right. and entre thou nat in to the feelde of faderles children. to putte them oute of their herita ge For almighty god that is their nigh frende shal mak their cause ful greuouse and ful hard apēst the Prouer. xxiii.

The ii. chapter.

We fynde in holy wrytte the thrid boke of kinges xxi. c. That ther was a kinge of israel that hight Achab/ and ther was a man duellyng by him that hizt naboth that hadde a faire vyne perd that lay nigh the kinges pa leis/ and therfore the kinge desy/ red gretly to haue it/ and saide to naboth. reue me thy vyneperde. and I shal yeue the a better ther fore. or elles as moche money as it is worthe Thāne naboth saide god forbede that I shulde chaū ge my faders heritage. I wole ne uir chaunge it ne selle it. Thāne the kinge was wroth and for ma lancoly leyde him on his bedde. & wolde nat ete ne drynke. The quene Jesabel his wyf come to him and ayed what him ayled The king saide that he had spo ken to naboth to haue his vyne perde/ and he wolde nat graunte it him Thāne Jesabel the ques ne saide Be of gode confort and take me thy tynge and I shal ye ue to the. the vyneperde Thāne she wrote lettres i the kinges na me to the principalis of the citee Ondre the kinges signet. And badde them gadre their courte to gidder and make a solempne fas tynge so to blynde the people w' ppocrisie and bad them ordeyne. two false wytnesses/which shuld accuse naboth. and say þ he spak euyl of god and of the king and so dampne him as gilty and sto ne him to the deth and so they did For it was the lawe that who so spake euyl of god or of the king or cursyd them he shulde be slayn ℂwhanne Jesabel hadde tidin ges þ naboth was slayne/ she ca me to the kinge and badde hym ryse vp & be mery & take the vyn perd to him for naboth was dede And anone the kinge rose & wete into the vyneperde & toke it to hi ℂThā at the bydding of god Ely the pphete met w' him & saide to him in goddes name Thou hast

Precepte.

slayn and thou hast that thou couetist. But I tel the it for sothe in the same place there the houndes haue lykked vp the blode of Nabothe/ houndes shal lyche vp thy blode, and houndes shall ete thy wyf Iesabel. and houndes & bridges shalle ete thy body/ and god shall distroye thyne housholde. and sle al thy kynred/ and thyne alpaunce/ and sone after it fel so And thus of false couetise/ came plurie/ false wytnesse. murdre/ & manslaughter and distruccione. of the kingdome. We rede also in the passion of seint Beatrice that there was a false couetouse man whos name was Lucres. And he coueytid moche the place of seynt Beatrice And for coueti ce to haue ye place he accused her to an hethen iuge. that she was a cristen woman And so by his accu sacion she was slayne. For she wolde nat forsake Criste ne Cri stes lawe. Whanne she was thus dede/ Lucres entryd into her pla ce to haue it in possession And for ioye of the place he made therin a grete feest to his frendes And whanne he was moost mery and iocunde in the myddes of the feest a yong soukyng childe that was there in his moders arme sayd al alowde that al men myght here it Audi Lucreci. Here nowe Lucres

Thou hast slayne/ & thou haste entryd falsly into this place and haste it at thy wylle. But nowe thou art youen into the nyghte & into possession of thy moste ene my And anone in tyme of the se est bifore al his freendes and his gestes/ the feende entryd within hym/ and iii. oures togidre so for trauelyd him and so rent him be fore them al til he slewe him and for his fals couetise bare his soul to helle Here thou myght se it that perel is to purchace any thing as mys by false couetise And ther fore if thou haue purchased any thing falsly/ or if thou occuppe a ny thing mys purchased looke þ thou make restitucion for salua cion of thy self/ and of thyne hey res For it is a comen prouerbe De male quesitis vix gaudet tercius heres. Of euyl goten gode ye thrid heire vnneth hath ioye.

The iii. chapter.

Dives. If I hadde oughte purchaced amys my self. I holde me bounden to restituci on/ But of my former faders pur chace haue I nought to do Whe ther it were rightful or nat right fulle. Butt that they lefte to me I wyl kepe it as the gode mi

The nynth.

Naboth dyd of whom thou spak full late Paup. Naboth wolde haue kept stylle his faders heritage that longyd to him by right / & by discent of heritage. But if thou kepe any thinge wyttingly that thy former faders purchasid fallsly. in that thou kepist nat thi faders heritage as naboth dyde. But thou kepist other mennys heritage to whiche neither thou ne thy fader hadde right And therfore but thou mak restitucōn thou shalt relese it and al thyne heires. as Achab dyd and his heires. Wt the loste nat only that they had mysgoten of naboth by murdre. and by gyle / but therto they lost their lif their worship and theire heritage for euir. ¶ I rede that ther was a grete man whiche did moche almesse / & for his almesse. god wolde haue him saued It byfell in an euenynge he rompd alone vndre his wode side by his place. ther came an aungel in a mannes lyknes & bad him go wt him Sodenly they were togidre I a depe valeye / and in the myddes of the valey was a depe pytt ful of fyre smoderinge medlyd with pit che and brymstone. ful foule stynkynge. Thanne the aungel bad this man loke into this pytt. He lokyd downe / and there he sawe thre galowes stonding in the fire

On the ferthest henge a man by the tunge. on the seconde henge a man by the hondes / but on the thridde henge no man. Thanne the aungel ayed him what he sawe. and he tolde him al the soth. Thanne saide the aungel. He þ hangith by the tūge is thy faders fader / which purchased the place that thou duellyst in / by gyle of his tunge / by false othes / by leesynges / by piurie / by false wytnesses / and dyd many mē forswere them / and therfore is he principaly punysshed in his tūge / and haungith by his tunge in this orrible fyre and shal do withouten ende for he wolde nat make restitucion. He that hangith on the seconde galowes by the hondis is thy fader whiche kept stylle by myghty hond that his fader mispurchased / and wolde nat make restitucion The thridde galowes in whiche hangithe no man been ordeyned for the But if thou amende the and make restitucion Anone the aungel passyd awey from him. and he was delyuered ayen vndre his woode syde.

The nexte daye after he sent after the heires of the plaace and made restitucion. His wyf and his children were fulle sory. and saide vnto him. Allas allas nowe been we alle beggers.

Precepte.

Thanne he aunswerid & said Leuer I haue that we begge in this worlde/thanne to bryngge you al and me into that endelesse peyne tha I sawe And better it is to ha for to lese a place in erthe to whiche we haue no right/thanne to lese oure place in heuene blisse wᵗ outen ende. Diues I assent wel to thy spech/say forth what thou wylt.

The iiii. chapter.

Pauper. Many harde ven/geaunces haue fallen for false couetise Giezi was smyten with foule miselrie For couetise made hym to sel the helth of Naman/whiche helth came only by the grace of god. iiii°. R. B. c. For couetise iudas solde Cryste. goddes sonne for thritty penys. and betrayed hym/& after he wet & henge hym self tyl his bely brast And there his bely braste/& there the beuyl that was in hym flewe oute and bare his soule with hym to helle. Diues. Why went natt the feende oute at his mouthe.

Paup. For his mouth hadde ouchyd cristes mouthe/whanne he kyssed crist in gile and sayde. Hayle maister. Diues. Thy reply is gode say forth what thou vylte. Pauper. Also for couetise anany and saphira his wif di

ed sodeyn deth & dispitouse bethe for they lyed to the holy ghoost. & forsoke their money to seint Petyr For couetise Nachor was stoned to the deth/ for he stale golde and clothe ayest goddes forbode Iosue viii. ☙ We fynde in the lyf of seint Barlaam pat on a tyme an archer toke a nightyngale and wolde haue slayne it God yaue speche to the nightyngale. whiche saide to the archer/ what shal it proufyt to the to slee me. Thou maist nat fylle thy wombe with me I am so lytel Saue my lawe and lett me fle and I shalle teche the thre wysdomes whiche if thou kepe wele they shal do ye moche proufyt. Thanne the archer was a woundryd of her speche and hight her sykerly that he let her fle. if she taughte hym the wysdomes. Thanne she said beswe the nat to take thinge þ thou might nat take. For thinge that is looste and may nat be recured ne goten ayen make no sorowe. Thinge that is nat semely to be sothe/ leue it nat The archer lete the nightyngale fle. whanne the nightyngale was vp in the ayre. she saide to the archer a feble coũsepl hast thou take For thou hast lost a grete treasoure For I haue a margery stone in my wõbe more thanne an ostriches ey.

The nynth.

Thāne the archer was sory and prayed the nightyngale come ageyn to hym & hight her wele Thā saide the nightyngale. Nowe I wote wele thou art a fole, and al my sore psiteth the nat. For thou makest moche sorowe. for thou hast lost me. and yit thou might nat gete me ayen Thou trauaylist to take me. and thou mighte nat take me, ne passe the Wepe þ I passe by And ouir that thou scurst that I hadde suche a precious stone in my body as moche. as an ostriches ey. and al my body is nat half so moche. Oiues. What is this to purpose. Pauy. By this nightyngale þ syngeth so swetly, I vnderstonde Criste. goddes sonne that songe to man kynde sōges of endles loue. And a nightyngale is in latyne philomena. þ is to saye in englisshe. a swete louer, as saith Catholicon And a sweter louer thāne Cryste was ther neuir none He taughte to us many Wysdomes, in which he taught us these iii. First, he badde that thou shuldest natt be besy to take thing þ thou mighte nat take. Whanne he bad the nat stele, ne coueyte thy neighboure gode with wronge. For as the sawe saith. Hoc solum possum9. quod de iure possumus. Only we may do that we may do law-fully And therfore if thou trauail to gete thing vnlaufully þ thou might nat haue by the lawe, be it house or londe worship or dignyte, thanne thou besiest the to gete a rthinge that thou mighte nat take. And therfore the wiseman saith Noli laborare vt diteris &c. Trauayle thou nat to moche to be riche. But putte measure and maner to thy wysdoome, and to thy slight, that though thou might gete a thinge by sleight or by soteltie, alwaye take hede to the right and to the lawe. Ne erigas oclōs tuos ad opes quas habere nō poteris. s. de iure &c. Lift nat vp thyn iye saith Salomon to richesses that thou might natt haue rightfully. For they shalle make them winges as of an egle and fle into heuene, that is to sey they shal fle alway from the, and accuse the bifore god of thy false hede, and of thy couetise Prouer xxiii. Also couetouse folk doo a peynst the secoūde lesson that this nightingale crist ihūs taught vs to kepe. For whā they lese thing by myshappe or by aduersite, or by deth of wif or children they make so moch sorowe. þ they reny god, & falle in ful harde sekenes Bothe of soule and of body. But dauid the king keping this wisdome dyd natt soo But while hi-

Precepte.

sone say sche. as long as he was of hope to haue his life: so longe he wept and fasted. and prayde for his life to god. But whanne the childe was dede, and he sesed of his weppynge and ete & dranke and made mery: For he wyst wel that he might not gete him ayen. ii°. R̃ xii°. c°. Also couetise maketh men to leeue thynge that is not semely to be soth, and to beleue many stronge lesynges. For thynge that is moch desired is sone leued. as sayth the master of stories. And for as moch as couetouse folk̃e desiren to haue moch thyng that they haue noo right to, therfor they bileue many false tales. and assenten to falsehede. For the couetise and the false accorden sone to gedre. For if a false man come and telle the couetise man a fals tale of wynnynge. or telleth him that he hath right to a thynge: he leueth him sone be it neuer so false. But therfore this nightyngale blessid Jesus sayde Qui cito credit leuis est corde &c. He that sone bileueth is light of herte and fulle chaungeable. fro vertue to vice. from treuth to falsnesse from charite to couetise. Et minorabitur And he that sone bileueth shalbe lessed in worship and litylset by. For sone leuyg of lesynges bryget people to moch foly. This maketh men to bigynne pleyes and brigges & one neighbore to hate another. the husbonde to hate his wyfe. the wife hir husbonde. the fader his sonne. the sonne his fader. the moder hir doughter. the brother his suster. this hath brought englond in bitter balis. Therfore the wise man saith Non omni verbo credas. Bileue not euery word Eccle. xiiii°. He þ leueth sone lesynges. his worde and his loue and his feith waluen about as the wynde. Therfore the grete clerke Seneca sayth in his epistle. that no wyse man bileueth any newe tales lightly.

The 8. chapter.

Also we rede in holy wrytt numeri xxii. That Balaā the false prophete wold haue cursed goddes people for couetise of the yiftis which Balaac kyng of moab profered him. natwitston, dyng that god forbad it him and bad him nat come there. Wherfor as he rode to the kyng Balac. his asse that he roode on vndername him and hurt his fote ayens a wal. For the asse sawe an aungel stondinge with a sswerd drawen ayēs him in the weye. and therfore the asse fled out of þe wey ito þe feld Balaā was wroth & smoote his

The eight.

asse ful harde with a stafe: for he bare him so oute of the weye And the as came in a strait wey bytwene two wallys. and there he saw also the aungel apens him And for drede he fled asyde and bare Balaam apens ye wal and hurt his fote apens the wal Thane Balaam bette eftsones ful euyl. Sone after the aungel stode apens him in so straite weye. that the asse might not flee on any syde. Butt felle doune and wolde no ferther thanne efte he smote the asse/ God openid the assis mouth and he sayde to Balaam. what haue I doo apens the. Why bytefte thou me nowe the thirde tyme/ I haue alwey be thy beest. and thou hast alwey reden on me. and I serued the neuer thus tyl nowe/ Thane god opened the iyen of Balaam. & he sawe the aungel stondynge apens him with a naked swerde which repreued him of hys false couetyse and of his wicked purpos. and for that he bete his asse withoute gilte and sayde. & Butt the asse had goon oute of the wey he shulde elles haue slayne hym for hys wey was apens the plesaunce of god: Diues. What bitokeneth thys tale Paup. Balaam is to saye in englisshe a deuourer of the people and sturblour of the folke Iterptatur deuorans pplm et turbans gentem And therfor Balaam bitokeneth false couetise of this worlde whiche deuoureth the pore peple and stourbelith euery nacion/ For nigh alle the debate in this worlde is for myn and thyn: And therfore sayde a philosofre. Tolle duo verba meum et tuum. et totus mundus erit in pace/ Put oute of this worlde two wordys myne and thyn. and al the world shalbe in pees. Balaam firste in his prophecie worshipped god des people and prophicied to them moche prosperitie as he was compelled by the might of god to say But at the laste with his shere wed counceile that he yaue to Balac to haue his yiftis. he disseyued goddes people and brought this to lechery and to ydolatrie. and so to offende god wherfore foure and twenty thousand of goddes people were slayne. and alle the princes of the peple were hangid vpon gebettes apens the sonne at the biddynge of god Right so couetyse of this worlde fyrste putteth men in hope of grete prosperitye. and hoteth them welthe and worship / See sayth couetise. suche a clerke is there that may spende so moche by yere / and yit he was but a pore mannys sone as thou art / Be of goode hert / for

440

Precepte.

suche as he is thou mighte be. And so couetise puttith example of knightes, of marchauntes, of prelates of lordes and of ladies. If thou haue richesse saith couetise, thou may do moche almesse and haue many prestis to pray for ye out of purgatorye. But be ware for by suche bihestes the feende & worldly couetise been aboute to disceyue the and to bringe the in glotonye and lecherye, and ydolatrie, as Balaam broughte goddes people to shenship. He wole make the more to trust in thy gode thā in thy god. For what thinge that man or woman loueth mooste & settith his hert moost therin, that is his god, as saith seint Jerom. Therfore seint poule saith, that auarice is seruage of malwmetry. For gold is god to the couetouse man, to whome he dothe mooste worship, whiche false god is betoknyd by the ymage of golde, þ was lx. cubites in hight and vi. in brede. Whiche the kinge Nabugodonosor reysed vp in the feeld of Durain, and cōpellyd al men to worship it. And who so wolde nat worship it, he dyd put theim in an ouen ful of fyre in token that who so worshipeth nat i this worlde the false god of gold and of false couetise, and yeueth noo tale of this worlde and wole nat

obeye to false couetise to serue it with gile falsshede and plury but lyue in treuth and in charite, yat man shal haue moche woo i this worlde. And therfore seint poule saith þ they that wole lyue mekely and goodly in criste shal suffre moch tribulacion i this worlde. Therfore seint Gregory saithe. This worlde is a furneys and a ouen to trye in goddes children. By anguysshe and tribulacion. Be ware of the bihestes of couetise. For faire bihestes make sottes blithe. He wole so entryh the in dett and in synne, that it shall be ful harde to the for to escape. and so to bryng the to die in dedly synne. And if thou dye in dedly synne, al the golde vnder the cope of heuene though it were thyne, ne alle the prestes vnder sōne may nat helpe the. Therfore seit poule Qui volunt diuites fieri i cidunt in temptationes et in laqum diaboli. &c. They that coueyte to be riche i this worlde fal into harde temptacions and into the feendes snare. and into wycked desires and vnproufitable. and fulle noyous, whiche drench men into the dethe of helle & brig them to perdicion. For why saith he, Roote of alle euyl is couetise Prima ad Thi. vi.

G i

The VI. chapiter.

Diues. I wene that all men might be holpen with her richesses after her deth. **Pauper.** It is nat soo But only they that be holpen with their goode, after their dethe, that deseruyd by ther lyf to be holpen with their richesses after their dethe. as they that do almesse after their staate, and spende wele the goode. that god hathe sentte to theym, and paye wele their dettes, and do such other gode dedys, and kepe theim from dedely synne to their lyues ende or namely thanne. Thus saith seynt Austyne In glosa prima ad thessalo. quarto sup illud. Nolumus vos ignorare de dormientibus. And therfore be ware and take hede to thre warnyngis and tokenes that god yaue to Balaam to slee the sverde Firste his asse went oute of his waye. After that he hurte his foote and diseasyd al his body At the laste he fel downe vndre him and wolde no ferther bere him. By the asse I vnderstonde welth of this world that stondith principaly in richesses and in bodily helthe. whiche beryth a man vp in this world as the asse bare Balaam. Butt be ware. for right as the asse is a ful dulle beest, and whanne a man hath moost nede and moost hast in his iourney, thanne he wol nat go but at his owne luste, and so disceyueth his master Right soo worldly welthe disceyueth them that trust therin, and fayleth the at nede. This asse of worldly welth firste gothe out of the wey that is whane god sendith a man aduersite, and his causes and his traueil goth nat forth as he wold ne as he wende they shulde doo. But whanne he wenyth to wyn. he seeith and spedith natt as he wende to spede. And there he wenyth to fynd frendes, he fyndeth enemyes. And in case if he wole passe the see, the wynde is agenst him, and dryueth him out of his weye. And if he plete, sume slyzt puttith him oute of his purpose, and if he wende to spede in a moneth he shal nat spede it in a yere. and parauenture neuir bringe his cause into the right wey there he wolde haue it. Whanne this asse gothe oute of the waye. take hede to thy waye and to thy purpose, and if thy way and purpose be agenst the plesaunce of god, as was the waye of Balaam thanne wende ayen and cese of thyn euil purpose. And if it be nat agenst the plesaunce of god, dispose the to pacience and thank god of al.

and take hede what the aungell sayde to Balaam. Butt the asse sayde he. hadde gone oute of the waye I hadde slayne the But welthe of the worlde wente sumtyme oute of the waye by ad uersite and by schenesse/ elles it shulde be cause to moche folke. of dethe. Bothe bodily and gostly. For if man hadde alway his welthe and his wyl in this worlde he shulde. peue no tale of god/ ne of man. ⁋The secounde token was that he hurte his foote. and soo diseased his bodye/ that is whanne god sendith man sekenesse and castith him downe i his bedde/ and maketh him so feble. that his feete may nat bere hym. thanne take thou hede to thy wey and to thy lyf. if it be ought contrarie to god/ and if it be amend the. ⁋The thridde token was. that the asse fel downe vndre his feet in a strept wey/ and wold no ferther bere him ⁋This strept wey & so narow a paas/ is deth where no man may flee ⁋Thanne welth of this worlde lykned to the asse. fallith downe to grounde & wole no leger bere mā vp in this world ⁋Thanne passith helth and welth and al lust of the flesshe And ther fore whanne thou cūmpst to the poynt/ take hede to thy wey and to thy lif. And if it be contrarie to god/ amende the thanne for euir as thou wylte fle goddes swerde Richesse and welth of this worlde is lykned to a iogulours horse.

⁋We fynde that on a tyme ca me a proud gettour into a stable and founde a mynstralles horse. stonding by his horse. And for it was better thanne his/ he toke it and rode away theron/ and lefte his feble horse there. ⁋The myn stral perceyued that/ and ranne by a nigh pathe. and mette with hi. in passyng ouir a water and cry= ed. Flectamus ianua. ⁋The hors knewe wele his maisters voyce. as he was wont to doo in prey he dyd thanne/ and knelyd downe i the water. ⁋Thanne the mynstral saide. Leuate. And anone the horse rose vp as he was taught and keste the proude iettor in the water/ and ranne ayen to his ma ster. ⁋This mynstral is the worlde whiche pleyeth with folk of this worlde as a mynstralle/ as a io= gulour and as a disour His hors is richesses of this worlde/ which ofte at the voyce of this worlde playeth Flectamus genua. and bringeth them lowe and to grete pouert & forsaketh them in theire moost nede/ & folowelth the play of this worlde and nat the wyll of coueitouse folk that wold ha= ue them/ but ful often they that

G ii.

traueyle moofte to be riche / been moofte poze And namely cupl goten goode sone plyepeth Flectam' genua. With them that haue mys goten them by myspurchace / oz by withholdyng of dett / oz by fals executorie. oz by mychherie oz rob berye Therfoze it is a comen pzouerbe. De male quesitio vix gaudet tercius heres. Of cupl goten gode vnneth ioyeth the thyrd heir

The vii. chapter

Dives. Thy speche is nat plesaunte to worldly couetouse men / and yit experience shewith that thou saiste sothe.

Pauper. It farith by many folke as it doth by many shepe. For many shepe be nat payed to go with their felawes in come pasture / but seke their mete amonges busshes thoznes & byymbles. to haue the better bytte / tyl they ben so wystred and snarled among busshes & thoznes that they may nat go away. Thanne cummeth the pie oz the rauene and pyketh oute the one iye. and afterwarde the other iye. Thanne cummeth the wolf oz any hounde oz summe other beest & sleeth him Right so it is of couetous folk For they wole nat lyue in playne pasture. amonges their neighbours / ne be nat payed with comen pasture that god hath sent to theym: But outrage and seke to be in higher degre of richesses and of worship thanne their nighbours ben. and seke their lyuyng amonges brimbles and thoznes / that is to saye amonges false richesses / as sayth Cryst i the gospel. They bozowe of one v. li. of a nother. xx. li. & so forth and thynk neuir to pay & thus they gete moche gode and lyue a mery lyf with other mennys gode Also they bicome executours and attourneys to summe riche man in his diyng. & hote him wel to be true to him But whan he is dede they kepe al to theself & thus they snarle theself so i dett & in false richesses to be holde grete in this worlde / that they maye nat pay ther dettes Tha cumeth the feend & pyketh out ther right iye & maketh them lese cscience. anentis god After he pyketh oute their left iye. & maketh them lese shame anentis the worlde So y' neither for dred of god / ne for shame ne for speche of the world / they cese nat to bozowe ne to gete falsly other mennys gode / & so falle depper & depper in dett / tyl at the last the feend sleeth them body & soule And therfore loke ÿ thou pay wele thy dettes. Whyle thou may/ for els thou shalt nat whā thou woldest For a shepe ꝑ gothe moche amonge thornes leeuyth sume of his flece in euery busshe. there he gothe. tyl he is naked Right so the thornes of fals richesses. and such dettes shal take thy flece fro the/ ꝑ is to saye/ thy true catel if thou any haue/ so ꝑ thou shalt haue right nought to helpe with thy self. tyl whā thou shalt go nakyd of gode/ and haue lesse than nought Therfore saith a grete clerke Tulius. li. ii. de officiis. that no thing saueth more a compnye than faith. But septhe may nat be saith he But men wol pay their dettes. And in the thrid boke. de officiis. he saith/ ꝑ it is a synne apenst kynde to tak alwey falsely a nother mannes gode/ ⁊ to make him riche with a nother mannys losse For ꝑ saith he/ distropeth charite and the felaushyp of mankynde For men dare nat compne their gode to gidre by lenyng/ for drede of false couetise. Diues. That is soth For I had leuyr haue my gode in other mennys bondes thanne in myne/ if I wyste that they wolde truly pay it apen But I fynd so many fals and so fewe true/ ꝑ I dare nat lene but to fulle fewe Saye for the what thou wylt.

The viii. chapter.

PAup. Two thinges principaly shulde abate couetise of mannys herte. Vnstablenesse of this worlde and drede of dethe. First Vnstablenesse of this worlde/ for this worlde. and the welth of this world is skyned to foure thinges ful vnstable To a whele aboute turnyng/ to a shyp in the se saylyng/ to a stoure that sone fadith and fallith to grou̇d. and to a shadow that alway passith and duellith but a stounde Firste welth of this world is likned to a whele aboute turnynge. for whan the whele gothe about that/ ꝑ is bynethe. anone it is aboue. and that ꝑ is aboue. anone it is bynethe. And that ꝑ is on thone syde anone it is on the other syde Right so it is in the whele of fortune of this worlde. For nowe a man is bynethe in his pouthe ⁊ in his begynnynge In myddel age he is aboue in his welthe ⁊ in his floures/ But anon the whele turneth downe apen to greter age to pouert/ to seknesse and feblenes. tyl at the last he fallith of ye whele/ ⁊ dieth/ ⁊ lyeth there as a clott of erthe by the walle. Therfore in the whele of fortune is writt this verse. Regnabo regno. regnaui. sū sine regno. Man in his youth

The nynthe.

whanne he is towarde in hope of welthe. he saith Regnabo. I shal reigne. But whanne he is in his mydday age and hath the world at wyll and so sytteth aboue on the whele. than he saith I his pryde. Regno. Nowe I regne. I am alse aboue But anone the whele turneth doulwarde anon cūmeth age sekenesse, feblenesse, losse of catel and aduersite than he may say Regnaui. I haue regned. sūtyme I was a man But whanne he speth on dyinge he may saye Sum sine regno. I am without kingdome. My reigne my kingdome. my welth is done. Also in the whele of fortune, that is the one syde, anone it is in the other syde For they that ben this daye a mannes frendes and stonde on his side to help him, the next day they shalbe his enemyes and stōde ayēst him with his aduersarie Of this whele speketh Dauid. In circuitu impii ambulāt. wicked couetouse folke goo aboute as a whele. Posuisti eos Vt rotā. et sicut stipulam ante faciē Vēti. Lorde saith he thou hast put thē as a whele, and a stoble bifor the face of the wynde For as the stoble whyle the wynde bloweth waueteth and fleeth aboue in theyr. nowe high, nowe lowe, But anon as the wynde passith it fallith a downe to the erth and lyeth there styll. Right so the proude couetous folke wauere in this wor̄ld in welthe and worship, nowe higher, nowe lower, And as the stoble and the strawe in his flight hespith noo certeyn waye, soo kepe they no wey of goddes lawe, tyll at the last the wynd passith oute. of their body and they fal downe into ther graue, and many of thē into the pytte of helle. Also this worlde is lykned to a shyp, in the see sayinge For be the ship euir so grete of him self and haue the wynde with him al at wylle. and bere he his saile neuir so high & go he neuir so yerne, Be he passed there is no tokē where he wēt Right so be a man neuir so grete in this worlde, and haue the wid of mennys mouthe neuir so wele w' him to bere his name. to pryse him and to flatere him, thoughe his name sprynge neuir so wyde and bere him neuir so high in pride, or be he so solepne & so mighty. v no man dare quyeche ayenst him ne do, Be he dede, and passed oute of this worlde, sone he is for getten. Men shal fynde no tokē of him within a felwe yeres. Vnnethes shal he fynde one frende. that wose do syng a messe for his soule. Go to the churchyerd and thou shalt knowe by the bodies.

the riche from the pore, the faire, from the foule, the wise from the folts, the free fro the bonde. But as they turne there to erth & asshē to wormes mete, to styncche and vncleñesse Al these grete kinges that were sūtym so grete of name Where ben they al bicome. Alexander. Julius cesar Nabugodonosor. Octoupan. Arthur. king charles & al suche other Where be they bicome. Therfore they may say that is writen in the Book of Wysdome Quid nobis pfuit sup'bia &c. What profited to vs oure grete pride. What halpe vs oure pope & oure grete richesses. All is passed away as a shadowe, & as a ship ꝑ passith the wawes of the see, of which be it passed mē may fynde no token Sap. v. c. Mannes lyf may wele be lykened to a ship whiche is strept & narowe at bothe endes, but in the myddes it is wyde & large. Right so is mānes lyf, for his byrth & his begynnyng is ful strayt & ful narowe. For he cūmeth into this worlde naked and pore, weppynge & wailyng, vnmightȳ. Vnwytty & nought may ne can helpe hym self, & with moche trauayle is brought forth, til by litel & litel he cūmeth to mānes age. There the ship of his lyf is sudele wyde & large, for in his myddel age he hath moost

his might, his wytte & his wyllel But anone the ship of this lif drawetḣ to another strayte ende. As none cūmpth age, feblenesse sekenes. aduersite, losse of catel, & pouert, & at the last dethe maketh a ful strayte ende, whāne he dyeth with bytter peyne & moche drede. & moche sorowe & wendith hens nakyd & pore right as he came, & nought berith wͭ him but his dedes gode & wycked. Of these ii. strepte endes saith Job thus.

Nudus egressus sum de vtero matris mee: et nudus reuertar il, luc. Nakyd I came oute of my moders wombe, & nakyd I shal turne ayen into the erth moder of all. And if a man wole stire wele a shyp or a bote, he may nat stōd in the myddes of the ship, ne i the former ende. But he muste stōde i the laste ende, & there he may stiͤ the ship as he wole. Right so he ꝑ wole styre wele the ship of his lyf in this worlde, he may nat stōde in the myddes of his ship, nat set his thoughte & his hert in welthē ꝑ he hath in his middel age, ne he shal nat stonde in the former ēde nat sett his hert ne his thoughte in his byrthe ne in his begynnīge to thynke moche of his kynrede. ne of alliaunce to stire him to pride. Butt he must stōde in the last ende of his shyppe. and of his lyf

G iiii.

The nynthe.

and thinke on his dethe, and on laste his ende. And howe myscheuously and howe perilously he shal wend hens, and how whedyr ne whanne, woit he neuir. And in that maner he shalle best stere the shyppe of his lyf to the sikyr hauene of heuyn blisse. Therfore the wyseman saith Memorare nouissima tua et in eternum non peccabis. Thynke inwardly of thy laste thinges & of thyne ende, and thou shalt neuir do syn. Ecclesiastes vii. In the begynnyng of euery dede, thynk on the ende what ende it may haue and what may falle therof.

The ix. chapter.

Also welth of this world is lykened to a floure that sone fadeth and falleth to ye groūd For as the rose floure is faire to the sight, swete in smellyng, soft in handlynge, soo welth of this worlde is faire to the sight of mā and likynge in the hauyng But right as the rose weyith alway amonges the thornes, and he that gadrith roses but he be more ware shal lightly hurte him & prych him. Right so welth and richesses of this world weyith al amōges thornes of harde trauayle of thought of besynesse and of many perels. Bothe bodily and gostly For a man hath moche traueil in the gettyng, moche drede i the keppyng, moche bytter sorowe in the lesyng. Diues diuicias nō congregat absq̅ labore. Non tenet absq̅ metu. nec deserit absq̅ dolore. Whanne a mā hath trauayled all his lyf tyme to gadre gode, and to haue welth and worship in this worlde, it wole sone welke fade and fall away as the rose. Sodeynly cūmeth moreyn and his beestes dye, cūmeth aduersite and losse of catel. and at last deth takith away euery deel And who soo wole be besy to gadre the rose of worldly welth and of richesses, But he be right ware he shal hurte him bothe bodily & gostly And therfore seint Poule saith that they that couepte to be riche in this worlde, they falle in the feendes snare & into ful harde temptacions For these sylles seint James saith y̅ the riche mā shal passe away as the floure of the grasse & of the hay For whan the sonne shyneth hote on the hey it welkith and drieth & his floure fadith. and his beaute passithe Right so saith he the rich mā welkith and fadith in his weyis that is to say in his spuyng Jacobi. i.

448

Precepte.

Also worldly welth is lykned to the shadowe alway passing For al oure lyuyng in this worlde is but a passynge and a wantynge of lyght of heuene blisse In the middes of the day whan the sone is hyghest/thanne is the shadowe shortest Right so whan a man weneth to be butt in the myddes of his lyf.and is hyghest in welthe.&c in his pride/thanne is his lif shortest/for thanne men dye sonest in their moste prosperite And the nygher euen and the end of the day. the lenger is a mannys shadowe. Right so these worldly couetous men the lenger that they lyue and whanne they been att their lyues ende/thanne they thynke moste to lyue lenger Thanne they purchace/than they house/than they begyn to plete tyl their lyf passe. sodenly alway as the shadowe at euē Therfore mannes lyf is lykned to a slyder wey For whanne a man goth by a slyder wey/the more that he gasith aboute/and the ferther that he loketh fro him the soner and the harder he shalle fal But if he loke wel to his feet. and to his way/he may kepe him on lofte/& though he fal. he shall take no grete harme. Right so it farithe by the lyf of this worlde. It is so slyder. that there myghte neuer man ne woman passe by this

wey/ But at the laste he slydethe into seknesse and myscheif/and fel downe and dyed.or elles shal come to the same end And comō ly whanne men loke ferthest fro them self and thynke to lyue lengest/& begynne mooste to house. & to purchace/ and purpose many shrewyd turnes/ and to lyue moste in welth & in delices thāne they dye sonest and passe awaye. sodenly/ as a shadowe at euen. Example Crist tellith in the gospel Luce. xii. Ther was saithe Criste sumtyme a riche man and hadde in a yere a plenteous crop. on his londe. in somoche that he hadde nat houses ynowe to ley it in He thākyd nat god of his yift butt turnyd him to proude couetous thoughtis/and saide to him self/ what shal I doo I haue no housyng to ley in my corne & my gode I shal distroy myn olde bernys and garneris and mak newe lenger and larger. and stuffe the ful of gode. and thanne shalle I say to my soule. Nowe soule thou haste goode enough for many yeres/nowe take thy reste. Now ete and drynke and make feest So he thought al of his lyf in this worlde and nought of the lyf in the other worlde. Anone god saide to him. Fole this night fendes shall take thy soule from the whos thanne shal be alle the godes þ thou hast araped and gadryd to gidder He might say that they shulde be their/ that traueyſed nat therfore.

The x. chapter

Clerkes that trete of kynd say that the fox in wynter whanne he goth to ſeke his pray if he cũme to a froſen water/ he lyeth his ere downe to the yce/ ⁊ if he here any water rynnynge vndrenethe/ he woſe nat paſſe ouyr that/ for the yce is nat ſyker But he ſekith hym a nother ſiker way. Thus I wolde þ al ſynful couetouſe men dyd/ whan they goo about to ſeke their pray of falſe coueytyſe/ of falſ purchas/ or to rob ⁊ begyle any man of his gode.

Thanne I wolde they leyd their eye to the yce and thought how frele a mannes lyf is For as the rũmeth of the water and turnyd ayen to the water/ righte ſo al we came of the erthe. ⁊ ſhalle turne ayen to the erthe/ ⁊ if they wolde thus ley their ere to this yce/ they ſhuld here water renyng They ſhuld here ſay/ there dyeth a pope/ there a kinge/ there a pryce. there a duyke. there dyethe a buſſhoppe. there a knighte. there

a ſquyer. They ſhulde here that aſſone dieth the riche/ as the pore/ the grete as the ſmalle/ the yonge as the olde. Therfore holy wrytte ſaith. Omnes morimur et in terrã quaſi aqua dilabimur Alle we dye and ſlyde into the erthe as water ii. Regũ viii. Therfore ſeint Bernarde in his meditacion repreueth the proud couetouſe folk of this worlde ⁊ ſaith thus. Vbi ſunt amatores ſeculi. qui nobiſcum ãte pauca tẽpora. fuerunt. Telle me nowe ſaith he where ben nowe theſ lordes and leders/ theſe proude iettours and theſe falſe couetouſe men þ were here with vs within a fewe yeres where be they now bicome Ther is no thing of them left but aſſhe pouder and wormes Thake hede what they wer and what they been They were men as thou art. ete ⁊ dranke as thou doſte/ ⁊ led their daies in moche myrth/ and tuynklynge of an iye many of them ſanke downe into the pytt of hel where their fleſſhe is youen vnto wormes/ and where their ſoule is put into endleſſe peyne. What help them their beyne glorye/ their pompe/ their pryde/ their myrth/ theire gaame and glee. Where is nowe ther game and their laugh ynge/ their booſt and their highe berynge/ al is paſt as a ſhadowe

Precepte.

From grete myrth they ben fall into endeles sorowe, from luste & likyng they be fal into bitt payn from plente into endeles myschief Diues. These wordes stire me. and so they may many other syttes to sett by welthe and worsshyp of this worlde But wele is he yt may haue helpe of his gode after his dethe. and thanne fynde frendes and true atturneys Paup. But moch better he is yt hath grace to help him self bifore his deth. with his owne gode For one peny shal profyt more bifore his deth thanne twenty penys after. And more profiteth one candel bifore a man than xx. besynd hym Therfore seynt Lucye taught her moder to do almesse by her lyf, & nat abyde tyl after her deth, & said to her moder Here ye my counsepl It is no gift ful plesaunt to god what man or woma yeueth thing yt he may nat use hi self therfore if ye wole yt god be plesyd with youre gift, yeue ye to him thig yt ye may use your self For yt ye yeue i your diynge therfore ye yeue it, for ye may nat bere it wt you And therfore moder while ye lyue & haue helth of your body, yeue to god. that ye haue.

℟ The xi. chapter.

Whanne a man wole natt do for him self while he maye. though his executoures & his attourneys do nought for him it is no grete wondre For eche man & woman is moste holden to him self But it sarith oft by hem that dye & by their executoures as it dyd onys by ii. fooles. that duellyd in a lordes courte. The oone was a fole sage the other was a naturel fole. It bifel on a daye. they came to giddre into a Bakeshouse Whanne folke were at the ouen, and the ouen was glowig hote Thanne saide the fole sage to the naturel foole. Whether the ouene be nowe hote as it semyth Wole we assaye saide the other. ye saide the fole sage But which of us shal go into the ouene for to assaye Than saide the naturel fole. I shal go in, and thou shalt haue a Bolle fulle of water. and stonde att the ouene mouthe. And if I fele hete and I cry cast caste. anone cast the water after me, and quenche the fyre aboute me It shalbe done said the other. foole. Thanne the foole naturel toke the foole sage a Bolle fulle of water in his honde, and he wente & crepte into the ouene. And anone as he was in. he began to brenne. And anoone he

The nynth.

cryed caste cast. Whane the other fole sawe his foly he laughed soo entercly at his foly þ vnnethes he myght stonde on his fete Thane the fole in the ouen cried cast ind cast I brenne to deth Thanne the other fole aunswered. Brenne if thou brenne wylte, die if thou dye wylt, I laugh so that I may nat caste. And so the fole brent to dethe in the ouen. By tho ii. foles I vnderstonde men þ dye & their false executoures, for bothe been they fooles. For the executours been greate foles in that, þ they bynde theim to helle peyne, for their falshede But they that dye been more foles, in that that they trust more to other men, thā to themself. For whanne they shal crepe into purgatorye, that is hoter thanne any ouene, than they take to their executoures a bolle fulle of water in their hond that is to say golde and syluer, & other richesses, for to do almesse for them, & by almesdede. By messes syngyng and holy praiers refresshe them in their peynes, & kele the syre aboute theym But comonly whan they haue this boll of water in their honde, and haue the godes at their wylle, they laughe so and make so mery and fare so wele wt the godes of the dede þ they may no thing cast after

them, for they be ful lothe to forgo any of the godes And therwhiles the synful soule lyeth in purgatory. & suffrith ful moch wo & crieth after helpe night & day sayeng in this maner. Miseremini mei miseremini mei, saltē Vos amici mei. qr manus dn̄i tetigit me Job. xix. Haue ye mercy on me Haue ye mercy on me, namely ye my frendis, for the hōde of god ful harde hath touched me And whā they fynde no help of thē þ shuld helpe them they aske vengeaunce on them night & day. A greate clerke turpinus de gestis karoli tellith, þ the kyng Charles hadde with him a knighte in his ooste. a man of gode conscience, & whā he shulde die he cleppd to him his neuewe prayinge him that whan he were dede he shuld sel his hors and his harneys and do almesse. and doo synge thritty messes for his loue. He behight him wel But kastyd him ful euyl, and kepte it stylle to his owne vse. and dyd nat as he badde him doo. Whanne the thritty daies were passed I the night folowyng the knight apperyd I slepe to his neuewe & ayed him why he had nat don as he bad him do. Than he excused hī by diuerse besynesses þ he feyned nat that he hadde And he ayed his eme howe he faryde.

Precepte.

And than he aunswered and said I shal telle the howe I fare and howe thou shalt fare. All these thritty daies I haue be in purgatory and suffred ful moche woo. a peyne for defaute of helpe But nowe thankyd be god I am passed purgatorye and go up to heuene blisse withouten ende. But for thou woldest nat helpe me as I badde the/ therfore er this day mydmorwe thou shalt dye & goo to helle withouten ende. On the next day folowyng as he rode in the ooste on the same hors & told these dreempts to his felawes. as for a iape/ at mydmorowe came sodenly a blake skye with thundre and lightnyng and grete nobre of feendis in lyknesse of rauenys and rokes & bent him up fro the hors in the middes of the oost and flewe away with hym/ so yᵗ they sawe nomore of him tyl that came foure daies iourney thens. amonges the mountes of nauerne. There they founde him all to rent and drawen lith from lythe.

Butte his soule was drawen to helle. By his cote armure they knewe wele that it was the same man. Diues be a man dede he syndeth selwe freendes.

The vii. chapter.

Mauy I rede in Vita Barlaam. ther was a riche man whiche had iii. frendes The first frede & the secounde he loupd wᵗ al his hert/ but the thrid frende he lo upd lytel or nought. This man fel in suche a daūger ayeſt his king yᵗ al his gode was forfetted and escheyted to the king/ & hiself wenyd to haue been slayne Than he went to his furst frede yᵗ he loupde so moche prayng him of help. & yᵗ he wolde go to the kinge & speke for him and saue his lyf if he might Than he aunswerpd & saide Fare wele fast I knowe the nat I haue other felawes and freendes ynowe with whome I haue my myrthes & solace. Natheleſſe if thou be slayne I shal yeue the a shete to burye the in. Than he wente to the secounde frende yᵗ he loupd so moch prayng him also of helpe And he excused him & said I pray the haue me excused for I am so besi & in tap nat at ed to the But yit for olde felauship I shal go with the on way to the yate. Thanne went he to the thridde freende that he loupd soo lytel. and prayed hym of helpe. and saide. Leue frende I am aſhampd to speke to the for I haue been to the ful unkynde and litel loue shewpd to the Butt I pray the haue reuthe on me. and for goddes saake. helpe me in this neede. And thanne.

The nynth.

he aunswerpd and saide. Leue frende welcome be thou/ and be of goode comforte/ for I am thy frende and wole be thy freende/ & to helpe the that I may do/ thou shalt fynde me redy. And anone he went and dyd so and spake to the kynge that he sauyd his lyf. and delyuered him oute of al his daunger. Diues. So it fareth these daies as longe as a man is in welthe/ so longe he shall haue fredes ynowe to take of hi what they may and to flater him/ and to please him. But if he begynne to go donwarde/ thanne fyndeth he felw freendes and many enemyes. Therfore saith the wyseman. Tempore felici multi numerantur amici. Cum fortuna perit nullus amicus erit. In tyme of welth a mā shal fynde fredes ynowe But whāne richesses & hap is gone. he shal fynde felw frendes and fele fone. Say forth thy tale. Pauper. By this riche man I vnderstōde euery man yt hath richesses and goodes of this world By his furst frende þ he loued so moche/ whiche paue hym But a shete to be buryed in/ I vnderstōde the worlde/ which world ly mē loue so moche/ that for loue therof they trauayle nyghte & day & put them in peril of body & soule/ & oft lese them self both bo

dy & soule. And yit at the last vnnethes yeueth it to them a shete to be buryed in For many of them whanne they die haue lesse thanne nought And if they haue ought yit their executoures wole saye that they haue noughte/ & þ they owe more than they haue By the seconde frende þ wente wt him to the pate I vnderstōde a mannys wyf/ his children and his bodily frendes And a womānes husbonde. her children. & her bodily frendes/ whiche whanne they ben dede/ shal go with them on wey to the pate and brynge thē to their graue/ & pauenture stōde and wepe on them But be man. or woman dede and doſuen vndre clay/ he is sone forjeten/ and oute of mynde passed alwaye Be the belles rūge and the messe sūge he is sone forjeten. Vnnethes shall he fynde oone freende that wole synge for him one messe vnnethes in the yere. By the thridde frende whiche he loued so lytel. and whiche halpe hym att his nede. I vnderstonde almesse dede. whiche the worldely coueytouse men loue fulle lytell. And yit att the dredeful doome whanne they shall stonde att the barre bifore the soueraigne iuge. Crist Ihesu/ thanne almessedede shalbe the beste frende. that they ſhal haue. For that ſhal ſpeke for them and pray for hem and ſaue hem if they ſhalbe ſaued And therfore ſalomon ſaithe Concluſde elimoſinam in ſinu paupis, et ipſa pro te exoraB it aB omni malo Eccleſiaſtici. xxix. Therfore leue frende do ye as Tobye taught his ſonne. Ex ſubſtancia tua fac elimoſinam. Do almeſſe of thy goode & of thy catel. and nyl thou turne away thy face from any pore man, & as thou might be thou merciable.

If thou haue mooche yeue thou mooche. Butt and if thou haue but lytel ſtudye thou to yeue litel with good wylle For tha thou treſoureſt to the a grete pift in the day of nede For almeſſe deliuereth ſoules from euery ſynne and from dethe, and ſuffreth nat the ſoule to go into derknes Tobie quarto.

The viii. chapter.
Diues To whom ſhal I do my almeſſe. Paup. Do as Criſt biddeth i the goſpel. Of petenti te tribue. yeue to euery nedye & ayiſh the, if thou might Luce vi. Diues. Cōtra Criſt in the goſpel Luce viii. ſaith thus. Whā thou makeſt a feſt nyl thou clepe therto thy frendes, thy nigh boures, thy coſyns and riche mē. But clepe thou pore mē feble blid and halt, By which wordes it ſemyth to me & I ſhuld do none almeſſe But to pore & ben feble blid & halt Paup Criſt forBeditth nat men to Bid their frēdes & their niȝhBoures & riche men to the feeſt But he Bad hem & they ſhuld nat only Byd their frēdes & the riche. But alſo pore folk, nedy & feBle. Alſo he Bad mē ſhulde nat Byd the riche folke & their frendes to feeſt with no wycked intencion. I hope of falſe wynnyng, for pōpe, for glutony, for lecchery, or to gete them a grete worldly name. But principaly for to noriſhe pece & charite And in token & feſtis made with gode itencion Both to riche & pore Ben pleſaunt to god. criſte clepith Bo al riche & pore to the endleſſe feeſt. And criſt him ſelf though he were pore. in our e mahede, he was nat feBle Blyndene halt Whā the phariſe to whō he ſayde tho wordes Bad hym to mete, ne whan he was at the Brydales with his moder in the chane of galile, ne whan mary magdaleyn & her ſuſtre martha, & zacheus made hī grete feeſtes, & yit they were pryſed of Criſt for ther dedys, and al that fedde Cryſte. and his apoſtles, and his diſciples Whanne they Wente about the worlde preching and teching Been prayſyde. And yitt the

apostlees and his disciples/ were strong men neither blynde ne halt And crist him self fedde his disciples neither blynde ne halte And sumtyme he fedde iiii. thousand of men/ sumtyme fyue thousande that folowed him fro cūtre to cūtre to here his prechyng/ and to se the woundres that he dyd/ & yit were they nat blynd ne halt For as the gospel saith he made them hole of their bodily sekenesse/ or he fed them Luce. ix. et M'. viii Also tho ii. disciples þ toke criste to herborowe in the lykenesse of a pilgryme on esterne day at euyn Ben praysed/ and yit was he neither blynde ne halt. Also abraham and Loth and many other holy men resceyued aungels in the liknesse of worshipful men neither blynde ne lame to mete and herborowe And seynt Petyr resceyued knightes & worshipful men to mete and to herborowe which came to him on message from the grete lorde cornely/ as we rede in holy wrytt/ actuū ix. c. And alle these been prised of god/ and had moch thanke of god for their almesdede. Therfore I saide firste Crist badde that men shuld do almes to al that nede bothe frende and foo And the apostle biddeth if thyne enemye haue hūgre fede him/ if he haue thurste. yeue him

drynke. The charite of cristen faith outaketh no persone man ne woman state ne degre/ ne secte. hethen ne criste/ from almesdede whanne they had nede. But us must haue pyte on all/ and helpe all at oure power Natheleese us must kepe ordre in yeuynge and takyng hede to the cause/ and to the maner of nede in theym. that we yeue almesse to. For why some be pore by their wylle and some ayenst their wylle And they þ ben pore by their wylle sūme ben pore for the loue of god/ and sūme for the loue of the worlde. They that been pore for the loue of god must be holpen passing other for their pouertie is medeful parfyte and vertuous. They þ been pore wylfully nat for god. But for the worlde. as the romanes were/ and as these daies moche folke dispytte them of their owne gode and tak it to ther children to make them greate in this worlde/ and moch folke take so moch hede to other mennys profyte/ that they take none hede to them self/ and so falle in pouerte and in nede/ such pore folk must principaly be holpen of them/ to whome their godes profityd and rather helpe theym thanne other. that been pore ayenst their wyll. But they sh al nat be putte bifore

Precepte.

them that be poze for the loue of god but the nede be the moze.

The ḋliiii. chapter

Of them that be poze apēst their wylle/ sume ben poze by fortune/ by myſauentures as they to whō fortune ſerueth nat at their wylle/ ne god multiplyeth nat their gode as thẽy wolde and that/ þ they haue they leſe by myſauentures/ and by the dome of god. And ſume been poze only by ſynne/ and for the loue of ſyn as they that waſt their gode in lechery and glutonye/ in pride and pleyyng/ and in myſuſe at the dyce in ryot and in vanite. Suche poze folke been laſte in the ozdre of almeſſe doynge/ but their nede be the moze And natḣleſſe if they haue pacience with their pouerte they ſhal haue mede for their pacience. if they repente theym. for their myſdedys. And in the ſame maner ſume been feble blynde. ꝇ lame for goddes cauſe ꝇ for goddes loue. Sume ayenſt their wyl by courſe of kynde. Sume ayēſt ther wyl for loue of ſynne as theves fighters baratoures/ whiche in fight and barett leſe their iyen. their feet/ their hondes/ and ofte ben punyſſhed by the lawe. God forbede þ ſuche poze folk blynde

ꝇ halt ſhuld be put in the ozdre of almes doing bifoze them þ be pore ꝇ feble by vertue. ꝇ for goddes ſake. Suche ſhalbe holpen natt to luſte of their fleſſhe/ ne to doo them worſhip/ but oonly to ſaue their kynde. tyl the dome of god paſſe vpon hem by preſſe of lawe ꝇ by goddes myniſtres. Diues. Moche folke thynke þ it is none almeſſe to do gode to ſuche folk. Pauper. phis forſothe For god woſe þ men help them/ ꝇ at the dome he ſhal ſay I was in priſone ꝇ ye viſited me/ ꝇ þ ye dyd to the leeſt of myne ye dyd it to me. Diues. Seint auſtyn de verbis dñi ſermone xxxv. ſaith. þ' god ſhal ſay the wozdes to them þ be poze in ſpiryt ꝇ lowe of hert/ and þ ſuche been cleppyd the brethernе of Criſt and leeſt for lowneſſe by whiche they ſet leeſt by them ſelf Paup. They ben no folke pore in ſpirite. But they that be poze for goddes ſake And ſo ſeint auſtyne ſhewyth there þ god ſhal accept moze the almes þ is done to them þ ben poze for goddes ſake. than to them þ been poze ayenſte their wylle ꝇ for ſynne ſake. what the concluſion alle though is be ſothe. yitt me thynketh þ Criſte ſhal ſay tho wozdes for tho wozdes for the almeſſe that he hathe done to al maner poze men both

The nynthe.

parfyte and Vnpfyte. For thanne he shal yeld mede for euery gode dede. For why wycked doers and synful pore men been cleppd the leest of goddes menye, for they be leest set by in the court of heuene. And therfore he saith in the gospel that who soo brekith one of his leest comaundementes and techich other by word or by euyl ensample, so to breke his comaundmentes he shalbe cleppd leeste in the kingdome of heuenes. God shal shewe at the dome grete pite and moche mercy, & banne thing that is done for his sake to his enemyes and to his leest seruantes, moste vnworthy, he shal accept it & rewarde it as it were done to his owne pfone, and say I thank you, For that ye did to the leest of myne, ye dydit to me. Diues. Why shal he clepe them bretherne that bi leest worthye, and many of theym to whō the almesse was done shalbe dampned. Pauper Er he shalle yeue the sentence of dampnacion he shal clepe al men bretherne for sybnesse of kynde. For in that he is man he is brother to vs al by sybnesse of kynd, but nat by grace ne by blysse, but only to them that ben in grace. That the meke iuge shal clepe alle men bretherne to confort of them that shalbe saued, and to grete discon-

forte of them that shalbe dampned. Whanne they shal see the meke iuge nat forȝete the brotherhede ne sybnesse in kynde. Which he hath w' them, and yit catched and in maner copellyd by his ryghtfulnesse to dampne theym. Grete mater shal they haue than to sygh and sorowe, whan they shal knowe their synnes so greeuous and so grete. and their vnkyndnesse so moche, that ther oure brother so meke a iuge muste dampne them. Diues. This opinion is more plesaunt to ryche men and to other synful wrecches. that hope than to be holpen by almesdede. For in many cuntrees. been but felwe pore folk in spirit. ne by their wyll felwe that forsaken the worlde for goddes sake. But many ther be that the worlde hath forsake, many that for synne ben ful pore, and many for their mysdedis lye bounde in pryson in grete pouert, hungre colde and bytter peynes. And to suche folke in many cuntrees men doo moste comonly their almes, I hope to be thankyd and rewardyd, therfore at the laste dome Paup They shalbe thanked and be medyd. therfore as I sayde firste. & sithen Criste ryghtful iuge shalle thanne thank men for the almes that they dyd for his loue to his

458

Precepte.

enemyes & wycked doers as many suche ben/ moche more he shal thanke them for the almesse that they dyd to his frendis and to his true seruauntes. And sithen they shalbe dampned that wolde nat yeue to his enemyes at nede. for his sake moche soner shal they be dampned þ wold nat helpe his frendes and his true seruauntes at nede for his sake. þ putt thē self for his loue to pouert and moche trauayle for helpe of mannes soule And if it be so plesaunt and medfull to yeue almesse to suche pore folke forsakinge the worlde/ of whiche many neither shalbe rescepued into endlesse tabernacles of blisse/ neither shall rescepue into that blisse. moche more it is plesaūt to god and meritorie to help them that ben pore in spirite. and in wyll for the loue of god. For as Crist saith in the gospell. the kigdome of heuenes is theirs and it is grauntyd to them to rescepue folk that haue holpen thē into endlesse tabernacles.

The .yi. chapter

And therfore leue freēd wytype it wele þ if man or womā haue more wyll to yeue to them that been pore ayenst their wylle and for the loue of synne/ thanne for to yeue to them that ben pore for goddes sake. and for goddes cause. they synne ful greuously. and lese the mede of their almesse in that they putt goddes enemyes bifore his frendes/ and vice bifore vertue. And therfore ye shal releue al the pore and nedy as ye may/ but principaly them that be nedy and pore for goddes sake & by wey of vertue. For if ye secue by false opinion the more almes. for the lesse. Whanne ye may doo bothe in gode maner/ ye lese mede bothe for the more and for the lesse. Therfore seint austyn saith thus. Thou shalt nat do to the pore precheoure of goddes worde. as thou dost to the begger passig by the wey. To the begger thou yeuest. for Crist biddith the that thou yeue to eche that ayith the. Butt to the pore precheoure thou owyst to yeue though he aye the nat. And therfore loke that the pore pechour goddes knight nede nat to aye the For if he nede to aye for thy defaute/ and thy defaute & thy laccheffe/ he shewit the the dampnable or he aye And right as it is saide of the begger. that sekith the/ yeue thou euery man that ayith the/ so it is saide of him that thou owyst to seke Let thyne almesse swete in thyne honde/ tyl thou fynd him to whō

H ii.

The nynthe.

thou muste yeue. ¶yeue thou to euery mā that axith the/ But moche rather and more yeue to goddes seruauntes/ to the knight of criste though he axe nat. Hec au-gustinus. et ponitur in glosa sup iſtud ⁊i. Producens fenū lumentis. And therfore saith the ſall e. that who so wol nat yeue almes to men that folowe the lyf of the apostles ī pouert and to the pore prechours for their nedeful vse. he dampneth him self. ⱱ̄i. q̄. i. apſicis. For as the apostle saith it is due dett to the pore prechour of goddes worde to lyue by his p̄chyng Therfore Reynylde de ho spīlitate ordinand. septh þ some aye almesse of dette, sūme only for nede to sustepne the bodye. ¶They that axe almesse of dett eith r̄ they be knowen for suche, or nat knowen for suche If they be knowen for suche they must ned ly be holpen. If they be nat knowen, they shalbe exampned wisely whether it be as they say. For it were grete peryl to sett them if it be so. For in that they yeue gostly thinges bodily thinges be due dett to them, as saith poule ⁊ the lawe. vlii. distinctione quiesca'. And if they axe only for sustenāce of the body. either thou might peue al for stede and tyme, either thou might nat peue all If thou

mayst peue al, thou oweſt to peue al after the nede that they pretende, and after their state we ſe ruled. Take ensample of Abraham and Loth which receyued folke indifferently to hospitalite a so they receyued āngelis And if they hadde putt sūme awaye, pauēture they shuld haue put all ey aungelis for men As saith Crisoſtom. sup epiſtm̄ ad hebreon. Therfore he saith that god shall nat yeld the thy mede, for the gode lyf of them which thou resceyueſt, But for thy gode wylle, and for the worship that thou dost to the for goddes sake, for thy mercy and thy godenesse. And therfore the lawe saith, that mē owe to yeue their almesse to cursed folk. ⁊ to synful folk. be they neuir so wycked. ⱱ̄i. q̄. iii. q̄m multos. et ⱱ. lxxxⱱi. pasce ⁊c. nō satis in fine. But they do the worse, for yᵉ they ben syker of their lyuelode. For as seint austeyn saith. if the sinner do the worse for mennyp almesse, it is better to withdraw e it from him thāne to yeue it him. B. q̄. ⱱ. nō oſs. Natheleſſe if he be in ⱱtter nede, he muſt be holpē. di. lxxxⱱi. pasce.

¶The xi. chapter.

And in case it han thou mizt nat helpe alle, thou muſte

Precepte.

take hede to ỹ thinges. To seith cause/ place. tyme. maner. nede. neighnesse of blode. ⁊ of affinite. age/ feblenesse. noblep. First tak hede hede to feith/ for I caas thou shalt put a cristen man bifore an hethen ma. Also take hede to the cause of his neede/ whether he is cost to nede for goddes cause. or by canse of synne Take hede also to the place as whan the rightful man is turmentyd in prison for dett/ ⁊ helpe him if thou may For sith we be boude to help al if we may/ moche more we be bou den to helpe the rightfull man/ ⁊ woman. Also take heede to the tyme/ for if he gete no thinge of the in tyme of his tribulacion, and in tyme of pell whanne he is led to his deth vnrightfully/ but thou settyst more by thy money. than thou dost by his lyf/ it is no light synne Also take hede to the maner of peuing/ that thou peue so one day that thou may peue a nother day/⁊ so to one that thou may peue to a nother. Butt thou wylte forsake the worlde alle at onys for goddes sake and for ỹ pfeccion Also take hede to nede ⁊ peue them after that they haue nede Also take hede to nighnesse of blode and of affinite For by wey of kynde they must be holpen ra ther thanne straugers if the nede

of bothe be euen Also take heede to age/ for old folk muste be put bifore yonge folke. Also ta ke hede to the feblenesse. for blide ⁊ lame and other feble folk must be holpen rather than hole folke. in euen nede Also take hede to ye noblep of the psone/namely I thē ꝟ withoutᵉ synne ben falle to po uertie and myschepf/ for comon ly suche ben shamfast to axe. di. lxxx vi. Non satis. Et eadᵐ di cit ambꝛ. libro de officiis vnde Versus. Causa/ fides. tēpus. sā guis/ locus/ ac modus etas De bilis ingenius/ Vetitudus factus egenᵘ. Hiis bona psonis prudēs erogare teneris. And seynt Au styne accordeth therto in. de doc trina xpiana libro primo c.decīo Diues. I suppose I mette wᵗ li. pore men straungers elyke ne dye/ bothe they aye/ and I haue nought that I may peue but on ly to the one of them. Pauper Seint Austyn in the same place. Biddeth that thou shuldest thāne peue it by lott. Diues. I assent. say forth what thou wylt Paup Also in thy peuyng thou must ta ke hede to the holpnes and to the profitablenesse/ and the nighnes of the psone that nedith help For to the holpen man and to him pat is or hath ben more profitable to to the compnte if he nede/ thou

The nynthe.

ſhalt peue rather and better/ thā to a pſone nigh of kyn or of affinite nat ſo holy ne ſo profitable. But thou haue the more ſpecialle cure of hym/ and but he be in the greter nede. Also to them that be pore for criſtis ſake and to the pore prechoures that preche principally for the worſhip of god and helpe of mannes ſoule. puttyng alway as ſpices of falſe couetiſe. thou ſhalt peue them that is nedeful to them after the tyme and after thy power, as to diſciples of criſt But to other pore folk that been pore ayenſt their wylle whiche the worlde hath forſake/ nat they the worlde/ it ſuffiſeth to peue of thy relif honeſt a holeſome. For it is ſynne to peue deyntees to ſuche pore comē beggers whā they ben nat conuenient to them As the lawe ſaith. di. xxv. Inſt. S. multi. et di. pli. Non cogant Of other pore men ſpekith ſeynt auſtyne. in a ſermone of clerkes lyf and ſaith thus If the rich mā haue but one child/ wene he that criſt be his other childe. If he haue two childrē/ wene he that criſt be the thrid. If he haue y. make he Criſt the elleuenth. that is ſay peue he to criſt that he ſhuld ſpēd on the elleuenth. xiiii. q ii. ſi quis traſcitur. And thus leue frende ye may ſe y riche men whiche be god

des reues and goddes baylies owe to ordeyne for them that ben pore for goddes ſone and wylfully haue forſaken the worlde for his ſake that they haue no nede But to comen beggers and nedy folk whiche the worlde hath forſake. it ſuffiſeth ſo to helpe theym and to peue hem that they periſſh nat Alſo leue frende as ſaith ſeint auſtyn in the boke of the cite of god li. 20. xvi. cᵒ. xxvi. they that wol nat amende their lyf. ne forſake their grete ſynnes/ done no pleaſaunt almeſſe. For why ſaith he. almeſſe ſhulde be done to gett foryeueneſſe of ſynnes that be paſt. nat to gette leue to duelle ſtyl in ſynne/ and to do a mys.

Here endith the .ix. precepte.
And begynneth the tenthe.

Dues. Me thynketh thy ſpeche ſtyplſulle. gode a proufitable/ a wele cōfermyd by grete auctorite. I thāke the for thy wordes and thy gode informacion in the nynthe precepte. Nowe I praye the enfourme me in the tenthe cōmaundment Pauper. The tenthe commaundmente is this. Non deſiderabis vxorem primi tui/nō seruū/nō ancillā. nō Bouē/nō asinū/nec omīa que illius sunt. Exodi. xx. Thou shalt nat desire thy neighbours wyf/nat his seruaūt nat his may den. nat his oxe/nat his asse/ne no thinge that to him longith. In the nynthe cōmaundemente. god forbidith couetise of a nother mannes gode nat mouable. In this laste he forbedith all maner false couetise of a nother mānes gode meuable Also in the nynthe pcept he forbedith couetise of the iye/ in this last principaly he for/ bedith couetise of the flessh. And therfore saith seynt austyne that the tenthe pcepte is this allone. thou shalt nat desire thy nighbou res wif. And all þ folowith after Whāne he saith nat his seruaūte. nat his oxe ne his asse/ne no thig þ to him logith/ it is of the nynth pcepte. And it is also a newe for/ bedynge of all maner mys coue= tise. Bothe of thing meuable and nat meuable bothe of couetise of the iye & of the flessh. And therfoꝛ if a may myscouept a nother mā nes seruaunt/ or his Wyf/ or his childe/ as for possession. and set= upce/ it is apenst the nynthe pres cepte/ and principally apenst co/ uetise of the iye And if he couepte theym for mysluste of the flesshe. thanne it is apenst the tenthe cō= maundement. Diues. I hope þ nat euery miscouetise is dedely synne apenst goddes precept For couetise both of the iye and of the flesshe fallith lightly in mannes hert And it is nat in our power al Waye to flee thoughtes of fals co uetise For as seynt poule saith. the flesshe couetith alway apenst the spirite Pauper. God forbe= dith nat such couetise that is nat in oure power to flee/ but he for= bedith alle maner myscouetyse. With assent to pfourme it a longe syking therin And therfore thou/ ghe men do nat in dede their fals couetise/ if they be in Wyl to doo it in dede if they might or durste. for drede of the World/ than they synne dedly apenst goddes heest. Diues Sith it is so that false co uetise with assent and wyll to p= fourme/ it is dedly synne/ and a= penst goddes pcepte/ & as seynte poule saith/ It is roote & Begyn= nyng of euery euyl. Radix oīm malorum est cupiditas. Sithen Wyckedwylle goth Bifore Wyc= ked dede/Why puttith nat god ye forbeding of fals couetise and of Wyckedwyll. in the ordre of ten. cōmaūdemētes bifore the forBe/ dyng of the dede of lecherye/ and of thefte/ sithen that false couetī/ se and euyl wylle is Begynnynge of Both. For Wycked wylle goth

H iiii.

463

The tenth.

biforē euery syn in somoche/ȳⁿne were nat wycked wyll. ther shuld no synne be. ¶Pauper. God gaue the tenthe commaundemente to the people as soueryne techer and as soueraigne leche. And euery teching must begynne at thinges that been moste easy to knowe/ and euery cut and lechecraft bothe of body and of soule muste begynne there the seknesseis felt moost greuous. ¶And for as moche as the Unwise peple hath more knowynge þ my dede was synne thanne myswylle/ and felt them more agreuyd by my dede than myswylle/ therfore god forbedith first the dede of false couetyse/ & after he forbedith the wyll and the assent to myscouetyse. ¶Diues. yit contra te God forbedith no thinge but synne. & synne of dede and wylle is all one. For synne begynneth at euyl wylle & endith in euyl dede. ¶As we rede in the seconde boke of kinges/ of kinge Dauid. Firste he desired the faire woman Bersabee. that was wyf to the true knighte Urie/ and fro that wycked desire he felle into auoutre/ and from auoutrie into glotonye/ and from glotonye into false traytourye/ & from traytourye into murdre/ and manslaughter/ and blasphempe. and to dispisyng of goddes high maieste/ Wherfore god punysshed him full harde/ for the childe so mys gote dyed sone after the birth. And his sonne Absolon lay openly by his wyues i sight of the people and droue him oute of his kyngdome. His other sone Amnsaye by his owne suster. thamar. And therfore absolon her brother and his sleue him. And salomon his sone slewe his brother Adony. And so dauid had litel ioy of his children/ bicause of his auoutrye. And was ther neuir after stabilite i his kingdome for þ auoutrye and murdre/ & other synnes þ came al of his wycked desire & euyl wyll/ for þ he so mys desired another mannes wyf. ayenst the hest of god whan he saith Non desidrabis vxorē ꝓximi tui. ¶Thou shalt nat desire thy neighboures wyf. Pauȳ. Whan wycked dede is knyt to wycked wyll/ it is one synne/ and bothe been forboden by the same comaundmēt in whiche he forbedith lechery & thefte. But whāne the wyl & the assente be nat doone in dede. thanne the synne stondeth only in euyl wyl & suche syn principaly is forbode by these ii. last comautdmentes in whiche god shewith openly þ euyl wyll withouten the dede is dedely synne.

¶The ii. chapter.

Precepte.

Dives. Whan god gaue the commaundementis in the monte of synay to moyses/there he forbade first couetise of the iye But whan moyses rehersid ayen the lawe to the children of israel. Whane they shulde entre into the londe of biheest/there moyses for bad first couetise of flesshe & puttith it bifore. as we rede Deutro. v. c. What was cause of this diuersite. Paup. Whan god gaue them the lawe in the mount of synay. they were in desert in greate myscheif/ and therfore they were more inclyned to robberye thane to lecherye. And therfore god for that tyme forbedith them first couetise of the iye rather than couetise of the flesshe But whan moyses rehercyd ayen the lawe to theim in his laste daies/ they were att the entre of the lode of biheest in a ful plenteuous cuntre/ where they were more enclyned to lecherye. for welfare than to robbery for mysfare And therfor moyses for that tyme forbade them first couetise. of the flesshe & thanne couetise of the iye. and of richesse Another skylle leue frende is this For all the pilgrymage of the childrē of israel pl. yere in desert betokneth our pilgrymage here i this world from oure begynnyng ūto oure endynge In token than that mā and woman in his youthe and in his begynnynge is sonner temptyde to couetise of the iye and of worldly gode/ thanne couetise of the flesshe/ and in his eldyng and in his age latter temptyd to. couetyse of the iye and of worldsly go/ de thanne to couetise of the flessh for in olde folk whanne al other temptaciones cese/ thanne is teptacion of couetyse of the iye and of worldly gode moost breme.

For righte as their bodye by age nighith to the erthe/ so their herte cleueth thanne mooste to erthlye thinges. And therfore in the begynnyng of their pilgrymage in deserte as to begynnynge folke. god forbadde them firste and principally couetise of the iye/ and in the ende of their pilgramage. as to folke nigh their ende/ he forbedeth them principaly and laste/ & moost openly withouten ofte rehersynge couetise of the iye. For comonly the more that men nigh ther ēde the more couetouse they been.

The iii. chapter.

Diues Thy skylles be gode say forth what thou wylte Pauper. God in the sixte biheest forbidith the dede of lechery and of spousebrech. and in this heest he forbedith the wylle. and the cōsent of hert to lecherie. and

465

The tenthe.

to spousebrecke. For as the dede of lechery is dedly synne, soo is the foule consent and the desyre of hert dedly synne. For as Crist saith in the gospel M'. v. He that seeth a woman & coueytith her by desire to doo lechery with her, he hath do lechery in his hert, though he do it nat in dede. And therfore eche man shulde take hede bisyly what thoughtes entre ito his hert & if any thoughtes ben about to drawe the reson of his soule to consent to synne, anone put he awey tho thoughtes mightyly, & let hi think on the bytter peynes þ crist suffred in his syde, hondes & feet & so turne his myssust into deuocion of cristes passion, & quenche the brennyng thoughtes of lichery with the blode and the water þ ranne out of cristes side, whan his hert was clouen a two w' þ sharp spere, & thynk on þ endles loue þ cryst shewyd than to him & to all mankynde. And so to turne his foule stinkinge loue þ he begynneth to falle in shame & shenship, ito the swete clene loue of ihū ful of ioye & worship. Tellith the master of kynd. li. vii. þ ther is a bird in egipt þ is cleppd a pellicane.

And of all foulis he is moost chere ouir his briddes & moste loueth tho. Ther is a grete enemyte bitwene him & the adder, wherfor

the adder waiteth whan the pellicane is oute of his neste to seeke mete for him & for his briddes, & than he gothe into the nest of the pellicane, & stingith his briddes. & enuenemyth them & sleeth them. Whā the pellicane cūmeth ayen. & fyndeth his briddes thus slayn he maketh moch sorowe & mone. & by wey of kynde thre daies and thre nightes he morneth for deth of his briddes. And at the thridde daies ende he settith him ayen ouir his briddes & with his bylle. he smytith him self in the syde, & settith his bode ful downe on the briddes. And anone as the blode toucheth his briddes, anoone by wey of kynde & by vertue of the blode they quyken ayen, & risen from dethe to lyf. By this pellicane b loueth soo wele his briddes. is vnderstonde Crist ihū goddes sonne þ loueth manes soule & wo mans more than euir dyd the pellicane his briddes. And he saithe hiself Similis factus sū pellicano solitudiniis. I am made like to the pellicaue of deserte. By the birdes I vndstōde adā. eue & all mākynd. By the nest I vndstōd the blisse of paradise For right as birdes be brouʒt forth i þe nest, so mākynde had his begynnynge, & was brought fortthe in paradise. By the adder I vndstōd the feed

Precepte.

whiche appered in the lykenesse of an adder. to eue a stange her full euyl a ad alſo w' his wyched ſō dyng a ſleweth them bothe body. a ſoul. And nat only he ſleweth them but alſo he ſleweth al mankynde i them/ For if adam hadde nat ſyn ned/ we ſhulde neuir haue dyed. ne haue wyſte of woo. Wherfore this pellicane Jeſus criſt ſeynge the myſcheif of mankynde was fal in be gyle of the feed/ he had ruth on mankynde. And for grete lo ueⱪ he had to mankynde/ as ſeint Poule ſaith. he auentiſſhed hym ſelf a toke fleſſh and blode of the mayden marye/ a bicame man in the lykeneſſe of a ſeruaunt/ and in oure maʒede. a in oure kynde ſuf fred to be taken and be bounde a beten/ forſpitted/ diſpyſed biſcour gyd at the pyler. be crowned with thornes/ be naled to the tree hon des a feet/ a hangyd on the croſſe as a theef amonges theuys/ a be ſtoge to the herte with the ſharpe ſpere. a ſo dyed bytter deth/ al for oure gilt a nat for his gilt. for he dyd neuir amyſſe in worde. ne in dede. as ſaith ſeint petyr in his py ſtel And thus for oure loue ⱪ ben to bliſful vnkynde/ he ſhed his p̄ cio' blode out of euery pte of his bliſful body borne of the mayde. And his Iner hert blode he ſhed ſo to waſſhe vs fro our ſynnes/ a to rayſe vs fro the dethe of ſyn into the lyf of grace. And after fro bo dily deth/ into the lyf of endleſſe bliſſe Therfore ſeint John ſaith. Dilexit nos. a lauit nos. a pctio ntis i ſāguine ſuo. apoc. i. c. He louyd vs ſo moche. ⱶ he waſſhed vs from our ſynnes w' his p̄cio' blode. Loue droue hi downe fro heuen ito erthe. loue led hym into the maydens boſom a brought hi into this wycked worlde Loue bode hi i cradyl a wode hym i clou tes ful pore a leyde hi in an oye ſtalle Loue heelde hym here in ſo rowe a care higre a thriſt a moch trauayl. xxxii. yere a more Atte laſte loue toke hi a bode hi a ſett him at the barre bifore the ſynful iuſtice poilce pylate loue ſeyde him on the croſſe a nayled him to the tre Loue led him to his dethe. a cleef his hert a two. And for whoſe loue leeue frende forſoth for loue of you a of me a of other ſynful wretches ⱶ neuir dyd hym gode but offendyd him nygte a day a been to him full vnkynde.

Therfore he may wele ſay the wordes that ſalomon ſaide For tis eſt vt mors dilectio Cant viii Loue is ſtronge as dethe yhe for ſothe moche ſtrenger than dethe. For loue ledde his lyf to his deth a he that neuir mygt die by wey of kynde. loue made him die for mankynde. And ſo ſaith ſalomō there. Broondes of his loue.

ben brondes of fire and of flames. both For the loue that he shewed to mankynde/ & also for the loue that we ought to shewe to hym. For right as the hete of the sunne. with his light whan he shyneth i the fyre in the house/ wastith the fyre and quenchith it/ so the loue of god and the endlesse charite of his passion if it shone in mannes soule with his hete it shulde quesche and waste the broondes & the fyre of lechery brennyng in mannes soule by foule luste and wycked desire. And therfore he sayth to euery cristen soule Pone me ut signaculū sup cor tuū Cant. viii Sett me as a token vpon thyne hert And seint poule saithe Spū luxurie & desidia carnis nō pficietis. ad gala. v. Goo ye with the the holy hoste þ is cleppyd well of gostly fire/ & ye shal nat do the desire of the flesshe For deuocion. & mynd of cristis passion is the best remedy ayēst tēptaciō of lechery

The liiii.. chapter

Also it is a gode remedye to man to thike on his deth & on his freelte & on the bitter peynes of helle euirlastyng/ & of the hygh offence of god/ & of the endelesse ioyes þ they lese/ if they assēt to lechery Therfor salomō saith Memorare nouissima tua & in eternū nō peccabis. Ecclesiastici vii. Thynke on thy last thinges & thou shalt neuir do synne. Ech man and woman/ shulde be wat þ neither by nyce contenaunce ne by foly speche/ ne by nyce arape. of body they stire any mā or womā to lechery. And though resonable arape and honestie be cōmendyd bothe in mā and womā after their state reuled by goddes lawe and reason/ & so they muste be wele ware that by suche arape they falle nat in pride ne in lechery. ne stire other to lecherye. wylsyng and wepynge. We rede in vitis patrum' that ther was a holy womā whose name was alexandre. and she was a ful faire woman/ and whānne she herde. saye that a man was fallen into harde temptacion of lecherye bycause of her beaute/ she closed her self in an house and neuir wolde se man after. ne come oute of þe house/ but toke her lyuynge in to her by a smalle wykket whē ayd her why she dyd so And she said that she hadde leuyr to shytte her self all quycke in the graue/ than to harme any soule þ god maade to his lyknesse/ and boughte soo dere with his preciouse bloode.

We rede also in the lif of seynte Bride, þ a man wolde haue weddyd her for her beaute, & she prayed god þ he wold sed her sume blemysshynge of her face, wherby þt mannes temptacion myght cese. Anoon her one iye braste oute of her hede, wherfore her fader made her a nunne, as a womān vnable to the world. And whan she was made a nunne and hadde forsake the worlde, anone she had her iye and her sight ayen. Thus shulde wymen besily kepe them in chastite & clennesse, maydens in chastite of maydenhode, widowes in chastite of widowehode, wyues in chastite of wedloc, & kepe ther body truly to their husbondes, & so the husbōdes truly to their wyues. Forsothe it is a dedly syn i̇ a man, to despre a nother mannes wyf or his mayden or his dough ter, to flesshely luste. Moch more it is dedly synne to opresse them, and defoule them & lye by them.

The 8. chapter.
Dvces. Seynt poule saith, þ the flesshe desireth & coueitith alway anenst the soule. And it is ful harde to withstonde his lustis & his desires. Paul therfore mā shuld gouerne & chastise his body, as a gode mā of armes gouerneth & chastiseth his horse,

For as Job saith Al oure spulge vpon erth, is knighthode & fightyng apenst the feende the world & the flesshe Job vii. And in this batayle oure bodye is oure horse which we muste chastise & rule, as a knight doth his horse. For if the horse be to proude & cupltacched, he may lightly lese his master & be cause of his dethe. And if he be tame to his maister, & wele tacched, it shall do hi worshyp, & helpe him at nede & in caas saue his lyf. Thre thinges been nedeful to the knight to rule wel his hors. He muste haue a brydell, & sadyl, and two spores. By the bridel I vnderstonde abstinence & trauayle, by the which the flesshe must be refrayned fro his lustes, & his cupltacched whā he begynneth to weye proude & wynsyng, & kikyng apenste his master þ is the soule. And if he be ouir proud & to rebell to his maister, he must haue a sharpe bridel of sharpe abstinence & of harde trauayle And if he be meke & tretable, pene him a smothe brydel of easy abstinēce & of compy trauayle. The raynes of thy bridel shulde be ii. pties of temporaunce þ is to say nei ther to moche ne to lytel knyt to gidre I a knot of gode discrecion

And thanne thyne horse shal goo ryghte forthe in the weye of lyf and bere the to heuenly blisse. Yf thou yeue thy flesshe to moch mete and drynke and eese, it wol be thy maister and slee the.

And if thou yeue it to lytel, it shalbe to feble & fayle the at nede and let the of thy iourney The sadyl of thy hors shalbe pacience and meeknesse & thou be paciente in aduersite & in seknesse & thou folowe nat the gruchynges & the steryuges of thy flesshe. The steroppes of thy sadel shulde be lownesse and sadnes Lownesse ayenst pride/ sadnesse ayenst the worlde and the flesshe That thou be nat to sory for no wo ne to glade for no wele ne for no welefare Sytt sadly in thy sadyl and kepe wele thy steroppes/ and for no pryde, ne for no wrathe/ for no seknesse for no aduersite/ let nat thy hors cast the downe out of ye sadyl of pacience But syt faste by the vertue of goostly strength. & kepe thy soule in the sadel of pacience as crist byddeth i the gospel whan he saith. In paciencia vestra possidebitis aias vestras. ye shal kepe your soules in your pacience And as the sadel maketh an hors semely and plesaunte to the sighte so pacience maketh a man plesant. to the sight of god & of men & maketh them haue loue in euery cumpany where they ben And wrath

& Ipacience & hastynesse, maketh a man vnplesaunt & withoute loue Of this sadyl god spak to caym whan he was wroth w^t his brother abel Why said god art thou wroy & why is thy face & thy chere soo fulle For he was falle out of the sadyl of pacience If thou do wel thou shalt resceyue of me goode mede And if thou do euyl anone thy synne cometh att the yate to be punysshed But the desire of syn shalbe vndre the & in thy power. as the horse vndre the knyst And thou shalt be lorde therof if thou wylt Gen̄ iiii. But caym by mysgouernaunce of his horse felle out of his sadyl of pacience. In to manslaughter of his brother. for he wolde nat kepe him in the sadyl of pacience/ ne restrayne the wycked desire of his flessh/ & therfore god cursed him first of al men Therfore leue freende kepe you wele in the sadyl of paciēce/ & let no angre/ no losse of catel/ ne dethe of frendes/ none aduersite/ no tribulacion/ no seknesse vnsadle you of pacience. But sytt ye fast as Job dyd/ & say ye as he sayde. Whan he hadde lost al his goode and al his children were slayne. and him self smyten with harde seknesse/ and orrible and foule. than he saide thus. If we haue taken goode thinges of goddes bonde/ Why shulde nat we suffre wycked thinges and peynful of his soonde. God yaue. and god hath taken alwaye/ as god wylle so it is done. Blessyd be our lordes name. Job i°. et ii°. c. Thus sytpe sadly in the sadel of pacience. & rule ye your horse by the brydel of abstinence/ & by the reynes of tempaunce/ & if your horse be soo dulle in goddes wey/ pryke him with ii. spores þ been drede of hel peyne. & loue of god. & of heuene blisse And so with drede & loue cōpell ye your hors to hie him forth in goddes wey. Let nat your hors þ is your flesshe be to carnalle by ease & welfare; ne to feble for misfare and ouirtrauayle.

The vi. chapter.

The master of kynde li. iiii. De qualitate elimētari tellith. that ther is a bridde that is clepyd a Bernak. This bridde weyth oute of a tre ouir the water. But as long as it hangith on the tree. it is dede/ But anon as it lousith from the tre. and fallith down into the water/ anone it quykneth & swymmeth forth. This bridde he saith hath lytel flesshe & lesse blode. By this tree I vnder/stonde mākynde þ came al of Adā & eue as the tre & his braūches

come al of the rote bynethe. By this bridde I vnderstonde euery mā & womā whiche whā they be first borne of their moder they be dede by original synne of Adam & nat able to the lif of grace ne of blisse for as seint Poule saith we ben alle borne children of wrath. & of dethe But anone as we fall into the fontstone. & in the water of baptyme & ben Baptised/ anon we resceyue the lyf of grace and be able to the lyf of heuen blysse. if we kepe vs besily from the blode of synne/ & from the carnalite of the bodye. and despyes of the flesshe for seint petyr biddeth vs Abstinete vos a carnalibus desideriis que militāt aduersus alaz. i. petri ii. Abstepne ye you from flesshely desires that fight ayenst the soule But for as moch as Job saith þ al mannes lyf vpon erthe is knyghthode & fightyng ayēste gostly enemyes. Milicia est vita hois sup terrā Job vii. Therfore it is nedeful to euery cristen man to gouerne wele the horse of his body as I haue saide. But more ouir as seynt Poule saithe. he must arme him with gostly armure ayenst the oyntes. and the dartes of the fendes temptacion For as seint poule saith. Ad eph. vi. Alle oure fightynge is ayenst the wycked spirites of derknessis

The tenthe.

Whiche be princes & powers & gouernoures of synful men. Therfore he saithe Arme ye you in the armure of god that ye may with stonde the busshement and the slightes of the deuyl/ and stonde pfyte in al thinges. Stonde ye saith he in treuthe/ and gyrde ye your lendes w' the gyrdel of chastite/ & do ye on the habergeon of rightfulnesse/ and shoo ye youre feet in dightyng of the gospell of peec. And in al thinges take ye to you the shelde of feith/ w' whiche ye may quenche al the brennyng dartes of the wycked feende And take ye you the baspnett of helth & the swerde of the holy gooste/ þ is goddes worde. Which as he saith in a nother place is sharper thā any ii. egged swerde. Ad hebreos iiii°. And by alle maner prayers & besechyng pray ye euery tyme & alway in spirite/ and Wake ye alway in him in all maner besynesse And thus seint poule by the lyknes of bodily armure/ techith vs gostly armure/ and techith vs Wele to arme oure lendes by the vertue of chastite/ Whan he byddeth vs gyrde Wele oure lendes. And thā he byddeth vs do on the habergeon of rightfulnesse in defence both of body & soule/ þ We do right to al and yelde to god & to euery creature þ longith to him.

Both to our soueraignes & to our felawes/ & to our subgettes. and to theim that been bifore vs past oute of this World/ by almesse ye vpnge/ and yeldyng of dettes for them that ben dede/ and to theim that ben behynde vs to cūme by sauyng of their right and of their due heritage. And thus arme We vs behynde and bifore and I euery syde With the habergeon of rightfulnes And right as in the habergeon euery ryng accordeth w' other & is knytt With other/ So shulde al our rightfulnes accord to gidder & so be knytt to gydder. þ We do right to alle/ soo that We do no man ne womā wronge. For if We do somoche rightte and fauoure to one þ it be byndynge to anothers right/ thā the ryngs in our habergeon of rightfulnes accorde nat ne be Wele knytte to gider But ther is an hole Wherby the feende may hurt oure soule Also he byddeth vs arme our feet & our legges With legge harneys þ is gostly pouert þ We Withdraw oure hertes & oure affections from erthly thinges/ & nat set our loue to moche in erthely thinges ne in Worldly godes/ nat to stryue/ nat to plete for no Worldly godes/ But the more nede cōpell vs therto/ But seke to lyue I peec w' all men if it may be. And thus

472

arme vs wtih goſtly pouert oure legges and our feet/that is to ſay oure loue and oure affections aʒpenſt the temptacions of falſe couetiſe. And therfore he byddeth vs ſhoe oure feet into the digḣtly of the goſpel of peas. For euery criſten man and woman owethe to haue goſtly pouert whicħ criſt taughte iṅ the goſpel/ and to for ther the goſpel of criſt that is the goſpel of pees ī wyl & dede to his power/ & to teċh it if he cā. And if he caṅ nat. helpe and forther thē that can iṅ techīg of the goſpel. and of goddes lawe/ & helpe thē wtih his gode to their nedeful ſuſtenāuce if he may & and they haue nede. Alſo he biddeth vs take to vs the ſhelde of feith/ for as ye ſhelde is a triangle & hath thre corners/ iṅ whicħe triangle if fro the myddes be drawen thre lynes. in to the thre corners/ ther ſhulde be thre triangles/ whicħe thre be but one triangle/ and yit none of thē is other   And therfore he ſaith. feith of the holy trinyte is likned to a ſhelde/ for ther been thre pſones iṅ the holy trinyte/ the fader. the ſonne. and the holy gooſte/ & ecħe of them is god. and none of theym is other.   And though they ben alle thre but one god iṅ maieſtie/ this ſhelde of feithe of the holy Trinyte. vs muſt

take to vs iṅ goſtly ſight & bileʒue iṅ the hooly trinyte & ſett alle oure feith & alle oure truſt iṅ one god iṅ trinyte/ and pray to the fadre almighty/ that he ſēde vs miġht. to the ſonne al witty that he graunte vs wytt and wyſdome. to the holy gooſte all gracious & ful of mercy/ that he graunte vs grace/ ſo that we may haue miȝt wytt and grace to withſtonde al goſtly enemyes. Alſo he byddeth vs to take to vs. the baſynett of helth.and of ſaluacion/ as ſaith the gloſe/ hope to haue the maiſtre of oure enemyes by the helpe of god/ and heuene bliſſe to oure mede for oure fightynge and for oure trauayle For ther wyl noo man put him to lauful fight/ but iṅ hope to haue the maiſtrie/ and mede for his trauayle And as the baſynet wel arayed is clene furʒbuſſhed from ruſt/ and made ſlyke and ſmothe.that ſhot may ſone glide of/ and it is higheſt of al armure goyng and gaderyng vp warde into a ſmalle poynte/ ſoo muſte oure hope and oure truſte. principaly go vp to god/and nat ſet oure hope ne oure truſt to moche iṅ mannes might ne iṅ erthly helpe/ whicħe is but ruſte waſtiġ the baſynet of hope that we owe to god. Therfore ſaith the pphet Ieremye. Curſed be the mā that

Ii

trustith in man/ and in flesshe lye might/ & settith his hert go all vp fro god And blissed be that man. Which settith his hope & his trust in oure lorde god Jeremye vpii. Also seint poule biddeth that we shulde take with vs rerebras and vabras and gloues of plate that is to say gode occupaciones & besynesse in gode werkes And therfore he biddeth vs wake in al maner besynesse of gode werkis For as the wise man saith &c. xxviii. Idelship & slouth is cause of moch wickednesse For an ydel man & lustles is lyke a man hondlesse/ & wepenles amonge his enemyes. and lyke a man in batteyl with naked armes and hondes which for nakednesse and for defaut of armure lesith both arme & honde Also we must do aboue the iacke or the acton of charite For as the iacke is softe and nessh & by his softnesse and nesshenesse softith & seyntith al strokes yat cumeth therayenst/ so charite softith and seyntith all the dyntes of the fendes temptacion. Therfore seint poule saith/ that charite suffreth al thinge pacientlly/ & maketh euery trauayle soft & berith al thinge easily. Omnia suffert. oīa sustinet. Prima ad cor. xiiii And therfore seyth the glose there that charite & pacience & benignyte. with compassion of otheres myscheif, been the principall armure that longith to cristen peple This iacke of charite is betokenyd by the clothe of crist without te seme all wone aboue into one which in tyme of his passion the knightes wold nat kyt/ but kept it hole/ and kest lott who shulde haue it hole In token that euery gode knight of god shuld be besy to arme him with the clothe & the iacke & the armure of charite/ and trauayle to saue peas & vnyte. & make no diuision For the end of euery bataple shulde be pees/ & to þende & for none other mē of armes shuld trauell & fight/ as saith seint austyn. Thus leue frede I pray you þ ye arme you in gostly armure. as goddes gode knight. For though ye be nat able to bodily bataple/ ye be yit able to gostly fight In that þ ye be cristen ye be cristes knight ordeyned to sizt in this gostly bateyl/ if ye wol be saued. And therfore arme ye you wel as I haue nowe sayed & gird ye you with the swerde of goddis worde/ by which ye shuld defede you from al gostly enemyes For as the swerde ysith/ kyttith a maketh sepacion/ so goddes worde. & prechinge techinge & redyng of goddes worde & of goddes lawe. ysith mannes hert/ & womans and maketh sepacion bitwene synful soules & their synne, & departith. & wynne wycked cūpany & maketh sepacion of mannnes herte, from erthely couetise. Therfore crist seith that he came nat to make sinful peas, But to sēde swerd of sepatione in erthe, to distroye wycked peas þ men haue in their synne Therfore leue frende as goddes gode knight gyde ye you with this swerde of goddes word þ is to say fastne ye it wel in your hert by heryng & reding, by teching & by dede doynge, & than take ye to you the spere of cristes passion & thynke howe he was smyten to the hert for your sake with þ sharpe spere. & his syde opned, & his hert clouen a two to shewe you howe moche he louyd you And thanne he shedde oute his hert blode and water in token. & if he hadde had more blode more he wolde haue shed. for your loue Moreouir ye shal vnderstōde þ in bodily fight a mā must chese him a gode grounde & a playn place to fight in For it is no gode fightyng in myres, ne amonge corne, in slidre wey, & pitty grounde, ne in stoble groūd And therfore seint poule biddeth vs stonde in treuthe & equite & in all oure doynge we loke to oure grounde & oure cause be true and rightful, clere & clene, & make no stryf in vncerteyne Also a wyse knight in his fight wole take with him the hyl & the sune & the wide if he may. & so must be in gostly fight take with vs the hyl of holy lyuyng þ we may say with the apostle. Mea couersatō in celis ē Oure liuyng & couesarione is in heuenes & in heuynsly thinges. And therfore seint poule biddeth vs stode pfite in alle thinges. Also we must take with vs in oure fight the sune & the lighte of goddes grace, & the wynde of holy ppēr. And therfore seint poule biddeth vs praye in euery tyme & al way, by al maner prayer & bisechyng in the holy gost, þ is to sey with the grace of the holy gooste In this maner leue frende. arme ye you in gostly armure, & dispose ye you to gostly batteyl ayēste al gostly enemyes, & gouerne ye wele your hors of your boody as I haf seyd Lete it nat be to feble by oūdone abstinēce & traueil, ne to wild by ouirdon rest, by gluto nye, by lechery, by wycked desyres of the flesshe & euyl wylles for in caas such wycked wylles & desires been dedly synne in goddes sight & ayēst this last pcept Therfore dauid saith god sueth and knowith mānes hert & his sedes þ is to say god knowith mannes wyll & his lust For he knowith more ꝑfetly the thoughtes of mēnes hertis & wpnies/ thanne any man may. knowithe othere werkes He seeth & knowith alle thig And therfore such as man or womā is in hert & in soule/ & in wpl suche he is bifore god þ knowyth bothe body and soule.

The vii. chapter.

NOwe leue frende I haue ī partie declared thou the x cōmaundementes. By whiche ye must gouerne your lif/ if ye wole be saupd For crist saith to ech mā and womā Si vis ad vitam īgredi serua mandata. Mᵗ. xix. If thou wylte entre euirlasting lyf. keepe goddes cōmaundmentes. And therfore do ye as salamon saithe. Deū time et mādata eius obserua. hoc est ois hō. Ec. xiiio Drede ye god & kepe his cōmaūdmentes. this is euery man & womā For asmoche as man or womā plesith god by kepinge of his heestis/ so moche is he in goddes sight. And asmoche as man or woman is in goddes sight/ so moche he is and no more. as saythe seint austyne de ciuitate. li. xxᵒ. c. iiii. For as he saith. ther is noo man ought but the keper of goddes cōmaūdmētes/ for as he seith Who so is nat keper of goddes cō

maūdemētes/ he is nought. For he is nat reformyd ayē to the lyknesse of treuthe/ þ he was made after/ but duellith stylle in the lyknesse of vanitye þ he was nat made to. Therfore dauyd saide Maledicti q̄ declināt a mādatis tuis. Cursed be they þ bowe away fro thy cōmaūdmētis/ & wose nat the pᵗ them. ¶We rede in holy wrpt Deutro. xxvii. þ god badde the chil'oren of israel þ whan they came newly into the londe of beheest vi. hpnredes of iacob/ þ is to say Symeon. leup. iuda. ysachar/io seph. & beniamyn/ shulde stonde on the hyl of garizym. ther to thā ke god/ & to blesse. alle the kepers of goddes lawe And ayenst them shulde stonde other vi. hpnredes of iacob. þ is to say Ruben/ gad. aser/ zabulon. Dan/ & Neptisym on the hyll þ hight ebal. and curs wᵗ high voyce al that breke goddes hestis & say in this wyse. Cursed be þ man & womā þ maketh any graue ymage that is abhomi/ nacyon to god/ werke of the hondes of men of crafte to worship it outward with his body/ & settith it in pryue place/ þ is to say. his hert. to sette his feith & his truste. therin/ soo to worship it with his hert īwarde/ and at goddes bydyng al the people shuld answere & sey amen. So mote it be. Curs

Precepte.

ſyd be he ɏ nat worſhipeth fader
& moder. amē ſeide the peple Cur
ſyd be he ɏ flitteth the boundes &
the doles or termes of his neigh=
boure/ and puttith him out of his
right/ amen ſeyde all the people.
Curſed be he ɏ maketh the blide.
to wyl or to erre iŋ his wey. amē
ſeyde al the people. Curſyd be he
ɏ perttith the rightfull doome of
the comelyng and of the ſtraun=
ger. & of the faderleſſe childe and
of the moderleſſe chylde/ and of
the widowe. Amen ſaide al the
peple. Curſed be he that lyeth by
his faders wyf/ or by any of his
nigh kynred/ or of nigh affinitie.
Amen ſaide al the people. Cur=
ſed be he that medlith fleſſhely wᵗ
any vnreaſonable beeſte/ Amen
ſaide al the people. Curſed be he
ɏ lyeth by his nighboures wif A=
men ſaide al the people. Curſyd.
be he that priuely ſleeth and mur
dreth his nighboure/ amen ſayde
alle the people. Curſed be he that
takith giftes to ſlee bl that is nat
gilty. amen ſaide all the people.
Curſed be he ɏ duellith nat in the
wordes of goddes lawe. ne dothe
them nat iŋ dede. Amen ſaide all
the peole. This is the high curſe.
& the ſolēpne ſentence which god
beueth to al tho ɏ wole nat kepe
his heeſtis & lawe/& what curſe &
miſcheif ſhuld fall to them ɏ wyl

tyngly or wylfyng breke his heſ=
tes/ he ſhellyth iŋ the ſame boke
the nexte chapter where he ſaithe
thus.

The viii. chapter.

IF thou wylte nat here the
voyce of thy lord god. to
kepe and to do al his cōmaunde
mentes & his ſtatuteo/ al theſe cur
ſeo & myſcheups ſhal fall to the.
& take the. Thou ſhalt be curſed
iŋ cite. iŋ towne iŋ feld/ thy bern
thy gerner. & thy ſeller ſhalbe cur
ſyd. & that ɏ ſeueth the cuir the pe
te ſhalbe curſed. The fruyt of thi
body ſhalbe curſed/ & the fruyt of
thy lond ſhalbe curſed/ thy beſtis
thy ſhepe ſhalbe curſed. Thou
ſhalt be curſed whā thou cōmeſt
iŋ & whā thou w̄ eſt out. God
ſhal ſede vpoŋ the hūgre & myſ=
cheif & myſhap/& blame to al thy
werkes ɏ thou doſte He ſhal ſmy
te the with peſtilence/tyl he ſhall
waſte the & diſtroye the. He ſhall
ſmyte the with harde feuers both
colde & hote/ & with benemouſe.
eyr. God ſhal make heuene and
the eyre aboue the braſſe/ & therth
vpneth the prenp. that is to ſaye
bareyne for defaute of reyne For
thy reyne ſhalbe pouder & aſſhes.
& myldewe to diſtroye the. God
ſhalle take the into thy enemyes
hondes/ & thou ſhalt falle bifore
thyn enemyes. Thou ſhalte goo

I iiii.

The tenth.

agenst them by one wepe/ and fle awey by vii. wepes/ ⁊ briddes/ ⁊ beestis shal ete thy body in the felde God shal smyte the with sekenesse that may nat be helpd God shal smyte the with woodenesse. ⁊ blyndnesse of wytte. and so bisot the that thou shalt nat wit what is for to do/ ne cunne no rede ne counseyl. Thou shalt house ⁊ other shal duell therin Thou shalt tyl and other shal in that thou tylest Thy oxe/ thyne asse/ thy horse. thy shepe and thy beestis/ shalbe take fro the/ and thy wyf and thy children ledde away prisoners. God shal smyte the with sekenes incurable from the sole of thy fete unto the top of the hede. that is to say god shal punysshe the peple that wole nat cunne. ne kepe his lawes from the lowest staate to the highest And but thou wylt kepe his lawes and amende the. He shal lede the and thy kynge pt thou shalt make vpon the/ prisoners into ferre cuntre pt thou neuir knewe ne thy faders bifore the. Al these curses ⁊ many mo therto Whiche be writen in the same place shal take the. ⁊ pursue the. tyl thou be distroyed For thou herdist nat the voice of thy lord god ne kepist nat his beestis ⁊ his lawes pt he bad the kepe And at the day of doome he shal yeue to all

tho pt dispise his lawes/ his endlesse curse bitterest of alle. Whanne he shal say to them. Discedite a me maledicti in ignem eternu. Mt. ppd. Go ye hens fro me ye cursed wretches into the fire of hell/ ther to duell wt the feede ⁊ his angels withoute ende. Diues. pt last curse is moste for to drede/ for other curses of temporal mischeif fal as sone to the gode as to the wicked

Paup. Temporal mischeif sumtyme fallith to psone in special/ sumtyme to comunte in general. In special. it fallith sum tyme for synne/ sumtyme withouten synne/ to encreasyng of a mannes mede But than pt mischeif is noo curse But a soueryn of god. Butt comen mischeif fallith nat to the comuntie/ but for synne of the comuntie And of suche comen myscheues pt shuld fall to the people. if they dispised goddes beestis spekeþ god in pt place And suche comune myscheups pt fall to the comunte for comen synne Be clepid curses. Diues. Why were tho vi. kynredes of Jacob so assigned of god to curse the brekers of goddes lawe/ ⁊ the other vi. assigned to blesse the kepers of goddes lawe Paup. Them pt were most vngentyl of birthe god assignyde to curse For al tho vi. sones of Jacob. were borne of the secundarye

478

Precepte.

wyues that were but seruauntes to his cheif wyues/ lya. & rachel. suaf. ruben. whiche lost his worshippe/ for that he laye by his faders secundarie wyf. that highte bala. The other vi. kynredes were borne gentyl of birthe/ for thei were borne of the principal & more gentyl wyues/ lya & rachel. foure of lya/ & ii. of rachel. And therfore god ordeyned theym to blesse/ in token þ no mā shuld be chosen to preesthode. But he were gentyl by wantyng of cursed cōdicions. And also in tokē that it is more kyndely to worshipfuly sones as al prestes shulde be/ to blesse than to curse. And therfore Busshopes & other pstes shuld nat curse but for a full greuouse opē syn & for grete nede. Therfore poule saith. to mē of pfeccion as al pstes shulde be. Benedicite. et nolite maledicere. Blesse ye and be ye nat in wylle ne redy to curs But for grete nede/ and that it be done in charite to worship For cursyng in the self is a dede of impfeccion. And therfore god chose theim that were mooste impfyte. and leest worshipful of the birth to pnounce the curse/ & the moste pfite & worshipful in birthe to pnounce his blessing to þe kepers of his lawe. whiche seyde thus/ & goddes name to the people.

The ix. chapter.

IF thou here the voyce. of thy lorde god. to cūne and to kepe al his heestes þ I byd the kepe/ thy lorde god shalle make the hygher thanne al nacioūs þ duelle vpon erthe And al these blessinges shal come to the & takē the. so that thou kepe goddes heestes. thou shalt be blessed in cyte. in towne & in feelde The frute of thy body/ the frupt of thy londe. the frupte of thy beestes shalle be blessed/ thy berne/ thy garner/thy seller shalbe blessed/& al thy feulges shalbe blessyd. Thou shalte. be blessyd cūmyng in and goyng oute. God shalle make thyn enmyes that rise ayenst the. to fall in sight bifore the. They shal come ayenst the by one wey. & they shal fle away by vii. weyes. God shal yeue his blessing psprite & spede to al thy werkes. soe þ thou kepe goddes heestis & go in his weyes & in his lawes/ þ al pe ple on erthe shal se and knowe þ the name of oure lorde is cleppyd on the/ and they shal drede the/ & worship the/ & oure lord god shal make the plenteouse in al godes God shal vndo his beest tresour. aboue from heuene. and yeue the reyne in tyme. Thou shalt lene

J iiii

℈he tenth.

to other nacions/ ⁊ thou shalt haue no nede to borowe of other nacions God shal make the ito the hede ⁊ nat into the tayle. For he shal putt the alway aboue ⁊ nat bynethe so ꝑ thou kepe his heestis and his lawes. And at the day of dome he shal yeue to al the kepers of his lawes his endlesse blissing. of euirlasting ioye/ ⁊ say to them in this wyse. Venite b͂ndicti p͞tris mei. possidete paratū uobis regnū a constitut͡oe mūdi. M᷑ ꝑp͞s. Come ye with me ye blissed children of my fadris/ ⁊ take ye i possessione the kingdome of heuene arayed ⁊ ordeyned to you. from the setlig or makig of the worLd.

In whiche kingdome as saith austyn shalbe light without derkenesse/ endlesse ioy withoutē heuynesse/ endlesses lyf withouten wo. endlesse myrthe ⁊ gladnesse. w᷑ the blisful cūpany of aungelis apostles ⁊ al seintes. Ther saith he is light of light/ ⁊ wel of brizt shynynge There is the cite of seintes ꝑ is cleppd Jerusalem of heuē There is the grete couent of martires ⁊ of holy ꝓphetes ⁊ patriarkes abraham Jsaac ⁊ Jacob ⁊ of all seruntes There is noo sorowe ne heuynesse. after ioye. There shalbe no night/ none age/ no feblenesse. There is charite without ende ⁊ euirlasting peas/ no debate no discension. There euery man and woman hath ꝑ he loueth. and what he desireth Ther is al loue withouten wo ⁊ withouten sorowe ⁊ care. Ther shall we be aungels peris and felall es in blisse with the high potestatis cherubyn ⁊ seraphin/ ⁊ with alle nyne ordres of aūgels Ther shal be man̄a oure heuenly fode without corrupcion Ther shalbe aūgelis lyf/ and to say shortly. ther shalȝe sowne no sorowe no disese none euyl. and what may be thought of any godnes: ther shalbe founde.

℈he y. chapter.

The kingdome of heuen is cleppd in holy writte a cyte sett on a ful high hylle in stabilite and sikernesse withouten drede. and withouten peryl/ for ther may none enemye/ no peryl noo disease neigh therto It stondithe so high and in so grete welth For men haue in this cyte what euir they desire Ther is nouȝt to seke frō without/ it nedith noo helpe from without But al must seke help from within this cite. Therfore saith. psaie. the ꝓphete lx.c. Helth ⁊ sanacion occupy the walles of this cytee/ kepe theym and defende them ⁊ praisyng of god.

Precepte.

withoutē ceasyng. occupieth the yates & so kepith hem þ ther may no sorow entre. In this cite saith he shalt thou not nede to haue ye sūne to shyn to the by day, ne the light of the mone shal nat shyne to the by night, but thy lorde god crist ihesus þ bought the soo dere. shalbe light withouten ende, and thy god shalbe thy ioye. there thy sonne shal neuer go downe, & thy mone shall neuer wayne, for thy lord god shalbe thy light withoutē ende, & the daies of thy sorowe here in this worlde, there shalbe endyd. For god there shalle wype away the teris from the iyen of his seyntes. Ther shalbe no weping, no cryinge, none hūgre, no thurst no sorowe. For al the wo & diseases þ were bifore. Ben all past frō them þ come to this cyte. Alle the people of this citee shall be gode & rightful, there shalle no shrewe no bryger, no lechour. no wyched lyuer, entre into this cite. There euery mā & womā shall shyne as bright as the sūne. And whā many sūnes ben gadryd to gidder in cūpany wt the bigh sūne of rightfulnesse crist ihesus which saith in the gospel Ego sum lux mūdi Joh. viii. I am light of the worlde, there shalbe a faire cūpany. a blisful cūpany. god bring vs therto. Than the sūne shalbe

seuē sithes brighter thā it is now. & the mone as bright as the sūne is now. Than the sūne shal stōde in the Eest alway stylle. & the mone in the west alwey shynyng withoutē wanyng. So þ synful soules dāned to hel vnder therth shal no confort haue, neither by sonne ne by mone. In this kingdome in this cytee is noo wynde no storme, no tēpest. no thundre no lightnig no reyne, hayl froste ne snowe, no hete no colde. Ther be no strypes no cloudes to let our light, but alway mery somer: alway bright day. In this cite alle mē & wymē ben fre. The king of this cite axith no presaunces, ne yiftes of man ne of womun, but their hertis and their loue & þ thei fare wele. He puttith no man, ne womā there to trauayle, butt he wole that alle be in rest in peas & in ease. And what any man or woman there desireth to haue, he yeueth it to them anone. He axith no rent, noo tribute, no seruyce, none homage but gode loue and gode hert, and that we loue hym with ioye and myrthe, and gladnesse. He yeueth vs al that he axith of vs. Yeue thy self to this blysse. and thou shalte haue this blisse. Other pryce axith he none. For this blisse may nat be boughte. butt with loue. and

The tenthe.

charite In this cyte shalle euery man & womā haue so grete lordshyp þ' al they shall haue place ynough withoutē enuye/ & all be kinges & quenes. of asmoche as they desire. Ther shalbe no pleetyng for no lordshyp/ for no lōde There shalbe none enuye butt euery man and womā glade of others welfare Ther shalbe no wo noo disease. But endles ioye. and welthe. and endlesse helth.

In heryng swete songe. & melody. in sight/ endlesse fairnesse/ in tastyng & smellyng / endles swetnesse. in feling endlesse likyng w'outen woo.

The vi. chapter.

Of this cyte spekithe seynt Iohn in the boke of goddes priueties xxi°. c. and saithe thus The aungel ledde me in spirite by vision ito a ful high hylle & a ful grete. And there he shewid me the holy cite of Ierusalem or deyned of god/ & hauyng the brightnesse & the beaute of god The light of this cyte was lyke the p'cious stone iaspis & cristel which stone betokneth crist sonne of rightwysnesse. Whiche saith in the gospel Ego sū lux mūdi Io. viii I am light of the worlde This cyte had a wal ful grete & ful hiz & it had xii. yates/ & eche yate xii all yelis redy porters. to lede in al gode soules/ and I the yates were writē al the names of the xii. kiredes of israel. þ is to say/ of all þ shalbe saued & be able to se god his face For the names of alle þ shalbe saued been registred in the Boke of lif in heuene & redy writen I the yates of heuē/ a yest our cūmyng in tokē þ we shalbe welcome & siker of our blisse if we do our deuer. This cite stode I square & it had thre yates into the eest thre into the northe. thre into the south/ & iiii. into the west/ in tokē þ oute of iiii. ptes of the worlde. þ is to say/ out of euery pte of the worlde soules entre into heuene Blisse of yonge & olde riche & pore By the feyth of the hooly trinitye. þ is betoknyde by the thre yates. yonge folke ben vnderstonde by the eest/ there the day begynneth Olde folk by the weste there the day ēdith Rich folk by the south Pore folk by the northe. for þ cūtre is most sharpe & bareyne The wal of the cite was set & groūdid on vii. pcious stones. The firste was Iaspis. the ii. saphirus. the iii. calcidonius. the iiii. smaragd'. the v. sardenyx. the vi. sardin'. the vii. crisolit'. the viii. beril lus. the ix topasius/ the x. crisopassus. the elleuenthe iacinctus. the xii. amatistus And in tho stoones were writen the names

Precepts.

of the xii. apostles & of goddes sō be And al the wall was made of precious stones/ and the yates made of saphires & smaragdes. as to byē saith in his boke. xiii. c. And as seit Iohn saith. euery yate was as a margarite or margery stone The stretis of the cite were clene golde as clere as glasse And as toby seith the stretis of this cytee were pauyd with ful white clene stone/ and alway in the stretis is songe alleluya. Which song coude neuir clerke wele declare ne expowne to the vtterest/ for the ioy the myrth/ the melody/ & gladnes is there may no tunge telle/ ne herte thynke/ ne honde wryte/ ne wytte deuyse & declare In this citee seint Iohn sawe no teple/ for almighty and goddes lombe crist Ihesus verrey god & mā he is the temple of this cite. This cite as seith seint Iohn nedith neither sū ne ne mone. For the brightnesse of god wel of light & the sūne of rightfulnesse illumpneth this cyte. The lōbe crist ihesus is the lā terne & the light of this cite Alle nacions & peoples shal go in the light of this cyte. & bryng theire noblēy their blisse. theire worship. into this cite. The yates of this cite shal neuir be shytt Ther shal be no nighte But alway day/ al wey somer and neuir wynter In to this cite shall come noo foule thinge no false lier/ no forswerene none that doth abhomynacion. of dedly synne Ther shal no mā entre but they ϸ ben wryten in the boke of lyf and in the lyf of the lombe criste Iesus that boughte vs so dere with his blode·

The xii. chapter.

And as saith a grete clerke Doctor de spra. By the xii. precious stones. on whiche this cite is groundyd./ in which stones the names of the xii. apostles be wryten ben vndstonde the xii. articles of the feith. Which the xii. apostles gaderyd into one crede. in whiche xii. articles al oure saluacion is sett & groundyd And therfore seint poule saithe Fide statis. ye stonde in faith. for oure feith is grounde of oure saluacion By the twelue yatis ben vndstonde the x. cōmaundmentes. & the ii. preceptes of charite Of whiche yatis crist saith Si vis ad vitā ingredi. serua mādata M' vip

If thou wylt entre into the lyf of this blissfull cite there no may dieth. kepe thou the cōmaundementes This scripture is wretyn in euery yate of this citee, in token that into this cite cūmeth

The tenthe.

no man ne woman but the kepers of goddes comaundementis For the comaundementes ben the pates of heuene, by whiche vs must entre, and they ben also the weye ledyng to the pate of heuene And therfore dauid saide Viam mandatoru tuor cucurri: cū dilatasti cor meū. Po. Cxviii. I ran the weye of thy comaundmetes whan thou madest myne herte large by charite For whan men be to strait at the breest by false couetise and nygardship, they may natt wele renne in the weye of goddes heestes. For false couetise byndeth them so streit at the hert þ they haue no likynge in goddes heestes. Therfore dauid said. Deduc me dūe in semita mandatoru tuoru: qr ipam volui. Inclina cor meū deus in testimonia tua: et non in auariciā. Po Cxviii. Lorde lede thou me in the pathe of thy comaūdemētes, for it is my desire. & my wyll to go that wey Bowe myne herte into thy witnessingis & into thy comaundmētes, & nat into auarice & couetise Thus leue frende holy wrytt & holy men declare the blisse of heuene by thīges visible þ we may see at iye, so to lede vs into knowynge of the blisse that we may se with oure bodily iye while we lyue I the cōdes of erthe.   Butt leue freende

byleue ye it forsothe y' ther is an hundryd thousāde thousād folde more blisse than any tunge may telle. or any hert thynke.

The xiiii. chapter

Diues If men hadde sadde feith to haue such blisse for their gode dedes, ther wolde noo mā ne womā do amys. for drede to lese that blisse.   Pauper. It farith by folke borne in prisone. of the wycked worlde as it doth by a childe borne in the depe derk pytt of the prison whan it fallith a woman with childe be put I prisone. The moder that knowith the welfare þ she had oute of pryson is in moch sorowe & care and longith ful moche to be oute of prisone ayen in her welfare Butt the childe borne in the myscheyf of the prisone and neuir had knowyng of better fare reueth lytel tale of þ myscheif in prison. But as longe as he hath his moder wt hym & his sustenaunce though it be ful feble, he maketh no sorow ne care. He lōgith after no better fare. for he knowith no better. For if his moder telle him of the ioye and welfare oute of prisone of the sūne, mone & of the sterres. of the faire floures spryngynge vpon erth. of the briddes syngig

Precepte.

of myrtḫe/ of melodye/ of rich ar
raye/ of lordes of ladies/ ⁊ welth
þͭ is oute of prison. alſe hir tale is
but a dreme to the childe. He bile/
ueth it nat/ and therfore he longeth nat therafter. and wote natt
for al this bliſſe ⁊ the welefare pͭ
ſhe spekith of/ forſake his modre
ne the feble fare. that he hath wͭ
her/ and that is for he bileueth it
nat And yit it is as the modre tel
lith the childe But were the child
onys out of prison. and ſawe the
welthe ⁊ myrthe and the welfare
whiche his moder told him of. he
wold be ful ſory for to wēde aȝē
to prison there to ſpue wͭ his moder For al his lyf in prison þ was
firste likinge ynough to hī ſhuld
than be ful bytter. and he ſhulde
neuir haue ioye ne reſt in hert tyl
he came aȝen to that welefare. þ
he ſaw out of prison. Right thus
folke of this world borne ⁊ brou/
ght forth in ſorowe and care and
moche trauayle in the prisone of
this worlde/ they haue ſo moche
loue and likynge to theire erthly
moder and to ther cūpany/ þ is to
ſay in erth ⁊ in erthly thīges/ for
erth is moder of alle. þ they haue
no likyng in heuenly thinges/ ne
longe nat therafter And yit their
goſtly moder holy churche ⁊ ther
goſtly fader ⁊ god hīſelf fader of
al telliṫh them of the bliſſe of he-

uen It is to thē but a dreme/ as
is the moders tale to her childe in
priſō/ and they haue no ſad feith
therin And though it be ſo as our
moder holy church tellith þo tho/
ugh the childe bileue nat þ ſuche
welfare be out of prisone/ the wel
fare is neuir the leſſe. ⁊ though er/
thly couetouſe mē haue no likīg
but in erth ⁊ in erthly thinges bileue nat þ ſuche bliſſe be in heuen
yit ther is ſuche bliſſe. ⁊ neuir the
leſſe for their falſ bileue But had
they onys ſene and aſſayed a ſy-
tel of that bliſſe/ all the ioye and
likyng þ they haue in this world
⁊ in erthly thinges ſhuld be to thē
ful grete bytternes ful of ſorow.
⁊ care. Example we haue of ſeṫt
petyr. whom Criſte ledde vpon
the hylle of Thabor. with ſeynt
John ⁊ James. ⁊ there he ſhewid
thē but a litel of the bliſſe of his
manhode. His face ſhone as bright as the ſunne/ his clothes were
white as ſnowe. Moyſes ⁊ Hely
aperyd wͭ hī i grete bliſſe ⁊ maieſ
tie. Thā petyr ſaide to our ſore.
ihū Lord it is gode to vs to be her
Mak we her iii. tabernacles one
to ȝe. another to moiſes ⁊ anoþer
to hely. ⁊ let vs al duel her Luce
ix. And ⁊ ī ī ſight of litel bliſſe
he forȝat al the blis of this world
He cared neither for mete drik ne
clothing For ȝl thought he miȝt

haue spued withoutẽ ende by the blissful sight & w' that cũpany Also whan seint poule was rauyſſhed into heuene & hadde seen the vision of god/ afterwarde al his lif in this worlde was to hī a peyne. so moche he longyd ayẽ to ye blisse. And therfore he saide Infelix ego quis me liberabit de morte corporis huius. Ro. vii. I an vnsely man who shal deliuer me fro the deth of this body I coueit to be departed/ the soule fram the body & be withoutẽ ende w' crist. Moyses was w' god in the mount of synay xl. daies. and xl. nyghtes meteleſſe and drynkles/ fedde by the speche of god/ and by his pſence/ and yitt sawe he butt lytel of this blisse For he was nat able to see his blisse/ ne no mā liuyng in this worlde/ as god saide to hī that tyme Butt leue frende after oure deth if we kepe wele goddes cōmaundmentes & amende oure mysdedes by oure lyf/ we shal see his grete blisse which neither Petir ne poule ne moyses might se I erthe And we shalbe siker of that blisse withoutẽ ende/ which blisse as seint poule saith y none erthly iye may se/ ne ere here/ ne hert thīke. ne wytte compꝛhende In this blisse leue frend I hope to se you and duelle with you in the highe cite of ierusalē in the kīges court

of heuene. To whiche blisse he bring vs/ that for vs dyed on the rode tree. Amen.

Here endith a compendiouse tretise dyalogue. of Diues & paup. that is to say. the riche & the pore fructuously tretyng vpon the x. cōmaūdmentes/ fynisshed the. S. day of Iuyl. the yere of oure lord god. M.CCCC.lxxxxiii. Emprentyd by me Richarde Pynson at the temple barre. of london. Deo gracias.

BIBLIOGRAPHY

MANUSCRIPTS
Glasgow. University Library. Hunterian MS 270
Lichfield, Staffs. Cathedral Chapter Library. Lichfield MS 5.
London. British Museum. Harleian MS 149.
London. British Museum. Royal MS 17 C. 20.
London. British Museum. Royal MS 17 C. 21.
New Haven. Yale University Library. (Uncatalogued.)
Oxford. Bodleian Library. MS Douce 295.
Oxford. Bodleian Library. MS Eng.th.d.36.
Oxford. Bodleian Library. MS Eng.th.e.1. (Fragment.)

PRINTED EDITIONS
Dives and Pauper. London: Richard Pynson, 1493. (STC 19212.)
―――――. London: Wynken de Worde, 1496. (STC 19213.)
―――――. London: Thomas Berthelet, 1536. (STC 19214.)

SECONDARY SOURCES
Barnum, Priscilla Heath. "A Preliminary Edition of the 'Table,' The Prologue on 'Holy Poverty,' and "Commandment I' of *Dives et Pauper.*" Ph.D. dissertation, Syracuse University, 1967. (Order No. 68-13,811.)

Deanesly, Margaret. *The Lollard Bible and Other Medieval Biblical Versions.* Cambridge, 1966.

"Dives and Pauper," *Notes and Queries,* ser. 2, vol. 5, no. 106 (January 1858): 38.

Gage, Sister M. Anselm. "A Commentary on the 1536 Edition of *Dives and Pauper.*" M.A. thesis, Columbia University, 1947.

Gasquet, Cardinal. "How Our Fathers Were Taught in Catholic Days." *Dublin Review,* ser. 4, vol. 2, no. 120 (April 1897); 245-65.

Hodnett, Edward. *English Woodcuts: 1480-1535.* London, 1935.

Kolve, V. A. *The Play Called Corpus Christi.* Stanford: Stanford University Press, 1966.

Leland, John. *Commentarii de Scriptoribus, Britannicis.* Edited by A. Hall. Vol. 2. London, 1709.

Londes, William. *Bibliographer's Manual of English Literature.* Vol. 2. New ed. London: Henry Bohn, 1857.

Manual of the Writings in Middle English: 1050-1500. Vol. 3. Edited by Albert E. Hartung. Archon Books. Hamden, Ct.: Shoe String Press, 1972.

Morgan, Margery M. "Pynson's Manuscript of *Dives and Pauper.*" *Library,* 5th ser., vol. 8, no. 4 (December 1953): 217-28.

Owst, Gerald R. *Literature and Pulpit in Medieval England.* Oxford, 1961.

———. *Preaching in Medieval England.* London, 1926.

Pantin, D. W. A. *The English Church in the Fourteenth Century.* Notre Dame, Ind.: University of Notre Dame Press, 1962.

Pfander, H. G. "*Dives and Pauper.*" *Library*, 4th ser., no. 14 (1933): 299-312.

Plomer, Henry R. "Two Lawsuits of Richard Pynson." *Library*, 2d ser., no. 10 (1904): 115-33.

Richardson, H. G. "*Dives and Pauper.*" *Library*, 4th ser., no. 15 (1934): 31-37.

———. "*Dives and Pauper.*" *Notes and Queries*, 2d ser., no. 4 (21 October 1911): 321-23.

Sheeran, Francis. "An Edition of Wynken de Worde's 'Dives and Pauper,' Collated with Pynson's Edition, MSS Yale, Eng.th.d.36, and Lichfield 5; With the Alternate Prologue on 'Holy Poverty' in Hunterian MS 270, Collated with Royal MSS 17 C. 20 and 21, and MS Douce 295." Ph.D. dissertation, University of Nebraska, 1970. (Order No. 70-17,757.)

———. "Printing Errors in the Texts of *Dives and Pauper.*" *The Papers of the Bibliographical Society of America*, vol. 65, no. 2 (1971): 150-54.

———. "Ten Verse Fragments in *Dives and Pauper.*" *Neuphilologische Mitteilungen* (in press, 1973).

Tahney, Rev. Shane, O. Carm. "The Manuscripts and Editions of *Dives and Pauper*, A Medieval Treatise on the Ten Commandments." M.A. thesis. Catholic University of America, 1950.

White, Helen. *Social Criticism in Popular Religious Literature of the Sixteenth Century.* New York, 1944.

Woolf, Rosemary. "The Theme of Christ the Lover-Knight in Medieval English Literature." *Review of English Studies* 13 (1962): 1-16.

INDEX

This index includes the names of authorities (and their works if mentioned), general topics when not covered adequately by the "Table of Contents," and references to discussion about the English.

Abortion, 275
Absolom, 201-02
Achab and flattery, 251-52
Adam's rib, significance of, 294; sin, compared to Eve's, 337
Adulterers, hardships of, 281
Adultery, greater sin in man, 295; slaying wife permitted, 284; spiritual, 328
Agatha, Saint, 236
Ages of the world, sixth, 184
Ages for various temptations, 465
Agnes, Saint, 236
Alchemy, 112
Alexandre, *Vitas Patrum*, 468
Alms, giving, 457;
    of ill-gotten goods, 363;
    order of distribution, 461
Ambrose, *De Officiis*, 461;
    Super Beati Immaculati, 300;
    Super Lucam, 308, 399;
    Baptism of pagan children forbidden, 357;
    Clerks should pray, not fight, 279;
    Many make a great prayer, 119;
    No blame in riches, 365-66;
    On lying, 416
Amusements forbidden clerks, 274
Angels, 234
Apostles' Lots, 91
Aquinas, Thomas, *De Veritate Theologie*, on swearing, 143;
    on pains of hell, 321; on lying, 400;
    on baptising pagan children (In quadam questione de quolibet), 358
Aristotle, *De Somno et Vigilia*, 105;
    Ethics, 4. 17, 407; 4. 57, 225; 5, 282;
    Politics, 3, 389;
    I Perihermeneias (sic: peryamynias), speech is token of thoughts in heart, 405; "The Philosopher," time, 82; stealing, 376; avoid vice, 355; "thine and mine," 440
Arthur, King, 447
Astronomy, 62-67; 76 ff.; 85 ff.; judicial, 75
Augustine of Hippo; *City of God*, 10. 5 (Eve's fall), 59; 14. 11 (Eve's fall), 341-42; 20. 4 (Adam's fall), 308; 476; 21. 26, 462; City of Jerusalem, 479; on suicide, 283;
    Contra Mendacium, 405;
    De Decem Cordis, 265 ff.; 293 ff.
    De Doctrina Christiana, 1. 10, 461
    De Libro Arbiterio, 1, when manslaughter permitted, 271;
    De Mendacio, seven manners of lying, 401 ff.;
    De Natura Demonom, 87;
    Epistle to Casulanum, on lying, 401;
    Epistle ad Letum, 208
    Commentaries: Gloss on 1 Thess. 4:442;
    Gen. 11:14, 340-41;
    Psalter, worship, 56;
    Epistle to Macedonians, stolen goods, 367;
    First Epistle to Corinthians, 9
    Sermons (unnamed): on Decollacion of St. John, on lending, 149-50;
    "De Verbis Domini," 35; on alms, 457-59;
    on clerks' life, 462;

on found objects, 355;
souls should be found clean, 320
Subjects: Abraham's two wives, 334;
  Adam's sin, 341;
  Adultery, 294-96;
  All are spiritual beggars, 36;
  Alms to the evil destitute, 460;
  Apostle's money, 383;
  Christmas star, 75;
  Clergy hunting, 112;
  Commandment divisions, 195;
  Dancing and pagan plays, 191;
  Father as head of household, 218;
  Flattering, 245;
  Guilt in Christ's death, 244;
  Judicial astronomy, 75;
  Kingdom of Heaven, 483;
  Last Judgment, 426-27;
  Lawful to kill guilty men, 271;
  Lordship is God's gift, 350;
  Lying and feigned deeds, 400 ff.;
  Merchandising in temple, 135;
  Ownership, 348-49;
  Peace at the end of battle, 285;
  Prayer, 121;
  Praise, 247-48;
  Religious' duty to his parents, 208 f.;
  Rich and poor are necessary to each other, 31;
  Solomon's prayer glossed, 36;
  Swearing, 146;
  Tenth Commandment, 448;
  Theft and alms, 357-58;
  Wicked peoples' purpose, (on psalms), 224;
  Will of thief, 353;
  Work of Creation, 169; 173.

Balaam, "devourer of people," 440; gloss on, 442-43; ass, 269 ff.
Baptism of Jewish and pagan children, Sylvester and Ambrose, 358

Barlaam, Saint; Life of, 437; 453
Battle, three things necessary for rightful, 285
Beatrice, Passion of Saint; and Lucres, 435
Bede, *De Gemma (Gemitum) Anime*, Bk. 3, Good Friday Customs, 45
  De Officio Divino, significance of vestments, 414
  Adam and Eve tempted, 308
  Adulterers, 291
  Rich and poor, 27; 36
  Shape of man is a Cross, 45
Benedict, quoted in Gregory's *Dialogues*, 210-11
Benefices, 381; 237-39
Bernack, cf. Master of Kinds
Bernard, Saint, *Epistle ad Eugenium*, duties of benefice holder, 366
  Epistle ad Monacho, 233;
  Meditation on the Passion, 42-43;
  "Epistle" to a canon, 367;
  "Meditation" of vanity of man's life, 450;
  joyful praying, 127;
  Last Judgment, 430;
  Love God "dulciter, prudenter, fortiter," 197;
  Pains of hell, 321
Black Mass, 92
Boethius, *De Disciplina Scholarium*, tale, 355-56
Bonaventure, *Life of Saint Francis*, 211
Boniface's letter to King of England, 292
Book of Dreams, 91
Book of Painture, 42
Buryings, too costly, 132
Business practices, usury in, 391 ff.

Camel and Needle's eye exposition, 32-33
Catholycon, Philomena as "Sweet Lover," 438
Cato, 407
Cecilia, Saint; and Valerian, 235-36;
  Hairshirt under rich clothes, 314
Chastity not popular among men, 238

INDEX   493

Children, disciplined like young tree, 216;
  Begetting and raising, 70-72
Cicero, *De Officiis*, 3, sin to get rich on another's goods;
  2, faith binds a community, 445
Ciconia (stork), 203
Christ as archer, 427
Christmas, star, 74
  Twelve days of, 111
Chrysostom, *Opere Imperfecto*, Hom. 6 on Matthew, 75; 429;
  "In tractu" on Judas' power to work miracles, 130;
  on Epistle to the Hebrews, 460;
  on Last Judgment, 425-26;
  On Lying, 401;
  Christ's torture instruments, 425-26
Church services, cost, 115-118; decoration of, 114-16
Clerk, may bear weapon, 278
Clothing, English too fine, 315; of clergy, 412-13
Civil Law—killing one's wife, 284
Colchester, 205
Commandments, Two Great, 195; First table, 38; 195;
  Second table, 38; 199-200; Second table especially for the young, 39-41
Comet, of 1402, 85; token of woe, 84
Common Law, 85
Constitution, synodal, pay of annualers, 383-84;
  Lambeth, 384
Council Lugdonense, 399
Custom, expositor and determiner of positive law, 376

Dances and songs lawful, 191
De Celebratione Missarsum, 3, 2, 384
Devil, 86ff.; compelled to talk when enclosed in rings, 90
Dice playing, 98
Dockynge, on *Deuteronomy*, 367; 368 f.; 407
Doctor, patient dies through his fault, 275

Dreams, causes of, 194 ff.;
  meaning of, 106
Dress, leading to lechery, 314; of clergy, too rich, 367
Dyana or Herodyana, 92

Eagle, looks at sun, 216
Elves, 334
Emperor, "Qui omnibus pre est: omnibus indiget," 366
England, Martyrs in, 128;
  Perjury in, 160, 408;
  Sports in, 274
English, known as adulterous, 292;
  love war, 120-21;
  making of churches, 114;
  moral shortcomings, 113-15;
  pillage in war, 398;
  worship God before king, 126
Execution, lawful, 253; 270 ff.;
  forbidden to clergy, 271 f.
Exempla, Christian deceiving Jew, 148;
  Do not force perjury, 150;
  Joshua and swearing, 165;
  Proud getter, 113

Fairs and markets in churchyard, 89; 134
Feast of Tabernacles, 173-75
Figures, armor and grace, 471-75;
  body and knight's horse, 469 ff.;
  bow as doom of God, 427;
  Forty-year exile as man's life, 467;
  fox crossing ice and Christian soul, 451;
  Holy Trinity as shield, 473;
  lion is chastised by beating whelp, 338;
  mother treasurers only child, 129;
  narrow way and man's life, 449;
  nightingale, 437;
  sheep as covetous soul, 444-45;
  wheel, ship, flower, shadow as instability, 445 ff.
Fishing lawful, 187
Flatterer, as chameleon and as ape, 409-10
Flattering,
  of false preachers, 251;

as chief sin of English, 251;
kinds of, 244-46
Fornication, ghostly, 335
Francis, Saint, giving away altar clothes, 211;
Life of, 211
Free will and planetary influence, 65-66

Galahad, moral meaning of, 412
Galoches controversy, 49
Gesta Karoli, Turpin's bloody shirt tale, 320-22
Golden trental, 383; 386
Good Friday liturgy, 45
Gratian, *Decretals*, on support of clergy, 378
Gregory, *Dialogues*, 3 and 4, 386; 4, 385-86;
  Moralium, 8, 18, on lying, 401, 403; 8, faith in dreams, 106; 8, on flatterers, 246
  Homilies, God looks at man's heart, 114; man turns good things into bad, 423; "on Epiphany," only destiny is God, 72; on churchmen lying, 257
  Subjects: blames old man full of sins, 222; clergy as witnesses, 413; covetise, 441; gives to poor man who is angel, 211; God tests him to be Pope, 211; Last Judgment (on use of riches), 431; lecherous priests, 327; Mass releases his monk from Purgatory, 385; Obligations of the rich, 29; origin of his Mass (to free mother from purgatory), 385; overcome lechery by meditation on Passion, 320; Peter's denial caused by lechery, 310; Pope's letter to bishop in defense of images, 42; Saturday hallowed, 184; sing for souls day by day, 386
Guydo in Rosario, 373

Halis, on reverence, 56
Haymo, 289
Heretic burning, 276

Herodyana, 92
Homicides, no mass for, 362
Hostiensis, on covenants, 362
Hymns, happy, not appropriate in Lent, 52

Image, three uses of, 41-42; angels, 41; 49-50; Apostles, 48-49; Bernard, 42-43; crucifix, 42; 44-46; of evangelists, 50-52; hidden in Lent, 52; John the Baptist, 48; John the Evangelist, 48; Katherine, 48; lewd people's book, 42; 47; Margaret, 48; Mary, 47; Mass, 44; not too rich, 49; Paul and Peter, 48; of Saint when alive, as compared to array of statue, 53; token by which a knight or lord may be recognized, 46
Imagery, of Good Friday, 45; of Passion Sunday, 46; and painting, 42
Incubi, 335
Irregularity, causes of, 329 ff.
Isidore, *De Summo Bono*, Bk. 2, 342

Jerome,
  Ad Nepocianum, priest lives by tithes, 369;
  Ad Rusticum Monachum, 320;
  Epistle ad Paulam et Eustochium, 264;
  Prologue, Super Actus Apostolorum, 126;
  Avarice, 98; Balaam and covetise, 441; good angels, 234, Good of church are for all, 366
Josephus, 140
Judas' death, 437
Judgment, two, 428; Last, 424
Just price, 360 ff.

Katherine, buried by angels, 236; image of, 48
Knight rules well his horse, figure, 469

Lady's Day Fast, 102-04; falling in Lent, 385
Lambeth, Constitution of, 384
Last Judgment, 424

Lay Fee, 239
Law, Civil, 284
Lechery, nine species of, 287; and clergy in the New Law, 325-26; remedies for, 317 ff.
Leo, Pope, sermon, 63
Liturgy, Passion Sunday, 46; Good Friday, 45; Images covered in Lent, 52
Lordship, kinds of, 28-29; 349-50
Lots, casting, 98
Lucy, Saint, refuses suicide, 282-83; teaches mother charity, 451
Lyra, on Abraham's Sara, 316; on Solomon's prayer, 36; on twelve jewels of Heavenly City, 438

Magic, using lots, 98
Manslaughter, 270-71
Marriage, symbols of, 329-30; sexual proscriptions in, 285 ff.
Martyrs in England, 128
Mass vestments, symbolism of, 413-14
Master of Kinds, *De qualitate elementariis*, 4, Bernake, 471; Chameleon as flatterer, 409-10; crisolitus, 243; dypsa (18), 246; taxus (brok or bawsym) in 18, 319; tyrus, 247
Master of Properties, ciconia (stork), 203; pellican, 203
Master of Sentences, 2. 22, 242
Master of stories, David and Gabonites, 166-67; Fall of Adam and Eve, 304; Jept, 138-40; Sodom and punishment of women and children, 325
Matrimony, two reasons for, 288-89; three main good things, 289; symbolism of, 190
Media Villa, Richard de; *Super Tercium Sentencia*, on worship, 55 f.; *Super Sentencias*, 3. 28. 4, 407
Miracle plays, 191; feigned, 347; lacking in present day, 129; not so needful now, 130
Misshapen children as signs, 335

Nabugodonosor, 229
Natural wonders in England as signs, 84

Nicholas, Life of Saint, 148
Number symbolism, six, 169; 184 f.; seven, 185; ten, 376

Obedience, to bad ruler in lawful things, 226-27; to ghostly fathers, 220; to husband telling wife to break vow, 232-33; to parents in choosing marriage partner, 228; to priest under bishop in undecided questions, 229-30; to religious superiors, 229 ff.; subject cannot do illegal things, 228
Origin, on *Leviticus*, 176
Ornaments, three belonging to wife are ring, brooch, garland, 290
Oxford, story about tyrant of, 263

Parents, story of father receiving ill treatment, 205; old man fooling son with bushel of earth, 205-06; tree crop metaphor and discipline, 207
Peasant Uprising, 242
Patron, three kinds of, 337; and prelates, 338; and advancement in church, 239
Pelican and adder, figures, 466
Perjury, realm of England noted for, 399; 408
Philomena, derivation, 455
Planets, under God's control, 66
Poor folk and tyrants, 254
Portents and falling stars, 131
Prayer, two manners of 124
Preacher, Poor, is God's knight, 459; is God's mouth, 258
Prelates, shortcomings of English, 114
Properties, kinds of, 350
Prophecy on England, 84-85
Prince, definition of lawful, 285

Raymond, *De Furtis*, 344-56; buying and selling free men, 356; gift may be given for five causes, 378 f.; paying a delayed tithe, 371; priest cannot take money to move mass of day, 384; restitution, 357; 375; 417; source of tithes, 371; tithes personales and prediales, 371 f.; *Summa Confessiorum*, ubiquitous

Rich and poor, exposition of "needle's eye," 32-34
Rich men, in Old Testament, 34; are God's bailiffs, 349
Ring, symbolism of wedding, 289
Robin Hood, songs of, 114
Rosamund, mistress of King Henry, 320 f.

Sabboth, change from Saturday to Sunday, 169-70; be merry on, 193; four reasons for observing, 168-69; four sabboths: day, month, year, fifth year, 180-81; hallow seventh day, 169; 180; meaning in English, 171; occurrences on that day, 170; plays and dances allowed on, 191; sins on Sunday, 177-79; Sunday laws, 176; work on, 179; 187 f.
Sacrileges, kinds of, 360
Sathanas, 187
Scrolls for magic, 91
Selling price, just, 360 f.
Seneca, *De Beneficiis* 4, 227; "epistle," 439; on flatterers, 249
Sermon, better to hear than a mass, 259
Servant's behavior, 222-24
Seven, meaning of, 185; blisses, 185 f.
Simony, definition, 376; three manners of, 377 f.; selling Church offices, 390; in agreements, 381; trental, 384
Sins of youth and old age, 40
Six, perfect number, 184; ages of the world, 169; 184; 185
Solinus, *De Mirabilibus Mundi*, well of Sardinia, 399
Sovereigns, obedience to, 226-28
Sphere of Pithagoras, 91
Spirits walking, 102
Stars, are takens, not causes, 65; and planets' size, 74
Statutes in England too rich, 52
Stealing, four manners without sin, 352; children of heathens to baptise, 358
Steracles (plays), 191
Succubi, 335
Superstitions, first day of year, 110; hunting with men of religion, 112; kites and puttocks, 109; luck follows dream about devil, 108; meeting frogs and toads, 109; meeting monk on left side, 113; satanic, 80 f.; step on wax of holy candle, 95; tale of "proud gettour" and horse, 443-44; twelve days of Christmas, 111
Swearing, by one's own body, 153; by parts of Christ's body, 152; excuses for, 142; foreswearing in six manners, 149; lawful causes for, 143; miracle of Mary appearing to swearing judge, 151; on inanimate objects and creatures, 146; on parents' souls, 147; Punishments for: in Canon Law, 162; in Almayne, 151; in Imperial Law, 151; Scotsman who would not before a judge, 161; use of Bible in, 147; wives, 156; 159
Sylvester, not to baptise pagan children, 357
Synodals of England, 384

Tales, Archer and nightingale, 437-38; child born in prison wants to stay, 482; love of gooseflesh, 355-56; man given vision of three gallows in hell, 436; minstrel and his horse ("Flectamus ianua"), 443-44; son bites off father's nose, 355; swearing judge, 151; test for three friends, 453-54; two fools in furnace, 451-52; two lawyers, 410-11; tyrant of Oxford, 263
Tarentinus, Peter, *Super Quartum Sent.*, on church patronage, 381; men of church have spiritual sword, 280
Ten, as perfect number, 264; analysis of, 376
Theft, species of, 348
Thomas Becket's grave, 158
Tides, 81
Tithes, clerks should fix church tithe, 372 f.; definition of, 255; division into four parts, 372; Guydo in Rosario—follow custom of country in repairing churches, 373; Guydo in Rosario—cannot give tithe to whom one wishes, 373; Hostiensis, on

INDEX 497

source of, 371; Innocent III on tithes personales and prediales, 375; not all things should be tithed, 372; curate should serve personally, 375; to evil clergy, 373
Tokens, of repentance and reverence, 55-56; of droughts and tempests, 79; of lay lords, 46
Tournaments and jousts, 274
Trade practices, restrictive, 391
Trentals, golden, 384; Gregorys', 385; invented by devil, 386
Turpin, *De Gestis Karoli*, monitory tale, 452-53

Urban, Pope, 235
Usurers, three months to move on, 396
Usury, Definition of, 389; permitted by emperor, 394; piunishment for 395; why allowed to Jews, 391

Veneration, three kinds of, 54-56
Verse fragments,
  "Adam, Sampsonem," 305;
  "Cerne cicatrices," 319-20;
  "Crux splendidior," 45;
  "Reminiscens," 320;
  "Rosa mundi," 320;
  "There is no man worthy," 88;
  Trenorum, "The joy of our heart," 427
Vestments, symbolism of, 413-14; bishop's cross, 415
Vitas Patrem, Alexandre fleeing temptation, 468
Vow, definition, 389

War, English attitude, 84; why allowed, 285
Weather, tokens of, 79-81
William, *Gloss*, 383
Witchcraft, definition, 99; charming animals, 100; manners of, 96-97; necromancy, geomancy, pyromancy. aeromancy, hydromancy, 96-97; return of dead, 100-01
Witches, remedies against, 92; and Imperial Law, 92; and devil, 95-96; and minstrels, 363; ride at night, 92
Witnesses, degree and number, 419-21; forty, 423; three kinds, 422
Woman, why made from rib of Adam, 294
Worship, De Halis on Kneeling to God, 58; green trees, 57; incensing, 59-61; king's son not to kneel to churl, 49; Latria, dulia, hyperdulia, 53-60; two manners of, 53; why facing east, 61, 63